Elements of Claims and Defenses in Nevada
by Day R. Williams, Attorney at Law

Preface

My son, an All-American cross-country runner, has reminded me how important it is to practice the fundamentals. To run well, you must run hard during the week, eat right, drink lots of liquids, take a day of rest each week, and stay focused. In the practice of law, as with participation in sports, you must return to the fundamentals again and again. This book is about the fundamentals, the elements, in the practice of law. "An 'element' of a claim is a 'part of a claim that must be proved for the claim to succeed.'" [1]

A little about me: Since 1991 I've been a licensed Nevada attorney, which is an honor and a privilege. As I grew up in Reno, I delivered the morning paper, the *Nevada State Journal*, and on my three-speed bike, I delivered the evening paper, the *Reno Evening Gazette*. I attended Hunter Lake Elementary School, Swope Junior High School, and Reno High School. After I graduated from Reno High School as a National Merit Scholar, I earned a B.A. in English Literature at Reed College in Portland, Oregon.

Before I went to law school, I drove a tractor and moved wheel lines on a farm; I worked as a taxi driver for Whittlesea in Reno; I worked as a cashier at Harrah's and Eddie's Fabulous Fifties in Reno; and I photographed models, actresses, and wagon trains. In law school I scored top of my classes (each class had more than 100 students) in Evidence and Constitutional Law. I enjoyed studying torts under Professor Dan B. Dobbs at the University of Arizona School of Law in Tucson, Arizona, now named the James E. Rogers College of Law. (Nevada had no law school when I began law school.) Professor Dobbs produced an excellent textbook on torts, and he taught us to learn the elements of each tort.

I began my practice as a solo Nevada lawyer in 1993. This book began with a list I kept as a practicing lawyer. When drafting a Complaint or an Answer, a Motion for Summary Judgment, and other pleadings, having a list of possible claims and affirmative defenses gave me a head start in writing my pleading.

I provide here a partial list of claims and affirmative defenses. The lists are also only "partial," because the Nevada Revised Statutes cover a multitude of topics and because the law develops every day. Creative lawyers often come up with new claims and affirmative defenses.

This work focuses mainly on contracts, torts, and civil rights. Due to space limitations, important areas are omitted. These include family law, real estate law, elections law, and utilities law.

May this be helpful to you, the practicing lawyer.

(Please post your positive reviews on amazon.com, and send your comments and suggestions to me at day_williams@sbcglobal.net.)

~Day R. Williams, Attorney at Law, Carson City, Nevada
cclegal.pro
"The Client is Number One"®

January 2016 A.D.

Day Williams

---

[1] *Mitchell v. District Court*, 131 Nev., Advance Opinion 21 (2015 (en banc), citing Black's Law Dictionary 559 (8th ed. 2004).

Work by Day Williams

Amazon.com:

1001 Quotations®: Bible Passages
http://tinyurl.com/cx8dctj

1001 Quotations®: The Future
http://tinyurl.com/9wvacdw

1001 Quotations®: Military Maxims
http://tinyurl.com/d3yq2hv

1001 Quotations®: Money Matters
http://tinyurl.com/d3g7yh4

1001 Quotations®: Sports Sayings
http://tinyurl.com/ccvschj

The Case of the Secret Silver
http://tinyurl.com/cl75rz3

David the King
http://tinyurl.com/d9bffzc

Elements of Claims and Defenses in Nevada
http://www.tinyurl.com/c6s5wlh
youtube: youtube.com/watch?v=qaPWDpXK48A

Light of Day: Short Christian Poems
http://tinyurl.com/p9bda9h

Masons and Mystery at the 33rd Parallel
http://tinyurl.com/bk7v86w

The Minor Prophets in Blank Verse
http://tinyurl.com/otftker

New Testament in Blank Verse
Part I Gospels
http://tinyurl.com/o38mnc5

New Testament in Blank Verse
Part II Letters
http://tinyurl.com/pccs2wz

A Treasury of Christian Poetry
http://tinyurl.com/c7c83c7

Virginia Street and Other Poems
http://tinyurl.com/cfyfxyh

We the People: Presidential Quotations and Milestone Documents
http://tinyurl.com/nlndfrv

Blog: http://www.daysworld.org/daysworldblog/

Blurb.com:
Bridgeport's Fourth of July
        http://www.blurb.com/bookstore/detail/3371491

First Thursday
        http://www.blurb.com/b/4498810-first-thursday
        http://www.youtube.com/watch?v=HGh-QGHA-20

2

Leadville Parade July 28, 2012 A.D.
    http://www.blurb.com/bookstore/detail/3481910
    On youtube: www.youtube.com/watch?v=daUtgxdtycw

Yes!
    http://www.blurb.com/b/4143344-yes

Legal website:
http://www.carsontrialattorney.com

Photographs and art:
http://www.fineartamerica.com/art/all/Day+Williams/all
Stock photography agent: http://www.sciencesource.com
Youtube: "Bestsellers": www.youtube.com/watch?v=Bmjw8Z7yHX8
    or tinyurl.com/bsh2e5g
    Bill of Rights: http://youtu.be/Ub68CAS0Z10
    "Highway 50": http://www.youtube.com/watch?v=ZqtvoHcqp7s
    "Yes":www.youtube.com/watch?v=kXO_iM-7wrw
http://www.zazzle.com/daysrays
    "First Thursday": http://www.youtube.com/watch?v=HGh-QGHA-20
        "Hot August Nights": http://www.youtube.com/watch?v=Vg0HNRdy8Pc&feature=youtu.be

Movie:
    Grandpa's Trunk: http://www.youtube.com/watch?v=RIhwSKOjp0I

twitter: @Owlmanyeyes, @DaysWorld1

Disclaimer

This is a guide and a starting point for lawyers, who must always do independent research and exercise independent judgment under Rule 11 and the Rules of Professional Conduct. This is a book with Nevada civil law for Nevada lawyers. All other jurisdictions—use common sense and do your own research. While this book may provide a good jumping off point, your laws may be different.

The author and publisher does not provide any warranty of the item whatsoever—whether express, implied, or statutory—including, but not limited to, any warranty of merchantability or fitness for a particular purpose or any warranty that the contents of the item will be error-free. In no respect shall the author and publisher incur any liability for any damages, including, but not limited to, direct, indirect, special, or consequential damages arising out of, resulting from, or in any way connected to the use of the item, whether or not based upon warranty, contract, tort, or otherwise; whether or not injury was sustained by persons or property or otherwise; and whether or not loss was sustained from, or arose out of, the results of, the item, or any services that may be provided by the author or publisher.

The Nevada Supreme Court
Carson City, Nevada
(Day Williams Photo)

Acknowledgements

Thank you to the Nevada Supreme Court, which keeps developing our case law. As always, thank you to my loving wife, family, and friends.

Nevada Supreme Court Justices
(Back, from left to right) Justices Pickering, Gibbons,
Parraguire, and Hardesty
(Front, from left to right) Justices Douglas, Cherry, and Saitta

Nevada Court of Appeals
Justices Gibbons, Silver and Tao

Table of Contents

7

11

CLAIMS

Abuse of Process

Abuse of process is not when a defendant tears up the summons or swears at the process server. The elements of an abuse of process claim are: "(1) an **ulterior** purpose by the defendants other than resolving a legal dispute, and (2) a willful act in the use of the legal process not proper in the regular conduct of the proceeding." Abuse of process can arise from both civil and criminal proceedings. The claimant must provide facts, rather than conjecture, showing that the party intended to use the legal process to further an ulterior purpose.[2] The utilized process must be judicial, as the tort protects the integrity of the court.[3] The tort requires a "willful act," and merely filing a complaint and proceeding to properly litigate the case does not meet this requirement.[4]

Malice, want of probable cause, and termination in favor of the person initiating or instituting proceedings are not necessary elements for a prima facie abuse of process claim.[5] An abuse of process claim may not be supported by a complaint to an administrative agency.[6] However, Nevada law clearly holds that "the mere filing of a complaint is insufficient to establish the tort of abuse of process."[7]

Accord and Satisfaction

To successfully establish the fact of an accord and satisfaction with regard to an unliquidated claim, a litigant must satisfy three elements: (1) a bona fide dispute over the unliquidated amount; (2) a payment tendered in full settlement of the entire dispute; and (3) an understanding by the creditor of the transaction as such, and acceptance of the payment. While certain conduct by a creditor may imply an accord and satisfaction as a matter of law, the parties' intent to make a settlement is generally a question of fact.

NRS 104.3311, "Accord and satisfaction by use of instrument," provides as follows:

1. If a person against whom a claim is asserted proves that he or she in good faith tendered an instrument to the claimant as full satisfaction of the claim, the amount of the claim was unliquidated or subject to a bona fide dispute, and the claimant obtained payment of the instrument, subsections 2, 3 and 4 apply.

2. Unless subsection 3 applies, the claim is discharged if the person against whom the claim is asserted proves that the instrument or an accompanying written communication contained a conspicuous statement to the effect that the instrument was tendered as full satisfaction of the claim.

3. Except as otherwise provided in subsection 4, a claim is not discharged under subsection 2 if either of the following applies:

(a) The claimant, if an organization, proves that:

(1) Within a reasonable time before the tender, the claimant sent a conspicuous statement to the person against whom the claim is asserted that communications concerning disputed debts, including an instrument tendered as full satisfaction of a debt, are to be sent to a designated person, office or place; and

(2) The instrument or accompanying communication was not received by that designated person, office or place.

(b) The claimant, whether or not an organization, proves that within 90 days after payment of the instrument, the claimant tendered repayment of the amount of the instrument to the person against whom the claim is asserted. This paragraph does not apply if the claimant is an organization that sent a statement complying with subparagraph (1) of paragraph (a).

---

[2] *Land Baron Investments v. Bonnie Springs Family Limited Partnership*, 131 Nev., Advance Opinion 69 at 15 (2015).

[3] *Id.*

[4] *Id.*

[5] *LaMantia v. Redisi*, 118 Nev. 27, 38 P.3d 877 (2002).

[6] *Land Baron Investments v. Bonnie Springs Family Limited Partnership*, 131 Nev., Advance Opinion 69 (2015).

[7] *Laxalt v. McClatchy*, 622 F.Supp. 737, 752 (D. Nev. 1985).

4. A claim is discharged if the person against whom the claim is asserted proves that within a reasonable time before collection of the instrument was initiated, the claimant, or an agent of the claimant having direct responsibility with respect to the disputed obligation, knew that the instrument was tendered in full satisfaction of the claim.

Accounting

The action for an accounting is equitable in nature and may be brought to compel the defendant to account to the plaintiff for money where a fiduciary relationship exists.[8] The elements of a claim for accounting are (1) a fiduciary relationship and (2) a balance due from the defendant to the plaintiff that can only be determined by an accounting—that is, the sum is not certain and cannot be made certain by calculations.[9]

The Nevada case of *Eikelberger v. Tolotti*[10] had an action for accounting, but the elements of an accounting are not presented in it.

An account of profits (sometimes referred to as an accounting for profits or simply an accounting) is a type of equitable remedy most commonly used in cases of breach of fiduciary duty.[11] It is an action taken against a defendant to recover the profits taken as a result of the breach of duty, in order to prevent unjust enrichment. In conducting an account of profits, the plaintiff is treated as if they were conducting the business of the defendant, and made those profits which were attributable to the defendant's wrongful actions. This can be rather complex in practice, because the defendant's accounting records must be examined (sometimes by a forensic accountant) to determine what portion of his gross profits were derived from the wrongful act in question.[12]

Historically an account was not an equitable remedy, but was an action at common law, and is therefore technically an instrument of law, though it arose at a time before the distinction between law and equity was marked.[13] Co-owners in concurrent estates also have the right to an accounting of profits, in order to properly apportion income from the use or leasing of the property.

Case law has shown roughly two approaches to assessing the extent of an account of profits:

1) To account, not of the entire business, but of the particular benefits which flowed to him in breach of his duty;
2) to account for the entire business and its profits, due allowance being made for the time, energy, skill and financial contribution of the fiduciary (the approach in *Boardman v. Phipps*).[14]

The right to an accounting by a partner during disputes or at the dissolution of a partnership has long been recognized.[15] "[A] breach of the partnership agreement does not necessarily result in a forfeiture of the partner's interest or deprive him of his right to an accounting." *B.K.K. Co. v. Schultz*, 7 Cal.Ct.App.3d 786, 797, 86 Cal.Rptr. 760 (1970) (defendant's breach of partnership agreement was not a sufficient basis for denying his request for an accounting, and trial court made no other findings of fact which would support any theory divesting defendant of his interest in the business; because appellate court could not determine whether defendant was refused an accounting on proper factual grounds or upon an erroneous interpretation of law, judgment was reversed and remanded for further proceedings).

The right of a member of a limited liability company (LLC) to an accounting has not been as clear, even though LLCs have been widely used for more than two decades. Although many state statutes are silent as to the right of an accounting in disputes involving LLCs, recent case law seems to be trending towards similar rights of members for accountings in some circumstances. The LLC's operating agreement may require an accounting.

---

[8] 5 Witkin, Cal. Procedure (4th ed. 1997) Pleading, § 775, p. 233.

[9] 5 Witkin, supra, § 776, p. 233.

[10] 90 Nev. 463, 530 P.2d 104 (1974).

[11] *Black's Law Dictionary* 20 (7th ed. 1999).

[12] Leigh Ellis, *Theory into Action: Calculating Damages Payments and Accounts of Profits in Patent Cases.*

[13] *National Trust Co. v. H & R Block Canada, Inc.*, 2003 SCC 66.

[14] *Boardman v. Phipps* UKHL 2 (1966) is a landmark English trusts law case concerning the duty of loyalty and the duty to avoid conflicts of interest.

[15] Posted by Ted Zwyer, *The Right to an Accounting in Disputes among Members or During Dissolution of LLCs.*

The Pleading Lawyer
By Honoré Daumier

Other states have more law than Nevada on the action for accounting. The Indiana Business Flexibility Act, Burns Ind. Code Ann. § 23-18-1-1 *et seq.*, which governs LLCs, is silent on the right to an accounting by a member. The Court of Appeals of Indiana ruled, however,[16] that a trial court erred when it failed to order an accounting of an LLC's finances in order to determine the proper distribution to the LLC's creditors and the members upon dissolution of the LLC. The LLC was an executive search firm that was owned by two members. When the defendant member proposed to change the LLC's compensation so that the compensation was not split equally between the members, plaintiff member refused, and the plaintiff then began to receive less information as to the finances of the LLC. The plaintiff sought dissolution of the LLC, and the trial court granted the dissolution and awarded a distribution amount to the plaintiff from the LLC and the defendant based upon the plaintiff's testimony. The defendant then appealed the failure of the trial court to order an accounting before approving the distribution. The Court of Appeals held that it was an error for the trial court to determine the amount of the distribution that the plaintiff was due in the dissolution of the LLC without ordering an accounting of the LLC's finances.

Similarly, the Kentucky Limited Liability Company Act, KRS § 275.001, *et seq.*, is silent as to a court's power to order an accounting. The Court of Appeals of Kentucky has ruled that a trial court could grant a member's request for an accounting and subsequent judicial dissolution of an LLC.[17] The two members formed the LLC to run a used car lot. After only two months, the plaintiff member sought an accounting and dissolution. The trial court ordered an accounting, rejected defendant member's proffered accounting, and then approved the LLC's dissolution without approving any accounting. The Court of Appeals held as follows: "The circuit court erred by entering summary judgment at this stage in the accounting. After rendering an order to account, the court must then conduct the accounting and render final judgment."

In a two-paragraph opinion, the Supreme Court of New York, Appellate Division, ruled that "members of a limited liability company may seek an equitable accounting under common law."[18] The appellate division found that the right to an accounting existed even though no explicit right to an accounting exists in the New York Limited Liability Company Law, NY CLS LLC § 101 *et seq.* A year earlier, another department of the appellate division had stated without explanation that a member of an LLC had a right to demand an accounting.[19]

A Pennsylvania court ruled in 2008 that a member of an LLC had a right to an accounting if certain allegations were shown. In *Baird v. Macklin*, 2008 Pa. Dist. & Cnty. Dec. LEXIS 130 (Pa. County Ct. 2008), the court found that the plaintiff failed to sufficiently plead "any of required elements of the cause of action for an accounting." The court initially stated that there was no case law specifically granting the right to an accounting: "Defendants argue that Count I of the Plaintiff's Complaint inappropriately asserts a separate cause of action for an 'accounting.' Defendants' brief is devoid of any Pennsylvania case law to support their claim, and our research found no cases from this jurisdiction regarding members of an LLC alleging a claim for accounting." The court proceeded to rule, though, that a member could properly state a cause of action at law for an accounting if the member asserted a breach of contract claim or any other claim for assumpsit. Furthermore, a member could properly "assert a separate action for an accounting in equity, provided there is a sustainable underlying equity claim. Thus, Plaintiff must state another valid equitable cause of action

---

[16] *Perkins v. Brown*, 901 N.E.2d 63 (Ind. Ct. App. 2009).

[17] *Gentry v. Cremeens*, 2009 Ky. App. Unpub. Lexis 139 (Ky. Ct. App. 2009).

[18] *Gottlieb v. Northriver Trading Co. LLC*, 58 A.D.3d 550 (N.Y. App. Div. 1st Dep't 2009).

[19] *East Quogue Jet, LLC v. East Quogue Members, LLC*, 50 A.D.3d 1089 (N.Y. App. Div. 2nd Dep't 2008).

in order to proceed with a claim for accounting." The court granted the plaintiff leave of court for thirty days in which to file an amended complaint that stated a legally sufficient equity claim for an accounting.

Although it found that a full accounting was not the appropriate remedy in the case before it because "a full financial accounting would unnecessarily prolong this otherwise simple matter," the Supreme Court of South Carolina held that an accounting of an LLC could be proper in some circumstances under S.C. Code Ann. § 33-44-410 of the South Carolina Limited Liability Company Act.[20] Similarly, the Court of Appeals of Tennessee held that, although a member was not entitled to an additional expanded accounting of the LLC, the Court of Appeals had earlier ruled that she had been entitled to an initial accounting, which was completed.[21]

The State of Nevada has no statute on point as to accounting. The State of Montana does have a statute, Montana Code Annotated 201182-10-101, which provides for an action for accounting for royalty as follows:

(1) Whenever an owner of a royalty interest in or attaching to lands producing natural gas, oil, or other minerals or in or to the natural gas, oil, or other mineral production from said lands, whether said royalty is payable in kind out of the product of the lands or out of the money proceeds from the sale of the product of said lands, shall make a written demand upon the person or persons obligated to deliver or pay such royalty for an accounting of the natural gas, oil, or other minerals produced from said lands and makes written demand for delivery or payment of such owner's royalty as may then be due and the person or persons obligated for the delivery or payment of said royalty fail to make the accounting demanded and the payment or delivery of the royalty due within a period of 60 days following the date upon which said demand is made, then the owner of said royalty may file an action in the district court of the county wherein said lands are located to compel the accounting demanded and to recover the payment or delivery of the royalty due against the person or persons obligated as aforesaid.

(2) In said action the successful party or parties recovering judgment against the person or persons obligated shall, in addition to relief by way of accounting and recovery of the royalty due as hereinabove provided, also recover judgment for a sum of money by way of reasonable attorney fees to be allowed by the court together with the costs allowed to successful parties by law in actions generally in said court.

(3) Whenever the same person or persons is or are obligated for delivery or payment of said royalty to separate owners of royalty in or to a tract of land or any portion of said land or the product of the whole or any part of said land, then any number of said owners of royalty may join their separate causes of action as parties plaintiff in the action herein provided for, and in their complaint filed in said action, each cause of action of each of the several plaintiffs shall be set forth separately in said complaint, and the judgment given, made, and rendered upon said complaint shall adjudge the relief to one or more of the plaintiffs and deny relief to any one or more of said plaintiffs accordingly as the evidence may establish.

(4) If the defendant or defendants prevail in said action against any one or more of said plaintiffs, the court shall adjudge and allow to such defendant or defendants and against the unsuccessful plaintiff or plaintiffs recovery of a sum of money as reasonable attorney fees to be allowed by the court and adjudge and allow costs to said defendant to be recovered from the said unsuccessful plaintiff or plaintiffs in said action, as provided for by law in actions generally in said court.

Recovery of an unjust enrichment is an equitable remedy.[22] Seeking an accounting, where the accounting is not provided for by contract, is also an equitable remedy.[23] Because laches is an equitable defense,[24] laches can bar an unjust enrichment and accounting claims. See *McKesson*, 339 F.3d at 1093 (rejecting the plaintiff's unjust enrichment claim based on the equities); Ronald E. Dimock, Dimock: *Intellectual Property Disputes: Resolutions and Remedies* § 18.2(a)(i) (2008) ("since an accounting of profits is an equitable remedy, the plaintiff may be refused the remedy upon equitable grounds," such as a "long delay in commencing the proceedings") (footnotes omitted)).

Action against Killer of Decedent

General Provisions

NRS 41B.010, "Definitions," provides as follows:

---

[20] *Historic Charleston Holdings, LLC v. Mallon*, 381 S.C. 417 (S.C. 2009).

[21] *Braden v. Strong*, 2009 Tenn. App. Lexis 54 (Tenn. Ct.App. 2009).

[22] *See McKesson HBOC, Inc. v. New York State Common Ret. Fund, Inc.*, 339 F.3d 1087, 1093 (9th Cir. 2003).

[23] See *Dairy Queen, Inc. v. Wood*, 369 U.S. 469, 478 (1962).

[24] See *Jarrow Formulas, Inc. v. Nutrition Now, Inc.*, 304 F.3d 829, 835 (9th Cir. 2002).

As used in this Chapter, unless the context otherwise requires, the words and terms defined in NRS 41B.020 to 41B.160, inclusive, have the meanings ascribed to them in those sections.

NRS 41B.020, "'Acquitted' defined," provides as follows:

"Acquitted" includes, without limitation, a finding of not guilty by reason of insanity or diminished capacity.

NRS 41B.030, "'Agent' defined," provides as follows:

"Agent" means a person who is authorized to represent or act for another person. The term includes, without limitation, an attorney-in-fact under a durable or nondurable power of attorney or a person who is authorized pursuant to the provisions of a governing instrument to make decisions concerning the provision of health care to another person.

NRS 41B.040, "'Beneficiary' defined," provides as follows:

"Beneficiary" means a person who is entitled to accrue, acquire or receive any property, interest or benefit pursuant to the provisions of a governing instrument or the laws of intestate succession.

NRS 41B.050, "'Community property' defined," provides as follows: "Community property" has the meaning ascribed to it in NRS 123.220.

NRS 41B.060, "'Community property with right of survivorship' defined," provides as follows:

"Community property with right of survivorship" means community property in which a right of survivorship exists pursuant to NRS 111.064 or 115.060 or any other provision of law.

NRS 41B.070, "'Convicted' and 'conviction' defined," provides as follows:

"Convicted" and "conviction" mean a judgment based upon:
1. A plea of guilty, guilty but mentally ill or nolo contendere;
2. A finding of guilty or guilty but mentally ill by a jury or a court sitting without a jury;
3. An adjudication of delinquency or finding of guilty or guilty but mentally ill by a court having jurisdiction over juveniles; or
4. Any other admission or finding of guilty or guilty but mentally ill in a criminal action or a proceeding in a court having jurisdiction over juveniles.

NRS 41B.080, "'Culpable actor in the felonious and intentional killing of a decedent' defined," provides as follows:

"Culpable actor in the felonious and intentional killing of a decedent" means a person who:
1. Causes or perpetrates the felonious and intentional killing of the decedent;
2. Aids, abets, commands, counsels, encourages, hires, induces, procures or solicits another person to cause or perpetrate the felonious and intentional killing of the decedent; or
3. Is a principal in any degree, accessory before the fact, accomplice or conspirator to the felonious and intentional killing of the decedent.

NRS 41B.090, "'Governing instrument' defined," provides as follows:

"Governing instrument" means any of the following:
1. A deed or any other instrument that transfers any property, interest or benefit.
2. An annuity or a policy of insurance.
3. A trust, whether created by an instrument executed during the life of the settlor, a testamentary instrument or any other instrument, judgment or decree, including, without limitation, any of the following:
(a) An express trust, whether private or charitable, and any additions to such a trust.

(b) A trust created or determined by a judgment or decree under which the trust is to be administered in the manner of an express trust.

4. A will, a codicil or any other testamentary instrument, including, without limitation, a testamentary instrument that:

(a) Appoints a person to serve in a fiduciary or representative capacity, nominates a guardian or revokes or revises another will, codicil or testamentary instrument; or

(b) Excludes or limits the right of a person or class of persons to succeed to any property, interest or benefit pursuant to the laws of intestate succession.

5. Any account or deposit that is payable or transferable on the death of a person or any instrument that provides for the payment or transfer of any property, interest or benefit on the death of a person.

6. A security registered as transferable on the death of a person.

7. Any instrument creating or exercising a power of appointment or a durable or nondurable power of attorney.

8. Any instrument that appoints or nominates a person to serve in any fiduciary or representative capacity, including, without limitation, an agent, guardian, executor, personal representative or trustee.

9. Any public or private plan or system that entitles a person to the payment or transfer of any property, interest or benefit, including, without limitation, a plan or system that involves any of the following:

(a) Pension benefits, retirement benefits or other similar benefits.

(b) Profit-sharing or any other form of participation in profits, revenues, securities, capital or assets.

(c) Industrial insurance, workers' compensation or other similar benefits.

(d) Group insurance.

10. A partnership agreement or an agreement concerning any joint adventure, enterprise or venture.

11. A premarital, antenuptial or postnuptial agreement, a marriage contract or settlement or any other similar agreement, contract or settlement.

12. Any instrument that declares a homestead pursuant to Chapter 115 of NRS.

13. Any other dispositive, appointive, nominative or declarative instrument.
(Added to NRS by 1999, 1349; A 2011, 1417)

NRS 41B.100, "'Interest' defined," provides as follows:

"Interest" means:

1. Any interest, in whole or in part, in any property or estate, whether such interest is legal or equitable, present or future, or contingent or vested;

2. A right, power or privilege to appoint, consume, exercise, transfer or use any such interest; or

3. Any other right, power or privilege relating to any such interest.
(Added to NRS by 1999, 1350)

NRS 41B.110, "'Interested person' defined," provides as follows:

"Interested person" means:

1. A parent, spouse, child or sibling of a decedent;

2. A beneficiary or a person who would be a beneficiary if another person were found to be a killer of a decedent;

3. A person who serves in any fiduciary or representative capacity with respect to any property, interest or benefit that is in any way related to a decedent, the decedent's estate or a governing instrument or a person who would be entitled to serve in such a capacity if another person were found to be a killer of a decedent; or

4. A person who has a right to or claim against any property, interest or benefit that is in any way related to a decedent, the decedent's estate or a governing instrument or a person who would have such a right or claim if another person were found to be a killer of a decedent.

NRS 41B.120, "'Joint tenants with right of survivorship' defined," provides as follows:

"Joint tenants with right of survivorship" means two or more persons who hold any property, interest or benefit under circumstances that entitle one or more of the persons to the whole of the property, interest or benefit on the death of one or more of the other persons.

NRS 41B.130, "'Killer' defined," provides as follows;

"Killer" means a person who is deemed to be a killer of a decedent pursuant to NRS 41B.250 or 41B.260.
(Added to NRS by 1999, 1350)

NRS 41B.140, "'Payor' defined," provides as follows:

"Payor" means a person who is authorized or obligated by law or a governing instrument to pay or transfer any property, interest or benefit to another person.
(Added to NRS by 1999, 1350)

NRS 41B.150, "'Person' defined," provides as follows:

"Person" means any of the following:
1. A natural person.
2. Any form of business or social organization and any other nongovernmental legal entity, including, without limitation, a corporation, partnership, association, trust or unincorporated organization.
3. A government, a political subdivision of a government or an agency or instrumentality of a government or a political subdivision of a government.
(Added to NRS by 1999, 1350)

NRS 41B.160, "'Property' defined," provides as follows:

"Property" means anything that may be the subject of ownership, including, without limitation, any real or personal property or any estate in such property.
(Added to NRS by 1999, 1351)

Applicability of Chapter
NRS 41B.200, "General rule; killer cannot profit or benefit from wrong; anti-lapse statute and right of representation; contingent, residuary and other beneficiaries; common law," provides as follows:

1. Notwithstanding any other provision of law, the provisions of this Chapter apply to any appointment, nomination, power, right, property, interest or benefit that accrues or devolves to a killer of a decedent based upon the death of the decedent. If any such appointment, nomination, power, right, property, interest or benefit is not expressly covered by the provisions of this Chapter, it must be treated in accordance with the principle that a killer cannot profit or benefit from his or her wrong.
2. The provisions of this Chapter do not abrogate or limit the application of:
(a) The anti-lapse provisions of NRS 133.200 or the right of representation, as defined and applied in Chapter 134 of NRS, with respect to a person who is not a killer of the decedent; or
(b) Any provision of a governing instrument that designates:
(1) A contingent or residuary beneficiary who is not a killer of the decedent; or
(2) Any other beneficiary who is not a killer of the decedent.
3. The provisions of this Chapter do not abrogate or limit any principle or rule of the common law, unless the principle or rule is inconsistent with the provisions of this Chapter.

NRS 41B.210, "Acts constituting felonious and intentional killing; insanity or diminished capacity," provides as follows:

For the purposes of this Chapter:
1. A killing is "felonious" if it is committed without legal excuse or justification.
2. A killing is "intentional" if it is caused by or occurs during the commission of any act which involves a degree of culpability that is greater than criminal negligence.
3. Insanity or diminished capacity shall be deemed not to be a legal excuse or justification and must not be considered in determining whether a killing is felonious or intentional.

NRS 41B.250, "Criminal action: Conclusive effect of judgment of conviction; admissibility of judgment of conviction in civil action," provides as follows:

1. If a court in this state or any other jurisdiction enters a judgment of conviction against a person in which the person is found to have been a culpable actor in the felonious and intentional killing of a decedent:
    (a) The conviction conclusively establishes for the purposes of this Chapter that the person feloniously and intentionally killed the decedent; and
    (b) The person shall be deemed to be a killer of the decedent.
2. Notwithstanding the provisions of NRS 48.125 or 51.295 or any other provision of law, a judgment of conviction described in subsection 1, including, without limitation, a judgment of conviction based upon a plea of nolo contendere, is admissible in any civil action brought pursuant to the provisions of this Chapter.
3. For the purposes of this section:
    (a) A court in "any other jurisdiction" includes, without limitation, a tribal court or a court of the United States or the Armed Forces of the United States.
    (b) A court "enters" a judgment of conviction against a person on the date on which guilt is admitted, adjudicated or found, whether or not:
        (1) The court has imposed a sentence, a penalty or other sanction for the conviction; or
        (2) The person has exercised any right to appeal the conviction.
    (c) A killing in this state that constitutes murder of the first or second degree, as defined in NRS 200.010, 200.020 and 200.030, or voluntary manslaughter, as defined in NRS 200.040, 200.050 and 200.060, shall be deemed to be a felonious and intentional killing.
    (Added to NRS by 1999, 1351)

NRS 41B.260, "Civil action: Parties; burden of proof; evidence; stay of proceedings; limitation on time for commencement," provides as follows:

1. For the purposes of this Chapter, an interested person may bring a civil action alleging that a person was a culpable actor in the felonious and intentional killing of a decedent. An interested person may bring such a civil action whether or not any person who is alleged to be a killer in the civil action or any other person is or has been, in a separate criminal action, charged with or convicted or acquitted of being:
    (a) A culpable actor in the felonious and intentional killing of the decedent; or
    (b) A culpable actor in any other offense arising out of the facts surrounding the killing of the decedent.
2. If an interested person brings a civil action pursuant to this section, the court shall determine, by a preponderance of the evidence, whether a person who is alleged to be a killer of the decedent was a culpable actor in the felonious and intentional killing of the decedent. If the court finds by a preponderance of the evidence that a person who is alleged to be a killer of the decedent was a culpable actor in the felonious and intentional killing of the decedent:
    (a) The finding of the court conclusively establishes for the purposes of this Chapter that the person feloniously and intentionally killed the decedent; and
    (b) The person shall be deemed to be a killer of the decedent.
3. If, in a separate criminal action, a person is charged with being a culpable actor in the felonious and intentional killing of a decedent or with any other offense arising out of the facts surrounding the killing of the decedent and:
    (a) The person is acquitted of the charge;
    (b) The charge is dismissed; or
    (c) A verdict or judgment is not reached or entered on the charge for any reason,
evidence concerning any such matter is not admissible in a civil action brought pursuant to this section.
4. Upon its own motion or the motion of an interested person, the court may, in whole or in part, stay the proceedings in a civil action brought pursuant to this section during the pendency of any separate criminal action that has been brought against a person who is alleged to be a killer in the civil action. The provisions of this subsection do not limit the power of the court to stay the proceedings in the civil action for any other reason.

5. A civil action described in this section may not be commenced by an interested person more than 5 years after the interested person discovers or through the use of reasonable diligence should have discovered the material facts that constitute the cause of action.

Scope of Forfeiture

NRS 41B.300, "Estate of decedent," provides as follows:

1. A killer of a decedent forfeits any appointment, nomination, power, right, property, interest or benefit that, pursuant to the provisions of title 12 of NRS or the common law, accrues or devolves to the killer from or through the estate of the decedent, including, without limitation:
(a) An intestate share.
(b) An elective share.
(c) The share of an omitted spouse or child.
(d) A family allowance.
(e) A homestead allowance.
(f) Any exempt property.
2. The intestate estate of the decedent passes as if the killer had predeceased the decedent, and any other appointment, nomination, power, right, property, interest or benefit described in subsection 1 must be treated as if the killer had predeceased the decedent.
(Added to NRS by 1999, 1353)

NRS 41B.310, "Governing instruments," provides as follows:

1. Except as otherwise provided in NRS 41B.320, a killer of a decedent forfeits any appointment, nomination, power, right, property, interest or benefit that, pursuant to the provisions of a governing instrument executed by the decedent or any other person, accrues or devolves to the killer based upon the death of the decedent.
2. In addition to any forfeiture required by subsection 1, if a governing instrument provides for the payment of certain benefits only upon the death of a decedent, a killer of the decedent forfeits any right or interest that the killer is entitled to assert against those benefits on the basis that community property was used, in whole or in part, to purchase the governing instrument or to pay one or more contributions or premiums that were related to the governing instrument.
3. If a killer of a decedent forfeits any appointment, nomination, power, right, property, interest or benefit pursuant to this section, the provisions of each governing instrument affected by the forfeiture must be treated as if the killer had predeceased the decedent.

NRS 41B.320, "Community property with right of survivorship and joint tenants with right of survivorship," provides as follows:

1. A killer of a decedent forfeits any right of survivorship in property that, at the time of the killing, was held by the decedent and the killer as community property with right of survivorship or as joint tenants with right of survivorship.
2. If a killer forfeits any right of survivorship pursuant to subsection 1:
(a) The respective interests in the property held by the decedent and the killer:
(1) Shall be deemed to be severed and transformed into tenancies in common; and
(2) Are presumed to be undivided equal interests in the property, unless a personal representative of the decedent establishes that the contributions made by the decedent concerning the property exceeded the contributions made by the killer; and
(b) The interest of the decedent passes as the separate property of the decedent and as if the killer had predeceased the decedent.

NRS 41B.330, "Action for wrongful death," provides as follows:

1. A killer of a decedent may not:
(a) Bring an action for wrongful death of the decedent pursuant to NRS 41.085; or

(b) Benefit in any way from such an action brought by a personal representative of the decedent.

2. Each person who may bring or benefit from an action for wrongful death of the decedent pursuant to NRS 41.085 must be determined as if the killer had predeceased the decedent.

(Added to NRS by 1999, 1354)

The Widow at a Consultation
By Honoré Daumier

Liability

NRS 41B.400, "Payor or other third person who pays or transfers forfeited property, interest or benefit," provides as follows:

Except as otherwise provided by specific statute, if a payor or other third person, in good faith, pays or transfers any property, interest or benefit to a beneficiary in accordance with the provisions of a governing instrument, the payor or other third person is not liable to another person who alleges that the payment or transfer to the beneficiary violated the provisions of this Chapter unless, before the payment or transfer, the payor or other third person had actual knowledge that the beneficiary was prohibited from acquiring or receiving the property, interest or benefit pursuant to the provisions of this Chapter.

(Added to NRS by 1999, 1354)

NRS 41B.410, "Person who acquires or receives forfeited property, interest or benefit without legal right or authorization," provides as follows:

1. Except as otherwise provided in subsection 2, if a person, without legal right or authorization, acquires or receives any property, interest or benefit forfeited by a killer pursuant to the provisions of this Chapter, the person is required to transfer the property, interest or benefit to the beneficiary who is entitled to it pursuant to the provisions of this Chapter, or the person is liable to such beneficiary for the value of the property, interest or benefit.

2. The provisions of subsection 1 do not apply to a person who:

(a) Acquired the property, interest or benefit for value and without notice; or

(b) Received the property, interest or benefit in full or partial satisfaction of a legally enforceable obligation and without notice.

(Added to NRS by 1999, 1354)

NRS 41B.420, "Killer who transfers forfeited property, interest or benefit to third person; effect of preemption by federal law," provides as follows:

1. If a killer, for value or otherwise, transfers to a third person any property, interest or benefit forfeited by the killer pursuant to the provisions of this Chapter, the killer is required to recover and transfer the property, interest or benefit to the beneficiary who is entitled to it pursuant to the provisions of this Chapter, or the killer is liable to such beneficiary for the value of the property, interest or benefit.

2. If any federal law preempts any provision of this Chapter requiring a killer to forfeit any property, interest or benefit and the property, interest or benefit accrues or devolves to the killer because of the preemption, the killer is required to transfer the property, interest or benefit to the beneficiary who, in the absence of the preemption, would have been entitled to it pursuant to the provisions of this Chapter, or the killer is liable to such beneficiary for the value of the property, interest or benefit.

Nevada Cases

Absent a statute to the contrary, a murderer may inherit from the victim. In the absence of a statute preventing a murderer from inheriting from his victim (cf. NRS ch. 41B), heir at law may inherit from his victim, because the right of inheritance is a civil right which becomes vested upon the death of the decedent, and RL § 6278 (cf. NRS 212.010) provides that a conviction of crime shall not work a forfeiture of any property or of any right or interest therein.[25]

Daumier: A Criminal Case

A former section of the probate code pre-empted common law. At common law, a person who feloniously and intentionally killed a decedent could still succeed to the estate of the decedent. By enacting former NRS 134.007 of the probate code, legislature chose to pre-empt common law. Any statutory bar to inheritance can only be extended by the legislature, and legislative intent to disinherit must be clearly reflected in a slayer statute and will not be implied. (N.B., NRS 111.067, 134.007 and 688A.420, Nevada's former slayer statutes, were repealed and superseded by the enactment of NRS ch. 41B in 1999.)[26]

A former section of insurance code pre-empted the common law. At common law, a person who feloniously and intentionally killed decedent could not recover as beneficiary of decedent under policy of life insurance. By enacting former NRS 688A.420 of the insurance code, the legislature chose to pre-empt common law. (N.B., NRS 111.067, 134.007 and 688A.420, Nevada's former slayer statutes, were repealed and superseded by the enactment of NRS ch. 41B in 1999.)[27]

An act abolishing the insanity defense and authorizing a plea of "guilty but mentally ill" is unconstitutional. The provisions of Senate Bill No. 314 of the 1995 Legislative Session (see ch. 637, Stats. 1995), which abolished exculpation by reason of insanity and authorized a plea of "guilty but mentally ill" in criminal proceedings, are unconstitutional. "Legal insanity," pursuant to which a person is not culpable for a criminal act if he cannot form the

---

[25] *Wilson v. Randolph*, 50 Nev. 371, 261 Pac. 654 (1927), cited, *In re Estate of Torres*, 61 Nev. 156, at 160, 120 P.2d 816 (1942), *Voorhees v. Spencer*, 89 Nev. 1, at 9, 504 P.2d 1321 (1973), *Salisbury v. List*, 501 F. Supp. 105, at 108 (D. Nev. 1980).

[26] *Holliday v. McMullen*, 104 Nev. 294, 756 P.2d 1179 (1988), cited, *Life Ins. Co. of North America v. Wollett*, 104 Nev. 687, at 691, 766 P.2d 893 (1988), *Sheriff, Washoe County v. Marcus*, 116 Nev. 188, at 192, 995 P.2d 1016 (2000).

[27] *Life Ins. Co. of North America v. Wollett*, 104 Nev. 687, 766 P.2d 893 (1988).

necessary *mens rea*, is a fundamental principle under the due process clauses of both the U.S. and Nevada constitutions (see Nev. Const. art. 1, § 8). Furthermore, although certain provisions of the 1995 act could be construed in a constitutional fashion, they cannot be severed without defeating the whole scope and object of the law, and thus the provisions of Senate Bill No. 314 of the 1995 Legislative Session must be rejected in their entirety. (N.B., this case was decided before the amendment of NRS 41B.070 in 2003.)[28]

      See also NRS 286.669, "Public employees' retirement, murderer ineligible to receive benefits accrued from victim."

Aiding and Abetting

      Under the RESTATEMENT (SECOND) OF TORTS, liability attaches for civil aiding and abetting if the defendant substantially assists or encourages another's conduct in breaching a duty to a third person.[29] California has adopted the common law rule for subjecting a defendant to liability for aiding and abetting a tort. "'Liability may . . . be imposed on one who aids and abets the commission of an intentional tort if the person (a) knows the other's conduct constitutes a breach of duty and gives substantial assistance or encouragement to the other to so act or (b) gives substantial assistance to the other in accomplishing a tortious result and the person's own conduct, separately considered, constitutes a breach of duty to the third person.'"[30]

      A cause of action for aiding and abetting a breach of fiduciary duty requires (1) breach by a fiduciary of a duty owed to a plaintiff, (2) a defendant's knowing participation in the breach, and (3) damages.[31]

Alter Ego

      NRS 78.747, "Liability of stockholder, director or officer for debt or liability of corporation," provides as follows:

> 1. Except as otherwise provided by specific statute, no stockholder, director or officer of a corporation is individually liable for a debt or liability of the corporation, unless the stockholder, director or officer acts as the alter ego of the corporation.
> 2. A stockholder, director or officer acts as the alter ego of a corporation if:
> (a) The corporation is influenced and governed by the stockholder, director or officer;
> (b) There is such unity of interest and ownership that the corporation and the stockholder, director or officer are inseparable from each other; and
> (c) Adherence to the corporate fiction of a separate entity would sanction fraud or promote a manifest injustice.
> 3. The question of whether a stockholder, director or officer acts as the alter ego of a corporation must be determined by the court as a matter of law.[32]

Therefore the requirements for finding alter ego, which must be established by a preponderance of the evidence, are as follows:

> (1) The corporation must be influenced and governed by the person asserted to be its alter ego; (2) There must be such unity of interest and ownership that one is inseparable from the other; and (3) The facts must be such that adherence to the fiction of separate entity would, under the circumstances, sanction a fraud or promote injustice.[33]

It should be noted, however, that " '[t]he corporate cloak is not lightly thrown aside' and that the alter ego doctrine is an exception to the general rule recognizing corporate independence."[34] The Nevada Supreme court "will

---

    [28] *Finger v. State*, 117 Nev. 548, 27 P.3d 66 (2001), *cert. denied*, 122 S.Ct. 1063 (2002), cited, *O'Guinn v. State*, 118 Nev. 849, at 852, 59 P.3d 488 (2002).

    [29] *Dow Chemical Co. v. Mahlum*, 114 Nev. 1468, 970 P.2d 98 (1998).

    [30] *Saunders v. Superior Court*, 27 Cal.Ct.App.4th 832, 846 (Ca. Ct. App.4th 1994); RESTATEMENT (SECOND) OF TORTS, § 876; *Fiol v. Doellstedt*, 50 Cal.Ct.App.4th 1318, 1325-1326 (1996).

    [31] *Holmes v. Young*, 885 P.2d 305 (Colo. Ct.App. 1994).

    [32] See *Lorenz v. Beltio, Ltd.*, 114 Nev. 795, 807, 963 P.2d 488, 496 (1998).

    [33] *Truck Ins. Exch. v. Palmer J. Swanson, Inc.*, 124 Nev. 629, 189 P.3d 656 (2008).

    [34] *LFC Mktg. Group, Inc. v. Loomis*, 116 Nev. 896, 903-04, 8 P.3d 841, 846 (2000) (quoting *Baer v. Amos J. Walker, Inc.*, 85 Nev. 219, 220, 452 P.2d 916, 916 (1969)).

uphold a district court's determination with regard to the alter ego doctrine if substantial evidence exists to support the decision."[35] "[T]he 'essence' of the alter ego doctrine is to 'do justice' whenever it appears that the protections provided by the corporate form are being abused."[36] " 'Reverse piercing' is particularly appropriate . . . when the controlling party uses the controlled entity to hide assets or secretly conduct business to avoid the pre-existing liability of the controlling party."[37]

Nevada allows such piercing "in certain limited circumstances . . . to recover an individual debt from the assets of a corporation determined to be the alter ego of the individual debtor."[38] Piercing the corporate cloak is appropriate, however, only "where the particular facts and equities . . . require that the corporate fiction be ignored so that justice may be promoted."[39] In furtherance of that standard, Nevada courts examine the parties' reasonable expectations and reliance. See id. at 847 (noting that courts must look to the equities of other parties such as shareholders and other creditors to determine whether they might be harmed if the corporate form is ignored.)[40]

In order to apply the alter ego doctrine, the party seeking to pierce the corporate veil must establish by a preponderance of the evidence that (1) the entity was influenced and governed by the person asserted to be its alter ego, (2) such a unity of interest and ownership that one is inseparable from the other, and (3) facts that establish that "adherence to the fiction of a separate entity would, under the circumstances, sanction a fraud or promote injustice."[41]

There is no litmus test for determining when the alter ego doctrine should apply. Rather, the application of the doctrine depends on the circumstances presented in the case.[42] In determining whether a unity of interest exists, courts have considered whether there was a "commingling of funds, undercapitalization, treatment of corporate assets as the individual's own, and failure to observe corporate formalities."[43] Other factors the court may consider in determining whether piercing the corporate veil is proper include the following:

> [C]ommingling of funds and other assets, failure to segregate funds of the separate entities, and the unauthorized diversion of corporate funds or assets to other than corporate uses; the treatment by an individual of the assets of the corporation as his own; the failure to obtain authority to issue stock, or to subscribe to or issue stock; the holding out by an individual that he is personally liable for the debts of the corporation; the failure to maintain minutes or adequate corporate records, and the confusion of the records of the separate entities; identical equitable ownership in the two entities; the identification of the equitable owners thereof with the domination and control of the two entities; identification of the directors and officers of the two entities in the responsible supervision and management; sole ownership of all of the stock in a corporation by one individual or the members of a family; the use of the same office or business location; the employment of the same employees and/or attorney; the failure to capitalize a corporation adequately; the total absence of corporate assets, and undercapitalization; the use of the corporation as a mere shell, instrumentality, or conduit for a single venture or the business of an individual or another corporation; the concealment and misrepresentation of the identity of the responsible ownership, management, and financial interest, or concealment of personal business activities; the disregard of legal formalities and the failure to maintain arm's length relationships among related entities; the use of the corporate entity to procure labor, services, or merchandise for another person or entity; the diversion of assets from a corporation by or to a stockholder or other person or entity, to the detriment of creditors, or the manipulation of assets and liabilities in another; the contracting with another with intent to avoid performance by use of a corporate entity as a shield against personal liability, or the use of a corporation as a subterfuge in illegal transactions; and the formation and use of a corporation to transfer to it the existing liability of another person or entity.[44]

Where it is clearly shown, undercapitalization is an important factor in determining whether the alter ego

---

[35] Id.

[36] LFC Mktg. Group, Inc. v. Loomis, 116 Nev. 896, 903-04, 8 P.3d 841, 846 (2000).

[37] Id.

[38] Id.

[39] Id. at 846.

[40] In re Twin Lakes Village, Inc., 2 B.R. 532, 542 (Bankr. D. Nev. 1980) (applying the reasonable reliance standard to a judgment creditor's quest to pierce the corporate veil).

[41] McCleary Cattle, 73 Nev. at 282, 317 P.2d at 959.

[42] Polaris Industrial Corp. v. Kaplan, 103 Nev. 598, 747 P.2d 884 (1987).

[43] Lorenz v. Beltio, Ltd., 114 Nev. 795, 808, 963, P.2d 488, 497 (1998).

[44] North Arlington Medical Bldg., Inc. v. Sanchez Const. Co., 86 Nev. 515, 523 n.3, 471 P.2d 240, 245 n.3 (1970).

doctrine is appropriate.[45] Where there is no resulting fraud or injustice, undercapitalization is "not an absolute ground for disregarding the corporate entity."[46]

A mere showing that one entity is owned by another entity, or that two entities share interlocking directors or officers "is insufficient to support a finding of alter ego."[47] Further, a simple showing of a mutuality of interest is insufficient to support the application of the alter ego doctrine absent "evidence of commingling of funds or property interests, or of prejudice to creditors."[48] Nevada courts also focus on the reasonable reliance of the person seeking to pierce the corporate veil on the alleged alter egos when determining whether adherence to the corporate fiction would sanction a fraud or promote injustice.[49] Further, "simply not being paid . . . is not, in and of itself sufficient injustice" to justify piercing the corporate veil.[50] However, the arbitrary and unprincipled use of corporate funds for personal use resulting in nonpayment is sufficient injustice to support a finding of injustice.[51]

A defendant member or manager of a limited liability company may argue that the alter ego doctrine does not apply to limited liability companies. Under NRS 86.371, members and managers of a Nevada limited liability company are generally not liable for the debts and liabilities of the company. The defendants may find further support for this argument based on amendments to Nevada's corporation statutory law. In 2001, Nevada statutory law formally codified the alter ego doctrine as it relates to corporations.[52] While the alter ego doctrine was codified as to corporations, the doctrine was not codified as to limited liability companies. The fact that the alter ego doctrine was not codified as to limited liability companies "arguably creates a negative inference that there is no alter ego exception for limited liability companies."[53] The Nevada Supreme Court has not considered this issue, but the Bankruptcy Court for the District of Nevada has considered the issue, and the reasoning contained in its decision is persuasive.[54]

In that case, the Bankruptcy Court noted that "[t]he varieties of fraud and injustice that the alter ego doctrine was designed to redress can be equally exploited through limited liability companies."[55] Further, the court noted that in codifying the alter ego doctrine in relation to corporations, the legislative history behind NRS 78.747 "indicates that legislators were interested in increasing corporate franchise fees, and were prepared to codify corporate alter ego liability as a price for that increase."[56] Against this legislative background, the court determined that the common law alter ego doctrine would still apply to limited liability companies.[57] But the court noted that some jurisdictions apply the factors to limited liability companies in the same manner as corporations, but that, in the context of limited liability companies, the principles used to apply corporate alter ego may apply with different weight due to the fact that limited liability companies are permitted by statute to have its members manage the company.[58]

Nevada limited liability companies are often managed and owned by the same people, and that, in and of itself, horizontally and vertically integrated companies do not necessarily establish that each is the alter ego of the other.[59] Just the same, based on the persuasive reasoning in *In Re Giampietro*,[60] a plaintiff may submit that the alter ego doctrine applies to Nevada limited liability companies.

The doctrine of "piercing the corporate veil" is an equitable remedy which allows a court to disregard the separate and distinct nature of a corporation or LLC in order to hold the shareholders of that corporation or LLC directly liable for the debts of that corporation or LLC. Claims brought under the doctrine of piercing the corporate veil are often referred to as "alter ego" claims. These claims can have either a consensual basis, such as the claims of the corporation or

---

[45] *Rowland v. Lepire*, 99 Nev. 308, 662 P.2d 1332 (1983).

[46] *Id.*

[47] *Bonanza Hotel Gift Shop, Inc. v. Bonanza No. 2*, 95 Nev. 463, 466, 596 P.2d 227, 229 (1979) (citing *Lipshie v. Tracy Investment Co.*, 93 Nev. 370, 566 P.2d 819 (1977)).

[48] *Id.* (*citing First Nat. Bank v. Walton*, 262 P. 984 (Wash. 1928)).

[49] *See In Re Giampietro*, 317 B.R. 841 (Bkrtcy. D. Nev. 2004), see also *Matter of Twin Lakes Village, Inc.*, 2 B.R. 532 (Bkrtcy. D.Nev. 1980); see also *Lipshie v. Tracy Investment Co.*, 93 Nev. 370, 379, 566 P.2d 819, 824-25 (1977).

[50] *In Re Giampietro*, 317 B.R. at 853 (citing *Twin Lakes, Inc.*, 2 B.R. 532, 542 (Bkrtcy.D. Nev. 1980); *Lipshie*, 93 Nev. at 378, 566 P.2d at 824).

[51] See *Polaris Industrial Corp. v. Kaplan*, 103 Nev. at 603, 747 P.2d at 888 (1987).

[52] See NRS 78.747, *In Re Giampietro*, 317 B.R. 841 (Bkrtcy.D. Nev. 2004).

[53] *In Re Giampietro*, 317 B.R. at 846.

[54] *Id.*

[55] *Id.*

[56] *Id.* at 847.

[57] *Id.* at 848.

[58] *Id.* at 848 n. 9-10.

[59] See *Bonanza Hotel Gift Shop, Inc. v. Bonanza No. 2*, 95 Nev. 463, 596 P.2d 227 (1979).

[60] *In Re Giampietro*, 317 B.R. 841 (Bkrtcy. D. Nev. 2004).

LLC's trade creditors or they can be of a nonconsensual nature, such as the claim held by a tort victim injured by a product manufactured by the corporation or LLC. Alter ego claims take on special significance when the corporation or LLC liable for a debt has become insolvent or has insufficient assets to pay the debt. This is especially so in the case of a closed corporation or LLC where there are very few shareholders. In these cases, an alter ego claim may represent a plaintiff's only chance to recover on a debt based on the plaintiff's transaction with the corporation or LLC.

Americans with Disabilities Act (ADA)

In enacting the ADA, Congress declared as follows:

It is the purpose of this chapter—

(1) to provide a clear and comprehensive national mandate for the elimination of discrimination against individuals with disabilities;

(2) to provide clear, strong, consistent, enforceable standards addressing discrimination against individuals with disabilities;

(3) to ensure that the Federal Government plays a central role in enforcing the standards established in this chapter on behalf of individuals with disabilities; and

(4) to invoke the sweep of congressional authority, including the power to enforce the fourteenth amendment and to regulate commerce, in order to address the major areas of discrimination faced day-to-day by people with disabilities.[61]

The ADA's goal is twofold.[62] Congress intended not only to remedy discrimination against disabled individuals but to prevent it, too. "To effectuate its sweeping purpose," the ADA has a comprehensive scope covering discriminatory practices that disabled persons face "in major areas of public life," including access to public accommodations.[63] But Congress was not simply concerned with intentional discrimination when it enacted the ADA.[64] It also specifically designed the provisions of the ADA to prevent discrimination stemming from neglect and indifference. As such, regardless of the intent of an owner of a place of public accommodation, such as when a facility is not constructed to be readily accessible to individuals with disabilities, the owner is liable for unlawful discrimination.[65] Notably, however, with the exception of landlord-tenant relationships,[66] the ADA and its regulations contain no provisions that permit indemnification or the allocation of liability among the various entities that are subject to the ADA.

Arrest and Bail

NRS 31.470, "Arrest in civil cases," provides as follows: "No person shall be arrested in a civil action except as prescribed by this Chapter." The writ of *ne exeat*[67] was abolished by the statutory substitution of civil arrest. Under code provisions similar to NCL § 8643 (cf. NRS 31.470), which provides that no person shall be arrested in a civil action except as prescribed by an act relating to arrest and bail in civil actions, it has uniformly been held that a common-law writ of *ne exeat* has been abolished by statutory substitution.[68]

---

[61] 42 U.S.C. § 12101(b) (2006).

[62] *Rolf Jensen & Associates v. Dist. Ct.*, 128 Nev. Adv. Op. No. 42 (August 9, 2012).

[63] *PGA Tour, Inc. v. Martin*, 532 U.S. 661, 675 (2001).

[64] *See id.*

[65] 42 U.S.C. § 12183(a)(1) (2006) (explaining that "discrimination" for purposes of the ADA includes "a failure to design and construct facilities for first occupancy . . . that are readily accessible to and usable by individuals with disabilities"); see 42 U.S.C § 12182(a) (2006) (prohibiting the discrimination against disabled individuals "in the full and equal enjoyment of . . . facilities . . . or accommodations of any place of public accommodation by any person who owns . . . or operates a place of public accommodation");

[66] 28 C.F.R. § 36.201(b) (2010).

[67] *Ne exeat republica*, also known by its shortened form of *ne exeat*, is or was a chancery writ in common law countries, a writ in equity, issued under a court's equitable jurisdiction. The writ's name comes from the Latin phrase for "let him not exit the republic." No longer widely used in many jurisdictions, the aim of the writ is to prevent the removal of a party or of disputed property from a court's jurisdiction. In the United States it is still provided for in the Internal Revenue Code at 26 U.S.C. § 7402(a), and is also used in child custody cases to refer to a parent's right to control the child's place of residence. *Black's Law Dictionary* 1054 (7th ed. 1999).

[68] *Summers v. District Court*, 68 Nev. 99, 227 P.2d 201 (1951).

NRS 31.480, "Cases in which defendant may be arrested," provides as follows:

The defendant may be arrested, as hereinafter prescribed, in the following cases:

1. In an action for the recovery of money or damages on a cause of action arising upon contract, express or implied, when the defendant is about to depart from the State with intent to defraud the defendant's creditors, or when the action is for libel or slander.

2. In an action for a fine or penalty, or for money or property embezzled, or fraudulently misapplied or converted to his or her own use by a public officer, or an officer of a corporation, or an attorney, factor, broker, agent or clerk in the course of his or her employment as such or by any other person in a fiduciary capacity, or for misconduct or neglect in office, or in professional employment, or for a willful violation of duty.

3. In an action to recover the possession of personal property unjustly detained, when the property, or any part thereof, has been concealed, removed, or disposed of so that it cannot be found or taken by the sheriff.

4. When the defendant has been guilty of a fraud in contracting the debt or incurring the obligation for which the action is brought, or in concealing or disposing of the property, for the taking, detention or conversion of which the action is brought.

5. When the defendant has removed or disposed of the defendant's property, or is about to do so, with intent to defraud the defendant's creditors.

A defendant's previous voluntary surrender does not prevent a subsequent civil arrest. The fact that the defendant voluntarily surrendered himself into custody before any order for his arrest and detention was entered and thereafter voluntarily departed from custody after the plaintiff had stated to the sheriff that he did not demand arrest and detention did not, under the provisions of B §§ 416, 424 and 1143 (cf. NRS 31.740, NRS 31.820 and NRS 31.580), prevent his subsequent arrest and detention under B § 1135 (cf. NRS 31.480).[69]

A civil arrest applies in an action on a tort judgment. The provisions of B § 1135 (cf. NRS 31.480), authorizing the arrest and detention of a defendant who has disposed of his property in an effort to defraud creditors, are not confined in their application to cases arising from a contract, and do apply in an action on a tort judgment. Such provisions do not conflict with the provisions of Nev. Const. art. 1, § 14.[70]

Civil arrest is authorized for costs. The arrest and detention of a defendant under B § 1135 (cf. NRS 31.480) is authorized for costs incurred in an action on a judgment, as well as for the amount of the original judgment.[71]

A civil arrest is a coercive means to enforce the collection of a judgment. The arrest and detention of a defendant for attempting to defraud creditors, which is authorized by B § 1135 (cf. NRS 31.480) is a coercive means, given by statute and sanctioned by the constitution, to enforce the collection of a judgment.[72] A civil arrest applies to certain acts performed outside the state. The fact that some of the acts whereby a defendant disposed of his property with the intent to defraud his creditors were committed outside the state during the temporary absence of the defendant did not prevent his arrest and detention under B § 1135 (cf. NRS 31.480).[73]

The court may order a civil arrest for recently discovered acts committed before the judgment. The arrest and detention of a defendant under B § 1135 (cf. NRS 31.480) is authorized in an action on a judgment as well as in an original action on an obligation. The fact that the fraudulent acts on which the arrest is based were committed before the rendition of the judgment in the first action does not divest the court of the authority to cause the arrest in the second action where the commission of fraudulent acts was not known until after the entry of the judgment in the first action.[74]

An order for arrest may be based on verified complaint and affidavit. Under RL §§ 5088 and 5090 (cf. NRS 31.480 and 31.500), providing for the arrest of a defendant in a civil action if he is about to depart the state or dispose of or remove his property with the intent to defraud creditors, the order of arrest can be based both upon a verified complaint and an affidavit for arrest, and if both taken together are sufficient to justify the order, it is not improperly issued.[75]

NRS 31.490, "Order for arrest," provides as follows: "An order for the arrest of the defendant shall be obtained from a judge of the court in which the action is brought."

---

[69] *Ex parte Bergman*, 18 Nev. 331, 4 Pac. 209 (1884).
[70] *Id.*
[71] *Id.*
[72] *Id.*
[73] *Id.*
[74] *Id.*
[75] *In re Boyd*, 36 Nev. 162, 134 Pac. 455 (1913).

NRS 31.500, "Order for arrest made when plaintiff's affidavit shows a sufficient cause; requisites and filing of affidavit," provides as follows:

> The order may be made whenever it shall appear to the judge, by the affidavit of the plaintiff or some other person, that a sufficient cause of action exists, and the case is one of those mentioned in NRS 31.480. The affidavit shall be either positive or upon information and belief; and when upon information and belief it shall state the facts upon which the information and belief are founded. If an order of arrest be made, the affidavit shall be filed with the clerk of the court.

The order for arrest may be based upon both a verified complaint and an affidavit. Under RL §§ 5088 and 5090 (cf. NRS 31.480 and 31.500), providing for the arrest of a defendant in a civil action if he is about to depart the state or dispose of or remove his property with the intent to defraud creditors, the order of arrest can be based both upon a verified complaint and an affidavit for arrest, and if both taken together are sufficient to justify the order, it is not improperly issued.[76]

Honoré Daumier, "The Two Lawyers"

NRS 31.510, "Undertaking from plaintiff," provides as follows:

> Before making the order the judge shall require a written undertaking, payable in lawful money of the United States, on the part of the plaintiff, with sureties, to the effect that if the defendant recover judgment, the plaintiff will pay all costs and charges that may be awarded to the defendant, and all damages which the defendant may sustain by reason of the arrest, not exceeding the sum specified in the undertaking, which shall be at least $500. Each of the sureties shall annex to the undertaking an affidavit that the surety is a resident and householder or freeholder within the State, and worth double the sum specified in the undertaking over and above all the surety's debts and liabilities, exclusive of property exempt from execution. The undertaking shall be filed with the clerk of the court.

NRS 31.520, "Order and arrest; return of order," provides as follows:

> The order may be made to accompany the summons, or any time afterwards before judgment. It shall require the sheriff of the county where the defendant may be found forthwith to arrest the defendant and hold the defendant to bail in a specified sum, naming the money or currency in which it is payable, and to return the order at a time therein mentioned to the clerk of the court in which the action is pending.

NRS 31.530, "Delivery of affidavit and order to sheriff and defendant," provides as follows:

> The order of arrest, with a copy of the affidavit upon which it is made, shall be delivered to the sheriff, who, upon arresting the defendant, shall deliver to the defendant the copy of the affidavit, and also, if desired, a copy of the order of arrest.

NRS 31.540, "Arrest of defendant," provides as follows: "The sheriff shall execute the order by arresting the defendant and keeping the defendant in custody until discharged by law."

---

[76] *Id.*

NRS 31.550, "Defendant to be discharged on bail or deposit," provides as follows: "The defendant, at any time before execution, shall be discharged from the arrest either upon giving bail or upon depositing the amount mentioned in the order of arrest in the money or currency therein named, as provided in this Chapter."

NRS 31.560, "Defendant may give bail," provides as follows:

The defendant may give bail by causing a written undertaking, payable in the money of the contract (if any be named), and in other cases as directed by the judge, to be executed by two or more sufficient sureties, stating their places of residence and occupations, to the effect that they are bound in the amount mentioned in the order of arrest; that the defendant shall at all times render himself or herself amenable to the process of the court during the pendency of the action, and to such as may be issued to enforce the judgment therein; or that they will pay to the plaintiff the amount of any judgment which may be recovered in the action.

NRS 31.570, "Bail may surrender defendant," provides as follows: "At any time before judgment, or within 10 days thereafter, the bail may surrender the defendant in their exoneration; or the defendant may surrender to the sheriff of the county where the defendant was arrested."

NRS 31.580, "Arrest, delivery and surrender of defendant by bail; exoneration of bail," provides as follows:

For the purpose of surrendering the defendant, the bail at any time or place before they are finally charged may themselves arrest the defendant; or by a written authority, endorsed on a certified copy of the undertaking, may empower the sheriff to do so. Upon the arrest of the defendant by the sheriff, or upon delivery of the defendant to the sheriff by the bail, or upon the defendant's own surrender, the bail shall be exonerated; provided, such arrest, delivery or surrender shall take place before the expiration of 10 days after judgment; but if such arrest, delivery or surrender be not made within 10 days after judgment, the bail shall be finally charged on their undertaking, and be bound to pay the amount of the judgment within 10 days thereafter.

A previous voluntary surrender does not prevent subsequent civil arrest. The fact that the defendant voluntarily surrendered himself into custody before any order for his arrest and detention was entered and thereafter voluntarily departed from custody after the plaintiff had stated to the sheriff that he did not demand arrest and detention did not, under the provisions of B §§ 416, 424 and 1143 (cf. NRS 31.740, NRS 31.820 and NRS 31.580), prevent his subsequent arrest and detention under B § 1135 (cf. NRS 31.480).[77]

NRS 31.590, "Action against bail," provides as follows: "If the bail neglect or refuse to pay the judgment within 10 days after they are finally charged, an action may be commenced against bail for the amount of the original judgment."

NRS 31.600, "Bail exonerated by death, imprisonment or discharge of defendant," provides as follows: "The bail shall also be exonerated by the death of the defendant, or by the defendant's imprisonment in a state prison, or by the defendant's legal discharge from the obligation to render himself or herself amenable to the process."

NRS 31.610, "Return of order; plaintiff may except to bail," provides as follows:

Within the time limited for that purpose, the sheriff shall file the order of arrest in the office of the clerk of the court in which the action is pending, with the sheriff's return endorsed thereon, together with a copy of the undertaking of the bail. The sheriff shall retain the original undertaking in the sheriff's possession until filed, as herein provided. The plaintiff, within 10 days thereafter, may serve upon the sheriff a notice that the plaintiff does not accept the bail, or the plaintiff shall be deemed to have accepted them, and the sheriff shall be exonerated from liability. If no notice be served within 10 days, the original undertaking shall be filed with the clerk of the court.

NRS 31.620, "Notice of justification of bail," provides as follows:

---

[77] *Ex parte Bergman*, 18 Nev. 331, 4 Pac. 209 (1884).

Within 5 days after the receipt of notice, the sheriff or defendant may give to the plaintiff or the plaintiff's attorney notice of the justification of the same, or other bail (specifying the places of residence and occupations of the latter), before the judge of the court, or clerk, at a specified time and place; the time to be not less than 5 nor more than 10 days thereafter, except by consent of parties. In case other bail be given, there shall be a new undertaking.

NRS 31.630, "Qualifications of bail," provides as follows:

The qualifications of bail shall be as follows:
1. Each of them shall be a resident and householder, or freeholder, within the county.
2. Each shall be worth the amount specified in the order of arrest, or the amount to which the order is reduced, as provided in this Chapter, over and above all debts and liabilities of the bail, exclusive of property exempt from execution; but the judge, or clerk, on justification, may allow more than two sureties to justify severally in amounts less than that expressed in the order, if the whole justification be equivalent to that of two sufficient bail.

NRS 31.640, "Examination of bail," provides as follows:
For the purpose of justification, each of the bail shall attend before the judge, or clerk, at the time and place mentioned in the notice, and may be examined on oath, on the part of the plaintiff, touching the bail's sufficiency, in such manner as the judge, or clerk, in the exercise of discretion may think proper. The examination shall be reduced to writing, and subscribed by the bail, if required by the plaintiff.

NRS 31.650, "Allowance of bail exonerates sheriff," provides as follows:

If the judge, or clerk, find the bail sufficient, the judge or clerk shall annex the examination to the undertaking, endorse the judge's or clerk's allowance thereon, and cause them to be filed, and the sheriff shall thereupon be exonerated from liability.

NRS 31.660, "Deposit by defendant in lieu of bail," provides as follows:

.   The defendant may, at the time of the defendant's arrest, instead of giving bail, deposit with the sheriff the amount mentioned in the order. In case the amount of the bail be reduced, as provided in this Chapter, the defendant may deposit such amount instead of giving bail. In either case the sheriff shall give the defendant a certificate of the deposit made, and the defendant shall be discharged from custody.

NRS 31.670, "Sheriff must pay deposit into court," provides as follows:

The sheriff shall, immediately after the deposit, pay the same into court, and take from the clerk receiving the same two certificates of such payment; the one of which the sheriff shall deliver or transmit to the plaintiff or the plaintiff's attorney and the other to the defendant. For any default in making such payment, the same proceedings may be had on the official bond of the sheriff to collect the sum deposited as in other cases of delinquency.

NRS 31.680, "Undertaking may be substituted for deposit," provides as follows:

If the money be deposited, as provided in NRS 31.660 and 31.670, bail may be given and may justify upon notice at any time before judgment; and on the filing of the undertaking and justification with the clerk the money deposited shall be refunded by such clerk to the defendant.

NRS 31.690, "Disposition of deposit," provides as follows:

Where money shall have been deposited, if it remain on deposit at the time of a recovery of a judgment in favor of the plaintiff, the clerk shall, under the direction of the court, apply the same in satisfaction thereof, and after satisfying the judgment shall refund the surplus, if any, to the defendant. If the judgment be in favor of the defendant, the clerk shall, under like direction of the court, refund to the defendant the whole sum deposited and remaining unapplied.

NRS 31.700, "Liability of sheriff for escape or rescue," provides as follows:

> If, after being arrested, the defendant escape or be rescued, the sheriff shall be liable as bail; but the sheriff may discharge himself or herself from such liability by the giving and justification of bail at any time before judgment.

NRS 31.710, "Recovery on official bond of sheriff," provides as follows:

> If a judgment be recovered against the sheriff, upon the sheriff's liability as bail, and an execution thereon be returned unsatisfied, in whole or in part, the same proceedings may be had on the sheriff's official bond for the recovery of the whole or any deficiency, as in other cases of delinquency.

NRS 31.720, "Defendant may move to vacate arrest or reduce bail; hearing," provides as follows:

> A defendant arrested may, at any time before the justification of bail, apply to the judge who made the order, or the court in which the action is pending, upon reasonable notice to the plaintiff, to vacate the order of arrest or to reduce the amount of bail. If the application be made upon affidavits on the part of the defendant, but not otherwise, the plaintiff may oppose the same by affidavits or other proofs in addition to those on which the order of arrest was made.

Grounds for motion to vacate arrest. Under RL §§ 5112 and 5113 (cf. NRS 31.720 and 31.730), providing that a defendant arrested in a civil action may apply to the court to vacate an order of arrest, if the only ground of the motion to vacate is because the affidavit upon which the order for arrest was based was insufficient, the court will look only to the affidavit, and if insufficient, the defendant will be discharged. If the motion contains a further ground that the facts do not justify his arrest, he will not be discharged unless all evidence at the hearing so warrants.[78]

NRS 31.730, "Vacation of order of arrest and reduction of bail," provides as follows:

> If, upon such application, it shall satisfactorily appear that there was not sufficient cause for the arrest, the order shall be vacated, or if it satisfactorily appear that the bail was fixed too high, the amount shall be reduced.

Grounds for motion to vacate arrest. Under RL §§ 5112 and 5113 (cf. NRS 31.720 and 31.730), providing that a defendant arrested in a civil action may apply to the court to vacate an order of arrest, if the only ground of the motion to vacate is because the affidavit upon which the order for arrest was based was insufficient, the court will look only to the affidavit, and if insufficient, the defendant will be discharged. If the motion contains a further ground that the facts do not justify his arrest, he will not be discharged unless all evidence at the hearing so warrants.[79]

Assault

The tort of assault is defined as the willful threat or attempt to harm or touch another offensively, which threat or attempt reasonably places the other in fear of such contact. The threat or attempt must be coupled with a definitive act by one who has the apparent ability to do the harm or to commit the offensive touching. An essential element of the tort of assault is that the actor knew with substantial certainty that his or her act would bring about harmful or offensive contact.[80]

"Assault and battery" is a state law tort claim.[81] An "assault" in tort law is the threat or use of force on another that causes that person to have a reasonable apprehension of imminent harmful or offensive contact; the act of putting another person in reasonable fear or apprehension of an immediate battery by means of an act amounting to an attempt or threat to commit a battery.[82] A "battery" in tort law is an intentional and offensive touching of another without lawful justification.[83] A plaintiff is entitled to damages when he or she suffers the trauma of apprehension.[84]

---

[78] *In re Boyd*, 36 Nev. 162, 134 Pac. 455 (1913).

[79] *Id.*

[80] *Smith v. John Deere Co.*, 83 Ohio App.3d 398, 614 N.E.2d 1148, 1154 (Ohio 1993).

[81] See *Smith's Food & Drug Cntrs. v. Bellegarde*, 114 Nev. 602, 605, 958 P.2d 1208, (1998), overruled on other grounds by *Countrywide Home Loans v. Thitchener*, 124 Nev. 725, 192 P.3d 243 (2008).

[82] *Black's Law Dictionary* 109 (7th ed. 1999).

[83] *Id.*

Assumpsit ("he has undertaken," from Latin, *assumere*) is a form of action at common law for the recovery of damages caused by the breach or non-performance of a simple contract, either express or implied, and whether made orally or in writing.[85] Assumpsit was the word a plaintiff used in pleadings to set forth the defendant's undertaking or promise, hence the name of the action. Claims in actions of assumpsit were ordinarily divided into the following classes:

      (a) common or *indebitatus* assumpsit,[86] brought usually on an implied promise, and

      (b) special assumpsit, founded on an express promise.[87]

The actual "causes of action" that could be pleaded through assumpsit were known as the "common counts," and could be pleaded in a terse, compact style.

Daumier: The Pleading Lawyer

The development of the action of assumpsit in the fourteenth century gave rise to the enforceability of the oral promise.[88] Although parties to an action could not be witnesses, the alleged promise could be enforced on the strength of oral testimony of others not concerned with the litigation. To maintain the action of assumpsit for money had and received, the defendant must have made an express or implied promise to pay the plaintiff.[89] An action of assumpsit is founded on a contract relation between the parties—a promise to pay, either express or implied.[90]

The Common Law Procedure Act of 1852 abolished the common law forms of action in England and Wales. Furthermore, assumpsit as a form of action became obsolete in the United Kingdom after the Judicature Acts of 1873 and 1875 were passed. In the United States, assumpsit, like the other forms of action, became obsolete in the federal courts after the adoption of the Federal Rules of Civil Procedure in 1938. Thirty-five states have moved to rules similar to the Federal Rules of Civil Procedure, which have replaced the various forms of action with the civil action. However, many states continue to recognize assumpsit as a common law or statutory cause of action or allow the use of the old "common counts" as causes of action. For example, California has a special "common counts" cause of action form (to be attached to an optional form complaint) based directly on the old common counts that were pleaded in assumpsit.[91]

See "Money Had and Received."

---

[84] See *State v. Eaton*, 101 Nev. 705, 713, 710 P.2d 1370, 1375 (1985) (quoting *Dillon v. Legg*, 68 Cal.2d 728, 441 P.2d at 915) (Cal. 2008).

[85] This article incorporates text from a publication now in the public domain: Chisholm, Hugh, ed., *Encyclopædia Britannica* (11th ed.). Cambridge University Press (1911).

[86] The Latin phrase means "being indebted he promised," or more literally "he undertook, or he assumed the duty [to pay]."

[87] See Lionel D. Smith, *et al., The Law of Restitution in Canada: Cases, Notes, and Materials*, pp. 72-75 (Emond Montgomery Publications 2004) (avail. Google Books).

[88] *Azevedo v. Minister*, 86 Nev. 576, 578, 471 P.2d 661 (1970).

[89] *Humboldt County v. Lander County*, 24 Nev. 461, 463 (1899).

[90] *Horgan v. Indart*, 41 Nev. 228, 229-30, 168 Pac. 953 (1917).

[91] Form PLD-C-001(2), "Cause of Action-Common Counts," Judicial Council of California (Rev. Jan. 1, 2009); www.courts.ca.gov/documents/pldc0012.pdf.

Pershing County Courthouse

Attachment

The statutes for attachment are set forth in NRS Chapter 31.

NRS 31.010, "Application to court for writ of attachment: Timing; requirements when Department of Taxation has taken over management of local government," provides as follows:

> 1. Except as otherwise provided in subsection 2, the plaintiff at the time of issuing the summons, or at any time thereafter, may apply to the court for an order directing the clerk to issue a writ of attachment and thereby cause the property of the defendant to be attached as security for the satisfaction of any judgment that may be recovered, unless the defendant gives security to pay such judgment as provided in this Chapter.
>
> 2. If the Department of Taxation has taken over the management of a local government pursuant to the provisions of NRS 354.686, and if a plaintiff is allowed by law to apply to a court for an order directing the clerk to issue a writ of attachment, the plaintiff must comply with the applicable provisions of NRS 354.701 before applying for such an order.

Garnishment is treated as the attachment of money and credits. Because §§ 123-144, ch. 112, Stats. 1869 (cf. NRS 31.010 and 31.240), treated garnishment as the attachment of moneys and credits and made no distinction as to the kind of property which might be released from attachment by giving of undertaking by the defendant, an objection on appeal from an order discharging a writ of attachment that only the property in the hands of the sheriff could be released, but not moneys garnished and remaining in a bank, was without merit.[92]

The proceedings for an attachment are statutory. Attachment proceedings are purely statutory, and to ascertain the right of attachment, recourse must be had to NCL §§ 8703 and 8704 (cf. NRS 31.010 *et seq.*), providing procedures to authorize the issuance of a writ.[93]

The plain language of the section allows a writ of attachment to be used postjudgment. Although a writ of attachment is used typically as a prejudgment remedy, and although some language set forth in NRS 31.010 suggests that a writ of attachment applies only with respect to the satisfaction of a judgment which "may be" recovered, other, more specific language in NRS 31.010 states that a plaintiff may, at the time of issuing the summons "or at any time thereafter," apply for an order directing the issuance of a writ of attachment. Thus, the plain language of NRS 31.010 allows a writ of attachment to be used postjudgment.[94]

The sheriff may require indemnity from a plaintiff. Although an attachment creates a lien on the property seized, and, under § 123, ch. 112, Stats. 1869 (cf. NRS 31.010 *et seq.*), property is thereafter held as security for any judgment a plaintiff may recover, a sheriff may give up property and abandon the levy if a plaintiff refuses to indemnify the sheriff upon his reasonable demand, where the ownership of the property is doubtful.[95]

The summons must be issued on a nonjudicial day. Under B § 955 (cf. NRS 1.130), which provides that a writ of attachment may be issued on a nonjudicial day if the plaintiff makes an affidavit stating that a lien cannot be obtained unless a writ is issued immediately, where a person makes an affidavit without having previously commenced an action,

---

[92] *Goldfield-Mohawk Mining Co. v. Frances-Mohawk Mining & Leasing Co.*, 31 Nev. 348, 102 Pac. 963 (1909).

[93] *Johnson v. Lee Fong*, 62 Nev. 249, 147 P.2d 884 (1944).

[94] *LFC Mktg. Group, Inc. v. Loomis*, 116 Nev. 896, 8 P.3d 841 (2000).

[95] *Gaudette v. Roeder*, 13 Nev. 341 (1878).

a complaint not only may, but must, be filed and a summons issued on a nonjudicial day on which the writ is issued, because B § 1184 *et seq.* (cf. NRS 31.010 *et seq.*), relating to attachments, provides that an action must be commenced or pending to authorize the issuance of a writ of attachment.[96]

The action must be commenced or pending at the time a writ of attachment is issued. B § 955 (cf. NRS 1.130[97]), which provides that a writ of attachment may be issued on Sunday or a holiday, must be construed in connection with B 1184 *et seq.* (cf. NRS 31.010 *et seq.*), relating to attachments, which requires that an action must be commenced or pending at the time a writ of attachment is issued, and when so construed it neither authorizes the issuance of a writ first and commencement of action afterward, nor limits the issuance of a writ on a nonjudicial day to cases in which an action has already been commenced.[98]

The remedy of attachment is statutory. In the examination of an applicant for admission to the bar, a question on attachment could not be answered without a reference to statutes, because this remedy as recognized in the western states was unknown to common law and depends for effectiveness entirely on compliance with the legislative requirements.[99]

Equitable relief is not appropriate if a bond affords sufficient protection. In an action by the maker of a note for adjudication of the balance due, where an action on the note was pending and attachment of the maker's property was threatened, and the plaintiff did not allege an inability to pay the installments due and had not tendered payment, NRS 31.030 requiring a bond of the plaintiff on attachment, and NRS 31.040 and 31.180 providing for the prevention of attachment and release of property on the giving of a bond by the defendant, afforded sufficient protection, and the court was not justified in substituting equitable relief under NRS 33.010 providing for the granting of injunctions. (See also NRS 31.010.)[100]

NRS 31.013, "Issuance of writ of attachment after notice and hearing," provides as follows:

> The court may, after notice and hearing, order the clerk to issue a writ of attachment in the following cases:
> 1. In an action upon a judgment or upon a contract, express or implied, for the direct payment of money:
> (a) If the judgment is not a lien upon or the contract is not secured by mortgage, lien or pledge upon real or personal property situated in this state; or
> (b) If such lien or security has, without any act of the plaintiff or the person to whom the security was given, become valueless or insufficient in value to secure the sum due the plaintiff, in which case the attachment shall issue only for the unsecured portion of the amount due the plaintiff, which is equal to the excess of the amount due the plaintiff above the value of the security.
> 2. In any case where the attachment of the property of the defendant is allowed pursuant to this Chapter or other provision of law.
> 3. In any other case where the court finds that extraordinary circumstances exist which will make it improbable for the plaintiff to reach the property of the defendant by execution after the judgment has been entered.

---

[96] *Levy v. Elliott*, 14 Nev. 435 (1880).

[97] NRS 1.130, "Nonjudicial days; transaction of judicial business," provides in relevant part as follows:
> 1. No court except a justice court or a municipal court shall be opened nor shall any judicial business be transacted except by a justice court or municipal court on Sunday, or on any day declared to be a legal holiday according to the provisions of NRS 236.015, except for the following purposes:
> . . .
> (e) For the issue of a writ of attachment, which may be issued on each and all of the days above enumerated upon the plaintiff, or some person on behalf of the plaintiff, setting forth in the affidavit required by law for obtaining the writ the additional averment as follows:
> That the affiant has good reason to believe, and does believe, that it will be too late for the purpose of acquiring a lien by the writ to wait until subsequent day for the issuance of the same.

[98] *Id.*

[99] See NRS 31.010; *In re Loer*, 68 Nev. 1, 226 P.2d 272 (1951).

[100] *Aronoff v. Katleman*, 75 Nev. 424, 345 P.2d 221 (1959), cited, *Cooper v. Liebert*, 81 Nev. 341, at 344, 402 P.2d 989 (1965).

The writ may be issued only for the amount to which the plaintiff is entitled. In an action to recover a share of the profits from land development and housing construction, where under 2 of 10 situations grouped under the first cause of action the plaintiff was entitled to receive direct payment of money as required by former provisions of NRS 31.010 (cf. NRS 31.013), but under the remaining situations of the first cause of action and under the second cause of action, he was not, but a writ of attachment was issued for the entire amount claimed, the writ should have been discharged.[101]

Second trust deeds are not equivalent to money. In an action to recover a share of the profits from land development and housing construction, where the affidavit for attachment recited that the action was based on a contract for direct payment of money but the contract actually provided for payment of this share either in money or in second trust deeds, these deeds were not equivalent to money, as required by former provisions of NRS 31.010 (cf. NRS 31.013) to justify the attachment, and a writ of attachment should have been discharged.[102]

It is not sufficient for an attachment that the amount of damages can be computed. Under former provisions of NRS 31.010 (cf. NRS 31.013) that an attachment may be had in an action based on a contract for direct payment of money, it is not sufficient that the amount of damages can be computed or ascertained.[103]

Plaintiff must establish the lack of value of a lien or security. Before an action on a note with ancillary attachment was permitted as provided in former provisions of NRS 31.010 (cf. NRS 31.013), the holder of the note secured by a trust deed was required under NRS 40.430 to exhaust the security by sale under the trust deed or show that the security, without fault of the beneficiary, had become valueless. The creditor's affidavit of value did not establish such lack of value.[104]

An opinion of value must be shown by a qualified witness. On an appeal from an order discharging an attachment in a judicial foreclosure action under NRS 40.430, where the affidavit of attachment stated only the sum by which counsel believed indebtedness exceeded the value of the security, the order of a lower court was affirmed, because the affidavit was merely conclusory and did not show the value of the security was insufficient to secure the sum due as required by former provisions of NRS 31.010 (cf. NRS 31.013). While an ancillary remedy of attachment afforded by that section is available in a judicial foreclosure action under NRS 40.430, the affidavit must contain an opinion of the value by a qualified witness and show that the security has decreased in value since the security interest was created.[105]

NRS 31.017, "Issuance of writ of attachment without notice and hearing," provides as follows:

> The court may order the writ of attachment issued without notice to the defendant only in the following cases:
>
> 1. In an action by a resident of this State against a defendant not residing in this State. For purposes of this subsection only, domestic corporations and foreign corporations who are doing business in this State and who have qualified to do business in this State as required in Chapter 80 of NRS shall be deemed residents of this State. Alien corporations and foreign corporations who have not qualified to do business shall be deemed nonresidents.
>
> 2. In an action upon a foreign judgment for the direct payment of money.
>
> 3. In an action for the recovery of the value of personal property, where such personal property is owned by the plaintiff and has been taken or converted by the defendant without the consent of the plaintiff.
>
> 4. In an action by a resident of this State, where the defendant is about to remove the defendant's money or property, or any part thereof, from this State, and the defendant's property which may remain within this State, if any, will be insufficient to satisfy plaintiff's claim. For purposes of this subsection only, a foreign corporation qualified to do business in this State as provided in Chapter 80 of NRS shall be deemed a resident of this State.
>
> 5. Where the defendant is about to give, assign, hypothecate, pledge, dispose of or conceal the defendant's money or property or any part thereof and the defendant's money or property remaining in this State or that remaining unconcealed will be insufficient to satisfy the plaintiff's claim.
>
> 6. In an action for the recovery of money or property, or the proceeds thereof, obtained

---

[101] *Clarence E. Morris, Inc. v. Vitek*, 80 Nev. 408, 395 P.2d 521 (1964).

[102] *Id.*

[103] *Id.*

[104] *McMillan v. United Mortgage Co.*, 82 Nev. 117, 412 P.2d 604 (1966), cited, *Nevada Land & Mortgage Co. v. Hidden Wells Ranch, Inc.*, 83 Nev. 501, at 504, 435 P.2d 198 (1967); see also *Bonicamp v. Vazquez*, 120 Nev. 377, at 380, 91 P.3d 584 (2004), distinguished, *Paramount Ins., Inc. v. Rayson & Smitley*, 86 Nev. 644, at 647, 472 P.2d 530 (1970).

[105] *Paramount Ins., Inc. v. Rayson & Smitley*, 86 Nev. 644, 472 P.2d 530 (1970).

from the plaintiff by the defendant through embezzlement, forgery, larceny or extortion.

    7. In an action brought under Chapter 112 of NRS.

    8. In an action by the State, or a political subdivision thereof, brought under Chapter 130 of NRS.

    9. In an action where jurisdiction in this State can only be obtained by the attachment of the defendant's property.

Plaintiff could not challenge the constitutionality of those provisions of NRS 31.017 from which he suffered no injury. In an action for a declaratory judgment that NRS 31.017 was unconstitutional on the ground that it violated the right to due process guaranteed by the U.S. 14th amendment, the plaintiff had standing to challenge only the provisions of subsection 5 of that section because the opposing party who brought a state court action against the plaintiff sought and obtained a prejudgment writ of attachment against the plaintiff solely under the provisions of that subsection. The plaintiff, therefore, suffered no injury from, and did not have standing to challenge, any other provisions of NRS 31.017. (N.B., this case was not appropriate for publication and may not be cited to or by the courts for the Ninth Circuit except as provided in Ninth Circuit Rule 36-3.)[106]

The federal court was instructed to abstain from ruling on the constitutionality of NRS 31.017 until the state courts construed the statute. On appeal from an action for a declaratory judgment that NRS 31.017 was unconstitutional on the ground that it violated the right to due process guaranteed by the U.S. 14th amendment, the federal district court was instructed to abstain from deciding the federal constitutional issues that were presented under *Pullman*[107] because:

(1) the Nevada Supreme Court had not construed the statute and it was possible that the Nevada courts would construe the statute, along with other statutes governing prejudgment writs of attachment, in a manner that would comply with federal constitutional requirements, thereby avoiding the necessity to address the plaintiff's claims; and

(2) a pending state court action provided an opportunity for the Nevada courts to resolve the issues presented. (N.B., this case was not appropriate for publication and may not be cited to or by the courts for the Ninth Circuit except as provided in Ninth Circuit Rule 36-3.)[108]

NRS 31.020, "Affidavit for attachment: Contents," provides as follows:

    1. All applications to the court for an order directing the clerk to issue a writ of attachment without notice to the defendant shall be accompanied by the affidavit of the plaintiff or any other person having personal knowledge of the facts constituting one or more of the grounds for attachment, which affidavit or affidavits shall:

    (a) Set forth clearly the nature of the plaintiff's claim for relief and that the same is valid.

    (b) Set forth the amount which the affiant believes the plaintiff is entitled to recover from the defendant, and if there is more than one plaintiff or more than one defendant, the amount the affiant believes each plaintiff is entitled to recover or the amount that the plaintiff is entitled to recover from each defendant.

    (c) Describe in reasonable and clear detail all the facts which show the existence of any one of the grounds for an attachment without notice to the defendant.

    (d) Describe in reasonable detail the money or property sought to be attached and the location thereof if known.

    (e) If the property sought to be attached is other than money, set forth to the best knowledge and information of the affiant, the value of such property less any prior liens or encumbrances.

    (f) Name all third persons upon whom a writ of garnishment in aid of the writ of attachment will be served.

    (g) In an action upon a foreign judgment attach a copy of the judgment to the affidavit for attachment as an exhibit.

    (h) State whether, to the best information and belief of the affiant, the money or property sought to be attached is exempt from execution.

    2. All applications to the court for an order directing the clerk to issue a writ of attachment with notice to the defendant shall be accompanied by an affidavit setting forth the item required by subsection 1, except that such affidavit may show the existence of any one of the grounds for attachment with notice.

---

[106] *Fetish & Fantasy Halloween Ball, Inc. v. Ahern Rentals*, 45 Fed. Appx. 585 (9th Cir. 2002).

[107] *Railroad Commission v. Pullman*, 312 U.S. 496, 61 S.Ct. 643 (1941).

[108] *Fetish & Fantasy Halloween Ball, Inc. v. Ahern Rentals*, 45 Fed. Appx. 585 (9th Cir. 2002).

Strictness is not required in the affidavit. Great strictness is not required in setting out the facts authorizing the issuance of a writ of attachment in an affidavit required of an attaching creditor by sec. 121, ch. 103, Stats. 1861 (cf. NRS 31.020).[109]

Belief in the existence of facts may be based on information from third persons. Under sec. 121, ch. 103, Stats. 1861 (cf. NRS 31.020), relating to the affidavit required of an attaching creditor, the attaching creditor is required to swear to his belief in the existence of certain facts and to state the facts upon which such belief is founded. Such belief may be founded on information derived from third persons, but affidavits from such third persons are not required.[110]

An affidavit may be based on a presumption of fraud. Under sec. 121, ch. 103, Stats. 1861 (cf. NRS 31.020), relating to an affidavit required of an attaching creditor, where the creditor is informed by the debtor that such debtor has disposed of all his property and will satisfy the debt at his own convenience, the creditor may draw the conclusion that fraud has been committed and base his affidavit upon such presumption.[111] The affidavit may be filed before an application for a writ of attachment. An affidavit filed under sec. 121, ch. 103, Stats. 1861, as amended by sec. 2, ch. 70, Stats. 1864-1865 (cf. NRS 31.020), will support the issuance of a writ of attachment, if otherwise sufficient, even though made 11 days before filing.[112]

Where an affidavit made by one of two plaintiffs in a Justice Court action showed that the action was brought to recover $56.99 for goods furnished the defendant at his request, that defendant owed such sum over and above all setoffs and counterclaims, and that two statutory grounds for attachment existed, such affidavit satisfied the requirements of sec. 124, ch. 112, Stats. 1869, as amended by sec. 2, ch. 48, Stats. 1887 (cf. NRS 31.020), and warranted the issuance of an attachment by the justice of the peace under another statute which made such section applicable to proceedings in Justice Courts.[113]

An allegation of a just claim is required. In setting out grounds for the issuance of a writ of attachment, no particular language is required, and it is sufficient substantially to follow language of the statute. The allegation that the claim "is just" satisfied the requirement of NCL § 8704 (cf. NRS 31.020).[114]

NRS 31.022, "Procedure when notice and hearing not required," provides as follows:

> The court shall, without delay, examine the plaintiff's application and affidavit and receive additional evidence if necessary, and shall order the clerk to issue a writ of attachment without notice to the defendant if:
> 1. The plaintiff's affidavit, alone or as supplemented by additional evidence, meets the requirements of subsection 1 of NRS 31.020; and
> 2. The court determines, specifically, that there exist one or more grounds for attachment without notice as indicated in such affidavit or by additional evidence.

A Famous Cause
By Daumier

---

[109] *Bowers v. Beck*, 2 Nev. 139 (1866).
[110] *Id.*
[111] *Id.*
[112] *O'Neil v. New York & Silver Peak Mining Co.*, 3 Nev. 141 (1867).
[113] *Pratt v. Stone*, 25 Nev. 365, 60 Pac. 514 (1900).
[114] *Johnson v. Lee Fong*, 62 Nev. 249, 147 P.2d 884 (1944).

NRS 31.024, "Procedure when notice and hearing required: Order to show cause," provides as follows:

If the plaintiff's application is for an order directing the clerk to issue a writ of attachment after notice and hearing, and the plaintiff's affidavit, alone or as supplemented by additional evidence received by the court, meets the requirements of subsection 2 of NRS 31.020, the court shall issue an order directed to the debtor to show cause why the order for attachment should not be issued. The order must:

1. Fix the date and time for hearing on the order, which must not be set sooner than 3 days after the service of the order.

2. Direct the time within which service of the order must be made upon the defendant or the defendant's attorney.

3. Fix the manner in which service of the order must be made, which may be by personal service upon the defendant or service upon the defendant's attorney. If such service cannot be made, service may be by publication or in such a manner as the court determines is reasonably calculated to afford notice to the defendant under the circumstances set forth in the plaintiff's affidavit.

4. State that the debtor:

(a) Is entitled to certain exemptions, describe those exemptions in the manner set forth in subsection 2 of NRS 31.045 and explain that the debtor may claim an exemption if it appears that exempt property may be seized;

(b) Has the right to file affidavits on the debtor's behalf; and

(c) May appear personally or by way of an attorney, and present testimony on the debtor's behalf at the time of hearing.

5. State that if the defendant fails to appear the defendant shall be deemed to have waived his or her right to the hearing and that in such case the court may order the clerk to issue a writ of attachment.

NRS 31.026, "Procedure when notice and hearing required: Hearing," provides as follows:

A hearing on the order to show cause shall be conducted by the court without a jury. The court at such hearing shall consider all affidavits, testimony and other evidence presented and shall make a determination of the probable validity of the plaintiff's underlying claim against the defendant. If the court determines such claim is probably valid it shall order the clerk to issue a writ of attachment.

NRS 31.028, "Contents of order for attachment," provides as follows:

The court or judge issuing any order for attachment with or without notice shall set forth in the order:

1. The ground or grounds for attachment relied upon for the issuance of the order.

2. The facts or reasons why the court believes the ground or grounds exist.

3. The fact that the plaintiff has alleged a meritorious claim for relief.

4. The amount for which the attachment will issue.

5. The amount of security which must be given by the plaintiff before the writ will issue.

6. The names of all third persons upon whom writs of garnishment in aid of attachment may be served.

7. A description in reasonable detail of the money or property to be attached, and, if property, the value of the property based upon the evidence or affidavits presented to the court. The writ of attachment shall demand the amount for which attachment will issue, as specified in the order, and the court may order several writs to be issued at the same time to the sheriffs of different counties.

NRS 31.030, "Written undertaking on attachment; additional bond; exception to sufficiency of sureties; vacation of writ," provides as follows:

1. The court, in its order for attachment, shall require a written undertaking on the part of the plaintiff payable in lawful money of the United States in a sum not less than the amount claimed by the plaintiff or the value of the property to be attached, whichever is less, with two or more sureties to the effect that if the plaintiff dismiss such action or if the defendant recover judgment the plaintiff will pay in lawful money of the United States all costs that may be awarded to the defendant, and all damages which the defendant may sustain by reason of the attachment including attorney's fees, not exceeding the sum specified

in the undertaking. Each of the sureties shall annex to the undertaking an affidavit that the surety is a resident and householder or freeholder within the State, and worth double the sum specified in the undertaking over and above all the surety's debts and liabilities, exclusive of property exempt from execution. In the case of an attachment issued with notice to the defendant, or in any case upon showing by the defendant after notice to the plaintiff, the court may require an additional bond. No bond may be required of the State or of an officer or agency thereof.

  2. Before issuing the writ of attachment the clerk shall require the filing by the plaintiff of the written undertaking required by the court pursuant to subsection 1.

  3. At any time after the issuing of the attachment, but not later than 5 days after actual notice of the levy thereof, the defendant may except to the sufficiency of the sureties. If the defendant fails to do so, the defendant is deemed to have waived all objections to them. When excepted to, the plaintiff's sureties, within 5 days from service of written notice of exception, upon notice to the defendant of not less than 2 nor more than 5 days, must justify before the judge, justice, or clerk of the court in which the action is pending; and upon failure to justify, or if others in their place fail to justify, at the time and place appointed, the writ of attachment must be vacated.

The undertaking shall be produced at trial. Under sec. 122, ch. 103, Stats. 1861 (cf. NRS 31.030), relating to the plaintiff's written undertaking on attachment, it is immaterial who has custody of such an undertaking when a suit is brought. It is sufficient if such an undertaking is produced at trial.[115]

The costs of litigation are recoverable as damages for wrongful attachment. In an action against a surety on an attachment undertaking required by NRS 31.030, to recover the costs and expense of litigating the prior action in which the attachment was had, if the attachment was defective and subject to being dissolved regardless of the merits of the principal action, the expenses of litigation could be regarded as damages for wrongful attachment, because had there been no attachment, no expenses would have been incurred.[116]

The expenses of prior litigation are not recoverable as damages for wrongful attachment. In an action against a surety on an attachment undertaking, required by NRS 31.030, to recover the costs and expenses of litigation for the attorney and witnesses in defending the prior action in which the attachment was had, where the attachment was not defective and its wrongfulness was due only to the lack of a cause of action, the expenses of litigation were incurred not because of the attachment but because the principal action was brought. The costs were proper damages for wrongful attachment, but the expenses of the prior litigation could not be recovered because they were damages resulting from bringing the suit, which was not a malicious prosecution where it was brought in good faith.[117]

Equitable relief is not appropriate if a bond affords sufficient protection. In an action by the maker of a note for the adjudication of a balance due, where the action on the note was pending and the attachment of the maker's property threatened, and the plaintiff did not allege an inability to pay the installments due and had not tendered payment, NRS 31.030 requiring a bond of the plaintiff on attachment, and NRS 31.040 and 31.180 providing for the prevention of attachment and release of property on giving of a bond by a defendant, afforded sufficient protection, and the court was not justified in substituting equitable relief under NRS 33.010 providing for the granting of injunctions.[118]

Damages for wrongful attachment are premature if the action is still pending. Where an attachment was obtained and later discharged as improper, the action was still pending, and the attachment bond, written under NRS 31.030, was expressly conditioned upon the dismissal of such action, an action for damages for wrongful attachment was premature and was properly dismissed by the trial court.[119]

NRS 31.040, "Sheriff to attach and keep property; undertaking by defendant," provides as follows:

  The writ must be directed to the sheriff of any county in which property of the defendant may be and require the sheriff to attach and keep safely all the money or property of the defendant described in the order for attachment within the county not exempt from execution, or so much thereof as is sufficient to satisfy the amount demanded by the writ of attachment, whichever is less, unless the defendant gives the sheriff security by the undertaking of at least two sufficient sureties in an amount equal to the amount demanded by the writ or

---

[115] *Bowers v. Beck*, 2 Nev. 139 (1866).

[116] *Great American Indem. Co. v. Sweetwater Mining Co.*, 74 Nev. 219, 326 P.2d 1105 (1958).

[117] *Id.*

[118] *Aronoff v. Katleman*, 75 Nev. 424, 345 P.2d 221 (1959), cited, *Cooper v. Liebert*, 81 Nev. 341, at 344, 402 P.2d 989 (1965).

[119] *Clarence E. Morris, Inc. v. Vitek*, 85 Nev. 652, 461 P.2d 864 (1969).

the value of the property levied upon, whichever is less, apart from costs, in lawful money of the United States, in which case the writ must require the sheriff to take such an undertaking.

The surety's liability is limited. A surety who executed an undertaking as provided for in sec. 126, ch. 112, Stats. 1869 (cf. NRS 31.040), to prevent the attachment of property which, unknown to the surety, had already been attached, was not liable on the undertaking, even though the attachment was subsequently discharged, because the discharge was not what the surety bargained for, or benefit accruing to or accepted by him, and there was a total failure of consideration.[120]

The statute authorizing service of process by the sheriff is to be construed in connection with contemporaneous acts of the legislature. Under the statute which authorized the sheriff of one county to serve all papers in another county where the counties were attached to form one judicial district for judicial purposes, it did not follow that because two or more counties composed one judicial district they were attached for judicial purposes, and the statute had to be construed in connection with others passed at the same session, including the act which defined judicial districts, and sec. 123, ch. 103, Stats. 1861 (cf. NRS 31.040), which provided that a writ of attachment should be directed to the sheriff of any county in which the defendant had property.[121]

The statutes concerning service of process by sheriff were reconcilable. The statute which authorized the sheriff of one county to serve all papers in another county where the counties were attached to form one judicial district for judicial purposes, and sec. 123, ch. 103, Stats. 1861 (cf. NRS 31.040), which provided that a writ of attachment should be directed to the sheriff of any county in which the defendant had property, were easily reconcilable under the view that the sheriff of one county could serve process, issued by the district court of his county, in another county in the same judicial district only where both counties were treated as one county in all matters regarding district and probate courts.[122]

A bond against future attachments is a valid consideration for an undertaking. On an appeal from the denial of relief from a judgment to a surety on an attachment bond, where the bond was entitled "undertaking for return of property to defendants" and recited the levy of the attachment and the desire of the defendant for the return of the property and no further attachments, it had to be construed as an undertaking to prevent the attachment under NRS 31.040, rather than to discharge the attachment under NRS 31.180-31.220, and there was no failure of consideration in that the sheriff had not taken possession of any property, because the bond against future attachments furnished a valid consideration, and the undertaking was valid at common law.[123]

Equitable relief is not appropriate if a bond affords sufficient protection. In an action by the maker of a note for adjudication of the balance due, where an action on the note was pending and the attachment of the maker's property threatened, and the plaintiff did not allege an inability to pay the installments due and had not tendered payment, NRS 31.030 requiring a bond of a plaintiff on attachment, and NRS 31.040 and 31.180 providing for the prevention of attachment and release of property on giving of a bond by the defendant, afforded sufficient protection, and the court was not justified in substituting equitable relief under NRS 33.010 providing for the granting of injunctions.[124]

The modification of the effect of the statute must be made by the legislature. In an action by the maker of a note for adjudication of an amount due, where an action on the note was pending and the attachment of the maker's property threatened, preliminary injunctive relief against the attachment was not justified on the ground of harshness of the attachment statutes, NRS 31.040 and 31.190, fixing the amount of the bond required of a defendant in an attachment to prevent the attachment or obtain the release of property, because the statutes had to be considered as having received the attention of the legislature at the time of the last amendment 2 years earlier, and any modification had to be by legislative enactment.[125]

The defendant was not insulated from damages by the sheriff's failure to protect property. In an action for abuse of process resulting from an attachment of heavy equipment, the award for damages resulting from the failure of the sheriff to protect the property was proper despite the fact that under NRS 31.040 the duty to protect the property lay with the sheriff, and he was not the agent of the defendant. The sheriff's failure to protect the property did not insulate the defendant from the consequences of the initial tort.[126]

---

[120] *Laveaga & Hawley v. Wise & Levy*, 13 Nev. 296 (1878).

[121] *Sadler v. Celso Tatti & Co.*, 17 Nev. 429, 30 Pac. 1082 (1883).

[122] *Id.*

[123] *Covrig v. Powers*, 74 Nev. 348, 332 P.2d 650 (1958).

[124] *Aronoff v. Katleman*, 75 Nev. 424, 345 P.2d 221 (1959), cited, *Cooper v. Liebert*, 81 Nev. 341, at 344, 402 P.2d 989 (1965).

[125] *Aronoff, supra.*

[126] *Nevada Credit Rating Bureau, Inc. v. Williams*, 88 Nev. 601, 503 P.2d 9 (1972), cited, *Elliott v. Denton & Denton*, 109 Nev. 979, at 986, 860 P.2d 725 (1993) (dissenting opinion).

NRS 31.045, "Notice of execution on writ of attachment: Service required; form; contents," provides as follows:

1. Execution on the writ of attachment by attaching property of the defendant may occur only if:

(a) The judgment creditor serves the defendant with notice of the execution when the notice of the hearing is served pursuant to NRS 31.013; or

(b) Pursuant to an ex parte hearing, the sheriff serves upon the judgment debtor notice of the execution and a copy of the writ at the same time and in the same manner as set forth in NRS 21.076.

If the attachment occurs pursuant to an ex parte hearing, the clerk of the court shall attach the notice to the writ of attachment at the time the writ is issued.

2. The notice required pursuant to subsection 1 must be substantially in the following form:

NOTICE OF EXECUTION

YOUR PROPERTY IS BEING ATTACHED OR
YOUR WAGES ARE BEING GARNISHED

Plaintiff, ... (name of person), alleges that you owe the plaintiff money. The plaintiff has begun the procedure to collect that money. To secure satisfaction of judgment, the court has ordered the garnishment of your wages, bank account or other personal property held by third persons or the taking of money or other property in your possession.

Certain benefits and property owned by you may be exempt from execution and may not be taken from you. The following is a partial list of exemptions:

1. Payments received pursuant to the federal Social Security Act, including, without limitation, retirement and survivors' benefits, supplemental security income benefits and disability insurance benefits.

2. Payments for benefits or the return of contributions under the Public Employees' Retirement System.

3. Payments for public assistance granted through the Division of Welfare and Supportive Services of the Department of Health and Human Services or a local governmental entity.

4. Proceeds from a policy of life insurance.

5. Payments of benefits under a program of industrial insurance.

6. Payments received as disability, illness or unemployment benefits.

7. Payments received as unemployment compensation.

8. Veteran's benefits.

9. A homestead in a dwelling or a mobile home, not to exceed $550,000, unless:

(a) The judgment is for a medical bill, in which case all of the primary dwelling, including a mobile or manufactured home, may be exempt.

(b) Allodial title has been established and not relinquished for the dwelling or mobile home, in which case all of the dwelling or mobile home and its appurtenances are exempt, including the land on which they are located, unless a valid waiver executed pursuant to NRS 115.010 is applicable to the judgment.

10. All money reasonably deposited with a landlord by you to secure an agreement to rent or lease a dwelling that is used by you as your primary residence, except that such money is not exempt with respect to a landlord or the landlord's successor in interest who seeks to enforce the terms of the agreement to rent or lease the dwelling.

11. A vehicle, if your equity in the vehicle is less than $15,000.

12. Seventy-five percent of the take-home pay for any workweek, unless the weekly take-home pay is less than 50 times the federal minimum hourly wage, in which case the entire amount may be exempt.

13. Money, not to exceed $500,000 in present value, held in:

(a) An individual retirement arrangement which conforms with the applicable limitations and requirements of section 408 or 408A of the Internal Revenue Code, 26 U.S.C. §§ 408 and 408A;

(b) A written simplified employee pension plan which conforms with the applicable limitations and requirements of section 408 of the Internal Revenue Code, 26 U.S.C. § 408;

(c) A cash or deferred arrangement that is a qualified plan pursuant to the Internal Revenue Code;

(d) A trust forming part of a stock bonus, pension or profit-sharing plan that is a qualified plan pursuant to sections 401 et seq. of the Internal Revenue Code, 26 U.S.C. §§ 401 et seq.; and

(e) A trust forming part of a qualified tuition program pursuant to Chapter 353B of NRS, any applicable regulations adopted pursuant to Chapter 353B of NRS and section 529 of the Internal Revenue Code, 26

U.S.C. § 529, unless the money is deposited after the entry of a judgment against the purchaser or account owner or the money will not be used by any beneficiary to attend a college or university.

14. All money and other benefits paid pursuant to the order of a court of competent jurisdiction for the support, education and maintenance of a child, whether collected by the judgment debtor or the State.

15. All money and other benefits paid pursuant to the order of a court of competent jurisdiction for the support and maintenance of a former spouse, including the amount of any arrearages in the payment of such support and maintenance to which the former spouse may be entitled.

16. Regardless of whether a trust contains a spendthrift provision:

(a) A present or future interest in the income or principal of a trust, if the interest has not been distributed from the trust;

(b) A remainder interest in the trust whereby a beneficiary of the trust will receive property from the trust outright at some time in the future under certain circumstances;

(c) A discretionary power held by a trustee to determine whether to make a distribution from the trust, if the interest has not been distributed from the trust;

(d) The power to direct dispositions of property in the trust, other than such a power held by a trustee to distribute property to a beneficiary of the trust;

(e) Certain powers held by a trust protector or certain other persons;

(f) Any power held by the person who created the trust; and

(g) Any other property of the trust that has not been distributed from the trust. Once the property is distributed from the trust, the property is subject to execution.

17. If a trust contains a spendthrift provision:

(a) A mandatory interest in the trust in which the trustee does not have discretion concerning whether to make the distribution from the trust, if the interest has not been distributed from the trust;

(b) A support interest in the trust in which the standard for distribution may be interpreted by the trustee or a court, if the interest has not been distributed from the trust; and

(c) Any other property of the trust that has not been distributed from the trust. Once the property is distributed from the trust, the property is subject to execution.

18. A vehicle for use by you or your dependent which is specially equipped or modified to provide mobility for a person with a permanent disability.

19. A prosthesis or any equipment prescribed by a physician or dentist for you or your dependent.

20. Payments, in an amount not to exceed $16,150, received as compensation for personal injury, not including compensation for pain and suffering or actual pecuniary loss, by the judgment debtor or by a person upon whom the judgment debtor is dependent at the time the payment is received.

21. Payments received as compensation for the wrongful death of a person upon whom the judgment debtor was dependent at the time of the wrongful death, to the extent reasonably necessary for the support of the judgment debtor and any dependent of the judgment debtor.

22. Payments received as compensation for the loss of future earnings of the judgment debtor or of a person upon whom the judgment debtor is dependent at the time the payment is received, to the extent reasonably necessary for the support of the judgment debtor and any dependent of the judgment debtor.

23. Payments received as restitution for a criminal act.

24. Personal property, not to exceed $1,000 in total value, if the property is not otherwise exempt from execution.

25. A tax refund received from the earned income credit provided by federal law or a similar state law.

26. Stock of a corporation described in subsection 2 of NRS 78.746 except as set forth in that section.

These exemptions may not apply in certain cases such as proceedings to enforce a judgment for support of a child or a judgment of foreclosure on a mechanic's lien. You should consult an attorney immediately to assist you in determining whether your property or money is exempt from execution. If you cannot afford an attorney, you may be eligible for assistance through .... (name of organization in county providing legal services to the indigent or elderly persons).

PROCEDURE FOR CLAIMING EXEMPT PROPERTY

If you believe that the money or property taken from you is exempt or necessary for the support of you or your family, you must file with the clerk of the court on a form provided by the clerk a notarized affidavit claiming the exemption. A copy of the affidavit must be served upon the sheriff and the judgment creditor within 8 days after the notice of execution is mailed. The property must be returned to you within 5 days after you file the affidavit unless the judgment creditor files a motion for a hearing to determine the issue of exemption. If this happens, a hearing will be held to determine whether the property or money is exempt. The hearing must be held within 10 days after the motion for a hearing is filed.

IF YOU DO NOT FILE THE AFFIDAVIT WITHIN THE TIME SPECIFIED, YOUR PROPERTY MAY BE SOLD AND THE MONEY GIVEN TO THE JUDGMENT CREDITOR, EVEN IF THE PROPERTY OR MONEY IS EXEMPT.

If you received this notice with a notice of a hearing for attachment and you believe that the money or property which would be taken from you by a writ of attachment is exempt or necessary for the support of you or your family, you are entitled to describe to the court at the hearing why you believe your property is exempt. You may also file a motion with the court for a discharge of the writ of attachment. You may make that motion any time before trial. A hearing will be held on that motion.

IF YOU DO NOT FILE THE MOTION BEFORE THE TRIAL, YOUR PROPERTY MAY BE SOLD AND THE MONEY GIVEN TO THE PLAINTIFF, EVEN IF THE PROPERTY OR MONEY IS EXEMPT OR NECESSARY FOR THE SUPPORT OF YOU OR YOUR FAMILY.

NRS 31.050, "Attachment of shares of stock, debts due defendant and other property," provides as follows:

Subject to the order for attachment and the provisions of NRS 78.746 and Chapter 104 of NRS, the right of shares which the defendant may have in the stock of any corporation or company, together with the interest and profits therein, and all debts due such defendant, and all other property in this State of such defendant not exempt from execution, may be attached, and if judgment be recovered, be sold to satisfy the judgment and execution.

An interest in property subject to a conditional sale is an attachable interest. The interest of a vendee in property the subject of a conditional sale contract is an attachable interest under RL § 5151 (cf. NRS 31.050) and RL § 5287 (cf. NRS 21.080), relating to property subject to attachment and execution.[127]

NRS 31.060, "Execution of writ of attachment, Manner in which property is to be attached," provides as follows:

Subject to the requirements of NRS 31.045, the sheriff to whom the writ is directed and delivered shall execute it without delay, and if the undertaking mentioned in NRS 31.040 is not given, as follows:
1. Real property must be attached by leaving a copy of the writ with the occupant of the property or, if there is no occupant, by posting a copy in a conspicuous place on the property and recording the writ, together with a description of the property attached, with the recorder of the county.
2. Personal property must be attached:
(a) By taking it into immediate custody, and, if directed by the plaintiff, using the services of any company which operates a tow car, as defined in NRS 706.131, or common motor carrier, as defined in NRS 706.036, to transport it for storage in a warehouse or storage yard that is insured or bonded in an amount not less than the full value of the property; or
(b) By placing a keeper in charge of a going business where the property is located, with the plaintiff prepaying the expense of the keeper to the sheriff, during which period, the defendant, by order of the court or the consent of the plaintiff, may continue to operate in the ordinary course of business at the defendant's own expense if all sales are for cash and the full proceeds are paid to the keeper for the purpose of the attachment.
If the property is stored pursuant to paragraph (a), the property must be segregated from other property and marked by signs or other appropriate means indicating that it is in the custody of the sheriff.
3. Any mobile home, as defined in NRS 40.215, must be attached by:
(a) Posting a copy of the writ in a conspicuous place on the mobile home;
(b) Taking it into immediate custody, subject to the provisions of subsection 2; or
(c) Placing a keeper in charge of the mobile home for 2 days, with the plaintiff prepaying the expense of the keeper to the sheriff:

---

[127] *Nevada Motor Co. v. Bream*, 51 Nev. 89, 269 Pac. 602 (1928).

(1) During which period, the defendant may continue to occupy the mobile home; and

(2) After which period, the sheriff shall take the mobile home into the sheriff's immediate custody, subject to the provisions of subsection 2, unless other disposition is made by the court or the parties to the action.

4. Debts and credits, due or to become due, and other personal property in the possession or under the control of persons other than the defendant must be attached by service of a writ of garnishment as provided in NRS 31.240 to 31.460, inclusive.

Evidence that a sheriff, in executing a writ of attachment, rounded up and counted certain cattle, kept them together for three-quarters of an hour and in his sight for several hours, and refused to permit the claimant to take them away until an undertaking was given to secure their release, was sufficient to sustain the finding that the sheriff took and maintained possession of the cattle.[128]

The attaching officer is to retain and assert power and control over the property. Under RL § 5152 (cf. NRS 31.060), relating to the execution of a writ of attachment, the custody required of the attaching officer should be such as to enable the officer to retain and assert his power and control over the property in order that it cannot be withdrawn or taken by another without his knowing it.[129]

There must be actual taking of possession required for certain property. Under NCL § 8708 (cf. NRS 31.060), which relates to the manner in which property is to be attached, in order to constitute a levy under a writ of attachment upon personal property capable of manual delivery, there must be actual taking of possession of the property.[130]

Where a sheriff left bulky machinery which was the subject of an attachment in the debtor's equipment yard but examined the machinery, recorded the serial and identification numbers, placed a seal on the machinery and told the debtor not to use it and the debtor did not use it, the attachment lien continued in force between the debtor and creditor even though the sheriff permitted the attached property to remain in the debtor's possession when NRS 31.060 requires a sheriff to take personal property into immediate possession upon the execution of a writ of attachment.[131]

A writ of attachment of real property must be recorded.[132]

NRS 31.065, "Deposits by plaintiff of money with sheriff to pay expenses of taking, transporting and keeping certain personal property; liability of sheriff," provides as follows:

1. In cases where the sheriff is instructed to take into possession easily transportable personal property, whether it is to be placed in a warehouse or storage yard or in the custody of a keeper, the sheriff shall require, as prerequisite to the taking of the property, that in addition to written instructions the plaintiff or the plaintiff's attorney of record deposit with the sheriff a sum of money sufficient to pay the expenses of taking, transporting and keeping safely the property for a period not to exceed 30 days.

2. If a further detention of the property is required, the sheriff shall make written demands upon the plaintiff or the plaintiff's attorney for further deposits to cover estimated expenses for periods not to exceed 30 days each. If the attaching party desires to make a greater deposit, the attaching party may do so. Such demand must be personally served on the plaintiff or the plaintiff's attorney or left with a responsible person or in a proper receptacle at the office or residence of the plaintiff or the plaintiff's attorney or the demand must be deposited in the post office in a sealed envelope, as first-class registered or certified mail postage prepaid, addressed to the person on whom it is served or the person's attorney at the last known office or place of residence.

3. If the money so demanded is not paid, the sheriff shall notify the defendant within 5 days after money for storing and handling the property is no longer available and shall release the property to the persons from whom it was taken. Failure so to notify the defendant imposes liability on the sheriff for the expenses unless sufficient money can be obtained from the plaintiff.

---

[128] *Lightle v. Berning*, 15 Nev. 389 (1880).

[129] *Green v. Hooper*, 41 Nev. 12, 167 Pac. 23 (1917), cited, *Beemer v. Seaborn*, 54 Nev. 459, at 463, 22 P.2d 356 (1933), *Peterson v. Wiesner*, 62 Nev. 184, at 195, 146 P.2d 789 (1944).

[130] *Beemer v. Seaborn*, 54 Nev. 459, 22 P.2d 356 (1933), cited, *Crystal Bay Corp. v. Schmitt*, 58 Nev. 378, at 394, 81 P.2d 1070 (1938).

[131] *Nevada Credit Rating Bureau, Inc. v. Williams*, 88 Nev. 601, 503 P.2d 9 (1972).

[132] AGO 351 (10-29-1954).

NRS 31.070, "Third-party claims in property levied on; undertaking by plaintiff; liability of sheriff; exception to sufficiency of sureties; hearing to determine title to property," provides as follows:

1. If the property levied on is claimed by a third person as the person's property by a written claim verified by the person's oath or that of the person's agent, setting out the person's right to the possession thereof, and served upon the sheriff, the sheriff must release the property if the plaintiff, or the person in whose favor the writ of attachment runs, fails within 7 days after written demand to give the sheriff an undertaking executed by at least two good and sufficient sureties in a sum equal to double the value of the property levied on. If such undertaking be given, the sheriff shall hold the property. The sheriff, however, shall not be liable for damages to any such third person for the taking or keeping of such property if no claim is filed by any such third person.

2. Such undertaking shall be made in favor of and shall indemnify such third person against loss, liability, damages, costs and counsel fees by reason of such seizing, taking, withholding or sale of such property by the sheriff. By entering into such an undertaking the sureties thereunder submit themselves to the jurisdiction of the court and irrevocably appoint the clerk of the court as agent upon whom any papers affecting liability on the undertaking may be served. Liability on such undertaking may be enforced on motion to the court without the necessity of an independent action. The motion and such reasonable notice of the motion as the court prescribes may be served on the clerk of the court, who shall forthwith mail copies to the sureties if their addresses are known.

3. Exceptions to the sufficiency of the sureties and their justification may be had and taken in the same manner as upon an undertaking given in other cases under titles 2 and 3 of NRS. If they, or others in their place, fail to justify at the time and place appointed, the sheriff must release the property; but if no exception is taken within 7 days after notice of receipt of the undertaking, the third person shall be deemed to have waived any and all objections to the sufficiency of the sureties.

4. The sheriff may demand and exact the undertaking herein provided for notwithstanding any defect, informality or insufficiency of the verified claim served upon the sheriff.

5. Whenever a verified third-party claim is served upon the sheriff upon levy of the writ of attachment, the plaintiff or the third-party claimant is entitled to a hearing within 10 days therefrom before the court having jurisdiction of the action, in order to determine title to the property in question, which hearing must be granted by the court upon the filing of an application or petition therefor. Seven days' notice of such hearing must be given to all parties to the action and all parties claiming an interest in the property, or their attorneys, which notice must specify that the hearing is for the purpose of determining title to the property in question. The court may continue the hearing beyond the 10-day period, but good cause must be shown for any such continuance.

Where, in proceedings following the rendition of judgment for plaintiff, a third person testified that he refused to surrender the automobile attached by plaintiff because defendant had delivered the automobile to him as security for his claims against the defendant, the court exceeded its jurisdiction in ordering the third person to surrender the automobile, and properly set aside such order subsequently, because the third person was not a party to the action, and to hold that the court could destroy his asserted lien on the automobile upon plaintiff's unsupported affidavit would violate Nev. Const. art. 1, § 8, under which no person may be deprived of property without due process of law.[133]

Taking of possession is not an exercise of a right of ownership. In an action for conversion, where the plaintiff had attached property in a previous action, the defendant had filed a third-party claim against such property in a previous action under NRS 31.070, alleging ownership, and had taken possession of it when the plaintiff failed to post the required bond, and the property was found not to belong to the defendant, it was not wrongful or tortious in the absence of malice to engage in litigation over the title to the property, and taking of possession was a lawful procedural step under the statute, not an exercise of the right of ownership adverse to the rights of the other parties to the previous action.[134]

Possession by a third party under the statute was not a conversion of the property. In an action for conversion, where the plaintiff had attached property in a previous action, the defendant had filed a third-party claim against such property in a previous action, alleging ownership, and had taken possession of it when the plaintiff failed to post bond under NRS 31.070, and the property was found not to belong to the defendant, the facts did not constitute conversion,

[133] *Persing v. Reno Stock Brokerage Co.*, 30 Nev. 342, 96 Pac. 1054 (1908), cited, *State v. Fouquette*, 67 Nev. 505, at 514, 221 P.2d 404 (1950), *Greene v. Eighth Judicial Dist. Court*, 115 Nev. 391, at 394, 990 P.2d 184 (1999).
[134] *Wantz v. Redfield*, 74 Nev. 196, 326 P.2d 413 (1958), cited, *Great American Indem. Co. v. Sweetwater Mining Co.*, 74 Nev. 219, at 222, 326 P.2d 1105 (1958), *Kulik v. Albers, Inc.*, 91 Nev. 134, at 138, 532 P.2d 603 (1975).

which is defined as a distinct act of dominion wrongfully exerted over the personal property of another in denial or derogation of or inconsistent with the rights of the owner.[135]

Statute provides the complete and exclusive remedy. Where a third-party claim to attached real property and notice to furnish undertaking were filed under NRS 31.070, a motion to discharge the claim was properly denied, because this statute provides complete and exclusive remedy and under former provisions of NRS 28.010 (cf. NRS 28.070), "property" includes both real and personal property.[136]

A third party was liable for damages sustained as a result of attachment. In an action for damages based on a third-party undertaking executed by the defendant, where the plaintiff purchased a truck from a debtor and notified the defendant, but the defendant attached the truck and executed a third-party undertaking promising to pay for any damages sustained as a result of the attachment. The plaintiff could properly bring an action against the defendant for damages sustained as a result of the attachment because the defendant's liability growing out of the third-party undertaking was not only contractual but also mandatory under NRS 31.070, which is the exclusive remedy for third persons whose property has been attached. Wrongful attachment is not a condition precedent to an action based on a third-party undertaking. The defendant could preclude the plaintiff's recovery only by showing a bar by estoppel to the plaintiff's action.[137]

CONSTRUCTION

The term "writ of execution" is interchangeable with "writ of attachment." 1931 NCL § 8708 (cf. NRS 21.120 and 31.070) provides that if property which is levied on is claimed by a third person, and a written claim is served on the sheriff, the sheriff must release the property if the plaintiff fails within 5 days after the written demand to give the sheriff the undertaking with sufficient sureties in a sum equal to double the value of the property levied on, and although reference is made to "writ of attachment," the statute requires a written demand by the sheriff on the plaintiff in either attachment or execution because the terms "writ of attachment" and "writ of execution" are interchangeable in the statute.[138]

The construction of the statute is not controlled by a subsequent California decision. Where a third-party claim statute, NRS 31.070, was enacted before a California decision construing a similar statute, that decision did not control the construction of the Nevada statute, because the legislature could not have had such a decision in mind.[139]

PROCEDURE

The defense of the lack of service of a third-party claim must be made at trial. In attachment proceedings, an appellate court would not consider the plaintiff's contention that the trial court lacked jurisdiction to hear the petition of third-party claimants because there was no showing which verified that the third-party claim was served upon the sheriff as required by NCL § 8708.01 (cf. NRS 31.070) where the plaintiffs failed to assert such defense in trial court.[140]

Compliance with statute is not a condition precedent for an action against the original plaintiff by a third person. Compliance with 1931 NCL § 8708.01 (cf. NRS 31.070), providing for the release of attached property by the sheriff upon a verified claim by a third person, is not a condition precedent to the right of action by an owner against a party who as the plaintiff in the original action caused the attachment to be levied.[141]

---

[135] *Wantz v. Redfield*, 74 Nev. 196, 326 P.2d 413 (1958), cited, *Great American Indem. Co. v. Sweetwater Mining Co.*, 74 Nev. 219, at 222, 326 P.2d 1105 (1958), *Bader v. Cerri*, 96 Nev. 352, at 356, 609 P.2d 314 (1980), *Pelletier v. Pelletier*, 103 Nev. 408, at 411, 742 P.2d 1027 (1987), *Ferreira v. P.C.H. Inc.*, 105 Nev. 305, at 308, 774 P.2d 1041 (1989), *Evans v. Dean Witter Reynolds, Inc.*, 116 Nev. 598, at 606, 5 P.3d 1043 (2000), *Custom Teleconnect v. International Tele-Services, Inc.*, 254 F.Supp.2d 1173, at 1182 (D. Nev. 2003), *Edwards v. Emperor's Garden Rest.*, 122 Nev. 317, at 328, 130 P.3d 1280 (2006).

[136] *Cooper v. Liebert*, 81 Nev. 341, 402 P.2d 989 (1965), cited, *All Nite Garage, Inc. v. A.A.A. Towing, Inc.*, 85 Nev. 193, at 196, 452 P.2d 902 (1969), *Kulik v. Albers, Inc.*, 91 Nev. 134, at 137, 532 P.2d 603 (1975), *Elliott v. Denton & Denton*, 109 Nev. 979, at 981, 860 P.2d 725 (1993), but see *Elliott v. Denton & Denton*, 109 Nev. 979, at 985, 860 P.2d 725 (1993) (dissenting opinion).

[137] *All Nite Garage, Inc. v. A.A.A. Towing, Inc.* 85 Nev. 193, 452 P.2d. 902 (1969), cited, *Elliott v. Denton & Denton*, 109 Nev. 979, at 981, 860 P.2d 725 (1993).

[138] *Bowler v. Vannoy*, 67 Nev. 80, 215 P.2d 248 (1950).

[139] *Cooper v. Liebert*, 81 Nev. 341, 402 P.2d 989 (1965).

[140] *Chiatovich v. Young*, 61 Nev. 286, 127 P.2d 218 (1942).

[141] *Peterson v. Wiesner*, 62 Nev. 184, 146 P.2d 789 (1944), cited, *Elliott v. Denton & Denton*, 109 Nev. 979, at 986, 860 P.2d 725 (1993) (dissenting opinion).

LIABILITY OF SHERIFF

The sheriff's liability accrues on the date of the levy. Where a third person claimed ownership of cattle levied upon on a writ of execution, and the sheriff did not demand, and the execution plaintiff did not furnish, the indemnity bond as required under 1931 NCL § 8708.01 (cf. NRS 21.120 and 31.070), liability in tort for the wrongful conversion of such cattle accrued on the date of the levy and not the date a third-party claim was executed, served and filed.[142]

A cause of action by a third party existed from the date of the levy. Where a third person claimed ownership of cattle levied upon on a writ of execution, and the sheriff did not demand, and the execution plaintiff did not furnish, the indemnity bond as required under 1931 NCL § 8708.01 (cf. NRS 21.120 and 31.070), damages for the alleged conversion were not waived, nor was conversion stayed from the date of levy until the third-party claim was filed and served on the sheriff, because the claim was not necessary to establish a cause of action which existed and continued to exist until an action was filed and proved or became barred by the statute of limitations.[143] Sheriff was required to release property to a third party. Where a third person claimed cattle that had been levied upon on a writ of execution, but the sheriff did not demand and the execution plaintiff did not furnish the indemnity, the bond required under 1931 NCL § 8708.01 (cf. NRS 21.120 and 31.070), and the person who claimed the cattle filed a third-party claim, the sheriff was required to release the cattle to such third person.[144]

Where the execution plaintiff was advised by her attorneys and others to cause the removal of cattle by the sheriff from a ranch of persons who were not parties to the action, and the cattle were delivered to the plaintiff before the ranch owners filed a third-party claim, such facts did not absolve the sheriff or plaintiff from the obligation to return the cattle to the claimant ranch owners in the absence of a demand by the sheriff for, or filing by the plaintiff of, the indemnity bond as required under 1931 NCL § 8708.01 (cf. NRS 21.120 and 31.070).[145]

NRS 31.100, "Examination of person served with copy of writ and defendant; delivery and memoranda of personal property," provides as follows:

> After the writ has been issued, any person owing debts to the defendant or having in the person's possession or under the person's control any credits or other personal property belonging to the defendant, may, by subpoena, be required to give a deposition or attend before the court, or judge, or a master appointed by the court or judge, and be examined on oath respecting the same. After the writ has been issued, the defendant may also be required to give a deposition or attend for the purpose of giving information respecting the defendant's property, and may be examined on oath. The court or judge may, after such examination, order personal property capable of manual delivery to be delivered to the sheriff on such terms as may be just, having reference to any liens thereon or claims against the same, and a memorandum to be given of all other personal property, containing the amount and description thereof.

Examination applies to the property in the possession of the defendant as well as the garnishee. Under sec. 131, ch. 112, Stats. 1869 (cf. NRS 31.100), which provides for examination of garnishees and defendants in attachment proceedings, the defendant may be examined not only as to the property in the possession of the garnishee, but also as to the property in his own possession, and discovery may be had of property concealed on his person.[146]

A court may order delivery of stock to the sheriff. Where the defendant in an action on a promissory note was examined concerning his property in attachment proceedings under sec. 131, ch. 112, Stats. 1869 (cf. NRS 31.100), and the court ordered the mining stock found upon his person to be delivered to the sheriff pending the outcome of the action, the order was upheld as within the jurisdiction of the district court on application for a writ of certiorari to the Supreme Court.[147]

An order of delivery was not reviewable on certiorari. Where the court had jurisdiction of the subject matter and person in garnishment proceedings brought under sec. 131, ch. 112, Stats. 1869 (cf. NRS 31.100), its order directing payment of money to the sheriff to be applied to the judgment, if recovered, was not reviewable on certiorari, no matter how erroneous.[148]

An examination is not an appropriate procedure to acquire possession of property after a judgment against the defendant is entered. Where the plaintiff attached the defendant's property, which was in the hands of a third person who

---

[142] *Bowler v. Vannoy*, 67 Nev. 80, 215 P.2d 248 (1950).
[143] *Id.*
[144] *Id.*
[145] *Id.*
[146] *Bivins v. Harris*, 8 Nev. 153 (1872).
[147] *Id.*
[148] *Birchfield v. Harris*, 9 Nev. 382 (1874), cited, *In re Wixom*, 12 Nev. 219, at 222 (1877).

refused to surrender the property on the ground that he held a valid, prior lien on it, the plaintiff, upon securing a judgment against the defendant, should have instituted proceedings supplemental to execution against the third person, and was not entitled under sec. 131, ch. 112, Stats. 1869 (cf. NRS 31.100), relating to examination of garnishees, to acquire possession of such property by citing the third person into court and having the court take the property from the third person notwithstanding his claim of right therein accruing before attachment.[149]

NRS 31.110, "Sheriff's return of writ; certificate," provides as follows:

> The sheriff shall return the writ of attachment within 25 days after its receipt, with a certificate of the sheriff's proceeding endorsed thereon or attached thereto. The certificate must contain the date, time and place of each levy upon real or personal property, a full inventory of the personal property attached, a description of all real property attached, and the date, time and place where each writ of garnishment was served. The sheriff shall also attach to the writ of attachment a true and correct copy of each writ of garnishment served.

Imposition of certain costs on a garnishee is not appealable. An order of a Justice Court under sec. 132, ch. 112, Stats. 1869 (cf. NRS 31.110), requiring the garnishee to pay the costs of the proceeding to obtain information respecting the amount and description of debt due the defendant, was not an order to pay the tax, impost or municipal fine within the meaning of former provisions of Nev. Const. art. 6, § 4, or § 5, Chapter 19, Stats. 1865, conferring appellate jurisdiction on the Supreme Court in cases at law involving "the legality of any tax, impost, assessment, toll or municipal fine," and the appeal of such an order to the Supreme Court after affirmance by a district court was dismissed for lack of jurisdiction.[150]

Imposition of certain costs on garnishee is not punishment. The general requirement is that costs in a legal proceeding fall upon the party in the wrong or in default, and costs imposed upon a garnishee by a justice of the peace under sec. 132, ch. 112, Stats. 1869 (cf. NRS 31.110), in a proceeding to obtain information respecting the amount and description of debt due the defendant, are not imposed as punishment, but because of the failure of the garnishee to furnish such information to the sheriff, thereby compelling the plaintiff to institute legal proceedings to acquire it.[151]

NRS 31.120, "Sale of attached perishable property; sheriff to retain proceeds and attached property to answer judgment," provides as follows:

> If any of the property attached is perishable, the sheriff shall sell it in the manner prescribed by the court. The proceeds and other property attached by the sheriff shall be retained by the sheriff to answer any judgment that may be recovered in the action, unless sooner subject to execution upon another judgment recovered previous to the issuing of the attachment. Debts and credits attached may be collected by the sheriff, if the same can be done without suit. The sheriff's receipt shall be a sufficient discharge for the amount paid.

The sale is not permitted when the expense of keeping the property exceeds its value. Although the expense of keeping property under attachment is frequently more than its value, sec. 133, ch. 112, Stats. 1869 (cf. NRS 31.120), which relates to the sale of perishable property by sheriffs, does not permit the sale in such a case. Relief should be sought under sec. 292, ch. 112, Stats. 1869 (cf. NRS 31.130), which provides for a court order for the sale where it is in the best interests of the parties.[152]

NRS 31.130, "Sale of attached property; proceeds to be deposited in court," provides as follows:

> Whenever property has been taken by an officer under a writ of attachment, and it is made to appear satisfactorily to the court, or a judge thereof, that the interest of the parties to the action will be subserved by a sale thereof, the court or judge may order such property to be sold in the same manner as property is sold under an execution, and the proceeds to be deposited in the court to abide the judgment of the action. Such order can be made only upon notice to the adverse party or the adverse party's attorney.

---

[149] *Persing v. Reno Stock Brokerage Co.*, 30 Nev. 342, 96 Pac. 1054 (1908), cited, *Greene v. Eighth Judicial Dist. Court*, 115 Nev. 391, at 394, 990 P.2d 184 (1999).

[150] *Wearne v. Haynes*, 13 Nev. 103 (1878).

[151] *Id.*

[152] *Newman v. Kane*, 9 Nev. 234 (1874).

A sale is not permitted when the expense of keeping the property exceeds its value. Although the expense of keeping property under attachment is frequently more than its value, sec. 133, ch. 112, Stats. 1869 (cf. NRS 31.120), which relates to the sale of perishable property by sheriffs, does not permit the sale in such a case. Relief should be sought under sec. 292, ch. 112, Stats. 1869 (cf. NRS 31.130), which provides for a court order for the sale where it is to the best interests of the parties.[153]

NRS 31.140, "Satisfaction of judgment by sales of attached property," provides as follows:

> If judgment be recovered by the plaintiff, the sheriff shall satisfy the same out of the property attached by the sheriff which has not been delivered to the defendant or a claimant, as hereinafter provided, or subjected to execution on another judgment recovered previous to the issuing of the attachment, if it be sufficient for that purpose:
> 1. By paying to the plaintiff the proceeds of all sales of perishable property sold by the sheriff or of any debts or credits collected by the sheriff, or so much as shall be necessary to satisfy the judgment.
> 2. If any balance remain due, and an execution shall have been issued on the judgment, the sheriff shall sell under the execution so much of the property, real or personal, as may be necessary to satisfy the balance, if enough for that purpose remain in the sheriff's hands. Notice of the sales shall be given, and the sales conducted as in other cases of sales on execution.

A cause of action on a bond was stated where sheriff allegedly sold attached property under judgment. Where the principal and sureties executed a bond in favor of the sheriff conditioned on the retention of attached property, a complaint in an action on the bond did not fail to state the cause of action by reason of showing that the property was sold to satisfy the judgment where it was also alleged that the sheriff kept the property under attachment until the judgment was rendered, because sec. 135, ch. 112, Stats. 1869 (cf. NRS 31.140), required the sheriff to satisfy the judgment out of the attached property, and the obligors contracted under and with reference to such section.[154]

NRS 31.150, "Deficiency after sale of attached property; sheriff to collect balance as upon an execution," provides as follows:

> If, after selling all the property attached by the sheriff remaining in the sheriff's hands, and applying the proceeds, together with the proceeds of any debts or credits collected by the sheriff, deducting the fees, to the payment of the judgment, any balance shall remain due, the sheriff shall proceed to collect such balance as upon an execution in other cases. Whenever the judgment shall have been paid, the sheriff, upon reasonable demand, shall deliver over to the defendant the attached property remaining in the sheriff's hands, and any proceeds of the property attached unapplied on the judgment.

NRS 31.160, "Plaintiff may prosecute undertaking if execution returned unsatisfied," provides as follows:

> If the execution be returned unsatisfied, in whole or in part, the plaintiff may prosecute any undertaking given under NRS 31.040 or 31.190, or the plaintiff may proceed as in other cases upon the return of an execution.

NRS 31.170, "Discharge of attachment after judgment for defendant or dismissal of action; stay of release pending appeal," provides as follows:

> If the defendant recovers judgment against the plaintiff, or if the claim for relief upon which the attachment is based is dismissed, then any undertaking received in the action, all the proceeds of sales and money collected by the sheriff, and all the property attached remaining in the sheriff's hands, shall be delivered to the defendant or the defendant's agent, and the order of attachment shall be discharged and the property released therefrom; but if an appeal is taken from an order dissolving or discharging the attachment, from a final judgment in favor of the defendant or from an order dismissing the claim for relief upon which the attachment is based, the court may, upon such terms as are just, stay or enjoin the release by the sheriff and the dissolution of the writ pending the appeal.

---

[153] *Id.*
[154] *Gaudette v. Roeder*, 13 Nev. 341 (1878).

Under sec. 138, ch. 112, Stats. 1869 (cf. NRS 31.170), providing that an attachment is discharged if the defendant recovers judgment, from the moment such judgment is rendered the attachment is dissolved, the lien created by it is vacated, the property is released from custody of law, and where the sheriff refuses to surrender the property, the remedy is an action against him for such property or its value.[155]

An order refusing dissolution of an attachment is not appealable. Where the defendant recovered judgment in an action in which his property was attached, although sec. 2, ch. 89, Stats. 1887 (cf. NRAP 3A(b)) provided for appeals from orders refusing to dissolve attachments, he was precluded from appealing from such order by sec. 138, ch. 112, Stats. 1869 (cf. NRS 31.170), providing that an attachment is discharged if the defendant recovers judgment, because the judgment dissolved the attachment without a court order, the order was void, and the proper remedy was against the attaching officer.[156]

The sheriff acquires the special property in chattels. Under sec. 138, ch. 112, Stats. 1869 (cf. NRS 31.170) providing that an attachment is discharged if the defendant recovers judgment when the property is attached, the sheriff acquires special property in chattels, defeasible by the plaintiff failing in his action. The general property remains with the defendant, and if he recovers, the attachment is *ipso facto* dissolved and the special property of the sheriff ceases. He is answerable in trover if he detains chattels after the demand.[157]

Discharge of attachment is not delayed by new trial. Where sec. 138, ch. 112, Stats. 1869 (cf. NRS 31.170) provided that an attachment was discharged if the defendant recovered judgment, without requiring that such judgment be the final one in the sense of ending litigation, the fact that there was a motion for a new trial pending did not keep the attachment in force after the defendant recovered judgment in the trial court.[158]

NRS 31.180, "Defendant, having appeared in action, may move for discharge of attachment upon giving undertaking; stipulations for release of attachments," provides as follows:

> 1. Whenever the defendant shall have appeared in the action, the defendant may apply, upon reasonable notice to the plaintiff, to the court in which the action is pending, or to the judge thereof, for an order to discharge the attachment, wholly or in part, upon the execution and filing of the undertaking mentioned in NRS 31.190. Such order may be granted directing the release from the operation of the attachment, upon the filing of such undertaking and the justification of the sureties thereon, if required by the plaintiff, of all or any part of the property, money, debts or credits attached, as the case may be. All the proceeds of sales and moneys collected by the sheriff, and all the property attached remaining in the sheriff's hands, so released, shall be delivered or paid to the defendant upon the filing of such undertaking and making such justification, if required by the plaintiff.
>
> 2. The plaintiff and defendant may stipulate in writing that the attachment of defendant's property may be released wholly or in part. Upon the filing of such a stipulation, the sheriff shall release the property pursuant to the stipulation.

Defendant may move for discharge at any time after appearing. Under sec. 139, ch. 112, Stats. 1869 (cf. NRS 31.180), providing that "whenever the defendant shall have appeared in the action" he may apply to the court for an order to discharge the attachment, the defendant may apply for a discharge at any time after appearing.[159]

Bond against future attachments is a valid consideration for undertaking. On an appeal from the denial of relief from a judgment to surety on an attachment bond, where the bond was entitled "undertaking for return of property to defendants" and recited the levy of the attachment and the desire of the defendant for the return of the property and no further attachments, it had to be construed as an undertaking to prevent the attachment under NRS 31.040, rather than to discharge the attachment under NRS 31.180-31.220, and there was no failure of consideration in that the sheriff had not taken possession of any property, because the bond against future attachments furnished a valid consideration, and the undertaking was valid at common law.[160]

Equitable relief not appropriate if a bond affords sufficient protection. In an action by the maker of a note for adjudication of a balance due, where the action on the note was pending and the attachment of the maker's property

---

[155] *Ranft v. Young*, 21 Nev. 401, 32 Pac. 490 (1893), cited, *Turner v. Dorland*, 89 Nev. 408, at 410, 514 P.2d 210 (1973).

[156] *Ranft, supra.*

[157] *Id.*

[158] *Id.*

[159] *Goldfield-Mohawk Mining Co. v. Frances-Mohawk Mining & Leasing Co.*, 31 Nev. 348, 102 Pac. 963 (1909).

[160] *Covrig v. Powers*, 74 Nev. 348, 332 P.2d 650 (1958).

threatened, and the plaintiff did not allege an inability to pay the installments due and had not tendered payment, NRS 31.030 requiring a bond of the plaintiff on attachment, and NRS 31.040 and 31.180 providing for the prevention of attachment and release of property on giving of a bond by the defendant, afforded sufficient protection, and the court was not justified in substituting equitable relief under NRS 33.010 providing for the granting of injunctions.[161]

NRS 31.190, "Undertaking of defendant; determination of disputed value of property; justification by sureties," provides as follows:

> 1. On granting an order for discharge of attachment pursuant to NRS 31.180, the court or the judge shall require an undertaking on behalf of the defendant, with at least two sureties, residents and freeholders, or householders, in the county, which shall be filed:
>   (a) To the effect, in case the value of the property or the amount of money, debts, or credits sought to be released equals or exceeds the demand of the writ, that the defendant will pay to the plaintiff the amount of the judgment which may be recovered in favor of the plaintiff in the action or the demand of the writ, whichever is less; or
>   (b) To the effect, in case the value of the property or the amount of money, debts, or credits sought to be released is less than the demand of the writ, that the defendant will pay the amount of money, debts or credits, or value of the property sought to be released, in lawful money of the United States.
>   2. The value of the property sought to be released, if disputed, shall be determined by the court or judge thereof, upon proof or by a sworn appraiser or sworn appraisers, not exceeding three, to be appointed by the court or judge for that purpose.
>   3. Before filing the undertaking, the defendant shall serve a copy thereof upon the plaintiff, and if the plaintiff require a justification by the sureties, the plaintiff shall give notice thereof to the defendant within 2 days; or at the time of giving notice of motion for an order to discharge the attachment, the defendant may in the defendant's notice name the sureties, and if the plaintiff require them to justify the plaintiff shall give notice thereof at the hearing of the motion. If required, the sureties shall justify before the court in which the suit is pending, or the judge thereof, after reasonable notice.

A bond is not voided by showing an attachment was void. Where the defendant has given a bond, as required by sec. 137, ch. 103, Stats. 1861 (cf. NRS 31.190), to secure the release of property from an attachment, such bond is not voided by showing that the attachment was void. Such bond will be voided only where it is against public policy to support it or where the defendant shows that it was given under duress.[162]

Property of sureties may consist of stock. On an appeal from an order discharging the attachment issued against a corporation, the fact that the property of the sureties on the bond for the discharge of the attachment consisted of stock in the corporation did not disqualify them under sec. 140, ch. 112, Stats. 1869 (cf. NRS 31.190), relating to the requirements for sureties.[163]

The collateral question of superior title in a freeholder is not tried by the court. Courts do not try the collateral question of superior title in determining whether a person is a freeholder under sec. 140, ch. 112, Stats. 1869 (cf. NRS 31.190), relating to sureties on bonds for discharge of attachments.[164]

"Freeholder" construed: Under sec. 140, ch. 112, Stats. 1869 (cf. NRS 31.190), requiring that sureties on bonds for the discharge of attachments be residents and freeholders in the county, persons whose rights depended upon quitclaim deed and possession, and who were not shown to have secured government title, were freeholders and qualified as sureties.[165]

"Householder" construed: Under sec. 140, ch. 112, Stats. 1869 (cf. NRS 31.190), requiring that sureties on bonds for the discharge of attachments be residents and freeholders or householders in the county, a person with a hired servant residing in the house which he rented from a corporation bearing his name was a householder within the meaning of the statute and qualified as a surety.[166]

---

[161] *Aronoff v. Katleman*, 75 Nev. 424, 345 P.2d 221 (1959), cited, *Cooper v. Liebert*, 81 Nev. 341, at 344, 402 P.2d 989 (1965).

[162] *Bowers v. Beck*, 2 Nev. 139 (1866), cited, *Covrig v. Powers*, 74 Nev. 348, at 354, 332 P.2d 650 (1958).

[163] *Goldfield-Mohawk Mining Co. v. Frances-Mohawk Mining & Leasing Co.*, 31 Nev. 348, 102 Pac. 963 (1909).

[164] *Id.*

[165] *Id.*

[166] *Id.*

A judgment creditor brought an action against the judgment debtor's surety who joined in execution of bond for release of judgment debtor's attached property and for prevention of further levy on the writ of attachment, to recover remainder of judgment debt after partial satisfaction of judgment debt by execution sale of judgment debtor's automobile. The trial court entered judgment for judgment creditor against the surety, and the surety appealed. The Nevada Supreme Court held that the surety would not be heard to inquire whether the attachment was regular and, therefore, would not be heard to contend that an irregularity of the levy destroyed consideration for the execution of the bond.[167]

Modification of the effect of the statute must be made by legislature. In an action by the maker of a note for adjudication of the amount due, where an action on the note was pending and the attachment of the maker's property was threatened, preliminary injunctive relief against the attachment was not justified on the ground of harshness of the attachment statutes, NRS 31.040 and 31.190, fixing the amount of a bond required of the defendant in the attachment to prevent the attachment or obtain release of the property, because the statutes had to be considered as having received the attention of the legislature at the time of last amendment 2 years earlier, and any modification had to be by legislative enactment.[168]

The trial court was under no duty to determine which type of bond would be in the best interest of the surety. Where the proffered bond fully protected the plaintiff, the trial court properly accepted it without inquiring as to whether the surety had properly protected his contractual interest. The provisions for the bond when the value of the property sought to be released is less than the demand of writ would not be read into statutory provisions for a bond when the amount sought to be released equals or exceeds the demand of the writ, so as to limit the surety's liability to the value of the property actually released.[169]

NRS 31.200, "Grounds for discharge of attachment," provides as follows:

> 1. The defendant may also, at any time before trial, apply by motion, upon reasonable notice to the plaintiff, to the court in which the action is brought or to the judge thereof, for a discharge of the attachment, or the money or property attached through the use of a writ of garnishment, on the following grounds:
>   (a) That the writ was improperly or improvidently issued.
>   (b) That the property levied upon is exempt from execution or necessary and required by the defendant for the support and maintenance of the defendant and the members of the defendant's family.
>   (c) That the levy is excessive.
> 2. If the court or the judge thereof on the hearing of such motion shall find that any of the grounds stated in subsection 1 exist, the attachment and levy thereof shall be discharged. If the motion is based upon paragraph (c) of subsection 1 only, and the fact is found to exist, the discharge of attachment shall be only as to the excess.

The merits of the case will not be considered on a motion to discharge. A motion to discharge an attachment under BH § 3163 (cf. NRS 31.200) should be denied where the affidavit in support of the motion consists of denials of the general facts constituting the cause of action set forth in the complaint. Matters involving the merits of a case will not be considered on such a motion.[170]

A bond against future attachments is a valid consideration for an undertaking. On an appeal from the denial of relief from a judgment to a surety on an attachment bond, where the bond was entitled "undertaking for return of property to defendants" and recited the levy of the attachment and the desire of the defendant for the return of the property and no further attachments, it had to be construed as an undertaking to prevent the attachment under NRS 31.040, rather than to discharge the attachment under NRS 31.180–31.220, and there was no failure of consideration in that the sheriff had not taken possession of any property, because the bond against future attachments furnished a valid consideration, and the undertaking was valid at common law.[171]

A writ of mandate is not available for the release of property. Where a casino obtained a writ of attachment upon its chips taken by the sheriff from a prisoner in the county jail, the prisoner was not entitled to a writ of mandate for

[167] *Covrig v. Powers*, 74 Nev. 348, 332 P.2d 650 (1958).

[168] *Aronoff v. Katleman*, 75 Nev. 424, 345 P.2d 221 (1959).

[169] *United Pac. Ins. Co. v. Chism Homes, Inc.*, 102 Nev. 494, 728 P.2d 809 (1986).

[170] *Kuehn v. Paroni*, 20 Nev. 203, 19 Pac. 273 (1888), cited, *McMillan v. United Mortgage Co.*, 82 Nev. 117, at 125, 412 P.2d 604 (1966) (dissenting opinion).

[171] *Covrig v. Powers*, 74 Nev. 348, 332 P.2d 650 (1958).

their release because under NRS 34.170 a writ is available only in the absence of a remedy at law and the prisoner could have applied for a discharge of the attachment under NRS 31.200.[172]

The remedy under the statute is not exclusive. In an action for abuse of process, the fact that the plaintiff had not sought the release of attached property under the provisions of NRS 31.200 did not preclude the recovery of damages, because the remedy under the statute is not exclusive, and an action under it is not a condition precedent to an action for malicious prosecution, wrongful attachment or abuse of process.[173]

NRS 31.210, "When motion to discharge attachment made on affidavits, plaintiff may oppose by affidavits," provides as follows: "If the motion is made upon affidavits on the part of the defendant, the plaintiff may oppose it by affidavits or other evidence, in addition to those on which the writ of attachment was issued."

NRS 31.220, "Improperly, improvidently or irregularly issued writ must be discharged; issuance of new writ," provides as follows: "If upon such application it satisfactorily appears that the writ of attachment was improperly, improvidently or irregularly issued, it must be discharged; but the release of the property shall not be ordered if, at or before the hearing on such application, the court orders a new writ to be issued as provided in NRS 31.024 and 31.026, in which case the sheriff shall relevy upon the property under the new writ."

A bond against future attachments is a valid consideration for an undertaking. On an appeal from the denial of relief from a judgment to a surety on an attachment bond, where the bond was entitled "undertaking for return of property to defendants" and recited the levy of the attachment and the desire of defendant for the return of the property and no further attachments, it had to be construed as an undertaking to prevent the attachment under NRS 31.040, rather than to discharge the attachment under NRS 31.180-31.220, and there was no failure of consideration in that the sheriff had not taken possession of any property, because the bond against future attachments furnished a valid consideration, and the undertaking was valid at common law.[174]

An original attachment was not amendable after the entry of the court order dissolving it. A defect or an irregularity in attachment papers must be corrected by amendment before discharge of the attachment.[175]

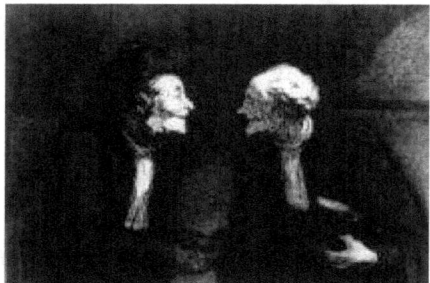

Two Lawyers The Handshake
By Honoré Daumier (1808–1879)

Attorney's Fees

The American Rule

Nevada follows the American Rule that attorney fees may not be awarded absent a statute, rule, or contract authorizing such award.[176] Statutes and rules include NRS 17.115, NRCP 68, NRS 18.020, and NRS 69.050. Generally,

[172] *State ex rel. Gutting v. Lamb*, 86 Nev. 36, 464 P.2d 27 (1970).
[173] *Nevada Credit Rating Bureau, Inc. v. Williams*, 88 Nev. 601, 503 P.2d 9 (1972), cited, *Elliott v. Denton & Denton*, 109 Nev. 979, at 986, 860 P.2d 725 (1993) (dissenting opinion).
[174] *Covrig v. Powers*, 74 Nev. 348, 332 P.2d 650 (1958).
[175] *Fireman's Fund Ins. Co. v. Shawcross*, 84 Nev. 446, 442 P.2d 907 (1968).
[176] *Thomas v. City of North Las Vegas*, 122 Nev. 82, 90, 127 P.3d 1057 (2006).

"the district court may not award attorney fees absent authority under a statute, rule, or contract."[177] "[A]s an exception to the general rule, attorney fees may be awarded as special damages in limited circumstances."[178]

NRS 17.115, "Offer of Judgment," was repealed, effective October 1, 2015. It had provided as follows:

1. At any time more than 10 days before trial, any party may serve upon one or more other parties a written offer to allow judgment to be taken in accordance with the terms and conditions of the offer of judgment.

2. Except as otherwise provided in subsection 7, if, within 10 days after the date of service of an offer of judgment, the party to whom the offer was made serves written notice that the offer is accepted, the party who made the offer or the party who accepted the offer may file the offer, the notice of acceptance and proof of service with the clerk. Upon receipt by the clerk:

    (a) The clerk shall enter judgment according to the terms of the offer unless:

        (1) A party who is required to pay the amount of the offer requests dismissal of the claim instead of entry of the judgment; and

        (2) The party pays the amount of the offer within a reasonable time after the offer is accepted.

    (b) Regardless of whether a judgment or dismissal is entered pursuant to paragraph (a), the court shall award costs in accordance with NRS 18.110 to each party who is entitled to be paid under the terms of the offer, unless the terms of the offer preclude a separate award of costs.

Any judgment entered pursuant to this section shall be deemed a compromise settlement.

3. If the offer of judgment is not accepted pursuant to subsection 2 within 10 days after the date of service, the offer shall be deemed rejected by the party to whom it was made and withdrawn by the party who made it. The rejection of an offer does not preclude any party from making another offer pursuant to this section. Evidence of a rejected offer is not admissible in any proceeding other than a proceeding to determine costs and fees.

4. Except as otherwise provided in this section, if a party who rejects an offer of judgment fails to obtain a more favorable judgment, the court:

    (a) May not award to the party any costs or attorney's fees;

    (b) May not award to the party any interest on the judgment for the period from the date of service of the offer to the date of entry of the judgment;

    (c) Shall order the party to pay the taxable costs incurred by the party who made the offer; and

    (d) May order the party to pay to the party who made the offer any or all of the following:

        (1) A reasonable sum to cover any costs incurred by the party who made the offer for each expert witness whose services were reasonably necessary to prepare for and conduct the trial of the case.

        (2) Any applicable interest on the judgment for the period from the date of service of the offer to the date of entry of the judgment.

        (3) Reasonable attorney's fees incurred by the party who made the offer for the period from the date of service of the offer to the date of entry of the judgment. If the attorney of the party who made the offer is collecting a contingent fee, the amount of any attorney's fees awarded to the party pursuant to this subparagraph must be deducted from that contingent fee.

5. To determine whether a party who rejected an offer of judgment failed to obtain a more favorable judgment:

    (a) If the offer provided that the court would award costs, the court must compare the amount of the offer with the principal amount of the judgment, without inclusion of costs.

    (b) If the offer precluded a separate award of costs, the court must compare the amount of the offer with the sum of:

        (1) The principal amount of the judgment; and

        (2) The amount of taxable costs that the claimant who obtained the judgment incurred before the date of service of the offer.

As used in this subsection, "claimant" means a plaintiff, counterclaimant, cross-claimant or third-party plaintiff.

6. Multiple parties may make a joint offer of judgment pursuant to this section.

---

[177] *Albios v. Horizon Cmtys., Inc.*, 122 Nev. 409, 417, 132 P.3d 1022, 1028 (2006).

[178] *Liu v. Christopher Homes, LLC*, 130 Nev. Adv. Op. 17, 321 P.3d 875, 878 (2014) (internal quotations omitted).

7. A party may make to two or more other parties pursuant to this section an apportioned offer of judgment that is conditioned upon acceptance by all the parties to whom the apportioned offer is made. Each party to whom such an offer is made may serve upon the party who made the offer a separate written notice of acceptance of the offer. If any party rejects the apportioned offer:

(a) The action must proceed as to all parties to whom the apportioned offer was made, whether or not the other parties accepted or rejected the offer; and

(b) The sanctions set forth in subsection 4:

(1) Apply to each party who rejected the apportioned offer.

(2) Do not apply to any party who accepted the apportioned offer.

8. If the liability of one party to another party has been determined by verdict, order or judgment, but the amount or extent of the liability of the party remains to be determined by further proceedings, the party found liable may, not later than 10 days before commencement of the proceedings to determine the amount or extent of the liability, serve upon the party to whom he or she is liable a written offer of judgment. An offer of judgment made pursuant to this subsection shall be deemed to have the same effect as an offer of judgment made before trial.

9. The sanctions set forth in subsection 4 do not apply to:

(a) An offer of judgment made to multiple defendants unless the same person is authorized to decide whether to settle the claims against all the defendants to whom the offer is made and:

(1) There is a single common theory of liability against all the defendants to whom the offer is made;

(2) The liability of one or more of the defendants to whom the offer is made is entirely derivative of the liability of the remaining defendants to whom the offer is made; or

(3) The liability of all the defendants to whom the offer is made is entirely derivative of a common act or omission by another person.

(b) An offer of judgment made to multiple plaintiffs unless the same person is authorized to decide whether to settle the claims of all the plaintiffs to whom the offer is made and:

(1) There is a single common theory of liability claimed by all the plaintiffs to whom the offer is made;

(2) The damages claimed by one or more of the plaintiffs to whom the offer is made are entirely derivative of an injury to the remaining plaintiffs to whom the offer is made; or

(3) The damages claimed by all the plaintiffs to whom the offer is made are entirely derivative of an injury to another person.

(Added to NRS by 1971, 1129; A 1979, 829; 1987, 1027; 1999, 1102; 2005, 116)

NRCP 68, "Offers of Judgment," provides as follows:

(a) The Offer. At any time more than 10 days before trial, any party may serve an offer in writing to allow judgment to be taken in accordance with its terms and conditions.

(b) Apportioned Conditional Offers. An apportioned offer of judgment to more than one party may be conditioned upon the acceptance by all parties to whom the offer is directed.

(c) Joint Unapportioned Offers.

(1) Multiple Offerors. A joint offer may be made by multiple offerors.

(2) Offers to Multiple Defendants. An offer made to multiple defendants will invoke the penalties of this rule only if (A) there is a single common theory of liability against all the offeree defendants, such as where the liability of some is entirely derivative of the others or where the liability of all is derivative of common acts by another, and (B) the same entity, person or group is authorized to decide whether to settle the claims against the offerees.

(3) Offers to Multiple Plaintiffs. An offer made to multiple plaintiffs will invoke the penalties of this rule only if (A) the damages claimed by all the offeree plaintiffs are solely derivative, such as that the damages claimed by some offerees are entirely derivative of an injury to the others or that the damages claimed by all offerees are derivative of an injury to another, and (B) the same entity, person or group is authorized to decide whether to settle the claims of the offerees.

(d) Judgment Entered Upon Acceptance. If within 10 days after the service of the offer, the offeree serves written notice that the offer is accepted, either party may then file the offer and notice of acceptance together with proof of service. The clerk shall enter judgment accordingly. The court shall allow costs in accordance with NRS 18.110 unless the terms of the offer preclude a separate award of costs. Any judgment entered pursuant to this section shall be expressly designated a compromise settlement. At his option, a defendant may within a reasonable time pay the amount of the offer and obtain a dismissal of the claim, rather than a judgment.

(e) Failure to Accept Offer. If the offer is not accepted within 10 days after service, it shall be considered rejected by the offeree and deemed withdrawn by the offeror. Evidence of the offer is not admissible except in a proceeding to determine costs and fees. The fact that an offer is made but not accepted does not preclude a subsequent offer. With offers to multiple offerees, each offeree may serve a separate acceptance of the apportioned offer, but if the offer is not accepted by all offerees, the action shall proceed as to all. Any offeree who fails to accept the offer may be subject to the penalties of this rule.

(f) Penalties for Rejection of Offer. If the offeree rejects an offer and fails to obtain a more favorable judgment,

(1) the offeree cannot recover any costs or attorney's fees and shall not recover interest for the period after the service of the offer and before the judgment; and

(2) the offeree shall pay the offeror's post-offer costs, applicable interest on the judgment from the time of the offer to the time of entry of the judgment and reasonable attorney's fees, if any be allowed, actually incurred by the offeror from the time of the offer. If the offeror's attorney is collecting a contingent fee, the amount of any attorney's fees awarded to the party for whom the offer is made must be deducted from that contingent fee.

(g) How Costs Are Considered. To invoke the penalties of this rule, the court must determine if the offeree failed to obtain a more favorable judgment. Where the offer provided that costs would be added by the court, the court must compare the amount of the offer with the principal amount of the judgment, without inclusion of costs. Where a defendant made an offer in a set amount which precluded a separate award of costs, the court must compare the amount of the offer together with the offeree's pre-offer taxable costs with the principal amount of the judgment.

(h) Offers After Determination of Liability. When the liability of one party to another has been determined by verdict, order or judgment, but the amount or extent of the liability remains to be determined by further proceedings, the party adjudged liable may make an offer of judgment, which shall have the same effect as an offer made before trial if it is served within a reasonable time not less than 10 days prior to the commencement of hearings to determine the amount or extent of liability.
[Replaced; effective October 27, 1998.]

NRS 18.020, "Cases in which costs allowed prevailing party," provides as follows:

Costs must be allowed of course to the prevailing party against any adverse party against whom judgment is rendered, in the following cases:
1. In an action for the recovery of real property or a possessory right thereto.
2. In an action to recover the possession of personal property, where the value of the property amounts to more than $2,500. The value must be determined by the jury, court or master by whom the action is tried.
3. In an action for the recovery of money or damages, where the plaintiff seeks to recover more than $2,500.
4. In a special proceeding, except a special proceeding conducted pursuant to NRS 306.040.
5. In an action which involves the title or boundaries of real estate, or the legality of any tax, impost, assessment, toll or municipal fine, including the costs accrued in the action if originally commenced in a Justice Court.

NRS 69.050, "Award of costs to prevailing party by district court on appeal from justice court," provides as follows:

> In the event of an appeal, the district court is authorized to award to the prevailing party all costs of court as now allowed by law incurred by such party, and also a reasonable attorney fee to be fixed and allowed by the district court for all services rendered in [sic] behalf of the prevailing party.

A judicially created exception to the American Rule is the substantial benefit doctrine, which allows recovery of attorney fees when a successful party confers a substantial benefit on the members of an ascertainable class, and where the court's jurisdiction over the subject matter of the suit makes possible an award that will operate to spread the costs proportionately among them. To recover fees under the substantial benefit doctrine, a successful party must demonstrate that: (1) the class of beneficiaries is small in number and easily identifiable; (2) the benefit [can] be traced with some accuracy; and (3) the costs can be shifted with some exactitude to those benefiting.[179] To qualify for the substantial benefit exception to the American Rule that parties generally must bear their own attorney fees, the prevailing party must show that the losing party has received a benefit from the litigation.[180]

In general, for costs and disbursements, see NRS Chapter 18. For fees and costs in justices' courts, see NRS Chapter 69.

Class Actions

Class actions are not exempt from the provisions of NRCP 68 for the award of attorney fees following a pretrial offer of judgment if the judgment finally obtained by offeree is not more favorable than the offer, despite the claimed difficulty inherent in notifying members of a large class of a settlement offer within the allotted ten days.[181] It is within the discretion of the trial judge to allow attorney fees under NRCP 68, based on the failure of the offeree to obtain a judgment more favorable than the pretrial offer of judgment. In exercising that discretion, the trial court must evaluate whether the plaintiff's claim was brought in good faith, whether defendant's offer of judgment was brought in good faith both in timing and amount, whether plaintiff's decision to reject the offer and proceed to trial was grossly unreasonable or in bad faith, and whether the fees sought by the offeror are reasonable and justified in amount.[182] An award of attorney fees to a defendant who prevailed at trial after making a pretrial offer of judgment was not subject to being disturbed on appeal where it could not be said that the trial court's exercise of discretion was arbitrary or capricious.[183]

Trial Court's Discretion and Beattie Factors

The decision to award attorney fees is within the sound discretion of the district court and will not be overturned absent a manifest abuse of discretion.[184] A party who rejects an offer of judgment yet fails to obtain a more favorable judgment may be ordered to pay attorney fees. NRS 17.115(4)(d); NRCP 68(f)(2). An offeree may accept the offer within ten days, but such offer will lapse after that time. NRS 17.115(2)-(3); NRCP 68(e)-(f). The "offer of judgment pursuant to NRCP 68 and NRS 17.115 is irrevocable during the ten-day period."[185] If the offer of judgment is not accepted within 10 days after the date of service, then the offer shall be deemed rejected by the party to whom it was made.[186]

The Nevada Supreme Court has set forth factors established by *Beattie v. Thomas*,[187] in assessing motions for attorney fees under NRS 17.115 and NRCP 68. In exercising its discretion regarding allowance of fees and costs under NRCP 68 providing for the payment of costs and attorney fees by the offeree when the judgment finally obtained by the offeree is not more favorable than offer, the trial court must evaluate whether plaintiff's claim was brought in good faith, whether defendants' offer of judgment was reasonable and in good faith in both timing and amount, whether plaintiff's decision to reject the offer and proceed to trial was grossly unreasonable or in bad faith, and whether the fees sought by

---

[179] *Thomas v. City of North Las Vegas*, 122 Nev. 82, 91, 127 P.3d 1057 (2006).
[180] *Id.*
[181] See *Schouweiler v. Yancey*, 101 Nev. 827, 833, 712 P.2d (1985).
[182] *Id.*
[183] *Id.*, see NRCP 68.
[184] *County of Clark v. Blanchard Constr. Co.*, 98 Nev. 488, 492, 653 P.2d 1217, 1220 (1982).
[185] *Nava v. Dist. Ct.*, 118 Nev. 396, 398, 46 P.3d 60, 61 (2002).
[186] NRS 17.115(3); NRCP 68(e).
[187] 99 Nev. 579, 588-89, 668 P.2d 268, 274 (1983).

offeror are reasonable and justified in amount.[188] Where the court has failed to consider those factors, it is abuse of discretion for court to award full amount of fees requested.[189]

There "is no bright-line rule that qualifies an offer of judgment as per se reasonable in amount; instead, the district court is vested with discretion to consider the adequacy of the offer and the propriety of granting attorney fees." *Certified Fire Prot. v. Precision Constr.*, 128 Nev. Adv. Op. No. 35 (August 9, 2012), citing State Drywall v. Rhodes Design & Dev., 122 Nev. 111, 119 n.18, 127 P.3d 1082, 1088 n.18 (2006). Nor are explicit findings on every *Beattie* factor required for the district court to adequately exercise its discretion. See *id.*; *Wynn v. Smith*, 117 Nev. 6, 13, 16 P.3d 424, 428 (2001) ("Although explicit findings with respect to these factors are preferred, the district court's failure to make explicit findings is not a per se abuse of discretion.").

Self-Represented Parties Are Ineligible for Attorney Fees

A party that represents itself is not eligible for attorney fees.[190] The Nevada Supreme Court has held that another attorney fee provision, NRS 69.030, which provides that a prevailing party shall receive reasonable attorney fees and costs, does not authorize an award of attorney fees to a prevailing proper person litigant, even if that litigant is an attorney.[191] The reasoning for that decision is that "an attorney proper person litigant must be genuinely obligated to pay attorney fees before he may recover such fees."[192]

Other Rules

Courts must make findings of reasonableness on awards of attorney fees under the *Brunzell* factors.[193] The basic elements to be considered in determining the reasonable value of an attorney's services may be classified under four general headings (1) the qualities of the advocate: his ability, his training, education, experience, professional standing and skill; (2) the character of the work to be done: its difficulty, its intricacy, its importance, time and skill required, the responsibility imposed and the prominence and character of the parties where they affect the importance of the litigation; (3) the work actually performed by the lawyer: the skill, time and attention given to the work; (4) the result: whether the attorney was successful and what benefits were derived.[194] Furthermore, good judgment would dictate that each of these factors be given consideration by the trier of fact and that no one element should predominate or be given undue weight.[195] Nonattorney staff costs are recoverable because they are part of a reasonable attorney fee and promote cost-effective litigation.[196]

Any memorandum of costs and disbursements must comply with the requirements of *Berosini v. PETA*[197] and *Bergmann v. Boyce*.[198]

When a secured entity incurs attorney fees in direct litigation with the surety over the bond, attorney fees may be awarded under NRS 17.115, NRCP 68, and NRS 18.010.[199]

Offers of judgment made before a second "trial" in a bifurcated trial were not untimely and did not preclude the application of a court rule and statute providing that the offeree may be required to pay offeror's attorney fees when the offeree receives judgment at the trial that is not more favorable than offer.[200]

Attorney fees could be awarded for the defense of a fraudulent claim under the statute permitting an award of fees to the prevailing party when court finds that the claim of the opposing party was brought without reasonable ground or to harass prevailing party.[201] A claim is groundless if the allegations in the complaint are not supported by any credible evidence at trial.[202] Certainly, if the record reveals that counsel or any party has brought, maintained, or defended an action in bad faith, the rationale for awarding attorney fees is even stronger. Bad faith may include conduct aimed at

---

[188] *Beattie*, 99 Nev. 579 at 588-589.

[189] *Id.* at 589.

[190] *Settelmeyer & Sons v. Smith & Harmer*, 124 Nev. 1206, 1220, 197 P.3d 1051 (2008).

[191] *Sellers v. Dist. Ct.*, 119 Nev. 256, 259, 71 P.3d 495, 498 (2003).

[192] *Id.* at 259, 71 P.3d at 497-98.

[193] *Brunzell v. Golden Gate National Bank*, 85 Nev. 345, 349, 455 P.2d 31 (1961).

[194] *Id.*

[195] *Id.* at 349-350.

[196] *LVMP v. Yeghiazarian*, 129 Nev., Advance Opinion 81, p. 11 (Nov. 7, 2013).

[197] *Bobby Berosini, Ltd. v. PETA*, 114 Nev. 1348, 1352, 971 P.2d 383, 385 (1998).

[198] *Bergmann v. Boyce*, 109 Nev. 670, 856 P.2d 560 (1993).

[199] See *Trustees v. Developers Surety*, 120 Nev. 56, 61, 84 P.3d 59 (2004).

[200] *Allianz Ins. Co. v. Gagnon*, 109 Nev. 990, 993-995, 860 P.2d 720, 724 (1993).

[201] *Allianz Ins. Co. v. Gagnon*, 109 Nev. 990, 995-996, 860 P.2d 720, 724 (1993).

[202] *Id.* at 996 (citation omitted).

unwarranted delay or disrespectful of truth and accuracy.[203] Thus, the bad faith of a party in bringing fraudulent claims makes the case for awarding attorney's fees even stronger.[204] To the extent that a claim is fraudulent, *i.e.*, an intentional perversion of the truth, it must also be groundless. Therefore, a district court may award attorney's fees under NRS 18.010(2)(b) for the defense of a fraudulent claim.[205]

The district court may award attorney fees in a post-divorce action as part of its continuing jurisdiction.[206] Moreover, under NRS 18.010(2)(b), a court may award attorney fees to the prevailing party if the court finds that the opposing party's claim was brought or maintained without reasonable grounds.

The clear majority rule is that attorney fees incurred in removing spurious clouds from a title qualify as special damages in an action for slander of title.[207]

For a civil rights action, 42 U.S.C. § 1988, "Proceedings in vindication of civil rights," applies to award attorney's fees to a "prevailing party" as follows:

(a) Applicability of statutory and common law

The jurisdiction in civil and criminal matters conferred on the district courts by the provisions of titles 13, 24, and 70 of the Revised Statutes for the protection of all persons in the United States in their civil rights, and for their vindication, shall be exercised and enforced in conformity with the laws of the United States, so far as such laws are suitable to carry the same into effect; but in all cases where they are not adapted to the object, or are deficient in the provisions necessary to furnish suitable remedies and punish offenses against law, the common law, as modified and changed by the constitution and statutes of the State wherein the court having jurisdiction of such civil or criminal cause is held, so far as the same is not inconsistent with the Constitution and laws of the United States, shall be extended to and govern the said courts in the trial and disposition of the cause, and, if it is of a criminal nature, in the infliction of punishment on the party found guilty.

(b) Attorney's fees

In any action or proceeding to enforce a provision of sections 1981, 1981a, 1982, 1983, 1985, and 1986 of this title, title IX of Public Law 92-318 [20 U.S.C. § 1681 *et seq.*], the Religious Freedom Restoration Act of 1993 [42 U.S.C. § 2000bb *et seq.*], the Religious Land Use and Institutionalized Persons Act of 2000 [42 U.S.C. § 2000cc *et seq.*], title VI of the Civil Rights Act of 1964 [42 U.S.C. § 2000d *et seq.*], or section 13981 of this title, the court, in its discretion, may allow the prevailing party, other than the United States, a reasonable attorney's fee as part of the costs, except that in any action brought against a judicial officer for an act or omission taken in such officer's judicial capacity such officer shall not be held liable for any costs, including attorney's fees, unless such action was clearly in excess of such officer's jurisdiction.

(c) Expert fees

In awarding an attorney's fee under subsection (b) of this section in any action or proceeding to enforce a provision of section 1981 or 1981a of this title, the court, in its discretion, may include expert fees as part of the attorney's fee.

Lien for Attorney's Fees

A lawyer may assert a lien for attorney's fees under NRS 18.015, "Lien for attorney's fees: Amount, perfection; enforcement," which provides as follows:

1. An attorney at law shall have a lien upon any claim, demand or cause of action, including any claim for unliquidated damages, which has been placed in the attorney's hands by a client for suit or collection, or upon which a suit or other action has been instituted. The lien is for the amount of any fee which has been agreed upon by the attorney and client. In the absence of an agreement, the lien is for a reasonable fee for the services which the attorney has rendered for the client on account of the suit, claim, demand or action.

---

[203] *Id.*

[204] *Id.*

[205] *Id.*

[206] *Halbrook v. Halbrook*, 114 Nev. 1455, 971 P.2d 1262 (1998) (recognizing that a district court has the authority to award attorney fees in post-divorce proceedings involving child custody); see also NRS 125.150(3) (providing that the district court may award attorney fees in a divorce proceeding when fees are in issue in the pleadings).

[207] *Id.*

2. An attorney perfects the lien by serving notice in writing, in person or by certified mail, return receipt requested, upon his or her client and upon the party against whom the client has a cause of action, claiming the lien and stating the interest which the attorney has in any cause of action.

3. The lien attaches to any verdict, judgment or decree entered and to any money or property which is recovered on account of the suit or other action, from the time of service of the notices required by this section.

4. On motion filed by an attorney having a lien under this section, the attorney's client or any party who has been served with notice of the lien, the court shall, after 5 days' notice to all interested parties, adjudicate the rights of the attorney, client or other parties and enforce the lien.

5. Collection of attorney's fees by a lien under this section may be utilized with, after or independently of any other method of collection.

NRS 18.015 allows an attorney to enforce a charging lien even if that attorney withdrew before her client secured some form of recovery.[208]

The lien is subject to an exception for an award of industrial insurance. 1911 CPA § 434 (cf. NRS 18.015), which states the general law as to attorneys' liens, is subject to the exceptions contained in ch. 111, Stats. 1913, as amended by sec. 10, ch. 190, Stats. 1915 (cf. NRS 616C.205), which provides that the award of workers' compensation is to be paid only to the claimant.[209]

Where a complaint by an attorney alleged that he was employed by a woman in a divorce action, that he rendered the service, that she obtained a judgment for money, that she failed to pay him, that the husband received notice of the attorney's lien, and that, despite the notice, the husband paid the wife, the action was within the purview of NCL § 8923 (cf. NRS 18.015), which provides for attorneys' liens, and was sufficient to charge the husband with liability.[210]

The statute allows an independent action to enforce a lien. NCL § 8923 (cf. NRS 18.015), which gives attorneys at law a lien for their services, is to be so construed as to allow an independent action by an attorney for enforcement of a lien against a judgment debtor of his client.[211]

An attorney's lien under the statute is distinguished from a lien on papers in attorney's possession. In a certiorari proceeding challenging part of a substitution order requiring the former attorneys to deliver to a substituted attorney papers belonging to the client, a lien of the attorney upon papers in his possession, which depends on possession, relates to professional services generally, and cannot be enforced by proceedings to foreclose, and it had to be distinguished from a lien conferred by NCL § 8923 (cf. NRS 18.015) on the proceeds of the judgment, which does not depend on possession, relates only to services in a particular action, and can be enforced directly. The former is a retaining, the latter a charging, lien.[212]

The statute is inapplicable to a retaining lien on papers in the attorney's possession. Enactment of NCL § 8923 (cf. NRS 18.015), giving an attorney a lien on a cause of action and the proceeds of judgment, did not affect his retaining a lien on papers in his possession, because both a retaining lien and a charging lien on the judgment were recognized at common law, and the statute affects only the charging lien.[213]

The court in an action where the services were rendered may enforce or determine validity of lien. Under the former provisions of NRS 18.010 (cf. NRS 18.015), an attorney has a lien for services rendered to a client, and by reason of its control over its processes and parties, a court has power, in an action in which such services are rendered, to enforce or determine the validity of a lien claimed by an attorney, and to protect the attorney against any improper attempt to defeat such a lien.[214]

The recourse of a withdrawing attorney is not limited to a statutory lien; the court in the pending action may bind the litigant by personal judgment. Where judgment for attorneys' fees in favor of attorneys who withdrew from a pending action pursuant to a court order was rendered in such action, recourse of the attorneys was not limited to a statutory lien, (see former provisions of NRS 18.010, cf. NRS 18.015), and personal judgment was proper without resort

[208] *MacDonald Carano Wilson LLP v. The Bourassa Law Group, LLC*, 131 Nev. Advance Opinion 90 (2015).

[209] *Dunseath v. Nevada Industrial Commission,* 52 Nev. 104, 282 Pac. 879 (1929), cited, *Bero-Wachs v. Law Office of Logar & Pulver*, 123 Nev., Advance Opinion 10, at ___, 157 P.3d 704 (2007).

[210] *Berrum v. Georgetta*, 60 Nev. 1, 93 P.2d 525 (1939).

[211] *Id.,* distinguished, *Morse v. Eighth Judicial Dist. Court*, 65 Nev. 275, at 281, 284, 195 P.2d 199 (1948).

[212] *Morse v. Eighth Judicial Dist. Court*, 65 Nev. 275, 195 P.2d 199 (1948), cited, *In re Kaufman*, 93 Nev. 452, at 457, 567 P.2d 957 (1977), *Figliuzzi v. Eighth Judicial Dist. Court*, 111 Nev. 338, at 342, 890 P.2d 798 (1995), see also *Michel v. Eighth Judicial Dist. Court*, 117 Nev. 145, at 149, 17 P.3d 1003 (2001).

[213] *Morse, supra.*

[214] *Earl v. Las Vegas Auto Parts, Inc.*, 73 Nev. 58, 307 P.2d 781 (1957).

by the attorneys to an independent action, because a lien is merely security for a right founded on a contract, and jurisdiction to bind a litigant by an award of fees includes jurisdiction to bind by personal judgment.[215]

The power of a court to fix a fee and give a judgment against a client is independent from a statutory lien. The right of a discharged attorney to be paid is not based upon or limited to either a statutory charging lien, under former provisions of NRS 18.010 (cf. NRS 18.015), or a common-law retaining lien, but is based upon a contract, express or implied. The power of a court to fix a fee and enter a judgment against a client is independent of the nature or assertion of the lien.[216]

An offset of attorney's fees and costs takes priority over an attorney's lien. In a civil action, the offset of attorney's fees and costs awarded to the defendant under NRS 17.115 is part of a trial judgment and takes priority over a lien filed by the plaintiff's attorney under NRS 18.015. Where the offset was greater than the damages awarded to the plaintiff, an attorney's lien could not be enforced because there was no judgment or fund available to the client to which it could attach.[217]

A lien for attorney's fees became unenforceable upon a consent judgment being entered against the attorney for malpractice. An appellant hired a respondent law firm to represent her in a personal injury action, but became dissatisfied and replaced them with another law firm. After transferring the case file, the respondents notified the other law firm that the respondents claimed a lien for attorney's fees upon any recovery received by the appellant (see NRS 18.015). The appellant filed an action for malpractice against the respondents and accepted an offer of judgment from the respondents. The consent judgment settling the action for malpractice provided that the judgment constituted adjudication of all claims of the parties in any way arising out of or relating to the subject matter of the case. The court held that a lien for attorney's fees became unenforceable after the consent judgment was entered in an action for malpractice because (1) both actions were founded upon the same events and, therefore, the lien was extinguished by the terms of the consent judgment, and (2) it would be inconsistent to allow the respondent to collect attorney's fees for the same services that formed the foundation for a substantial judgment against the respondent for malpractice.[218]

The section does not apply to fee agreements between attorneys which are not based on fee agreement between client and attorney. A Nevada attorney was retained as local counsel by a California attorney who represented a party in a personal injury case filed in Nevada. The personal injury case was settled out of court and when the California attorney failed to remit payment to the Nevada attorney, the Nevada attorney filed a motion to adjudicate an attorney's lien under NRS 18.015 against proceeds of the settlement of the personal injury case. The Supreme Court held that the district court erred in entertaining the motion to adjudicate an attorney's lien because (1) there was no fee agreement between the client in the personal injury case and the Nevada attorney, (2) dispute over payment was based solely on the agreement between the California attorney and the Nevada attorney, and (3) NRS 18.015 was inapplicable to fee agreements between attorneys which were not based on a fee agreement between a client and an attorney.[219]

In a civil action, where an attorney filed a notice of an attorney's lien for fees and costs under NRS 18.015 and the district court ordered the attorney's fees stricken from the lien and granted the attorney only his costs, the attorney had no right of appeal under NRAP 3A(a) because he was not a party to the underlying action. The proper remedy for the attorney was a petition to the Supreme Court for extraordinary relief.[220]

Liens for attorney's fees take priority over liens for medical care providers. Where: (1) an arbitration award was insufficient to pay the liens of plaintiff's medical care providers; (2) the plaintiff's attorney deducted his attorney's fees from the arbitration award and filed an interpleader action for the remaining amount; and (3) one of the medical care providers contended that the attorney should return the amount he deducted because all the liens should be treated the same, with all the lienholders given a pro rata share of the arbitration award, the court held that liens for attorney's fees (see NRS 18.015) have priority over liens for medical care providers and that liens for attorney's fees are not subject to pro rata distribution.[221]

---

[215] *Gordon v. Stewart*, 74 Nev. 115, 324 P.2d 234 (1958), cited, *Sarman v. Goldwater, Taber & Hill*, 80 Nev. 536, at 540, 396 P.2d 847 (1964), *Van Cleave v. Osborn, Jenkins & Gamboa, Chtd.*, 108 Nev. 885, at 888, 840 P.2d 589 (1992).

[216] *Sarman v. Goldwater, Taber & Hill*, 80 Nev. 536, 396 P.2d 847 (1964), cited, *Bero-Wachs v. Law Office of Logar & Pulver*, 123 Nev., Advance Opinion 10, at ___, 157 P.3d 704 (2007).

[217] *Muije v. A North Las Vegas Cab Co.*, 106 Nev. 664, 799 P.2d 559 (1990), cited, *Michel v. Eighth Judicial Dist. Court*, 117 Nev. 145, at 149, 17 P.3d 1003 (2001).

[218] *Van Cleave v. Osborn, Jenkins & Gamboa, Chtd.*, 108 Nev. 885, 840 P.2d 589 (1992), cited, *Michel v. Eighth Judicial Dist. Court*, 117 Nev. 145, at 152, 17 P.3d 1003 (2001).

[219] *Harvey L. Lerer, Inc. v. Eighth Judicial Dist. Court*, 111 Nev. 1165, 901 P.2d 643 (1995), cited, *Michel v. Eighth Judicial Dist. Court*, 117 Nev. 145, at 151, 17 P.3d 1003 (2001).

[220] *Albert D. Massi, Ltd. v. Bellmyre*, 111 Nev. 1520, 908 P.2d 705 (1995).

[221] See also NRS 108.600; *Michel v. Eighth Judicial Dist. Court*, 117 Nev. 145, 17 P.3d 1003 (2001).

An attorney's lien does not attach to exempt assets awarded in a divorce decree. The Nevada Supreme Court concluded that an attorney's lien does not attach to alimony and to qualified retirement accounts awarded in a divorce decree that are exempt from execution by creditors. The Court determined that NRS 18.015, which allows an attorney's lien to attach to a client's interest in the judgment or decree, must yield to NRS 21.090, which exempts alimony and certain retirement accounts from execution. NRS 21.090 arises out of a constitutional mandate that debtors shall enjoy certain exemptions from payment of any debts.[222] Exemption statutes promulgated in response to a constitutional mandate are to be strictly construed, and any apparently conflicting legislation must be subordinated to the clear intent of those statutes.[223]

The Nevada Supreme Court concluded that an attorney could not include a forensic accountant's fees in his attorney's lien when the client had an independent retainer agreement with the accountant. NRS 18.015 provides that only an "attorney at law"—not another professional—may have an attorney's lien on his client's "claim, demand or cause of action." An attorney may include costs in his lien to the extent such costs were incurred in furtherance of the client's litigation. In this case, the client independently contracted with the accountant to pay the fees. Consequently, the attorney was not a principal under the contract, and his act of recommending the accountant's services did not create joint and several liability with the client for payment of the fees. Thus, the attorney could not include those fees in an attorney's lien.[224]

There was no lien on land secured in a proceeding before federal agency. Under RL § 5376 (cf. NRS 18.015), an attorney does not have a lien upon land, title to which was secured by him for a client in a proceeding before the United States Department of the Interior, because such a proceeding was not an "action" within the meaning of the statute and was not within the jurisdiction of Nevada.[225]

A trustee in bankruptcy could avoid an attorney's lien of which notice was served after a proceeding in bankruptcy was commenced, because under NRS 18.015 a lien is not perfected until notice is served.[226]

It was proper for the district court to deny dismissal of an attorney from an interpleader action under the circumstances. Where a plaintiff's attorney deducted his attorney's fees from an arbitration award and filed an interpleader action for the remaining amount (see NRCP 22), the Court held that it was proper for the district court to deny dismissal of the attorney from the interpleader action because before a court enforces an attorney lien under NRS 18.015, the full amount of the funds in dispute must be submitted for judicial distribution and the court must determine: (1) whether the attorney may use NRS 18.015 to obtain the fees claimed; (2) whether the amount claimed by the lien stems from a judgment or settlement, as required by NRS 18.015; (3) whether the lien is enforceable; (4) whether the lien has been properly perfected under NRS 18.015; (5) whether there are any setoffs reducing the net amount subject to the lien; (6) whether equitable factors, such as a child support garnishment, affect the net amount of the judgment or the priority of the lien; and (7) based upon the net amount subject to the lien, the amount the attorney is due calculated under NRS 18.015.[227]

Daumier: Testimony of a Minor

Bad Faith

The Nevada Supreme Court has concluded that a policy-holder's "failure-to-inform theory" was a viable basis

---

[222] See Nev. Const. art. 1, § 14.

[223] *Bero-Wachs v. Law Office of Logar & Pulver*, 123 Nev., Advance Opinion 10, at ___, 157 P.3d 704 (2007).

[224] See also RPC 1.8; *Bero-Wachs v. Law Office of Logar & Pulver*, 123 Nev., Advance Opinion 10, at ___, 157 P.3d 704 (2007).

[225] *Gates v. Columbia-Knickerbocker Trust Co.*, 233 Fed. 359 (9th Cir. 1916).

[226] *In re Nicholson*, 57 B.R. 672 (Bankr. D. Nev. 1986).

[227] *Michel v. Eighth Judicial Dist. Court*, 117 Nev. 145, 17 P.3d 1003 (2001).

for bad faith by itself. Other courts have held that "an insurer can be liable for bad faith failure to settle even where a demand exceeds policy limits if the insured is willing and able to pay the amount of the proposed settlement that exceeds policy coverage."[228]

A claim for bad faith in California has two elements. First, an insurer must withhold some kind of benefit under the policy. Second, the tort requires that the reason for the withholding of benefits must be "without proper cause."[229] Texas also recognizes the tort of bad faith. In order for an insured to establish the tort of bad faith in Texas, proof must include: (1) the absence of a reasonable basis for denying or delaying payment of benefits under the policy, and (2) that the carrier knew or should have known that there was no reasonable basis for denying the claim or delaying payment of the claim. However, as long as the insurer has a reasonable basis to deny or delay payment of the claim, even if that basis is eventually determined by the fact-finder to be erroneous, the insurer is not liable for the tort of bad faith.[230]

In Nevada, a bad faith cause of action can be brought under statutory grounds or under common law. Nevada has the Unfair Claims Settlement Practices Act ("UCSPA") which sets forth the specific actions taken by an insurer deemed to be unfair to the policyholder.[231] An insurer violates the UCSPA if it, among other things, misrepresents insurance policy provisions, fails to communicate promptly with the insured about the claim, and dare I say, advising an insured not to seek legal counsel. If the insurer commits one of the acts prohibited in the UCSPA, then the policyholder is given a private right of action against the insurer and can seek any damages sustained as a result of any unfair practice. A claim brought under the UCSPA must be brought within three years of the violation.[232]

As for common law bad faith, Nevada recognizes an implied covenant of good faith and fair dealing in every contract. A breach of the covenant gives rise to a bad faith tort claim.[233] "Bad faith is established where the insurer acts unreasonably and with knowledge that there is no reasonable basis for its conduct."[234] So, how long does a Nevada policyholder have to sue the insurer when the insurance company unreasonably denies the claim or unreasonably withholds the policy benefits? Under Nevada law, a complaint for a bad faith tort must be filed within four years of the adverse action by the insurer.[235]

Bailment

A "bailment" is a non-ownership transfer of possession.[236] The word "bailment" derives from a Latin verb, *bajulare*, meaning "to bear a burden," and then from French, "bailler," which means "to deliver" (i.e., into the hands or possession of someone). Under English Common Law, the right to possess a thing is separate and distinct from owning the thing.[237] In some jurisdictions, an owner of an object can steal his own property, a curious result of the distinction.[238] In context, an owner who lends someone else an article, then secretly takes it back, can be stealing.[239] When a bailment is created, the article is said to have been "bailed."[240] One who delivers the article is the "bailor." One who receives a "bailed" article is the "bailee."[241] Usually there is an agreement in which the holder (bailee) is responsible for the safekeeping and return of the property. Examples include securities left with a bank, vehicles parked in a garage, animals lodged with a kennel, or a storage facility (as long as the goods can be moved and are under the control of the custodian).

Another definition is that a "bailment" is a delivery of personal property by one person the bailor to another (the bailee) who holds the property for a certain purpose, usually under an express or implied-in-fact contract. Black's Law Dictionary 162 (9th ed. 2009). Breach of the bailment contract may be asserted by the bailor when there is a failure to return that which was bailed. A bailee, the person who received the property, is not an insurer of the goods left in his possession. That is to say, she is not absolutely responsible if she does not redeliver the goods. She is only responsible if the failure to redeliver is caused by her negligence. When the goods are lost, destroyed or damaged by accident, without

---

[228] *Allstate Insurance Co. v. Miller*, 212 P.3d 318 (2009).

[229] *Love v. Fire Ins. Exchange*, 221 Cal.App. 1136, 1151 (1990).

[230] See *Lyons v. The Miller Ins. Co. of Texas*, 866 S.W. 2d 597 (Tex. 1993).

[231] NRS 686A.310.

[232] *Schumacher v. State Farm Fire & Casualty Co.*, 467 F. Supp. 2d 1090 (D.Nev. 2006).

[233] *Allstate Ins. Co. v. Miller*, 125 Nev. Adv. Op. No. 28, 212 P.3d 318 (2009).

[234] *Guaranty Nat'l Ins. Co. v. Potter*, 912 P.2d 267, 272 (1996).

[235] *Schumacher* at 1094-95.

[236] Retrieved from "http://www.law.cornell.edu/wex/index.php/Bailment". Content is available under a Creative Commons Attribution-ShareAlike 2.5 License.

[237] *Id.*

[238] *Id.*

[239] *Id.*

[240] *Id.*

[241] *Id.*

any fault on the part of the bailee, the loss must fall on the bailor.[242]   But once a bailor has proved the existence of a bailment, the defendant/bailee has the burden to establish by a preponderance of the evidence all of the facts necessary to prove that the loss of the items occurred without negligence on the part of defendant. where it was declared that if the burden remains with the bailor, "he will be faced in many cases with insuperable difficulties in securing and presenting evidence."[243] It was concluded as follows:

> [W]hen a bailee who is under the duty of exercising ordinary care is unable to redeliver the subject of the bailment, it is not enough for him [or her] to show that the property was lost, stolen or destroyed, but that if he relies upon such fact to excuse his failure, he must go further and show that the loss occurred without negligence on his part. As heretofore stated, a contrary rule would place upon the plaintiff [bailor], in many cases, an impossible burden. It is just and fair that one who undertakes for reward to care for a chattel should have the burden of explaining its loss or destruction while in his custody and of negativing an inference of negligence on his part arising from such loss or destruction.[244]

There are different types of bailments, such as "bailments for hire" in which the custodian (bailee) is paid, "constructive bailment," where the circumstances create an obligation on the custodian to protect the goods, and "gratuitous bailment" in which there is no payment, but the bailee is still responsible.

Although bailment has often been said to arise only through a contract, the modern definition does not require that there be an agreement. One widely quoted definition holds that a bailment is "the rightful possession of goods by one who is not the owner. It is the element of lawful possession, however created, and the duty to account for the thing as the property of another, that creates the bailment, regardless of whether such possession is based upon contract in the ordinary sense or not."[245]

There is a lower standard of care imposed upon the bailee in a gratuitous bailment, and the parties may contract to hold the bailee free from liability in any bailment. As the law of bailments establishes a lower standard of care for the bailee in a gratuitous bailment agreement, such an agreement or receipt should indicate explicitly that the bailee is acting without compensation.

When a bailment is for the exclusive benefit of the bailee, the bailee owes a duty of extraordinary care. If the bailment is for the mutual benefit of the bailee and bailor, the bailee owes a duty of ordinary care. A gratuitous bailee must use only slight care and is liable only for gross negligence.

To create a bailment, the alleged bailee must have actual physical control with the intent to possess. Physical control and intent to possess will be interpreted according to the parties' expectations. If a court thinks that liability would be unexpected or unfair, it can usually find that the defendant did not have "physical control" or "intent to possess." For example, courts are more likely to find a bailment of a car exists in a garage with an attendant than in a park-and-lock garage.

A 1703 English case delineated the types of bailments as follows:

> I must show the several sorts of bailments. And there are six sort of bailments. The first sort of bailment is, a bare, naked bailment of goods, delivered by one man to another to keep for the use of the bailor; and this I call a depositum, and it is that sort of bailment which is mentioned in Southcote's case. The second sort is, when goods or chattels that are useful are lent to a friend gratis, to be used by him; that is called commodatum because the thing is to be restored in specie. The third sort is, when goods are left with the bailee to be used by him for hire; this is called locatio el conductio, and the lender is called locator, and the borrower conductor. The fourth sort is, when goods or chattels are delivered to another as a pawn, to be a security to him for money borrowed of him by the bailor; and this is called in Latin, vadium, and in English, a pawn or a pledge. The fifth sort is when goods or chattels are delivered to be carried, or something is to be done about them for a reward to be paid by the person who delivers them to the bailee, who is to do the thing about them. The sixth sort is, when there is a delivery of goods or chattels to somebody who is to carry them, or to do something about them gratis, without any reward for such his work or carriage, which is this present case. I mention these things, not so much that they are all of them so necessary in order to maintain the proposition which is to be proved, as to clear the reason of the obligation which is upon

---

[242] *Gebert v. Yank*, 172 Cal. App. 3d 544, 218 Cal. Rptr. 585 (Cal.App.Dist.2 1985).

[243] *Downey v. Martin Aircraft Service*, 96 Cal. App. 2d 94, 97 [214 P.2d 581] (1950).

[244] *Id.* at 99-100.

[245] *Zuppa v. Hertz*, 268 A.2d 364 (N.J. 1970).

persons in cases of trust.[246]

The State of Nevada has a statute that limits an innkeeper's liability for a bailment. NRS 651.010, "Civil liability of innkeepers limited," provides as follows:

> 1. An owner or keeper of any hotel, inn, motel, motor court, boardinghouse or lodging house in this State is not civilly liable for the theft, loss, damage or destruction of any property brought by a patron upon the premises or left in a motor vehicle upon the premises because of theft, burglary, fire or otherwise, in the absence of gross neglect by the owner or keeper.
>
> 2. An owner or keeper of any hotel, inn, motel, motor court, boardinghouse or lodging house in this State is not civilly liable for the theft, loss, damage or destruction of any property of a guest left in a guest room if:
>
> > (a) The owner or keeper provides a fireproof safe or vault in which guests may deposit property for safekeeping;
> >
> > (b) Notice of this service is personally given to a guest or posted in the office and the guest's room; and
> >
> > (c) The property is not offered for deposit in the safe or vault by a guest,
>
> unless the owner or keeper is grossly negligent.
>
> 3. An owner or keeper is not obligated to receive property to deposit for safekeeping which exceeds $750 in value or is of a size which cannot easily fit within the safe or vault.
>
> 4. The liability of the owner or keeper does not exceed the sum of $750 for any property, including, but not limited to, property which is not deposited in a safe or vault because it cannot easily fit within the safe or vault, of an individual patron or guest, unless the owner or keeper receives the property for deposit for safekeeping and consents to assume a liability greater than $750 for its theft, loss, damage or destruction in a written agreement in which the patron or guest specifies the value of the property.

In a 2011 case, the Nevada Supreme Court held that NRS 651.010 does not apply to motor vehicles and that the statues does not abrogate common law bailment liability as it related to motor vehicles.[247] The Court wrote as follows:

> *Arguello* asserts that NRS 651.010 also does not shield a hotel from liability for breach of bailment, as opposed to other forms of civil liability. In *Nadjarian*, we concluded that NRS 651.010 does not limit common law bailment liability. 111 Nev. at 766, 895 P.2d at 1293. That conclusion, however, was based upon a version of NRS 651.010 that only limited liability from the loss of property left in guests' rooms, which differs substantially from the current version of NRS 651.010. *Id.* at 764 n.1, 895 P.2d at 1292 n.1. Thus, we have not determined whether the current version of NRS 651.010 abrogates common law bailment liability. Because we conclude that NRS 651.010 does not apply to motor vehicles, it follows that the statute does not abrogate common law bailment liability as it relates to motor vehicles. We need not reach the issue of whether NRS 651.010 abrogates common law bailment liability as it concerns other property.

Battery

A California court of appeal recently noted that, "[e]ven though the statutory definition of battery requires 'force or violence,' this has the special legal meaning of a harmful or offensive touching."[248] "It has long been established, both in tort and criminal law, that 'the least touching' may constitute battery. In other words, force against the person is enough, it need not be violent or severe, it need not cause bodily harm or even pain, and it need not leave any mark."[249]

At common law, battery is the tort of intentionally and voluntarily bringing about an unconsented harmful or offensive contact with a person or to something closely associated with them (*e.g.*, a hat, a purse). Unlike assault, battery involves an actual contact. The contact can be by one person (the tortfeasor) of another (the victim), or the contact may

---

[246] *Coggs v. Bernard*, 2 Ld.Raym 909 (1703).

[247] *Arguello v. Sunset Station*, 127 Nev., Advance Opinion 29, fn. 4 (2011).

[248] *People v. Page*, 20 Cal. Rptr. 3d 857, 863 n.1 (Ct. App. 2004) (citation omitted).

[249] *People v. Colantuono*, 865 P.2d 704, 709 n.4 (Cal. 1994) (quoting *People v. Rocha*, 479 P.2d 372, 377 n.12 (Cal. 1971)).

be by an object brought about by the tortfeasor. For example, the intentional contact by a car is a battery.

Battery is a form of trespass to the person and as such no actual damage (*e.g.,* injury) needs to be proved. Only proof of contact (with the appropriate level of intention or negligence) needs to be made. If there is an attempted battery, but no actual contact, that may constitute a tort of assault.

The common law requires the contact for battery be "harmful or offensive." The offensiveness is measured against a 'reasonable person' standard. Looking at a contact objectively, as a reasonable person would see it, would this contact be offensive? Thus, a hypersensitive person would fail on a battery action if jostled by fellow passengers on a subway, as this contact is expected in normal society and a reasonable person would not find it offensive. "Harmful" is defined by any physical damage to the body.

Battery need not require body-to-body contact. Any volitional movement, such as throwing an object toward another, can constitute battery. Touching an object "intimately connected" to a person (such as an object he or she is holding) can also be battery.[250] Intent can be transferred with battery, *i.e.,* a person swings to hit one person and misses and hits another. He or she is still liable for a battery.[251]

The standard defenses to trespass to the person, namely necessity and consent, apply to battery. As practical examples, under the first, a physician may touch a person without that person's consent to render medical aid to him or her in an emergency. Under the second, a person who has, either expressly or impliedly, consented to participation in a contact sport cannot assert a batter claim against other participants for a contact permitted by the rules of that sport.

Breach of Confidence

The tort of breach of confidence, is a common law tort that protects private information that is conveyed in confidence. A claim for breach of confidence typically requires the information to be of a confidential nature, which was communicated in confidence, and was disclosed to the detriment of the claimant.

Establishing breach of confidentiality depends on proving the existence and breach of a duty of confidentiality. Courts in the US look at the nature of the relationship between the parties. Most commonly, breach of confidentiality applies to the patient-physician relationship but it can also apply to relationships involving banks, hospitals, and insurance companies and many others. For example, under Pennsylvania law, a breach of physician-patient confidentiality gives rise to a distinct cause of action.[252] See "Invasion of Privacy."

Breach of Contract

To prevail on a claim for breach of contract in Nevada, a plaintiff must prove the following elements:

(1) the existence of a valid contract,
(2) a breach by the defendant, and
(3) damage as a result of the breach.[253]

"[W]hether a contract exists is [a question] of fact, requiring this court to defer to the district court's findings unless they are clearly erroneous or not based on substantial evidence."[254] A contract must be sufficiently definite to be enforced.[255] "Basic contract principles require, for an enforceable contract, an offer and acceptance, meeting of the minds, and consideration."[256] A meeting of the minds exists when the parties have agreed upon the contract's essential terms.[257] Which terms are essential "depends on the agreement and its context and also on the subsequent conduct of the parties, including the dispute which arises and the remedy sought."[258] "When essential terms such as these have yet to be

---

[250] See *Fisher v. Carrousel* [sic] *Motor Hotel, Inc.* 424 S.W.2d 627 (Tex. 1967).

[251] See *Talmage v. Smith*, 59 N.W. 656, 101 Mich. 370 (Mich. 1894).

[252] See *Haddad v. Gopal*, 787 A.2d 975, 980-981 (Pa.Super.2001) (recognizing a cause of action for breach of physician-patient confidentiality in situations where a physician discloses privileged treatment information that is unrelated to any judicial proceedings); *Grimminger v. Maitra*, 887 A.2d 276, 280 (Pa.Super.2005).

[253] See *Cohen-Breen v. Gray Television Group, Inc.*, 661 F. Supp. 2d 1158, 1171 (D. Nev. 2009).

[254] *May*, 121 Nev. at 672-73, 119 P.3d at 1257. See generally *Certified Fire Prot. v. Precision Constr.*, 128 Nev. Adv. Op. No. 35 (August 9, 2012).

[255] *Chung v. Atwell*, 103 Nev. 482, 484, 745 P.2d 370, 371 (1987).

[256] *May v. Anderson*, 121 Nev. 668, 672, 119 P.3d 1254, 1257 (2005).

[257] *Roth v. Scott*, 112 Nev. 1078, 1083, 921 P.2d 1262, 1265 (1996).

[258] RESTATEMENT (SECOND) OF CONTRACTS § 131 cmt. g (1981).

agreed upon by the parties, a contract cannot be formed."[259]

Generally, when a contract is clear on its face, it will be construed from the written language and enforced as written.[260] In interpreting a contract, "the court shall effectuate the intention of the parties, which may be determined in light of the surrounding circumstances if not clear from the contract itself."[261] Unambiguous contractual construction is a question of law.[262] A court may consider trade usage and industry custom to interpret a contract.[263]

A settlement agreement is governed by principles of contract law.[264] A settlement agreement must be supported by consideration in order to be enforceable.[265] Consideration is the exchange of a promise or performance, bargained for by the parties.[266] If the settlement agreement is reduced to a writing signed by the party that it is being enforced against, or by his or her attorney, then it is enforceable under D.C.R. 16.[267] As such, a settlement agreement is an enforceable contract when there is "an offer and acceptance, meeting of the minds, and consideration."[268]

Any employee in Nevada is presumed to be at-will, but "[a]n employee may rebut this presumption by proving by a preponderance of the evidence that there was an express or implied contract of employment that provided for termination only for cause."[269] Again, employees are presumed to be employed "at-will" unless the employee can prove facts legally sufficient to show a contrary agreement was in effect.[270]

NRS 99.040(1) applies to all contracts and requires interest to be paid on all sums from the time they become due.[271]

Breach of Duty of Fair Representation

A school principal filed suit against the school administrators' union and against the attorney who was hired by the union to represent the principal during an investigative interview and a subsequent arbitration hearing, and who was simultaneously retained by the school district to represent the school district's assistant general counsel in a separate federal lawsuit. The Nevada Supreme Court held that the school principal could not bring a legal malpractice claim against the attorney but rather had to pursue a claim against the union for breach of the duty of fair representation.[272]

The Nevada Supreme Court agrees with federal law that the duty of fair representation governs the relationship between union members and union representatives.[273] The duty of fair representation governs the relationship between union members and union representatives.[274] When a collective bargaining agreement is in place, the union and its bargaining representatives owe a duty of fair representation to its members.[275] The duty of fair representation requires that when the union represents or negotiates on behalf of a union member, it must conduct itself in a manner that is not arbitrary, discriminatory, or in bad faith.[276] If the union's conduct is deemed to be within the duty of fair representation, liability will not lie against the union for acts undertaken in representing a union member.[277]

---

[259] See *Nevada Power Co. v. Public Util. Comm'n*, 122 Nev. 821, 839-40, 138 P.3d 486, 498-99 (2006).

[260] *Buzz Stew v. City of North Las Vegas*, 131 Nev., Advance Opinion 1 (2015), (Gibbons, J., with whom Cherry, J., agrees, dissenting).

[261] *Anvui, LLC v. G.L. Dragon*, LLC, 123 Nev. Adv. Op. 25, 163 P.3d 405, 407 (2007).

[262] *Ellison v. C.S.A.A.*, 106 Nev. 603, 797 P.2d 975, 977 (1990) (noting that contracts lacking ambiguity or factual complexities are suitable for determination by summary judgment).

[263] *Galardi v. Naples Polaris, LLC*, 192 Nev., Advance Opinion 33 (2013).

[264] *May v. Anderson*, 121 Nev. 668, 672, 119 P.3d 1254, 1257 (2005).

[265] *Id.*

[266] *Pink v. Busch*, 100 Nev. 684, 688, 691 P.2d 456, 459 (1984) (citing RESTATEMENT (SECOND) OF CONTRACTS § 71(1), (2) (1981)).

[267] See *Resnick v. Valente*, 97 Nev. 615, 616-17, 637 P.2d 1205, 1206 (1981) (reversing a district court's enforcement of a settlement agreement when the agreement was not reduced to a signed writing or entered in the court minutes following a stipulation); see *Jones v. SunTrust Mortgage, Inc.*, 128 Nev. Adv. Op. No. 18 (2012).

[268] *May*, 121 Nev. at 672, 119 P.3d at 1257 (citing *Keddie v. Beneficial Insurance, Inc.*, 94 Nev. 418, 421, 580 P.2d 955, 956 (1978) (Batjer, C. J., concurring)).

[269] *Southwest Gas v. Vargas*, 111 Nev. 1064, 1071, 901 P.2d 693, 697 (1995).

[270] *Dillard Department Stores v. Beckwith*, 115 Nev. 372, 373 (1999).

[271] *Paradise Homes v. Central Surety*, 84 Nev. 109, 437 P.2d 78 (1968); *Close v. Isbell Constr. Co.*, 86 Nev. 524, 471 P.2d 257 (1970).

[272] *Weiner v. Beatty*, 121 Nev. 243, 116 P.3d 829 (2005).

[273] *Id.* at 249, fn. 31, citing *Steelworkers v. Rawson*, 495 U.S. 362, 372 (1990).

[274] *Weiner v. Beatty*, 121 Nev. at 249, 116 P.3d 829 (2005); see NRS Chapter 288.

[275] *Weiner, supra.*

[276] *Id.*

[277] *Id.*

Breach of Fiduciary Duty

Under the RESTATEMENT (SECOND) OF TORTS, a "fiduciary relation exists between two persons when one of them is under a duty to act for or to give advice for the benefit of another upon matters within the scope of the relation." In Nevada, a claim for breach of fiduciary duty has three elements:

1. Existence of a fiduciary duty;
2. Breach of the duty; and
3. The breach proximately caused the damages.[278]

A fiduciary relationship is deemed to exist when one party is bound to act for the benefit of the other party. Such a relationship imposes a duty of utmost good faith.[279] "An agency relationship is a fiduciary one, obliging the agent to act in the interest of the principal."[280] Because "the subagent owes the same duties to the principal as does the agent"[281] it follows that the relationship between subagent and principal is a fiduciary one.

A helpful California definition of a fiduciary is as follows: "[A]ny relation existing between parties to a transaction wherein the vulnerability of one party to the other results in the empowerment of the stronger party by the weaker which empowerment has been solicited or accepted by the stronger party and prevents the weaker party from effectively protecting itself."[282]

A breach of fiduciary duty is analogous to fraud, and thus, Nevada applies the three-year statute of limitations set forth in NRS 11.190(3)(d).[283] The statute of limitations for a claim for breach of fiduciary duty does not begin "to run until the aggrieved party knew, or reasonably should have known, of the facts giving rise to the breach."[284] When a fiduciary "fails to fulfill his obligations" and keeps that failure hidden, the statute of limitations will not begin to run until the failure of the fiduciary is "discovered, or should have been discovered, by the injured party."[285] "Mere disclosure of a transaction by a director, without disclosure of the circumstances surrounding the transaction, is not sufficient, as a matter of law, to commence the running of the statute."[286]

A claim for breach of fiduciary duty arising from an attorney-client relationship is a legal malpractice claim and is therefore subject to the statute of limitations contained in NRS 11.207(1).[287]

Breach of Implied Covenant of Good Faith and Fair Dealing

An implied covenant of good faith and fair dealing exists in every Nevada contract and essentially forbids arbitrary, unfair acts by one party that disadvantage the other.[288] It is well established within Nevada that every contract imposes upon the contracting parties the duty of good faith and fair dealing.[289] Moreover, it is recognized that a wrongful act which is committed during the course of a contractual relationship may give rise to both tort and contractual remedies.[290]

---

[278] *Klein v. Freedom Strategic Partners, LLC*, 595 F. Supp. 2d 1152 (D. Nev. 2009).

[279] *Hoopes v. Hammargren*, 102 Nev. 425, 725 P. 2d 238 (1986).

[280] *Engalla v. Permanente Medical Group, Inc.*, 15 Cal.4th 951, 977 (1977).

[281] *Streit v. Covington & Crowe*, 82 Cal.Ct.App.4th at p. 446, fn. 3 (Cal. Ct.App. 2000).

[282] *Richelle L. v. Roman Catholic Archbishop*, 106 Cal.Ct.App.4th 257, 130 Cal.Rptr.2d 601, 611 (Cal.Ct.App. 1 Dist. 2003).

[283] *Nevada State Bank v. Jamison Partnership*, 106 Nev. 792, 799, 801 P.2d 1377, 1382 (1990).

[284] *Id.* at 800, 801 P.2d at 1382.

[285] *Golden Nugget, Inc. v. Ham*, 95 Nev. 45, 48-49, 589 P.2d 173, 175 (1979).

[286] *Id.* at 48, 589 P.2d at 175. See also *In re AMERCO Derivative Litigation*, 127 Nev. ___, ___ r.6, 252 P.3d 681, 697 n.6 (2011).

[287] *Stalk v. Mushkin*, 125 Nev., Advance Opinion 3 (2009).

[288] *See Consolidated Generator v. Cummins Engine*, 114 Nev. 1304, 1311-12, 971 P.2d 1251, 1256 (1998).

[289] See *A.C. Shaw Construction v. Washoe County*, 105 Nev. 913, 914, 784 P.2d 9, 9-10 (1989); *Ainsworth v. Combined Ins. Co.*, 104 Nev. 587, 592 n.1, 763 P.2d 673, 676 (1988), *cert. denied*, 493 U.S. 958 (1989) (covenant applies to every commercial contract).

[290] *Hilton Hotels v. Butch Lewis Productions*, 109 Nev. 1043, 1046-47 (1993).

"When one party performs a contract in a manner that is unfaithful to the purpose of the contract and the justified expectations of the other party are thus denied, damages may be awarded against the party who does not act in good faith."[291] As the implied covenant applies to every contract or duty in the Nevada Uniform Commercial Code, it thus applies to warranties.[292] The Nevada Supreme Court has held that good faith is a question of fact.[293] "Good faith" is a state of mind consisting in 1) honesty in belief and purpose, 2) faithfulness to one's duty or obligation, 3) observance of reasonable commercial standards of fair dealing in a given trade or business, or 4) absence of intent to defraud or to seek unconscionable advantage.[294]

The implied covenant of good faith and fair dealing does not apply during the negotiation or formation phase of a contract.[295] See RESTATEMENT (SECOND) OF CONTRACTS § 205 cmt. c (1981) ("Bad faith in negotiation, although not within the scope of [the implied covenant of good faith and fair dealing], may be subject to sanctions. Particular forms of bad faith in bargaining are the subjects of rules as to capacity to contract, mutual assent and consideration and of rules as to invalidating causes of such as fraud and duress."); see also *Threshold Techs., Inc. v. United States*, 117 Fed. Cl. 681, 708 (2014) ([T]he covenant of good faith and fair dealing cannot attach until the *start* of plaintiff's implied-in-fact contract with the government" (emphasis added)).[296] Bad faith in negotiations is covered by other concepts like [such as] fraud, mistake, or duress.[297]

Breach of Implied Warranty to Perform in a Workmanlike Manner

The Nevada Supreme Court has held that a party's liability may be founded upon an implied duty to perform in a workmanlike manner, and that it is sufficient to instruct the jury that appellant had an implied duty to perform in a workmanlike manner.[298] To prove the breach of duty, expert testimony is not necessarily required. "It is well settled that the standard of care must be determined by expert testimony unless the conduct involved is within the common knowledge of laypersons.[299] . . . Where, as in the instant case, the service rendered does not involve esoteric knowledge or uncertainty that calls for the professional's judgment, it is not beyond the knowledge of the jury to determine the adequacy of the performance."[300]

Civil Conspiracy

Actionable civil conspiracy consists of a combination of two or more persons who, by some concerted action, intend to accomplish an unlawful objective for the purpose of harming another, and damage results from the act or acts.[301] An actionable conspiracy consists of a combination of two or more persons, who, by some concerted action, intend to accomplish an unlawful objective for the purpose of harming another, and damage results from the act or acts.[302]

Civil Conspiracy to Defraud

An actionable civil conspiracy-to-defraud claim exists when there is (1) a conspiracy agreement, *i.e.*, a combination of two or more persons who, by some concerted action, intend to accomplish an unlawful objective for the purpose of harming another; (2) an overt act of fraud in furtherance of the conspiracy; and (3) resulting damages to the plaintiff.[303]

Claim and Delivery

NRCP 64, "Seizure of Person or Property," provides as follows:

---

[291] *Id.*

[292] NRS 104.1203.

[293] *Mitchell v. Bailey & Selover, Inc.*, 96 Nev. 147, 150, 605 P.2d 1138, 1139 (1980).

[294] *Black's Law Dictionary* 762 (9th ed. 2009).

[295] *Hollier Trust v. Shack*, 131 Nev., Advance Opinion 59, p.7, n.1 (2015).

[296] *Id.*

[297] *Id.*

[298] *Daniel v. Hilton Hotels Corp.*, 98 Nev. 113, 115, 642 P.2d 1086 (1982).

[299] *Id.*

[300] *Id.*

[301] *Consolidated Generator v. Cummins Engine*, 114 Nev. 1304, 1306, 971 P.2d 1251 (1998).

[302] *Collins v. Union Fed. Savings & Loan*, 99 Nev. 284, 303, 662 P.2d 610, 622 (1983).

[303] *Jordan v. State, Dep't of Motor Vehicles*, 121 Nev. 44, 75-76, 110 P.3d 30, 41, 42 n.23 (2005).

At the commencement of and during the course of an action, all remedies providing for seizure of person or property for the purpose of securing satisfaction of the judgment ultimately to be entered in the action are available under the circumstances and in the manner provided by the law of the State. The remedies thus available include arrest, attachment, garnishment, replevin, sequestration, and other corresponding or equivalent remedies, however designated.

NRS 31.840, "Delivery may be claimed before answer," provides as follows:

Except as provided in NRS 179.1171, the plaintiff in an action to recover the possession of personal property may, at the time of issuing the summons, or at any time before answer, claim the delivery of such property to the plaintiff as provided in this Chapter.

Claim and delivery is analogous to replevin. An action for claim and delivery under §§ 99-110, ch. 103, Stats. 1861 (cf. NRS 31.840-31.950), is analogous to the common-law action of replevin.[304]

A demand for recovery of personal property from tortfeasor need not be proved. In an action to recover possession of personal property from one who acquired it tortiously, no demand need be proved.[305] Demand for return of personal property need not be proved when answer admits detention. Where the answer in action for possession of personal property admits detention but claims title, it is not necessary for the plaintiff to prove the demand for the return of the property.[306]

A demand for the return of personal property need not be proved if an unlawful detention can be shown. In an action to recover possession of personal property from one who acquired possession rightfully, it is not necessary to prove the demand for the return of the property if unlawful detention can be shown in some other way.[307]

The plaintiff must show that the defendant possesses the property at the time of an action. To establish a case in claim and delivery under sec. 99, ch. 112, Stats. 1869 (cf. NRS 31.840), the plaintiff must show that defendant has possession of the demanded property when the action begins, for detention is the gist of the action, and recovery of possession of property is its primary object.[308]

No cause of action is established if defendant did not have possession of property at time of action. The plaintiff failed to establish a cause of action in claim and delivery, brought under sec. 99, ch. 112, Stats. 1869 (cf. NRS 31.840), where the proof showed the defendant no longer had possession of the demanded property when the action began.[309]

A demand for return of property is unnecessary where a conversion is shown. In an action of claim and delivery under RL § 5124 (cf. NRS 31.840), the demand for the return of the property and the refusal establish conversion, but where conversion is otherwise shown by evidence, demand is unnecessary.[310]

Claim and delivery was a provisional remedy in an action to replevy property. In an action to replevy a neon display sign which was leased by the plaintiff to the defendant, where the sign continued in the possession of the defendant, the plaintiff could have recovered possession of the sign before the judgment through the provisional remedy of claim and delivery under NRCP 64 and NRS 31.840.[311]

NRS 31.850, "Requisites of affidavit by plaintiff," provides as follows:

Where a delivery is claimed, an affidavit shall be made by the plaintiff, or by someone in [or on] the plaintiff's behalf, and filed with the court showing:
1. That the plaintiff is the owner of the property claimed (particularly describing it), or is lawfully entitled to the possession thereof.

---

[304] *Perkins v. Barnes*, 3 Nev. 557 (1868).

[305] *Id.,* cited, *Ward v. Carson River Wood Co.*, 13 Nev. 44, at 62 (1878), *Studebaker Bros. Co. v. Witcher*, 44 Nev. 442, at 461, 195 Pac. 334 (1921).

[306] *Perkins v. Barnes*, 3 Nev. 557 (1868).

[307] *Id.,* cited, *Whitman Gold & Silver Mining Co. v. Tritle*, 4 Nev. 494, at 498, 504 (1869) (concurring opinion), *Studebaker Bros. Co. v. Witcher*, 44 Nev. 442, at 461, 195 Pac. 334 (1921).

[308] *Gardner v. Brown*, 22 Nev. 156, 37 Pac. 240 (1894), cited, *Fapp v. McQuillan*, 38 Nev. 117, at 118, 145 Pac. 962 (1914), *Nielsen v. Rebard*, 43 Nev. 274, at 279, 183 Pac. 984 (1919), distinguished, *Studebaker Bros. Co. v. Witcher*, 44 Nev. 442, at 463, 195 Pac. 334 (1921).

[309] *Gardner v. Brown, supra.*

[310] *Studebaker Bros. Co. v. Witcher*, 44 Nev. 442, 195 Pac. 334 (1921).

[311] *Adelson, Inc. v. Young Elec. Sign Co.*, 76 Nev. 367, 355 P.2d 173 (1960).

2. That the property is wrongfully detained by the defendant.

3. The alleged cause of the detention thereof according to the plaintiff's best knowledge, information and belief.

4. That the same has not been taken for a tax, assessment or fine pursuant to a statute, or seized under an execution or an attachment against the property of the plaintiff, or, if so seized, that it is by statute exempt from such seizure.

5. The actual value of the property.

The affidavit must state the value of the property. In an action of claim and delivery, the affidavit required by NCL § 8681 (cf. NRS 31.850) must state the value of the property, but it is not required that the value be alleged in the complaint.[312]

An affidavit must state that the property has not been taken for tax, fine or execution. In an action of claim and delivery, where the plaintiff claims delivery of property pending the action, the affidavit required by NCL § 8681 (cf. NRS 31.850) must state, among other things, that the property has not been taken for tax, fine or execution, but such matters need not be stated in the complaint in the absence of a statute requiring it.[313]

NRS 31.853, "Order to show cause; contents; service," provides as follows:

The court shall promptly examine the affidavit, and if it is satisfied that it meets the requirements of NRS 31.850, shall issue an order directed to the defendant to show cause why the property should not be taken from the defendant and delivered to the plaintiff. Such order shall:

1. Fix the date and time for the hearing thereon, which shall be no sooner than 10 days from the date of issuance of the order.

2. Inform the defendant that the defendant may file affidavits on the defendant's behalf with the court and may appear and present testimony on the defendant's behalf at the hearing, or that the defendant may, at or prior to such hearing, file with the court a written undertaking to stay delivery of the property pursuant to NRS 31.890.

3. Inform the defendant that if the defendant fails to appear, the plaintiff will apply to the court for a writ of possession.

4. Require service of the affidavit and order upon the defendant, and fix the time and manner within which such service shall be made, which shall be by personal service or in such other manner as the court may determine to be reasonably calculated to afford notice of the proceeding to the defendant under the circumstances appearing from the affidavit.

NRS 31.856, "Issuance of writ of possession without hearing; order shortening time for hearing; undertaking by plaintiff," provides as follows:

1. A writ of possession may be issued prior to the hearing provided by NRS 31.853 if the plaintiff, by affidavit or by presentation of other evidence, establishes reasonable cause to believe the probability of any one of the following:

(a) The defendant gained possession of the property by the commission of any criminal act forbidden by Chapter 205 of NRS.

(b) The property possessed by the defendant consists of one or more negotiable instruments or credit cards.

(c) The property sought to be returned either:

(1) Is perishable, and will perish before any hearing upon notice can be had; or

(2) By reason of threatened action by the holder, such property is in immediate danger of destruction, serious harm, concealment, removal from this state or sale to an innocent purchaser.

2. Where a writ of possession has been issued prior to hearing under the provisions of this section, the defendant or other person from whom possession of such property has been taken may apply to the court for an order shortening the time for hearing on the order to show cause, and the court may, upon such application, shorten the time for such hearing, and direct that the matter shall be heard on not less than 48 hours' notice to the plaintiff.

---

[312] *Johnson v. Johnson*, 55 Nev. 109, 27 P.2d 532 (1933).
[313] *Id.*

3. No writ of possession may issue pursuant to this section until the plaintiff has filed with the court an approved written undertaking as required by NRS 31.863.

NRS 31.859, "Temporary restraining order in lieu of immediate issue of writ of possession," provides as follows:

In addition to the issuance of an order to show cause provided by NRS 31.853, and in lieu of the immediate issuance of a writ of possession provided by NRS 31.856, the court may issue such temporary restraining orders directed to the defendant prohibiting such acts with respect to the property as may appear necessary for the preservation of rights of the parties and the status of the property.

NRS 31.863, "Hearing on order to show cause; undertaking by plaintiff," provides as follows:

1. Upon the hearing on the order to show cause, the court shall consider the showing made by the parties appearing, and shall make a preliminary determination which party, with reasonable probability, is entitled to possession, use, and disposition of the property pending final adjudication of the claims of the parties. If the court determines that the action is one in which a prejudgment writ of possession should issue, it shall direct the issuance of such writ.
2. A writ of possession shall not issue until plaintiff has filed with the court a written undertaking executed by two or more sufficient sureties, approved by the court, to the effect that they are bound to the defendant in double the value of the property, as determined by the court, for the return of the property to the defendant if return thereof is ordered, and for the payment to the defendant of any sum as may from any cause be recovered against the plaintiff, except that if there is reasonable cause to believe that the plaintiff is a secured party, as defined in Chapter 104 of NRS, no undertaking shall be required for the issuance of the writ of possession.

NRS 31.866, "Writ of possession," provides as follows:

1. The writ of possession shall be directed to the sheriff within whose jurisdiction the property is located. It shall describe the specific property to be seized, and shall specify the location or locations where, as determined by the court from all the evidence, there is probable cause to believe the property or some part thereof will be found. It shall direct the levying officer to seize it if it is found, and to retain it in the officer's custody. There shall be attached to such writ a copy of the written undertaking filed by the plaintiff, and such writ shall inform the defendant that the defendant has the right to except to the sureties upon such undertaking or to file a written undertaking for the redelivery of such property, as provided in NRS 31.890.
2. Upon probable cause shown by further affidavit or declaration by plaintiff or someone on the plaintiff's behalf, filed with the court, a writ of possession may be endorsed by the court, without further notice, to direct the levying officer to search for the property at another location or locations and to seize it, if found.

NRS 31.870, "Sheriff to take property described in writ; service of writ and undertaking on defendant," provides as follows:

Upon receipt of the writ of possession, with a copy of the written undertaking attached, the sheriff shall forthwith take the property described in the writ, if it be in the possession of the defendant or the defendant's agent, and retain it in the sheriff's custody. The sheriff shall also, without delay, serve on the defendant a copy of the writ and undertaking, by delivering the same to the defendant personally, if the defendant can be found, or to the defendant's agent, from whose possession the property is taken, or, if neither can be found, by leaving them at the usual place of abode of either, with some person of suitable age and discretion; or, if neither have any known place of abode, by putting them in the nearest post office, directed to the defendant.

The sheriff is to retain the property in his custody until delivery. In an action of claim and delivery, the law requires a sheriff, upon receipt of an affidavit, notice and written undertaking of the plaintiff provided for in RL § 5127 (cf. NRS 31.870), immediately to take the property of the defendant described in the affidavit and retain it in his custody until he delivers it to the plaintiff or to the defendant, if the defendant makes a demand for its return and complies with the provisions of RL §§ 5129 and 5130 (cf. NRS 31.890 and 31.900).[314]

NRS 31.880, "Defendant may except to sufficiency of sureties," provides as follows:

> The defendant may, within 2 days after the service of the writ and the undertaking, give notice to the sheriff that the defendant excepts to the sufficiency of the sureties. If the defendant fails to do so, the defendant shall be deemed to have waived all objection to them. When the defendant excepts, the sureties shall justify on notice in like manner as upon bail on arrest; and the sheriff shall be responsible for the sufficiency of the sureties until the objection to them is either waived, as above provided, or until they justify. If the defendant excepts to the sureties the defendant cannot reclaim the property, as provided in NRS 31.890.

A defendant who fails to except to sureties is deemed to waive his objections to sureties. In an action of claim and delivery, where the sheriff duly took possession of personal property of the defendant, and the defendant did not except to the sufficiency of the plaintiff's sureties within 2 days after service upon him of the affidavit and undertaking, as provided in RL § 5128 (cf. NRS 31.880), he was deemed to have waived all objections to the sureties offered on the undertaking of the plaintiff.[315]

NRS 31.890, "Return of property to defendant upon giving written undertaking." provides as follows:

> At any time before the delivery of the property to the plaintiff, the defendant may, if the defendant does not except to the sureties of the plaintiff, require the return thereof, upon the filing with the court, and serving of a copy upon the plaintiff or the plaintiff's attorney, of a written undertaking, approved by the court and executed by two or more sufficient sureties, to the effect that they are bound in double the value of the property, as stated in the affidavit of the plaintiff, for the delivery thereof to the plaintiff, if such delivery be adjudged, and for payment to the plaintiff of such sum as may for any cause be recovered against the defendant. If a return of the property is not so required within 5 days after the taking thereof and the serving of the writ of possession and undertaking upon the defendant, it shall be delivered to the plaintiff, except as provided in NRS 31.940.

The sheriff receives the undertaking for plaintiff's benefit. A sheriff who receives an undertaking from the defendant in an action of claim and delivery under § 104, ch. 112, Stats. 1869 (cf. NRS 31.890), receives the undertaking for the benefit of the plaintiff. The sheriff has no interest in the undertaking and is not a proper party in an action against the sureties.[316]

The sheriff is to retain the property in his custody until delivery. In an action of claim and delivery, the law requires a sheriff, upon the receipt of an affidavit, notice and written undertaking of the plaintiff provided for in RL § 5127 (cf. NRS 31.870), immediately to take the property of the defendant described in the affidavit and retain it in his custody until he delivers it to the plaintiff or to the defendant, if the defendant makes a demand for its return and complies with the provisions of RL §§ 5129 and 5130 (cf. NRS 31.890 and 31.900).[317]

The plaintiff is not required to except to defendant's sureties. In an action of claim and delivery, where a sheriff duly takes possession of personal property of the defendant, and the defendant requires the return of his property, he must, under RL § 5129 (cf. NRS 31.890), give the sheriff a written undertaking executed by two or more sufficient sureties, and the plaintiff need not except to the sufficiency of the sureties because under RL § 5130 (cf. NRS 31.900), it is the defendant's duty to take the initiative by giving the plaintiff notice and having his sureties justify either before a judge or clerk in the same manner as upon bail on arrest.[318]

The sheriff is to retain custody of the property until the expiration of the defendant's time to demand return. In an action of claim and delivery, after a sheriff has taken possession of personal property of the defendant, he is required by RL §§ 5129 and 5130 (cf. NRS 31.890 and 31.900) to retain possession of the property until the time has expired in

---

[314] *State ex rel. Sugarman v. Lamb*, 37 Nev. 19, 138 Pac. 907 (1914).

[315] *Id.*

[316] *McBeth v. Van Sickle*, 6 Nev. 134 (1870), cited, *Nevada Cornell Silver Mines v. Hankins*, 51 Nev. 420, at 428, 279 Pac. 27 (1929), distinguished, *Mandlebaum v. Gregovich*, 24 Nev. 154, at 158, 50 Pac. 849 (1897).

[317] *Id.*

[318] *Id.*

which the defendant may take advantage of the provisions of these sections and demand the return of his property by filing his undertaking, giving notice to the plaintiff, and having his sureties justify.[319]

The sheriff is to deliver the property to the plaintiff unless demanded by the defendant or claimed by a third party. In an action of claim and delivery, if the defendant does not require the return of his property from the sheriff within the time prescribed, or if, having made demand, he fails to notify the plaintiff and fails to justify his sureties on the undertaking, the sheriff must, under the provisions of RL §§ 5129 and 5130 (cf. NRS 31.890 and 31.900), deliver the property to the plaintiff unless it is claimed by a third party, in which case RL § 5134 (cf. NRS 31.940) prescribes the procedure to be followed.[320]

Plaintiff may appeal the refusal of a sheriff to deliver property. In an action of claim and delivery, where the sheriff refused to deliver the property of the defendant to the plaintiff, although the defendant failed to comply with RL §§ 5129 and 5130 (cf. NRS 31.890 and 31.900) prescribing the procedure to be followed for the return of his property, and the trial court refused to grant the application of the plaintiff for a writ of mandamus ordering the sheriff to deliver the property to him, the plaintiff had exhausted his remedies in the trial court and was entitled to have the matter heard and determined by an appellate court.[321]

Defendant may demand return of property upon compliance with statute. In an action of claim and delivery, where the sheriff duly took possession of personal property of the defendant, and the defendant did not except to the sufficiency of the sureties on the plaintiff's undertaking, the defendant had the right to demand the return of his property as soon as he complied with RL §§ 5129 and 5130 (cf. NRS 31.890 and 31.900) by giving the sheriff a written undertaking executed by two or more sufficient sureties, notifying the plaintiff that the sureties would justify, and having them justify before a judge or clerk in the same manner as upon bail on arrest.[322]

NRS 31.900, "Justification of defendant's sureties," provides as follows:

The defendant's sureties, upon notice to the plaintiff of not less than 2 nor more than 5 days, shall justify before the judge or the clerk in the same manner as upon bail on arrest; and upon such justification, the sheriff shall deliver the property to the defendant. The sheriff shall be responsible for the defendant's sureties until they justify, or until the justification is completed or expressly waived, and may retain the property until that time. If they or others in their place, fail to justify at the time and place appointed, the sheriff shall deliver the property to the plaintiff.

The sheriff is to retain the property in his custody until delivery. In an action of claim and delivery, the law requires a sheriff, upon receipt of an affidavit, notice and written undertaking of the plaintiff provided for in RL § 5127 (cf. NRS 31.870), immediately to take the property of the defendant described in the affidavit and retain it in his custody until he delivers it to the plaintiff or to the defendant, if the defendant makes a demand for its return and complies with the provisions of RL §§ 5129 and 5130 (cf. NRS 31.890 and 31.900).[323]

The sheriff shall deliver property to plaintiff upon payment of fees and expenses. In an action of claim and delivery, where the defendant failed to comply with the provisions of RL § 5130 (cf. NRS 31.900), in that he gave no notice to the plaintiff, and the sureties on his undertaking did not justify, it was the duty of the sheriff, upon receipt of his lawful fees for taking the property of the defendant and necessary expenses for keeping it, to deliver the property to the plaintiff.[324]

The sheriff is to deliver property to plaintiff unless demanded by defendant or claimed by third party. In an action of claim and delivery, if the defendant does not require the return of his property from the sheriff within the time prescribed, or if, having made demand, he fails to notify the plaintiff and fails to justify his sureties on the undertaking, the sheriff must, under the provisions of RL §§ 5129 and 5130 (cf. NRS 31.890 and 31.900), deliver the property to the plaintiff unless it is claimed by a third party, in which case RL § 5134 (cf. NRS 31.940) prescribes the procedure to be followed.[325]

The plaintiff may appeal the refusal of a sheriff to deliver property. In an action of claim and delivery, where the sheriff refused to deliver the property of the defendant to the plaintiff, although the defendant failed to comply with RL §§ 5129 and 5130 (cf. NRS 31.890 and 31.900) prescribing the procedure to be followed for the return of his

---

[319] *State ex rel. Sugarman v. Lamb*, 37 Nev. 19, 138 Pac. 907 (1914).

[320] *Id.*

[321] *Id.*, cited, *Bowler v. Vannoy*, 67 Nev. 80, at 112, 215 P.2d 248 (1950) (concurring opinion).

[322] *Sugarman, supra.*

[323] *State ex rel. Sugarman v. Lamb*, 37 Nev. 19, 138 Pac. 907 (1914).

[324] *Id.*, cited, *Bowler v. Vannoy*, 67 Nev. 80, at 107, 215 P.2d 248 (1950).

[325] *State ex rel. Sugarman v. Lamb*, 37 Nev. 19, 138 Pac. 907 (1914).

property, and the trial court refused to grant the application of the plaintiff for a writ of mandamus ordering the sheriff to deliver the property to him, the plaintiff had exhausted his remedies in the trial court and was entitled to have the matter heard and determined by an appellate court.[326]

The sheriff to retain custody of property until the expiration of the defendant's time to demand return. In an action of claim and delivery, after a sheriff has taken possession of personal property of the defendant, he is required by RL §§ 5129 and 5130 (cf. NRS 31.890 and 31.900) to retain possession of the property until the time has expired in which the defendant may take advantage of the provisions of these sections and demand the return of his property by filing his undertaking, giving notice to the plaintiff, and having his sureties justify.[327]

The plaintiff is not required to except to the defendant's sureties. In an action of claim and delivery, where a sheriff duly takes possession of personal property of the defendant, and the defendant requires the return of his property, he must, under RL § 5129 (cf. NRS 31.890), give the sheriff a written undertaking executed by two or more sufficient sureties, and the plaintiff need not except to the sufficiency of the sureties because under RL § 5130 (cf. NRS 31.900), it is the defendant's duty to take the initiative by giving the plaintiff notice and having his sureties justify either before a judge or clerk in the same manner as upon bail on arrest.[328]

Defendant may demand the return of his property upon his compliance with the statute. In an action of claim and delivery, where the sheriff duly took possession of personal property of the defendant, and the defendant did not except to the sufficiency of the sureties on the plaintiff's undertaking, the defendant had the right to demand the return of his property as soon as he complied with RL §§ 5129 and 5130 (cf. NRS 31.890 and 31.900) by giving the sheriff a written undertaking executed by two or more sufficient sureties, notifying the plaintiff that the sureties would justify, and having them justify before a judge or clerk in the same manner as upon bail on arrest.[329]

NRS 31.910, "Qualifications of sureties and manner of justification," provides as follows: "The qualifications of sureties and their justification shall be such as are prescribed by this Chapter in respect to bail upon an order of arrest."

NRS 31.920, "Sheriff may take concealed property by force after demand," provides as follows:

> If the property, or any part thereof, be concealed in a building or enclosure, the sheriff shall publicly demand its delivery. If it be not delivered, the sheriff shall cause the building or enclosure to be broken open, and take the property into the sheriff's possession, and, if necessary, the sheriff may call to the sheriff's aid the power of the sheriff's county.

NRS 31.930, "Sheriff to keep property in secure place; to deliver upon receipt of fees and expenses," provides as follows:

> When the sheriff shall have taken property, as in this Chapter provided, the sheriff shall keep it in a secure place, and deliver it to the party entitled thereto upon receiving the sheriff's lawful fees for taking and necessary expenses for keeping the same.

The sheriff may retain the property until the payment of fees and expenses. In an action of claim and delivery, if the party entitled to receive possession of property from the sheriff fails or refuses to pay the sheriff his lawful fees for taking the property and the necessary expenses incurred in keeping the property, under RL § 5133 (cf. NRS 31.930), it is the privilege of the sheriff to retain possession until such fees and expenses are paid.[330]

NRS 31.940, "Claim by third party; undertaking by plaintiff; determination of title," provides as follows:

> 1. If the property taken is claimed by any other person than the defendant or the defendant's agent, and such person makes an affidavit of the person's title thereto, or right to possession thereof, stating the grounds of such title or right, and files the affidavit with the court and serves a copy upon the sheriff, the sheriff is not bound to keep the property or deliver it to the plaintiff, unless the plaintiff, on demand of the sheriff or the sheriff's agent, indemnifies the sheriff against such claim by an undertaking by two sufficient sureties, accompanied by their affidavits that they are each worth double the value of the property, as specified

---

[326] *Id.,* cited, *Bowler v. Vannoy,* 67 Nev. 80, at 112, 215 P.2d 248 (1950) (concurring opinion).
[327] *State ex rel. Sugarman v. Lamb,* 37 Nev. 19, 138 Pac. 907 (1914).
[328] *Id.*
[329] *Id.*
[330] *State ex rel. Sugarman v. Lamb,* 37 Nev. 19, 138 Pac. 907 (1914).

in the affidavit of the plaintiff, over and above their debts and liabilities, exclusive of property exempt from execution, and are freeholders or householders in the county. No claim to such property by any other person than the defendant or the defendant's agent is valid against the sheriff unless so made.

        2. The title to such property shall be determined in the manner provided for in cases of third-party claims after levy under a writ of execution or attachment.

The sheriff is to deliver the property to the plaintiff unless demanded by the defendant or claimed by a third party. In an action of claim and delivery, if the defendant does not require the return of his property from the sheriff within the time prescribed, or if, having made demand, he fails to notify the plaintiff and fails to justify his sureties on the undertaking, the sheriff must, under the provisions of RL §§ 5129 and 5130 (cf. NRS 31.890 and 31.900), deliver the property to the plaintiff unless it is claimed by a third party, in which case RL § 5134 (cf. NRS 31.940) prescribes the procedure to be followed.[331]

NRS 31.950, "Sheriff to make return within 20 days after taking property," provides as follows:

        The sheriff shall file the writ of possession and undertaking with the sheriff's proceedings thereon, with the clerk of the court in which the action is pending, within 20 days after taking the property mentioned therein.

See "Replevin."

Concert of Action

Concert of action may also be known as "concerted action," which is an action "that has been planned, arranged, and agreed on by the parties acting together to further some scheme or cause, so that all involved are liable for the actions of one another.[332] Under the RESTATEMENT (SECOND) OF TORTS, liability for concert of action attaches if two persons commit a tort while acting in concert with one another, or pursuant to a common design.[333] While concert of action resembles the tort of civil conspiracy, the theories of recovery differ in that civil conspiracy requires that defendants have an intent to accomplish an unlawful objective for purpose of harming another, while concert of action merely requires that defendants commit a tort while acting in concert.

To be jointly and severally liable under the concert of action exception to the comparative fault statute, the defendants must have agreed to engage in conduct that is inherently dangerous or poses a substantial risk of harm to others.[334] This requirement is met when the defendants agree to engage in an inherently dangerous activity, with a known risk of harm, that could lead to the commission of a tort; mere joint negligence, or an agreement to act jointly, does not suffice.[335]

The Nevada Supreme Court discussed the meaning of "concert of action" in *Dow Chemical Co. v. Mahlum*[336] and explained that this doctrine requires more than just an agreement to act.

Under the RESTATEMENT (SECOND) OF TORTS, liability attaches for concert of action if two persons commit a tort while acting in concert with one another or pursuant to a common design.[337] The tort of concert of action has traditionally been quite narrow in the scope of its application. The classic application of concert of action is drag racing, where one driver is the cause-in-fact of plaintiff's injury and the fellow racer is also held liable for the injury.[338] Similarly, one court remarked that application of the doctrine of concert of action "is largely confined to isolated acts of adolescents in rural society,"[339] and another court observed that this theory is meant to "deter antisocial or dangerous behavior."[340]

Concert of action resembles the tort of civil conspiracy.[341] "An actionable [civil] conspiracy consists of a combination of two or more persons who, by some concerted action, intend to accomplish an unlawful objective for the

---

[331] *Id.*

[332] *Black's Law Dictionary* 328 (9th ed. 2009).

[333] *Dow Chemical Co. v. Mahlum*, 114 Nev. 1468, 1472 (1998).

[334] *GES, Inc. v. Corbitt*, 117 Nev. 265, 271, 21 P.3d 11 (2001).

[335] NRS 41.141(5)(d).

[336] *Dow Chemical Co. v. Mahlum*, 114 Nev. 1468, 970 P.2d 98 (1998).

[337] § 876(a).

[338] *Santiago v. Sherwin-Williams Co.*, 794 F. Supp. 29, 31 (D. Mass. 1992), *aff'd*, 3 F.3d 546 (1st Cir. 1993).

[339] *Halberstam*, 705 F.2d at 489.

[340] *Juhl v. Airington*, 936 S.W.2d 640, 644 (Tex. 1996).

[341] *Halberstam*, 705 F.2d at 477.

purpose of harming another, and damage results from the act or acts."[342] Civil conspiracy in Nevada differs from concert of action as defined in § 876 in that civil conspiracy requires that the defendants have an intent to accomplish an unlawful objective for the purpose of harming another, while concert of action merely requires that the defendants commit a tort while acting in concert.

Both causes of action require an agreement. To prevail in a civil conspiracy action, a plaintiff must prove an agreement between the tortfeasors, whether explicit or tacit.[343] Similarly, when § 876 refers to acting in concert with another tortfeasor or pursuant to a common design, it refers to this concept of agreement.[344] Proof of an agreement alone is not sufficient, however, because it is essential that the conduct of each tortfeasor be in itself tortious.[345]

Construction Defects

Construction defects, or "constructional defects," are covered by NRS 11.202-11.206, and NRS 40.600-40.695.

Constructive Dismissal

Constructive Dismissal is also known as Constructive Discharge in Violation of Public Policy or Constructive Retaliatory Discharge Against Public Policy.

Tortious constructive discharge is shown to exist upon proof that: (1) the employee's resignation was induced by action and conditions that are violative of public policy; (2) a reasonable person in the employee's position at the time of resignation would have also resigned because of the aggravated and intolerable employment actions and conditions; (3) the employer had actual or constructive knowledge of the intolerable actions and conditions and their impact on the employee; and (4) the situation could have been remedied.[346]

In *Hansen v. Harrah's*,[347] former employees brought separate actions alleging retaliatory discharge by their former employers stemming from the former employees' filing of workmen's compensation claims. The district courts dismissed the complaints and the former employees appealed. The cases were consolidated. The Nevada Supreme Court held that: (1) retaliatory discharge by the employer stemming from the filing of workmen's compensation claim by the injured employee is actionable in tort; (2) since such a cause of action and its remedy are governed by tort law, there is no need for administrative relief within the framework of the state industrial insurance system and no need to exhaust the purported administrative remedies before bringing such actions; and (3) in an action for retaliatory discharge, punitive damages are appropriate in cases where the former employees can demonstrate malicious, oppressive or fraudulent conduct on the part of their former employers, in causes of action arising subsequent to the present opinion.

Although some federal laws recognize a cause of action for third-party retaliatory discharge, Nevada does not.[348]

Examples of actions potentially justifying resignation:

Failing to pay wages due.
Putting managers into excessively difficult work situations without supporting their decisions.
Harassment or humiliation, particularly in front of less senior staff.
Victimization of the staff member.
Unilaterally changing the employee's job content or terms of employment.
Significantly changing the employee's job location at short notice.
Falsely accusing an employee of misconduct or of not being capable of carrying out their job.
Undue demotion or disciplinary procedures.
Sabotage of employee's work product either directly or indirectly with repeated interruption, confusing or inaccurate direction, or uncommunicated deadline changes.
Vandalizing the employee's workspace, home or other personal property. Such tactics could range from minor destruction of immaterial items to more severe acts of vandalism.

---

[342] *Sutherland v. Gross*, 105 Nev. 192, 196, 772 P.2d 1287, 1290 (1989).
[343] See *Eikelberger v. Tolotti*, 96 Nev. 525, 528 n.1, 611 P.2d 1086, 1088 n.1 (1980).
[344] See § 876(a), comment a; *Halberstam v. Welch*, 705 F. 2d 472, 477 (D.C. Cir. 1983).
[345] Section 876(a), comments b & c.
[346] *Martin v. Sears, Roebuck and Co.*, 111 Nev. 923, 926, 899 P.2d 551, 553 (1995).
[347] 100 Nev. 60, 675 P.2d 394, 397 (1984).
[348] *Brown v. Eddie World, Inc.*, 131 Nev., Advance Opinion 19 (2015).

Constructive Fraud

Under Nevada law, a fiduciary relationship is an element of a claim for constructive fraud.[349] Constructive fraud is the breach of some legal or equitable duty which, irrespective of moral guilt, the law declares fraudulent because of its tendency to deceive others or to violate confidence.[350] Constructive fraud may arise when there has been "a breach of duty arising out of a fiduciary or confidential relationship."[351] Such a relationship exists where "one reposes a special confidence in another so that the latter, in equity and good conscience, is bound to act in good faith and with due regard to the interests of the one reposing the confidence."[352] "Good faith" is a state of mind consisting in 1) honesty in belief and purpose, 2) faithfulness to one's duty or obligation, 3) observance of reasonable commercial standards of fair dealing in a given trade or business, or 4) absence of intent to defraud or to seek unconscionable advantage.[353]

In *Long*, the Nevada Supreme Court noted that "[g]enerally, no fiduciary obligations exist between a buyer and seller of property" and concluded, on the facts at issue in that case, that the buyer had "reposed no special confidence" in the seller."[354] In that case, the buyer stated that she did not trust the seller.[355] Furthermore, in *Long* the Nevada Supreme Court concluded that the seller had not "misrepresented or concealed any material fact."[356]

The elements of constructive fraud are 1) a duty existing by virtue of the relationship between the parties, 2) representations or omissions made in violation of that duty, 3) reliance thereon by the complaining party, 4) injury to the complaining party as a proximate result thereof, and 5) the gaining of an advantage by the party to be charged at the expense of the complaining party.[357] In constructive fraud, the law infers fraud from the relationship of the parties and the circumstances which surround them.[358] A constructive fraud may arise in the absence of a confidential relationship where: 1) a seller makes unqualified statements in order to induce another to make a purchase; 2) the buyer relies upon the statements; and 3) the seller has professed to the buyer that he has knowledge of the truth of the statements.[359] The law recognizes that in a buyer-seller relationship one party may be in the unique possession of knowledge not possessed by the other and may thereby enjoy a position of superiority over the other. The relationship is therefore one which invokes a duty of good faith and fair dealing.

Constructive Trust

For plaintiff to impose a constructive trust, Plaintiff must establish that "(1) a confidential relationship exists between the parties; (2) retention of legal title by the holder thereof against another would be inequitable; and (3) the existence of such a trust is essential to the effectuation of justice."[360] Proof of the circumstances needed to impose a constructive trust must be shown by clear and convincing evidence.[361]

A confidential relationship exists where there is evidence of a special trust.[362] Such a relationship exists where "one reposes a special confidence in another so that the latter, in equity and good conscience, is bound to act in good faith and with due regard to the interests of the one reposing the confidence."[363] Further, federal district courts have noted that the Nevada Supreme Court has not found a special or confidential relationship exists between a lender and a borrower, or between a lender and guarantor.[364]

---

[349] *Long v. Towne*, 98 Nev. 11, 639 P.2d 528, 530 (1982).

[350] *Executive Mgmt. v. Ticor Title Ins. Co.*, 114 Nev. 823, 841 (1998).

[351] *Id.* at 13, 639 P.2d at 530.

[352] *Id.*

[353] *Black's Law Dictionary* 762 (9th ed. 2009).

[354] *Id.*; see also *Mullen v. Cogdell*, 643 N.E.2d 390, 401 (Ind. Ct.App. 1994) (recognizing that a fiduciary relationship does not exist between a buyer and seller in an arm's length transaction).

[355] *Long*, 98 Nev. at 13, 639 P.2d at 530.

[356] *Id.* at 13, 639 P.2d at 530. See *Mullen*, 643 N.E.2d at 401 (holding that the existence of a fiduciary relationship is not the only basis for a claim of constructive fraud and that such a claim may arise between buyers and sellers).

[357] *Nestor v. Kapetanovic*, 573 N.E.2d 457 (Ind. Ct.App. 1991).

[358] *Scott v. Bodor*, 571 N.E.2d 313 (Ind. 1991).

[359] *Id.*

[360] *Locken v. Locken*, 98 Nev. 369, 372, 650 P.2d 803, 805 (1982).

[361] *Randono v. Turk*, 86 Nev. 123, 466 P.2d 218 (1970).

[362] *Id.* at 129, 466 P.2d at 222.

[363] *Executive Management, Ltd. v. Ticor Title Ins. Co.*, 114 Nev. 823, 841 963 P.2d 465, 477 (1988) (internal citations omitted).

[364] See *Yerington Ford, Inc. v. General Motors Acceptance Corp.*, 359 F.Supp.2d 1075 (D. Nev. 2004)

In Nevada, imposition of a constructive trust requires: (1) that a confidential relationship exists between the parties; (2) retention of legal title by the holder thereof against another would be inequitable; and (3) the existence of such a trust is essential to the effectuation of justice. The requirement that a confidential relationship exist is based on the idea that the existence of the relationship creates an inference of fraud or undue influence when property is obtained without consideration. We have stated, however, that constructive trust as a remedy is not limited to fraud and misconduct cases; it redresses unjust enrichment, not wrongdoing.[365]

Consumer Fraud

NRS 41.600, "Actions by victims of fraud," provides as follows:

1. An action may be brought by any person who is a victim of consumer fraud.
2. As used in this section, "consumer fraud" means:
(a) An unlawful act as defined in NRS 119.330;
(b) An unlawful act as defined in NRS 205.2747;
(c) An act prohibited by NRS 482.36655 to 482.36667 inclusive;
(d) An act prohibited by NRS 482.351; or
(e) A deceptive trade practice as defined in NRS 598.0915 to 598.0925, inclusive.
3. If the claimant is the prevailing party, the court shall award the claimant:
(a) Any damages that the claimant has sustained; and
(b) The claimant's costs in the action and reasonable attorney's fees.
4. Any action brought pursuant to this section is not an action upon any contract underlying the original transaction.

Contributory Infringement

"[O]ne who, with knowledge of the infringing activity, induces, causes or materially contributes to the infringing conduct of another, may be held liable as a 'contributor' infringer."[366]

Conversion

Conversion is defined as "a distinct act of dominion wrongfully exerted over another's personal property in denial of, or inconsistent with his title or rights therein or in derogation, exclusion, or defiance of such title or rights."[367] A conversion is the wrongful possession or disposition of another's property as if it were one's own; an act or series of acts of willful interference, without lawful justification, with an item of property as if it were one's own.[368] Conversion is an act or series of acts of willful interference, without lawful justification, with an item of property in a manner inconsistent with another's right, whereby that other person is deprived of the use and possession of the property.[369] There are three distinct methods by which one man may deprive another of his property, and so be guilty of a conversion and liable in an action for trover – (1) by wrongful taking it, (2) by wrongly detaining it, and (3) by wrongly disposing of it.[370]

"A conversion is defined as a distinct act of dominion wrongfully exerted over another's personal property in denial of, or inconsistent with, his title or rights therein or in derogation, exclusion, or defiance of such title or rights." "Dominion" means "control; possession."[371] "[A]n act, to be a conversion, must be essentially tortious; a conversion imports an unlawful act, or an act which cannot be justified or excused in law."[372] Liability for a claim of conversion is predicated upon an act of general intent, which does not require wrongful intent and is not excused by care, good faith, or

---

(reversed on other grounds by Giles v. General Motors Corp., 494 F.3d 865 (9th Cir. 2007)).

[365] Waldman v. Maini, 124 Nev., Advance Opinion 93, 195 P.3d 850 (2008) (citations omitted).

[366] Fonovisa, Inc. v. Cherry Auction, Inc., 76 F.3d 259, 264 (9th Cir. 1996).

[367] Evans v. Dean Witter Reynolds, Inc., 116 Nev. 598, 606, 5 P.3d 1043, 1048 (2000) (internal quotations omitted).

[368] Black's Law Dictionary 381 (9th ed. 2009).

[369] Id.

[370] Id., citing R.F.V. Heuston, Salmond on the Law of Torts 94 (17th ed. 1977).

[371] Black's Law Dictionary 502 (7th ed. 1999); Wiggins v. Houston Oil Co. of Tex., 203 S.W.2d 252 (Tex. Civ. Ct. App. 1947) ("the word 'dominion' means perfect control in right of ownership").

[372] Ferreira v. P.C.H. Inc., 105 Nev. 305, 308 (1989) (citations omitted).

lack of knowledge.[373] Conversion generally is limited to those severe, major, and important interferences with the right to control personal property that justify requiring the actor to pay the property's full value.[374]

Conversion is the wrongful exercise of dominion over the property of another. The elements of a conversion claim are: (1) the plaintiff's ownership or right to possession of the property; (2) the defendant's conversion by a wrongful act or disposition of property rights; and (3) damages.[375] Conversion is a strict liability tort. The foundation of the action rests neither in the knowledge nor the intent of the defendant. Instead, the tort consists in the breach of an absolute duty; the act of conversion itself is tortious. Therefore, questions of the defendant's good faith, lack of knowledge, and motive are ordinarily immaterial. The basis of a conversion action "'rests upon the unwarranted interference by defendant with the dominion over the property of the plaintiff from which injury to the latter results. Therefore, neither good nor bad faith, neither care nor negligence, neither knowledge nor ignorance, are the gist of the action.[376] The unauthorized transfer of property constitutes a conversion.[377] Money may be the subject of conversion if the claim involves a specific, identifiable sum; it is not necessary that each coin or bill be earmarked.[378]

Copyright Infringement

U.S. copyright law is set forth in Title 17 of the United States Code.

Deceit or Misrepresentation

The tort action of deceit or misrepresentation requires the plaintiff to establish that the defendant made a false representation to him, with knowledge or belief that the representation was false or without a sufficient basis for making the representation. Further, the plaintiff must establish that he was damaged as a result of his reliance.[379] (Generally, an action in deceit will not lie for nondisclosure.[380] Plaintiff must show a duty to disclose.)

See "Fraud/ Misrepresentation."

Deceptive Trade Practice

See NRS 598.0915 to 598.0925.

NRS 41.600 Actions by victims of fraud.
1. An action may be brought by any person who is a victim of consumer fraud.
2. As used in this section, "consumer fraud" means:

. . .

(e) A deceptive trade practice as defined in NRS 598.0915 to 598.0925, inclusive.

NRS 598.0915, " 'Deceptive trade practice' defined," provides as follows:

A person engages in a "deceptive trade practice" if, in the course of his or her business or occupation, he or she:

1. Knowingly passes off goods or services for sale or lease as those of another person.

2. Knowingly makes a false representation as to the source, sponsorship, approval or certification of goods or services for sale or lease.

3. Knowingly makes a false representation as to affiliation, connection, association with or certification by another person.

4. Uses deceptive representations or designations of geographic origin in connection with goods or services for sale or lease.

5. Knowingly makes a false representation as to the characteristics, ingredients, uses, benefits, alterations or quantities of goods or services for sale or lease or a false representation as to the sponsorship, approval, status, affiliation or connection of a person therewith.

---

[373] *Dynamic Transit Company v. Trans Pacific Ventures, Inc.*, 128 Nev., Advance Opinion 69 (12/27/12).

[374] *Edwards v. Emperor's Garden Rest.*, 122 Nev. 317, 328-29, 130 P.3d 1280 (2006).

[375] *Los Angeles Federal Credit Union v. Madatyan*, 209 Cal.App.4th 1383, 1387 (Cal. Ct.App. 2012); see CACI 2100.

[376] *Los Angeles Federal Credit Union v. Madatyan*, supra, 209 Cal.App.4th at p. 1387; see *PCO, Inc. v. Christensen, Miller, Fink, Jacobs, Glaser, Weil & Shapiro, LLP*, 150 Cal.App.4th 384, 395 (Cal. Ct.App. 2007).

[377] See 5 Witkin, Summary of Cal. Law (10th ed. 2005) Torts, § 711(2), p. 1035 (Witkin).

[378] *Haigler v. Donnelly*, 18 Cal.2d 674, 681 (1941).

[379] *Epperson v. Roloff*, 102 Nev. 206, 210-211, 719 P.2d 799 (1986).

[380] *Id.* at 213.

6. Represents that goods for sale or lease are original or new if he or she knows or should know that they are deteriorated, altered, reconditioned, reclaimed, used or secondhand.

7. Represents that goods or services for sale or lease are of a particular standard, quality or grade, or that such goods are of a particular style or model, if he or she knows or should know that they are of another standard, quality, grade, style or model.

8. Disparages the goods, services or business of another person by false or misleading representation of fact.

9. Advertises goods or services with intent not to sell or lease them as advertised.

10. Advertises goods or services for sale or lease with intent not to supply reasonably expectable public demand, unless the advertisement discloses a limitation of quantity.

11. Advertises goods or services as being available free of charge with intent to require payment of undisclosed costs as a condition of receiving the goods or services.

12. Advertises under the guise of obtaining sales personnel when the purpose is to first sell or lease goods or services to the sales personnel applicant.

13. Makes false or misleading statements of fact concerning the price of goods or services for sale or lease, or the reasons for, existence of or amounts of price reductions.

14. Fraudulently alters any contract, written estimate of repair, written statement of charges or other document in connection with the sale or lease of goods or services.

15. Knowingly makes any other false representation in a transaction.

16. Knowingly falsifies an application for credit relating to a retail installment transaction, as defined in NRS 97.115.

(Added to NRS by 1973, 1483; A 1983, 881; 1985, 2256; 1995, 1094; 1997, 1375; 1999, 3280; 2001, 489, 2149)

NRS 598.0916, " 'Deceptive trade practice' defined," provides as follows:

A person engages in a "deceptive trade practice" when, in the course of his or her business or occupation, he or she disseminates an unsolicited prerecorded message to solicit a person to purchase goods or services by telephone and he or she does not have a preexisting business relationship with the person being called unless a recorded or unrecorded natural voice:

1. Informs the person who answers the telephone call of the nature of the call; and

2. Provides to the person who answers the telephone call the name, address and telephone number of the business or organization, if any, represented by the caller.

(Added to NRS by 1999, 3332)

NRS 598.0917, " 'Deceptive trade practice' defined," provides as follows:

A person engages in a "deceptive trade practice" when in the course of his or her business or occupation he or she employs "bait and switch" advertising, which consists of an offer to sell or lease goods or services which the seller or lessor in truth may not intend or desire to sell or lease, accompanied by one or more of the following practices:

1. Refusal to show the goods advertised.

2. Disparagement in any material respect of the advertised goods or services or the terms of sale or lease.

3. Requiring other sales or other undisclosed conditions to be met before selling or leasing the advertised goods or services.

4. Refusal to take orders for the sale or lease of goods or services advertised for delivery within a reasonable time.

5. Showing or demonstrating defective goods for sale or lease which are unusable or impractical for the purposes set forth in the advertisement.

6. Accepting a deposit for the goods or services for sale or lease and subsequently switching the purchase order or lease to higher priced goods or services.

7. Tendering a lease of goods advertised for sale or a sale of goods advertised for lease or tendering terms of sale or lease less favorable than the terms advertised.

(Added to NRS by 1985, 2255; A 1993, 1959; 1999, 3281)

NRS 598.0918, " 'Deceptive trade practice' defined," provides as follows:

A person engages in a "deceptive trade practice" if, during a solicitation by telephone or sales presentation, he or she:

1. Uses threatening, intimidating, profane or obscene language;

2. Repeatedly or continuously conducts the solicitation or presentation in a manner that is considered by a reasonable person to be annoying, abusive or harassing;

3. Solicits a person by telephone at his or her residence between 8 P.M. and 9 A.M.;

4. Blocks or otherwise intentionally circumvents any service used to identify the caller when placing an unsolicited telephone call; or

5. Places an unsolicited telephone call that does not allow a service to identify the caller by the telephone number or name of the business, unless such identification is not technically feasible.

(Added to NRS by 2001, 659; A 2003, 2875)

NRS 598.092, " 'Deceptive trade practice' defined," provides as follows:

A person engages in a "deceptive trade practice" when in the course of his or her business or occupation he or she:

1. Knowingly fails to identify goods for sale or lease as being damaged by water.

2. Solicits by telephone or door to door as a lessor or seller, unless the lessor or seller identifies himself or herself, whom he or she represents and the purpose of his or her call within 30 seconds after beginning the conversation.

3. Knowingly states that services, replacement parts or repairs are needed when no such services, replacement parts or repairs are actually needed.

4. Fails to make delivery of goods or services for sale or lease within a reasonable time or to make a refund for the goods or services, if he or she allows refunds.

5. Advertises or offers an opportunity for investment and:

(a) Represents that the investment is guaranteed, secured or protected in a manner which he or she knows or has reason to know is false or misleading;

(b) Represents that the investment will earn a rate of return which he or she knows or has reason to know is false or misleading;

(c) Makes any untrue statement of a material fact or omits to state a material fact which is necessary to make another statement, considering the circumstances under which it is made, not misleading;

(d) Fails to maintain adequate records so that an investor may determine how his or her money is invested;

(e) Fails to provide information to an investor after a reasonable request for information concerning his or her investment;

(f) Fails to comply with any law or regulation for the marketing of securities or other investments; or

(g) Represents that he or she is licensed by an agency of the State to sell or offer for sale investments or services for investments if he or she is not so licensed.

6. Charges a fee for advice with respect to investment of money and fails to disclose:

(a) That he or she is selling or offering to lease goods or services and, if he or she is, their identity; or

(b) That he or she is licensed by an agency of any state or of the United States to sell or to offer for sale investments or services for investments or holds any other license related to the service he or she is providing.

7. Notifies any person, by any means, as a part of an advertising plan or scheme, that he or she has won a prize and that as a condition of receiving the prize he or she must purchase or lease goods or services.

8. Knowingly misrepresents the legal rights, obligations or remedies of a party to a transaction.

9. Fails, in a consumer transaction that is rescinded, cancelled or otherwise terminated in accordance with the terms of an agreement, advertisement, representation or provision of law, to promptly restore to a person entitled to it a deposit, down payment or other payment or, in the case of property traded in but not available, the agreed value of the property or fails to cancel within a specified time or an otherwise reasonable time an acquired security interest. This subsection does not apply to a person who is holding a deposit, down payment or other payment on behalf of another if all parties to the transaction have not agreed to the release of the deposit, down payment or other payment.

10. Fails to inform customers, if he or she does not allow refunds or exchanges, that he or she does not allow refunds or exchanges by:

(a) Printing a statement on the face of the lease or sales receipt;

(b) Printing a statement on the face of the price tag; or

(c) Posting in an open and conspicuous place a sign at least 8 by 10 inches in size with boldface letters,

specifying that no refunds or exchanges are allowed.

11. Knowingly and willfully violates NRS 597.7118 or 597.7125.

(Added to NRS by 1985, 2256; A 1987, 87; 1993, 1959; 1999, 3281; 2005, 1426; 2009, 2443)

NRS 598.0921, " 'Deceptive trade practice' defined," provides as follows:

1. A person engages in a "deceptive trade practice" if, in the course of his or her business or occupation:

(a) He or she issues a gift certificate that expires on a certain date, unless either of the following is printed plainly and conspicuously on the front or back of the gift certificate in at least 10-point font and in such a manner that the print is readily visible to the buyer of the gift certificate before the buyer purchases the gift certificate:

(1) The expiration date of the gift certificate; or

(2) A toll-free telephone number accompanied by a statement setting forth that the buyer or holder of the gift certificate may call the telephone number to obtain the balance of the gift certificate and the expiration date of the gift certificate;

(b) He or she imposes upon the buyer or holder of a gift certificate a service fee, unless each of the following is printed plainly and conspicuously on the front or back of the gift certificate in at least 10-point font and in such a manner that the print is readily visible to the buyer of the gift certificate before the buyer purchases the gift certificate:

(1) The amount of the service fee;

(2) The event or events that will cause the service fee to be imposed;

(3) The frequency with which the service fee will be imposed; and

(4) If the service fee will be imposed on the basis of inactivity, the duration of inactivity, which must not be less than 3 continuous years of nonuse, that will cause the service fee to be imposed; or

(c) Regardless of the notice provided, he or she imposes upon the buyer or holder of a gift certificate:

(1) A service fee or a combination of service fees that exceed a total of $1 per month; or

(2) A service fee that commences or is imposed within the first 12 months after the issuance of the gift certificate.

2. The provisions of this section do not apply to:

(a) A gift certificate that is issued as part of an award, loyalty, promotional, rebate, incentive or reward program and for which issuance the issuer does not receive money or any other thing of value;

(b) A gift certificate that is sold at a reduced price to an employer or nonprofit or charitable organization, if the expiration date of the gift certificate is not more than 30 days after the date of sale; and

(c) A gift certificate that is issued by an establishment licensed pursuant to the provisions of Chapter 463 of NRS.

3. As used in this section:

(a) "Gift certificate" means an instrument or a record evidencing a promise by the seller or issuer of the instrument or record to provide goods or services to the holder of the gift certificate for the value shown in, upon or ascribed to the instrument or record and for which the value shown in, upon or ascribed to the instrument or record is decreased in an amount equal to the value of goods or services provided by the issuer or seller to the holder. The term includes, without limitation, a gift card, certificate or similar instrument. The term does not include:

(1) An instrument or record for prepaid telecommunications or technology services, including, without limitation, a card for prepaid telephone services, a card for prepaid technical support services and an instrument for prepaid Internet service purchased or otherwise distributed to a consumer of such services, including, without limitation, as part of an award, loyalty, promotional or reward program; or

(2) An instrument or record, by whatever name called, that may be used to obtain goods or services from more than one person or business entity, if the expiration date is printed plainly and conspicuously on the front or back of the instrument or record.

(b) "Issue" means to sell or otherwise provide a gift certificate to any person and includes, without limitation, adding value to an existing gift certificate.

(c) "Record" means information which is inscribed on a tangible medium or which is stored in an electronic or other medium, including, without limitation, information stored on a microprocessor chip or magnetic strip, and is retrievable in perceivable form.

(d) "Service fee" means any charge or fee other than the charge or fee imposed for the issuance of the gift certificate, including, without limitation, a service fee imposed on the basis of inactivity or any other type of charge or fee imposed after the sale of the gift certificate.

(Added to NRS by 2005, 1226; A 2007, 308)

NRS 598.0922, " 'Deceptive trade practice' defined," provides as follows:

1. Except as otherwise provided in subsection 2, a person engages in a "deceptive trade practice" if the person advertises or conducts a live musical performance or production in this State through the use of a false, deceptive or misleading affiliation, connection or association between a performing group and a recording group.

2. A person does not engage in a "deceptive trade practice" pursuant to subsection 1 if:

(a) The performing group is the authorized registrant and owner of a federal service mark comprising in whole or dominant part the mark or name of that group registered in the United States Patent and Trademark Office;

(b) At least one member of the performing group was a member of the recording group and has a legal right by virtue of use or operation under the group name without having abandoned the name or affiliation with the group;

(c) The live musical performance or production is identified in all advertising and promotion as a salute or tribute and the name of the performing group is not so closely related or similar to that used by the recording group that it would tend to confuse or mislead the public;

(d) The advertising does not relate to a live musical performance or production taking place in this State; or

(e) The performance or production is expressly authorized in writing by the recording group.

3. As used in this section:

(a) "Performing group" means a vocal or instrumental group seeking to use the name of another group that has previously released a commercial sound recording under that name.

(b) "Person" means the performing group or its promoter, manager or agent. The term does not include the performance venue or its owners, managers or operators unless the performance venue has a controlling or majority ownership interest in and produces the performing group.

(c) "Recording group" means a vocal or instrumental group at least one of whose members has previously released a commercial sound recording under that group's name and in which the member or members have a legal right by virtue of use or operation under the group name without having abandoned the name or affiliation with the group.

(d) "Sound recording" means a work that results from the fixation on a material object of a series of musical, spoken or other sounds regardless of the nature of the material object, such as a cassette tape, compact disc or phonograph album, in which the sounds are embodied.

(Added to NRS by 2007, 737)

NRS 598.0923, " 'Deceptive trade practice' defined," provides as follows:

A person engages in a "deceptive trade practice" when in the course of his or her business or occupation he or she knowingly:

1. Conducts the business or occupation without all required state, county or city licenses.

2. Fails to disclose a material fact in connection with the sale or lease of goods or services.

3. Violates a state or federal statute or regulation relating to the sale or lease of goods or services.

4. Uses coercion, duress or intimidation in a transaction.

5. As the seller in a land sale installment contract, fails to:

(a) Disclose in writing to the buyer:

(1) Any encumbrance or other legal interest in the real property subject to such contract; or

(2) Any condition known to the seller that would affect the buyer's use of such property.

(b) Disclose the nature and extent of legal access to the real property subject to such agreement.

(c) Record the land sale installment contract pursuant to NRS 111.315

within 30 calendar days after the date upon which the seller accepts the first payment from the buyer under such a contract.

(d) Pay the tax imposed on the land sale installment contract pursuant to Chapter 375 of NRS.

(e) Include terms in the land sale installment contract providing rights and protections to the buyer that are substantially the same as those under a foreclosure pursuant to Chapter 40 of NRS.

As used in this subsection, "land sale installment contract" has the meaning ascribed to it in paragraph (d) of subsection 1 of NRS 375.010.

(Added to NRS by 1985, 2256; A 1999, 3282; 2009, 1118)

NRS 598.0925, " 'Deceptive trade practice' defined," [Effective July 1, 2011] provides as follows:

1. Except as otherwise provided in this section, a person engages in a "deceptive trade practice" when, in the course of his or her business or occupation, he or she:

(a) Makes an assertion of scientific, clinical or quantifiable fact in an advertisement which would cause a reasonable person to believe that the assertion is true, unless, at the time the assertion is made, the person making it has possession of factually objective scientific, clinical or quantifiable evidence which substantiates the assertion; or

(b) Fails upon request of the Commissioner or Attorney General to produce within 6 working days the substantiating evidence in his or her possession at the time the assertion of scientific, clinical or quantifiable fact was made.

2. This section does not apply to general assertions of opinion as to quality, value or condition made without the intent to mislead another person.

(Added to NRS by 1989, 649; A 1997, 3195; 2009, 2712, effective July 1, 2011)

NRS 598.0927, " 'Director' defined [Effective July 1, 2011]," provides as follows:

"Director" means the Director of the Department of Business and Industry.

(Added to NRS by 1983, 881; A 1993, 1799; R temp. 2009, 2732, expires by limitation on June 30, 2011)—(Substituted in revision for NRS 598.415)

NRS 598.0933, " 'Elderly person' defined," provides as follows:

"Elderly person" means a person who is 60 years of age or older.

(Added to NRS by 1993, 1978; A 2003, 2569)

NRS 598.0934, " 'Goods' defined," provides as follows:

"Goods" includes, without limitation, a mobile or manufactured home which:

1. Is not affixed to land; or

2. Is affixed to land and sold, leased or offered for sale or lease separately from the land to which it is affixed.

(Added to NRS by 2003, 587)

NRS 598.0935, " 'Mark' defined," provides as follows:

"Mark" means a word, name, symbol, device or any combination of the foregoing in any form or arrangement.

(Added to NRS by 1973, 1484)—(Substituted in revision for NRS 598.420)

NRS 598.0936, " 'Person with a disability' defined," provides as follows:

"Person with a disability" means a person who:

1. Has a physical or mental impairment that substantially limits one or more of the major life activities of the person;

2. Has a record of such an impairment; or

3. Is regarded as having such an impairment.

(Added to NRS by 1993, 1978)—(Substituted in revision for NRS 598.093)

Declaratory Judgments

Actions for declaratory relief are covered by NRS 30.010 to NRS 30.160, inclusive, and NRCP 57. NRS 30.010, "Short title," provides as follows: "NRS 30.010 to 30.160, inclusive, may be cited as the Uniform Declaratory Judgments Act."

Declaratory relief is available only if a justiciable controversy exists between persons with adverse interests, the party seeking declaratory relief has a legally protectable interest in the controversy, and the issue is ripe for judicial determination.[381] The declaratory relief statute should not be used for the purpose of anticipating and determining an issue which can be determined in the main action.[382] Additionally, whether a determination is proper in an action for declaratory relief is a matter within the trial judge's discretion that will not be disturbed on appeal unless abused.[383] Finally, it must clearly appear that the asserted alternative remedies are available to the plaintiff seeking the declaratory relief, and that such remedies are speedy and adequate or as well suited to the plaintiff's needs as is declaratory relief.[384]

The powers of courts under the Uniform Declaratory Judgments Act, NCL § 9440 et seq. (cf. NRS 30.010), are not restricted by special enumerations in the act. Any relief which will terminate the controversy or remove uncertainty may be granted.[385]

A claim for relief is required. A complaint seeking to vacate a Nevada divorce decree on the ground that the court which granted it was without jurisdiction because of the lack of domiciliary intention on the part of the plaintiff did not present a claim for relief under the Uniform Declaratory Judgments Act (see NRS 30.010–30.160). No justiciable issue as to the parties' marital status in Nevada existed, because the decree, which was not appealed from, was a final determination of the marital status by the court acting within its jurisdiction, and was not subject to attack for extrinsic fraud.[386]

NRS 30.020, " 'Person' defined," provides as follows:

"Person" wherever used in NRS 30.010 to 30.160, inclusive, shall be construed to mean any person, partnership, joint stock company, unincorporated association or society, or municipal or other corporation of any character whatsoever.
[13:22:1929; NCL § 9452]

NRS 30.030, "Scope," provides as follows:

Courts of record within their respective jurisdictions shall have power to declare rights, status and other legal relations whether or not further relief is or could be claimed. No action or proceeding shall be open to objection on the ground that a declaratory judgment or decree is prayed for. The declaration may be either affirmative or negative in form and effect; and such declarations shall have the force and effect of a final judgment or decree.

The effect of the adoption by Nevada of the Uniform Declaratory Judgment Act, ch. 22, Stats. 1929 (cf. NRS Chapter 30), was to permit adjudication of innumerable complaints and controversies not previously capable of judicial relief, including the vindication of challenged rights, the clarification and stabilization of unsettled legal relations, and the removal of legal clouds which create insecurity and fear.[387]

Conditions precedent to declaratory relief. In an action for a declaratory judgment under ch. 22, Stats. 1929 (cf. NRS Chapter 30), the conditions precedent to declaratory relief are: (1) a justiciable controversy must exist in which a claim of right is asserted against one who has an interest in contesting it; (2) the controversy must be between persons whose interests are adverse; (3) the party seeking the declaratory relief must have a legally protectable interest in the

---

[381] *Cnty. of Clark, ex rel. Univ. Med. Ctr. v. Upchurch*, 114 Nev. 749, 752, 961 P.2d 754, 756 (1998) [citations omitted].

[382] *Capitan Club v. Fireman's Fund Ins. Co.*, 89 Nev. 65, 69, 506 P.2d 426, 428 (1973).

[383] *Id.* at 68.

[384] *Id.* at 70.

[385] NCL § 9444 (cf. NRS 30.070). *Woods v. Bromley*, 69 Nev. 96, 241 P.2d 1103 (1952).

[386] *Colby v. Colby*, 78 Nev. 150, 369 P.2d 1019 (1962).

[387] *Kress v. Corey*, 65 Nev. 1, 189 P.2d 352 (1948), cited, *Woods v. Bromley*, 69 Nev. 96, at 106, 241 P.2d 1103 (1952), *Cox v. Glenbrook Co.*, 78 Nev. 254, at 271, 371 P.2d 647 (1962) (concurring opinion).

controversy; and (4) the issue involved in the controversy must be ripe for judicial determination.[388]

The requirements for joinder. On appeal from a judgment dismissing an action for declaratory judgment under ch. 22, Stats. 1929 (cf. NRS Chapter 30), and for injunctive and other relief, by the plaintiff purchaser of a business under a contract calling for assignment or sublease against the seller demanding contract payment, the lessor demanding possession of the premises, and the bank escrow agent, where the case met the requirements for declaration of rights, all relief prayed for could be coupled in one action, and all defendants were properly joined, judgment was reversed and the case remanded.[389]

A declaratory judgment does not compel a party to satisfy the declared rights and may be coupled with injunctive relief. A declaratory judgment does not carry with it an element of coercion as to either party. It determines their legal rights without undertaking to compel either party to pay money or to take some other action to satisfy such rights as are determined to exist by declaratory judgment, but under the appropriate circumstances, a declaratory judgment may be coupled with injunctive relief.[390]

The court was without power to issue declaratory judgment that did not involve a declaration of any right, status or other legal relation. A claimant in a medical malpractice action filed an affidavit of an expert witness with a screening panel (see former NRS 41A.039) in response to an answer of the defendant. The defendant filed in district court a complaint for declaratory and injunctive relief. In entering a declaratory judgment in favor of the defendant and permanently enjoining the insurance commissioner and the screening panel from considering the affidavit, the district court exceeded its jurisdiction because the decision of a screening panel did not involve a substantial right of any party to a medical malpractice action and, therefore, an alleged declaratory judgment action on behalf of the defendant did not involve a declaration of any right, status or legal relation.[391]

An action for declaratory relief presented no justiciable controversy ripe for judicial determination where a judgment in a civil action had not been obtained. Plaintiff brought a civil action against defendant alleging that the defendant, while driving a car belonging to another person, negligently struck the plaintiff as she stood in a crosswalk. Before judgment was obtained in the civil action, the plaintiff filed an amended complaint seeking a declaratory judgment (see NRS 30.030) against the defendant's insurer after the insurer denied the plaintiff's claim under the defendant's policy of motorcycle insurance because, according to the insurer, the policy excluded coverage for the defendant's use of the vehicle. The district court dismissed the plaintiff's action against the insurer for failure to state a claim upon which relief could be granted. On appeal, the Supreme Court held that plaintiff's action for declaratory relief presented no justiciable controversy ripe for judicial determination. Because plaintiff's rights against the insurer were contingent on her successful litigation of the pending civil action against the defendant, the plaintiff could assert no legally protectable interest creating justiciable controversy ripe for declaratory relief.[392]

Declaratory relief was properly granted to address the issue of whether statutory limitation on governmental tort liability applies separately to each governmental entity in an action or applies in the aggregate to all those governmental entities. Where:

(1) the plaintiffs brought negligence actions against multiple governmental entities and settled with some of the governmental entities for $50,000 each (the limit set forth in NRS 41.035) [now $100,000], but had not settled with the defendants;

(2) the question of the defendants' liability in a pending negligence action brought by the plaintiffs was unresolved; and

(3) the district court granted declaratory relief in favor of the plaintiffs with respect to the issue of whether the statutory limitation on governmental tort liability applies separately to each governmental entity involved in an action or applies in the aggregate to all governmental entities involved in the action (see also NRS 30.030), the Supreme Court determined that the issue at bar was an issue of first impression that could profoundly affect public treasuries and would likely arise again and that resolution of the issue would promote judicial economy by preventing future litigation and by possibly ending the pending negligence action between the parties. The Supreme Court held that NRS 30.040 suggests that immediate review of the rights of the parties pursuant to NRS 41.031 and 41.035 was appropriate and that the district

---

[388] *Heller v. Legislature*, 120 Nev. 456, at 473, 93 P.3d 746 (2004).

[389] *Kress v. Corey*, 65 Nev. 1, 189 P.2d 352 (1948), cited, *Woods v. Bromley*, 69 Nev. 96, at 106, 241 P.2d 1103 (1952), *Dredge Corp. v. Wells Cargo, Inc.*, 80 Nev. 99, at 101, 389 P.2d 394 (1964).

[390] *Aronoff v. Katleman*, 75 Nev. 424, 345 P.2d 221 (1959).

[391] *Phelps v. Second Judicial Dist. Court*, 106 Nev. 917, 803 P.2d 1101 (1990), cited, *Barrett v. Baird*, 111 Nev. 1496, at 1501, 1513, 908 P.2d 689 (1995), distinguished, *Ashokan v. State, Dep't of Ins.*, 109 Nev. 662, at 666, 856 P.2d 244 (1993).

[392] *Knittle v. Progressive Cas. Ins. Co.*, 112 Nev. 8, 908 P.2d 724 (1996), cited, *Heller v. Legislature*, 120 Nev. 456, at 473, 93 P.3d 746 (2004), *Herbst Gaming, Inc. v. Heller*, 122 Nev. 877, at 887, 141 P.3d 1224 (2006).

court did not abuse its discretion in granting declaratory relief.[393]

The issue of whether employment of State Legislators in the Executive Branch violates separation of powers may be raised in a proper action in the district court. Although the judiciary may not review whether state executive branch employees are qualified to sit in the Nevada Legislature (see Nev. Const. art. 4, § 6), the judiciary may review whether it is constitutional for State Legislators to hold positions in the Executive Branch under the doctrine of separation of powers (see Nev. Const. art. 3, § 1). This dichotomy exists because unlike Nev. Const. art. 4, § 6, which expressly gives to each house the authority to judge the qualifications, elections and returns of its members, no constitutional provision gives the Executive Branch the exclusive authority to judge the qualifications of its officers and employees. Thus, the dual service issue may be raised as a separation-of-powers challenge to Legislators working in the Executive Branch if the challenge is brought in a proper action in the district court. A proper action may be: (1) a quo warranto action brought by the Attorney General against a Legislator seeking to oust the Legislator from an executive branch position invested with sovereign power (see NRS 35.010, NRS 35.040, NRS 35.050, NRS 35.060 and Nev. Const. art. 6, §§ 4 and 6); or (2) an action for declaratory and injunctive relief brought by a person with standing against a Legislator seeking to enjoin the Legislator from continuing to work in an executive branch position (see NRS 30.030, 30.130 and 33.010). Such actions should be brought in the district court to allow a full record to be developed regarding the nature and scope of the Legislator's duties and position in the Executive Branch.[394]

The district court lacked authority at the preelection stage to interpret a voter initiative. Opponents of a proposed initiative restricting smoking in business establishments argued that because of the district court's preelection conclusion that the initiative would encompass hotel and motel rooms, contrary to the statements of initiative proponents, the initiative's title was unconstitutionally misleading. The Supreme Court did not consider the argument, ruling that the district court lacked authority at the preelection stage to interpret the initiative. The district court improperly attempted to apply the measure to a hypothetical set of facts, essentially rendering an advisory opinion, which thus was void.[395]

NRS 30.040, "Questions of construction or validity of instruments, contracts and statutes," provides as follows:

1. Any person interested under a deed, written contract or other writings constituting a contract, or whose rights, status or other legal relations are affected by a statute, municipal ordinance, contract or franchise, may have determined any question of construction or validity arising under the instrument, statute, ordinance, contract or franchise and obtain a declaration of rights, status or other legal relations thereunder.

2. A maker or legal representative of a maker of a will, trust or other writings constituting a testamentary instrument may have determined any question of construction or validity arising under the instrument and obtain a declaration of rights, status or other legal relations thereunder. Any action for declaratory relief under this subsection may only be made in a proceeding commenced pursuant to the provisions of title 12 or 13 of NRS, as appropriate.
[2:22:1929; NCL § 9441]—(NRS A 2009, 1636)

In an action for declaratory judgment under ch. 22, Stats. 1929 (cf. NRS Chapter 30), where plaintiff alleged a demand by the defendant seller of a business and assignor of an unexpired lease for payment of rent and installments of the purchase price under threat of forfeiture, and service of notice to vacate by the defendant lessor on the ground that assignment to the plaintiff was in violation of the lease, the rule that declaratory relief may not be had where danger is merely apprehended did not apply to such claims, demands and threats.[396]

On appeal from a judgment dismissing an action for declaratory judgment under ch. 22, Stats. 1929 (cf. NRS Chapter 30), and for injunctive and other relief, by plaintiff purchaser of a business under a contract calling for assignment or sublease against the seller demanding contract payment, the lessor demanding possession of the premises, and the bank escrow agent, where the case met the requirements for declaration of rights, all relief prayed for could be coupled in one action, and all defendants were properly joined, judgment was reversed and the case remanded.[397]

In an action by a county for a declaration of rights under the statute providing that any county in which is situated any federal hydroelectric project may commence action against the state and have determined whether the

---

[393] *County of Clark ex rel. Univ. Med. Ctr. v. Upchurch*, 114 Nev. 749, 961 P.2d 754 (1998).

[394] *Heller v. Legislature*, 120 Nev. 456, 93 P.3d 746 (2004).

[395] See Nev. Const. art. 6, § 6; see also NRS 30.030 and Nev. Const. art. 19, § 2; *Herbst Gaming, Inc. v. Heller*, 122 Nev. 877, 141 P.3d 1224 (2006).

[396] *Kress v. Corey*, 65 Nev. 1, 189 P.2d 352 (1948), cited, *Cox v. Glenbrook Co.*, 78 Nev. 254, at 271, 371 P.2d 647 (1962) (concurring opinion).

[397] *Kress v. Corey*, 65 Nev. 1, 189 P.2d 352 (1948), cited, *Woods v. Bromley*, 69 Nev. 96, at 106, 241 P.2d 1103 (1952), *Dredge Corp. v. Wells Cargo, Inc.*, 80 Nev. 99, at 101, 389 P.2d 394 (1964).

county is entitled to any money paid the state under an act of Congress, dismissal on the sustaining of a demurrer and refusal to amend, where trial court based the ruling on the construction of the act of Congress, was a declaration of rights of the parties within the meaning of NCL § 9440 (cf. NRS 30.030), providing that declaration may be either affirmative or negative in form, and NCL § 9441 (cf. NRS 30.040), providing for the construction of and determination of rights under the statutes.[398]

Future use of easement could not be the subject of a declaratory judgment. Whether future use of an easement in connection with a proposed subdivision would cause an unreasonable burden on a servient estate could not be the subject of a declaratory judgment, because under NRS 30.110, the determination of such issue would depend upon the facts as to the actual use existing in the future, and there was presently no justiciable controversy.[399]

A review of discretionary orders was appropriate. Where an insurance company challenged the interpretation of a premium tax statute (cf. NRS 680B.027 et seq.) by the commissioner of insurance, an action for declaratory judgment was appropriate under NRS 30.040. The purpose of the provisions of former NRS 680.230 (cf. NRS 679B.370) is to provide judicial review of discretionary orders of the commissioner, based on factual material presented to him.[400]

A legal interest is required for standing. Absent evidence of third-party beneficiary status, an assignment of contract rights or delegation of contract duties, the heirs lacked the necessary legal interest in an agreement between the decedent, the family corporation and other stockholders concerning the purchase of decedent's stock to give them standing to challenge an agreement in a declaratory judgment action under NRS 30.040 and 30.130, even though the agreement may have affected their inheritance in a practical, as distinguished from a legal, sense.[401]

A member of the board of regents of a university had the requisite standing to bring an action for a declaratory judgment challenging the constitutionality of the statute which extended the terms of the members of the board from 4 to 6 years because, pursuant to NRS 30.040 he was a "person . . . whose rights, status or other legal relations are affected by a statute."[402]

Actions for declaratory relief are governed by the same liberal standards of pleading that are applied in other civil actions. Actions for declaratory relief (see NRS 30.040) are governed by the same liberal standards of pleading that are applied in other civil actions.[403]

Section suggests that immediate review of the parties' rights concerning statutory limitations on governmental tort liability was appropriate. Where: (1) the plaintiffs brought negligence actions against multiple governmental entities and settled with some of the governmental entities for $50,000 each (the limit set forth in NRS 41.035), but had not settled with the defendants; (2) the question of the defendants' liability in a pending negligence action brought by the plaintiffs was unresolved; and (3) the district court granted declaratory relief in favor of the plaintiffs with respect to the issue of whether the statutory limitation on governmental tort liability applies separately to each governmental entity involved in an action or applies in the aggregate to all governmental entities involved in the action (see also NRS 30.030), the Supreme Court determined that the issue at bar was an issue of first impression that could profoundly affect public treasuries and would likely arise again and that resolution of the issue would promote judicial economy by preventing future litigation and by possibly ending the pending negligence action between the parties. The Supreme Court held that NRS 30.040 suggests that immediate review of the rights of the parties under NRS 41.031 and 41.035 was appropriate and that the district court did not abuse its discretion in granting declaratory relief.[404]

NRS 30.050, "Contract may be construed before or after breach," provides as follows: "A contract may be construed either before or after there has been a breach thereof."
[3:22:1929; NCL § 9442]

NRS 30.060, "Declaration of rights in certain cases," provides as follows:
1. Any person interested as or through an executor, administrator, trustee, guardian or other fiduciary, creditor, devisee, legatee, heir, next of kin or cestui que trust, in the administration of a trust, or of the estate of a decedent, an infant, lunatic or insolvent, may have a declaration of rights or legal relations in respect thereto:
(a) To ascertain any class of creditors, devisees, legatees, heirs, next of kin or others;

[398] County of Clark v. State, 65 Nev. 490, 199 P.2d 137 (1948).
[399] See also NRS 30.040; Cox v. Glenbrook Co., 78 Nev. 254, 371 P.2d 647 (1962), cited, Breliant v. Preferred Equities Corp., 109 Nev. 842, at 848, 858 P.2d 1258 (1993), distinguished, Sievers v. Zenoff, 94 Nev. 53, at 57, 573 P.2d 1190 (1978).
[400] Prudential Ins. Co. v. Insurance Comm'r, 82 Nev. 1, 409 P.2d 248 (1966).
[401] Wells v. Bank of Nevada, 90 Nev. 192, 522 P.2d 1014 (1974).
[402] Tam v. Colton, 94 Nev. 452, 581 P.2d 447 (1978).
[403] Breliant v. Preferred Equities Corp., 109 Nev. 842, 858 P.2d 1258 (1993).
[404] County of Clark ex rel. Univ. Med. Ctr. v. Upchurch, 114 Nev. 749, 961 P.2d 754 (1998).

(b) To direct the executors, administrators or trustees to do or abstain from doing any particular act in their fiduciary capacity; or

(c) To determine any question arising in the administration of the estate or trust, including questions of construction of wills, trusts and other writings.

2. Any action for declaratory relief under this section may only be made in a proceeding commenced pursuant to the provisions of title 12 or 13 of NRS, as appropriate.

[4:22:1929; NCL § 9443]—(NRS A 2009, 1636)

Declaratory relief is not precluded by a cause for equitable relief. Under the Uniform Declaratory Judgments Act, NCL § 9443 (cf. NRS 30.060), an executor may seek a declaratory judgment, and the fact that a complaint alleges a cause for equitable relief does not preclude declaratory relief.[405]

NRS 30.070, "Enumeration not exclusive," provides as follows:

The enumeration in NRS 30.040, 30.050 and 30.060 does not limit or restrict the exercise of the general powers conferred in NRS 30.030 in any proceeding where declaratory relief is sought, in which a judgment or decree will terminate the controversy or remove an uncertainty.

[5:22:1929; NCL § 9444]

Declaratory relief is not precluded by a cause for equitable relief. Under the Uniform Declaratory Judgments Act, NCL § 9443 (cf. NRS 30.060), an executor may seek declaratory judgment, and the fact that a complaint alleges cause for equitable relief does not preclude declaratory relief, NCL § 9444 (cf. NRS 30.070).[406]

Relief is not restricted by special enumerations. The powers of courts under the Uniform Declaratory Judgments Act, NCL § 9440 et seq. (cf. NRS 30.010), are not restricted by special enumerations in the act. Any relief which will terminate controversy or remove uncertainty may be granted.[407]

NRS 30.080, "Discretion of court to render or enter judgment," provides as follows: "The court may refuse to render or enter a declaratory judgment or decree where such judgment or decree, if rendered or entered, would not terminate the uncertainty or controversy giving rise to the proceeding."

The court has discretion to refuse declaratory relief. Where an insured sought declaratory relief in an action against an insurer for purposes of determining whether an insurance policy provided coverage against liabilities asserted against the insured by third parties in numerous actions in another state, it was an abuse of discretion to dismiss the action as premature, because the fact that no judgment had been recovered against the insured in the other actions did not render the action premature. Before a court may properly exercise discretion to refuse declaratory relief on the ground that other remedies are available, it must clearly appear that the asserted alternative remedies are available and are as speedy and adequate or as well suited to the plaintiff's needs as is declaratory relief.[408]

NRS 30.090, "Review," provides as follows: "All orders, judgments and decrees under NRS 30.010 to 30.160, inclusive, may be reviewed as other orders, judgments and decrees."

NRS 30.100, "Supplemental relief," provides as follows:

Further relief based on a declaratory judgment or decree may be granted whenever necessary or proper. The application therefor shall be by petition to a court having jurisdiction to grant relief. If the application be deemed sufficient, the court shall, on reasonable notice, require any adverse party whose rights have been adjudicated by the declaratory judgment or decree, to show cause why further relief should not be granted forthwith.

A prayer for injunctive relief need not be included in the initial complaint for declaratory relief, and may be in the form of a petition or motion. A homebuilder's association filed a complaint seeking to have a city ordinance declared

---

[405] NCL § 9444 (cf. NRS 30.070). *Woods v. Bromley*, 69 Nev. 96, 241 P.2d 1103 (1952).

[406] *Woods v. Bromley*, 69 Nev. 96, 241 P.2d 1103 (1952).

[407] *Id.*

[408] *El Capitan Club v. Fireman's Fund Ins. Co..*, 89 Nev. 65, 506 P.2d 426 (1973), cited, *County of Clark ex rel. Univ. Med. Ctr. v. Upchurch*, 114 Nev. 749, at 752, 961 P.2d 754 (1998).

invalid. The district court granted summary judgment for the association and declared the ordinance invalid. The association moved for supplemental relief, seeking an injunction prohibiting the city from collecting any further revenue under the ordinance, and the district court entered an injunction. On appeal, the city argued that: (1) the district court erred in entering the injunction because no prayer for such relief was made in the initial complaint; and (2) supplemental relief was inappropriate because NRS 30.100 requires that such relief be sought by petition, and the association sought the injunction by motion. In rejecting the city's arguments, the Supreme Court held that: (1) a prayer for injunctive relief need not be included in the initial complaint for declaratory relief, since NRS 30.100 specifically allows supplemental relief based on a declaratory judgment whenever necessary or proper; and (2) relief from the previously declared invalid ordinance was necessary and proper, whether in the form of a petition or motion, and the city was attempting to draw a meaningless distinction within the context and purpose of NRS 30.100.[409]

NRS 30.110, "Jury trial," provides as follows: "When a proceeding under NRS 30.010 to 30.160, inclusive, involves the determination of an issue of fact, such issue may be tried and determined in the same manner as issues of fact are tried and determined in other civil actions in the court in which the proceeding is pending."
[9:22:1929; NCL § 9448]

A justiciable controversy is required. Whether the future use of an easement in connection with a proposed subdivision would cause an unreasonable burden on a servient estate could not be the subject of a declaratory judgment, because under NRS 30.110 the determination of such an issue would depend upon the facts as to the actual use existing in the future, and there was presently no justiciable controversy.[410]
A limitation on facts shall be considered. A declaratory judgment should deal with the present, ascertained or ascertainable state of facts.[411]

NRS 30.120, "Costs," provides as follows: "In any proceeding under NRS 30.010 to 30.160, inclusive, the court may make such award of costs as may seem equitable and just."

NRS 30.130, "Parties," provides as follows:

When declaratory relief is sought, all persons shall be made parties who have or claim any interest which would be affected by the declaration, and no declaration shall prejudice the rights of persons not parties to the proceeding. In any proceeding which involves the validity of a municipal ordinance or franchise, such municipality shall be made a party, and shall be entitled to be heard, and if the statute, ordinance or franchise is alleged to be unconstitutional, the Attorney General shall also be served with a copy of the proceeding and be entitled to be heard.
[11:22:1929; NCL § 9450]

The Attorney General is not required to be made a party. Under NRS 30.130, which requires that the Attorney General be served with a copy of the proceedings and be given an opportunity to be heard in a constitutional attack on any statute, ordinance or franchise in any proceeding, it was not necessary to make the Attorney General a party to the action.[412]
Legal interest required for standing. Absent evidence of third-party beneficiary status, the assignment of contract rights or the delegation of contract duties, heirs lacked the necessary legal interest in agreement between the decedent, family corporation and other stockholders concerning the purchase of the decedent's stock to give them standing to challenge the agreement in a declaratory judgment action under NRS 30.040 and 30.130, even though the agreement may have affected their inheritance in a practical, as distinguished from a legal, sense.[413]
District court and county were necessary parties in a declaratory relief action brought by an attorney seeking to invalidate a contract which set the fees of court-appointed attorneys at less than statutory rate. Persons who are required to be made parties to a declaratory relief action are specified in provisions of NRS 30.130. Therefore, in an action for declaratory relief brought by a court-appointed attorney against the deputy clerk of a county and the court administrator, wherein the attorney sought to invalidate the contract he entered into with the district court which provided for

---

[409] *Southern Nevada Homebuilders Ass'n v. City of N. Las Vegas*, 112 Nev. 297, 913 P.2d 1276 (1996).
[410] *Cox v. Glenbrook Co.*, 78 Nev. 254, 371 P.2d 647 (1962), cited, *Breliant v. Preferred Equities Corp.*, 109 Nev. 842, at 848, 858 P.2d 1258 (1993), distinguished, *Sievers v. Zenoff*, 94 Nev. 53, at 57, 573 P.2d 1190 (1978).
[411] *Cox v. Glenbrook Co.*, 78 Nev. 254, 371 P.2d 647 (1962).
[412] *City of Reno v. Saibini*, 83 Nev. 315, 429 P.2d 559 (1967).
[413] *Wells v. Bank of Nevada*, 90 Nev. 192, 522 P.2d 1014 (1974).

compensation of a court-appointed attorney who defended indigent criminal defendants at a rate less than that provided in NRS 7.125, the Supreme Court ruled that the district court and county were necessary parties to the action. The district court was a party to the contract and presumably supplied or approved the terms of compensation to be paid to court-appointed attorneys. Because a declaratory judgment concerning the validity of a contract could prejudice or otherwise affect the rights of the court and county, the district court and county should have been made parties to the proceedings.[414]

Issue of whether employment of State Legislators in the Executive Branch violates separation of powers may be raised in a proper action in the district court. Although the judiciary may not review whether state executive branch employees are qualified to sit in the Nevada Legislature (see Nev. Const. art. 4, § 6), the judiciary may review whether it is constitutional for State Legislators to hold positions in the Executive Branch under the doctrine of separation of powers (see Nev. Const. art. 3, § 1). This dichotomy exists because unlike Nev. Const. art. 4, § 6, which expressly gives to each house the authority to judge the qualifications, elections and returns of its members, no constitutional provision gives the Executive Branch the exclusive authority to judge the qualifications of its officers and employees. Thus, the dual service issue may be raised as a separation-of-powers challenge to Legislators working in the Executive Branch if the challenge is brought in a proper action in the district court. A proper action may be:

(1) a quo warranto action brought by the Attorney General against a Legislator seeking to oust the Legislator from an Executive Branch position invested with sovereign power (see NRS 35.010, 35.040, 35.050, 35.060 and Nev. Const. art. 6, §§ 4 and 6); or

(2) an action for declaratory and injunctive relief brought by a person with standing against a Legislator seeking to enjoin the Legislator from continuing to work in an executive branch position (see NRS 30.030, 30.130 and 33.010). Such actions should be brought in the district court to allow a full record to be developed regarding the nature and scope of the Legislator's duties and position in the Executive Branch.[415]

Joinder of Parties

Related controversies are required. A complaint alleged that the plaintiffs contracted to purchase a restaurant business and an unexpired term of lease. The plaintiffs entered into possession but the lessees had failed further to perform. The lessors threatened dispossession for breach by the lessees of the covenant against the assignment without the lessor's consent. A purchase-money note was held by a bank as security for the indebtedness of the lessees. The Nevada Supreme Court held that the complaint stated a cause of action for a declaratory judgment, and it held that the defendants were properly joined because both controversies related to the same premises, and the determination of one was necessary in order to determine the other.[416]

Lack of prejudice is required. In an action for declaratory judgment under ch. 22, Stats. 1929 (cf. NRS Chapter 30), where the plaintiff purchaser of a business under a contract calling for the assignment of or possession under the unexpired lease joined as the defendant's seller, lessor, and the bank escrow agent holding the note of the plaintiff payable to the defendant seller, all the defendants were properly joined under the Declaratory Judgments Act and Civil Practice Act, NCL § 8556 (cf. NRCP 20(a)), because neither the seller nor lessor was prejudiced by making the bank a party, and the bank, by permitting entry of default, accomplished the same result as an interpleader in holding the note and escrow subject to the order of the court.[417]

The granting of summary judgment for nonjoinder of parties was erroneous under the circumstances. Where an attorney, who had entered into a contract with the district court whereby the attorney would receive a certain amount of fees after appointment by the court to represent indigent criminal defendants, filed a complaint for declaratory relief against the deputy county clerk and county court administrator seeking judicial declaration of contractual invalidity because his contract compensated court-appointed attorneys at a rate less than that specified in NRS 7.125, the district court improperly granted summary judgment on the basis that the defendants were not proper parties to the action. Misjoinder or nonjoinder of parties did not justify entry of summary judgment against the attorney. The district court should have denied the motion for summary judgment and allowed the attorney to amend his complaint to delete the party or parties, or the district court should have effectuated the amendment sua sponte.[418]

NRS 30.140, "Construction," provides as follows:

NRS 30.010 to 30.160, inclusive, are declared to be remedial; their purpose is to settle and to afford

---

[414] *Crowley v. Duffrin*, 109 Nev. 597, 855 P.2d 536 (1993).

[415] *Heller v. Legislature*, 120 Nev. 456, 93 P.3d 746 (2004).

[416] *Kress v. Corey*, 65 Nev. 1, 189 P.2d 352 (1948).

[417] *Id.*

[418] See also NRS 30.130 and NRCP 21.); *Crowley v. Duffrin*, 109 Nev. 597, 855 P.2d 536 (1993), cited, *Civil Serv. Comm'n v. Second Judicial Dist. Court*, 118 Nev. 186, at 190, 42 P.3d 268 (2002).

relief from uncertainty and insecurity with respect to rights, status and other legal relations; and are to be liberally construed and administered.

A broad and liberal concept of the purposes of the declaratory judgment act is to be adopted.[419]

NRS 30.150, "Severability," provides as follows:

The several sections and provisions of NRS 30.010 to 30.160, inclusive, except NRS 30.030 and 30.040, are hereby declared independent and severable, and the invalidity, if any, or part or feature thereof shall not affect or render the remainder of such sections invalid or inoperative.

NRS 30.160, "Uniformity of interpretation," provides as follows:

NRS 30.010 to 30.160, inclusive, shall be so interpreted and construed as to effectuate their general purpose to make uniform the law of those states which enact them, and to harmonize, as far as possible, with federal laws and regulations on the subject of declaratory judgments and decrees.

In a declaratory judgment action, where the complaint alleged that the defendant had claimed exorbitant storage charges for logs on its property and had caused them to be sold to it for such charges, and the plaintiff sought a declaration of ownership and determination of proper charges if any, a good cause of action was stated under the Uniform Declaratory Judgments Act, NRS Chapter 30 and NRCP 57, providing that the existence of other adequate remedies does not defeat the right to declaratory judgment.[420]

The action must commence in the district court. An action for declaratory judgment under NRS ch. 30 must be commenced in a district court, and a petition may not be filed initially in the Supreme Court.[421]

Some limitations on injunctive relief. An applicant for a determination of suitability to be associated with a gaming enterprise could not circumvent the provisions of NRS 463.343, which provided that the district court had no jurisdiction to grant injunctive relief to the applicants in certain gaming matters by petitioning the district court under the Uniform Declaratory Judgments Act (see NRS ch. 30) for declaratory relief and a stay of proceedings.[422]

Provisional Remedies

Injunctions pendente lite. In an action for declaratory judgment under ch. 22, Stats. 1929 (cf. NRS ch. 30), and for injunctive relief, by the purchaser of a business under contract for assignment or sublease of an unexpired lease against a seller demanding payment and a lessor demanding possession, it was not improper for the trial court to enjoin both defendants pendente lite in order to preserve the status quo, because a prayer for injunctive relief may be joined with declaratory judgment, but where many months had passed since the injunction was dissolved, and the appeal was confined to judgment, no ruling on those proceedings was required.[423]

Temporary injunctions. In an action for declaratory judgment under NRS ch. 30, where the complaint alleged that the defendant had claimed exorbitant storage charges for logs on its property and had caused them to be sold to it for such charges, and the plaintiff sought a declaration of his ownership, a prayer for a temporary injunction to restrain the defendant from transferring, encumbering or changing the nature of the logs was a proper provisional remedy to maintain the status quo.[424]

The existence of a Uniform Act was a compelling reason for a federal court to decline to assert jurisdiction over actions for declaratory relief. Where the insureds were sued in personal injury actions in a state court and the insurer brought separate diversity actions in federal court to obtain a declaratory judgment that an "assault and battery" exclusion in policies absolved the insurer of the responsibility to defend and indemnify the insureds, the United States District

[419] *Woods v. Bromley*, 69 Nev. 96, 241 P.2d 1103 (1952).

[420] *Nevada Management Co. v. Jack*, 75 Nev. 232, 338 P.2d 71 (1959), cited, *City of Boulder City v. Miles*, 85 Nev. 46, at 48, 449 P.2d 1003 (1969).

[421] *Beko v. Kelly*, 78 Nev. 489, 376 P.2d 429 (1962).

[422] *State v. Glusman*, 98 Nev. 412, 651 P.2d 639 (1982), cited, *Cohen v. State*, 113 Nev. 180, at 187, 930 P.2d 125 (1997) (dissenting opinion).

[423] *Kress v. Corey*, 65 Nev. 1, 189 P.2d 352 (1948), cited, *Woods v. Bromley*, 69 Nev. 96, at 106, 241 P.2d 1103 (1952), *Nevada Management Co. v. Jack*, 75 Nev. 232, at 236, 338 P.2d 71 (1959), *Dredge Corp. v. Wells Cargo, Inc.* 80 Nev. 99, at 101, 389 P.2d 394 (1964).

[424] *Nevada Management Co. v. Jack*, 75 Nev. 232, 338 P.2d 71 (1959), cited, *Dredge Corp. v. Wells Cargo, Inc.*, 80 Nev. 99, at 101, 389 P.2d 394 (1964).

Court, in granting the insureds' motion to dismiss actions for a declaratory judgment, held that the existence of Nevada's Uniform Declaratory Judgments Act (see NRS 30.010 *et seq.*) was a compelling reason for the
court to decline to assert jurisdiction over actions for declaratory relief because the insurer could have sought declaratory relief from the same state court that would decide the underlying tort actions against the insureds.[425]

NRCP 57, "Declaratory Judgments," provides as follows:

The procedure for obtaining a declaratory judgment pursuant to statute, shall be in accordance with these rules, and the right to trial by jury may be demanded under the circumstances and in the manner provided in Rules 38 and 39. The existence of another adequate remedy does not preclude a judgment for declaratory relief in cases where it is appropriate. The court may order a speedy hearing of an action for a declaratory judgment and may advance it on the calendar.

In a declaratory judgment action, where the complaint alleged that defendant had claimed exorbitant storage charges for logs on its property and had caused them to be sold to it for such charges, and plaintiff sought a declaration of ownership and a determination of proper charges if any, good cause of action was stated under the Uniform Declaratory Judgments Act, NRS ch. 30 and NRCP 57, providing that the existence of other adequate remedies does not defeat the right to a declaratory judgment.[426]

Defamation

An action for defamation requires the plaintiff to prove four elements: (1) a false and defamatory statement; (2) an unprivileged publication to a third person; (3) fault, amounting to at least negligence; and (4) actual or presumed damages.[427] However, if the defamatory communication imputes a "person's lack of fitness for trade, business, or profession," or tends to injure the plaintiff in his or her business, it is deemed defamation per se and damages are presumed.[428] "Defamation is a publication of a false statement of fact."[429] An opinion cannot be defamatory because "there is no such thing as a false idea."[430] If a plaintiff is defamed and the damage to that person's reputation caused the denial of a federally protected right or the damage was inflicted in connection with a federally protected right, that person is entitled to damages under a "stigma-plus" defamation theory.[431]

A statement is actionable as "mixed type" statement of opinion and fact when they imply the existence of information which would tend to lower the plaintiff's reputation. A "mixed-type" theory requires an "inference that the source has based the opinion on underlying, undisclosed defamatory facts."[432]

A defamatory communication is defined as follows: "A communication is defamatory if it tends so to harm the reputation of another as to lower him in the estimation of the community or to deter third persons from associating or dealing with him."[433]

Article 1, § 9, of the Nevada Constitution provides that "[e]very citizen may freely speak, write and publish his sentiments on all subjects, being responsible for the abuse of that right." The Nevada Supreme Court has observed that the "constitutional right to free speech . . . embraces every form and manner of dissemination of ideas held by our people."[434] "Free speech . . . must be given the greatest possible scope and have the least possible restrictions imposed upon it, for it is basic to representative democracy."[435]

The burden of proof as to a defamation claim is set forth in RESTATEMENT (SECOND) OF TORTS § 613 in relevant part as follows:

In an action for defamation the plaintiff has the burden of proving, when the issue is properly raised,

---

[425] *Diamond State Ins. Co. v. Fame Operating Co.*, 917 F. Supp. 736 (D. Nev. 1996).

[426] *Nevada Management Co. v. Jack*, 75 Nev. 232, 338 P.2d 71 (1959), cited, *City of Boulder City v. Miles*, 85 Nev. 46, at 48, 449 P.2d 1003 (1969).

[427] *Pope v. Motel 6*, 121 Nev. 307 at 315, 114 P.3d at 282; see *Lubin v. Kunin*, 117 Nev. 107, 111, 17 P.3d 422, 425 (2001).

[428] *K-Mart Corporation v. Washington*, 109 Nev. 1180, at 1192, 866 P.2d at 282 (1993).

[429] *Pegasus v. Reno Newspapers, Inc.*, 118 Nev. 706, 714, 57 P.3d 82, 87 (2002).

[430] *Id.* (quoting *Gertz v. Robert Welch, Inc.*, 418 U.S. 323, 339-40 (1974) (internal quotation mark omitted)).

[431] *Cooper v. Dupnick*, 924 F.2d 1520, 1532 (9th Cir. 1991).

[432] *Lubin v. Kunin*, 117 Nev. 107, 113, 17 P.3d 422, 426 (2001) (quoting *Nevada Ind. Broadcasting Corp. v. Allen*, 99 Nev. 404, 411, 664 P.2d 337, 342 (1983) (internal quotation marks omitted)).

[433] RESTATEMENT (SECOND) OF TORTS § 559.

[434] *Culinary Workers Union v. Eighth Judicial Dist. Court*, 66 Nev. 166, 173, 207 P.2d 990, 993 (1949).

[435] *Id.* at 173, 207 P.2d at 994 (citations omitted).

i.	the defamatory character of the communication;
ii.	its publication by the defendant;
iii.	its application to the plaintiff;
iv.	the recipient's understanding of its defamatory meaning;
v.	the recipient's understanding of it as intended to be applied to the plaintiff;
vi.	special harm resulting to the plaintiff from its publication;
vii.	the defendant's negligence, reckless disregard or knowledge regarding the truth or falsity and the defamatory character of the communication; and
viii.	the abuse of a conditional privilege.

THE RESTATEMENT (SECOND) OF TORTS § 614, provides that:

(1)The court determines
(a) whether a communication is capable of bearing a particular meaning, and
(b) whether that meaning is defamatory.

A defamation action does not lie for the expression of a mere opinion.[436] THE RESTATEMENT (SECOND) OF TORTS § 580B states that, with respect to the defamation of a private person, one who publishes a false and defamatory communication concerning a private person . . . is subject to liability, if, but only if, he:

(a) knows that the statement is false and that it defames the other;
(b) acts in reckless disregard of these matters, or
(c) acts negligently in failing to ascertain them.[437]

The United States Supreme Court has specifically held that the First Amendment to the Constitution does not permit the imposition of "liability without fault" on "a publisher or broadcaster of defamatory falsehood injurious to a private individual."[438] Comment c to § 580B states in part: "A significant measure of fault on the part of the defendant in regard to the falsity of the communication is required." Malice and damages are necessary elements of the tort.[439] Truth is a defense to a defamation claim. THE RESTATEMENT (SECOND) OF TORTS § 581A states: "One who publishes a defamatory statement of fact is not subject to liability if the statement is true."

Slander per se is an oral statement "which would tend to injure the plaintiff in his or her trade, business, profession or office."[440] With slander per se, the plaintiff is entitled to presumed, general damages.[441]

General damages are presumed upon proof of the defamation alone because that proof establishes that there was an injury that damaged plaintiff's reputation and because of the impossibility of affixing an exact monetary amount for present and future injury to plaintiff's reputation, wounded feelings and humiliation, loss of business, and any consequential physical illness or pain. See NRS 41.334, which provides as follows: "'General damages' are damages for loss of reputation, shame, mortification and hurt feelings."

Slander per se is slander "for which special damages need not be proved because it imputes to the plaintiff any one of the following: (1) a crime involving moral turpitude, (2) a loathsome disease (such as a sexually transmitted disease), (3) conduct that would adversely affect one's business or profession, or (4) unchastity (esp. of a woman)."[442]

In order to fit within the business category, the slanderous utterance must prejudice the person in the profession, trade or business in which he is actually engaged. This means that the statement must be of or concerning one in his business capacity.[443] Words which are merely injurious to one regardless of his occupation do not qualify as slander per se.[444]

Slanderous imputations affecting business, trade, profession or office are defined as follows: "One who publishes a slander that ascribes to another conduct, characteristics or a condition that would adversely affect his fitness

---

[436] RESTATEMENT (SECOND) OF TORTS § 566.
[437] RESTATEMENT (SECOND) OF TORTS § 580B.
[438] *Gertz v. Robert Welch, Inc.*, 418 U.S. 323 (1974).
[439] *Chowdhry v. NLVH, Inc.*, 109 Nev. 478, 483, 851 P.2d 459, 462 (1993).
[440] *Bongiovi v. Sullivan*, 122 Nev. 556, 577, 138 P.3d 433 (2006).
[441] *Id.*
[442] *Black's Law Dictionary* 1514 (9th ed. 2009).
[443] See 53 C.J.S. Libel and Slander §§ 32-33 (1948); *Lady Windsor Hairdressers, Inc. v. Calvo*, 35 Misc.2d 739, 231 N.Y.S.2d 221 (N.Y. 1962).
[444] *Gunsberg v. Roseland Corp.*, 34 Misc.2d 220, 225 N.Y.S.2d 1020 (N.Y. 1962).

fo: the proper conduct of his lawful business, trade or profession . . . is subject to liability without proof of special harm."
Comment e to § 573 states as follows:

> Disparaging words, to be actionable per se under the rule stated in this Section, must affect the plaintiff in some way that is peculiarly harmful to one engaged in his trade or profession. Disparagement of a general character, equally discreditable to all persons, is not enough unless the particular quality disparaged is of such a character that it is peculiarly valuable in the plaintiff's business or profession. It is not necessary that the defamer refer to the other as engaged in the particular professional or calling in question. It is enough if the statement is of such a character to be particularly disparaging of one engaged in such an occupation. Thus, a statement that a physician consorts with harlots is not actionable per se, although a charge that he makes improper advances to his patients is actionable; the one statement does not affect his reputation as a physician whereas the other does so affect it.

NRS 11.190(4) provides a two-year statute of limitations for defamation.
"The false light privacy action differs from a defamation action in that the injury in privacy actions is mental distress from having been exposed to public view, while the injury in defamation actions is damage to reputation."[445]
See also "Invasion of Privacy."

Defense of Property

Defense of property is a justification defense by the defendant that s/he should not be held liable because the ac:ion was taken in defense of the defendant's premises or personal property. This defense is available, if one harms or threatens another when defending one's property.

Dental Malpractice

See *Physicians Insurance Co. v. Williams*, 128 Nev. Adv. Op. No. 30 (2012) (in a claims-made insurance coverage case, the Nevada Supreme Court held that a court may not rewrite a policy under the guise of construing it. For a "report" of a potential demand for damages to qualify as a "claim" requires sufficient specificity to alert the insurer's cla:im department to the existence of a potential demand for damages arising out of an identifiable incident, involving an identified or identifiable claimant or claimants, with actual or anticipated injuries.). Although it is an insurance case more than a dental malpractice case, the facts that led to the claim of dental malpractice are worth a read. See "Medical Malpractice or Dental Malpractice" and "Professional Negligence."

Detinue

Detinue is the name of an action for the recovery of a personal chattel in specie. This action may be considered: 1. With reference to the nature of the thing to be recovered; 2. The plaintiff's interest therein; 3. The injury; 4. The pleadings; 5. The judgment.

The goods which it is sought to recover, must be capable of being distinguished from all others, as a particular horse, a cow, etc., but not for a bushel of grain. Detinue cannot be maintained where the property sued for had ceased to exist when the suit was commenced.

To support this action, the plaintiff must have a right to immediate possession, although he never had actual possession; a reversioner cannot, therefore, maintain it. A bailee, who has only a special property, may nevertheless support it when he delivered the goods to the defendant, or they were taken out of the bailee's custody.

The gist of the action is the wrongful detainer, and not the original taking. The possession must have been acquired by the defendant by lawful means, as by delivery, bailment or finding, and not tortiously. But a demand is not requisite, except for the purpose of entitling the plaintiff to damages for the detention between the time of the demand and that of the commencement of the action.

The plaintiff may declare upon a bailment or a trover; but the practice, by the ancient common law, was to allege, simply, that the goods came to the hands, etc., of the defendant without more. The trover, or finding, when alleged, was not traversable, except when the defendant alleged delivery over of a chattel actually found to a third person, before action brought, in excuse of the detinue. Nor is the bailment traversable, but the defendant must answer to the detinue. In describing the things demanded, much certainty is requisite, owing to the nature of the execution. A

---

[445] *Rinsley v. Brandt*, 700 F.2d 1304, 1307 (l0th Cir. 1983), cited in *PETA v. Bobby Berosini, Ltd.*, 111 Nev. 615, 622, fn. 4, 895 P.2d 1269 (1995).

declaration for 'a red cow with a white face,' is not supported by proof that the cow was a yellow or sorrel cow.

In this action the defendant frequently prayed garnishment of a third person, whom he alleged owned or had an interest in the thing demanded; but this he could not do without confessing the possession of the thing demanded, and made privity of bailment. If the prayer of garnishment was allowed, a sci. fac. issued against the person named as garnishee. If he made default, the plaintiff recovered against the defendant the chattel demanded, but no damages. If the garnishee appeared and the plaintiff made default, the garnishee recovered. If both appeared, and the plaintiff recovered; he had judgment against the defendant for the chattel demanded, and against the garnishee a judgment for damages, and a fi. fa.[446] in execution. The verdict and judgment must be such that a special remedy may be had for the recovery of the goods detained, or a satisfaction in value for each parcel, in case they, or either of them, cannot be returned. The judgment is in the alternative, that the plaintiff recover the goods or the value thereof and his damages for the detention and full costs, if he cannot have the goods themselves. This action has yielded to the more practical and less technical action of trover.

Detrimental Reliance

A cause of action for detrimental reliance requires the following elements: 1) A promise was made; 2) by a defendant who knows or who has reason to know; 3) that the promise will induce the plaintiff to rely; 4) to his detriment; and 5) provided the reliance is reasonable.[447] No Nevada case establishes a cause of action for detrimental reliance. See "Promissory Estoppel."

Disparate Treatment

Title VII makes it an unlawful employment practice to "discriminate against any individual with respect to his compensation, terms, conditions, or privileges of employment, because of such individual's race, color, religion, sex, or national origin."[448] To prevail, the plaintiff must establish a prima facie case of discrimination by presenting evidence that "gives rise to an inference of unlawful discrimination."[449] A plaintiff can establish a prima facie case of discrimination through either the burden shifting framework set forth in *McDonnell Douglas* or with direct or circumstantial evidence of discriminatory intent.[450]

Elder Exploitation

NRS 41.1395, "Action for damages for injury or loss suffered by older or vulnerable person from abuse, neglect or exploitation; double damages; attorney's fees and costs," provides in relevant part as follows:

1. Except as otherwise provided in subsection 3, if an older person or a vulnerable person suffers a personal injury or death that is caused by abuse or neglect or suffers a loss of money or property caused by exploitation, the person who caused the injury, death or loss is liable to the older person or vulnerable person for two times the actual damages incurred by the older person or vulnerable person.

2. If it is established by a preponderance of the evidence that a person who is liable for damages pursuant to this section acted with recklessness, oppression, fraud or malice, the court shall order the person to pay the attorney's fees and costs of the person who initiated the lawsuit.

. . .

4. For the purposes of this section:

. . .

---

[446] "fieri facias," [Medieval Latin, literally, "may you cause it to be done," from words used in the writ, typically *de terris et cattalis fieri facias* may you raise from the lands and chattels (of the defendant) (a given sum)] : a writ authorizing a sheriff to seize and sell certain items of the property of a debtor in order to satisfy a creditor's judgment against the debtor. Findlaw Legal Dictionary.

[447] *Becnel v. Whirley Indus.,* 2003 U.S. Dist. Lexis 21575; 2003 WL 22852215 (E.D. La. 2003).

[448] 42 U.S.C. § 2000e-2.

[449] *Cordova v. State Farm Ins. Co.,* 124 F.3d 1145, 1148 (9th Cir. 1997); see also *McDonnell Douglas Corp. v. Green,* 411 U.S. 792, 802 (1973).

[450] See *Metoyer v. Chassman,* 504 F.3d 919, 931 (9th Cir. 2007) ("When responding to a summary judgment motion . . . [the plaintiff] may proceed using the *McDonnell Douglas* framework, or alternatively, may simply produce direct or circumstantial evidence demonstrating that a discriminatory reason more likely than not motivated [the employer]") (citation omitted) (alterations in original).[450]

(b) "Exploitation" means any act taken by a person who has the trust and confidence of an older person or a vulnerable person or any use of the power of attorney or guardianship of an older person or a vulnerable person to:

(1) Obtain control, through deception, intimidation or undue influence, over the money, assets or property of the older person or vulnerable person with the intention of permanently depriving the older person or vulnerable person of the ownership, use, benefit or possession of his money, assets or property; or

(2) Convert money, assets or property of the older person with the intention of permanently depriving the older person or vulnerable person of the ownership, use, benefit or possession of his money, assets or property.

As used in this paragraph, "undue influence" does not include the normal influence that one member of a family has over another.

. . .

(d) "Older person" means a person who is 60 years of age or older.

(e) "Vulnerable person" means a person who:

(1) Has a physical or mental impairment that substantially limits one or more of the major life activities of the person; and

(2) Has a medical or psychological record of the impairment or is otherwise regarded as having the impairment.

The term includes, without limitation, a person who is mentally retarded, a person who has a severe learning disability, a person who suffers from a severe mental or emotional illness or a person who suffers from a terminal or catastrophic illness or injury.

Equal Pay Claim

The Equal Protection Act "prohibits discrimination in wages 'between employees on the basis of sex . . . for equal work, on jobs the performance of which requires equal skill, effort, and responsibility, and which are performed under similar working conditions.' "[451] However, each job requirement "must be substantially equal to state a claim."[452] Employers "may consider the marketplace value of the skills of a particular individual when determining his or her salary," and "[u]nequal wages that reflect market conditions of supply and demand are not prohibited."[453]

Equitable Estoppel

Equitable estoppel consists of the following elements: (1) the party to be estopped must be apprised of the true facts, (2) that party must intend that his conduct shall be acted upon or must so act that the party asserting estoppel has the right to believe it was so intended, (3) the party asserting estoppel must be ignorant of the true state of the facts, and (4) the party asserting estoppel must have detrimentally relied on the other party's conduct.[454]

Equitable estoppel is where a court will not grant a judgment or other legal relief to a party who has not acted fairly; for example, by having made false representations or concealing material facts from the other party. This illustrates the legal maxim: "He who seeks equity, must do equity."[455] Example: Larry Landlord rents space to Diana Dressmaker in his shopping center but falsely tells her a Sears store will be a tenant and will draw customers to the project. He does not tell her a new freeway is going to divert traffic from the center. When she failed to pay her rent due to lack of business, Landlord sues her for breach of lease. Diana Dressmaker may claim that he is equitably estopped from collecting her rent .

Equitable Lien

"An equitable lien is a right to subject property not in the possession of the lienor to the payment of a debt as a charge against that property. It may arise from a contract which reveals an intent to charge particular property with a debt or 'out of general considerations of right and justice as applied to the relations of the parties and the circumstances of their dealings.' . . . 'The basis of equitable liens is variously placed on the doctrines of estoppel, or unjust enrichment, or

---

[451] *Stanley v. University of Southern California*, 13 F.3d 1313, 1321 (9th Cir. 1994) (quoting 29 U.S.C. § 206(d)(1) (1988)).

[452] *Id.*

[453] *Id.* at 1322.

[454] *LVCVA v. Secretary of State*, 124 Nev. 669, 673, 191 P.3d 1138 (2008).

[455] *Lyerla v. Watts*, 87 Nev. 58, 62 (1971).

on the principle that a person having obtained an estate of another ought not in conscience to keep it as between them; and frequently it is based on the equitable maxim that equity will deem as done that which ought to be done, or that he who seeks the aid of equity must himself do equity.' " [Citations omitted.][456]

Under equitable lien principles, the homestead exemption did not apply to a judgment debtor's real property purchased from funds obtained from judgment creditor by fraudulent means.[457]

Equitable Subrogation

"Equitable subrogation" is an equitable remedy to avoid a person's receiving an unearned windfall at the expense of another.[458] Equitable subrogation permits a person who pays off an encumbrance to assume the same priority position as the holder of the previous encumbrance.[459] This is permitted so long as the (1) payor reasonably expected to receive a security interest in the real estate with the priority of the mortgage being discharged, and [(2)] subrogation [does] not materially prejudice the holders of intervening interests in the real estate."[460] "The payor is subrogated only to the extent that the funds disbursed are actually applied toward payment of the prior lien. There is no right of subrogation with respect to any excess funds."[461]

If there were no subrogation, a junior lien holder would be promoted in priority, giving that creditor/lien holder an unwarranted and unjust windfall.[462] For purposes of equitable subrogation, neither negligence nor constructive notice of an existing lien is relevant as to whether the junior lien holder will be unjustly enriched or prejudiced when a lender pays off a prior note.[463] Subrogation will not be granted if it would result in injustice or prejudice to an intervening lienor.[464]

In *Houston v. Bank of America*[465], a mortgagee intervened in a lien holders' action to enforce a judgment against a property owner's former husband by writ of execution and sale of the property. The district court entered an order enjoining the sale and granted summary judgment in favor of the mortgagee on its claim that it held the priority lien on the property because it succeeded to the rights of former lender. The lien holders appealed, and the Nevada Supreme Court affirmed the lower court. The Nevada Supreme Court held that a subsequent lender who pays off a prior note succeeds to the prior lender's priority lien position and, thus, is equitably subrogated to the former lender's priority lien position, as long as an intervening lien holder is not prejudiced, adopting the RESTATEMENT (THIRD) OF PROPERTY: MORTGAGES § 7.6. and (2) the mortgagee was equitably subrogated to the former lender's priority lien position.

In *American Sterling Bank v. Johnny Mgmt. LV*,[466] the Nevada Supreme Court considered whether an intervening lienholder suffers an injustice or prejudice precluding equitable subrogation where the terms, including the maturity date, of the refinancing loan are materially different than the terms and maturity date of the senior obligation. The court concluded that material differences in interest rates and payment terms do not cause prejudice to the intervening lienholder because equitable subrogation generally limits the paying lender's priority to the amount and terms of the retired senior obligation. However, a materially accelerated maturity date for the paying lender's loan can, and did in this case, prejudice the intervening lienholder, precluding equitable subrogation.[467]

---

[456] *Farmers Ins. Exchange v. Zerin*, 53 Cal.Ct.App.4th 445, 453 (1997).

[457] *Maki v. Chong*, 119 Nev. 390, 391, 75 P.3d 376 (2003).

[458] *Houston v. Bank of America*, 119 Nev. 488, 290, 78 P.3d 71 (2003).

[459] *Id.* at 488.

[460] *Recontrust v. Countrywide*, 130 Nev., Advance Opinion 1, p. 7 (2014); see RESTATEMENT (THIRD) OF PROP.: MORTGAGES § 7.6(b)(4).

[461] *Id.*, cmt. e, cited in *Recontrust, supra.*

[462] *Id.* at 490.

[463] *Id.*

[464] *Id.* at 491.

[465] 119 Nev. 485, 487 (2003).

[466] 126 Nev., Advance Opinion 41 (2010).

[467] *Id.*

Equitable Tolling

Equitable tolling operates to suspend the running of a statute of limitations when the only bar to a timely filed claim is a procedural technicality.[468] Even when the claim's untimeliness is due to a procedural technicality, application of the doctrine is appropriate only when "the danger of prejudice to the defendant is absent" and "the interests of justice so require."[469]

Like other statutes of limitations, NRS 288.110(4)'s deadline is subject to the equitable defenses of waiver, estoppel, and tolling.[470]

Equitable tolling focuses on "whether there was excusable delay by the plaintiff: If a reasonable plaintiff would not have known of the existence of a possible claim within the limitations period, then equitable tolling will serve to extend the statute of limitations for filing suit until the plaintiff can gather what information he needs."[471]

Equitable tolling is defined as "[t]he doctrine that the statute of limitations will not bar a claim if the plaintiff, despite diligent efforts, did not discover the injury until after the limitations period had expired"). The EMRB's reasonable conclusion that equitable tolling is permitted with respect to claims that are before it is entitled to deference.[472]

The Nevada Supreme Court has recognized equitable tolling for discrimination claims addressed to the Equal Rights Commission under NRS Chapter 613.[473] In *Copeland*, the Nevada Supreme Court stated that the following factors, among any other relevant considerations, should be analyzed when determining whether equitable tolling will apply: the claimant's diligence, knowledge of the relevant facts, reliance on misleading authoritative agency statements and/or misleading employer conduct, and any prejudice to the employer.[474]

Failure to Properly Supervise or Train under 42 U.S.C. § 1983

If the officers' conduct in seeking or in executing the warrant was sufficiently unreasonable to violate constitutional standards, then it is possible that the responsible supervisors might face liability under 42 U.S.C. § 1983. It is clear that the supervisors are not subject to vicarious liability, but are liable only for their own conduct.[475] The causal link between the supervisors' conduct and the deprivation of a right is key because "[a]nyone who 'causes' any citizen to be subjected to a constitutional deprivation is also liable."[476] In cases in which plaintiffs allege there is an official policy condoning or authorizing unconstitutional acts, the Supreme Court has indicated that to prevail the plaintiffs must demonstrate an "affirmative link" between their deprivation and "the adoption of a plan or policy by the supervisor–express or otherwise–showing their authorization or approval of such misconduct."[477]

In a 42 U.S.C. § 1983 claim for failure to supervise or train, the plaintiff must show that: "(1) the supervisor either failed to supervise or train the subordinate official; (2) a causal link exists between the failure to train or supervise and the violation of the plaintiff's rights; and (3) the failure to train or supervise amounts to deliberate indifference."[478]

See "Section 1983 Claims."

False Arrest

False arrest is an unlawful taking, seizing or detaining of a person, either by touching or putting hands on him or her, or by any other act that indicates an intention to take him or her into custody and subjects the person arrested to the actual control and will of the person making the arrest. The act must have been performed with the intent to make an arrest and must have been so understood by the person arrested. In order to prove false arrest, a plaintiff must show the

---

[468] *Copeland v. Desert Inn Hotel*, 99 Nev. 823, 826, 673 P.2d 490, 492 (1983) ("We therefore adopt the doctrine of equitable tolling . . . ; procedural technicalities that would bar claims . . . will be looked upon with disfavor.")

[469] *Seino v. Employers Ins. Co. of Nevada*, 121 Nev. 146, 152, 111 P.3d 1107, 1112 (2005) (quoting *Azer v. Connell*, 306 F.3d 930, 936 (9th Cir. 2002); *State, Dep't of Taxation v. Masco Builder,* 127 Nev. Adv. Op. No. 67 (2011).

[470] See *Zipes v. Trans World Airlines*, Inc., 455 U.S. 385, 393, 395 n.11 (1982) (explaining that because Title VII claims (like NRS Chapter 288 claims) were modeled after the NLRA's remedial provisions, Title VII, like the NLRA, includes a statute of limitations subject to equitable defenses).

[471] *Lukovsky v. City and County of San Francisco*, 535 F.3d 1044, 1051 (9th Cir. 2008) (see also *Black's Law Dictionary* 618 (9th ed. 2009).

[472] *Local Gov't Emp. v. General Sales*, 98 Nev. 94, 98, 641 P.2d at 480 (1982).

[473] *Copeland v. Desert Inn Hotel*, 99 Nev. 823, 826, 673 P.2d 490, 492 (1983) (providing that "procedural technicalities that would bar claims of discrimination will be looked upon with disfavor").

[474] *Id.*

[475] *Monell v. Department of Social Services*, 436 U.S. 658, 694 n.58, 56 L. Ed. 2d 611, 98 S. Ct. 2018 (1978).

[476] *Johnson v. Duffy*, 588 F.2d 740, 743 (9th Cir. 1978).

[477] *Rizzo v. Goode*, 423 U.S. 362, 370-71, 46 L. Ed. 2d 561, 96 S.Ct. 598 (1976).

[478] *Smith v. Brenoettsy*, 158 F.3d 908, 911–12 (5th Cir. 1998).

defendant instigated or effected an unlawful arrest.[479]

See "False Imprisonment."

False Imprisonment

The Nevada Supreme Court has stated that false arrest is part of a claim for false imprisonment. To establish false imprisonment of which false arrest is an integral part, it is only necessary to prove that the person be restrained of his liberty under the probable imminence of force without any legal cause or justification therefor.[480]

See also *Hernandez v. Reno*, 97 Nev. 429, 433, 634 P.2d 668, 671 (1981). An actor is subject to liability to another for false imprisonment if (a) he acts intending to confine the other or a third person within boundaries fixed by the actor, and (b) his act directly or indirectly results in such a confinement of the other, and c) the other is conscious of the confinement or is harmed by it. See RESTATEMENT (SECOND) OF TORTS § 35 (1965).

See "False Arrest."

First Amendment Retaliation

To assert a First Amendment retaliation claim, a public employee must demonstrate that he or she "engaged in constitutionally protected speech" and that the employer "took adverse employment action against the employee" in which the "employee's speech was a substantial or motivating factor in the adverse action."[481]

Fraud on the Court

In a judicial proceeding, fraud on the court is a lawyer's or a party's misconduct so serious that it undermines or is intended to undermine the integrity of the proceeding.[482] Examples are bribery of a juror and introduction of fabricated evidence.[483] True fraud on the court is rare and requires "egregious misconduct."[484] Nevada Rule of Civil Procedure 9(b) provides as follows: "In all averments of fraud or mistake, the circumstances constituting fraud or mistake shall be stated with particularity. Malice, intent, knowledge, and other condition of mind of a person may be averred generally."

"Fraud upon the court" has been recognized for centuries as a basis for setting aside a final judgment, sometimes even years after it was entered.[485] It is, of course, true that "in most instances society is best served by putting an end to litigation after a case has been tried and judgment entered."[486] For this reason, a final judgment, once entered, normally is not subject to challenge. However, the policy of repose yields when "the court finds after a proper hearing that fraud has been practiced upon it, or the very temple of justice has been defiled."[487] "[A] case of fraud upon the court [calls] into question the very legitimacy of the judgment."[488] Put another way, "[w]hen a judgment is shown to have been procured" by fraud upon the court, "no worthwhile interest is served in protecting the judgment."[489]

The problem lies in defining what constitutes "fraud upon the court." Obviously, it cannot mean any conduct of a party or lawyer of which the court disapproves; among other evils, such a formulation "would render meaningless the [time] limitation on motions under [Rule] 60(b)(3)."[490] The most widely-accepted definition holds that the concept embrace[s] only that species of fraud which does, or attempts to, subvert the integrity of the court itself, or is a fraud perpetrated by officers of the court so that the judicial machinery cannot perform in the usual manner its impartial task of

---

[479] *Nau v. Sellman*, 104 Nev. 248, 251, 757 P.2d 358 (1988).

[480] *Garton v. City of Reno*, 102 Nev. 313, 314-315, 634 P.2d 668 (1986).

[481] *Posey v. Lake Pend Oreille School Dist. No. 84*, 546 F.3d 1121, 1126 (9th Cir. 2008) (quoting *Freitag v. Avers*, 468 F.3d 528, 543 (9th Cir. 2006)) (internal quotation marks omitted).

[482] *Black's Law Dictionary* 732 (9th ed. 2009).

[483] *Id.*

[484] *Occhiuto v. Occhiuto*, 97 Nev. 143, 146 n.2, 625 P.2d 568, 570 n.2 (1981).

[485] See *NC-DSH, Inc. v. Garner*, 125 Nev., Advance Opinion 50, 218 P.3d 853 (2009); *Hazel-Atlas Co. v. Hartford Co.*, 322 U.S. 238, 245 (1944) (discussing "the historic power of equity to set aside fraudulently begotten judgments" and canvassing cases and treatises and vacating a judgment entered nine years earlier), overruled on other grounds by *Standard Oil Co. of Cal. v. United States*, 429 U.S. 17, 18 (1976).

[486] *Hazel-Atlas Glass Co. v. Hartford-Empire Co.*, 322 U.S. 238, 64 S.Ct. 997, 88 L.Ed. 1250 (1944).

[487] *Universal Oil Co. v. Root Rfg. Co.*, 328 U.S. 575, 580 (1946).

[488] *Calderon v. Thompson*, 523 U.S. 538, 557 (1998).

[489] RESTATEMENT (SECOND) OF JUDGMENTS § 70 cut. b (1982).

[490] *Kupferman v. Consolidated Research & Mfg. Corp.*, 459 F.2d 1072, 1078 (2d Cir. 1972) (Friendly, J.), cited with approval in *Occhiuto*, 97 Nev. at 146 n.2, 625 P.2d at 570 n.2, and *Murphy*, 103 Nev. at 186, 734 P.2d at 739.

adjudging cases . . . and relief should be denied in the absence of such conduct.[491]

An attorney is an officer of the court. "Where a judgment is obtained by fraud perpetrated by an attorney acting as an officer of the court, the judgment may be attacked for fraud on the court."[492] The United States Supreme Court has long recognized the damage that lawyer dishonesty can inflict on courts and litigants:

> [W]here an attorney fraudulently or without authority assumes to represent a party and connives at his defeat; or where the attorney regularly employed corruptly sells out his client's interest to the other side,– these, and similar cases which show that there has never been a real contest in the trial or hearing of the case, are reasons for which a new suit may be sustained to set aside and annul the former judgment or decree, and open the case for a new and a fair hearing.[493]

In addition to his duties to his clients, a lawyer also owes a duty of "loyalty to the court, as an officer thereof, [that] demands integrity and honest dealing with the court. And when he departs from that standard in the conduct of a case he perpetrates fraud upon the court."[494]

The general rule is that "a judgment in a contested action may be avoided if the judgment . . . [r]esulted from corruption of . . . the attorney for the party against whom the judgment was rendered."[495] Although not present in all fraud on the court cases, attorney involvement in the fraud is a signal characteristic of many of them.[496] The Nevada Supreme Court recognizes the substantial countervailing argument that a client who hires a lawyer establishes an agency relationship and that, ordinarily, the sins of an agent are visited upon his principal, not the innocent third party with whom the dishonest agent dealt.[497] However, courts "do not treat the attorney-client relationship as they do other agent-principal relationships . . . when the question is whether a settlement agreed to by the attorney binds the client."[498] While a lawyer has apparent authority to handle procedural matters for a client, "[m]erely retaining a lawyer does not create apparent authority in the lawyer" to settle her client's case.[499]

The Nevada Supreme Court has held that a lawyer's professional and psychiatric disintegration due to substance abuse justified an order vacating the final judgment against his client after the lawyer failed to appear for trial.[500] If a lawyer's addictive disorder can justify vacating a judgment against his neglected client, notwithstanding the imposition on his adversary, a lawyer's criminal conduct should permit a claim to relief from judgment by a victimized client as well.

Fraud in the Inducement

To establish fraud in the inducement (or fraudulent inducement), plaintiff must prove by clear and convincing evidence each of the following elements: (1) a false representation made by defendant, (2) defendant's knowledge or belief that the representation was false (or knowledge that it had an insufficient basis for making the representation), (3) defendant's intention to therewith induce plaintiff to consent to the contract's formation, (4) plaintiff's justifiable reliance

---

[491] *Demjanjuk v. Petrovsky*, 10 F.3d 338, 352 (6th Cir. 1994) (citing 7 *Moore's Federal Practice* § 60.33 (2d ed. 1978) (now at 12 *Moore's Federal Practice*, § 60.21 (3rd ed. 2009)); *Kupferman*, 459 F.2d at 1078 (noting the Second Circuit adopted *Moore's* formulation); *In re Intermagnetics America, Inc.*, 926 F.2d 912, 916 (9th Cir. 1991) (also adopting *Moore's* formulation); see *Occhiuto*, 97 Nev. at 146 n.2, 625 P.2d at 570 n.2 (citing this section of *Moore's* but without referring to the passage quoted in *Demjanjuk*).

[492] *In re Tri-Cran, Inc.*, 98 B.R. 609, 616 (Bankr. D. Mass. 1989).

[493] *United States v. Throckmorton*, 98 U.S. 61, 66 (1878). See *Savage v. Salzmann*, 88 Nev. 193, 195, 495 P.2d 367, 368 (1972) (citing *Throckmorton* and noting that fraud on the court involves situations where, as a result of the fraud, a "party is kept away from the court by . . . such conduct as prevents a real trial upon the issues involved").

[494] *Demjanjuk*, 10 F.3d at 352 (citing 7 *Moore's Federal Practice*, supra, § 60.33) (now at 12 *Moore's Federal Practice*, § 60.21).

[495] See RESTATEMENT (SECOND) OF JUDGMENTS § 70(1)(a).

[496] *Demjanjuk*, 10 F.3d at 352 (noting that "[c]ases dealing with fraud on the court often turn on whether the improper actions are those of parties alone, or if the attorneys in the case are involved"); *Eastern Financing Corp. v. JSC Alchevsk Iron*, 258 F.R.D. 76, 85 (S.D.N.Y. 2008) (analyzing *Hazel-Atlas*, *Kupferman*, and *H. K. Porter Co.* in these terms).

[497] *Rothman v. Fillette*, 469 A.2d 543, 545 (Pa. 1983); *Flowers v. Rigdon*, 655 N.E.2d at 237-38 (Jones, P.J., dissenting).

[498] Grace M. Giesel, *Client Responsibility for Lawyer Conduct: Examining the Agency Nature of the Lawyer-Client Relationship*, 86 Neb. L. Rev. 346, 348 (2007).

[499] RESTATEMENT (THIRD) OF THE LAW GOVERNING LAWYERS § 27 cmt. d (2000); see *id.* § 22(1).

[500] *Passarelli v. J-Mar Development*, 102 Nev. 283, 720 P.2d 1221 (1986).

upon the misrepresentation, and (5) damage to plaintiff resulting from such reliance.[501] Nevada Rule of Civil Procedure 9(b) provides as follows: "In all averments of fraud or mistake, the circumstances constituting fraud or mistake shall be stated with particularity. Malice, intent, knowledge, and other condition of mind of a person may be averred generally."

When a fraudulent inducement claim contradicts the express terms of the parties' integrated contract, it fails as a matter of law.[502]

Fraud/ Intentional Misrepresentation

Fraud

To establish fraud, the plaintiff must show that the defendant provided a false representation of a material fact, which he knew to be false; that the defendant intended the plaintiff to rely on the misrepresentation; that the plaintiff detrimentally relied on the misrepresentation; and that the misrepresentation proximately caused damages.[503] Nevada Rule of Civil Procedure 9(b) provides as follows: "In all averments of fraud or mistake, the circumstances constituting fraud or mistake shall be stated with particularity. Malice, intent, knowledge, and other condition of mind of a person may be averred generally."

Fraud for Concealment

In order to establish a claim of fraud for concealment (or fraudulent concealment), the plaintiff must show by clear and convincing evidence that:

1. The defendant assumed the responsibility to give information;
2. The defendant concealed or suppressed a material fact;
3. The defendant was under a duty to disclose the fact to the plaintiff;
4. The defendant knew [he] [she] [it] was concealing the fact;
5. The defendant intended to induce the plaintiff to act or refrain from acting in a manner different than the plaintiff would had [he] [she] [it] known the truth;
6. The plaintiff was unaware of the fact and would not have acted as [he] [she] [it] did had [he] [she] [it] known of the concealed or suppressed fact; and
7. The concealment or suppression of the fact caused the plaintiff to sustain damage.[504]

The omission of a material fact which a party is bound in good faith to disclose is equivalent to a false representation.[505] A defendant may be found liable for misrepresentation even when the defendant does not make an express misrepresentation, but instead makes a representation which is misleading because it partially suppresses or conceals information.[506] "Typically, a plaintiff would raise evidence of fraudulent concealment in response to a defendant's argument that the statute of limitations was a defense to the plaintiff's claims."[507]

A plaintiff alleging fraud may also ground its case on negative misrepresentations, omissions or fraudulent concealment. A defendant may be found liable for misrepresentation even when the defendant does not make an express misrepresentation, but instead makes a representation which is misleading because it partially suppresses or conceals information.[508] Once a party undertakes to give information, he has a duty to speak the whole truth and not by concealments make his statements untruthful and misleading.[509]

There are five essential elements for a fraudulent concealment under Nevada law: (1) The defendant must have concealed or suppressed a material fact; (2) The defendant must have been under a duty to disclose the fact to the plaintiff; (3) The defendant must have intentionally concealed or suppressed the fact with the intent to defraud the plaintiff, that is, he must have concealed or suppressed the fact for the purpose of inducing the plaintiff to acted differently than he would if he knew the fact; (4) The plaintiff must have been unaware of the fact and would not have act as he did if he had known of the concealed or suppressed fact; (5) as a result of the concealment or suppression of the fact, the plaintiff must have sustained damages.[510]

A defendant may be found liable for misrepresentation even when the defendant does not make an express

---

[501] *J.A. Jones Construction Co. v. Lehrer McGovern Bovis*, 120 Nev. 277, 290, 89 P.3d 1009 (2004).

[502] *Road & Highway Builders v. N. Nev. Rebar*, 128 Nev. Adv. Op. No. 36 (August 9, 2012).

[503] *Chen v. Nevada State Gaming Control Bd.*, 116 Nev. 282, 284, 994 P.2d 1151 (2000).

[504] *Nevada Civil Jury Instructions*, Fraud Instruction 10FR.4

[505] *Midwest Supply, Inc. v. Waters*, 89 Nev. 210, 510 P.2d 876, 878 (1973).

[506] *Epperson v. Roloff*, 102 Nev. 206, 212, 719 P.2d 799, 803 (1986).

[507] *Palmer v. Borg-Warner Corp.*, 838 P.2d 1243 (Alaska 1992).

[508] *Blanchard v. Blanchard*, 108 Nev. 908, 911, 839 P.2d 1320 (1992).

[509] *Northern Nev. Mobile Home v. Penrod*, 96 Nev. 394, 398, 610 P.2d 724 (1980).

[510] *Nevada Power Co. v. Monsanto Co.*, 891 F. Supp. 1406, 1415 (D. Nev. 1995).

misrepresentation, but instead makes a representation which is misleading because it partially suppresses or conceals information.[511]

Fraud for False Promise

In order to establish a claim of fraud for a false promise, the plaintiff must show clear and convincing evidence that establishes:

1. The defendant made a promise as to a material matter; and
2. At the time it was made, the defendant did not intend to perform;
3. The defendant made the promise with the intent to induce plaintiff to rely upon it and act or refrain from acting accordingly;
4. The plaintiff was unaware of the defendant's intention not to perform the promise;
5. The plaintiff acted in reliance upon the promise;
6. The plaintiff was justified in relying upon the promise; and
7. The plaintiff sustained damages as a result of plaintiff's reliance on defendant's promise.

See *Balsamo v. Sheriff, Clark County*, 93 Nev. 315, 316, 565 P.2d 650 (1977) ("A promise made without intention to perform is a misrepresentation of a state of mind, and thus a misrepresentation of existing fact, and a false pretense within the meaning of NRS 205.380."); see also NRS 205.380 (2005) ("A person who knowingly and designedly by any false pretense obtains from any other person any chose in action, money, goods, wares, chattels, effects or other valuable thing, including rent or the labor of another person not his employee, with the intent to cheat or defraud the other person is a cheat and unless otherwise prescribed by law, shall be punished.").

Intentional Misrepresentation

Intentional misrepresentation is established by three factors: (1) a false representation that is made with either knowledge or belief that it is false or without a sufficient foundation, (2) an intent to induce another's reliance, and (3) damages that result from this reliance.[512] With respect to the false-representation element of intentional-misrepresentation claim, the suppression or omission of a material fact which a party is bound in good faith to disclose is equivalent to a false representation, since it constitutes an indirect representation that such fact does not exist.[513] "Good faith" is a state of mind consisting in 1) honesty in belief and purpose, 2) faithfulness to one's duty or obligation, 3) observance of reasonable commercial standards of fair dealing in a given trade or business, or 4) absence of intent to defraud or to seek unconscionable advantage.[514]

Proximate cause limits liability to foreseeable consequences that are reasonably connected to both the defendant's intentional misrepresentation or omission and the harm that the misrepresentation or omission created.[515]

Intentional misrepresentation imposes a burden on the plaintiff to show that the defendant made a false representation to him, with knowledge or belief that the representation was false or without a sufficient basis for making the representation. Further, the plaintiff must establish that the defendant intended to induce the plaintiff to act or refrain from acting on the representation, and that the plaintiff justifiably relied on the representation. Finally, the plaintiff must establish that he was damaged as a result of his reliance.[516]

Nevada Jury Instruction 9.01 provides that the elements of intentional misrepresentation are as follows:

1. A false representation made by the defendant;
2. Knowledge or belief on the part of the defendant that the representation was false or that he had an insufficient basis of information to make the representation;
3. An intention on the part of the defendant to induce the plaintiff to act or to refrain from acting in reliance upon the misrepresentation;
4. Justifiable reliance upon the misrepresentation on the part of the plaintiff in taking action or refraining from it;
5. Damage to the plaintiff, resulting from such reliance.

In an equitable action based upon intentional misrepresentation, the plaintiff's reliance need not be

---

[511] *Blanchard v. Blanchard*, 108 Nev. 908, 911, 839 P.2d 1320, 1322 (1992).
[512] *Nelson v. Heer*, 123 Nev. 217, 225, 163 P.3d 420 (2007).
[513] *Id.*
[514] *Black's Law Dictionary* 762 (9th ed. 2009).
[515] *Id.* at 225-226.
[516] *Blanchard v. Blanchard*, 108 Nev. 908, 910-911, 839 P.2d 1320 (1992).

justifiable.[517]

Fraudulent Conveyance/ Fraudulent Transfer

Fraudulent Transfers, or fraudulent conveyances, are covered by Nevada Revised Statutes Chapter 112, Fraudulent Transfers (Uniform Act). Nevada Rule of Civil Procedure 9(b) provides as follows: "In all averments of fraud or mistake, the circumstances constituting fraud or mistake shall be stated with particularity. Malice, intent, knowledge, and other condition of mind of a person may be averred generally."

NEVADA CASES.

Recordation does not give notice to the existing creditors. In an action by a creditor seeking to have a deed from husband to wife declared void under the Uniform Fraudulent Conveyance Act (see NRS 112.140 et seq.), the recording of the deed did not impart notice to creditor so as to start running of the statute of limitations because NRS 111.320, governing constructive notice, applies only to subsequent purchasers and mortgagees, and not to existing creditors.[518]

A fraudulent conveyance under NRS ch. 112 does not require proof of intent to defraud.[519]

NRS 112.140, "Short title," provides as follows: "This chapter may be cited as the Uniform Fraudulent Transfer Act."

(Added to NRS by 1987, 8)

NRS 112.150, "Definitions," provides as follows:

As used in this chapter, unless the context otherwise requires:
1. "Affiliate" means:
(a) A person who directly or indirectly owns, controls or holds with power to vote, 20 percent or more of the outstanding voting securities of the debtor, other than a person who holds the securities:
(1) As a fiduciary or agent without sole discretionary power to vote the securities; or
(2) Solely to secure a debt, if the person has not exercised the power to vote;
(b) A corporation 20 percent or more of whose outstanding voting securities are directly or indirectly owned, controlled or held with power to vote, by the debtor or a person who directly or indirectly owns, controls or holds with power to vote, 20 percent or more of the outstanding voting securities of the debtor, other than a person who holds the securities:
(1) As a fiduciary or agent without sole power to vote the securities; or
(2) Solely to secure a debt, if the person has not in fact exercised the power to vote;
(c) A person whose business is operated by the debtor under a lease or other agreement, or a person substantially all of whose assets are controlled by the debtor; or
(d) A person who operates the debtor's business under a lease or other agreement or controls substantially all of the debtor's assets.
2. "Asset" means property of a debtor, but the term does not include:
(a) Property to the extent it is encumbered by a valid lien;
(b) Property to the extent it is generally exempt under nonbankruptcy law; or
(c) An interest in property held in tenancy by the entireties or as community property to the extent it is not subject to process by a creditor holding a claim against only one tenant.
3. "Claim" means a right to payment, whether or not the right is reduced to judgment, liquidated, unliquidated, fixed, contingent, matured, unmatured, disputed, undisputed, legal, equitable, secured or unsecured.
4. "Creditor" means a person who has a claim.
5. "Debt" means liability on a claim.
6. "Debtor" means a person who is liable on a claim.
7. "Insider" includes:
(a) If the debtor is a natural person:
(1) A relative of the debtor or of a general partner of the debtor;
(2) A partnership in which the debtor is a general partner;

---

[517] *Pacific Maxon, Inc. v. Wilson*, 96 Nev. 867, 619 P.2d 816 (1980).
[518] *Crescent v. White*, 88 Nev. 71, 493 P.2d 1323 (1972), cited, City of Reno v. Goldwater, 92 Nev. 698, at 702, 558 P.2d 532 (1976).
[519] *Sportsco Enterprises v. Morris*, 112 Nev. 625, 917 P.2d 934 (1996).

(3) A general partner in a partnership described in subparagraph (2); and

(4) A corporation of which the debtor is a director, officer or person in control;

(b) If the debtor is a corporation:

(1) A director of the debtor;

(2) An officer of the debtor;

(3) A person in control of the debtor;

(4) A partnership in which the debtor is a general partner;

(5) A general partner in a partnership described in subparagraph (4); and

(6) A relative of a general partner, director, officer or person in control of the debtor;

(c) If the debtor is a partnership:

(1) A general partner in the debtor;

(2) A relative of a general partner in, a general partner of, or a person in control of the debtor;

(3) Another partnership in which the debtor is a general partner;

(4) A general partner in a partnership described in subparagraph (3); and

(5) A person in control of the debtor;

(d) An affiliate, or an insider of an affiliate as if the affiliate were the debtor; and

(e) A managing agent of the debtor.

8. "Lien" means a charge against or an interest in property to secure payment of a debt or performance of an obligation, and includes a security interest created by agreement, a judicial lien obtained by legal or equitable process or proceedings, a common-law lien and a statutory lien.

9. "Person" includes a government and a governmental subdivision or agency.

10. "Property" means anything that may be the subject of ownership.

11. "Relative" means a natural person related by consanguinity within the third degree as determined by the common law, a spouse, or a natural person related to a spouse within the third degree as so determined, and includes a natural person in an adoptive relationship within the third degree.

12. "Transfer" means every mode, direct or indirect, absolute or conditional, voluntary or involuntary, of disposing of or parting with an asset or an interest in an asset, and includes payment of money, release, lease and creation of a lien or other encumbrance.

13. "Valid lien" means a lien that is effective against the holder of a judicial lien subsequently obtained by legal or equitable process or proceedings.

(Added to NRS by 1987, 8)

NEVADA CASES.

Respondent's interest in a private sports box was a lease and therefore property subject to the Uniform Fraudulent Transfer Act. Respondent's interest in a private sports box which was used to view athletic events at the university was a lease where: (1) respondent was able to sell part of his interest in the box to a friend; (2) interest included the right to exclusive use of the box during basketball games and other public events; (3) owner of interest had the right to demand payment for use of the box when used during conventions; (4) owner of interest was entitled to the sole and exclusive right of access to the box, subject to approval by the university; and (5) owner of interest had the right to furnish and improve the box. Therefore, respondent's interest was property pursuant to NRS 112.150, and the district court erred in concluding that respondent's rights in the box were not property for the purposes of the Uniform Fraudulent Transfer Act.[520]

FEDERAL AND OTHER CASES.

"Creditor" includes a person to whom a contingent obligation is owed. Creditors are not those persons only to whom debts are due, but also those to whom contingent obligation is owed by way of surety, guaranty or the like and any such creditor may set aside fraudulent conveyance.[521]

NRS 112.160, "Insolvency," provides as follows:

1. A debtor is insolvent if the sum of the debtor's debts is greater than all of the debtor's assets at a fair valuation.

2. A debtor who is generally not paying his or her debts as they become due is presumed to be insolvent.

---

[520] *Sportsco Enterprises v. Morris*, 112 Nev. 625, 917 P.2d 934 (1996).

[521] *Thomson v. Crane*, 73 Fed. 327 (C.C.D. Nev. 1896).

3. A partnership is insolvent under subsection 1 if the sum of the partnership's debts is greater than the aggregate, at a fair valuation, of all of the partnership's assets and the sum of the excess of the value of each general partner's nonpartnership assets over the partner's nonpartnership debts.

4. Assets under this section do not include property that has been transferred, concealed or removed with intent to hinder, delay or defraud creditors or that has been transferred in a manner making the transfer voidable under this chapter.

5. Debts under this section do not include an obligation to the extent it is secured by a valid lien on property of the debtor not included as an asset.

(Added to NRS by 1987, 10)

NRS 112.170, "Value; reasonably equivalent value; present value," provides as follows:

1. Value is given for a transfer or an obligation if, in exchange for the transfer or obligation, property is transferred or an antecedent debt is secured or satisfied, but value does not include an unperformed promise made otherwise than in the ordinary course of the promisor's business to furnish support to the debtor or another person.

2. For the purposes of paragraph (b) of subsection 1 of NRS 112.180 and NRS 112.190, a person gives a reasonably equivalent value if the person acquires an interest of the debtor in an asset pursuant to a regularly conducted, noncollusive foreclosure sale or execution of a power of sale for the acquisition or disposition of the interest of the debtor upon default under a mortgage, deed of trust or security agreement.

3. A transfer is made for present value if the exchange between the debtor and the transferee is intended by them to be contemporaneous and is in fact substantially contemporaneous.

(Added to NRS by 1987, 710)

NEVADA CASES.

"Fair consideration" given by satisfaction of antecedent debt and buyer's assumption of debts of seller. In an action by a creditor against a buyer to set aside the sale of a well-drilling rig made by a deceased seller on the ground that the sale was made to defraud the creditor, where the seller owed an antecedent debt to the buyer and the buyer agreed in exchange for the rig to release the debt and to pay the encumbrance due on the rig and another one due on the seller's automobile, the satisfaction of the antecedent debt and assumption of debts comprising encumbrances was considered as "fair consideration" under former NRS 112.050 (cf. NRS 112.190), which provides that a conveyance made without fair consideration by person who will thereby be rendered insolvent is fraudulent as against his creditors, because former NRS 112.040 (cf. NRS 112.170) defines "fair consideration" as including satisfaction of antecedent debt and it is well established that assumption of liability or debt of seller by buyer may be considered when determining whether consideration paid was fair.[522]

FEDERAL AND OTHER CASES.

Fair consideration not given where a large debt was incurred to pay the obligation of the transferor's parent corporation. Where parent corporation, in partial payment of its own obligation, caused subsidiary corporation to borrow from the same creditor an amount approximating 90 percent of its retained earnings and to give security interest in its property, the bankruptcy court properly held security agreement fraudulent under former NRS 112.060 (cf. NRS 112.180), which so characterized every conveyance made without fair consideration which left transferor with unreasonably small capital, and former NRS 112.040 (cf. NRS 112.170), which defined "fair consideration" in terms of benefit to transferor and good faith of transferee. Here, the benefit of agreement went to parent corporation and its creditor gained advantage.[523]

NRS 112.180, "Transfer made or obligation incurred with intent to defraud or without receiving reasonably equivalent value; determination of intent," provides as follows:

1. A transfer made or obligation incurred by a debtor is fraudulent as to a creditor, whether the creditor's claim arose before or after the transfer was made or the obligation was incurred, if the debtor made the transfer or incurred the obligation:
   (a) With actual intent to hinder, delay or defraud any creditor of the debtor; or
   (b) Without receiving a reasonably equivalent value in exchange for the transfer or obligation, and the debtor:

---

[522] *Matusik v. Large*, 85 Nev. 202, 452 P.2d 457 (1969), cited, *Sportsco Enterprises v. Morris*, 112 Nev. 625, at 632, 917 P.2d 934 (1996).

[523] *Wells Fargo Bank v. Desert View Bldg. Supplies, Inc.*, 475 F. Supp. 693 (D. Nev. 1978).

(1) Was engaged or was about to engage in a business or a transaction for which the remaining assets of the debtor were unreasonably small in relation to the business or transaction; or

(2) Intended to incur, or believed or reasonably should have believed that the debtor would incur, debts beyond his or her ability to pay as they became due.

2. In determining actual intent under paragraph (a) of subsection 1, consideration may be given, among other factors, to whether:

(a) The transfer or obligation was to an insider;

(b) The debtor retained possession or control of the property transferred after the transfer;

(c) The transfer or obligation was disclosed or concealed;

(d) Before the transfer was made or obligation was incurred, the debtor had been sued or threatened with suit;

(e) The transfer was of substantially all the debtor's assets;

(f) The debtor absconded;

(g) The debtor removed or concealed assets;

(h) The value of the consideration received by the debtor was reasonably equivalent to the value of the asset transferred or the amount of the obligation incurred;

(i) The debtor was insolvent or became insolvent shortly after the transfer was made or the obligation was incurred;

(j) The transfer occurred shortly before or shortly after a substantial debt was incurred; and

(k) The debtor transferred the essential assets of the business to a lienor who transferred the assets to an insider of the debtor.

(Added to NRS by 1987, 11)

NEVADA CASES.

Actual delivery is generally required. Delivery contemplated by sec. 66, ch. 9, Stats. 1861 (see NRS 112.180), which provides that the sale of personal property without immediate delivery of such property, is conclusive evidence of fraud upon the vendor's creditors, is actual delivery, and symbolic delivery will be sufficient only where actual delivery is impossible or extremely inconvenient.[524]

The purpose of the section is to prevent fraud. Purpose of sec. 64, ch. 9, Stats. 1861 (see NRS 112.180), which provides that the sale of personal property without immediate delivery of such property is conclusive evidence of fraud upon the vendor's creditors, is prevention of frauds which may result from permitting right of property to be in one person and possession and indicia of ownership of such property to be in another.[525]

Evidence concerning a conveyance to plaintiff's grantor was admissible. Where a person brings an action in the nature of ejectment to recover possession of property held under a sheriff's deed by creditors of grantor of plaintiff's grantor, evidence offered by such creditors to establish the nature of the transaction between the first and second grantor is material in showing the chain of circumstances resulting in fraud in the sale of such property and is admissible.[526]

A declaration concerning the fact of the conveyance admissible. Where a person conveys his interest in an unfinished mill, retains possession of such mill and subsequent to conveyance declares that he has not conveyed such interest, such declaration is admissible as part of res gestae to show the nature of such person's possession.[527]

A transferor's retention of possession is not always evidence of fraudulent intent. Where a person conveys real property and retains possession of such property to gather crops or to remove furniture or by renting such property, such possession does not necessarily create suspicion that the conveyance was made in attempt to delay the creditors of such person.[528]

Declaration of grantor concerning intention admissible. Declaration of grantor, made before the sale of real property, of his intention to make transfer to delay his creditors is admissible in action in the nature of ejectment brought by his grantee against grantor's creditors in possession of such property under a sheriff's deed.[529]

The intention of both parties must be shown. In order to establish fraud in a transaction, the motives and intentions of both parties to the transaction must be proven.[530]

---

[524] (See also NRS 104.2402.) *Doak v. Brubaker*, 1 Nev. 218 (1865), cited, *Sharon v. Shaw*, 2 Nev. 289, at 293 (1866), *Lawrence v. Burnham*, 4 Nev. 361, at 367 (1868), distinguished, *Gray v. Sullivan*, 10 Nev. 416, at 423 (1876).

[525] *Doak v. Brubaker*, 1 Nev. 218 (1865), cited, *Wilson v. Hill*, 17 Nev. 401, at 406, 30 Pac. 1076 (1883), *Hoffman v. Owens*, 31 Nev. 481, at 489, 103 Pac. 414 (1909)

[526] *Gregory v. Frothingham*, 1 Nev. 253 (1865).

[527] *Id.*

[528] *Id.*

[529] *Id.*

[530] *Id.*

Under sec. 64, ch. 9, Stats. 1861 (cf. NRS 112.180), which provides that the sale of personalty without immediate delivery followed by actual and continued change of possession is conclusive evidence of fraud, the change of possession must be actual and bona fide and must continue for such time as will, under the circumstances of each case, operate as general advertisement of the sale or change of title.[531]

Statement concerning sale not sufficient delivery. Under sec. 64, ch. 9, Stats. 1861 (cf. NRS 112.180), which provides that the sales of personalty are fraudulent as to creditors of the vendor unless accompanied by immediate delivery, a statement by the vendor before witnesses that certain grain had been sold was not sufficient delivery where the grain remained in the same bin as before and the vendor had access to the bin.[532]

Proof of management and control of property is evidence of change of possession. Under sec. 64, ch. 9, Stats. 1861 (cf. NRS 112.180), which provides that a sale made by a vendor of goods and chattels in his possession, unless accompanied by immediate delivery, and followed by continued change of possession, is conclusive evidence of fraud as against his creditors and subsequent purchasers in good faith, there is no better evidence of continued change of possession than proof that purchaser has assumed management and control of the property, and it is error to exclude evidence of such acts of ownership.[533]

Intent may be found as matter of law. Sec. 72, ch. 9, Stats. 1861 (cf. NRS 112.180), which provided that the question of fraudulent intent in conveyances shall be deemed a question of fact, did not preclude the court from holding the mortgage void as a matter of law, without regard to extrinsic facts, where the facts of fraud were expressly shown in the provisions of the mortgage.[534]

FEDERAL AND OTHER CASES.

A conveyance is not subject to attack where the property that is conveyed is exempt from execution. Creditors cannot be defrauded by the conveyance of a homestead without consideration because, since the homestead was exempt from execution, creditors are not prejudiced by the transfer.[535]

Conveyance between spouses for consideration not fraudulent where no intent to defraud. Preferential conveyance from insolvent husband to wife for valuable consideration is not fraudulent as to creditors where there is no intent to defraud, though the relationship may be considered in determining intent. C §§ 2708 and 2711 (cf. NRS 112.180 and 112.190).[536]

Relocation of mining claims for benefit of judgment creditor fraudulent. Where execution had issued against certain mining claims, subsequent relocation of the claims by a third person for the benefit of judgment debtor, which relocation was based on failure to do annual assessment work, was fraudulent conveyance and void as against creditors, where it was shown that annual assessment work for the preceding year had been performed on some of the claims.[537]

Mortgage given to spouse, for debt contracted before marriage, was invalid. Where husband gave wife chattel mortgage on stock and equipment as security for debt contracted 12 years before the mortgage, and for the purpose of protecting husband from other creditors, the mortgage was invalid as against husband's trustee in bankruptcy.[538]

Security agreement fraudulent where debt equal to majority of retained earnings incurred for benefit of parent corporation. Where parent corporation, in partial payment of its own obligation, caused subsidiary corporation to borrow from the same creditor an amount approximating 90 percent of its retained earnings and to give security interest in its property, bankruptcy court properly held security agreement fraudulent under former NRS 112.060 (cf. NRS 112.180), which so characterized every conveyance made without fair consideration which left transferor with unreasonably small capital, and former NRS 112.040 (cf. NRS 112.170), which defined fair consideration in terms of benefit to transferor and good faith of transferee. Here the benefit of agreement went to parent corporation and its creditor gained advantage.[539]

NRS 112.190, "Transfer made or obligation incurred by insolvent," provides as follows:

---

[531] (See also NRS 104.2402.) *Carpenter v. Clark*, 2 Nev. 243 (1866), cited, *Gray v. Sullivan*, 10 Nev. 416, at 424 (1876).

[532] (See also NRS 104.2402.) *Lawrence v. Burnham*, 4 Nev. 361 (1868), cited, *Wilson v. Hill*, 17 Nev. 401, at 407, 30 Pac. 1076 (1883).

[533] (See NRS 104.2201 and 104.2402.) *Conway v. Edwards*, 6 Nev. 190 (1870).

[534] *Lutz v. Kinney*, 24 Nev. 38, 49 Pac. 453, 50 Pac. 1031 (1897).

[535] *Thomson v. Crane*, 73 Fed. 327 (C.C.D. Nev. 1896).

[536] *Vansickle v. Wells, Fargo & Co.*, 105 Fed. 16 (C.C.D. Nev. 1900).

[537] *Wailes v. Davies*, 164 Fed. 397 (9th Cir. 1908).

[538] *In re Petersen*, 252 Fed. 849 (D. Nev. 1917).

[539] *Wells Fargo Bank v. Desert View Bldg. Supplies, Inc.*, 475 F. Supp. 693 (D. Nev. 1978).

1. A transfer made or obligation incurred by a debtor is fraudulent as to a creditor whose claim arose before the transfer was made or the obligation was incurred if the debtor made the transfer or incurred the obligation without receiving a reasonably equivalent value in exchange for the transfer or obligation and the debtor was insolvent at that time or the debtor became insolvent as a result of the transfer or obligation.

2. A transfer made by a debtor is fraudulent as to a creditor whose claim arose before the transfer was made if the transfer was made to an insider for an antecedent debt, the debtor was insolvent at that time, and the insider had reasonable cause to believe that the debtor was insolvent.

(Added to NRS by 1987, 11)

NEVADA CASES.

"Fair consideration" given by satisfaction of antecedent debt and buyer's assumption of debts of seller. In an action by a creditor against a buyer to set aside the sale of a well-drilling rig made by a deceased seller on the ground that the sale was made to defraud the creditor, where the seller owed antecedent debt to the buyer and the buyer agreed in exchange for the rig to release the debt and to pay an encumbrance due on the rig and another one due on the seller's automobile, satisfaction of antecedent debt and assumption of debts comprising encumbrances was considered as "fair consideration" under former NRS 112.050 (cf. NRS 112.190), which provides that conveyance made without fair consideration by person who will thereby be rendered insolvent is fraudulent as against his creditors, because former NRS 112.040 (cf. NRS 112.170) defines "fair consideration" as including satisfaction of antecedent debt and it is well established that the assumption of liability or debt of a seller by a buyer may be considered when determining whether consideration paid was fair.[540]

Burden of proof In an action to set aside a sale under former NRS 112.050 (cf. NRS 112.190), which provides that conveyance made without fair consideration by a person who will thereby be rendered insolvent is fraudulent as against his creditors without regard to actual intent of seller, creditor bore the burden of proof both with respect to insolvency of seller existing at the time or resulting from conveyance and with respect to absence or inadequacy of consideration.[541]

Possession obtained by a fraudulent conveyance does not perfect a security interest. Where holder of unperfected security interest had obtained possession of collateral by fraudulent conveyance under former NRS 112.050 (cf. NRS 112.190), possession did not serve to perfect security interest under former NRS 104.9302 (cf. NRS 104.9310), and security interest was subordinated to claim of subsequent lien creditor by virtue of former NRS 104.9301 (cf. NRS 104.9308).[542]

In action for medical malpractice, substitution of grandmother as guardian ad litem for child was not a fraudulent transfer of the claim of the child. The father of a child brought an action for medical malpractice after the child was born severely retarded as result of mother taking acne drug prescribed for her by defendant during the early stages of pregnancy. The initial complaint was filed by father on behalf of son as his parent and natural guardian. Before trial, the complaint was amended to allege that child's grandmother had been appointed guardian and guardian ad litem of child for purposes of prosecuting the action. The jury returned verdict in favor of the child, finding defendant 60 percent negligent and mother 40 percent negligent. On appeal, the supreme court held that the substitution of the grandmother as guardian ad litem was not an assignment of the claim from the father and mother to the grandmother and did not constitute a fraudulent transfer of claim (see NRS 112.190). The comparative negligence of the mother would not have been imputed to child even if she were the parent who asserted the cause of action of child. By allowing the complaint to be amended to reflect the grandmother as the new guardian ad litem pursuing the action for the child, the district court did nothing more than recognize the change of the individual responsible for the action.[543]

Defendant has the burden to come forward with rebuttal evidence. Where a creditor establishes existence of certain indicia or badges of fraud, the burden shifts to the defendant to come forward with rebuttal evidence showing that the transfer was not made to defraud creditor. The defendant must show that debtor was solvent at the time of the transfer and was not rendered insolvent by that transfer or show that the transfer was supported by fair consideration.[544]

FEDERAL AND OTHER CASES.

Conveyance made without consideration fraudulent, though made in good faith. Conveyance made in good

---

[540] *Matusik v. Large*, 85 Nev. 202, 452 P.2d 457 (1969), cited, *Sportsco Enterprises v. Morris*, 112 Nev. 625, at 632, 917 P.2d 934 (1996).

[541] *Matusik v. Large*, 85 Nev. 202, 452 P.2d 457 (1969), cited, *Sportsco Enterprises v. Morris*, 112 Nev. 625, at 632, 917 P.2d 934 (1996)

[542] *Kulik v. Albers, Inc.*, 91 Nev. 134, 532 P.2d 603 (1975).

[543] (See also NRS 12.080.) *Hogle v. Hall*, 112 Nev. 599, 916 P.2d 814 (1996).

[544] (See NRS 112.190.) *Sportsco Enterprises v. Morris*, 112 Nev. 625, 917 P.2d 934 (1996).

faith and for laudable purpose but without valuable consideration is fraudulent by operation of law where the facts clearly show existing creditors are prejudiced by the conveyance.[545] A conveyance between spouses for consideration is not fraudulent where there was no intent to defraud. Preferential conveyance from insolvent husband to wife for valuable consideration is not fraudulent as to creditors where there is no intent to defraud, though the relationship may be considered in determining intent.[546]

NRS 112.200, "Time at which transfer or obligation deemed made or incurred," provides as follows:

For the purposes of this chapter:
1. A transfer is made:
(a) With respect to an asset that is real property other than a fixture, but including the interest of a seller or purchaser under a contract for the sale of the asset, when the transfer is so far perfected that a good faith purchaser of the asset from the debtor against whom applicable law permits the transfer to be perfected cannot acquire an interest in the asset that is superior to the interest of the transferee; and
(b) With respect to an asset that is not real property or that is a fixture, when the transfer is so far perfected that a creditor on a simple contract cannot acquire a judicial lien otherwise than under this chapter that is superior to the interest of the transferee.
2. If applicable law permits the transfer to be perfected as provided in subsection 1 and the transfer is not so perfected before the commencement of an action for relief under this chapter, the transfer is deemed made immediately before the commencement of the action.
3. If applicable law does not permit the transfer to be perfected as provided in subsection 1, the transfer is made when it becomes effective between the debtor and the transferee.
4. A transfer is not made until the debtor has acquired rights in the asset transferred.
5. An obligation is incurred:
(a) If oral, when it becomes effective between the parties; or
(b) If evidenced by a writing, when the writing executed by the obligor is delivered to or for the benefit of the obligee.
(Added to NRS by 1987, 12)

NRS 112.210, "Rights of creditor in action for relief against transfer or obligation," provides as follows:

1. In an action for relief against a transfer or obligation under this chapter, a creditor, subject to the limitations in NRS 112.220, may obtain:
(a) Avoidance of the transfer or obligation to the extent necessary to satisfy the creditor's claim;
(b) An attachment or garnishment against the asset transferred or other property of the transferee pursuant to NRS 31.010 to 31.460, inclusive; and
(c) Subject to applicable principles of equity and in accordance with applicable rules of civil procedure:
(1) An injunction against further disposition by the debtor or a transferee, or both, of the asset transferred or of other property;
(2) Appointment of a receiver to take charge of the asset transferred or of other property of the transferee; or
(3) Any other relief the circumstances may require.
2. If a creditor has obtained a judgment on a claim against the debtor, the creditor, if the court so orders, may levy execution on the asset transferred or its proceeds.
(Added to NRS by 1987, 12)

NRS 112.220, "Avoidance of transfer or obligation: Protection of good faith transferee or obligee; recovery of judgment for value of asset transferred; certain transfers not voidable," provides as follows:

1. A transfer or obligation is not voidable under paragraph (a) of subsection 1 of NRS 112.180 against a person who took in good faith and for a reasonably equivalent value or against any subsequent transferee or obligee.
2. Except as otherwise provided in this section, to the extent a transfer is voidable in an action by a creditor under paragraph (a) of subsection 1 of NRS 112.210, the creditor may recover judgment for the value of the asset transferred, as adjusted under subsection 3 of this section, or the amount necessary to satisfy the creditor's claim,

---

[545] *Thomson v. Crane*, 73 Fed. 327 (C.C.D. Nev. 1896).
[546] C §§ 2708 and 2711 (cf. NRS 112.180 and 112.190). *Vansickle v. Wells, Fargo & Co.*, 105 Fed. 16 (C.C.D. Nev. 1900).

whichever is less. The judgment may be entered against:

(a) The first transferee of the asset or the person for whose benefit the transfer was made; or

(b) Any subsequent transferee other than a transferee who took in good faith for value or from any subsequent transferee.

3. If the judgment under subsection 2 is based upon the value of the asset transferred, the judgment must be for an amount equal to the value of the asset at the time of the transfer, subject to adjustment as the equities may require.

4. Notwithstanding voidability of a transfer or an obligation under this chapter, a transferee or obligee who took in good faith is entitled, to the extent of the value given the debtor for the transfer or obligation, to:

(a) A lien on or a right to retain any interest in the asset transferred;

(b) Enforcement of any obligation incurred; or

(c) A reduction in the amount of the liability on the judgment.

5. A transfer is not voidable under paragraph (b) of subsection 1 of NRS 112.180 or NRS 112.190 if the transfer results from:

(a) Termination of a lease upon default by the debtor when the termination is pursuant to the lease and applicable law; or

(b) Enforcement of a security interest in compliance with NRS 104.9101 to 104.9709, inclusive.

6. A transfer is not voidable under subsection 2 of NRS 112.190:

(a) To the extent the insider gave new value to or for the benefit of the debtor after the transfer was made unless the new value was secured by a valid lien;

(b) If made in the ordinary course of business or financial affairs of the debtor and the insider; or

(c) If made pursuant to a good faith effort to rehabilitate the debtor and the transfer secured present value given for that purpose as well as an antecedent debt of the debtor.

(Added to NRS by 1987, 12; A 1999, 389)

NEVADA CASES.

Imposing a constructive trust was improper under the circumstances. Where the record showed that jury had rejected respondent's argument at trial that appellant had imputed knowledge of alleged fraudulent transfer, it was error for the trial judge to award equitable relief in favor of respondent by imposing constructive trust upon the money in appellant's bank account, because in deciding whether to grant equitable relief, district court is prohibited from reconsidering any issues necessarily and actually decided by jury. Absent imputed knowledge, appellant stood in position of bona fide purchaser for value and the imposition of a constructive trust was improper under NRS 112.220.[547]

FEDERAL AND OTHER CASES.

Burden of proof: A plaintiff attempting to set aside a preference as a fraudulent conveyance has the burden of proving that defendant knew, or had reason to know, that the conveyance was intended as a preference.[548]

NRS 112.230, "Limitation of actions," provides as follows:

Except as otherwise provided in NRS 166.170, a claim for relief with respect to a fraudulent transfer or obligation under this chapter is extinguished unless action is brought:

1. Under paragraph (a) of subsection 1 of NRS 112.180, within 4 years after the transfer was made or the obligation was incurred or, if later, within 1 year after the transfer or obligation was or could reasonably have been discovered by the claimant;

2. Under paragraph (b) of subsection 1 of NRS 112.180 or subsection 1 of NRS 112.190, within 4 years after the transfer was made or the obligation was incurred; or

3. Under subsection 2 of NRS 112.190, within 1 year after the transfer was made or the obligation was incurred.

(Added to NRS by 1987, 13; A 1999, 1239)

NRS 112.240, "Supplementary general provisions of law applicable," provides as follows: "Unless displaced by the provisions of this chapter, the principles of law and equity, including the law merchant and the law relating to principal and agent, estoppel, laches, fraud, misrepresentation, duress, coercion, mistake, insolvency or other validating or invalidating cause, supplement its provisions."

---

[547] *Brown v. Federal Sav. and Loan Ins. Corp.*, 105 Nev. 409, 777 P.2d 361 (1989).

[548] *Alter v. Clark*, 193 Fed. 153 (D. Nev. 1911).

NRS 112.250 Construction of chapter. This chapter must be applied and construed to effectuate its general purpose to make uniform the law with respect to the subject of this chapter among states enacting it.

(Added to NRS by 1987, 14)

NEVADA CASES.

Recordation does not give notice to existing creditors. In an action by creditor seeking to have deed from husband to wife declared void under the Uniform Fraudulent Conveyance Act (see NRS 112.140 *et seq.*), recording of deed did not impart notice to creditor so as to start running of the statute of limitations because NRS 111.320, governing constructive notice, applies only to subsequent purchasers and mortgagees, and not to existing creditors.[549]

A fraudulent conveyance pursuant to NRS ch. 112 does not require proof of an intent to defraud.[550]

NEVADA CASES.

Respondent's interest in private sports box was lease and therefore property subject to Uniform Fraudulent Transfer Act. Respondent's interest in a private sports box which was used to view athletic events at the university was a lease where: (1) respondent was able to sell part of his interest in the box to a friend; (2) interest included the right to exclusive use of the box during basketball games and other public events; (3) owner of interest had the right to demand payment for use of the box when used during conventions; (4) owner of interest was entitled to the sole and exclusive right of access to the box, subject to approval by the university; and (5) owner of interest had the right to furnish and improve the box. Therefore, respondent's interest was property pursuant to NRS 112.150, and the district court erred in concluding that respondent's rights in the box were not property for the purposes of the Uniform Fraudulent Transfer Act.[551]

FEDERAL AND OTHER CASES.

"Creditor" includes a person to whom a contingent obligation is owed. Creditors are not those persons only to whom debts are due, but also those to whom a contingent obligation is owed by way of surety, guaranty or the like and any such creditor may set aside such a fraudulent conveyance.[552]

NEVADA CASES.

Actual delivery generally is required. The delivery contemplated by sec. 66, ch. 9, Stats. 1861 (see NRS 112.180), which provides that the sale of personal property without immediate delivery of such property is conclusive evidence of fraud upon the vendor's creditors, is actual delivery, and symbolical delivery will be sufficient only where actual delivery is impossible or extremely inconvenient.[553] Purpose of section is to prevent fraud. Purpose of sec. 64, ch. 9, Stats. 1861 (see NRS 112.180), which provides that the sale of personal property without immediate delivery of such property is conclusive evidence of fraud upon the vendor's creditors, is prevention of frauds which may result from permitting right of property to be in one person and possession and indicia of ownership of such property to be in another.[554]

Evidence concerning conveyance to plaintiff's grantor admissible. Where a person brings an action in the nature of ejectment to recover possession of property held under a sheriff's deed by creditors of grantor of plaintiff's grantor, evidence offered by such creditors to establish the nature of the transaction between the first and second grantor is material in showing the chain of circumstances resulting in fraud in the sale of such property and is admissible.[555]

Declaration concerning the fact of the conveyance was admissible. Where a person conveys his interest in an unfinished mill, retains possession of such mill and subsequent to conveyance declares that he has not conveyed such interest, such declaration is admissible as part of res gestae to show the nature of such person's possession.[556]

Retention of possession by transferor not always evidence of fraudulent intent. Where a person conveys real property and retains possession of such property to gather crops or to remove furniture or by renting such property, such

---

[549] *Crescent v. White*, 88 Nev. 71, 493 P.2d 1323 (1972), cited, *City of Reno v. Goldwater*, 92 Nev. 698, at 702, 558 P.2d 532 (1976)

[550] *Sportsco Enterprises v. Morris*, 112 Nev. 625, 917 P.2d 934 (1996).

[551] *Id.*

[552] *Thomson v. Crane*, 73 Fed. 327 (C.C.D. Nev. 1896).

[553] (See also NRS 104.2402.) *Doak v. Brubaker*, 1 Nev. 218 (1865), cited, *Sharon v. Shaw*, 2 Nev. 289, at 293 (1866), *Lawrence v. Burnham*, 4 Nev. 361, at 367 (1868), distinguished, *Gray v. Sullivan*, 10 Nev. 416, at 423 (1876).

[554] *Doak v. Brubaker*, 1 Nev. 218 (1865), cited, *Wilson v. Hill*, 17 Nev. 401, at 406, 30 Pac. 1076 (1883), *Hoffman v. Owens*, 31 Nev. 481, at 489, 103 Pac. 414 (1909).

[555] *Gregory v. Frothingham*, 1 Nev. 253 (1865).

[556] *Id.*

possession does not necessarily create a suspicion that the conveyance was made in attempt to delay the creditors of such person.[557]

Declaration of grantor concerning intention admissible. Declaration of grantor, made before the sale of real property, of his intention to make transfer to delay his creditors is admissible in action in the nature of ejectment brought by his grantee against grantor's creditors in possession of such property under a sheriff's deed.[558] Intention of both parties must be shown. In order to establish fraud in a transaction, the motives and intentions of both parties to the transaction must be proven.[559]

Change of possession. Under sec. 64, ch. 9, Stats. 1861 (cf. NRS 112.180), which provides that the sale of personalty without immediate delivery followed by actual and continued change of possession is conclusive evidence of fraud, change of possession must be actual and bona fide and must continue for such time as will, under circumstances of each case, operate as general advertisement of the sale or change of title.[560] Statement concerning sale not sufficient delivery. Under sec. 64, ch. 9, Stats. 1861 (cf. NRS 112.180), which provides that the sales of personalty are fraudulent as to creditors of the vendor unless accompanied by immediate delivery, a statement by the vendor before witnesses that certain grain had been sold was not sufficient delivery where the grain remained in the same bin as before and the vendor had access to the bin.[561] Proof of management and control of property is evidence of change of possession. Under sec 64, ch. 9, Stats. 1861 (cf. NRS 112.180), which provides that a sale made by a vendor of goods and chattels in his possession, unless accompanied by immediate delivery, and followed by continued change of possession, is conclusive evidence of fraud as against his creditors and subsequent purchasers in good faith, there is no better evidence of continued change of possession than proof that purchaser has assumed management and control of the property, and it is error to exclude evidence of such acts of ownership. (See NRS 104.2201 and 104.2402.)[562]

Intent may be found as matter of law. Sec. 72, ch. 9, Stats. 1861 (cf. NRS 112.180), which provided that the question of fraudulent intent in conveyances shall be deemed a question of fact, did not preclude the court from holding the mortgage void as a matter of law, without regard to extrinsic facts, where the facts of fraud were expressly shown in the provisions of the mortgage.[563]

FEDERAL AND OTHER CASES.

A conveyance was not subject to attack where the property conveyed was exempt from execution. Creditors cannot be defrauded by the conveyance of a homestead without consideration because, since the homestead was exempt from execution, creditors are not prejudiced by the transfer.[564]

Conveyance between spouses for consideration not fraudulent where no intent to defraud. Preferential conveyance from insolvent husband to wife for valuable consideration is not fraudulent as to creditors where there is no intent to defraud, though the relationship may be considered in determining intent. C §§ 2708 and 2711 (cf. NRS 112.180 and 112.190).[565]

The relocation of mining claims for the benefit of the judgment creditor was fraudulent. Where execution had issued against certain mining claims, the subsequent relocation of the claims by a third person for the benefit of the judgment debtor, which relocation was based on the failure to do annual assessment work, was a fraudulent conveyance and void as against creditors, where it was shown that annual assessment work for the preceding year had been performed on some of the claims.[566]

A mortgage given to a spouse, for a debt contracted before marriage, was invalid. Where a husband gave his wife a chattel mortgage on stock and equipment as security for a debt contracted 12 years before the mortgage, and for the purpose of protecting the husband from other creditors, the mortgage was invalid as against the husband's trustee in bankruptcy.[567]

---

[557] *Id.*

[558] *Id.*

[559] *Id.*

[560] (See also NRS 104.2402.) *Carpenter v. Clark*, 2 Nev. 243 (1866), cited, *Gray v. Sullivan*, 10 Nev. 416, at 424 (1876).

[561] (See also NRS 104.2402.) *Lawrence v. Burnham*, 4 Nev. 361 (1868), cited, *Wilson v. Hill*, 17 Nev. 401, at 407, 30 Pac. 1076 (1883).

[562] *Conway v. Edwards*, 6 Nev. 190 (1870).

[563] *Lutz v. Kinney*, 24 Nev. 38, 49 Pac. 453, 50 Pac. 1031 (1897).

[564] *Thomson v. Crane*, 73 Fed. 327 (C.C.D. Nev. 1896).

[565] *Vansickle v. Wells, Fargo & Co.*, 105 Fed. 16 (C.C.D. Nev. 1900).

[566] *Wailes v. Davies*, 164 Fed. 397 (9th Cir. 1908).

[567] *In re Petersen*, 252 Fed. 849 (D. Nev. 1917).

Security agreement fraudulent where debt equal to majority of retained earnings incurred for benefit of parent corporation. Where parent corporation, in partial payment of its own obligation, caused subsidiary corporation to borrow from the same creditor an amount approximating 90 percent of its retained earnings and to give security interest in its property, bankruptcy court properly held security agreement fraudulent under former NRS 112.060 (cf. NRS 112.180), which so characterized every conveyance made without fair consideration which left transferor with unreasonably small capital, and former NRS 112.040 (cf. NRS 112.170), which defined fair consideration in terms of benefit to transferor and good faith of transferee. Here the benefit of agreement went to parent corporation and its creditor gained advantage.[568]

Garnishment Proceedings

Garnishment proceedings are generally considered special proceedings.[569] NRS Chapter 31 governs, among other things, pre- and post-judgment garnishment proceedings.[570] Under that Chapter, writs of garnishment must be served in the same manner as a summons in a civil action, which gives the court jurisdiction to proceed against the "garnishee defendant."[571] Accordingly, garnishees who are properly served or appear formally become parties of record to the garnishment proceeding.[572]

Gross Negligence

"Gross negligence" signifies "more than ordinary inadvertence or inattention, but less than conscious indifference to the consequences."[573] Nevada cases which have had gross negligence claims include *Executive Management, Ltd. v. Ticor Title Ins. Co.*, 114 Nev. 823, 963 P.2d 465 (1998), *Maduike v. Agency Rent-A-Car*, 114 Nev. 1, 953 P.2d 24 (1998); and *Nadjarian v. Desert Palace, Inc*., 111 Nev. 763, 895 P.2d 1291 (1995). Gross negligence can be defined as reckless indifference or deliberate disregard of a trustee's fiduciary duty.[574] Note that, under NRS 42.001(1), to justify punitive damages, the defendant's conduct must have exceeded "mere recklessness or gross negligence."[575]

Hostile Work Environment

Although not explicitly included in the text of Title VII, claims based on a hostile work environment fall within Title VII's protections.[576] To state an actionable claim under Title VII, Plaintiff must show that (1) she was subjected to verbal or physical conduct based on her religion; (2) the conduct was unwelcome; and (3) the conduct was "sufficiently severe or pervasive to alter the conditions of her employment and create an abusive working environment."[577]

A plaintiff may establish a sex hostile work environment claim by showing that he was subjected to verbal or physical harassment that was sexual in nature, that the harassment was unwelcome and that the harassment was sufficiently severe or pervasive to alter the conditions of the plaintiff's employment and create an abusive work environment.[578] A plaintiff must establish that the conduct at issue was both objectively and subjectively offensive: he must show that a reasonable person would find the work environment to be "hostile or abusive," and that he in fact did perceive it to be so.[579] Where an employee is allegedly harassed by co-workers, the employer may be liable if it knows or should know of the harassment but fails to take steps "reasonably calculated to end the harassment."[580]

---

[568] *Wells Fargo Bank v. Desert View Bldg. Supplies, Inc.*, 475 F. Supp. 693 (D. Nev. 1978).

[569] *Settelmeyer & Sons v. Smith & Harmer*, 124 Nev. 1206, 1215, 197 P.3d 1051, 1057 (2008).

[570] *Id.*

[571] *Id.*

[572] *Id.*

[573] PROSSER AND KEETON ON TORTS, Fifth Edition, p. 212. See *Nist v. Tudor*, 407 P.2d 798 (1965), *Wager v. Pro*, 603 F.2d 1005 (D.C. 1979) ("an extreme departure from ordinary care").

[574] See, *e.g.*, W. Page Keeton *et al.*, PROSSER AND KEETON ON TORTS, 209, 212 (5th ed. 1984) (defining gross negligence as "a failure to exercise even that care which a careless person would use.")

[575] *Countrywide Home Loans v. Thitchener*, 124 Nev. 725, 192 P.3d 243 (2008).

[576] *Harris v. Forklift Sys.*, 510 U.S. 17, 21 (1993).

[577] *Galdamex v. Potter*, 415 F.3d 1015, 1023 (9th Cir. 1995) (quoting *Meritor Savings Bank, FSB v. Vinson*, 477 U.S. 57, 67 (1986)).

[578] See *Gregory v. Widnall*, 153 F.3d 1071, 1074 (9th Cir. 1998).

[579] *Faragher v. City of Boca Raton*, 524 U.S. 775, 787 (1998).

[580] *Nichols v. Azteca Rest. Enter., Inc.*, 256 F.3d 864, 875 (9th Cir. 2001) (internal quotation marks omitted).

Implied Waiver

Implied waiver applies when the other party's conduct clearly shows an intention to waive a right or when that party's neglect to insist upon the right prejudices the invoking party.[581]

Implied Warranty of Habitability

Nevada statutorily follows the national direction in residential leases and recognizes the implied warranty of habitability. This approach is based on consumer protection and related public policy grounds. This is so, although the Nevada courts have not expressly adopted it outside the realm of new construction litigation.

At common law, the real estate lease developed in the field of real property law, not contract law. Under property law concepts, a lease was considered a conveyance or sale of the premises for a term of years, subject to the ancient doctrine of caveat emptor.[582] Thus, under traditional common law rules, the landlord owed no duty to place leased premises in a habitable condition and no obligation to repair the premises.[583] These original common law precepts perhaps suited the agrarianism of the early Middle Ages which was their matrix; at such time, the primary value of a lease lay in the land itself and whatever simple living structures may have been included in the leasehold were of secondary importance and were readily repairable by the typical "jack-of-all-trades" lessee farmer. Furthermore, because the law of property crystallized before the development of mutually dependent covenants in contract law, a lessee's covenant to pay rent was considered at common law as independent of the lessor's covenants. Thus even when a lessor expressly covenanted to make repairs, the lessor's breach[584] did not justify the lessee's withholding of the rent.[585]

Rather than "caveat lessee," Nevada's statutes found at NRS 118A follow modern notions of leases as contracts for the possession of property, and not as conveyances under classic property theory. This is consistent with the thinking in a landmark case familiar to first-year law students, which stated as follows: "When American city dwellers, both rich and poor, seek 'shelter' today, they seek a well-known package of goods and services—a package which includes not merely walls and ceilings, but also adequate heat, light and ventilation, serviceable plumbing facilities, secure windows and doors, proper sanitation, and proper maintenance."[586]

Javins recognized modern society's transformation from agrarian to urbanized tenant interests in buildings on the land and not on the land itself. Moreover, *Javins* recognized that urban tenants lack an agrarian dweller's self-sufficiency and are unable to make repairs themselves. Moreover, given the short duration of residential leaseholds, the tenants lack incentives to make repairs. Additionally, tenants are limited in their abilities to gain access or to make complex repairs. Finally, having no long-term interests in the property, tenants cannot obtain financing for significant repairs.[587]

In *Radaker v. Scott*,[588] the Nevada Supreme Court held that the implied warranty of habitability reflects a naturally expected and sound public policy. The Court held that the owner/builder/vendor of house was subject to the implied warranty of habitability, as was the contractor who constructed the house, both of whom were liable for breach of the implied covenant of habitability because of their status as joint venturers.

In *Calloway v. City of Reno*, the Court, citing a Florida case, further confirmed that the common law warranty of habitability exists side-by-side with statutory warranties. The Court stated as follows:

> Buying a house is the largest investment many consumers ever make, and homeowners are an appealing, sympathetic class. If a house causes economic disappointment by not meeting a purchaser's expectations, the resulting failure to receive the benefit of the bargain is a core concern of contract, not tort, law. There are protections for homebuyers, however, such as statutory warranties, the general warranty of habitability, and the duty of sellers to disclose defects, as well as the ability of purchasers to inspect houses for defects.[589]

---

[581] *Dickinson v. American Medical Response*, 124 Nev. 460, 468 186 P.3d 878 (2008).

[582] See generally *Green v. Superior Court*, 10 Cal.3d 616 (Cal. 1974).

[583] See 3 Holdsworth, *A History of English Law* (5th ed. 1966) pp. 122-23; see, *e.g.*, *Brewster v. DeFremery* 33 Cal. 341, 345-346 (1867).

[584] 10 Cal.3d 623.

[585] See 6 Williston, *Contracts* (3rd ed. 1962) § 890, pp. 580-589; *Arnold v. Krigbaum*, 169 Cal. 143, 145 [146 P. 423] (Cal. 1915).

[586] *Javins v. First Nat'l Realty Corp.*, 428 F.2d 1071, 1074, *cert. denied*, 400 U.S. 925 (1970).

[587] *Id.*

[588] 109 Nev. 653, 655 (1993).

[589] *Calloway v. City of Reno*, 116 Nev. 250, 261, 993 P.2d 1259 (2000).

The common law imposes an implied warranty of workmanlike manner, which has been defined as a duty to perform to a reasonably skillful standard.[590]

Indemnity

Non-contractual or implied indemnity is an equitable remedy that allows a defendant to seek recovery from other potential tortfeasors whose negligence primarily caused the injured party's harm.[591] "At the heart of the doctrine is the premise that the person seeking to assert implied indemnity–the indemnitee–has been required to pay damages caused by a third party–the indemnitor."[592] Implied indemnification has been developed by the courts to address the unfairness which results when one party, who has committed no independent wrong, is held liable for the loss of a plaintiff caused by another party.[593] Generally, the remedy of indemnity is available after the defendant has extinguished its own liability through settlement or by paying a judgment.[594]

A cause of action for indemnity accrues when payment has been made.[595] A claimant seeking equitable indemnity must plead and prove that: (1) it has discharged a legal obligation owed to a third party; (2) the party from whom it seeks liability also was liable to the third party; and (3) as between the claimant and the party from whom it seeks indemnity, the obligation ought to be discharged by the latter.[596]

Indemnity is not available in a case involving joint tortfeasors having no legal relation to one another, and each owing a duty of care to a third party.[597]

The Nevada Supreme Court has analyzed implied indemnity in depth as follows:

Implied Indemnity

Non-contractual or implied indemnity is an equitable remedy that allows a defendant to seek recovery from other potential tortfeasors whose negligence primarily caused the injured party's harm. At the heart of the doctrine is the premise that the person seeking to assert implied indemnity–the indemnitee–has been required to pay damages caused by a third party–the indemnitor. Implied indemnification has been developed by the courts to address the unfairness which results when one party, who has committed no independent wrong, is held liable for the loss of a plaintiff caused by another party.

Generally, the remedy is available after the defendant has extinguished its own liability through settlement or by paying a judgment. This court has stated that "a cause of action for indemnity . . . accrues when payment has been made." A claimant seeking equitable indemnity must plead and prove that: (1) it has discharged a legal obligation owed to a third party; (2) the party from whom it seeks liability also was liable to the third party; and (3) as between the claimant and the party from whom it seeks indemnity, the obligation ought to be discharged by the latter.

We previously recognized that there is a split of authority whether a party entitled to indemnity may also recover from the indemnitor reasonable attorney fees and costs incurred in defending the primary tort action. We determined that a party is entitled to recover through indemnification at least some of the attorney fees and court costs incurred in defending an action. However, the right to fees and costs remains limited. We restricted the recovery of attorney fees and costs through indemnification to those "fees and expenses attributable to the making of defenses which are not primarily directed toward rebutting charges of active negligence.

Additionally, we also required some nexus or relationship between the indemnitee and indemnitor. We adopted the warning found in [a Florida case] that implied indemnification should not be construed as permission to open a floodgate for cross-claims seeking indemnification where there is no connection between the cross-claimant and the party from whom indemnification is sought.

Our previous opinions concerning implied indemnification addressed appeals in which a trial had been conducted on the merits and apportioned liability to each party. However, we have not

---

[590] *Olson v. Richard*, 120 Nev. 247, 89 P.3d 31 (2004) (Becker, J., dissenting).

[591] *Doctors Company v. Vincent*, 120 Nev. 644, 650, 98 P.3d 681, 686 (2004).

[592] *Harvest Capital v. West Virginia Dept. of Energy*, 560 S.E.2d 509, 513 (W. Va. 2002).

[593] *Id.* at 512.

[594] *Doctors Company v. Vincent*, 120 Nev. at 651, 98 P.3d at 686 (2004).

[595] *Aetna Casualty & Surety v. Aztec Plumbing*, 106 Nev. 474, 476, 796 P.2d 227, 229 (1990) (citing *Southern Maryland Oil Co. v. Texas Co.*, 203 F. Supp. 449, 452 (D. Md. 1962)).

[596] 41 Am. Jur. 2d Indemnity § 20 (2005).

[597] *Central Telephone Co. v. Fixtures Mfg.*, 103 Nev. 298, 300, 738 P.2d 510, 512 (1987).

addressed the issue of indemnity when the underlying liability claim is resolved through summary judgment without a finding of fault on behalf of the third-party defendant from whom the claimant seeks indemnity.

On this point, the West Virginia Supreme Court has provided persuasive reasoning that comports with our general authority concerning implied indemnity. In particular, the West Virginia Supreme Court, in *Harvest Capital*, held that a claimant is entitled to indemnity from a third-party defendant for attorney fees and costs only after it is established that the plaintiff in the original action has sustained an injury for which the third-party defendant is responsible. The fact that the party charged may be innocent of the claimed wrong and can successfully defend against such a suit does not entitle [the party] to pass the burden on to some equally innocent party. Thus, to prevent one innocent party from passing its burden on to an equally innocent party, a prerequisite to the recovery of attorney fees from a potential indemnitor is a finding of liability to the plaintiff by the potential indemnitor on the underlying claim. Therefore, when a district court has disposed of the underlying liability claim, but has not established that the potential indemnitor was at fault, no right to equitable indemnity exists.

In this case, the district court entered summary judgment in favor of the defendant, Primadonna, on the underlying negligence claim and subsequently concluded that the indemnity action was rendered moot by the termination of the underlying claim. Although we agree with the ultimate decision of the district court and conclude that the indemnity action should have been dismissed, we do not agree that it was rendered moot simply by granting summary judgment on the underlying negligence claim. Rather, the indemnity claim should have been dismissed because Marlene has not been found liable for the injuries sustained by Fabian. It is an established principle of implied indemnity that the potential indemnitor must be liable for the injuries to the plaintiff. We see no compelling reason to transfer the costs of defending the claim from one innocent party to another without an adjudication of liability against the indemnitor.

Furthermore, there exists no nexus or special relationship between the parties that would allow the application of implied indemnification in this case. Implied indemnification is not a license to assert a cross-claim against any third party in hope of alleviating the burden of costs associated with defending litigation. Primadonna failed to demonstrate any nexus or relationship with Marlene, and we see none.

We therefore conclude that the district court's order denying the motion for summary judgment was correct although not because the motion was moot. A district court's correct result will not be disturbed on appeal even though its decision was reached by relying on different grounds. Rather, we conclude that the motion for summary judgment was properly denied in this case because implied indemnification may not be asserted without determined liability of the third party to the injured party and the showing of a nexus or special relationship between the indemnitee and proposed indemnitor. Therefore, we conclude that the district court's denial of Primadonna's motion for summary judgment was proper.[598]

An Independent Action

The indispensable elements of such a cause of action are (1) a judgment which ought not, in equity and good conscience, to be enforced; (2) a good defense to the alleged cause of action on which the judgment is founded; (3) fraud, accident, or mistake which prevented the [party seeking to undo] the judgment from obtaining the benefit of his defense; (4) the absence of fault or negligence on the part of [said party]; and (5) the absence of any adequate remedy at law.[599]

Nevada's pre-Civil Rules formulation was that to entitle a party to relief from a judgment or decree, it must be made evident that he had a defense upon the merits; and that such defense has been lost to him, without such loss being attributable to his own omission, neglect, or default. The loss of a defense, to justify a court of equity in removing a judgment, must, in all cases, be occasioned by the fraud or act of the prevailing party, or by mistake or accident on the part of the losing party, unmixed with any fault of himself or his agent.[600]

The United States Supreme Court comprehensively reviewed Rule 60(b) in its 1998 decision in *United States v. Beggerly*, focusing, in particular, on the independent action for relief from judgment preserved by its "savings clause." As *Beggerly* notes, the 1946 amendments to Federal Rule 60(b) expressly abolished "nearly all of the old forms of obtaining relief from judgment, *i.e.*, coram nobis, coram vobis, audita querela, bills of review, and bills in the nature of

---

[598] *Rodriguez v. Primadonna Company, LLC*, 216 P.3d 793 (Nev. 10/01/2009) (citations omitted).

[599] *Bonnell v. Lawrence*, 128 Nev. Adv. Op. No. 37 (August 9, 2012).

[600] (Citations omitted.) See generally *Bonnell v. Lawrence, supra.*

review"; only "one of the old forms, *i.e.*, the 'independent action,' still survived."[601] Because it was preserved by a "savings clause," not created by grant, Rule 60(b) did not specify the requirements for a viable independent action. The Advisory Committee notes acknowledged, though, that the time limits imposed on motions for relief for judgment did not apply to the independent action preserved by Rule 60(b)'s savings clause. See Fed. R. Civ. P. 60 advisory committee's note (1946 amendment) ("If the right to make a motion is lost by the expiration of the time limits fixed in these rules, the only other procedural remedy is by a new or independent action to set aside a judgment upon those principles which have heretofore been applied in such an action.")[602]

Rule 60(b) thus contains an inherent dichotomy: "If relief may be obtained through an independent action in a [routine] case . . . , where the most that may be charged against the [judgment victor] is a failure to furnish relevant information that would at best form the basis for a Rule 60(b)(3) motion, the strict 1-year [in Nevada, six-month] time limit on such motions would be set at naught."[603] Addressing this dichotomy, *Beggerly* holds that "[i]ndependent actions must, if Rule 60(b) is to be interpreted as a coherent whole, be reserved for those cases of 'injustices which, in certain instances, are deemed sufficiently gross to demand a departure' from rigid adherence to the doctrine of res judicata."[604] "[U]nder the Rule, an independent action should be available only to prevent a grave miscarriage of justice."[605]

Rule 60(b) of the Nevada Rules of Civil Procedure is modeled on Rule 60(b) of the Federal Rules of Civil Procedure, as written before the latter's amendment in 2007.[606] Like its federal counterpart, NRCP 60(b) permits relief from judgment by motion or by independent action. Addressing motions, the rule specifies both the permissible grounds, see NRCP 60(b)(1)-(5), and the time deadlines that apply, see NRCP 60(b) (a motion under Rule 60(b) "shall be made within a reasonable time, and for reasons (1), (2), and (3) not more than 6 months after . . . written notice of entry of the judgment or order was served"). The rule's reference to relief by independent action, by contrast, provides no specifics. It appears in a "savings clause," which states only: "This rule [i.e., NRCP 60(b)] does not limit the power of a court to entertain an independent action to relieve a party from a judgment, order, or proceeding, or to set aside a judgment for fraud upon the court."

Because NRCP 60(b)'s text makes its time deadlines applicable only to motions, not independent actions,[607], Bonnell argued that she could proceed by independent action to set aside the summary judgment and associated fee award, despite her delay. In essence, Bonnell argued that a litigant who seeks relief from a final judgment but lets the time for doing so by motion under NRCP 60(b)(1)-(3) expire, can do so by independent action, so long as she alleges facts that might qualify for motion-based relief under NRCP 60(b)(1)-(3).[608]

But, held the Nevada Supreme Court, this is not the law. "Resort to an independent action may be had only rarely, and then only under unusual and exceptional circumstances."[609] To obtain relief by independent action after a judgment has become final and otherwise unreviewable, a claimant must meet the traditional requirements of such an equitable action, which are considerably more exacting than required for relief by motion under NRCP 60(b)(1)-(3). Furthermore, "under the Rule, an independent action [is] available only to prevent a grave miscarriage of justice."[610] This is a "demanding standard."[611]

Of note, applying review appropriate to summary judgment does not lessen the "demanding" substantive law

---

[601] 524 U.S. at 45 (footnote omitted).

[602] Quoted in *Beggerly*, 524 U.S. at 45; accord *Pickett v. Comanche Construction, Inc.*, 108 Nev. 422, 426-27, 836 P.2d 42, 45 (1992).

[603] *Beggerly*, 524 U.S. at 46.

[604] *Id.* (quoting *Hazel-Atlas Co.*, 322 U.S. at 244). See also *NC-DSH*, 125 Nev. at 654, 218 P.3d at 858 (upholding, under NRCP 60's savings clause, relief from judgment for "fraud upon the court" but limiting it to " 'that species of fraud which does, or attempts to, subvert the integrity of the court itself' "; rejecting argument that "fraud upon the court" means "any conduct of a party or lawyer of which the court disapproves; among other evils, such a formulation 'would render meaningless the [time] limitation on motions under [Rule] 60(b)(3)' " (alterations in original) (quoting *Demjanjuk v. Petrovsky*, 10 F.3d 338, 352 (6th Cir. 1993); *Kupferman v. Consolidated Research & Mfg. Corp.*, 459 F.2d 1072, 1078 (2d Cir. 1972) (Friendly, J.))).

[605] *Beggerly*, 524 U.S. at 47.

[606] See *NC-DSH, Inc. v. Garner*, 125 Nev. 647, 650-51 nn.1 & 2, 218 P.3d 853, 856 nn.1 & 2 (2009).

[607] See *Nevada Industrial Dev. v. Benedetti*, 103 Nev. 360, 365, 741 P.2d 802, 805 (1987) ("[t]he only time limitations on independent actions under Rule 60(b) are laches or a relevant statute of limitations").

[608] *Bonnell v. Lawrence*, 128 Nev. Adv. Op. No. 37 (August 9, 2012).

[609] 11 Charles Alan Wright, Arthur R. Miller & Mary Kay Kane, Federal Practice and Procedure § 2868, at 397-98 (2d ed. 1995).

[610] *United States v. Beggerly*, 524 U.S. 38, 47 (1998).

[611] *Id.*

that applies to independent actions seeking review from judgment.[612] The policy supporting the finality of judgments recognizes that, " 'in most instances society is best served by putting an end to litigation after a case has been tried and judgment entered.' "[613] Similar to a qualified immunity or other privilege defense, the bar against relitigation of already-decided issues is, in essence, "an entitlement not to stand trial or face the other burdens of litigation" and "should be resolved at the earliest possible stage in litigation."[614] "Summary judgment is appropriate when [claim or] issue preclusion bars a claim."[615]

Injunction

NRS 33.010, "Cases in which injunction may be granted," provides as follows:

An injunction may be granted in the following cases:
    1. When it shall appear by the complaint that the plaintiff is entitled to the relief demanded, and such relief or any part thereof consists in restraining the commission or continuance of the act complained of, either for a limited period or perpetually.
    2. When it shall appear by the complaint or affidavit that the commission or continuance of some act, during the litigation, would produce great or irreparable injury to the plaintiff.
    3. When it shall appear, during the litigation, that the defendant is doing or threatens, or is about to do, or is procuring or suffering to be done, some act in violation of the plaintiff's rights respecting the subject of the action, and tending to render the judgment ineffectual.
    [1911 CPA § 195; RL § 5137; NCL § 8693]

A party may not complain of error unless he shows a cause of action or a ground of defense. No party may complain of an error on appeal from a decision of a trial court unless he shows by his pleading that he has some cause of action or ground of defense.[616]

Requirements for injunction. Allegations by a plaintiff trustee for a stockholder that a trustee and officer of a mining corporation had ousted the one who was president and trustee, seized books and property of the corporation, moved its offices, cancelled stock of the corporation, issued stock to himself, refused to pay claims against the corporation, applied for a patent for the corporation's mining claims and was operating the corporation without supervision of the board of trustees or stockholders were insufficient to entitle the plaintiff to an injunction because the plaintiff had no standing to complain, there was adequate remedy at law on some counts and sufficient facts were not alleged to show probable injury to the plaintiff, the corporation or the stockholders.[617]

A reasonable probability of real injury is required. Injunction will issue only if there is a reasonable probability that real injury will occur if injunction does not issue.[618] No injunction to issue where complete and adequate remedy at law. Injunction will not issue where there is a complete and adequate remedy at law.[619] An injunction will issue only to prevent injury or mischief and affords no redress for wrongs already committed, but a remedy for an injury already committed will sometimes be given as an incident to an injunction.[620]

A preliminary injunction is available when the moving party can demonstrate that the nonmoving party's conduct, if allowed to continue, will cause irreparable harm for which compensatory relief is inadequate and that the moving party has a reasonable likelihood of success on the merits.[621] Plaintiff need not clearly be entitled to relief sought to obtain a preliminary injunction. Under sec. 112, ch. 112, Stats. 1869 (cf. NRS 33.010), providing that an injunction may issue where it appears from a complaint that the plaintiff is entitled to the relief demanded, or that the commission or continuance of some act during litigation would cause the plaintiff great or irreparable injury or render the judgment

---

[612] *Id.*

[613] *NC-DSH*, 125 Nev. at 653, 218 P.3d at 858 (quoting *Hazel-Atlas Co. v. Hartford Co.*, 322 U.S. 238, 244 (1944), abrogated on other grounds by *Standard Oil Co. of Cal. v. United States*, 429 U.S. 17 (1976)).

[614] *Butler v. Bayer*, 123 Nev. 450, 458, 168 P.3d 1055, 1061 (2007) (internal quotations omitted).

[615] *Elyousef v. O'Reilly & Ferrario, LLC*, 126 Nev. ___, ___, 245 P.3d 547, 548 (2010).

[616] *Sherman v. Clark*, 4 Nev. 138 (1868).

[617] *Id.*

[618] *Id., Hansen v. Eighth Judicial Dist. Court*, 116 Nev. 650, at 658, 6 P.3d 982 (2000).

[619] *Id.*, cited, *Conley v. Chedic*, 6 Nev. 222, at 224 (1870), *Phenix* [sic] *v. Frampton*, 29 Nev. 306, at 318, 90 Pac. 2 (1907), distinguished, *Czipott v. Fleigh*, 87 Nev. 496, at 498, 489 P.2d 681 (1971).

[620] *Sherman v. Clark*, 4 Nev. 138 (1868), cited, *Phenix v. Frampton*, 29 Nev. 306, at 318, 90 Pac. 2 (1907), distinguished, *Memory Gardens of Las Vegas, Inc. v. Pet Ponderosa Memorial Gardens, Inc.*, 88 Nev. 1, at 3, 492 P.2d 123 (1972).

[621] *Boulder Oaks Cmty. Ass'n v. B & J Andrews*, 125 Nev. 397, 403, 215 P.3d 27, 31 (2009).

ineffectual, in order for a preliminary injunction to issue the plaintiff need not clearly be entitled to the relief sought, because the appellate court has adopted a more liberal rule under which the trial court, in its discretion and as circumstances warrant, may better protect the right of the parties.[622]

The issuance of a preliminary injunction is in the discretion of the district court. Whether a preliminary injunction (see NRS 33.010 and NRCP 65(a)) should be granted or denied rests in the sound judicial discretion of the district court and will be reversed only where the district court abused its discretion.[623] Equitable relief is not appropriate if the bond affords sufficient protection. In an action by the maker of a note for adjudication of balance due, where an action on the note was pending and attachment of the maker's property threatened, and the plaintiff did not allege an inability to pay the installments due and had not tendered payment, NRS 31.030 requiring a bond of the plaintiff on attachment, and NRS 31.040 and 31.180 providing for prevention of the attachment and release of the property on giving of the bond by the defendant, afforded sufficient protection, and the court was not justified in substituting equitable relief under NRS 33.010 providing for granting of injunctions.[624]

The right of the court to restrain a breach of contract is well-recognized. In an action by a creditor to enjoin a debtor from interfering with the operation by the creditor of the debtor's business under an agreement giving the creditor full control until repaid out of profits or proceeds from the sale of the business for advances made under an earlier agreement for advances secured by inventory and receivables, the requisites for an injunction under NRS 33.010 were met. The right of the court to restrain a breach of contract under proper circumstances is well-recognized.[625]

Preliminary injunction: Factors to be established by party seeking issuance. A preliminary injunction to preserve the status quo (see also NRS 33.010) is normally available upon a showing that: (1) the party seeking the preliminary injunction enjoys a reasonable probability of success on the merits; and (2) the defendant's conduct, if allowed to continue, will result in irreparable harm for which compensatory damages is an inadequate remedy.[626]

Additional standard for preliminary injunction. In considering whether to grant a preliminary injunction, a court may also weigh the public interest and the relative hardships of the parties in deciding whether to grant a preliminary injunction.[627]

The decision whether to grant a preliminary injunction is within the discretion of the trial court and will be reversed on appeal only if an abuse of discretion is demonstrated. Where the trial court denied a motion for a preliminary injunction to enjoin the enforcement of a default judgment against the defendants, the Supreme Court reversed and held that even though the decision whether to grant a preliminary injunction (see NRS 33.010) is within the discretion of the trial court and will be reversed on appeal only if an abuse of discretion is demonstrated, the trial court abused its discretion in denying the preliminary injunction because the default judgment was entered without adequate notice to the defendants.[628]

A prima facie case sufficient to establish the probability of success is required for a preliminary injunction. In an action to enjoin foreclosure of a deed of trust, where the escrow agent had paid money owing under the deed of trust to a mortgage company which had made the loan and collected payments for several months but the mortgage company went bankrupt without paying the beneficiary to whom the note and deed of trust were assigned, the debtor showed the

---

[622] *Rhodes Mining Co. v. Belleville Placer Mining Co.*, 32 Nev. 230, 106 Pac. 561 (1910), cited, *Berryman v. International Bhd. of Elec. Workers*, 82 Nev. 277, at 280, 416 P.2d 387 (1966), *Harrison v. Department of Highways*, 87 Nev. 183, at 185, 484 P.2d 716 (1971), *Dangberg Holdings, LLC v. Douglas County*, 115 Nev. 129, at 146, 978 P.2d 311 (1999).

[623] *Rhodes Mining Co. v. Belleville Placer Mining Co.*, 32 Nev. 230, 106 Pac. 561 (1910), *Edwards v. Emperor's Garden Rest.*, 122 Nev. 317, at 326, 130 P.3d 1280 (2006), *Labor Comm'r v. Littlefield*, 123 Nev. 35, at 38, 153 P.3d 26 (2007), but see *Clark County School Dist. v. Buchanan*, 112 Nev. 1146, at 1150, 924 P.2d 716 (1996).

[624] *Aronoff v. Katleman*, 75 Nev. 424, 345 P.2d 221 (1959), cited, *Cooper v. Liebert*, 81 Nev. 341, at 344, 402 P.2d 989 (1965).

[625] *Chisholm v. Redfield*, 75 Nev. 502, 347 P.2d 523 (1959).

[626] *Number One Rent-A-Car v. Ramada Inns, Inc.*, 94 Nev. 779, 587 P.2d 1329 (1978), cited, *Christensen v. Chromalloy Am. Corp.*, 99 Nev. 34, at 36, 656 P.2d 844 (1983), *Labor Comm'r v. Littlefield*, 123 Nev. 35, at 39, 153 P.3d 26 (2007), distinguished, *State ex rel. Attorney Gen. v. NOS Communications, Inc.*, 120 Nev. 65, at 68, 84 P.3d 1052 (2004).

[627] *Ellis v. McDaniel*, 95 Nev. 455, 596 P.2d 222 (1979), cited, *Clark County School Dist. v. Buchanan*, 112 Nev. 1146, at 1150, 924 P.2d 716 (1996), see also *University Sys. v. Nevadans for Sound Gov't.*, 120 Nev. 712, at 721, 100 P.3d 179 (2004).

[628] See NRCP 55(b)(2); *Franklin v. Bartsas Realty, Inc.*, 95 Nev. 559, 598 P.2d 1147 (1979), cited, *Guerin v. Guerin*, 114 Nev. 127, at 134, 953 P.2d 716 (1998), see also *Dangberg Holdings, LLC v. Douglas County*, 115 Nev. 129, at 142, 978 P.2d 311 (1999), *S.O.C., Inc. v. Mirage Casino-Hotel*, 117 Nev. 403, at 407, 23 P.3d 243 (2001), *Labor Comm'r v. Littlefield*, 123 Nev. 35, at 38, 153 P.3d 26 (2007).

agency, actual or apparent, on the part of the mortgage company sufficient prima facie to establish the probability of success required for a preliminary injunction.[629] The appellate court reversed the order of the trial court denying a preliminary injunction.[630]

The burden of showing great or irreparable injury to support a preliminary injunction was met. In an action to enjoin foreclosure of a deed of trust, where the plaintiff showed erection of a log house worth $127,000 which he would be unable to redeem upon foreclosure for a debt of $59,000, the burden of showing great or irreparable injury to support a preliminary injunction under NRS 33.010 was met, because the unique nature of real property as such usually makes loss of interest in it irreparable and the disproportion of debt to value made compensatory damages inadequate.[631]

It was no abuse of discretion to order a preliminary injunction preventing the finalization of a settlement agreement for property to which other parties held rights. The trial court did not abuse its discretion in ordering a preliminary injunction preventing the parties in an action for the specific performance of a purchase agreement for property from finalizing their settlement agreement because the parties seeking intervention, who held real and personal property rights related to the property, demonstrated a reasonable probability of success in enforcing their property rights and made the requisite showing of the probability of irreparable harm to their property rights as a result of the settlement agreement.[632]

Statutory enforcement actions: Equitable considerations normally required to justify injunctive relief will be presumed when statutory conditions of enforcement action have been satisfied. To obtain injunctive relief in a statutory enforcement action, such as under NRS 598.0963, a state or government agency need only show, through competent evidence, a reasonable likelihood that the statute was violated and that the statute specifically allows injunctive relief. Traditional equitable considerations for the granting of injunctive relief, such as irreparable harm and an inadequate legal remedy, are presumed in a statutory enforcement action.[633]

The issue of whether employment of State Legislators in the Executive Branch violates the separation of powers may be raised in a proper action in the district court. Although the judiciary may not review whether state executive branch employees are qualified to sit in the Nevada Legislature,[634] the judiciary may review whether it is constitutional for State Legislators to hold positions in the Executive Branch under the doctrine of separation of powers.[635] This dichotomy exists because unlike Nev. Const. art. 4, § 6, which expressly gives to each house the authority to judge the qualifications, elections and returns of its members, no constitutional provision gives the Executive Branch the exclusive authority to judge the qualifications of its officers and employees. Thus, the dual service issue may be raised as a separation-of-powers challenge to Legislators working in the Executive Branch if the challenge is brought in a proper action in the district court. A proper action may be: (1) a quo warranto action brought by the Attorney General against a Legislator seeking to oust the Legislator from an executive branch position invested with sovereign power[636] or (2) an action for declaratory and injunctive relief brought by a person with standing against a Legislator seeking to enjoin the Legislator from continuing to work in an executive branch position.[637] Such actions should be brought in the district court to allow a full record to be developed regarding the nature and scope of the Legislator's duties and position in the Executive Branch.[638]

In order to obtain injunctive relief in a statutory enforcement action, a likelihood of future violations must be shown. Though irreparable injury and an inadequate legal remedy need not be shown for injunctive relief in a statutory enforcement action, the plaintiff must still demonstrate a likelihood of future violations to obtain an injunction. In assessing this question, the court must consider the totality of the circumstances, including the gravity of any harm caused, the extent of and motivation behind the violator's participation in the wrongful conduct, the isolated or recurrent nature of the violation, and whether the violator has recognized culpability and/or sincerely promised that future

---

[629] See NRS 33.010.

[630] *Dixon v. Thatcher*, 103 Nev. 414, 742 P.2d 1029 (1987), *Thirteen South Ltd. v. Summit Village, Inc.*, 109 Nev. 1218, at 1220, 266 P.2d 257 (1993), see also *Clark County School Dist. v. Buchanan*, 112 Nev. 1146, at 1150, 924 P.2d 716 (1996).

[631] *Dixon v. Thatcher*, 103 Nev. 414, 742 P.2d 1029 (1987), cited, *Pickett v. Comanche Constr., Inc.*, 108 Nev. 422, at 426, 836 P.2d 42 (1992), *Hansen v. Eighth Judicial Dist. Court*, 116 Nev. 650, at 658, 6 P.3d 982 (2000), see also *Dangberg Holdings Nevada, L.L.C. v. Douglas County*, 115 Nev. 129, at 142, 978 P.2d 311 (1999).

[632] *Dangberg Holdings Nevada, LLC v. Douglas County*, 115 Nev. 129, 978 P.2d 311 (1999).

[633] See NRS 33.010; *State ex rel. Attorney Gen. v. NOS Communications, Inc.*, 120 Nev. 65, 84 P.3d 1052 (2004), cited, *Edwards v. Emperor's Garden Rest.*, 122 Nev. 317, at 325, 130 P.3d 1280 (2006).

[634] See Nev. Const. art. 4, § 6.

[635] See Nev. Const. art. 3, § 1.

[636] See NRS 35.010, 35.040, 35.050, 35.060 and Nev. Const. art. 6, §§ 4 and 6.

[637] See NRS 30.030, 30.130, and 33.010.

[638] *Heller v. Legislature*, 120 Nev. 456, 93 P.3d 746 (2004).

violations will not occur. [639]

Injunction, Covenant Not to Compete, and Trade Secrets

Once a covenant not to compete has expired, the injunctive provisions that restricted the employee's business activities based on his likely violations of the Agreement should be dissolved once the Agreement is no longer enforceable. However, that does not necessarily mean that the injunctive provisions that applied to prevent likely trade secret violations should be dissolved.[640]

With respect to likely trade-secret violations, an injunction entered under Nevada's Uniform Trade Secrets Act "must be terminated when the trade secret has ceased to exist, but the injunction may be continued for an additional reasonable period of time to eliminate commercial or other advantage that otherwise would be derived from the misappropriation." NRS 600A.040(1). NRS 600A.040(1) requires that an injunction be terminated when the trade secret no longer exists. Assuming that trade secrets are found to exist, an injunction may only be extended for a "reasonable period of time" pursuant to NRS 600A.040(1). The comments to the Uniform Trade Secrets Act indicate that "an injunction should last for as long as is necessary, but no longer than is necessary, to eliminate the commercial advantage or 'lead time' with respect to good faith competitors that a person has obtained through misappropriation."[641] Accordingly, such a determination should be made on a case-by-case basis by the district courts.[642]

NRS 33.015, "Injunction to restrain unlawful act against witness or victim of crime," provides as follows:

> Whenever it appears that a defendant or other person is doing, about to do, threatening to do or procuring to be done some act against a victim of a crime or a witness in violation of any provision of NRS 199.230, 199.240 or 199.305, a court of competent jurisdiction may issue an injunction restraining the defendant or other person from the commission or continuance of that act.
> (Added to NRS by 1983, 1683; A 1985, 225)

Preliminary Injunction

A preliminary injunction is available when the moving party can demonstrate that the nonmoving party's conduct, if allowed to continue, will cause irreparable harm for which compensatory relief is inadequate and that the moving party has a reasonable likelihood of success on the merits.[643] A district court has discretion in deciding whether to grant a preliminary injunction.[644] The district court's decision " 'will be reversed only where the district court abused its discretion or based its decision on an erroneous legal standard or on clearly erroneous findings of fact.' "[645] Questions of law are reviewed de novo, even in the context of an appeal from a preliminary injunction.[646]

Intentional Infliction of Emotional Distress

The elements of this claim are: 1) extreme and outrageous conduct with either the intention of, or reckless disregard for, causing emotional distress; 2) the Plaintiffs having suffered severe or extreme emotional distress; and 3) actual or proximate causation.[647]

The Nevada Supreme Court has required a plaintiff to demonstrate that he or she has suffered some physical manifestation of emotional distress in order to support an award of emotional damages.[648] ("[I]n cases where emotional distress damages are not secondary to physical injuries, but rather, precipitate physical symptoms, either a physical impact must have occurred or, in the absence of physical impact, proof of 'serious emotional distress' causing physical

---

[639] *Edwards v. Emperor's Garden Rest.*, 122 Nev. 317, 130 P.3d 1280 (2006).

[640] *Finkel v. Cashman Professional, Inc.*, 128 Nev. Adv. Op. No. 6 (2012).

[641] Uniform Trade Secrets Act § 2 cmt., 14 U.L.A. 620 (2005).

[642] *Id.*

[643] *University Sys. v. Nevadans for Sound Gov't*, 120 Nev. 712, 721, 100 P.3d 179, 187 (2004); *Dangberg Holdings, LLC v. Douglas County*, 115 Nev. 129, 142, 978 P.2d 311, 319 (1999).

[644] *University Sys.*, 120 Nev. at 721, 100 P.3d at 187.

[645] *Attorney General v. NOS Communications*, 120 Nev. 65, 67, 84 P.3d 1052, 1053 (2004) (quoting *U.S. v. Nutri-cology, Inc.*, 982 F.2d 394, 397 (9th Cir. 1992)); see *S.O.C., Inc. v. The Mirage Casino-Hotel*, 117 Nev. 403, 407, 23 P.3d 243, 246 (2001).

[646] *University Sys.*, 120 Nev. at 721, 100 P.3d at 187; S.O.C., Inc., 117 Nev. at 407, 23 P.3d at 246.

[647] *Olivero v. Lowe*, 116 Nev. 395, 400, 995 P.2d 1023, 1026 (2000) (citing *Star v. Rabello*, 97 Nev. 124, 125, 625 P.2d 90, 91-92 (1981)).

[648] See, e.g., *Barmettler v. Reno Air, Inc.*, 114 Nev. 441, 448, 956 P.2d 1382, 1387 (1998).

injury or illness must be presented.").[649] The Nevada Supreme Court has relaxed the physical manifestation requirement in a few limited instances,[650] but the Nevada Supreme Court declined to conclude that a claim for emotional distress damages resulting from deceptive trade practices in connection with a failed real estate and lending transaction should be exempted from the physical manifestation requirement.

Evidence that a self-insured employer demoted an injured area sales manager because of her workers' compensation claim, that other employees openly speculated as to reason for the demotion, and that the manager's complaints to employer that her job situation was having adverse effect on her health established the employer's intentional infliction of emotional distress.[651]

Intentional Interference with Contractual Relations

To establish intentional interference with contractual relations, the plaintiff must show: (1) a valid and existing contract; (2) the defendant's knowledge of the contract; (3) intentional acts intended or designed to disrupt the contractual relationship; (4) actual disruption of the contract; and (5) resulting damages.[652] The tort of interference with contractual relations has its roots in the tort of inducing breach of contract. It is also referred to as the tort of interference with economic relations. Both the tort of interference with contract relations and the tort of interference with prospective contract or business relations involve basically the same conduct–in one case the interference takes place when a contract is already in existence, in the other, when a contract would, with certainty, have been consummated but for the conduct of the wrongdoer.

The act of inducing the breach must be an intentional one. If the actor had no knowledge of the existence of the contract or his actions were not intended to induce a breach, he cannot be held liable, though an actual breach results from his lawful and proper acts. It is not enough that the actor intended to perform the acts which caused the result–he or she must have intended to cause the result itself. The claim can only be asserted against a stranger to the contractual relationship, if the person complained of was a party to the contract, the claim should be brought as a breach of contract claim. Proof that it is reasonably probable that the lost economic advantage would have been realized but for the defendant's interference is required to prevail on the claim. One can be held liable for intentionally or negligently interfering with the existing or prospective economic relationships of another (e.g., contractual/business relationships).

The RESTATEMENT (SECOND) OF TORTS defines the tort of Intentional Interference with Prospective Contractual Relations as follows: "One who intentionally and improperly interferes with another's prospective contractual relation (except a contract to marry) is subject to liability to the other for the pecuniary harm resulting from loss of the benefits of the relation, whether the interference consists of:

(a) inducing or otherwise causing a third person not to enter into or continue the prospective relation or
(b) preventing the other from acquiring or continuing the prospective relation."[653]

See *Stalk v. Mushkin*, 125 Nev., Advance Opinion 3 (2009), where the Nevada Supreme Court stated as follows:

Claims for intentional interference with a prospective business advantage and contractual relations seek compensation for damage to business interests.[654] Business interests include intangible assets and inchoate rights, as well as other rights incidental to business ownership.[655] Such interests are personal property. The classic example of this tort occurs when one party induces another party to breach a contract with a third party, in circumstances where the first party has no privilege to act as it does and acts with knowledge of the existence of the contract. Such conduct is termed tortious inducement of breach of contract.

---

[649] *Chowdhry v. NLVH, Inc.*, 109 Nev. 478, 482-83, 851 P.2d 459, 462 (1993).

[650] See *Olivero v. Lowe*, 116 Nev. 395, 400, 995 P.2d 1023, 1026 (2000) (explaining that the physical manifestation requirement is more relaxed for damages claims involving assault).

[651] *Dillard Department Stores v. Beckwith*, 115 Nev. 372, 378-379, 989 P.2d 882 (1999).

[652] *Ramona Manor Convalescent Hosp. v. Care Ent.*, 225 Cal.Rptr. 120, 124 (Cal. Ct.App. 1986). *Hilton Hotels v. Butch Lewis Productions*, 109 Nev. 1043, 862 P.2d 1207 (1993).

[653] See RESTATEMENT (SECOND) OF TORTS § 766B.

[654] See *Zimmerman v. Bank of America National T. & S. Ass'n.*, 12 Cal. Rptr. 319, 321 (1961) ("The actionable wrong lies in the inducement to break the contract or to sever the relationship, not in the kind of contract or relationship so disrupted, whether it is written or oral, enforceable or not enforceable.").

[655] See *Teller v. Teller*, 53 P.3d 240, 248 (Haw. 2002) (indicating that goodwill and trade secrets are intangible assets in which business owners have property rights). See also *Clark v. Figge*, 181 N.W.2d 211, 215 (Iowa 1970) (citing *Liggett Co. v. Baldridge*, 278 U.S. 105, 111 (1928), overruled on other grounds by *North Dakota Pharmacy Bd. v. Snyder's Stores*, 414 U.S. 156, 167 (1973)).

See NRS 11.190(2)(c); *Orr v. Bank of America, NT & SA*, 285 F.3d 764, 781 (9th Cir. 2002) (applying Nevada law and concluding that a claim for "intentional interference with prospective business relations [is] subject to Nevada's four-year limitations period").

Intentional Interference with Prospective Business Relations

The tort of intentional interference with prospective business relations, also known as intentional interference with prospective business advantage, contains the following elements: (1) A prospective contractual relationship between the plaintiff and a third party; (2) defendant's knowledge of this prospective relationship; (3) intent to harm the plaintiff by preventing the relationship; (4) absence of privilege or justification by the defendant; and, (5) actual harm to plaintiff as a result of defendant's conduct.[656]

To establish intentional interference with prospective economic advantage, the plaintiff must show the following:

> a prospective contractual relationship between the plaintiff and a third party;
> knowledge by the defendant of the prospective relationship;
> intent to harm the plaintiff by preventing the relationship;
> the absence of privilege or justification by the defendant; and
> actual harm to the plaintiff as a result of the defendant's conduct.

For the statute of limitations on this claim see: NRS 11.190(2)(c); *Orr v. Bank of America, NT & SA*, 285 F.3d 764, 781 (9th Cir. 2002) (applying Nevada law and concluding that a claim for "intentional interference with prospective business relations [is] subject to Nevada's four-year limitations period").

Intentional Misrepresentation

See "Fraud/ Intentional Misrepresentation."

Interpleader

Interpleader is an equitable proceeding to determine rights of rival claimants to property held by a third person having no interest therein; indeed, by bringing such action, plaintiff waives any defense it might have had to claims of interpled defendants.[657] NRCP 22, "Interpleader," provides as follows:

> Persons having claims against the plaintiff may be joined as defendants and required to interplead when their claims are such that the plaintiff is or may be exposed to double or multiple liability. It is not ground for objection to the joinder that the claims of the several claimants or the titles on which their claims depend do not have a common origin or are not identical but are adverse to and independent of one another, or that the plaintiff avers that the plaintiff is not liable in whole or in part to any or all of the claimants. A defendant exposed to similar liability may obtain such interpleader by way of cross-claim or counterclaim. The provisions of this rule supplement and do not in any way limit the joinder of parties permitted in Rule 20.
> [As amended; effective January 1, 2005.]

The former statute expanded the equitable doctrine of interpleader to include claims which do not have common origin or are not identical. RL § 5005 (cf. NRCP 22), providing for summary proceedings in cases where a bill of the interpleader would lie, contains an essential element of the equitable doctrine of the interpleader that there must be two or more persons claiming the same thing, except that the statute has enlarged the scope of remedy to include claimants whose titles or claims do not have a common origin, or are not identical, but are adverse to and independent of one another.[658]

---

[656] *Consolidated Generator v. Cummins Engine*, 114 Nev. 1304, 1305, 971 P.2d 1251 (1998). See also *In re AMERCO Derivative Litigation*, 127 Nev. ___, ___ n.6, 252 P.3d 681, 697 n.6 (2011). See also *Wichinsky v. Mosa*, 109 Nev. 84, 88, 847 P.2d 727 (1993); *Leavitt v. Leisure Sports, Inc.*, 103 Nev. 81, 88, 734 P.2d 1221, 1225 (1987).

[657] *Farmers Ins. v. Civil Serv. Emp. Ins.*, 94 Nev. 733, 734, 587 P.2d 420 (1978).

[658] *Rutherford v. Union Land & Cattle Co.*, 47 Nev. 21, 213 Pac. 1045 (1923), cited, *Bartlett v. Bishop of Nevada*, 59 Nev. 283, at 295, 91 P.2d 828 (1939), *Young Inv. Co. v. Reno Club, Inc.*, 66 Nev. 216, at 222, 208 P.2d 297 (1949), *Trustees of Plumbers & Pipefitters Union Local 525 Health & Welfare Trust Plan v. Developers Sur. & Indem. Co.*, 120 Nev. 56, at 64, 84 P.3d 59 (2004).

It was proper for the district court to deny dismissal of an attorney from an interpleader action under the circumstances. Where a plaintiff's attorney deducted his attorney's fees from an arbitration award and filed an interpleader action for the remaining amount (see NRCP 22), the Court held that it was proper for the district court to deny dismissal of the attorney from the interpleader action because before a court enforces an attorney lien pursuant to NRS 18.015, the full amount of the funds in dispute must be submitted for judicial distribution and the court must determine: (1) whether the attorney may use NRS 18.015 to obtain the fees claimed; (2) whether the amount claimed by the lien stems from a judgment or settlement, as required by NRS 18.015; (3) whether the lien is enforceable; (4) whether the lien has been properly perfected pursuant to NRS 18.015; (5) whether there are any setoffs reducing the net amount subject to the lien; (6) whether equitable factors, such as a child support garnishment, affect the net amount of the judgment or the priority of the lien; and (7) based upon the net amount subject to the lien, the amount the attorney is due calculated pursuant to NRS 18.015.[659]

An interpleader proceeding is proper when two or more claims exceed a surety bond's penal limit In a surety bond dispute where two or more claims will exceed the bond's penal limit, the surety may initiate an interpleader proceeding pursuant to NRCP 22 to avoid double or multiple liability whether or not the claims are identical or of common origin. In an appeal where the Supreme Court held that a surety can be required to pay attorney's fees even if the award of fees, in conjunction with the judgment, would exceed the penal limit of the bond, the court also noted that the surety may initiate an interpleader proceeding and the district court has discretion to disapprove or approve the interpleader and discharge the surety from any further liability after the deposit of the bond's remaining penal limits with the court.[660]

Limitations Periods for Contribution and Indemnity

The Nevada Supreme Court has clarified that NRS 41A.097(2)'s limitations period does not apply to equitable indemnity and contribution claims, and that such claims are instead subject to the limitations periods laid out in NRS 11.190(2)(c) and NRS 17.285, respectively.[661]

Availability of NRCP 14(a) for Contribution and Indemnity

The Nevada Supreme Court has explicitly stated that NRCP 14(a) is available for claims of contribution as well as indemnity.[662] NRCP 14(a) provides as follows:

(a) When Defendant May Bring in Third Party. At any time after commencement of the action a defending party, as a third-party plaintiff, may cause a summons and complaint to be served upon a person not a party to the action who is or may be liable to the third-party plaintiff for all or part of the plaintiff's claim against the third-party plaintiff. The third-party plaintiff need not obtain leave to make the service if the third-party plaintiff files the third-party complaint not later than 10 days after serving the original answer. Otherwise the third-party plaintiff must obtain leave on motion upon notice to all parties to the action. The person served with the summons and third-party complaint, hereinafter called the third-party defendant, shall make any defenses to the third-party plaintiff's claim as provided in Rule 12 and any counterclaims against the third-party plaintiff and cross-claims against other third-party defendants as provided in Rule 13. The third-party defendant may assert against the plaintiff any defenses which the third-party plaintiff has to the plaintiff's claim. The third-party defendant may also assert any claim against the plaintiff arising out of the transaction or occurrence that is the subject matter of the plaintiff's claim against the third-party plaintiff. The plaintiff may assert any claim against the third-party defendant arising out of the transaction or occurrence that is the subject matter of the plaintiff's claim against the third-party plaintiff, and the third-party defendant thereupon shall assert any defenses as provided in Rule 12 and any counterclaims and cross-claims as provided in Rule 13. Any party may move to strike the third-party claim, or for its severance or separate trial. A third-party defendant may proceed under this rule against any person not a party to the action who is or may be liable to the third-party defendant for all or part of the claim made in the action against the third-party defendant.

Intrusion upon Seclusion
See "Invasion of Privacy."

---

[659] *Michel v. Eighth Judicial Dist. Court*, 117 Nev. 145, 17 P.3d 1003 (2001).
[660] *Trustees v. Developers Surety*, 120 Nev. 56, 84 P.3d 59 (2004).
[661] *Saylor v. Arcotta*, 126 Nev. ___, ____, 225 P.3d 1276, 1278-79. (2010).
[662] *Pack v. LaTourette*, 128 Nev. Adv. Op. No. 25 (2012).

The four species of privacy tort are: (1) unreasonable intrusion upon the seclusion of another; (2) appropriation of the name or likeness of another; (3) unreasonable publicity given to private facts; and (4) publicity unreasonably placing another in a false light before the public.[663]

Unreasonable Intrusion upon the Seclusion of Another

To recover for the tort of intrusion, a plaintiff must prove the following elements: (1) an intentional intrusion (physical or otherwise); (2) on the solitude or seclusion of another; (3) that would be highly offensive to a reasonable person.[664] In order to have an interest in seclusion or solitude which the law will protect, a plaintiff must show that he or she had an actual expectation of seclusion or solitude and that that expectation was objectively reasonable.[665] Thus, not every expectation of privacy and seclusion is protected by the law.[666] "The extent to which seclusion can be protected is severely limited by the protection that must often be accorded to the freedom of action and expression of those who threaten that seclusion of others."[667] For example, it is no invasion of privacy to photograph a person in a public place;[668] or for the police, acting within their powers, to photograph and fingerprint a suspect.[669] Common law and tort theories of negligence and outrageous contact are often the basis of invasion of privacy complaints.

Appropriation of the Name or Likeness of Another

A common law cause of action for appropriation of name or likeness may be pleaded by alleging (1) the defendant's use of the plaintiff's identity; (2) the appropriation of plaintiff's name or likeness to defendant's advantage, commercially or otherwise; (3) lack of consent; and (4) resulting injury.[670]

Unreasonable publicity given to private facts.

See RESTATEMENT (SECOND) OF TORTS § 652D, "Publicity Given to Private Life," which provides as follows:

A person who gives publicity to a matter concerning the private life of another is subject to liability to the other for invasion of his privacy, if the matter published is of a kind that
(a) would be highly offensive to a reasonable person, and
(b) is not of legitimate concern to the public.

The elements of the tort are: (1) publicity, given to (2) private facts, (3) which would be highly offensive to a reasonable person and (4) is not of legitimate concern to the public.[671]

The element of "publicity" requires that the matter is made public, by communicating it to the public at large, or to so many persons that the matter must be regarded as substantially certain to become one of public knowledge.[672] Disclosure of information to only one person is insufficient.[673]

There is a legal distinction between "publication" as that term is used in connection with liability for defamation, and "publicity" as it is used in a § 652D action for invasion of privacy. While the intentional or negligent communication of defamatory matter to a single person (or to a newspaper) might constitute a "publication" in the context of an action for defamation, see RESTATEMENT (SECOND) OF TORTS § 577 and comment b, that does not concern us here. The "publicity" which we here examine requires that the matter is made public by communicating it to the public at large, or to so many persons that the matter must be regarded as substantially certain to become one of public knowledge. Where a communication involving private facts reaches, or is sure to reach, the public, then publicity has been given to that

---

[663] *PETA v. Bobby Berosini, Ltd.*, 111 Nev. 615, 629, 895 P.2d 1269 (1995).

[664] *Id.*

[665] *Id.*

[666] *Id.*

[667] *Fowler v. Harper, The Law of Torts,* § 9.6, at 636 (2d ed. 1986).

[668] See, *e.g., Gill v. Hearst Publishing Co.*, 253 P.2d 441 (Cal. 1953).

[669] See, *e.g., Norman v. City of Las Vegas*, 64 Nev. 38, 177 P.2d 442 (1947).

[670] *Eastwood v. Superior Court*, 149 Cal.App.3d 409, 198 Cal. Rptr. 342 (1983); see Prosser, Law of Torts (4th ed. 1971) § 117, pp. 804-807; 3 Witkin, Cal. Procedure (2d ed. 1971) Pleading, § 606, p. 2244.

[671] See, *e.g., Brown v. Mullarkey*, 632 S.W.2d 507 (Mo. Ct.App. 1982); *Forsher v. Bugliosi*, 26 Cal.3d 792, 163 Cal.Rptr. 628, 608 P.2d 716 (1980). This is according to Pennsylvania's Superior Court in *Harris v. Easton Pub. Co.*, 335 Pa. Super. 141; 483 A.2d 1377; Pa. Super (1984).

[672] RESTATEMENT (SECOND) OF TORTS § 652D, comment a. *Wells Thomas*, supra.

[673] *Nagy v. Bell Tel. Co. of Pa.*, supra. See also *Vogel v. W.T. Grant Co., supra* (disclosure to four persons held insufficient).

party's private life.

The second element requires that the publicity involve a private fact. A private fact is one that has not already been made public. Liability cannot be based upon that which the plaintiff himself leaves open to the public eye.[674] It also follows from the use of the term private fact that the reader or recipient of the private fact not have prior knowledge of that fact: there can be no liability where the publicity given involves facts with which the recipient is familiar.

The third element requires that a reasonable person of ordinary sensibilities would find such publicity highly offensive. In making this determination, the customs of the time and place, occupation of the plaintiff and habits of his neighbors and fellow citizens are material.[675] The act which constitutes the tortious invasion of privacy must be committed in such a manner as to outrage or cause mental suffering, shame or humiliation to a person of ordinary sensibilities.[676]

The final element exempts from liability those facts which are of legitimate concern to the public, such as official court records open to public inspection. *Cox Broadcasting Co. v. Cohn*, 420 U.S. 469, 95 S.Ct. 1029, 43 L.Ed.2d 328 (1975). This also applies to persons who, voluntarily or involuntarily, have become public figures, RESTATEMENT (SECOND) OF TORTS § 652D, comments e and f, and may also apply to certain private facts relating to those public figures, such as the life history of one accused of a sensational crime, *id.*, comment h, and even to the members of that person's family.[677] This could include the installation and use of camera, video, or other recording device without consent in a bathroom, locker room, bedroom, dressing room, tanning, salon, or other type of private area.

False Light. The false light privacy action differs from a defamation action in that the injury in privacy actions is mental distress from having been exposed to public view, while the injury in defamation actions is damage to reputation.[678] "[A] false light cause of action is necessary to fully protect privacy interests, and we now officially recognize false light invasion of privacy as a valid cause of action in connection with the other three privacy causes of action that this court has adopted."[679]

The Nevada Supreme Court defined false light invasion of privacy under the RESTATEMENT (SECOND) OF TORTS Section 652E (1977), which provides as follows:

652E. Publicity Placing Person in False Light

One who gives publicity to a matter concerning another that places the other before the public in a false light is subject to liability to the other for invasion of his privacy, if

(a) the false light in which the other was placed would be highly offensive to a reasonable person, and
(b) the actor had knowledge of or acted in reckless disregard as to the falsity of the publicized matter and the false light in which the other would be placed.

Judicial Notice

Judicial notice is not a "claim" per se. It is a rule of evidence. Still, it is helpful to remember judicial notice when drafting pleadings and when appearing in court. See NRS 47.130 and *Occhiuto v. Occhiuto*, 97 Nev. 143, 145, 625 P.2d 568, 569 (1981) (recognizing general rule but holding that the close relationship between the case and a previous divorce proceeding justified the district court taking judicial notice of the prior proceeding). The Court may properly take notice of a party's court filings, which are matters of public record.[680] The Court may take judicial notice of "matters of public record" and may consider documents on which the complaint "necessarily relies."[681]

NRS 47.130, "Matters of fact," provides as follows:

---

[674] RESTATEMENT (SECOND) OF TORTS § 652D, comment b.

[675] RESTATEMENT (SECOND) OF TORTS § 652D, comment c. *Aquino v. Bulletin Company*, 190 Pa.Super. 528, 154 A.2d 422 (1959).

[676] *Nagy v. Bell Tel. Co. of Pa.*, supra.

[677] *Id.*, comment i, *Corabi v. Curtis Publishing Co.*, 441 Pa. 432, 273 A.2d 899 (1971). See also Prosser, Handbook of the Law of Torts 809-12 (4th ed. 1971).

[678] *Rinsley v. Brandt*, 700 F.2d 1304, 1307 (10th Cir. 1983), cited in *PETA v. Bobby Berosini, Ltd*, 111 Nev. 615, 622, fn. 4, 895 P.2d 1269 (1995).

[679] *Franchise Tax Board of the State of California v. Hyatt*, 130 Nev., Advance Opinion 71 (9/18/14).

[680] See *Fierle v. Perez*, 125 Nev. 728, ___ fn. 6, 219 P.3d 906, 912 fn. 6 (2009); *Reyn's Pasta Bella, LLC v. Visa USA, Inc.*, 442 F.3d 741, 746 fn. 6 (9th Cir. 1998); see also 5A Charles A. Wright & Arthur R. Miller, *Federal Practice and Procedure*, Civil 2D § 1356-57 (2nd ed. 1990).

[681] *Lee v. City of Los Angeles*, 250 F.3d 668, 688 (9th Cir. 2001) (citations omitted).

1. The facts subject to judicial notice are facts in issue or facts from which they may be inferred.

2. A judicially noticed fact must be:

(a) Generally known within the territorial jurisdiction of the trial court; or

(b) Capable of accurate and ready determination by resort to sources whose accuracy cannot reasonably be questioned,

so that the fact is not subject to reasonable dispute.

NRS 47.140, "Matters of law," provides as follows:

The laws subject to judicial notice are:

1. The Constitution and statutes of the United States, and the contents of the Federal Register.

2. The Constitution of this State and Nevada Revised Statutes.

3. Any other statute of this State if brought to the attention of the court by its title and the day of its passage.

4. A county, city or town code which has been filed as required by NRS 244.118, 268.014, 269.168 or the city charter and any city ordinance which has been filed or recorded as required by the applicable law.

5. The Nevada Administrative Code.

6. A regulation not included in the Nevada Administrative Code if adopted in accordance with law and brought to the attention of the court.

7. The population category and organization of a city incorporated pursuant to general law.

8. The constitution, statutes or other written law of any other state or territory of the United States, or of any foreign jurisdiction, as contained in a book or pamphlet published by its authority or proved to be commonly recognized in its courts.

Nevada Cases

The reported opinions of Nevada courts are subject to judicial notice. The law of Nevada as found in reported court opinions is subject to judicial notice (see NRS 47.140), and where plaintiffs moved trial court to take judicial notice of a prior decision of appellate court as the law of the case[682] and provided a copy of the decision and order, it was error for trial court to deny the motion.[683]

The records of the Secretary of State. Where the status of appellant as a licensed real estate broker for a corporation may have been unclear from the transcript of the trial, the appellate court pursuant to NRS 47.130 took judicial notice of his status from the records of the Secretary of State.[684]

Evidence from a prior proceeding not appearing in the record. On appeal from a judgment terminating a mother's parental rights, the district judge could not properly take judicial notice of evidence which had been before him in a guardianship proceeding after the death of the child's father but was not in the record in the termination proceeding, and appellate court could not consider such evidence in determining whether the findings in the termination proceeding were supported by sufficient evidence.[685]

The location of an intersection in a certain county is sufficient to support a finding that an alleged offense was committed in the county. Testimony at a preliminary hearing that alleged that a crime occurred "at the parking lot of the Safeway store at Tropicana and Maryland Parkway" was sufficient to support a finding that an alleged offense was committed in Clark County, Nevada. The fact that this intersection is located in Clark County, Nevada, was not reasonably open to dispute and was judicially noticed by the appellate court in reversing the order of district court granting a pretrial petition for habeas corpus.[686]

NRS 47.150, "Discretionary and mandatory notice," provides as follows:

---

[682] The law of the case doctrine requires that "the law or ruling of a first appeal must be followed in all subsequent proceedings, both in the lower court and on any later appeal." *Hsu v. Cnty. Of Clark*, 123 Nev. 625, 629, 173 P.3d 724, 728 (2007).

[683] See *Masonry & Tile Contractors Ass'n v. Jolley, Urga & Wirth, Ltd.*, 113 Nev. 737, at 746, 941 P.2d 486 (1997) (dissenting opinion).

[684] *Jory v. Bennight*, 91 Nev. 763, 542 P.2d 1400 (1975), cited, *Ainsworth v. Combined Ins. Co.*, 105 Nev. 237, at 267, 774 P.2d 1003 (1989), *Whitehead v. Commission on Judicial Discipline*, 110 Nev. 380, at 418, 873 P.2d 946 (1994), *Mikohn Gaming v. Espinosa*, 122 Nev. 593, at 599, 137 P.3d 1150 (2006).

[685] *Chapman v. Chapman*, 96 Nev. 290, 607 P.2d 1141 (1980).

[686] *Sheriff, Clark County v. Kravetz*, 96 Nev. 919, 620 P.2d 868 (1980).

1. A judge or court may take judicial notice, whether requested or not.

2. A judge or court shall take judicial notice if requested by a party and supplied with the necessary information.

Where a former husband and wife reconciled (without remarriage) for a period of time after the divorce and then separated, and shortly thereafter the husband brought an action against the wife, the district court could properly take judicial notice of the parties' prior divorce proceeding despite the general rule that courts should not take judicial notice of their records in another and different case even though the cases are connected. A close relationship between the present case and the previous divorce proceeding brought it within the exception to the general rule.[687]

Prior decision as law of case. The law of Nevada as found in reported court opinions is subject to judicial notice (see NRS 47.140). Where plaintiffs moved the trial court to take judicial notice of a prior decision of the appellate court as the law of the case and provided a copy of the decision and order, it was error for the trial court to deny the motion.[688]

NRS 47.160, "Opportunity to be heard," provides as follows: "A party is entitled upon timely request to an opportunity to be heard as to the propriety of taking judicial notice and the tenor of the matter to be noticed."

NRS 47.170, "Time of taking notice," provides as follows: "Judicial notice may be taken at any stage of the proceeding prior to submission to the court or jury."

Legal Malpractice

Under Nevada law, to establish a claim for professional negligence, a plaintiff must show: (1) the defendant had a duty to use the skill, prudence, and diligence as other members of the profession commonly possess and exercise; (2) the defendant breached that duty; (3) the breach proximately caused the resulting injury; and (4) actual loss or damage resulting from the professional's negligence.[689] Similarly, a showing of negligence requires plaintiff to show duty, breach, causation, and damages.[690] "Proximate cause, or legal cause, consists of two components: cause in fact and foreseeability."[691] Cause in fact requires a showing that the defendant's negligence was a "substantial factor" in bringing about plaintiff's injury.[692] Foreseeability is a "policy concern" that limits a defendant's liability to only those harms with a reasonably close connection to its breach.[693]

The required elements of a legal malpractice claim are: (1) an attorney-client relationship; (2) a duty owed to the client by the attorney to use such skill, prudence, and diligence as lawyers of ordinary skill and capacity possess in exercising and performing the tasks which they undertake; (3) a breach of that duty; (4) the breach being the proximate cause of the client's damages; and (5) actual loss or damage resulting from the negligence.[694] An attorney's violation of professional rules of responsibility does not create a private right of action, but is relevant to the standard of care owed by an attorney.[695]

A claim for breach of fiduciary duty arising from an attorney-client relationship is a legal malpractice claim and is therefore subject to the statute of limitations contained in NRS 11.207(1).[696] As a general rule, a legal malpractice action does not accrue until the plaintiff knows, or should know, all the facts relevant to the foregoing elements, damage has been sustained, and the underlying litigation has concluded.[697] Non-adversarial bankruptcy proceedings do not constitute litigation for purposes of the litigation malpractice tolling rule.[698]

---

[687] *Occhiuto v. Occhiuto*, 97 Nev. 143, 625 P.2d 568 (1981), cited, *Hampton v. Washoe County*, 99 Nev. 819, at 822, 672 P.2d 640 (1983), *Geary v. State*, 112 Nev. 1434, at 1437, 930 P.2d 719 (1996).

[688] *Andolino v. State*, 99 Nev. 346, 662 P.2d 631 (1983), cited, *Castillo v. State*, 110 Nev. 535, at 548, 874 P.2d 1252 (1994) (concurring opinion), *Masonry & Tile Contractors Ass'n v. Jolley, Urga & Wirth, Ltd.*, 113 Nev. 737, at 746, 941 P.2d 486 (1997) (dissenting opinion).

[689] *Morgano v. Smith*, 110 Nev. 1025, 1029, 879 P.2d 735, 738 (1994).

[690] *Bower v. Harrah's Laughlin, Inc.*, 215 P.3d 709, 724 (Nev. 2009).

[691] *Doud v. Las Vegas Hilton Corp.*, 109 Nev. 1096, 864 P.2d 796, 801 (1993) (citation omitted).

[692] *Id.*

[693] *Bower*, 215 P.3d at 724.

[694] *Mainor v. Nault*, 120 Nev. 750, 774, 101 P.3d 308 (2004).

[695] *Id.* at 768-69.

[696] *Stalk v. Mushkin*, 125 Nev., Advance Opinion 3 (2009).

[697] *Hewitt v. Allen*, 118 Nev. 216, 221, 43 P.3d 345, 347-48 (2002).

[698] *Moon v. McDonald, Carano & Wilson, LLP*, 129 Nev., Advance Opinion 56 (2013).

Nevada's lemon law is NRS 579.630,
"Duties of manufacturer if motor vehicle cannot be conformed to express Warranties." The statute provides as follows:

1. If, after a reasonable number of attempts, the manufacturer, or its agent or authorized dealer is unable to conform the motor vehicle to any applicable express warranty by repair or correction and the defect or condition causing the nonconformity substantially impairs the use and value of the motor vehicle to the buyer and is not the result of abuse, neglect or unauthorized modifications or alterations of the motor vehicle, the manufacturer shall:

(a) Replace the motor vehicle with a comparable motor vehicle of the same model and having the same features as the replaced vehicle, or if such a vehicle cannot be delivered to the buyer within a reasonable time, then a comparable motor vehicle substantially similar to the replaced vehicle; or

(b) Accept return of the motor vehicle from the buyer and refund to him or her the full purchase price including all sales taxes, license fees, registration fees and other similar governmental charges, less a reasonable allowance for his or her use of the vehicle. A reasonable allowance for use is that amount directly attributable to use by the buyer before his or her first report of the nonconformity to the manufacturer, agent or dealer and during any subsequent period when the vehicle is not out of service for repairs. Refunds must be made to the buyer, and lienholder if any, as their interests may appear.

2. It is presumed that a reasonable number of attempts have been undertaken to conform a motor vehicle to the applicable express warranties where:

(a) The same nonconformity has been subject to repair four or more times by the manufacturer, or its agent or authorized dealer within the time the express warranty is in effect or within 1 year following the date the motor vehicle is delivered to the original buyer, whichever occurs earlier, but the nonconformity continues to exist; or

(b) The motor vehicle is out of service for repairs for a cumulative total of 30 or more calendar days within the time the express warranty is in effect or within 1 year following the date the motor vehicle is delivered to the original buyer, whichever occurs earlier, except that if the necessary repairs cannot be made for reasons which are beyond the control of the manufacturer or its agent or authorized dealer, the number of days required to give rise to the presumption must be appropriately extended.

(Added to NRS by 1983, 611)

Where a motor vehicle manufacturer reimburses a buyer of a defective motor vehicle the full purchase price, including sales tax, the manufacturer is not entitled to a refund because Nevada law does not allow for such a refund and because the Department of Taxation is not required to adhere to its prior erroneous interpretation of the law.[699]

For the purposes of NRS 597.630, to determine whether a reasonable number of attempts have been made to repair a motor vehicle, a single attempt, or no attempt, can be a reasonable number. If the manufacturer or dealer refuses to attempt to repair a defect or, after having attempted to repair the defect, refuses to make any further attempts, or where any repair will not restore the vehicle to its new condition, the buyer is not precluded from exercising his rights under NRS 597.600 to 597.670, inclusive.[700]

For the purposes of NRS 597.630, to determine whether a defect causing a nonconformity to a motor vehicle substantially impairs the use and value of the vehicle to the buyer, the court must examine the subjective desires, needs and circumstances of the buyer, and then make an objective determination as to whether the value of the vehicle to the buyer has been substantially impaired and whether the buyer's dissatisfaction is reasonable.[701]

If a motor vehicle that does not conform to the express warranty has been out of service for repairs for an aggregate of at least 30 days within the time the express warranty is in effect or within 1 year after the delivery date of the vehicle, whichever occurs earlier, the buyer of the vehicle may demand a refund from the manufacturer even though the nonconformity no longer exists.[702] (See NRS 597.630.)

Under NRS 597.630, the presumption that a reasonable number of attempts to conform a motor vehicle to the

---

[699] *State of Nevada, Department of Taxation v. Chrysler Group LLC*, 129 Nev. Advance Opinion 29, ___ P.3d ___ (May 2, 2013).

[700] *Milicevic v. Mercedes-Benz USA*, 256 F.Supp.2d 1168 (D. Nev. 2003).

[701] *Id.*

[702] *Id.*

express warranty have been made if the vehicle is out of service for repairs for at least 30 days does not require the vehicle to be out of service for only one nonconformity. The presumption applies if an aggregation of nonconformities requires the vehicle to be out of service for that time.[703]

Where (1) the buyer of a motor vehicle that did not conform to the express warranty left the vehicle with the dealer for repairs while the necessary parts required for the repair were being ordered after being told that the parts would arrive in a few days; (2) the dealer ordered the wrong parts; and (3) the vehicle was out of service for 33 days, the dealer failed to rebut the presumption set forth in NRS 597.630 that a reasonable number of attempts to repair the vehicle had been made by arguing that the buyer could have taken her vehicle and returned it when the parts arrived. Where a vehicle is out of service for at least 30 days because of the unavailability of parts, the presumption is met.[704]

The buyer of a motor vehicle that did not conform to the express warranty was not obligated to comply with the informal procedures for resolving disputes set forth in the written warranty in order to recover under NRS 597.630 because it would have been futile to do so and the manufacturer of the vehicle made it impossible to do so by failing to contact the buyer's counsel to resolve the problems after being notified in writing of the buyer's complaints.[705] The buyer of a motor vehicle that did not conform to the express warranty was entitled to a full refund of the purchase price of the vehicle and the registration fees paid for the vehicle under NRS 597.630 where defects in the seal of the rear window and molding sufficiently impaired the use and value of the vehicle to the buyer, even though the defects did not affect the vehicle's safety.[706]

Libel

See "Defamation."

Loss of Consortium

Consortium" is defined as "the benefits that one person, esp. a spouse, is entitled to receive from another, including companionship, cooperation, affection, aid, financial support, and (between spouses) sexual relations.[707] A finding of fault and causation does not necessitate an award of damages for a loss of consortium claim.[708] A jury's decision to award no damages on a loss of consortium claim is not necessarily inconsistent with its findings of fault and causation in light of the evidence, jury instructions, and applicable law.

Damages for spousal consortium claims compensate for the loss of intangible benefits, such as "company, cooperation, affection, and aid," in addition to "tangible benefits of general usefulness, industry, and attention within the home and family."[709] The value of a spouse's companionship, affection, and aid is difficult to measure.[710] Thus, the amounts of damages "are primarily for the trier of fact to determine."[711] An appellate court will consequently refrain from "disturb[ing] a jury verdict for damages unless it is 'flagrantly excessive or inadequate, so out of reason so as to shock the conscience, the result of passion or prejudice, or lacking in evidentiary support.'"[712] "Whether damages in a given case are adequate depends on the particular facts of the case."[713]

An action for loss of consortium can also be viewed as derivative of the primary harm to the physically injured spouse (parent).[714] "[A] husband's claim for loss of consortium is derivative only; if his wife's underlying tort claim fails, his claim for loss of consortium also fails."[715]

Because of the derivative nature of loss of consortium claims, the location of the marital domicile is irrelevant and the claim must be decided under the same law as the main claim.[716]

---

[703] *Id.*

[704] *Id.*

[705] *Id.*

[706] *Id.*

[707] *Black's Law Dictionary* 351 (9th ed. 2009).

[708] See, *e.g.*, *Stockburger v. Robinson*, 270 N.W.2d 453, 454 (Iowa 1978) (noting if the injured spouse "proves negligence and proximate cause in obtaining a favorable judgment," the spouse seeking recovery for loss of consortium must then prove "his injury and damages").

[709] *Gail v. Clark*, 410 N.W.2d 662, 667 (Iowa 1987).

[710] *Spaur v. Owens-Corning Fiberglas* [sic] *Corp.* 510 N.W.2d 854, 870 (Iowa 1994).

[711] *Beeck v. Aquaslide 'N' Dive Corp.*, 350 N.W.2d 149, 164 (Iowa 1984).

[712] *Kuta v. Newberg*, 600 N.W.2d 280, 284 (Iowa 1999) (citations omitted).

[713] *Fisher v. Davis*, 601 N.W.2d 54, 57 (Iowa 1999).

[714] *Miller v. Holiday Inns, Inc.*, 112 Nev. 1038, 1052 (1996).

[715] See *Kohler v. Fletcher*, 442 N.W.2d 169, 173 (Minn. Ct.App. 1989).

[716] *Id.*; but see *General Motors Corp. v. Dist. Ct.*, 122 Nev. 466, 467, 134 P.3d 111 (2006) (under the

In *Donaldson v. Anderson*, the Nevada Supreme Court held that an award of zero damages to parents for loss of consortium resulting from the death of a minor child in an automobile accident was shocking and clearly inadequate, and thus, the parents were entitled to a new trial limited to damages unless they agreed to accept a $400,000 additur representing their loss of consortium.[717]

Loss of Parental Consortium

Loss of parental consortium is a relatively new cause of action and much of the analysis concerning the place of injury regarding this claim would parallel that of its analogue, loss of spousal consortium. A minor child has a strong interest in his parent's society, an interest closely analogous to that of the spouse in a normal loss of consortium claim.[718]

Malicious Prosecution

Under Nevada law, the plaintiff must satisfy four elements to make out a prima facie case for malicious prosecution: (1) want of probable cause to initiate the prior criminal proceeding; (2) malice; (3) termination of the prior criminal proceedings; and (4) damage.[719] However, regardless of the absence of malice in the form of actually demonstrated ill will or bad faith, courts uniformly permit malice in malicious prosecution actions to be inferred from a want of probable cause.[720] As one commentator indicates, "[regardless] of the theory on which a court relies to find malice, a close factual analysis of the cases suggests that malice is almost always found from the same facts as those which establish lack of probable cause."[721]

Medical Malpractice or Dental Malpractice

Under Nevada law, to establish a claim for professional negligence, a plaintiff must show: (1) the defendant had a duty to use the skill, prudence, and diligence as other members of the profession commonly possess and exercise; (2) the defendant breached that duty; (3) the breach proximately caused the resulting injury; and (4) actual loss or damage resulting from the professional's negligence.[722] Similarly, a showing of negligence requires plaintiff to show duty, breach, causation, and damages.[723] "Proximate cause, or legal cause, consists of two components: cause in fact and foreseeability."[724] Cause in fact requires a showing that the defendant's negligence was a "substantial factor" in bringing about plaintiff's injury.[725] Foreseeability is a "policy concern" that limits a defendant's liability to only those harms with a reasonably close connection to its breach.[726]

NRS Chapter 41A covers actions for medical or dental malpractice.

NRS 41A.003, "Definitions," provides as follows:

> As used in this Chapter, unless the context otherwise requires, the words and terms defined in NRS 41A.004 to 41A.017, inclusive, have the meanings ascribed to them in those sections.
> (Added to NRS by 1985, 2006; A 1989, 419; 1991, 1609; 1995, 2344; 1999, 5; 2002 Special Session, 8; 2004 initiative petition, Ballot Question No. 3)

NRS 41A.004, " 'Dental malpractice' defined," provides as follows:

RESTATEMENT (SECOND) CONFLICT OF LAWS section applicable to personal injury actions, the law of the state where the injury took place applies, unless a party presents some evidence of a relationship between the nonforum state, the occurrence, and the parties, and if so, then the law of the state having the most significant relationship with the occurrence and the parties applies.

[717] *Donaldson v. Anderson*, 109 Nev. 1039, 862 P.2d 1204 (1993).

[718] *Motenko v. MGM Dist., Inc.*, 112 Nev. 1038, 1052 (1996).

[719] *Chapman v. City of Reno*, 85 Nev. 365, 369, 455 P.2d 619, 620 (1969); see also *Jordan v. Bailey*, 113 Nev. 1038, 1047, 994 P.2d 828, 834 (1997).

[720] *Singleton v. Singleton*, 68 Cal.Ct.App. 2d 681, 696, 157 P.2d 886.

[721] Comment, *Attorney Liability for Malicious Prosecution and Legal Malpractice: Do They Overlap?*, 8 Pacific L.J. 897, 904, fn. omitted.

[722] *Morgano v. Smith*, 110 Nev. 1025, 1029, 879 P.2d 735, 738 (1994).

[723] *Bower v. Harrah's Laughlin, Inc.*, 215 P.3d 709, 724 (Nev. 2009).

[724] *Doud v. Las Vegas Hilton Corp.*, 109 Nev. 1096, 864 P.2d 796, 801 (1993) (citation omitted).

[725] *Id.*

[726] *Bower*, 215 P.3d at 724.

"Dental malpractice" has the meaning ascribed to the term "malpractice" in NRS 631.075.
(Added to NRS by 1995, 2344; A 1999, 5)

NRS 631.075, " 'Malpractice' defined," provides as follows:

"Malpractice" means failure on the part of a dentist to exercise the degree of care, diligence and skill ordinarily exercised by dentists in good standing in the community in which he or she practices. As used in this section, "community" means the entire area customarily served by dentists among whom a patient may reasonably choose, not merely the particular area inhabited by the patients of that individual dentist or the particular city or place where the dentist has an office.
(Added to NRS by 1983, 1106)

NRS 41A.007, " 'Economic damages' defined," provides as follows:

"Economic damages" includes damages for medical treatment, care or custody, loss of earnings and loss of earning capacity.
(Added to NRS by 2002 Special Session, 6)

NRS 41A.009, " 'Medical malpractice' defined," provides as follows:

"Medical malpractice" means the failure of a physician, hospital or employee of a hospital, in rendering services, to use the reasonable care, skill or knowledge ordinarily used under similar circumstances.
(Added to NRS by 1985, 2006; A 1989, 425)

NRS 41A.045, "Several liability of defendants for damages; abrogation of joint and several liability," provides as follows:

1. In an action for injury or death against a provider of health care based upon professional negligence, each defendant is liable to the plaintiff for economic damages and noneconomic damages severally only, and not jointly, for that portion of the judgment which represents the percentage of negligence attributable to the defendant.

2. This section is intended to abrogate joint and several liability of a provider of health care in an action for injury or death against the provider of health care based upon professional negligence.

(Added to NRS by 2004 initiative petition, Ballot Question No. 3)

The Nevada Supreme Court has held that the provision of several liability found in NRS 41A.045 entitles a defendant in a qualifying action to argue the percentage of fault of settled defendants and to include the settled defendants' names on the jury verdict form where the jury could conclude that the settled defendants' negligence caused some or all of the plaintiff's injury.[727]

Nevada Cases.
The district court erred in dismissing claims based on intentional torts for the failure to submit the claims to a medical screening panel. A plaintiff brought a civil action against providers of health care alleging claims for negligence and intentional torts after several defendants, as part of an investigation conducted by the investigation division of the Department of Motor Vehicles and Public Safety (now the Department of Public Safety) which resulted in the filing of a criminal complaint against the plaintiff for unlawfully obtaining controlled substances, provided allegedly false information to the investigation division by signing affidavits stating that the plaintiff failed to inform them that she was receiving prescription medicines for pain from other sources at the time that the defendants prescribed pain medicines for her. The district court dismissed the plaintiff's complaint for lack of jurisdiction because the claims had not been reviewed by a medical screening panel pursuant to former NRS 41A.016. On appeal, the Nevada Supreme Court held that, to the extent that the plaintiff's complaint set forth allegations of intentional torts, her action was not a case of

---

[727] *Piroozi v. District Court*, 131 Nev., Advance Opinion 100 (12/31/15).

medical malpractice requiring the review of a medical screening panel because the plaintiff did not accuse the defendants of failing to use reasonable care, skill or knowledge when they diagnosed and treated the pain in her back, but rather the plaintiff alleged that the defendants falsely reported that she unlawfully obtained medicines by prescription. Furthermore, the defendants were not rendering services within the meaning of NRS 41A.009 when they signed affidavits which led to the criminal prosecution of the plaintiff.[728]

Statutes did not deny claimants equal protection of the law. NRS 41A.009 and former 41A.016, which prohibited filing of a claim for medical malpractice against a physician, hospital, or employee of a hospital until it had been submitted to a screening panel, did not deny claimants equal protection of the law in violation of Nev. Const. art. 4, § 21 on the ground that actions for malpractice filed against other providers of health care were not subject to the same requirement. The distinction was rationally related to a legitimate governmental interest as the legislature could have concluded that physicians and hospitals were more affected by a difficulty in obtaining insurance, higher rates for insurance, and frivolous lawsuits than were other providers of health care.[729]

A hospital is required to employ "that degree of skill and care expected of a reasonably competent hospital in the same or similar circumstance."[730]

Federal and Other Cases.

The provisions governing claims for medical malpractice were applicable to a claim for negligent misrepresentation brought by an employer against an injured employee's treating physician. Where the treating physician of an injured employee determined that the employee was unable to perform the essential functions of his job, the employer of the employee, based on that determination, dismissed the employee because he was not qualified for a reasonable accommodation under the Americans with Disabilities Act, 42 U.S.C. §§ 12101 *et seq.*, and, in an action brought by the employee against the employer for employment discrimination, the physician changed his opinion, the physician's actions constituted "rendering services" for the purposes of the definition of medical malpractice set forth in NRS 41A.009. Therefore, the employer's unsuccessful claim against the physician for negligent misrepresentation was properly characterized as one for medical malpractice and the provisions of former NRS 41A.056 requiring an award of attorney's fees to a prevailing physician were applicable to that claim.[731]

NRS 41A.011, " 'Noneconomic damages' defined," provides as follows:

"Noneconomic damages" includes damages to compensate for pain, suffering, inconvenience, physical impairment, disfigurement and other nonpecuniary damages.
(Added to NRS by 2002 Special Session, 6)

Nevada Case.

An award of damages for pain and suffering may include an element of hedonic damages. Hedonic damages, which are monetary remedies awarded to compensate injured persons for their noneconomic loss of life's pleasures or the loss of enjoyment of life, may be included as an element of a pain and suffering award of damages. The laws of the State of Nevada do not restrict a plaintiff's attorney from arguing hedonic damages.[732]

NRS 41A.013, " 'Physician' defined," provides as follows:

"Physician" means a person licensed pursuant to Chapter 630 or 633 of NRS.
(Added to NRS by 1985, 2006; A 1989, 425)

NRS 41A.015, " 'Professional negligence' defined," provides as follows:

"Professional negligence" means a negligent act or omission to act by a provider of health care in the rendering of professional services, which act or omission is the proximate cause of a personal injury or wrongful death. The term does not include services that are outside the scope of services for which the provider

---

[728] *Jones v. Wilkin*, 111 Nev. 1335, 905 P.2d 166 (1995), cited, *Johnson v. Incline Village Gen. Imp. Dist.*, 5 F. Supp. 2d 1113, at 1115 (D. Nev. 1998).

[729] *Barrett v. Baird*, 111 Nev. 1496, 908 P.2d 689 (1995).

[730] *Wickliffe v. Sunrise Hospital*, 101 Nev. 542, 548, 706 P.2d 1383, 1388 (1985).

[731] *Johnson v. Incline Village Gen. Imp. Dist.*, 5 F. Supp. 2d 1113 (D. Nev. 1998).

[732] *Banks v. Sunrise Hospital*, 120 Nev. 822, 102 P.3d 52 (2004).

of health care is licensed or services for which any restriction has been imposed by the applicable regulatory board or health care facility.
(Added to NRS by 2004 initiative petition, Ballot Question No. 3)

NRS 41A.017, " 'Provider of health care' defined," provides as follows:

"Provider of health care" means a physician licensed under Chapter 630 or 633 of NRS, dentist, licensed nurse, dispensing optician, optometrist, registered physical therapist, podiatric physician, licensed psychologist, chiropractor, doctor of Oriental medicine, medical laboratory director or technician, or a licensed hospital and its employees.
(Added to NRS by 2004 initiative petition, Ballot Question No. 3)

NRS 41A.035, "Limitation on amount of award for noneconomic damages," provides as follows

In an action for injury or death against a provider of health care based upon professional negligence, the injured plaintiff may recover noneconomic damages, but the amount of noneconomic damages awarded in such an action must not exceed $350,000.
(Added to NRS by 2004 initiative petition, Ballot Question No. 3)

This statue is not unconstitutional on the basis that it violates the plaintiff's constitutional right to trial by jury.[733] The statutory cap does not apply per plaintiff and per defendant.[734] "The noneconomic damages cap in NRS 41.035 applies per incident, regardless of how many plaintiffs, defendants, or claims are involved."[735] The statute applies both to professional negligence and medical malpractice.[736]

NRS 41A.045, "Several liability of defendants for damages; abrogation of joint and several liability," provides as follows:

1. In an action for injury or death against a provider of health care based upon professional negligence, each defendant is liable to the plaintiff for economic damages and noneconomic damages severally only, and not jointly, for that portion of the judgment which represents the percentage of negligence attributable to the defendant.
2. This section is intended to abrogate joint and several liability of a provider of health care in an action for injury or death against the provider of health care based upon professional negligence.
(Added to NRS by 2004 initiative petition, Ballot Question No. 3)

NRS 41A.061, "Dismissal of action for failure to bring to trial; effect of dismissal; adoption of court rules to expedite resolution of actions," provides as follows:

1. Upon the motion of any party or upon its own motion, unless good cause is shown for the delay, the court shall, after due notice to the parties, dismiss an action involving medical malpractice or dental malpractice if the action is not brought to trial within:
(a) Three years after the date on which the action is filed, if the action is filed on or after October 1, 2002, but before October 1, 2005.
(b) Two years after the date on which the action is filed, if the action is filed on or after October 1, 2005.
2. Dismissal of an action pursuant to subsection 1 is a bar to the filing of another action upon the same claim for relief against the same defendants.
3. Each district court shall adopt court rules to expedite the resolution of an action involving medical malpractice or dental malpractice.
(Added to NRS by 2002 Special Session, 7)

---

[733] *Tam v. Eighth Judicial District Court*, 131 Nev., Advance Opinion 80 (2015) (en banc).
[734] *Id.*
[735] *Id.* at 12.
[736] *Id.* at 16.

NRS 41A.071, "Dismissal of action filed without affidavit of medical expert supporting allegations," provides as follows:

> If an action for medical malpractice or dental malpractice is filed in the district court, the district court shall dismiss the action, without prejudice, if the action is filed without an affidavit, supporting the allegations contained in the action, submitted by a medical expert who practices or has practiced in an area that is substantially similar to the type of practice engaged in at the time of the alleged malpractice.
> (Added to NRS by 2002 Special Session, 8)

NRS 41A.071's affidavit-of-merit requirements applies to claims for medical malpractice and dental malpractice, but not to claims for professional negligence, such as a claim against a podiatrist.[737] Compliance with affidavit requirement: Leave to amend. Under NRS 41A.071, in the event of complete failure to attach an affidavit to the complaint, the section clearly mandates dismissal without leave to amend. However, where there is a legitimate dispute over whether a filed affidavit of merit complies with NRS 41A.071, a district court, within its sound discretion and considering the need for judicial economy, may grant leave to amend the malpractice complaint under circumstances where justice so requires.[738]

The section shall be construed liberally in accordance with Nevada Supreme Court's NRCP 12 jurisprudence. The provisions of NRS 41A.071 govern the threshold requirements for initial pleadings in medical malpractice cases, and not the ultimate trial of such matters. Thus, as a procedural rule of pleading, NRS 41A.071 must be construed liberally in a manner that is consistent with the Nevada Supreme Court's NRCP 12 jurisprudence.[739]

The district court erred in determining that a gastroenterologist could not submit an affidavit relating to the alleged misdiagnosis and allegedly deficient surgery involving abdominal disease. In a medical malpractice case, the district court determined pursuant to NRS 41A.071 that, in relevant part, the plaintiff's expert medical affiant (a gastroenterologist) did not practice in an area substantially similar to that of the defendant (a general surgeon). On appeal, the Nevada Supreme Court held that, at least with respect to the particular patient, the diagnosis and treatment rendered to the patient, which involved a diagnosis of Crohn's disease and a recommendation for surgical intervention, implicated the affiant's area of expertise. Thus, the provisions of NRS 41A.071 were not violated when the gastroenterologist drew conclusions about perceived deficiencies in the general surgeon's diagnosis, choice of treatment modality and the surgical result obtained.[740]

The provisions of NRS 41A.071 state that an expert medical affiant must practice or have practiced in an area that is "substantially similar" to the type of practice engaged in (by the defendant) at the time of the alleged malpractice. This does not mean that the affiant must practice in the same area of medicine as the defendant. Instead, Nevada's statutory scheme allows medical experts to testify in medical malpractice cases where their present or former practice reasonably relates to that engaged in by the defendant at the time of the alleged professional negligence.[741]

The purpose of requiring an affidavit of a medical expert was explained. The legislative measure pursuant to which NRS 41A.071 was enacted abolished the former practice of using medical-legal panels to prescreen medical malpractice complaints. The expert affidavit requirements of NRS 41A.071 are designed to account for the abolition of the screening panels and to ensure that parties file malpractice cases in good faith; that is, to prevent the filing of frivolous lawsuits.[742]

A medical expert affidavit is not required in medical malpractice action based solely on res ipsa loquitur doctrine. Under NRS 41A.071, a medical malpractice action filed in district court must be dismissed if it is filed without a medical expert's supporting affidavit. However, under NRS 41A.100, expert medical testimony is not required to prove medical malpractice under certain circumstances implicating the doctrine of res ipsa loquitur. Thus, where a medical malpractice action is based solely on the res ipsa loquitur doctrine, the expert affidavit requirement set forth in NRS 41A.071 does not apply. In contrast, if a medical malpractice action consists both of a res ipsa loquitur claim and other claims not based on that doctrine, the other claims are subject to the requirements of NRS 41A.071.[743]

---

[737] *Egan v. Chambers*, 129 Nev., Advance Opinion 25, April 25, 2013, overruling, in part, *Fierle v. Perez*, 125 Nev. 728, 219 P.3d 906 (2009).

[738] *Borger v. Eighth Judicial Dist. Court*, 120 Nev. 1021, 102 P.3d 600 (2004), cited, *Washoe Med. Ctr. v. Second Judicial Dist. Court*, 122 Nev. 1298, at 1304, 148 P.3d 790 (2006).

[739] *Borger, supra,* clarified, *Szydel v. Markman*, 121 Nev. 453, at 458, 117 P.3d 200 (2005).

[740] *Borger v. Eighth Judicial Dist. Court*, 120 Nev. 1021, 102 P.3d 600 (2004).

[741] *Id.*

[742] *Id.*; see also *Washoe Med. Ctr. v. Second Judicial Dist. Court*, 122 Nev. 1298, at 1304, 148 P.3d 790 (2006), clarified, *Szydel v. Markman*, 121 Nev. 453, at 459, 117 P.3d 200 (2005).

[743] *Szydel v. Markman*, 121 Nev. 453, 117 P.3d 200 (2005).

Medical malpractice: Res ipsa loquitur claims; duty of plaintiff to meet prima facie requirements upon challenge by defendant. In a medical malpractice action, any res ipsa loquitur claim (see NRS 41A.100(1) filed without the affidavit of a medical expert (see NRS 41A.071) must, when challenged by the defendant in a pretrial or trial motion, meet the prima facie requirements for a res ipsa loquitur case. Thus, in such an instance, the plaintiff must present facts and evidence that show the existence of one or more of the situations enumerated in NRS 41A.100(1)(a)-(e).[744]

A medical malpractice suit filed without an expert affidavit is void and cannot be amended. A plaintiff who sued a medical center for alleged negligence failed to file a medical expert affidavit with her complaint, as required by NRS 41A.071. When the medical center moved to dismiss the complaint and after the statute of limitations had expired, the plaintiff filed an amended complaint with an expert affidavit attached. When the medical center sought mandamus relief, the plaintiff argued that NRCP 15(a), which permits a plaintiff to amend a pleading once as a matter of course before a responsive pleading is served, superseded NRS 41A.071's dismissal requirement. The Supreme Court disagreed. Because NRS 41A.071 provides that the district court "shall" dismiss without prejudice a medical malpractice action if it is filed without an expert affidavit, the Court concluded that such a complaint is *void ab initio*. Thus, it cannot be amended but must be automatically dismissed. Therefore, NRCP 15(a)'s amendment provisions are inapplicable.[745]

NRS 41A.081, "Settlement conference: Persons required to participate; powers and duties of judge; failure to participate," provides as follows:

> 1. In an action for medical malpractice or dental malpractice, all the parties to the action, the insurers of the respective parties and the attorneys of the respective parties shall attend and participate in a settlement conference before a district judge, other than the judge assigned to the action, to ascertain whether the action may be settled by the parties before trial.
> 2. The judge before whom the settlement conference is held:
> (a) May, for good cause shown, waive the attendance of any party.
> (b) Shall decide what information the parties may submit at the settlement conference.
> 3. The judge shall notify the parties of the time and place of the settlement conference.
> 4. The failure of any party, the party's insurer or the party's attorney to participate in good faith in the settlement conference is grounds for sanctions, including, without limitation, monetary sanctions, against the party or the party's attorney, or both. The judges of the district courts shall liberally construe the provisions of this subsection in favor of imposing sanctions in all appropriate situations. It is the intent of the Legislature that the judges of the district courts impose sanctions pursuant to this subsection in all appropriate situations to punish for and deter conduct which is not undertaken in good faith because such conduct overburdens limited judicial resources, hinders the timely resolution of meritorious claims and increases the costs of engaging in business and providing professional services to the public.
> (Added to NRS by 2002 Special Session, 8; A 2003, 3478)

NRS 41A.085, "Recommendation of settlement for amount of limits of policy of insurance: When authorized; insurer to pay for opinion of independent counsel upon request," provides as follows:

> 1. In an action for damages for medical malpractice or dental malpractice in which the defendant is insured pursuant to a policy of insurance covering the liability of the defendant for a breach of the defendant's professional duty toward a patient:
> (a) At any settlement conference, the judge may recommend that the action be settled for the limits of the policy of insurance.
> (b) If the judge makes the recommendation described in paragraph (a), the defendant is entitled to obtain from independent counsel an opinion letter explaining the rights of, obligations of and potential consequences to the defendant with regard to the recommendation. The insurer shall pay the independent counsel to provide the opinion letter described in this paragraph, except that the insurer is not required to pay more than $1,500 to the independent counsel to provide the opinion letter.
> 2. The section does not:
> (a) Prohibit the plaintiff from making any offer of settlement.
> (b) Require an insurer to provide or pay for independent counsel for a defendant except as expressly provided in this section.
> (Added to NRS by 2003, 3372)

---

[744] *Id.*

[745] *Washoe Med. Ctr. v. Second Judicial Dist. Court*, 122 Nev. 1298, 148 P.3d 790 (2006).

NRS 41A.097, "Limitation of actions; tolling of limitation," provides as follows:

1. Except as otherwise provided in subsection 3, an action for injury or death against a provider of health care may not be commenced more than 4 years after the date of injury or 2 years after the plaintiff discovers or through the use of reasonable diligence should have discovered the injury, whichever occurs first, for:

(a) Injury to or the wrongful death of a person occurring before October 1, 2002, based upon alleged professional negligence of the provider of health care;

(b) Injury to or the wrongful death of a person occurring before October 1, 2002, from professional services rendered without consent; or

(c) Injury to or the wrongful death of a person occurring before October 1, 2002, from error or omission in practice by the provider of health care.

2. Except as otherwise provided in subsection 3, an action for injury or death against a provider of health care may not be commenced more than 3 years after the date of injury or 1 year after the plaintiff discovers or through the use of reasonable diligence should have discovered the injury, whichever occurs first, for:

(a) Injury to or the wrongful death of a person occurring on or after October 1, 2002, based upon alleged professional negligence of the provider of health care;

(b) Injury to or the wrongful death of a person occurring on or after October 1, 2002, from professional services rendered without consent; or

(c) Injury to or the wrongful death of a person occurring on or after October 1, 2002, from error or omission in practice by the provider of health care.

3. This time limitation is tolled for any period during which the provider of health care has concealed any act, error or omission upon which the action is based and which is known or through the use of reasonable diligence should have been known to the provider of health care.

4. For the purposes of this section, the parent, guardian or legal custodian of any minor child is responsible for exercising reasonable judgment in determining whether to prosecute any cause of action limited by subsection 1 or 2. If the parent, guardian or custodian fails to commence an action on behalf of that child within the prescribed period of limitations, the child may not bring an action based on the same alleged injury against any provider of health care upon the removal of the child's disability, except that in the case of:

(a) Brain damage or birth defect, the period of limitation is extended until the child attains 10 years of age.

(b) Sterility, the period of limitation is extended until 2 years after the child discovers the injury.

(Added to NRS by 1971, 366; A 1975, 407; 1977, 857, 954, 1082; 1985, 2011; 1989, 424; 1991, 1131; 1993, 2224; 1995, 2350; 1999, 5; 2001, 1107; 2002 Special Session, 8; 2004 initiative petition, Ballot Question No. 3)

The statute incorporates the "diligent discovery" rule applicable where the occurrence and the manifestation of damage may not be contemporaneous. On appeal from a summary judgment for the defendant in a products liability action involving water damage to real property from a plumbing and heating system where the defendant contended that the cause of action accrued when the damage physically occurred or began to occur and the applicable statute of limitations (see NRS 11.220) had therefore expired, the appellate court held that the term "accrued" as used in NRS 11.220 incorporates the same "diligent discovery" rule that is present in other statutes applicable where the occurrence and manifestation of damage may not be contemporaneous (see NRS 11.190(3), 11.207 and 41A.097). Thus the case was remanded to allow the trier of fact to determine when the plaintiff knew, or in the exercise of proper diligence should have known, of the damage.[746]

An "injury" was construed to mean a legal injury encompassing all essential elements of a cause of action. Under NRS 41A.097, which provides that an action for medical malpractice may not be commenced more than 2 years after the plaintiff discovers or, through the use of reasonable diligence, should have discovered the injury, the appellate court construed the term "injury" to mean a legal injury, encompassing all essential elements of the cause of action, including not only physical damage but also negligence causing damage. A patient "discovers" his legal injury when he

---

[746] *Oak Grove Investors v. Bell & Gossett Co.*, 99 Nev. 616, 668 P.2d 1075 (1983), cited, *Beazer Homes Nev., Inc. v. Eighth Judicial Dist. Court*, 120 Nev. 575, at 585, 97 P.3d 1132 (2004).

knows, or should know, of facts that would put a reasonable person on notice to inquire as to a possible cause of action.[747]

Period of limitation did not begin to run until plaintiff became aware or should have become aware of cause of action. Where a postoperative patient discovered numbness and paralysis of her foot in August 1976, but relied on her physician's assurances that the symptoms were not unusual or permanent under the circumstances and consequently did not name the physician in a medical malpractice action until August 1979, the trial court erred in granting summary judgment dismissing the claim against the physician on the ground that it was barred by the 2-year statute of limitations provided in NRS 41A.097 because the period of limitation does not begin to run until the plaintiff discovers, or should have discovered, that she suffered physical harm and that it resulted from the physician's negligence, and a question of fact existed as to when that occurred.[748]

The period of limitation began to run from time of decedent's death or discovery thereof. In an action for wrongful death under NRS 41.085 brought in 1981, where a decedent received improper medical treatment beginning in 1976 and, as result thereof, died in 1979, the 2-year statute of limitations provided in NRS 41A.097 did not run before the plaintiff filed his complaint because, as used in that statute, "injury" means a legal injury and since death is an essential element of cause of a action for wrongful death, there can be no legal injury until death has occurred, and the period of limitation, therefore, does not begin to run until the time of the decedent's death or the discovery thereof.[749]

The period of limitation in wrongful death medical malpractice action. In a wrongful death medical malpractice action, the 2-year period of limitation provided in NRS 41A.097 does not begin to run until the plaintiff discovers or reasonably should have discovered the legal injury, which includes both the fact of death and the negligent cause thereof.[750]

Section inapplicable in calculating prejudgment interest. The provisions of NRS 41A.097, under which a statute of limitations is tolled until the injured party discovers or reasonably should have discovered the injury, are inapplicable when calculating the prejudgment interest in an action for medical malpractice. For purposes of determining the prejudgment interest, the cause of action accrues the moment a plaintiff suffers the injury or wrong.[751]

NRS 41A.100, "Required evidence; exceptions; rebuttable presumption of negligence," provides as follows:

1. Liability for personal injury or death is not imposed upon any provider of medical care based on alleged negligence in the performance of that care unless evidence consisting of expert medical testimony, material from recognized medical texts or treatises or the regulations of the licensed medical facility wherein the alleged negligence occurred is presented to demonstrate the alleged deviation from the accepted standard of care in the specific circumstances of the case and to prove causation of the alleged personal injury or death, except that such evidence is not required and a rebuttable presumption that the personal injury or death was caused by negligence arises where evidence is presented that the personal injury or death occurred in any one or more of the following circumstances:

(a) A foreign substance other than medication or a prosthetic device was unintentionally left within the body of a patient following surgery;

(b) An explosion or fire originating in a substance used in treatment occurred in the course of treatment;

(c) An unintended burn caused by heat, radiation or chemicals was suffered in the course of medical care;

(d) An injury was suffered during the course of treatment to a part of the body not directly involved in the treatment or proximate thereto; or

(e) A surgical procedure was performed on the wrong patient or the wrong organ, limb or part of a patient's body.

---

[747] *Siragusa v. Brown*, 114 Nev. 1384, at 1393, 971 P.2d 801 (1998).

[748] *Massey v. Litton*, 99 Nev. 723, 669 P.2d 248 (1983), cited, *Siragusa v. Brown*, 114 Nev. 1384, at 1393, 971 P.2d 801 (1998).

[749] *Gilloon v. Humana, Inc.*, 100 Nev. 518, 687 P.2d 80 (1984), cited, *Pope v. Gray*, 104 Nev. 358, at 362, 706 P.2d 763 (1988), *Fernandez v. Kozar*, 107 Nev. 447, at 449, 814 P.2d 68 (1991), *State Indus. Ins. Sys. v. Lodge*, 107 Nev. 867, at 869, 822 P.2d 664 (1991).

[750] *Pope v. Gray*, 104 Nev. 358, 760 P.2d 763 (1988), cited, *Fernandez v. Kozar*, 107 Nev. 447, at 449, 814 P.2d 68 (1991).

[751] See NRS 17.130; *Jain v. McFarland*, 109 Nev. 465, 851 P.2d 450 (1993).

2. Expert medical testimony provided pursuant to subsection 1 may only be given by a provider of medical care who practices or has practiced in an area that is substantially similar to the type of practice engaged in at the time of the alleged negligence.

3. As used in this section, "provider of medical care" means a physician, dentist, registered nurse or a licensed hospital as the employer of any such person.

(Added to NRS by 1975, 406; A 1977, 955; 1985, 1754; 1997, 1219; 1999, 5; 2002 Special Session, 9)

Nevada Cases.

Summary judgment for defendants appropriate where supporting affidavit of a competent medical witness stating defendant had met applicable standard of care was uncontradicted by plaintiff. Under NRS 41A.100 and NRCP 56(e), summary judgment for the defendants in a medical malpractice action was appropriate regardless of the state of evidence as to causation of the injury where the supporting affidavit of a competent medical witness including that the defendants had met the applicable standard of care was uncontradicted by the plaintiff.[752]

The strict locality rule is no longer applicable where defendant is a board-certified specialist. In a medical malpractice action where the defendant was a specialist in internal medicine certified by the American Medical Board, the plaintiff's expert witness (see NRS 41A.100), who was a board-certified specialist in the same area of medicine as the defendant, was competent to testify as to the standard of care of internal specialists without reference to the standards prevailing in a particular locality. The appellate court reversed the order of the district court granting summary judgment to the defendant, holding that the strict locality rule is no longer applicable where the defendant is a board-certified specialist.[753]

Physician's duty to disclose to patient is measured by professional medical standard which plaintiff must establish with expert testimony. In a medical malpractice action it was proper to refuse the plaintiff's proposed instruction on informed consent where the instruction was not supported by sufficient expert testimony. Under the traditional view and NRS 41A.100, a physician's duty to disclose to the patient is measured by a professional medical standard which the plaintiff must establish with expert testimony. The standard is either the customary disclosure practice of physicians in the relevant community or what a reasonable physician would disclose under the circumstances.[754]

Medical experts: Reasonable degree of medical probability standard; exception. Normally, a medical expert is expected to testify (see also NRS 41A.100 and 50.275) only to matters that conform to the reasonable degree of medical probability standard. However, where a medical expert is testifying as to matters other than causation, a factor of causation or an inquiry involving medical probabilities, his testimony need not be to a reasonable degree of medical probability.[755]

Expert testimony is not required if the propriety of medical treatment, or lack thereof, is a matter of common knowledge of laymen. In a medical malpractice action based upon the failure of a doctor, who was a specialist in internal medicine, to detect cancer of the colon in the plaintiff, the standard of care was established through testimony of a surgeon and pathologist, neither of whom practiced as specialists in internal medicine, that the recognition of red blood bleeding from the rectum was an indication of potential colon cancer, because the general rule is that expert testimony must be used to establish medical malpractice, unless the propriety of treatment or lack thereof is a matter of common knowledge of laymen.[756]

Screening panel considered expert for purposes of giving testimony. In an action for medical malpractice, the screening panel required to review a claim was considered an expert and, as such, could give an opinion regarding the ultimate issue of negligence and, in formulating its opinion, could rely on evidence that was otherwise inadmissible at trial, even when testifying before a jury regarding the presence of negligence.[757]

It was error for the district court to refuse plaintiff's proposed jury instruction patterned on section where The plaintiff presented evidence of existence of circumstance specified in the section. In an action alleging medical malpractice, where the plaintiff presented evidence that the defendant injured her colon and ureter during a spinal

---

[752] *Bakerink v. Orthopaedic Assocs.*, 94 Nev. 428, 581 P.2d 9 (1978), cited, *Aviation Ventures v. Joan Morris, Inc.*, 121 Nev. 113, at 119, 110 P.3d 59 (2005), distinguished, *Orcutt v. Russell F. Miller, M.D., Ltd.*, 95 Nev. 408, at 412, 595 P.2d 1191 (1979).

[753] *Orcutt v. Russell F. Miller, M.D., Ltd.*, 95 Nev. 408, 595 P.2d 1191 (1979), *Mishler v. State Bd. of Medical Examiners*, 109 Nev. 287, at 293, 849 P.2d 291 (1993).

[754] *Bronneke v. Rutherford*, 120 Nev. 230, at 233, 89 P.3d 40 (2004).

[755] *Morsicato v. Sav-On Drug Stores, Inc.*, 121 Nev. 153, at 158, 111 P.3d 1112 (2005), see also *Prabhu v. Levine*, 112 Nev. 1538, at 1544, 930 P.2d 103 (1996).

[756] *Fernandez v. Admirand*, 108 Nev. 963, 843 P.2d 354 (1992).

[757] See NRS 41A.100, NRS 50.285 and NRS 50.295; *Barrett v. Baird*, 111 Nev. 1496, 908 P.2d 689 (1995).

laminectomy and operated at the wrong level of her spine, the trial court erred in refusing the plaintiff's proposed jury instruction patterned on NRS 41A.100, Nevada's statutory res ipsa loquitur rule for medical malpractice cases, which provided that the law creates a rebuttable presumption that personal injury was caused by negligence where the personal injury occurred under any circumstance set forth in NRS 41A.100, and that such a presumption operates to shift to the defendant the burden of proving, by a preponderance of evidence, that the personal injury was not caused by negligence. Provisions of NRS 41A.100 replace, rather than supplement, the classic res ipsa loquitur formulation in medical malpractice cases where it is factually applicable, and the presumption of negligence automatically applies where any of the enumerated factual circumstances are present. All that a plaintiff needs to do to warrant an instruction under NRS 41A.100 is present some evidence of the existence of any factual predicate enumerated in that section. If the trier of fact then finds that such factual predicate exists, the presumption must be applied.[758]

The court is required to give an instruction on res ipsa loquitur where a factual predicate existed for admission of the instruction. Where the evidence presented at trial indicated that during each of two surgeries performed upon the plaintiff a surgical procedure was performed on the wrong organ or the wrong part of the plaintiff's body, it was reversible error for the district court to rule as a matter of law that the doctrine of res ipsa loquitur, as codified in NRS 41A.100 for cases involving medical malpractice, did not apply. Because it was shown that the factual predicate existed for the admission of the instruction, the district court was obligated to give the instruction.[759]

A chiropractor's duty to disclose to her patient is measured by professional medical standard which plaintiff must establish with expert testimony. Although NRS 41A.100 does not refer to chiropractors, the reasoning for the adoption of the professional standard in a malpractice action applies to chiropractors. Thus, in a chiropractic malpractice action alleging lack of informed consent, a chiropractor's duty to disclose to the patient is measured by a professional medical standard which the plaintiff must, at a minimum, establish with expert testimony.[760]

An injury to the brain that was suffered during shoulder surgery justified a res ipsa loquitur instruction. During rotator cuff surgery, the patient's blood pressure dropped and, after receiving two administrations of ephedrine, the patient went into cardiac arrest. Physicians were able to stabilize the patient but, following surgery, the patient failed to regain consciousness and was left in a permanently vegetative state as a result of deprivation of oxygen to the brain. In relevant part, the complaint filed on behalf of the victim contained a "Doe/Roe allegation" of negligent maintenance of the anesthesia equipment used in the surgery. The complaint also alleged that the anesthesiologist assigned to the surgery had failed to adhere to proper protocols in addressing, and administering medication for, the patient's decrease in blood pressure.

On appeal, the hospital asserted that the district court had erred in submitting a res ipsa loquitur instruction to the jury. The Nevada Supreme Court held that because the patient underwent surgery for treatment to his shoulder, but suffered an injury to his brain which caused the patient's vegetative state, and because the patient's brain was not directly or proximately related to the rotator cuff surgery (see NRS 41A.100(1)(d)), the district court did not abuse its discretion when it submitted the res ipsa loquitur instruction to the jury.[761]

Expert's medical testimony was permissible, even though based on less than a reasonable degree of probability. At trial, in a medical malpractice suit, a medical expert for the plaintiffs testified as to possible causes of things that might have contributed to an adverse event in which a surgical patient was rendered permanently vegetative as a result of oxygen deprivation and in which a certain piece of anesthesia equipment was alleged to have malfunctioned (see also NRS 41A.100 and 50.275). The medical expert admitted that, under the circumstances, he could not determine whether the equipment contributed to the patient's injury because the hospital had failed to keep records by which the equipment involved in the patient's surgical procedure could be identified. Nonetheless, the medical expert testified as to the possible ways in which the anesthesia equipment could fail and also testified that everyone with whom he had spoken who had owned the particular type of anesthesia equipment for any length of time had experienced failures in the equipment's interlock system. On appeal, the defendant hospital argued that the district court had abused its discretion in admitting the testimony of the medical expert, which testimony the hospital characterized as speculative.

The Nevada Supreme Court held that although the district court allowed the medical expert to give opinion testimony based on less than a reasonable degree of probability, the district court had not abused its discretion because: (1) the expert's testimony and opinions established that the anesthesia equipment's interlock device could malfunction intermittently; (2) the expert's testimony was helpful to establish the standard of care for preserving the identity of the

[758] *Johnson v. Egtedar*, 112 Nev. 428, 915 P.2d 271 (1996), cited, *Born v. Eisenman*, 114 Nev. 854, at 859, 962 P.2d 1227 (1998), *Banks v. Sunrise Hosp.*, 120 Nev. 822, at 832, 102 P.3d 52 (2004), *Carver v. El-Sabawi*, 121 Nev. 11, at 13, 107 P.3d 1283 (2005).

[759] *Born v. Eisenman*, 114 Nev. 854, 962 P.2d 1227 (1998), cited, *Banks v. Sunrise Hosp.*, 120 Nev. 822, at 832-33, 102 P.3d 52 (2004), *Szydel v. Markman*, 121 Nev. 453, at 457, 117 P.3d 200 (2005).

[760] *Bronneke v. Rutherford*, 120 Nev. 230, 89 P.3d 40 (2004).

[761] *Banks v. Sunrise Hosp.*, 120 Nev. 822, 102 P.3d 52 (2004).

anesthesia equipment; and (3) the expert's testimony assisted the jury in understanding how the anesthesia equipment could have malfunctioned and why it was reasonable to draw an adverse inference from the fact that the hospital had not preserved or identified the anesthesia equipment involved in the patient's surgical procedure.[762]

A medical expert affidavit is not required in a medical malpractice action based solely on the doctrine of res ipsa loquitur. Under NRS 41A.071, a medical malpractice action filed in district court must be dismissed if it is filed without a medical expert's supporting affidavit. However, pursuant to NRS 41A.100, expert medical testimony is not required to prove medical malpractice under certain circumstances implicating the doctrine of res ipsa loquitur. Thus, where a medical malpractice action is based solely on the res ipsa loquitur doctrine, the expert affidavit requirement set forth in NRS 41A.071 does not apply. In contrast, if a medical malpractice action consists both of a res ipsa loquitur claim and other claims not based on that doctrine, the other claims are subject to the requirements of NRS 41A.071.[763]

Medical malpractice: Res ipsa loquitur claims; duty of plaintiff to meet prima facie requirements upon challenge by defendant. In a medical malpractice action, any res ipsa loquitur claim (see NRS 41A.100(1)) filed without the affidavit of a medical expert (see NRS 41A.071) must, when challenged by the defendant in a pretrial or trial motion, meet the prima facie requirements for a res ipsa loquitur case. Thus, in such an instance, the plaintiff must present facts and evidence that show the existence of one or more of the situations enumerated in NRS 41A.100(1)(a)-(e).[764]

"Inference" and "rebuttable presumption" contrasted. An "inference" and a "rebuttable presumption" are not the same things. A "rebuttable presumption" is a rule of law by which the finding of a basic fact gives rise to a presumed fact's existence, unless the presumption is rebutted. In contrast, an "inference" is a logical and reasonable conclusion of a fact not presented by direct evidence but which, by process of logic and reason, a trier of fact may conclude exists from the established facts. Although an inference may give rise to a rebuttable presumption in appropriate cases, an inference simply allows the trier of fact to determine, based on other evidence, that a fact exists. An inference is permissible, not required, and it does not shift the burden of proof.[765]

NRS 41A.110, "Consent of patient: When conclusively established," provides as follows:

> A physician licensed to practice medicine under the provisions of Chapter 630 or 633 of NRS, or a dentist licensed to practice dentistry under the provisions of Chapter 631 of NRS, has conclusively obtained the consent of a patient for a medical, surgical or dental procedure, as appropriate, if the physician or dentist has done the following:
> 1. Explained to the patient in general terms, without specific details, the procedure to be undertaken;
> 2. Explained to the patient alternative methods of treatment, if any, and their general nature;
> 3. Explained to the patient that there may be risks, together with the general nature and extent of the risks involved, without enumerating such risks; and
> 4. Obtained the signature of the patient to a statement containing an explanation of the procedure, alternative methods of treatment and risks involved, as provided in this section.
> (Added to NRS by 1975, 408; A 1997, 1219; 1999, 5; 2007, 273)

It was improper for the court to instruct the jury concerning conclusive consent when consent was not obtained in compliance with provisions of section. In a medical malpractice action based in part on the failure of a physician to obtain an informed consent from the plaintiff before performing surgery, it was reversible error for the court to give the jury instruction concerning conclusive consent when such consent was not obtained in conformity with the requirements of NRS 41A.110. As the consent form signed by the plaintiff before surgery did not contain an explanation of the procedure to be undertaken, alternative methods of treatment or the risks inherent in the procedure, jury instructions concerning conclusive consent created a source of confusion and misunderstanding for the jury, thereby warranting a reversal and remanding of the case for a new trial.[766]

NRS 41A.120, "Consent of patient: When implied," provides as follows:

> In addition to the provisions of Chapter 129 of NRS and any other instances in which a consent is implied or excused by law, a consent to any medical, surgical or dental procedure will be implied if:

---

[762] *Id.*, clarified, *Morsicato v. Sav-On Drug Stores, Inc.*, 121 Nev. 153, at 157, 111 P.3d 1112 (2005).
[763] *Szydel v. Markman*, 121 Nev. 453, 117 P.3d 200 (2005).
[764] *Id.*
[765] *Bass-Davis v. Davis*, 122 Nev. 442, 134 P.3d 103 (2006).
[766] *Allan v. Levy*, 109 Nev. 46, 846 P.2d 274 (1993).

1. In competent medical judgment, the proposed medical, surgical or dental procedure is reasonably necessary and any delay in performing such a procedure could reasonably be expected to result in death, disfigurement, impairment of faculties or serious bodily harm; and

2. A person authorized to consent is not readily available.

(Added to NRS by 1975, 408; A 1997, 1220; 1999, 5)

To make an award for future pain and suffering (see also NRS 41.130 and NRS ch. 41A), the award must be substantially supported by expert testimony to the effect that future pain and suffering is a probable, as contrasted to a possible, result. (N.B., the Nevada Supreme Court has explained that where evidence of future pain and suffering is objective and not subjective, an award for pain and suffering need not be supported by expert testimony as long as the finder of fact determines from substantial evidence that future pain and suffering is probable.)[767] The Nevada Supreme Court has limited the claim for future pain and suffering arising from subjective physical injury, and in such cases the claim must be substantially supported by expert testimony to the effect that future pain and suffering is a probable consequence rather than a mere possibility.[768]

The "loss of chance" doctrine must be used to determine the amount of damages recoverable in actions for medical malpractice. In actions for medical malpractice (see NRS ch. 41A), the court has adopted a "loss of chance" doctrine, under which an injury to be redressed is not defined as death itself, but rather as a decreased chance of survival caused by medical malpractice. Plaintiff cannot recover merely on the basis of a decreased chance of survival or of avoiding a debilitating injury, but must in fact suffer death or a debilitating injury before there can be an award of damages. Additionally, damages are to be discounted to the extent that a preexisting condition likely contributed to death or serious debilitation. Specifically, the amount of damages recoverable is equal to the percent of the chance of survival lost due to negligence multiplied by the total amount of damages which are ordinarily allowed in a wrongful death action.[769]

A cause of action was established for negligent failure to reveal severely deformed fetus. The mother of a child born with severe deformities may maintain action for medical malpractice under the law of this State (see NRS ch. 41A) where the mother's physician negligently failed to perform or interpret properly prenatal medical examinations and, as a result, negligently failed to discover and reveal the fact that she was carrying a severely deformed fetus, thereby denying her of the right to terminate pregnancy. If proven, the mother may recover damages for extraordinary medical and custodial expenses associated with caring for the child for the period the child is dependent upon her to provide that care, which are not required to be offset by the amount it would cost to raise a child who is not handicapped, and damages for emotional distress, which are not required to be offset by emotional benefits attributable to the birth of the child. However, the mother may not recover damages for lost services or companionship.[770]

No cause of action against the mother's physician for a child born with severe deformities. A child born with severe deformities had no personal cause of action against the mother's physician who negligently failed to perform or interpret properly prenatal examinations and, as a result, negligently failed to discover and reveal the fact that the mother was carrying a severely deformed fetus, thereby denying her of the right to terminate her pregnancy. The State does not recognize the claim by the child for harm the child claims to have suffered by virtue of having been born.[771] Physicians had no action for malicious prosecution against attorney who had brought action against them for medical malpractice.

A patient under the care of respondent physicians was treated and discharged, after which the patient's condition deteriorated. The patient's son then sought, and the patient received, treatment from a different doctor, whereupon the patient's condition improved and the doctor told the patient's son that the patient might not have lived without the doctor's timely treatment. The patient's attorney filed an action against the respondent physicians for medical malpractice after the attorney: (1) relied on information gleaned from interviews with the patient and the patient's son; (2) obtained and reviewed the patient's medical records; (3) researched legal authorities regarding malpractice actions; and (4) researched and reviewed medical literature on the patient's ailments. The attorney did not obtain an expert opinion. The Supreme Court concluded that a reasonable attorney would have believed that the action against the respondent physicians was legally tenable, that the attorney therefore had probable cause to file the complaint, and that the respondent physicians had no action for malicious prosecution against the attorney.[772]

---

[767] *Gutierrez v. Sutton Vending Serv.*, 80 Nev. 562, at 565-66, 397 P.2d 3 (1964).

[768] *University & Cmty. Coll. Sys. v. Sutton*, 120 Nev. 972, 990 n. 44, 103 P.3d 8 (2004).

[769] *Perez v. Las Vegas Medical Center*, 107 Nev. 1, 805 P.2d 589 (1991), cited, *Greco v. United States*, 111 Nev. 405, at 411, 893 P.2d 345 (1995).

[770] *Greco v. United States*, 111 Nev. 405, 893 P.2d 345 (1995).

[771] *Id.*

[772] *Dutt v. Kremp*, 111 Nev. 567, 894 P.2d 354 (1995), cited, *Jordan v. Bailey*, 113 Nev. 1038, at 1047, 944 P.2d 828 (1997), clarified, *LaMantia v. Redisi*, 118 Nev. 27, at 31, 38 P.3d 877 (2002).

Determination whether probable cause exists to initiate action for medical malpractice lies with court and not jury. A patient's attorney filed an action against the respondent physicians for medical malpractice. The facts upon which the attorney acted in filing the action were based on: (1) information gleaned from interviews with the patient and the patient's son; (2) the patient's medical records; (3) legal authorities regarding malpractice actions; and (4) medical literature on the patient's ailments. When determining whether there was probable cause to institute an action, the district court erred by submitting a question to the jury because existence of probable cause was a legal question which should have been decided by the court.[773]

An attorney may properly file a malpractice action without obtaining an expert medical opinion. There is no absolute requirement that an attorney obtain an expert medical opinion before filing a malpractice lawsuit.[774]

An objective test is an appropriate standard to determine whether probable cause existed for bringing an action for medical malpractice. An action for medical malpractice was filed by a patient's attorney against the respondent physicians. The action was subsequently dismissed and the physicians brought action against the attorney for malicious prosecution. In determining whether probable cause existed for bringing an action for medical malpractice, the Supreme Court determined that the appropriate standard was an objective test. Under this test, the court must determine whether, on the basis of facts known to the attorney, a reasonable attorney would have believed that the institution of a malpractice action was legally tenable. The degree of expertise and the belief of the attorney who brought the action are not relevant.[775]

The evidence was insufficient to support finding that an attorney filed a malpractice action to coerce a settlement. Where an attorney examined all the medical records of a client, consulted medical and legal authorities, made no formal demand for settlement, and dismissed the complaint shortly after receiving an independent medical report from a qualified organization, there was insufficient evidence to support the finding that the attorney filed the malpractice action to coerce a nuisance settlement.[776]

What the plaintiff must show to prevail in medical malpractice action. To prevail in a medical malpractice action (see also NRS ch. 41A), the plaintiff must establish that: (1) the doctor's conduct departed from the accepted standard of medical care or practice; (2) the doctor's conduct was both the actual and proximate cause of the plaintiff's injury; and (3) the plaintiff suffered damages.[777]

Federal and Other Cases.

Defendant's rights under the Chapter were not waived by a stipulation to transfer the action from California to Nevada. A defendant's rights pursuant to NRS ch. 41A were not waived by the stipulation to transfer an action from the federal district court in California to Nevada.[778]

Where an insurer brought an indemnity action against a doctor in federal district court in California and the parties stipulated to transfer to Nevada, the provisions of NRS 41A.016 relating to screening panels were held applicable because the interests of Nevada outweighed those of California in that NRS Chapter 41A is a legislative response to the problem of insurance costs for health care and if the provisions were not applied, the state's scheme of protection of health care providers would be circumvented by the fact that a diversity case was first filed in California.[779]

Misappropriation

See the Lanham (Trademark) Act, 15 U.S.C. § 1114, 1125(a), (c) (trademark infringement, trademark dilution, unfair competition and false designation of origin). These trademark actions require commercial use of the domain name (See 15 U.S.C. § 1125(c)(4)(B) (1999) (noncommercial use of a mark is not actionable under this section).

Money Had and Received

In an action for money had and received, findings that on or about a certain date defendant became indebted to plaintiff in sum of $500 for money had and received by defendant by reason of an advancement made of such sum of money by plaintiff, and that on or about certain date, and before commencement of action, plaintiff demanded payment

---

[773] *Dutt v. Kremp*, 111 Nev. 567, 894 P.2d 354 (1995).

[774] *Id.*

[775] See NRS Chapter 41A; *Dutt v. Kremp*, 111 Nev. 567, 894 P.2d 354 (1995), cited, *Jordan v. Bailey*, 113 Nev. 1038, at 1047, 944 P.2d 828 (1997), clarified, *LaMantia v. Redisi*, 118 Nev. 27, at 31, 38 P.3d 877 (2002).

[776] *Dutt v. Kremp*, 111 Nev. 567, 894 P.2d 354 (1995).

[777] *Perez v. Las Vegas Medical Center*, 107 Nev. 1, at 4, 805 P.2d 589 (1991).

[778] *Truck Ins. Exch. v. Tetzlaff*, 683 F. Supp. 223 (D. Nev. 1988).

[779] *Id.*, cited, *Heredia v. Johnson*, 835 F. Supp. 553, at 554 (D. Nev. 1993), *Wray v. Gregory*, 61 F.3d 1414, at 1417 (9th Cir. 1995).

thereof from defendant, but that no part of the $500 was repaid by defendant, were sufficient to support a judgment for the plaintiff.[780] See "Assumpsit."

Negligence

A claim for negligence must be based on an existing duty of care, breach, legal causation, and damages.[781] To prevail on a negligence theory, the plaintiff generally must show that: (1) the defendant had a duty to exercise due care towards the plaintiff; (2) the defendant breached the duty; (3) the breach was an actual cause of the plaintiff's injury; (4) the breach was the proximate cause of the injury; and (5) the plaintiff suffered damage.[782] To prevail on a negligence claim, a plaintiff must establish four elements: (1) the existence of a duty of care, (2) breach of that duty, (3) legal causation, and (4) damages.[783]

Five Key Cases on Negligence

1. Dear Mrs. Palsgraf was injured by a falling set of scales, after a box of fireworks fell onto the railroad tracks and exploded.[784] The box fell after a passenger, who was being shoved into a crowded train car by a guard, dropped the box of fireworks. Judge Benjamin Cardozo's opinion created the "foreseeability" test for negligence, recognizing that a chain of actions had to be cut off somewhere. Judge Cardozo chose "foreseeability."

2. Three men went hunting: two behind and one in front, forming a triangle.[785] The two behind saw a quail and shot. The man in front got hit with bird shot. Which of the two men behind him is at fault? Either or both, said the California Supreme Court. If the plaintiff can't figure out which defendant specifically caused his injury, then as long as he can show that both defendants were negligent, the plaintiff can recover against each of them or both of them, and it's up to the defendants to sort out their own liability between them. *Summers* has become more important over the years in product liability cases.

3. MacPherson involved a car whose wheels collapsed.[786] Buick claimed it wasn't liable because it didn't manufacture the wheel and wasn't in "privity" with the plaintiff. Not so, said Judge Cardozo: Buick's responsibility to make a safe car extended to making sure that the parts it used were safe as well. A plaintiff's recovery can't be foreclosed just because he didn't have a contract directly with the party that made the faulty part. Judge Benjamin N. Cardozo which removed the requirement of privity of contract for duty in negligence actions, reasoning as follows:

> If the nature of a thing is such that it is reasonably certain to place life and limb in peril when negligently made, it is then a thing of danger. Its nature gives warning of the consequence to be expected. If to the element of danger there is added knowledge that the thing will be used by persons other than the purchaser, and used without new tests, then, irrespective of contract, the manufacturer of this thing of danger is under a duty to make it carefully. That is as far as we need to go for the decision of this case . . . . If he is negligent, where danger is to be foreseen, a liability will follow.[787]

4. A misbehaving five-year-old boy pulled a lawn chair out from under an old lady as she was about to sit down.[788] She suffered injury and sued for battery. Did he act intentionally? Yes, said the Supreme Court of Washington in this important 1955 decision which established that acting with "substantial certainty" of resultant harm is enough to show intent. The absence of an intent to injure or play a joke is not sufficient to absolve the accused of liability.

---

[780] *Craig v. Harrah*, 66 Nev. 1, 2, 201 P. 2d 1081 (1949).

[781] *Turner v. Mandalay Bay Sports Entertainment LLC*, 124 Nev. Adv. Op. No. 20, 180 P.3d 1172 (2008).

[782] *Perez v. Las Vegas Medical Center*, 107 Nev. 1, 4, 805 P.2d 589 (1991).

[783] *Sanchez v. Wal-Mart Stores*, 125 Nev. ___, ___, 221 P.3d 1276, 1280 (2009).

[784] *Palsgraf v. Long Island Railroad Co.*, 248 N.Y. 339, 162 N.E. 99 (N.Y. Ct.App. 1928), cited in *Merluzzi v. Larson*, 96 Nev. 409, 413, 610 P.2d 739 (1980) (defendant's duty to protect against reasonably foreseeable harm to others did not extend to the injured plaintiff).

[785] *Summers v. Tice* 33 Cal.2d 80, 199 P.2d 1 (Cal. 1948), cited in *Kleitz v. Raskin*, 103 Nev. 325 fn.2, 738 P.2d 508 fn. 2(1987) (when two separate tortfeasors act near simultaneously and it is unclear which one of the two caused the injury, the burden shifts to the defendant to show not only apportionment of damages but causation).

[786] *MacPherson v. Buick Motor Co.*, 217 N.Y. 382, 111 N.E. 1050 (N.Y. Ct. App. 1916), cited in *Calloway v. City of Reno*, 116 Nev.Adv.Op.No.24 (Nev. 02/29/2000).

[787] *MacPherson, supra*, 217 N.Y. at 389.

[788] *Garratt v. Dailey*, 46 Wash. 2d 197, 279 P.2d 1091 (Wash. 1955).

5. A group of barges broke free from their moorings, hit another barge, and sank it.[789] The Second Circuit found Carroll Towing, which had secured the mooring lines, had not met its standard of care because the cost of potential damage, multiplied by the probability of damage, was greater than the expense to take adequate precautions (B < CP). Cost-benefit analysis is one the foundations of the Law and Economics school of thought.

A landowner owes a duty of reasonable care to entrants for risks that exist on the landowner's property.[790] The open and obvious nature of a dangerous condition does not automatically relieve a landowner from the general duty of reasonable care.[791] The fact that a dangerous condition may be open and obvious bears on the assessment of whether reasonable care was exercised by the landowner.[792] Premises liability is not limited to circumstances where a condition on the land caused an injury.[793] The Restatement sanctions such an application where the landowner has acted to increase the risk posed to entrants.[794]

With regard to the element of duty, under common-law principles, no duty is owed to control the dangerous conduct of another or to warn others of the dangerous conduct.[795] An exception to this general rule arises, however, and an affirmative duty to aid others is recognized when (1) a special relationship exists between the parties or between the defendant and the identifiable victim, and (2) the harm created by the defendant's conduct is foreseeable.[796] A crucial factor in establishing liability in the context of special relationships between national and local fraternity chapters and a third party is "the element of control."[797] In *Scialabba*, the Nevada Supreme Court noted that the rationale for imposing liability when one party controls another is as follows:

> [S]ince the ability of one of the parties to provide for his own protection has been limited in some way by his submission to the control of the other, a duty should be imposed upon the one possessing control (and thus the power to act) to take reasonable precautions to protect the other one from assaults by third parties which, at least, could reasonably have been anticipated.[798]

Such ability to exercise control "must be real and not fictional and, if exercised, would meaningfully reduce the risk of the harm that actually occurred."[799] In the absence of this degree of control, "there is no special relationship giving rise to a duty of reasonable care."[800]

A legal cause of injury, damage, loss, or harm is a cause which is a substantial factor in bringing about the injury, damage, loss or harm.[801] In *Klasch v. Walgreen*,[802] the Nevada Supreme Court concluded that when a pharmacist has knowledge of a customer-specific risk with respect to a prescribed medication, the pharmacist has a duty to exercise reasonable care in warning the customer or notifying the prescribing doctor of this risk.

"[A] business owes its patrons a duty to keep the premises in a reasonably safe condition for use."[803] Where a foreign substance causing a slip and fall is made to be on the floor by the business owner or one of its agents, then "liability will lie, as a foreign substance on the floor is usually not consistent with the standard of ordinary care."[804] Traditionally, where a foreign substance causing a slip and fall results from "the actions of persons other than the

---

[789] *United States v. Carroll Towing Co.*, 159 F.2d 169 (2d. Cir. 1947).

[790] *Foster v. Costco*, 128 Nev., Advance Opinion 71 (2012); RESTATEMENT (THIRD) OF TORTS: Physical and Emotional Harm § 51.

[791] *Foster*, supra.

[792] *Id.*

[793] *FCH1, LLC v. Rodriguez*, 130 Nev., Advance Opinion 46 (2014).

[794] See RESTATEMENT (THIRD) OF TORTS: PHYS. & EMOT. HARM § 51(a) (2012).

[795] See *Mangeris v. Gordon*, 94 Nev. 400, 402, 580 P.2d 481, 483 (1978).

[796] *Lee v. GNLV Corp.*, 117 Nev. 291, 295, 22 P.3d 209, 212 (2001); *Elko Enterprises v. Broyles*, 105 Nev. 562, 565-66, 779 P.2d 961, 964 (1989); *Mangeris*, 94 Nev. at 402, 580 P.2d at 483.

[797] *Scialabba v. Brandise Constr. Co.*, 112 Nev. 965, 969, 921 P.2d 928, 930 (1996).

[798] *Id.* (alteration in original) (internal quotation omitted).

[799] *Grand Aerie Fraternal Order v. Carneyhan*, 169 S.W.3d 840, 851 (Ky. 2005).

[800] *Id.* at 853; see *Sparks v. Alpha Tau Omega Fraternity*, 127 Nev., Advance Opinion 23 (2011).

[801] *County of Clark, ex rel. University Medical Center v. Upchurch*, 114 Nev. 749, 961 P.2d 754 (1998); RESTATEMENT (SECOND) OF TORTS § 431.

[802] 127 Nev. Adv. Op. No. 74 (2011).

[803] *Sprague v. Lucky Stores, Inc.*, 109 Nev. 247, 250, 849 P.2d 320, 322 (1993).

[804] *Id.*

business or its employees, liability will lie only if the business had actual or constructive notice of the condition and failed to remedy it."[805]

The "mode of operation" approach focuses on the nature of the business at issue.[806] Where an owner's chosen mode of operation makes it reasonably foreseeable that a dangerous condition will occur, a store owner could be held liable for injuries to an invitee if the plaintiff proves that the store owner failed to take all reasonable precautions necessary to protect invitees from these foreseeable dangerous conditions.[807] The rationale underlying the mode of operation approach is that an owner of a self-service establishment has, as a cost-saving measure, chosen to have his customers perform tasks that were traditionally performed by employees.[808] If a customer who is performing such a task negligently creates a hazardous condition, the owner is charged with the creation of this condition just as he would be charged with the responsibility for negligent acts of his employees because it was the owner's choice of mode of operation that created the risk.[809] Under the mode of operation approach, the plaintiff's burden to prove notice is not eliminated.[810] Instead, the plaintiff satisfies the notice requirement if he establishes that an injury was attributable to a reasonably foreseeable dangerous condition on the owner's premises that is related to the owner's self-service mode of operation.[811] Mode of operation liability does not generally extend to a sit-down restaurant.[812]

When a medical facility performs a nonmedical function, general negligence standards apply, such that the medical facility has a duty to exercise reasonable care to avoid foreseeable harm as a result of its actions.[813]

A plaintiff may state a cause of action for negligence with medical monitoring as the remedy without asserting that he or she has suffered a present *physical* injury.[814] An individual has a legally protected interest in avoiding expensive diagnostic examinations.[815]

Negligence Per Se

To state a claim for negligence per se, a plaintiff must allege that: (1) he or she belongs to a class of persons that a statute was intended to protect; (2) the defendant violated the relevant statute; (3) the plaintiff's injuries are the type against which the statute was intended to protect; (4) the violation was the legal cause of plaintiff's injury; and (5) plaintiff suffered damages.[816] Whether a particular statute establishes a standard of care in a negligence action is a question of law.[817] Under NRS 11.190, the relevant statute of limitations for negligence per se is three years.[818]

For example, NRS 212.020 creates a duty not to oppress or be willfully inhumane to a prisoner. NRS 212.020, "Inhumanity to prisoners," provides as follows:

> 1. A jailer or person who is guilty of willful inhumanity or oppression to any prisoner under his care or custody shall be punished:
> (a) Where the prisoner suffers substantial bodily harm from the inhumanity or oppression, for a category D felony as provided in NRS 193.130.
> (b) Where no substantial bodily harm results, for a gross misdemeanor.
> 2. Whether or not the prisoner suffers substantial bodily harm, any public officer guilty of willful inhumanity is guilty of a malfeasance in office.

A negligence per se claim is available when a defendant violates a statute that is designed to protect others against the type of injury that was incurred.[819]

---

[805] *Id.* at 250, 849 P.2d at 322-23.
[806] *FGA, Inc. v. Giglio*, 128 Nev. Adv. Op. No. 26 (2012).
[807] *Id.*
[808] *Id.*
[809] *Id.*
[810] *Id.*
[811] *Id.*
[812] *Id.*
[813] *DeBoer v. Sr. Bridges of Sparks Fam. Hosp.*, 128 Nev. Adv. Op. No. 38, (August 9, 2012).
[814] *Sadler v. Pacificare of Nevada*, 130 Nev., Advance Opinion 98, p. 13 (2014) (emphasis in original).
[815] *Id.* at p. 14.
[816] See *Anderson v. Baltrusaitis*, 944 P.2d 797, 799 (1997).
[817] *Vega v. E. Courtyard Assocs.*, 24 P.3d 219, 221 (Nev. 2001).
[818] *Torreabla v. Kesmetis*, 124 Nev. ___, ___, 178 P.3d 716 (2008).
[819] *Ashwood v. Clark County*, 113 Nev. 80, 86, 930 P.2d 740, 744 (1997).

Negligent Entrustment

A theory of liability is that of "negligent entrustment" of a motor vehicle. Under this doctrine, a person who knowingly entrusts a vehicle to an inexperienced or incompetent person, such as a minor child unlicensed to drive a motor vehicle, may be found liable for damages resulting thereby.[820] Under this theory of liability, the entrusting person need not have known that the motor vehicle was going to be driven on a public roadway. In fact, a parent who entrusts his child with a motor vehicle may be found liable under a theory of negligent entrustment even when the parent expressly instructs the child not to use the vehicle on a public roadway.[821] The key elements are whether an entrustment actually occurred, and whether the entrustment was negligent.[822]

Negligent Hiring, Training, Supervision, and Retention

To prevail on a negligence theory, the plaintiff generally must show that: (1) the defendant had a duty to exercise due care towards the plaintiff; (2) the defendant breached the duty; (3) the breach was an actual cause of the plaintiff's injury; (4) the breach was the proximate cause of the injury; and (5) the plaintiff suffered damage.[823]

The tort of negligent hiring imposes a general duty on the employer to conduct a reasonable background check on a potential employee to ensure that the employee is fit for the position.[824] An employer breaches this duty when it hires an employee even though the employer knew, or should have known, of that employee's dangerous propensities.[825] Liability for negligent hiring is predicated on the employer's hiring of a person under circumstances antecedently giving the employer reason to believe that the person, by reason of some attribute of character or prior conduct, would create an undue risk of harm to others in carrying out his or her employment responsibilities.[826] An employer breaches this duty when it hires an employee even though the employer knew, or should have known, of that employee's dangerous propensities.[827]

An employer may be liable to a third person for the employer's negligence in hiring or retaining an employee who is incompetent or unfit.[828] "Liability for negligent hiring . . . is based upon the reasoning that if an enterprise hires individuals with characteristics which might pose a danger to customers or other employees, the enterprise should bear the loss caused by the wrongdoing of its incompetent or unfit employees."[829] An employer is liable for negligence if it "knew or should have known that hiring the employee created a particular risk or hazard and that particular harm materializes."[830] The rule set forth in the RESTATEMENT (SECOND) OF AGENCY § 213 provides in pertinent part as follows: "A person conducting an activity through servants or other agents is subject to liability for harm resulting from his conduct if he is negligent or reckless: . . . [¶] (b) in the employment of improper persons or instrumentalities in work involving risk of harm to others[.]"[831] "Liability for negligent . . . retention of an employee is one of direct liability for negligence, not vicarious liability."[832]

Comment d to § 213 of the RESTATEMENT (SECOND) OF AGENCY explains at pages 459 to 460 as follows:

> The principal may be negligent because he has reason to know that the . . . agent, because of his qualities, is likely to harm others in view of the work or instrumentalities entrusted to him. If the dangerous quality of the agent causes harm, the principal may be liable under the rule that one initiating conduct having an undue tendency to cause harm is liable therefor. [Citation.] [¶] . . . An agent . . . may be incompetent because of his reckless or vicious disposition, and if a principal, without exercising due care in selection, employs a vicious person to do an act which necessarily brings him in contact with others while in the performance of a duty, he is subject to liability for harm caused by the vicious propensity . . . . [¶] One who employs another to act for him is not liable . . . merely because the one employed is incompetent, vicious, or

---

[820] *Zugel v. Miller*, 100 Nev. 525, 528, 688 P.2d 310 (1984). See also *Connell v. Carl's Air Conditioning*, 97 Nev. 436, 634 P.2d 673 (1981) (doctrine of negligent entrustment held not to apply under particular facts of case). See generally 7A Am.Jur.2d Automobiles and Highway Traffic SS 643-45 (1980).

[821] *Id.*

[822] *Zugel v. Miller*, 100 Nev. 525, 528, 688 P.2d 310 (1984).

[823] *Perez v. Las Vegas Medical Center*, 107 Nev. 1, 4, 805 P.2d 589 (1991).

[824] *Hall v. SSF, Inc.*, 112 Nev. 1384, 1392, 930 P.2d 94 (1996).

[825] *Id.*

[826] *Id.*

[827] *Kelley v. Baker Protective Services, Inc.*, 401 S.E.2d 585, 586 (Ga. Ct. App. 1991).

[828] *Roman Catholic Bishop v. Superior Court*, 42 Cal.Ct.App.4th 1556, 1564-1565 (Cal.Ct. App.1996).

[829] *Mendoza v. City of Los Angeles*, supra, 66 Cal.Ct.App.4th at p. 1339.

[830] *Doe v. Capital Cities*, 50 Cal.Ct.App.4th 1038, 1054 (1996).

[831] *Id., Evan F. v. Hughson United Methodist Church*, 8 Cal.Ct.App.4th 828, 836 (1992).

[832] See *Delfino v. Agilent Technologies, Inc.*, 145 Cal.Ct.App.4th 790, 815 (2006).

careless. If liability results it is because, under the circumstances, the employer has not taken the care which a prudent man would take in selecting the person for the business in hand . . . . [¶] Liability results . . . not because of the relation of the parties, but because the employer antecedently had reason to believe that an undue risk of harm would exist because of the employment . . . .

In 2006, the RESTATEMENT (THIRD) OF AGENCY was published, adopting § 7.05 as the counterpart to § 213 of the RESTATEMENT (SECOND) OF AGENCY, and stating:

> (1) A principal who conducts an activity through an agent is subject to liability for harm to a third party caused by the agent's conduct if the harm was caused by the principal's negligence in selecting, training, retaining, supervising, or otherwise controlling the agent . . ..[833]

"Liability under this rule is limited by basic principles of tort law, including requirements of causation and duty."[834] Furthermore, "[l]iability under this rule also requires some nexus or causal connection between the principal's negligence in selecting or controlling an actor, the actor's employment or work, and the harm suffered by the third party."[835] A cause of action for negligent supervision may be stated if the employer knew or should have known facts which would warn a reasonable person that the employee presented an undue risk of harm to third persons in light of the particular work to be performed.[836]

Negligent Infliction of Emotional Distress

Nevada recognizes the tort of negligent infliction of emotional distress.[837] The elements of a claim for negligent infliction of emotional distress are as follows: 1) a duty, 2) a breach of the duty, 3) the conduct caused Plaintiff's emotional distress, and (4) damages suffered from the conduct.[838]

The Nevada Supreme Court generally requires a plaintiff to demonstrate that he or she has suffered some physical manifestation of emotional distress in order to support an award of emotional damages.[839] "Generally, a claim of negligent infliction of emotional distress is inappropriate in the context of a legal malpractice suit when the harm resulted from pecuniary damages, even if the plaintiffs demonstrated physical symptoms."[840] However, "this court [has] recognized the rule that, in special cases involving peculiarity personal subject matters, mental anguish may be a foreseeable damage resulting from breach of contract."[841] Nevada law therefore does not preclude the recovery of emotional distress damages for a special case, such as when harm arises from legal malpractice in a highly personal representation advancing a non-pecuniary interest. While the Nevada Supreme Court has relaxed the physical manifestation requirement in a few limited instances,[842] the Nevada Supreme Court cannot conclude that a claim for emotional distress damages resulting from deceptive trade practices in connection with a failed real estate and lending transaction should be exempted from the physical manifestation requirement.[843]

Unlike in *Olivero*, where the Nevada Supreme Court stated that "the nature of a claim of assault is such that the

---

[833] RESTATEMENT (THIRD) OF AGENCY, § 7.05, p. 177.

[834] *Id.*, com. c, p. 180.

[835] RESTATEMENT (THIRD) OF AGENCY, § 7.05, com. c, illus. 5, p. 180.

[836] *Federico v. Superior Court*, 59 Cal.Ct.App.4th 1207, 1214-1215 (Ca. 1997); *Virginia G. v. ABC Unified School Dist.*, 15 Cal.Ct.App.4th 1848 (Ca. 1993).

[837] *Shoen v. Amerco, Inc.*, 111 Nev. 735, 749, 896 P.2d 469, 477 (1995).

[838] *Foster v. State*, No. CV-N-97-611-DWH (PHA) (D. Nev. August 14, 1998); RESTATEMENT (SECOND) OF TORTS § 313 (1965).

[839] See, *e.g.*, *Barmettler v. Reno Air, Inc.*, 114 Nev. 441, 448, 956 P.2d 1382, 1387 (1998) ("[I]n cases where emotional distress damages are not secondary to physical injuries, but rather, precipitate physical symptoms, either a physical impact must have occurred or, in the absence of physical impact, proof of 'serious emotional distress' causing physical injury or illness must be presented."); *Chowdhry v. NLVH, Inc.*, 109 Nev. 478, 482-83, 851 P.2d 459, 462 (1993).

[840] *Kahn v. Morse & Mowbray*, 121 Nev. 464, 478, 117 P.3d 227, 237 (2005).

[841] *Selsnick v. Horton*, 96 Nev. 944, 946, 620 P.2d 1256, 1257 (1980); see also *Burrus v. Nev.-Cal.-Or. Ry.*, 38 Nev. 156 162, 145 P. 926, 929 (1915) (stating that "[r]ecovery for mental suffering should be limited to special cases").

[842] See *Olivero v. Lowe*, 116 Nev. 395, 400, 995 P.2d 1023, 1026 (2000) (explaining that the physical manifestation requirement is more relaxed for damages claims involving assault).

[843] See *Betsinger v. D.R. Horton, Inc.*, 126 Nev., Advance Opinion 17 (2010).

safeguards against illusory recoveries mentioned in *Barmettler* and *Chowdhry* are not necessary,"[844] there is no guarantee of the legitimacy of a claim for emotional distress damages resulting from a failed real estate and lending transaction without a requirement of some physical manifestation of emotional distress.

But see *Boorman v. Nevada Mem'l Cremation Society*, 126 Nev., Advance Opinion 29 (2010) (close family members who were aware of the death of a loved one and to whom mortuary services were being provided may assert an emotional distress claim for the negligent handling of a deceased person's remains against a mortuary. Those persons do not need to observe or have any sensory perception of the offensive conduct, and do not need to present evidence of any physical manifestation of emotional distress.) Similarly, a nuisance claim seeking only emotional distress damages need to be supported by proof of physical harm.[845]

Negligent Inspection and Maintenance

Circumstantial evidence of a property owner's failure to inspect the premises before an accident is sufficient to infer the risk existed long enough for the property owner, in the exercise of due care, to have discovered and removed it. In other words, a property owner's failure to reasonably inspect can be used to infer constructive knowledge of the dangerous condition, providing a causal link between the accident and the time period between inspections. The determination of what constitutes a reasonable time period between inspections will necessarily vary according to the particular circumstances. For instance, "[a] person operating a grocery and vegetable store in the exercise of ordinary care must exercise a more vigilant outlook than the operator of some other types of business where the danger of things falling to the floor is not so obvious." "Thus, while a 15- to 30- minute interval between inspections at a busy commercial retail center may lead to an inference of negligence, the same inference might not be found elsewhere."[846]

Negligent Misrepresentation

Negligent misrepresentation is defined as follows: "One who, in the course of his business, profession, or employment, or in any other action in which he has a pecuniary interest, supplies false information for the guidance of others in their business transactions, is subject to liability for pecuniary loss caused to them by their justifiable reliance upon the information, if he fails to exercise reasonable care or competence in obtaining or communicating the information."[847]

Nevada Jury Instruction 9.05 sets forth the elements of negligent misrepresentation as follows:

1.   The defendant must have supplied information while in the course of his business, profession or employment, or any other transaction in which he had a pecuniary interest;
2.   The information must have been false;
3.   The information must have been supplied for the guidance of the plaintiff in his business transactions;
4.   The defendant must have failed to exercise reasonable care or competence in obtaining or communicating the information;
5.   The plaintiff must have justifiably relied upon the information by taking action or refraining from it;
6.   And, finally, as a result of his reliance upon the accuracy of the information, the plaintiff must have sustained damage.[848]

Negligent Performance of an Undertaking

The Restatement (Second) of Torts section 324A provides as follows:

---

[844] 116 Nev. at 400, 995 P.2d at 1026.

[845] *Land Baron Investments v. Bonnie Springs Family Limited Partnership*, 131 Nev., Advance Opinion 69 (2015).

[846] *Zipusch v. LA Workout, Inc.*, 66 Cal.Rptr.3d 704, 155 Cal.Ct.App.4th 1281 (Cal.Ct.App. Dist.2 2007) (citations omitted).

[847] *Barmettler v. Reno Air, Inc.*, 114 Nev. 441, 449, 956 P.2d 1381 (1998); see RESTATEMENT (SECOND) OF TORTS § 552.

[848] See *Bill Stremmel Mtrs. v. First Nat'l Bank*, 94 Nev. 131, 575 P.2d 938 (1978); *Eikelberger v. Rogers*, 92 Nev. 282, 549 P.2d 748 (1976).

One who undertakes, gratuitously or for consideration, to render services to another which he should recognize as necessary for the protection of a third person or his things, is subject to liability to the third person for physical harm resulting from his failure to exercise reasonable care to perform his undertaking if
      (a) his failure to exercise reasonable care increases the risk of such harm, or
      (b) he has undertaken to perform a duty owed by the other to the third person, or
      (c) the harm is suffered because of reliance of the other or the third person upon the undertaking.

This section reflects the "Good Samaritan" doctrine. In *Dow Chemical Co. v. Mahlum*,[849] the Mahlums successfully contended that Dow Chemical effectively undertook to test completely and adequately the safety of the liquid silicone used in Dow Corning's breast implants and negligently performed that undertaking.

Negligent Repair and the Deceptive Appearance of Safety

A mechanic will be liable if the mechanic negligently returns a vehicle as repaired or inspected, giving the vehicle a "deceptive appearance of safety" on which the owner relies, when in fact the vehicle is not in a safe condition.[850]

See *Swenson Trucking & Excavating, Inc. v. Truckweld Equipment Co.*, 604 P.2d 1113 (Ak. 1980), where a company inspected a ram assembly and installed it on a truck but failed to discover a defective weld in the assembly. The company returned the truck to the owner as repaired and, about five weeks later, the assembly collapsed, destroying the truck. The court held that the question whether the repair company exercised reasonable care in inspecting and installing the ram assembly was one of fact for the jury to decide.

A mechanic who does not complete a vehicle repair fulfills his duty not to negligently induce reliance on the safety of the vehicle by clearly informing the vehicle owner that the vehicle was not repaired. Even if a mechanic makes clear to the vehicle owner that the vehicle remains unrepaired, the mechanic may still be held liable under the third specific theory of negligence implicated by this case: a mechanic returning an unrepaired vehicle is liable for harm caused by the use of the vehicle if the mechanic fails to exercise reasonable care to warn the owner of any dangerous condition of which he knows or has reason to know unless he has reason to believe that the owner is aware of the dangerous condition.[851]

As a recapper of tires, Johnny Antonelli may have breached a duty in negligence owed to plaintiff's decedent. Johnny Antonelli undertook an obligation to inspect the casings of tires delivered to it by its customers to determine whether the tires were safe and fit for recapping. The fact that an unsafe tire is turned over by a recapper as rebuilt "gives it a deceptive appearance of safety."[852] Hence, even if the unsafe condition is not of the recapper's own making, the recapper owes a duty to use reasonable care not only to inspect the tire for defects, but also to warn intended users of any potential dangers in the use of the tire of which it knows or should know, and which are not obvious to the intended users. In this respect, it is in the same position as a repairer who fails to warn its customers of a dangerous condition which it undertook to repair.[853]

Negligent Security

The totality of circumstances, including evidence of prior general criminal activity on the hotel and casino's premises, raised a material issue of fact as to whether the attacker's attack on a patron was a superseding cause that precluded liability for hotel and casino's alleged negligence in failing to provide additional security. A jury could reasonably decide that a foreseeable risk of harm to patron had been created by allegedly negligent security, such that the

---

[849] *Dow Chemical Co. v. Mahlum*, 114 Nev. 1468, 1492, 970 P.2d 98, 107-08 (1998), overruled in part on other grounds by *GES, Inc. v. Corbitt*, 117 Nev. 265, 270-71, 21 P.3d 11, 14-15 (2001).

[850] *Timothy R. Lindsey v. E&E Automotive & Tire*, No. 6514 (Ak. 2010); RESTATEMENT (SECOND) OF TORTS § 403 cmt. b (1965); *Jewell v. Dell*, 284 S.W.2d 92, 96 (Ky. 1955) ("Actionable negligence of a repairman or serviceman from failure of the mechanism of a motor car upon which he has worked rests in part, at least, upon his assurance–more often implied than expressed–that the machine was safe for operation when in fact it was not"); *Block v. Fitts*, 274 So. 2d 811, 814 (La. Ct.App. 1973) ("If [a repairman] represents to the owner that he has repaired the defect and that the car is safe to drive, and he allows the owner to take and operate the car under that erroneous impression, then we think the repairman's negligence in failing to properly repair the car, coupled with his failure to warn the owner, may be a proximate cause of an accident attributable to that defect").

[851] *Timothy R. Lindsey v. E&E Automotive & Tire*, No. 6514 (Ak. 2010).

[852] RESTATEMENT (SECOND) OF TORTS § 403 comment b.

[853] See *Vermette v. Kenworth Truck Co.*, 111 A.D.2d 448, 488 N.Y.S.2d 507, *rev'd on other grounds*, 68 N.Y.2d 714, 506 N.Y.S.2d 313, 497 N.E.2d 680); *Beasock v. Dioguardi Enterprises*, 499 N.Y.S.2d 558; 117 A.D.2d 1015 (N.Y. 1986).

attacker's attack on patron was within the scope of hotel's initial negligence and would not negate hotel's liability.[854]

NRS 41.141 provides in pertinent part as follows:

> 1. In any action to recover damages for death or injury to persons or for injury to property in which comparative negligence is asserted as a defense, the comparative negligence of the plaintiff or his decedent does not bar a recovery if that negligence was not greater than the negligence or gross negligence of the parties to the action against whom recovery is sought.
> 2. In those cases, the judge shall instruct the jury that:
>> (a) The plaintiff may not recover if his comparative negligence or that of his decedent is greater than the negligence of the defendant or the combined negligence of multiple defendants.

The purpose of the comparative negligence statute is to eradicate the harsh effect of a plaintiff's contributory negligence whenever such negligence is not greater than that of the source against which recovery is sought.[855] See also Nev. J.I. 4.18-4.19.

Where a property owner hires security personnel to protect his or her premises and patrons, that property owner has a personal and non-delegable duty to provide responsible security personnel. Therefore, we conclude as a matter of law that the security personnel are the employees of the property owner, even if the property owner engaged a third party to hire the security personnel. In such a situation, we find an employer-employee relationship without evaluating whether the security personnel were under the control of the property owner, noting that the control analysis is only one of the methods available.

Nuisance

A nuisance is "[a]nything which is injurious to health, or indecent and offensive to the senses, or an obstruction to the free use of property, so as to interfere with the comfortable enjoyment of life or property."[856] A nuisance at law, also called a nuisance per se, is "a nuisance at all times and under any circumstances, regardless of location or surroundings."[857] A nuisance in fact, also[858] called a *nuisance per accidens*, is "one which becomes a nuisance by reasons of circumstances and surroundings."

The determination of whether an activity constitutes a nuisance is generally a question of fact.[859] To sustain a claim for private nuisance, an interference with one's use and enjoyment of land must be both substantial and unreasonable.[860] A nuisance claim seeking only emotional distress damages need not be supported by proof of physical harm.[861]

NRS 40.140, "Nuisance defined; action for abatement and damages; exceptions," provides as follows:

> 1. Except as otherwise provided in this section:
> (a) Anything which is injurious to health, or indecent and offensive to the senses, or an obstruction to the free use of property, so as to interfere with the comfortable enjoyment of life or property;
> (b) A building or place used for the purpose of unlawfully selling, serving, storing, keeping, manufacturing, using or giving away a controlled substance, immediate precursor or controlled substance analog;
> (c) A building or place which was used for the purpose of unlawfully manufacturing a controlled substance, immediate precursor or controlled substance analog and:
>> (1) Which has not been deemed safe for habitation by the board of health; or
>> (2) From which all materials or substances involving the controlled substance, immediate precursor or controlled substance analog have not been removed or remediated by an entity certified or licensed to do so within 180 days after the building or place is no longer used for the purpose of unlawfully

---

[854] *Doud v. Las Vegas Hilton Corp.*, 109 Nev. 1096, 864 P.2d 796 (1993).

[855] *Id.* at 190.

[856] NRS 40.140(1)(a).

[857] *Sowers v. Forest Hills Subdivision*, 129 Nev., Advance Opinion 9, p. 5 (Feb. 14, 2013); see 66 C.J.S. Nuisances § 4 (2013).

[858] *Id.*

[859] *Sowers*, supra, p. 7.

[860] *Id.*, citing *Lied v. County of Clark*, 94 Nev. 275, 278, 579 P.2d 171, 173 (1978).

[861] *Land Baron Investments v. Bonnie Springs Family Limited Partnership*, 131 Nev., Advance Opinion 69 (2015).

manufacturing a controlled substance, immediate precursor or controlled substance analog; or

(d) A building or place regularly and continuously used by the members of a criminal gang to engage in, or facilitate the commission of, crimes by the criminal gang,

Ê is a nuisance, and the subject of an action. The action may be brought by any person whose property is injuriously affected, or whose personal enjoyment is lessened by the nuisance, and by the judgment the nuisance may be enjoined or abated, as well as damages recovered.

2. It is presumed:

(a) That an agricultural activity conducted on farmland, consistent with good agricultural practice and established before surrounding nonagricultural activities is reasonable. Such activity does not constitute a nuisance unless the activity has a substantial adverse effect on the public health or safety.

(b) That an agricultural activity which does not violate a federal, state or local law, ordinance or regulation constitutes good agricultural practice.

3. A shooting range does not constitute a nuisance with respect to any noise attributable to the shooting range if the shooting range is in compliance with the provisions of all applicable statutes, ordinances and regulations concerning noise:

(a) As those provisions existed on October 1, 1997, for a shooting range in operation on or before October 1, 1997; or

(b) As those provisions exist on the date that the shooting range begins operation, for a shooting range that begins operation after October 1, 1997.

Ê A shooting range is not subject to any state or local law related to the control of noise that is adopted or amended after the date set forth in paragraph (a) or (b), as applicable, and does not constitute a nuisance for failure to comply with any such law.

4. As used in this section:

(a) "Board of health" has the meaning ascribed to it in NRS 439.4797.

(b) "Controlled substance analog" has the meaning ascribed to it in NRS 453.043.

(c) "Criminal gang" has the meaning ascribed to it in NRS 193.168.

(d) "Immediate precursor" has the meaning ascribed to it in NRS 453.086.

(e) "Shooting range" means an area designed and used for archery or sport shooting, including, but not limited to, sport shooting that involves the use of rifles, shotguns, pistols, silhouettes, skeet, trap, black powder or other similar items.

Facts showing special injury must be pleaded. A private person may not maintain an action to abate a public nuisance pursuant to BH § 3273 (cf. NRS 40.140) in the absence of a clear showing that he has sustained, or will sustain, a special and peculiar injury, irreparable in its nature, and different in kind from that sustained by the general public. A mere difference in the degree of injury suffered is not sufficient to confer a right of action. Facts showing such special injury must be specially pleaded.[862]

Both injury and damage may exist as a result of an act not recognizable as a nuisance. Sec. 251, ch. 112, Stats. 1869 (cf. NRS 40.140), adopts the common-law rule that anything which constitutes an unreasonable obstruction to the free use of property is an actionable nuisance, and, while injury and damage are essential elements of a nuisance, both may exist as a result of an act which the law will not recognize as a nuisance because such an act is a reasonable use of property.[863]

Use of certain ditch a nuisance and owner restrained from use until the boxes were restored. Where the owner of an easement for an irrigation ditch widened and deepened the ditch over the protest of the owner of a servient tenement, and the increased flow endangered the home of the latter unless the ditch was boxed up, the use of the ditch in an open condition was a nuisance under sec. 251, ch. 112, Stats. 1869 (cf. NRS 40.140), and the owner of the easement, who had the duty to place the boxes and keep them in repair, was restrained from flowing water in the ditch until she restored the boxes she had removed therefrom after their deterioration.[864]   Duty of board of county commissioners to abate nuisances not supplanted by charter power of a city to regulate houses of ill fame. The charter power of a city to regulate, prohibit, and prescribe the location of and suppress all houses of ill fame did not supplant the authority and duty of a board of county commissioners, under NCL § 2043 (cf. NRS 244.360), which provides for the abatement of nuisances defined in NCL § 9051 (cf. NRS 40.140), to institute and maintain abatement proceedings against the plaintiffs

---

[862] *Fogg v. Nevada-Cal.-Ore. Ry.*, 20 Nev. 429, 23 Pac. 840 (1890), cited, *Blanding v. City of Las Vegas*, 52 Nev. 52, at 70, 280 Pac. 644 (1929), *Holcomb Constr. Co. v. Armstrong*, 590 F.2d 811, at 813 (9th Cir. 1979) (dissenting opinion), distinguished, *City of Las Vegas v. Cragin Indus., Inc.*, 86 Nev. 933, at 939, 478 P.2d 585 (1970).

[863] *Bliss v. Grayson*, 24 Nev. 422, 56 Pac. 231 (1899).

[864] *Thomas v. Blaisdell*, 25 Nev. 223, 58 Pac. 903 (1899), cited, *Czipott v. Fleigh*, 87 Nev. 496, at 499, 489 P.2d 681 (1971).

for maintaining a bawdyhouse within 400 yards of a church in violation of NCL § 10193 (cf. NRS 201.380 and NRS 201.390).[865]

Allegations of violations of criminal statutes are irrelevant. In an action to enjoin the operation of a house of prostitution under NCL § 2043 (cf. NRS 244.360), providing for the abatement of nuisances by county commissioners, allegations of a violation of criminal statutes were irrelevant, because the action was limited to the abatement of a nuisance as defined in NCL § 9051 (cf. NRS 40.140).[866]

Criminal statutes merely recognized the deleterious tendency of the operation of a house of prostitution. In an action to enjoin the operation of a house of prostitution, where NCL § 9051 (cf. NRS 40.140) defined nuisance as anything injurious to health, or indecent and offensive to the senses, or an obstruction to the free use of property, operation of such a house was a nuisance, and statutes making it also a misdemeanor under certain circumstances merely recognized its deleterious tendency.[867]

Operation of house of prostitution in unincorporated area of county not a nuisance per se. A house of prostitution in an unincorporated area of a county was not a nuisance per se within the meaning of NRS 40.140 and was not subject to abatement by the board of county commissioners pursuant to NRS 244.360 because a provision of NRS 244.345, which prohibits licensing of houses of prostitution in counties having a population of 200,000 or more, when read in conjunction with a requirement in the same section that places of amusement, entertainment or recreation be licensed, manifests a statutory licensing scheme for houses of prostitution which is repugnant to and, by plain and necessary implication, repeals the common-law rule that a house of prostitution constitutes a nuisance per se.[868]

Under facts in case plaintiff stated claim for relief for special injury. In a civil action based upon the "Nevada Public Nuisance Law" (see NRS 40.140) an allegation that the defendant negligently rendered a bridge unusable which the plaintiff would have used in a performing contract to build a new bridge stated a claim for relief for special injury distinct from the public generally.[869]

Exceptionally sensitive plaintiff cannot recover for a nuisance which does not cause significant harm to a normal person in the community. In an action to abate a nuisance (see NRS 40.140), where only one of several plaintiffs testified that the noise generated by the defendant's geothermal power plant substantially and unreasonably interfered with his enjoyment of his property, and other plaintiffs conceded that the noise from the plant had not been a substantial problem, a summary judgment was granted for the defendant because exceptionally sensitive plaintiffs cannot recover for a nuisance which does not cause significant harm, of a kind that would be suffered by a normal person in the community.[870]

The development of property in the Lake Tahoe Basin was not a nuisance. Where the Tahoe Regional Planning Agency, pursuant to the Tahoe Regional Planning Compact (see NRS 277.200), prohibited the development of certain property in the Lake Tahoe Basin in order to prevent the pollution of Lake Tahoe from the resulting erosion runoff, the agency was not exempt from paying just compensation for the denial of the use of the property required by the U.S. 5th amendment (see also Nev. Art. 1, § 8) on the ground that the uses that were prohibited constituted nuisances that could be restricted without the need for just compensation because: (1) the development of the property was not a nuisance under common law (see NRS 40.140) as the eutrophication of Lake Tahoe was not a health hazard or otherwise indecent or offensive; and (2) the Nevada Water Pollution Control Law (see NRS 445A.300 et seq.) did not prohibit such development as the definitions of "contaminant" (see NRS 445A.325) and "pollutant" (see NRS 445A.400) did not encompass the erosion runoff that was intended to be prevented.[871]

ATTORNEY GENERAL'S OPINIONS.

A house of prostitution constitutes a public nuisance. Statutes regulating the location of houses of prostitution do not repeal the common-law rule that such houses, wherever located, constitute a public nuisance. Thus, it is

---

[865] *Kelley v. Clark County*, 61 Nev. 293, 127 P.2d 221 (1942), cited, *Cunningham v. Washoe County*, 66 Nev. 60, at 65, 203 P.2d 611 (1949), distinguished, *Kuban v. McGimsey*, 96 Nev. 105, at 110, 605 P.2d 623 (1980).

[866] *Cunningham v. Washoe County*, 66 Nev. 60, 203 P.2d 611 (1949), cited, *Nye County v. Plankinton*, 94 Nev. 739, at 740, 587 P.2d 421 (1978).

[867] *Cunningham v. Washoe County*, 66 Nev. 60, 203 P.2d 611 (1949), distinguished, *Nye County v. Plankinton*, 94 Nev. 739, at 741, 587 P.2d 421 (1978), *Kuban v. McGimsey*, 96 Nev. 105, at 109, 605 P.2d 623 (1980).

[868] *Nye County v. Plankinton*, 94 Nev. 739, 587 P.2d 421 (1978), cited, *Kuban v. McGimsey*, 96 Nev. 105, at 109, 605 P.2d 623 (1980), *Princess Sea Indus., Inc. v. State*, 97 Nev. 534, at 537, 635 P.2d 281 (1981), AGO 96-01 (2-7-1996).

[869] *Holcomb Constr. Co. v. Armstrong*, 590 F.2d 811 (9th Cir. 1979).

[870] *Layton v. Yankee Caithness Joint Venture*, L.P., 774 F. Supp. 576 (D. Nev. 1991).

[871] *Tahoe-Sierra Preservation Council, Inc. v. Tahoe Regional Planning Agency*, 34 F. Supp. 2d 1226 (D. Nev. 1999).

mandatory, under the law requiring county commissioners to abate nuisances, that the commissioners abate disorderly houses within the county.[872]

A county may not declare livestock grazing on the open range to be a public nuisance. Although a county, pursuant to NRS 244.360, is authorized to abate a public nuisance and by resolution to declare an activity to be a public nuisance if it comes within the definition set forth in NRS 40.140, a county may not, absent a legal prohibition against livestock grazing on the open range, declare such activity to be a public nuisance, because nothing which the law itself authorizes may be declared a public nuisance. Since Nevada law clearly recognizes the use of the open range as a part of the custom in this state with regard to livestock, any effort to declare such activity a public nuisance is irreconcilable with the stated legislative support for the livestock industry.[873]

Nuisance liability arises where conduct which violates a duty that one owes to another also interferes with the party's free use and enjoyment of his property. An action for nuisance "may be brought by any person whose property is injuriously affected, or whose personal enjoyment is lessened by the nuisance, and by the judgment the nuisance may be enjoined or abated, as well as damages recovered."[874] Interference is substantial if normal persons living in the community would regard the [alleged nuisance] as definitively offensive, seriously annoying or intolerable.[875] Interference is unreasonable when the gravity of the harm outweighs the social value of the activity alleged to cause the harm.[876]

For example, the operation of a cattle feeding lot with its accompanying odors and flies, was a nuisance to the residents of neighboring community.[877] Spur Industries ran a cattle feedlot that was originally in a rural area. Spur started operations in 1956, but people had been raising cattle in the area since at least 1911. Over time, nearby cities grew and people started moving closer and closer to the feedlot. In 1959, the Sun City housing development was built by Webb. Webb sued Spur because the smell from the feedlots was a nuisance to the residents of the houses he built. The trial Court found for Webb, finding that Spur's operation was an enjoinable public nuisance.

The appellate court affirmed in part and reversed in part. In general, the courts have held that if a homeowner or business enters an area reserved for industrial or agricultural use and is damaged by a nuisance, the homeowner or business cannot obtain relief due to the doctrine of coming to the nuisance. Here, Webb could not obtain relief based on Spur being a private nuisance. But courts have also held that a company such as Spur can be required to move–not because of any wrongdoing on the part of the company, but because of a proper and legitimate regard for the rights and the interest of the public.

Basically, Sun City could obtain relief on the basis of Spur being a public nuisance. However, since Webb brought the city to Spur, Webb was responsible for the nuisance. Therefore, since Webb caused the foreseeable detriment of Spur, Webb had to pay a reasonable amount of the costs to relocate Spur's business. This case also explained the difference between a private nuisance that annoys a particular landowner, and a public nuisance that annoys the general public at large. There are different standards for relief, depending on which nuisance you are causing. Spur was both a private and a public nuisance.

For conduct to constitute an actionable nuisance, it must operate "as an obstruction or injury to the right of another" and "interfere with the use and enjoyment of land."[878] A property owner in a residential district was afforded procedural due process with respect to the county's decision to remove inoperable automobiles or vehicles from his property as part of nuisance abatement, despite his argument that the terms "inoperative automobile" and "inoperative vehicle" were impermissibly vague. The notices from the county made owner aware that the abatement would include such items, and the owner neglected to challenge the county's decision through available administrative remedies, waiting instead until the items were removed and taken to a landfill to file the court action.[879]

---

[872] AGO 14 (1-31-1951), but see *Nye County v. Plankinton*, 94 Nev. 739, 587 P.2d 421 (1978).

[873] (See NRS 568.300.) AGO 98-22 (8-7-1998).

[874] NRS 40.140; see *Culley v. Elko County*, 101 Nev. 838, 711 P.2d 864 (1985) (use of an extended airport runway was a nuisance in that it created noise, dust, fumes and vibration which interfered with surrounding properties).

[875] *Sowers*, supra, p. 7 (citations omitted).

[876] *Id.* (citation omitted).

[877] *Spur Industries, Inc. v. Del E. Webb Development Co.*, 494 P.2d 700 (Az. 1972).

[878] *Jezowski v. City of Reno*, 71 Nev. 233, 241, 286 P.2d 257 (1955).

[879] *Ransdell v. Clark County*, 124 Nev. 847, 860, 192 P.3d 756 (2008).

United States Patent and Trademark Office
Alexandria, Virginia

Nondisclosure

Nondisclosure arises where a seller is aware of materially adverse facts that could not be discovered by the buyer after diligent inquiry.[880] When the defect is patent and obvious, and when the buyer and seller have equal opportunities of knowledge, a seller cannot be liable for nondisclosure.[881] Liability for nondisclosure is generally not imposed where the buyer either knew of or could have discovered the defects prior to the purchase.[882]

Patent Infringement

Patent infringement is covered by 35 U.S.C. § 271 as follows:

(a) Except as otherwise provided in this title, whoever without authority makes, uses, offers to sell, or sells any patented invention, within the United States, or imports into the United States any patented invention during the term of the patent therefor, infringes the patent.

(b) Whoever actively induces infringement of a patent shall be liable as an infringer.

(c) Whoever offers to sell or sells within the United States or imports into the United States a component of a patented machine, manufacture, combination, or composition, or a material or apparatus for use in practicing a patented process, constituting a material part of the invention, knowing the same to be especially made or especially adapted for use in an infringement of such patent, and not a staple article or commodity of commerce suitable for substantial noninfringing use, shall be liable as a contributory infringer.

(d) No patent owner otherwise entitled to relief for infringement or contributory infringement of a patent shall be denied relief or deemed guilty of misuse or illegal extension of the patent right by reason of his having done one or more of the following: (1) derived revenue from acts which if performed by another without his consent would constitute contributory infringement of the patent; (2) licensed or authorized another to perform acts which if performed without his consent would constitute contributory infringement of the patent; (3) sought to enforce his patent rights against infringement or contributory infringement; (4) refused to license or use any rights to the patent; or (5) conditioned the license of any rights to the patent or the sale of the patented product on the acquisition of a license to rights in another patent or purchase of a separate product, unless, in view of the circumstances, the patent owner has market power in the relevant market for the patent or patented product on which the license or sale is conditioned.

(e)

(1) It shall not be an act of infringement to make, use, offer to sell, or sell within the United States or import into the United States a patented invention (other than a new animal drug or veterinary biological product (as those terms are used in the Federal Food, Drug, and Cosmetic Act and the Act of March 4, 1913)

---

[880] *Land Baron Investments v. Bonnie Springs Family Limited Partnership*, 131 Nev., Advance Opinion 69 at 12 (2015).

[881] *Id.*

[882] *Id.*

which is primarily manufactured using recombinant DNA, recombinant RNA, hybridoma technology, or other processes involving site specific genetic manipulation techniques) solely for uses reasonably related to the development and submission of information under a Federal law which regulates the manufacture, use, or sale of drugs or veterinary biological products.

(2) It shall be an act of infringement to submit—

(A) an application under section 505(j) of the Federal Food, Drug, and Cosmetic Act or described in section 505(b)(2) of such Act for a drug claimed in a patent or the use of which is claimed in a patent, or

(B) an application under section 512 of such Act or under the Act of March 4, 1913 (21 U.S.C. §§ 151-158) for a drug or veterinary biological product which is not primarily manufactured using recombinant DNA, recombinant RNA, hybridoma technology, or other processes involving site specific genetic manipulation techniques and which is claimed in a patent or the use of which is claimed in a patent, if the purpose of such submission is to obtain approval under such Act to engage in the commercial manufacture, use, or sale of a drug or veterinary biological product claimed in a patent or the use of which is claimed in a patent before the expiration of such patent.

(3) In any action for patent infringement brought under this section, no injunctive or other relief may be granted which would prohibit the making, using, offering to sell, or selling within the United States or importing into the United States of a patented invention under paragraph (1).

(4) For an act of infringement described in paragraph (2)—

(A) the court shall order the effective date of any approval of the drug or veterinary biological product involved in the infringement to be a date which is not earlier than the date of the expiration of the patent which has been infringed,

(B) injunctive relief may be granted against an infringer to prevent the commercial manufacture, use, offer to sell, or sale within the United States or importation into the United States of an approved drug or veterinary biological product, and

(C) damages or other monetary relief may be awarded against an infringer only if there has been commercial manufacture, use, offer to sell, or sale within the United States or importation into the United States of an approved drug or veterinary biological product. The remedies prescribed by subparagraphs (A), (B), and (C) are the only remedies which may be granted by a court for an act of infringement described in paragraph (2), except that a court may award attorney fees under section 285.

(5) Where a person has filed an application described in paragraph (2) that includes a certification under subsection (b)(2)(A)(iv) or (j)(2)(A)(vii)(IV) of section 505 of the Federal Food, Drug, and Cosmetic Act (21 U.S.C. § 355), and neither the owner of the patent that is the subject of the certification nor the holder of the approved application under subsection (b) of such section for the drug that is claimed by the patent or a use of which is claimed by the patent brought an action for infringement of such patent before the expiration of 45 days after the date on which the notice given under subsection (b)(3) or (j)(2)(B) of such section was received, the courts of the United States shall, to the extent consistent with the Constitution, have subject matter jurisdiction in any action brought by such person under section 2201 of title 28 for a declaratory judgment that such patent is invalid or not infringed.

(f)

(1) Whoever without authority supplies or causes to be supplied in or from the United States all or a substantial portion of the components of a patented invention, where such components are uncombined in whole or in part, in such manner as to actively induce the combination of such components outside of the United States in a manner that would infringe the patent if such combination occurred within the United States, shall be liable as an infringer.

(2) Whoever without authority supplies or causes to be supplied in or from the United States any

161

component of a patented invention that is especially made or especially adapted for use in the invention and not a staple article or commodity of commerce suitable for substantial noninfringing use, where such component is uncombined in whole or in part, knowing that such component is so made or adapted and intending that such component will be combined outside of the United States in a manner that would infringe the patent if such combination occurred within the United States, shall be liable as an infringer.

(g) Whoever without authority imports into the United States or offers to sell, sells, or uses within the United States a product which is made by a process patented in the United States shall be liable as an infringer, if the importation, offer to sell, sale, or use of the product occurs during the term of such process patent. In an action for infringement of a process patent, no remedy may be granted for infringement on account of the noncommercial use or retail sale of a product unless there is no adequate remedy under this title for infringement on account of the importation or other use, offer to sell, or sale of that product. A product which is made by a patented process will, for purposes of this title, not be considered to be so made after −

(1) it is materially changed by subsequent processes; or

(2) it becomes a trivial and nonessential component of another product.

(h) As used in this section, the term "whoever" includes any State, any instrumentality of a State, any officer or employee of a State or instrumentality of a State acting in his official capacity. Any State, and any such instrumentality, officer, or employee, shall be subject to the provisions of this title in the same manner and to the same extent as any nongovernmental entity.

(i) As used in this section, an "offer for sale" or an "offer to sell" by a person other than the patentee or any assignee of the patentee, is that in which the sale will occur before the expiration of the term of the patent.

Prima Facie Tort

To prevail at common law on a theory of prima facie tort, a plaintiff must show that the defendant's conduct was "generally culpable and not justified under the circumstances."[883] A "prima facie tort" is discussed in two footnotes in one Nevada case.[884]

Product Liability or Strict Product Liability

The whole idea behind strict tort liability is that the manufacturer, not the consumer, should bear the responsibility for injuries, even when the product is ostensibly properly prepared and marketed and when the plaintiff is not in a position to prove the origin of the defect.[885]

The RESTATEMENT (SECOND) OF TORTS § 402A governs strict product liability.[886] The RESTATEMENT (SECOND) OF TORTS § 402A (1965) provides as follows:

(1) One who sells any product in a defective condition unreasonably dangerous to the user or consumer or to his property is subject to liability for physical harm thereby caused to the ultimate user or consumer, or to his property, if

(a) the seller is engaged in the business of selling such a product, and
(b) it is expected to and does reach the user or consumer without substantial change in the condition in which it is sold.

(2) The rule stated in Subsection (1) applies although:

(a) the seller has exercised all possible care in the preparation and sale of his product, and
(b) the user or consumer has not bought the product from or entered into any contractual relation with the seller.

---

[883] *National Ass'n of Prof'l Baseball Leagues, Inc. v. Very Minor Leagues, Inc.*, 223 F.3d 1143, 1151 (10th Cir. 2000) (citing RESTATEMENT (SECOND) OF TORTS § 870)).

[884] *Powers v. United Servs. Auto. Ass'n*, 114 Nev. 690, 734, fn. 15 and fn. 16, 962 P.2d 596 (1998).

[885] See *Stackiewicz v. Nissan Motors Corp.*, 100 Nev. 443, 686 P.2d 925 (1984).

[886] *Rivera v. Philip Morris, Inc.*, 125 Nev., Advance Opinion 181, 209 P.3d 271 (2009).

Comment k, § 402A, RESTATEMENT (SECOND) OF TORTS (1965) provides as follows:

> k. Unavoidably unsafe products. There are some products which, in the present state of human knowledge, are quite incapable of being made safe for their intended and ordinary use. These are especially common in the field of drugs. An outstanding example is the vaccine for the Pasteur treatment of rabies, which not uncommonly leads to very serious and damaging consequences when it is injected. Since the disease itself invariably leads to a dreadful death, both the marketing and the use of the vaccine are fully justified, notwithstanding the unavoidable high degree of risk which they involve. Such a product, properly prepared, and accompanied by proper directions and warning, is not defective, nor is it unreasonably dangerous. The same is true of many other drugs, vaccines, and the like, many of which for this very reason cannot legally be sold except to physicians, or under the prescription of a physician. It is also true in particular of many new or experimental drugs as to which, because of lack of time and opportunity for sufficient medical experience, there can be no assurance of safety, or perhaps even of purity of ingredients, but such experience as there is justifies the marketing and use of the drug notwithstanding a medically recognizable risk. The seller of such products, again with the qualification that they are properly prepared and marketed, and proper warning is given, where the situation calls for it, is not to be held to strict liability for unfortunate consequences attending their use, merely because he [or she] has undertaken to supply the public with an apparently useful and desirable product, attended with a known but apparently reasonable risk.[887]

The Nevada Supreme Court has recognized that alternative safer designs are a factor in determining the existence of a design defect.[888]

In *Allison v. Merck and Company*,[889] the Nevada Supreme Court concluded that a drug manufacturer will be liable if it fails to market a vaccine with a proper warning.[890] In so determining, this court cited the RESTATEMENT (SECOND) OF TORTS section 402A, comment j.[891] The Nevada Supreme Court noted that comment j was consistent with their conclusion that a fact-finder could conclude from the evidence that the manufacturer was liable for "underwarning" the product.[892]

In *Michaels v. Pentair Water Pool and Spa*,[893] the Court of Appeals of the State of Nevada summarized the law of products liability as set forth below.

In Nevada, a manufacturer or distributor of a product is strictly liable for injuries resulting from a defect in the product that was present when the product left its hands.[894] "[P]roducts are defective which are dangerous because they fail to perform in the manner reasonably to be expected in light of their nature and intended function."[895] "Reasonableness" may be determined with reference to such things as whether a safer design was possible or feasible, whether safer alternatives are commercially available, and other factors.[896]

Furthermore, manufacturers are not necessarily liable for injuries caused by a product that was substantially modified or misused by the consumer or by an intermediary. "Generally, a substantial alteration will shield a manufacturer from liability for injury that results from that alteration," but a product manufacturer remains liable if the alterations was insubstantial, foreseeable, or did not actually cause the injury.[897]

When the risk of danger associated with a product is such that it cannot be corrected or mitigated by a commercially feasible change in the product's design available at the time the product was placed in the stream of commerce, the manufacturer must give adequate warning to consumers of potential danger.[898] Where a plaintiff alleges that such warnings were not adequately given, the "plaintiff carries the burden of proving, in part, that the inadequate

---

[887] See *Allison v. Merck and Company*, 110 Nev. 762, 769-70 (1994).

[888] *McCourt v. J.C. Penney Co.*, 103 Nev. 101, 734 P.2d 696 (1987).

[889] 110 Nev. 762, 878 P.2d 948 (1994).

[890] *Id.* at 774, 878 P.2d at 956.

[891] See *id.* at 774 n.12, 878 P.2d at 956 n.12.

[892] *Id.*

[893] 131 Nev. Advance Opinion 81, 18-19 and fn. 8(Ct. App. 2015).

[894] *Allison v. Merck & Co., Inc.*, 110 Nev. 762, 767, 878 P.2d 948, 952 (1994).

[895] *Ginnis v. Mapes Hotel Corp.*, 86 Nev. 408, 413, 470 P.2d 135, 138 (1970) (internal quotations omitted).

[896] See *McCourt v. J.C. Penney Co., Inc.*, 103 Nev. 101, 104, 734 P.2d 696, 698 (1987) (stating that "[a]lternative design is one factor for the jury to consider when evaluating whether a product is unreasonably dangerous").

[897] *Robinson v. G.G.C., Inc.*, 107 Nev. 135, 140, 808 P.2d 522, 525 (1991).

[898] See *id.* at 138, 808 P.2d at 524.

warning caused his injuries."[899]

Because products liability claims allege strict liability, comparative negligence is not a defense to a prima facie case of such liability.[900]

Professional Negligence

Under Nevada law, to establish a claim for professional negligence, a plaintiff must show: (1) the defendant had a duty to use the skill, prudence, and diligence as other members of the profession commonly possess and exercise; (2) the defendant breached that duty; (3) the breach proximately caused the resulting injury; and (4) actual loss or damage resulting from the professional's negligence. Similarly, a showing of negligence requires plaintiff to show duty, breach, causation, and damages. "Proximate cause, or legal cause, consists of two components: cause in fact and foreseeability." Cause in fact requires a showing that the defendant's negligence was a "substantial factor" in bringing about plaintiff's injury. Foreseeability is a "policy concern" that limits a defendant's liability to only those harms with a reasonably close connection to its breach.

Promissory Estoppel

The doctrine of promissory estoppel applies whenever "unconscionable injury . . . would result from denying enforcement of the contract after one party has been induced by the other seriously to change his position in reliance on the contract. . . ."[901] Detrimental reliance sufficient to create an estoppel does not necessarily require a showing of financial or pecuniary loss. By merely abandoning his home and moving to the land of another in reliance upon the promise that the land will someday belong to him, a person can incur detriment.[902]

Promissory estoppel can be used as a "consideration substitute" to support the release of liability under a guaranty contract.[903] "To establish promissory estoppel four elements must exist: (1) the party to be estopped must be apprised of the true facts; (2) he must intend that his conduct shall be acted upon, or must so act that the party asserting estoppel has the right to believe it was so intended; (3) the party asserting the estoppel must be ignorant of the true state of facts; (4) he must have relied to his detriment on the conduct of the party to be estopped."[904]

Normally, a cause of action will not be supported by a mere promise of future conduct.[905] The promise giving rise to a cause of action for promissory estoppel must be clear and definite, unambiguous as to essential terms, and the promise must be made in a contractual sense.[906] A promisor will only be liable for conduct intended to induce reliance on a promise "if the action induced amounts to a substantial change of position."[907] "There can be no promissory estoppel where complainant's act is caused by his or her own mistake in judgment."[908]

Broadly speaking, Nevada follows the doctrine of promissory estoppel articulated in the RESTATEMENT (SECOND) OF CONTRACTS.[909] The RESTATEMENT describes promissory estoppel as follows:

> A promise which the promisor should reasonably expect to induce action or forbearance on the part of the promisee or a third person and which does induce such action or forbearance is binding if injustice can be avoided only by enforcement of the promise. The remedy granted for breach may be limited as justice requires.[910]

---

[899] *Rivera v. Phillip Morris, Inc.*, 125 Nev. 185, 190, 209 P.3d 271, 274 (2009).

[900] *Maduike v. Agency Rent-a-Car*, 114 Nev. 1, 7, 953 P.2d 24, 27 (1998) ("[C]omparative negligence reductions do not apply when the claim is based on strict liability.").

[901] *Monarco v. Lo Greco*, 220 P.2d 737, 739 (Cal. 1950).

[902] *Alpark Distributing, Inc. v. Poole*, 95 Nev. 605, 608, 600 P.2d 229 (1979).

[903] See *Tally v. Atlanta Nat. Real Estate Trust*, 246 S.E.2d 700 (Ga. Ct.App. 1978).

[904] *Cheqer* [sic]*, Inc. v. Painters & Decorators Joint Committee, Inc.*, 98 Nev. 609, 614, 655 P.2d 996, 998-999 (1982); see *Pink v. Busch*, 100 Nev. 684, 691 P.2d 456 (1984); see also *Dynalectric Company v. Clark & Sullivan*, 127 Nev. Adv. Op. No. 41 (2011) and *Torres v. Nevada Direct Insurance Company*, 131 Nev., Advance Opinion 54 (2015).

[905] *Torres v. Nevada Direct Insurance Company*, 131 Nev., Advance Opinion 54, pp. 12-13 (2015), citing 31 C.J.S. *Estoppel and Waiver* Section § 116 (2008).

[906] *Id.*, cited in *Torres*, supra, at 13.

[907] *Torres v. Nevada Direct Insurance Company*, 131 Nev., Advance Opinion 54 at 14 (2015), citing 28 Am Jur. 2d *Estoppel and Waiver* § 51 (2011) and *American Savings & Loan Ass'n v. Stanton-Cudahy Lumber Co.*, 85 Nev. 350, 354, 455 P.2d 39, 41-42 (1969).

[908] *Torres v. Nevada Direct Insurance Company*, 131 Nev., Advance Opinion 54 at 14 (2015), quoting 31 C.J.S. *Estoppel and Waiver* § 116 (2008).

[909] See *Vancheri v. GNLV Corp.*, 105 Nev. 417, 421, 777 P.2d 366, 369 (1989).

[910] RESTATEMENT (SECOND) OF CONTRACTS § 90(1) (1981).

Comment d elaborates further upon the remedies available for promissory estoppel as follows:

> A promise binding under this section is a contract, and full-scale enforcement by normal remedies is often appropriate. But the same factors which bear on whether any relief should be granted also bear on the character and extent of the remedy. In particular, relief may sometimes be limited to restitution or to damages or specific relief measured by the extent of the promisee's reliance rather than by the terms of the promise.[911]

Thus, under the RESTATEMENT, an award of expectation damages is often an appropriate remedy for promissory estoppel claims. But, in other instances, reliance damages or restitutionary damages may be more suitable. Following the lead of the RESTATEMENT, the Nevada Supreme Court has held that the district court may award expectation, reliance, or restitutionary damages for promissory estoppel claims. Although the doctrine of promissory estoppel is conceptually distinct from traditional contract principles, there is no rational reason for distinguishing the two situations in terms of the damages that may be recovered.[912] In sum, no single measure of damages will apply to each and every promissory estoppel claim; instead, to determine the appropriate measure of damages for promissory estoppel claims, the district court should consider the measure of damages that justice requires and that comports with the RESTATEMENT's general requirements that damages be foreseeable and reasonably certain.[913]

Punitive Damages

A common pleading for punitive damages states as follows: "Defendant has been guilty of oppression, fraud or malice, express or implied. Plaintiff, in addition to the compensatory damages, should recover damages for the sake of example and by way of punishing the defendant." NRS 42.005, "Exemplary and punitive damages: In general; limitations on amount of award; determination in subsequent proceeding," provides as follows:

> 1. Except as otherwise provided in NRS 42.007, in an action for the breach of an obligation not arising from contract, where it is proven by clear and convincing evidence that the defendant has been guilty of oppression, fraud or malice, express or implied, the plaintiff, in addition to the compensatory damages, may recover damages for the sake of example and by way of punishing the defendant. Except as otherwise provided in this section or by specific statute, an award of exemplary or punitive damages made pursuant to this section may not exceed:
>
> (a) Three times the amount of compensatory damages awarded to the plaintiff if the amount of compensatory damages is $100,000 or more; or
> (b) Three hundred thousand dollars if the amount of compensatory damages awarded to the plaintiff is less than $100,000.
> 2. The limitations on the amount of an award of exemplary or punitive damages prescribed in subsection 1 do not apply to an action brought against:
> (a) A manufacturer, distributor or seller of a defective product;
> (b) An insurer who acts in bad faith regarding its obligations to provide insurance coverage;
> (c) A person for violating a state or federal law prohibiting discriminatory housing practices, if the law provides for a remedy of exemplary or punitive damages in excess of the limitations prescribed in subsection 1;
> (d) A person for damages or an injury caused by the emission, disposal or spilling of a toxic, radioactive or hazardous material or waste; or
> (e) A person for defamation.
>
> 3. If punitive damages are claimed pursuant to this section, the trier of fact shall make a finding of whether such damages will be assessed. If such damages are to be assessed, a subsequent proceeding must be conducted before the same trier of fact to determine the amount of such damages to be assessed. The trier of fact shall make a finding of the amount to be assessed according to the provisions of this section. The findings required by this section, if made by a jury, must be made by special verdict along with any other required findings. The

---

[911] *Id.* § 90 cmt. d.

[912] See *Dynalectric Company v. Clark & Sullivan*, 17 Nev. Adv. Op. No. 41, 255 P.3d 286 (2011).

[913] See RESTATEMENT (SECOND) OF CONTRACTS §§ 351, 352 (1981); *Dynalectric Company v. Clark & Sullivan*, 17 Nev. Adv. Op. No. 41, 255 P.3d 286 (2011).

jury must not be instructed, or otherwise advised, of the limitations on the amount of an award of punitive damages prescribed in subsection 1.

4. Evidence of the financial condition of the defendant is not admissible for the purpose of determining the amount of punitive damages to be assessed until the commencement of the subsequent proceeding to determine the amount of exemplary or punitive damages to be assessed.

5. For the purposes of an action brought against an insurer who acts in bad faith regarding its obligations to provide insurance coverage, the definitions set forth in NRS 42.001 are not applicable and the corresponding provisions of the common law apply.

Enacted in 1995, NRS 42.007 was intended to limit employers' pure vicarious liability for the wrongful acts of employees committed within the scope of employment. Under NRS 42.007's three alternative theories, an employer may be liable for punitive damages based on an employee's wrongful acts if:

> (a) The employer had advance knowledge that the employee was unfit for the purposes of the employment and employed him with a conscious disregard of the rights or safety of others;
> (b) The employer expressly authorized or ratified the wrongful act of the employee for which the damages are awarded; or
> (c) The employer is personally guilty of oppression, fraud or malice, express or implied.

In this way, NRS 42.007 ensures that employers are subject to punitive damages only for their own culpable conduct and not for the misconduct of lower level employees. Generally, if it is an issue in a punitive damages case, the trier of fact determines whether an employee was acting within the scope of his or her employment when the tortious act occurred.[914]

The breach of fiduciary duty arising from a partnership agreement is a separate tort upon which punitive damages may be based.[915]

The 2003 U.S. Supreme Court ruling in *State Farm Mutual Automobile Insurance v. Campbell*, 538 U.S. 408, established that Courts should consider three factors in determining punitive damages as follows:

> The degree of reprehensibility of the defendant's misconduct;
> The disparity between the actual and potential harm suffered by the plaintiff and the punitive damages award,

and

> The difference between the punitive damages awarded by the jury and the civil penalties authorized or composed in comparable cases.

However, the U.S. Supreme Court stated: "Our jurisprudence and the principles it has now established demonstrate, however, that, in practice, few awards exceeding a single-digit ratio between punitive and compensatory damages, to a significant degree, will satisfy due process." This was the U.S. Supreme Court's third effort to reduce punitive damage awards. The other two cases were *BMW v. Gore*[916] and *Cooper Industries v. Leatherman Tool Group.*[917]

Quantum Meruit, Quasi Contract, or Unjust Enrichment

"Quantum meruit" [Latin "as much as he has deserved"] is the reasonable value of services; damages awarded in an amount considered reasonable to compensate a person who has rendered services in a quasi-contractual relationship.[918] It is a claim or right of action for the reasonable value of services rendered.[919] The doctrine of quantum meruit generally applies to an action for restitution involving work and labor performed which is founded on an oral promise on the part of the defendant to pay the plaintiff as much as the plaintiff reasonably deserves for his labor in the absence of an agreed-upon amount.[920]

To recover in quantum meruit, a party must establish legal liability on either an implied-in-fact contract or

---

[914] *Kornton v. Conrad, Inc.*, 119 Nev. 123, 125, 67 P.3d 316, 317 (2003).
[915] *Clark v. Lubritz*, 113 Nev. 1089, 1096, 944 P.2d 861 (1997).
[916] 517 U.S. 559 (1996).
[917] 532 U.S. 424 (2001).
[918] *Black's Law Dictionary* 1255 (7th ed. 1999).
[919] *Id.*
[920] *Sack v. Tomlin*, 110 Nev. 204, 871 P.2d 298 (1994).

unjust enrichment basis.[921] The distinction between the two theories, quantum meruit and unjust enrichment, can be unclear. "One source of confusion is that quantum meruit is a cause of action in two fields: restitution and contract."[922] Quantum meruit historically was one of the common counts—a subspecies of the writ of indebitatus or general assumpsit—available as a remedy at law to enforce implied promises or contracts.[923] A party who pleaded quantum meruit sought recovery of the reasonable value, or "as much as he has deserved,"[924] for services rendered.[925]

Thus, quantum meruit's first application is in actions based upon contracts implied-in-fact. A contract implied-in-fact must be "manifested by conduct."[926] It "is a true contract that arises from the tacit agreement of the parties."[927] To find a contract implied-in-fact, the fact-finder must conclude that the parties intended to contract and promises were exchanged, the general obligations for which must be sufficiently clear. It is at that point that a party may invoke quantum meruit as a gap-filler to supply the absent term.[928] Where such a contract exists, then, quantum meruit ensures the laborer receives the reasonable value, usually market price, for his services.[929]

Quantum meruit's other role is in providing restitution for unjust enrichment: "Liability in restitution for the market value of goods or services is the remedy traditionally known as quantum meruit."[930] When a plaintiff seeks "as much as he . . . deserve[s]" based on a theory of restitution (as opposed to implied-in-fact contract), he must establish each element of unjust enrichment.[931] Quantum meruit, then, is "the usual measurement of enrichment in cases where nonreturnable benefits have been furnished at the defendant's request, but where the parties made no enforceable agreement as to price."[932]

Unjust enrichment exists when the plaintiff confers a benefit on the defendant, the defendant appreciates such benefit, and there is " 'acceptance and retention by the defendant of such benefit under circumstances such that it would be inequitable for him to retain the benefit without payment of the value thereof.' "[933] A pleading of quantum meruit for

---

[921] *Certified Fire Prot. v. Precision Constr.*, 128 Nev. Adv. Op. No. 35 (August 9, 2012).

[922] Candace Saari Kovacic-Fleischer, *Quantum Meruit and the Restatement (Third) of Restitution and Unjust Enrichment*, 27 Rev. Litig. 127, 129 (2007); RESTATEMENT (THIRD) OF RESTITUTION AND UNJUST ENRICHMENT § 31 cmt. e (2011) (A pleading in quantum meruit, "[f]rom its 17th-century origins to the present day, . . . has been used to state two quite different claims"); *Martin v. Campanaro*, 156 F.2d 127, 130 n.5 (2d Cir. 1946) (addressing the ambiguity of a pleading in quantum meruit).

[923] Joseph M. Perillo, CORBIN ON CONTRACTS § 1.18(b), at 53 (rev. ed. 1993); 7 C.J.S. Action of Assumpsit § 2 (2004).

[924] *Black's Law Dictionary* 1361 (9th ed. 2009) (defining quantum meruit).

[925] See generally *Certified Fire Prot. v. Precision Constr.*, 128 Nev. Adv. Op. No. 35 (August 9, 2012).

[926] *Smith v. Recrion Corp.*, 91 Nev. 666, 668, 541 P.2d 663, 664 (1975); *Hay v. Hay*, 100 Nev. 196, 198, 678 P.2d 672, 674 (1984);

[927] Perillo, supra, § 1.20, at 64.

[928] See Kovacic-Fleischer, supra, at 129-30; 1 Dan B. Dobbs, *Dobbs' Law of Remedies* § 4.2(3) (2d ed. 1993) (quantum meruit fills price term when it is appropriate to imply the parties agreed to a reasonable price).

[929] RESTATEMENT (THIRD) OF RESTITUTION AND UNJUST ENRICHMENT § 31 cmt. e (2011); see *Sack v. Tomlin*, 110 Nev. 204, 208, 871 P.2d 298, 302 (1994) ("The doctrine of quantum meruit generally applies to an action . . . involving work and labor performed which is founded on a[n] oral promise [or other circumstances] on the part of the defendant to pay the plaintiff as much as the plaintiff reasonably deserves for his labor in the absence of an agreed upon amount."); see also *Paffhausen v. Balano*, 708 A.2d 269, 271 (Me. 1998) (discussing quantum meruit as a contract implied-in-fact).

[930] RESTATEMENT (THIRD) OF RESTITUTION AND UNJUST ENRICHMENT § 49 cmt. f (2011); id. § 31 cmt. e (2011) (quantum meruit's secondary use is as a pleading in the common law in cases "regarded in modern law as instances of unjust enrichment rather than contract"); *Ewing v. Sargent*, 87 Nev. 74, 79-80, 482 P.2d 819, 822-23 (1971) (discussing recovery in quantum meruit to prevent unjust enrichment). " 'Where unjust enrichment is found, the law implies a quasi-contract which requires the defendant to pay to plaintiff the value of the benefit conferred. In other words, the defendant makes restitution to the plaintiff in quantum meruit.' " *Lackner v. Glosser*, 892 A.2d 21, 34 (Pa. Super. Ct. 2006) (quoting *AmeriPro Search, Inc. v. Fleming Steel Co.*, 787 A.2d 988, 991 (Pa. Super. Ct. 2001)).

[931] *Black's Law Dictionary* 1361 (9th ed. 2009); see RESTATEMENT (THIRD) OF RESTITUTION AND UNJUST ENRICHMENT § 49(3)(c) & cmt. f (2011) ("[T]he market value of . . . services is the remedy traditionally known as quantum meruit." (emphasis added)); Doug Rendleman, *Quantum Meruit for the Subcontractor: Has Restitution Jumped Off Dawson's Dock?*, 79 Tex. L. Rev. 2055, 2073 (2001) ("A defendant's unjust enrichment is the major prerequisite for a plaintiff's quantum meruit").

[932] RESTATEMENT (THIRD) OF RESTITUTION AND UNJUST ENRICHMENT § 49 cmt. f (2011).

[933] *Unionamerica Mtg. v. McDonald*, 97 Nev. 210, 212, 626 P.2d 1272, 1273 (1981) (quoting *Dass v. Epplen*, 424 P.2d 779, 780 (Colo. 1967)).

unjust enrichment does not discharge the plaintiff's obligation to demonstrate that the defendant received a benefit from services provided.[934]

"[B]enefit" in the unjust enrichment context can include "services beneficial to or at the request of the other," "denotes any form of advantage," and is not confined to retention of money or property.[935] But while "[r]estitution may strip a wrongdoer of all profits gained in a transaction with [a] claimant . . . principles of unjust enrichment will not support the imposition of a liability that leaves an innocent recipient worse off . . . than if the transaction with the claimant had never taken place."[936]

Similarly, the Nevada Supreme Court has concluded that "[t]he basis of recovery on quantum meruit . . . is that a party has received from another a benefit which is unjust for him to retain without paying for it."[937] In *Thompson*, the defendant was to build a dam for the plaintiffs but the defendant's preliminary work failed to meet state regulations and thus was rendered useless.[938] Because the plaintiffs were required to hire a new laborer to completely rebuild the dam to code, this court held that the defendant could not recover on his counterclaim under a theory of quantum meruit because he had provided no benefit to the plaintiffs, *i.e.*, while he began the work the plaintiffs requested, he ultimately provided no advantage to them.[939]

In *Paterson v. Condos*, the Nevada Supreme Court specifically concluded that an action may be based upon quantum meruit even though an express contract exists: "The contractor may . . . base his action upon both the contract and upon a quantum meruit by setting up the former in one count, and the latter in another in his complaint."

To put all in other words, the essential elements of quasi contract are a benefit conferred on the defendant by the plaintiff, appreciation by the defendant of such benefit, and acceptance and retention by the defendant of such benefit under circumstances such that it would be inequitable for him to retain the benefit without payment of the value thereof.[940] Additionally, unjust enrichment occurs whenever a person has and retains a benefit which in equity and good conscience belongs to another.[941]

In a case with a quantum meruit or unjust enrichment theory of recovery, the proper measure of damages is the " 'reasonable value of [the] services.' "[942] In determining the proper measure of damages, the Nevada Supreme Court has acknowledged the "applicability of 'established customs' when determining the 'reasonable value' of . . . services."[943]

An action based on a theory of unjust enrichment is not available when there is an express written contract, because no agreement can be implied when there is an express agreement.[944] "The doctrine of unjust enrichment or recovery in quasi contract applies to situations where there is no legal contract but where the person sought to be charged is in possession of money or property which in good conscience and justice he should not retain but should deliver to another [or should pay for].[945]

See also "Unjust Enrichment." The statute of limitations for an unjust enrichment claim is four years.[946]

---

[934] RESTATEMENT (THIRD) OF RESTITUTION AND UNJUST ENRICHMENT § 31 cmt. e (2011); 1 Dan B. Dobbs, *Dobbs' Law of Remedies* § 4.2(3) (2d ed. 1993) (plaintiff pursuing quantum meruit under unjust enrichment theory must show benefit to defendant); 26 Richard A. Lord, *Williston on Contracts* § 68:1, at 24 (4th ed. 2003) (quantum meruit to avoid unjust enrichment applies "when a party confers a benefit with a reasonable expectation of payment"); *EPIC v. Salt Lake County*, 167 P.3d 1080, 1086 (Utah 2007) (first element of quantum meruit is showing a benefit has been conferred).

[935] See RESTATEMENT OF RESTITUTION § 1 cmt. b (1937); see also *Topaz Mutual Co. v. Marsh*, 108 Nev. 845, 856, 839 P.2d 606, 613 (1992) (citing § 1, cmt. b and noting that postponing foreclosure on a property benefits owner by providing additional time to negotiate a sale and reducing overall debt).

[936] RESTATEMENT (THIRD) OF RESTITUTION AND UNJUST ENRICHMENT § 1 cmt. d (2011); cf. *Heartland Health Systems v. Chamberlin*, 871 S.W.2d 8, 11 (Mo. Ct. App. 1993) (quantum meruit available for provision of emergency medical services).

[937] *Thompson v. Herrmann*, 91 Nev. 63, 68, 530 P.2d 1183, 1186 (1975).

[938] *Id.* at 64-67, 530 P.2d at 1183-85.

[939] *Id.* at 68, 530 P.2d at 1186. See generally *Certified Fire Prot. v. Precision Constr.*, 128 Nev. Adv. Op. No. 35 (August 9, 2012).

[940] *Unionamerica Mtg. v. McDonald*, 97 Nev. 210, 212, 626 P.2d 1272, 1273 (1981).

[941] *Id.*

[942] *Flamingo Realty v. Midwest Development*, 110 Nev. 984, 987, 879 P.2d at 71 (1994) (quoting *Morrow v. Barger*, 103 Nev. 247, 252, 737 P.2d 1153, 1156 (1991)).

[943] *Flamingo Realty*, 110 Nev. at 988, 879 P.2d at 71.

[944] 66 AM.JUR.2D RESTITUTION § 6 (1973).

[945] *Leasepartners Corp. v. Robert L. Brooks Trust Dated Nov. 12, 1975*, 113 Nev. 747, 755-56, 942 P.2d 182, 187 (1997).

[946] NRS 11.190(2)(c).

Quasi Contract
　　　　See "Quantum Meruit."

Receivership
　　　　NRS Chapter 32 covers receivers, who are not to be confused with wide receivers in football. NRS 32.010, "Cases in which receiver may be appointed," provides as follows:

> 1. In an action by a vendor to vacate a fraudulent purchase of property, or by a creditor to subject any property or fund to the creditor's claim, or between partners or others jointly owning or interested in any property or fund, on application of the plaintiff, or of any party whose right to or interest in the property or fund, or the proceeds thereof, is probable, and where it is shown that the property or fund is in danger of being lost, removed or materially injured.
> 2. In an action by a mortgagee for the foreclosure of the mortgage and sale of the mortgaged property, where it appears that the mortgaged property is in danger of being lost, removed or materially injured, or that the condition of the mortgage has not been performed, and that the property is probably insufficient to discharge the mortgage debt.
> 3. After judgment, to carry the judgment into effect.
> 4. After judgment, to dispose of the property according to the judgment, or to preserve it during the pendency of an appeal, or in proceedings in aid of execution, when an execution has been returned unsatisfied, or when the judgment debtor refuses to apply the judgment debtor's property in satisfaction of the judgment.
> 5. In the cases when a corporation has been dissolved, or is insolvent, or in imminent danger of insolvency, or has forfeited its corporate rights.
> 6. In all other cases where receivers have heretofore been appointed by the usages of the courts of equity.

[1911 CPA § 251; RL § 5193; NCL § 8749]

　　　　The court may determine the receiver's compensation. Where a receiver was appointed in an action by the trial court under the provisions of sec. 146, ch. 112, Stats. 1869 (cf. NRS 32.010), stating when a receiver may be appointed, and had not been discharged, the trial court had jurisdiction to determine and allow the amount of compensation to which such receiver was entitled for services pending an appeal after the appeal was completed.[947]
　　　　A receiver is an officer of the court. A receiver appointed by trial court in accordance with provisions of sec. 146, ch. 112, Stats. 1869 (cf. NRS 32.010), stating when a receiver may be appointed, is an officer of that court, and accountable to it for the trust imposed upon him.[948]
　　　　Where a statute, such as RL § 5193 (cf. NRS 32.010), which governs the appointment of a receiver by a court in which an action is pending, is taken from a statute of another state, the construction placed upon such statute by courts of the latter state are given great weight by courts of this state.[949] Posting a bond is not required. NCL § 8749 (cf. NRS 32.010), which governs appointment of receivers, does not require posting of a bond.[950]

Receiver: Jurisdiction
　　　　Sufficient reasons for appointment of receiver. Under sec. 246, ch. 103, Stats. 1861 (cf. NRS 40.430), inadequacy of property to satisfy a lien, insolvency of a mortgagor, a specific pledge of rents and profits to keep down interest, which rents and profits were afterwards diverted, permissive waste of property by mortgagor, and threats of mortgagor to destroy property constitute sufficient reasons for appointing a receiver.[951]
　　　　A receiver is to be appointed to prevent fraud, injustice or loss of security in foreclosure suit. Receivers will be appointed in foreclosure suits where it is necessary to prevent fraud, injustice or loss of security. *Hyman v. Kelly*, 1 Nev. 179 (1865).
　　　　Copartner entitled to appointment of receiver under the circumstances. Where an irresponsible partner ousts a copartner from a business, absconds with partnership funds and leaves irresponsible persons in possession of the business, the copartner is entitled to have a receiver appointed under sec. 143, ch. 103, Stats. 1861 (cf. NRS 32.010).[952]
　　　　A receiver's appointment is not authorized in an action after a judgment to recover on a money demand. In RL

---

[947] *McKenzie v. Coslett*, 28 Nev. 220, 80 Pac. 1070 (1905).
[948] *Id.*
[949] *Ex rel. Nenzel v. District Court*, 49 Nev. 145, 241 Pac. 317 (1925).
[950] *Bowler v. First Judicial Dist. Court*, 68 Nev. 445, 234 P.2d 593 (1951).
[951] *Hyman v. Kelly*, 1 Nev. 179 (1865).
[952] *Maynard v. Railey*, 2 Nev. 313 (1866).

§ 5193 (cf. NRS 32.010), governing the appointment of a receiver by a court in which an action is pending, paragraphs 3 and 4, which provide that a receiver may be appointed after judgment to carry the judgment into effect, and in proceedings in aid of an execution where the execution has been returned unsatisfied, do not authorize the appointment of a receiver in a separate proceeding instituted simply to obtain the appointment of a receiver after judgment in the action at law to recover on a money demand.[953]

The insolvency of a corporation is not sufficient to authorize the appointment of a receiver. Under par. 5 of RL § 5193 (cf. NRS 32.010), which authorizes the appointment of a receiver by a court in which an action is pending where a corporation has been dissolved, is insolvent, or has forfeited its corporate rights, the insolvency of the corporation is not in itself sufficient to give the court jurisdiction to appoint a receiver over the property of the corporation.[954]

No jurisdiction in proceeding instituted solely to obtain appointment of receiver. Under RL § 5193 (cf. NRS 32.010), which enumerates cases where a receiver may be appointed by a court in which an action is pending, the court has no jurisdiction to appoint a receiver in a proceeding instituted for the sole purpose of obtaining the appointment of a receiver.[955]

Property not subject to lien. In an action for debt by a contract creditor who has no lien upon the property of the debtor, and asserts no right to subject the property to payment of the debt, the court, in the absence of statutory authority, has no power to appoint a receiver of the assets of the debtor, or to enjoin prosecution of claims against him.[956]

Property not under jurisdiction of the court. In an action for wages, where no service of summons has been accomplished, and no property of the defendant has been brought under the jurisdiction of the court by proper process, the court has no authority to appoint a receiver for the property, nor does the appointment of a receiver give the court jurisdiction over the property.[957]

Court may appoint a receiver in an action for liquidation of a bank. Where district court had taken jurisdiction of an action by depositors for liquidation of a bank under sec. 68, ch. 190, Stats. 1933 (cf. NRS 667.210), which provides that such an action shall be governed by the civil practice act, the court was not limited to the provisions following sec. 68 of the statute which set forth plans for organization and reorganization of insolvent banks, but could appoint a receiver pursuant to NCL § 8749 (cf. NRS 32.010).[958]

The statute as to an insolvent corporation does not apply to the appointment of a receiver for an insolvent corporation. NCL § 8749 (cf. NRS 32.010), which enumerates situations in which receivers may be appointed where an action is pending, is not applicable to actions to appoint receivers under NCL § 1645 (cf. NRS 78.630), which provides for appointment of receivers to take control of insolvent corporations and does not require that there be an action pending before a receiver may be appointed.[959]

The court may order the sheriff to put the receiver in possession. Where a receiver has been appointed under sec. 143, ch. 103, Stats. 1861 (cf. NRS 32.010), to take possession of partnership property and the person in possession refuses to surrender the property, the court may order the sheriff to put a receiver in possession.[960]

The maintenance of an attachment lien gives the sheriff a right superior to a receiver. Where the court appointed a receiver under RL § 5193 (cf. NRS 32.010), which enumerates the cases where the appointment of a receiver may be made by a court in which an action is pending, the court had no authority to order a receiver to take charge of the property of a corporation which was in the possession of a sheriff under a levy under a writ of attachment, because maintenance of the attachment lien by virtue of possession of the property by the sheriff gave him a right superior to that of a receiver.[961]

All orders of the court were void where the court lacked jurisdiction to appoint a receiver. Where the court lacked jurisdiction under RL § 5193 (cf. NRS 32.010) to appoint a receiver to take possession of the assets of a corporation, all orders of the court in the receivership proceeding were void, including the order which required the sheriff to show cause why he should not be punished for contempt for refusing to surrender to the receiver the property of the corporation which the sheriff held under a writ of attachment, and a writ of prohibition was made permanent to

---

[953] *Ex rel. Nenzel v. District Court*, 49 Nev. 145, 241 Pac. 317 (1925).

[954] *Id.*

[955] *Id.*, distinguished, *International Life Underwriters, Inc. v. Second Judicial Dist. Court*, 61 Nev. 42, at 48, 113 P.2d 616 (1941).

[956] *Electrical Prods. Corp. v. Second Judicial Dist. Court*, 55 Nev. 8, 23 P.2d 501 (1933), cited, *Sterling Builders, Inc. v. Fuhrman*, 80 Nev. 543, at 548, 396 P.2d 850 (1964).

[957] *Id.*

[958] *Seaborn v. First Judicial Dist. Court*, 55 Nev. 206, 29 P.2d 500 (1934).

[959] *International Life Underwriters, Inc. v. Second Judicial Dist. Court*, 61 Nev. 42, 113 P.2d 616 (1941), distinguished, *Shelton v. Second Judicial Dist. Court*, 64 Nev. 487, at 492, 185 P.2d 320 (1947).

[960] *Maynard v. Railey*, 2 Nev. 313 (1866).

[961] *Ex rel. Nenzel v. District Court*, 49 Nev. 145, 241 Pac. 317 (1925).

restrain the court from adjudging the sheriff guilty of contempt.[962]

The failure of a plaintiff to show he had no adequate remedy at law. In proceedings by a creditor of a corporation for the appointment of a receiver, where plaintiff alleged that certain property of the corporation had been attached, but did not allege that the corporation lacked other property sufficient to discharge all of its debts, or that its board of directors was guilty of fraud or mismanagement, the plaintiff failed to show that he had no adequate remedy at law, and therefore the court was not authorized to appoint a receiver under par. 6 of RL § 5193 (cf. NRS 32.010), which provides for the appointment of a receiver in all cases where receivers have been appointed by usages of courts of equity.[963]

The appointment of a receiver is improper if an adequate remedy at law exists. An appointment of a receiver under NCL § 8749 (cf. NRS 32.010) pending litigation is improper if an adequate remedy at law exists, because receivership is generally regarded as a remedy of last resort.[964]

The trial court's action is not disturbed on appeal in the absence of an abuse of discretion. NCL § 8749 (cf. NRS 32.010) provides that a receiver may be appointed in all cases where receivers were previously appointed by courts of equity, and such appointment rests within the sound discretion of the trial court, to be exercised in the promotion of justice where no other adequate remedy exists, with a view to all circumstances, and in the absence of an abuse of discretion, an action of a trial court will not be disturbed on appeal.[965]

The requirement of security for performance of duty as a receiver is reasonable. In a divorce action, where plaintiff's wife obtained an order blocking transfer of title to a purchaser at a sale by a trustee of a motel which had once belonged to the plaintiff, had been purchased by the defendant at execution sale, and was managed by the plaintiff, under NRS 32.010, which provides for appointment of receivers according to usage of equity, the trial court had power to appoint a receiver for the motel, and because the plaintiff was appointed the receiver, the requirement that the furniture which was her separate property remain in the motel as security for performance of duty as a receiver and for possible damages to the purchaser kept out of possession was reasonable.[966]

An order denying intervention is not appealable. A receiver applied to the court for permission to sell the stock of a certain company which was held by the company in receivership. A third company petitioned to intervene on the ground that it was the equitable owner of the stock. The court denied the petition. This order denying intervention in these circumstances was not appealable because it is not a final judgment within the former NRCP 72(b)(1) (cf. NRAP 3A(b)), and no provision is made by rule or statute for its appealability.[967]

NRS 32.015, "Additional cases in which receiver may be appointed," provides as follows:

> 1. In addition to the cases enumerated in NRS 32.010, a court or judge may appoint a receiver in an action brought by a secured lender to enforce the right provided in NRS 40.507, or a similar right provided in a mortgage, to enter and inspect real collateral to determine the existence, location, nature and magnitude of any past, present or threatened release or presence of a hazardous substance from, in, into or onto it. A right provided in a mortgage is subject to the same limitations and requirement of notice as are provided in NRS 40.507.
>
> 2. As used in this section, "hazardous substance," "release" and "secured lender" have the meanings ascribed to them in NRS 40.504, 40.505 and 40.506, respectively.
>
> (Added to NRS by 1993, 151)

---

[962] *Id.*

[963] *Id.*, cited, *Bowler v. Leonard*, 70 Nev. 370, at 384, 269 P.2d 833 (1954).

[964] *Bowler v. Leonard*, 70 Nev. 370, 269 P.2d 833 (1954).

[965] *Id.*, cited, *Peri-Gil Corp. v. Sutton*, 84 Nev. 406, at 411, 442 P.2d 465 (1968), *Nishon's, Inc. v. Kendigian*, 91 Nev. 504, at 505, 538 P.2d 580 (1975), *Charmicor, Inc. v. Bradshaw Fin. Co.*, 92 Nev. 310, at 313, 550 P.2d 413 (1976), *Johnson v. Steel, Inc.*, 100 Nev. 181, at 183, 678 P.2d 676 (1984), see also *Medical Device Alliance, Inc. v. Ahr*, 115 Nev. 851, at 862, 8 P.3d 135 (2000).

[966] *Kraemer v. Kraemer*, 79 Nev. 287, 382 P.2d 394 (1963).

[967] *Christensen v. Insurance Comm'r*, 85 Nev. 335, 454 P.2d 891 (1969), cited, *Archie v. Pierce*, 88 Nev. 182, at 183, 495 P.2d 363 (1972).

NRS 32.020, "Reversion and disposition of unclaimed dividends in receivership," provides as follows:

1. In any receivership proceeding instituted in which a dividend has been declared and ordered paid to creditors, any dividend which remains unclaimed for 3 years reverts to the general fund of the estate and must be applied as follows:
(a) To the payment of costs and expenses of the administration of the estate and receivership.
(b) To a new dividend distributed to creditors whose claims have been allowed but not paid in full.
After those claims have been paid in full, the balance is presumed abandoned under Chapter 120A of NRS.
2. This section applies to any receivership proceeding which may be brought, and includes any bank, banking corporation, corporation, copartnership, company, association or natural person.

Replevin

In a replevin action, judgment must be in alternative, *i.e.*, for return of property or its value in case return cannot be had, and prevailing party does not have option to take judgment for value of property absolutely.
NRS 17.120, "Replevin; judgment to be in alternative and with damages," provides as follows:

1. In an action to recover the possession of personal property, judgment for the plaintiff may be for the possession or the value thereof, in case a delivery cannot be had, and damages for the detention or the value of the use thereof. If the property has been delivered to the plaintiff, and the defendant claim a return thereof, judgment for the defendant may be for a return of the property or the value thereof, in case a return cannot be had, and damages for taking and withholding the same or the value of the use thereof.
2. In an action on a contract or obligation for the direct payment of money, payable in a specified or agreed kind of money or currency, judgment for the plaintiff, whether the same be by default or after verdict, or decision of the court or master, may follow the contract or obligation, and be made payable in the kind of money or currency therein specified or thereby agreed.
3. In an action against any person for the recovery of money received by such person in a fiduciary capacity, or to the use of another, judgment for the plaintiff, whether the same be by default or after verdict, or decision of the court or master, may be made payable in the same kind of money or currency so received by such person.

Replevin, sometimes known as "claim and delivery," is an old-fashioned legal remedy in which a court requires a defendant to return specific goods to the plaintiff at the outset of the action. Although rarely used, replevin can be a very powerful weapon in a case where somebody is wrongly holding your property, because it deprives the defendant of the use of your property while the case is awaiting trial, which increases the likelihood of a quick settlement.
See "Claim and Delivery."

Rescission

Rescission is an equitable remedy which totally abrogates a contract and which seeks to place the parties in the position they occupied before executing the contract.[968] A party to a contract may seek a rescission of that contract based on fraud in the inducement. Whether rescission shall be granted rests largely in the sound discretion of the district court.[969]

Res Ipsa Loquitur

Res ipsa loquitur is an exception to the general negligence rule. It permits a party to infer negligence, as opposed to affirmatively proving it, when certain elements are met.[970] For the doctrine to apply, traditionally a party must show:

(1) the event must be of a kind which ordinarily does not occur in the absence of someone's negligence; (2) the event must be caused by an agency or instrumentality within the exclusive control of the defendant; and (3) the event must not have been due to any voluntary action or contribution on the part of the plaintiff.[971] For res ipsa loquitur to apply, Nevada also requires the defendant to have superior knowledge of or be in a better position to explain the

---

[968] See *Awada v. Shuffle Master, Inc.*, 123 Nev. 613, 173 P.3d 707 (2007).
[969] See *Havas v. Alger*, 85 Nev. 627, 631, 461 P.2d 857, 860 (1969).
[970] *Woosley v. State Farm Ins. Co.*, 117 Nev. 182, 188, 18 P.3d 317, 321 (2001).
[971] *Id.* at 188-189.

accident.[972] Once the elements of res ipsa loquitur are met, the burden shifts to the defendant to show that something other than its negligence caused the accident.[973] Whether sufficient evidence supports an inference of negligence under res ipsa loquitur is a question for the jury; however, the district court must first determine whether sufficient evidence has been adduced at trial to support the consideration of a res ipsa loquitur instruction and therefore whether the instruction should be given.[974]

In *Woosley*, the Nevada Supreme Court revised the third element to accord with contemporary comparative negligence law and NRS 41.141.[975] Although Nevada used to recognize the complete bar of a plaintiff's recovery under the theory of contributory negligence, NRS 41.141 replaced this harsh rule. The statute permits a plaintiff to recover as long as his or her comparative negligence is not greater than that of the defendant or defendants.[976]

Res ipsa loquitur allows a plaintiff to prove the defendant's negligence by circumstantial evidence "when the direct evidence concerning the cause of the injury is primarily within the knowledge and control of the defendant."[977] Common applications of the doctrine include situations where objects fall from the defendant's premises, or where objects under the defendant's control simply explode.[978] In Illinois, the plaintiff is entitled to a presumption of negligence under res ipsa loquitur if the "thing which caused the injury is shown to be under the control or management of the party charged with negligence," and if "the occurrence is such as in the ordinary course of things would not have happened if the person so charged had used proper care . . . ."[979] The trial court determines whether this presumption is applicable as a matter of law.[980] The burden of proof then shifts to the defendant who may rebut the inference of negligence if he proves either that he exercised due care, or that "the accident was caused by the intervention of someone or something else."[981] This issue is for the fact-finder.[982]

A medical expert affidavit is not required in a medical malpractice action based solely on the res ipsa loquitur doctrine. Under NRS 41A.071, a medical malpractice action filed in district court must be dismissed if it is filed without a medical expert's supporting affidavit. However, under NRS 41A.100, expert medical testimony is not required to prove medical malpractice under certain circumstances implicating the doctrine of res ipsa loquitur. Thus, where a medical malpractice action is based solely on the res ipsa loquitur doctrine, the expert affidavit requirement set forth in NRS 41A.071 does not apply. In contrast, if a medical malpractice action consists both of a res ipsa loquitur claim and other claims not based on that doctrine, the other claims are subject to the requirements of NRS 41A.071.[983]

In a medical malpractice action, any res ipsa loquitur claim (see NRS 41A.100(1)) filed without the affidavit of a medical expert (see NRS 41A.071) must, when challenged by the defendant in a pretrial or trial motion, meet the prima facie requirements for a res ipsa loquitur case. Thus, in such an instance, the plaintiff must present facts and evidence that show the existence of one or more of the situations enumerated in NRS 41A.100(1)(a)-(e).[984]

Respondeat Superior

An employer may be held vicariously liable for an employee's torts, regardless of the employee's motivation, if the actual occurrence was a generally "foreseeable" consequence of the activity. For these purposes, "foreseeable" means merely that, in the context of the particular enterprise, the employee's conduct was not so unusual or startling that it would seem unfair to include the loss resulting from it among other costs of the employer's business. But the employer is not liable if the employee substantially departs from his duties for purely personal reasons.[985]

The policy objectives underlying respondeat superior are to prevent torts from occurring, to give greater assurance of compensation for the victim, and to ensure that victim's losses will be equitably borne by those who benefit from the enterprise that gave rise to the injury.[986]

---

[972] *Id.* at 189, 18 P.3d 317 (2001).

[973] *Id.*

[974] *Id.*

[975] *Id.*

[976] *Id.*, 117 Nev. at 189-90.

[977] *Senase v. Johns*, 420 N.E.2d 1104, 1107 (Ill. 1981).

[978] See generally W. Page Keeton, *et al.*, PROSSER AND KEETON ON THE LAW OF TORTS § 39, at 244-45 (5th ed. 1984).

[979] *Metz v. Central Illinois Elec. & Gas Co.*, 207 N.E.2d 305, 307 (Ill. 1965).

[980] *Id.*

[981] *Senase*, 51 Ill.Dec. at 550, 420 N.E.2d at 1108.

[982] *Metz*, 207 N.E.2d at 307.

[983] *Szydel v. Markman*, 121 Nev. 453, 117 P.3d 200 (2005).

[984] *Id.*

[985] *State, Dep't Hum. Res. v. Jimenez*, 113 Nev. 356, 358, 935 P.2d 274 (1997).

[986] *Id.*; see *National Convenience Stores v. Fantauzzi*, 94 Nev. 655, 658, 584 P.2d 689, 691 (1978) (a

To determine whether respondeat superior liability is applicable, the trier of fact generally determines whether an employee was acting within the scope of his or her employment when the tortious act occurred.[987]

NRS 41.745, "Liability of employer for intentional conduct of employee; limitations," provides as follows:

1. An employer is not liable for harm or injury caused by the intentional conduct of an employee if the conduct of the employee:
(a) Was a truly independent venture of the employee;
(b) Was not committed in the course of the very task assigned to the employee; and
(c) Was not reasonably foreseeable under the facts and circumstances of the case considering the nature and scope of his or her employment.
For the purposes of this subsection, conduct of an employee is reasonably foreseeable if a person of ordinary intelligence and prudence could have reasonably anticipated the conduct and the probability of injury.
2. Nothing in this section imposes strict liability on an employer for any unforeseeable intentional act of an employee.
3. For the purposes of this section:
(a) "Employee" means any person who is employed by an employer, including, without limitation, any present or former officer or employee, immune contractor, an employee of a university school for profoundly gifted pupils described in Chapter 392A of NRS or a member of a board or commission or Legislator in this State.
(b) "Employer" means any public or private employer in this State, including, without limitation, the State of Nevada, a university school for profoundly gifted pupils described in Chapter 392A of NRS, any agency of this State and any political subdivision of the State.
(c) "Immune contractor" has the meaning ascribed to it in subsection 3 of NRS 41.0307.
(d) "Officer" has the meaning ascribed to it in subsection 4 of NRS 41.0307.

NRS 41.745 provides that public and private employers are not liable for harm caused by their employees' intentional conduct if that conduct was (1) "a truly independent venture of the employee," (2) "not committed in the course of the very task assigned to the employee," and (3) "not reasonably foreseeable under the facts and circumstances of the case considering the nature and scope of his employment."[988]

In the "particularized facts" of a 2015 case, the Nevada Supreme Court found that the employee's criminal conduct was reasonably foreseeable.[989] The reasonable foreseeability standard in NRS 41.745(1)(c) sets forth a factual inquiry.[990] Nevada will hold an employer vicariously liable for an employee's intentional tort—even though it was outside the scope of employment—if that intentional tort was "reasonably foreseeable under the facts and circumstances of the case considering the nature and scope of his or her employment."[991] Sexual assault can be reasonably foreseeable, either as party of a vicarious liability inquiry or a direct negligence inquiry.[992] Although unlawful conduct can interrupt and supersede the causation between a negligent act and injury, an unlawful act will not supersede causation if it was foreseeable.[993]

Resulting Trust

A resulting trust exists where the acts or expressions of the parties indicate an intent that a trust relation results from their transaction.[994] Specifically, a resulting trust may arise on the failure of an express trust.[995]

---

respondeat superior case).

[987] *Kornton v. Conrad, Inc.*, 119 Nev. 123, 67 P.3d 316 (2003).

[988] *Wood v. Safeway, Inc.*, 121 Nev. 724, 738-39, 121 P.3d 1026, 1035 (2005); *Hughey v. Washoe County*, 73 Nev. 22, 23, 306 P.2d 1115 (1957) (applying the respondeat superior doctrine to a government entity).

[989] *Anderson v. Mandalay*, 131 Nev., Advance Opinion 82 (2015).

[990] *Id.* at 7.

[991] *Id.* at 10, citing NRS 41.745(1)(c).

[992] *Id.* at 10-11.

[993] *Id.* at 12, citing *Bower v. Harrah's Laughlin, Inc.*, 125 Nev. 470, 491-92, 215 P.3d 709, 724-25 (2009).

[994] 76 Am.Jur.2d Trusts § 163 (1992).

[995] *Bemis v. Estate of Bemis*, 114 Nev. 1021, 1027 (1998), citing *Washburn v. Park East*, 795 F.2d 870, 872 (9th Cir. 1986).

Retaliation

Under § 2000e-3(a), it is unlawful "for an employer to discriminate against any of his employees . . . because he has opposed any practice made an unlawful employment practice by [Title VII], or because he has made a charge, testified, assisted, or participated in any manner in an investigation, proceeding, or hearing under this subchapter." 42 U.S.C. § 2000e-3(a). To establish a prima facie case of retaliation, a plaintiff must demonstrate that "(1) she engaged in an activity protected under Title VII; (2) her employer subjected her to an adverse employment action; and (3) a causal link exists between the protected activity and the adverse employment action."[996] If a plaintiff establishes a prima facie case of retaliation, the burden shifts to the defendant to demonstrate a legitimate, nondiscriminatory reason for its decision.[997] If the defendant demonstrates such a reason, the burden shifts back to the plaintiff to show that the defendant's reason was a mere pretext for discrimination.[998]

Retaliatory Termination for Whistleblowing

As one lawyer wrote me: "Regrettably, Nevada once again sides with the employers." While allowing that terminating an employee in retaliation for reporting "illegal conduct of his employer" violates Nevada's public policy, the Court disingenuously made this absurd distinction that going through one's chain of command within the organization is not cognizable. Rather, the employee's lawful act of reporting illegality on behalf of his employer and the public does not make him a whistleblower. The hapless, good-intentioned employee is only a Nevada whistleblower entitled to protection when he or she reports the misconduct to 'appropriate authorities,' which means authorities who are outside of the company. Additionally, the Nevada Supreme Court did not define 'public good' in *Wiltsie*."[999]

Nine years later, the Nevada Supreme Court narrowed the whistleblower's protection even further, almost rendering it inaccessible in Nevada. In *Allum*,[1000] the Court rejected the theory that a whistleblowing claim might be sustainable when the claim is only a part of what led to the employee's termination. The Court said this was insufficient. The employee's termination had to be "*the* proximate cause of his discharge" (emphasis in original).[1001] The Court then went on to say that such tortious discharge actions "are severely limited to those rare and exceptional cases where the employer's conduct violates strong and compelling public policy."[1002] This hardly protects an employee who seeks to report illegal conduct. Not satisfied with that, the *Allum* court further required "good faith" reporting "not motivated by malice, spite, jealousy, or personal gain."[1003] In an strange twist, the *Allum* court summarized with this sentence: "A claim for tortious discharge should be available to an employee who was terminated for refusing to engage in conduct that he, in good faith, reasonably believed to be illegal."[1004]

To summarize:

1) The employee must report alleged illegality to an appropriate authority outside of his company.

2) The employee must report in good faith not for spite or personal gain,

3) The reported illegality must violate strong and compelling public policy, and

4) The terminated employee must show that his whistleblowing was the sole cause of termination (not one part of the cause for his termination).

Sanity, Judicial Declaration of

Proceedings for a judicial declaration of sanity are covered by NRS 41.300 to NRS 41.330.

NRS 41.300, "Insane persons; presumption of legal capacity on discharge," provides as follows:

After a person's insanity has been judicially determined, such person can make no conveyance or other contract, or delegate any power or waive any right until the person's restoration to presumed legal

---

[996] *Dennis v. Nevada*, 282 F.Supp.2d 1177 (D. Nev. 2003).

[997] *Ray*, 217 F.3d at 1240.

[998] *Id.*

[999] *Wiltsie v. Baby Grand Corp.*, 105 Nev. 291, 774 P.2d 432 (1989).

[1000] *Allum v. Valley Bank of Nevada*, 114 Nev. 1313, 970 P.2d 1062 (1998).

[1001] *Id.* at 1320.

[1002] *Id.* at 1320-21.

[1003] *Id.* at 1321.

[1004] *Id.* at 1324.

capacity, or until the person has been judicially declared to be sane. A certificate from the superintendent or resident physician of the insane asylum to which such person may have been committed showing that such person had been discharged therefrom shall establish the presumption of legal capacity in such person from the time of such discharge.

NRS 41.310, "Adjudication of sanity," provides as follows:

The district courts of the several counties shall have jurisdiction to hear and determine the question as to whether or not a person, previously adjudicated to be insane, shall be adjudicated to be sane.

NRS 41.320, "Petition seeking restoration of status as sane; notice," provides as follows:

Any person, on behalf of an alleged insane person, may file a petition in the district court seeking an order restoring the alleged insane person to the status of a sane person. Upon the filing of the petition for that purpose, the clerk shall give such notice of the filing of the same as the court may order.

NRS 41.325, "Notice of adjudication of sanity to be given to Administrative Officer and Medical Director of Northern Nevada Adult Mental Health Services" provides as follows:

After any proceeding in which a person, previously adjudicated to be insane, is adjudicated to be sane, the clerk of the district court shall immediately notify the Administrative Officer and the Medical Director of Northern Nevada Adult Mental Health Services of the adjudication.

NRS 41.330, "Conduct of proceedings by county officers; no fees to be charged," provides as follows: "All proceedings under NRS 41.300 to 41.330, inclusive, shall be conducted by the appropriate county officials, including the district attorney, without cost or expense of any kind to the petitioner or alleged insane person."

Courts have inherent power to entertain proceedings to establish the competency of persons adjudged incompetent.[1005] A certificate of discharge from a mental hospital raises the presumption of sanity and would be indirect evidence in a court proceeding to adjudge a discharged person to be sane.[1006]

Section 1983 Claims

There are two elements to a 42 U.S.C. § 1983 claim: (1) the conduct complained of must have been under the color of state law; and (2) the conduct must have subjected the plaintiff to a deprivation of constitutional rights.[1007] A claim for excessive force is actionable under 42 U.S.C. § 1983. Excessive force is unreasonable conduct that is prohibited by the Fourth Amendment as follows: "The right of the people to be secure in their persons . . . against unreasonable . . . seizures, shall not be violated." Application of force by prison guards exceeding that which is reasonable and necessary under the circumstances states a claim under Section 1983.

The United States statute, 42 U.S.C.A. § 1983, "Civil action for deprivation of rights," provides in relevant part as follows:

Every person who, under color of any statute, ordinance, regulation, custom, or usage, of any State or Territory or the District of Columbia, subjects, or causes to be subjected, any citizen of the United States or other person within the jurisdiction thereof to the deprivation of any rights, privileges, or immunities secured by the Constitution and laws, shall be liable to the party.

All the defendants, as State employees acting in the course and scope of their employment, were acting under color of law. Acts are done "under color of . . . law" not only when government officials act within the bounds or limits of their lawful authority, but also when such officials act without and beyond the bounds of their lawful authority. In order for unlawful acts of an officer to be done "under color of any law," the acts must be done while the officer is acting, purporting, or pretending to act in the performance of her or his official duties; that is to say, the unlawful acts must consist in an abuse or misuse of power which is possessed by the officer only because she or he is an officer; and the unlawful acts must be of such a nature, and be committed under such circumstances, that they would not have occurred but for the fact that the person committing them was an officer, purporting to exercise her or his official powers.

[1005] AGO 249 (12-17-1945).
[1006] Id.
[1007] Jones v. Community Redevelopment Agency, 733 F.2d 646, 649 (9th Cir. 1984).

176

When an individual has a special relationship with the State, such as a custodial relationship, the State assumes an affirmative obligation to secure that individual's constitutional liberty. See *Monmouth County Correctional Institutional Inmates v. Lanzaro*, 834 F.2d 326, 341 (3rd Cir. 1987) (holding that prison officials must ensure that funding is available for women to choose to terminate their pregnancies, and distinguishing *Maher* and *Harris* on the ground that "whatever the government's constitutional obligations to the free world," the government has an affirmative constitutional obligation to aid the exercise of the fundamental rights of prisoners), *cert. denied*, 486 U.S. 1006, 108 S.Ct. 1731, 100 L.Ed. 2d 195 (1988); *Escamilla v. City of Santa Ana*, 796 F.2d 266, 269-70 (9th Cir. 1986) (observing that the State has an affirmative duty to protect when it has a custodial relationship with an individual).

The courts have clearly articulated the "special relationship" principle in cases involving prisoners. "Whatever the constitutional obligations to the free world, those obligations often differ radically in the prison context." The Third Circuit held that the government's obligation to accommodate the retained rights of inmates arises "because of the very fact of incarceration," which deprives prisoners of their abilities to care for themselves.[1008] Similarly, the courts have held that the government has an affirmative obligation under the Eighth Amendment to provide prisoners with adequate medical care, food, and housing. See *Estelle v. Gamble*, 429 U.S. 97, 103, 50 L. Ed. 2d 251, 97 S. Ct. 285 (1976) (holding that the Eighth Amendment mandates that the government provide medical care to inmates because incarceration renders inmates dependent upon prison authorities).

In America we respect the sanctity of human life, including those confined in penal institutions. The rights of the human person must be vindicated as part of the common good of our society.[1009]

See "Failure to Properly Supervise or Train under 42 U.S.C. § 1983."

Slander (Defamation)
See "Defamation."

Slander Per Se
See "Defamation."

Slander of Title
Slander of title involves false and malicious communications, disparaging to one's title in land, and causing special damage.[1010] In an action for slander of title, the plaintiff may recover as damages the expense of legal proceedings necessary to remove a cloud on the plaintiff's title.[1011] These holdings are based on the RESTATEMENT (SECOND) OF TORTS, which provides the circumstances under which one becomes liable for slander of title. Specifically, § 633 of the RESTATEMENT defines "recoverable pecuniary loss" as:

> (a) the pecuniary loss that results directly and immediately from the effect of the conduct of third persons, including impairment of vendibility or value caused by disparagement, and
> (b) the expense of measures reasonably necessary to counteract the publication, including litigation to remove the doubt cast upon vendibility or value by disparagement.

The clear majority rule is that attorney fees incurred in removing spurious clouds from a title qualify as special damages in an action for slander of title.[1012]

Specific Performance
Specific performance is available only when: (1) the terms of the contract are definite and certain; (2) the remedy at law is inadequate; (3) the appellant has tendered performance; and (4) the court is willing to order specific performance.[1013] If a purchaser of real property has not yet tendered the purchase price, the district court may still grant specific performance if the purchaser can "demonstrate that she is ready, willing, and able to perform."[1014]

[1008] *Id.*
[1009] *Barrera-Echavarria v. Rison*, 21 F.3d 314, 319 (9th Cir. 1994).
[1010] *Executive Mgmt. v. Ticor Title Ins. Co.*, 114 Nev. 823, 842, 963 P.2d 465 (1998).
[1011] *Horgan v. Felton*, 123 Nev., Advance Opinion 53, 170 P.3d 982, 985 (2007).
[1012] *Id.*
[1013] *Serpa v. Darling*, 107 Nev. 299, 305, 810 P.2d 778, 782 (1991).
[1014] *Id.* at 304, 810 P.2d at 782.

Strict Liability

To present a prima facie case for strict liability in tort, a plaintiff must establish that her injuries were caused by a defect in the product, and that the defect existed when the product left the defendant's control.[1015] Under Nevada law, "strict liability may be imposed even though the product is faultlessly made if it was unreasonably dangerous to place the product in the hands of the user without suitable and adequate warning concerning safe and proper use."[1016] Inherent in this doctrine is that "a product must include a warning that adequately communicates the dangers that may result from its use or foreseeable misuse." More particularly, in *Fyssakis v. Knight Equipment Corp.*,[1017] the Nevada Supreme Court held that adequacy of warnings was an issue of fact for the jury where an industrial strength soap manufacturer's warnings did not alert the user that the soap could cause blindness.

Allison v. Merck and Company,[1018] a district court entered summary judgment in favor of a manufacturer of a children's vaccine. The Nevada Supreme Court reversed in light of their conclusion that the drug manufacturer was required to adequately warn parents of possible side effects of immunization, including blindness, deafness or mental retardation. Accordingly, the Nevada Supreme Court held that a general warning that an inoculated child could encounter rashes and possible brain inflammation was arguably inadequate and issues of fact remained as to the sufficiency of the warnings given. In remanding the *Allison* case for trial on the adequacy of the warnings, the Nevada Supreme Court rejected the notion that a drug manufacturer could, via a general warning, avoid liability as a matter of law, even where the product was either reasonably or unavoidably unsafe.

Warnings in the context of products liability claims must be (1) designed to reasonably catch the consumer's attention, (2) that the language be comprehensible and give a fair indication of the specific risks attendant to use of the product, and (3) that warnings be of sufficient intensity justified by the magnitude of the risk.[1019]

Survival of Causes of Action

NRS 41.100 covers the survival of cause of action. This is not a claim per se, but it tells a lawyer when and how an action may survive.

NRS 41.100, "Cause of action not lost by reason of death; damages; recovery for loss arising out of unfair practice regarding policy of life insurance; subrogation," provides as follows:

1. Except as otherwise provided in this section and NRS 179A.230 [see statute below], no cause of action is lost by reason of the death of any person, but may be maintained by or against the person's executor or administrator.

2. In an action against an executor or administrator, any damages may be awarded which would have been recovered against the decedent if the decedent had lived, except damages awardable under NRS 42.005 or 42.010 or other damages imposed primarily for the sake of example or to punish the defendant.

3. Except as otherwise provided in this subsection, when a person who has a cause of action dies before judgment, the damages recoverable by the decedent's executor or administrator include all losses or damages which the decedent incurred or sustained before the decedent's death, including any penalties or punitive and exemplary damages which the decedent would have recovered if the decedent had lived, and damages for pain, suffering or disfigurement and loss of probable support, companionship, society, comfort and consortium. This subsection does not apply to the cause of action of a decedent brought by the decedent's personal representatives for the decedent's wrongful death.

4. The executor or administrator of the estate of a person insured under a policy of life insurance may recover on behalf of the estate any loss, including, without limitation, consequential damages and attorney's fees, arising out of the commission of an act that constitutes an unfair practice pursuant to subsection 1 of NRS 686A.310.

5. This section does not prevent subrogation suits under the terms and conditions of an uninsured motorists' provision of an insurance policy.

NRS 179A.230, "When person who is subject of notice of information may bring action for damages; when child who is victim of offense committed by employee may bring action for damages against employer; statute of limitations," provides as follows:

[1015] *Shoshone Coca-Cola Bottling Co. v. Dolinski*, 82 Nev. 439, 420 P.2d 855 (1966).

[1016] *Lewis v. Sea Ray Boats, Inc.*, 119 Nev. 100, 107, 65 P.3d 245 (2003).

[1017] 108 Nev. at 214, 826 P.2d at 571-72.

[1018] 110 Nev. 762, 878 P.2d 948 (1994).

[1019] *Lewis v. Sea Ray Boats, Inc.*, 119 Nev. 100, 107, 65 P.3d 245 (2003).

1. A person who is the subject of a request for notice of information pursuant to NRS 179A.180 to 179A.240, inclusive, may recover actual damages in a civil action against:

(a) The Central Repository for an intentional or grossly negligent:

(1) Dissemination of information relating to the offenses listed in subsection 4 of NRS 179A.190 not authorized for dissemination; or

(2) Release of information relating to the offenses listed in subsection 4 of NRS 179A.190 to a person not authorized to receive the information;

(b) The Central Repository for an intentional or grossly negligent failure to correct any notice of information relating to the offenses listed in subsection 4 of NRS 179A.190 which was disseminated pursuant to NRS 179A.180 to 179A.240, inclusive; or

(c) An employer, representative of an employer or employee for an intentional or grossly negligent violation of NRS 179A.110. Punitive damages may be awarded against an employer, representative of an employer or employee whose violation of NRS 179A.110 is malicious.

2. An employer is liable to a child served by the employer for damages suffered by the child as a result of an offense listed in subsection 4 of NRS 179A.190 committed against the child by an employee if, at the time the employer hired the employee, the employee was the subject of information relating to the offenses for which notice was available for dissemination to the employer and the employer:

(a) Failed, without good cause, to request notice of the information pursuant to NRS 179A.180 to 179A.240, inclusive; or

(b) Was unable to obtain the information because the employee refused to consent to the search and release of the information, and the employer hired or retained the employee despite this refusal.

The amount of damages for which an employer is liable pursuant to this subsection must be reduced by the amount of damages recovered by the child in an action against the employee for damages sustained as a result of an offense listed in subsection 4 of NRS 179A.190.

3. An action pursuant to this section must be brought within 3 years after:

(a) The occurrence upon which the action is based; or

(b) The date upon which the party bringing the action became aware or reasonably should have become aware of the occurrence, whichever was earlier, if the party was not aware of the occurrence at the time of the occurrence.

4. This section does not limit or affect any other rights, claims or causes of action arising by statute or common law.

(Added to NRS by 1987, 1763; A 1989, 993; 2003, 2843)

Nevada Cases

The former statute did not conflict with the Supreme Court rule concerning the substitution of a representative upon the death of party pending appeal. Sec. 16, ch. 112, Stats. 1869 (cf. NRCP 25 and NRS 41.100), providing that an action shall not abate by death or disability of any party if the cause of action survives, but may be continued by his representative or successor in interest, is not in conflict with the rule of the Supreme Court providing that upon the death of a party pending appeal, his representative shall be substituted, but the statute goes further and directs that the action may be continued by or against his successor in interest or person to whom he has transferred his interest.[1020]

The survival of a tort action is not nullified by the application of the dead man's statute. In a personal injury action arising from an automobile accident, where the driver died before trial, the court rejected the argument of plaintiff that application of the dead man's statute, former NRS 48.010, to his testimony concerning the collision, to which there were no other witnesses, nullified the provisions of former NRS 41.110 (cf. NRS 41.100), which provided for survival of tort actions against estates of decedents, because physical evidence is usually available, and any determination of policy as between the possibility of injustice to individual claimants and protection of estates from fraudulent claims is for the legislature and not the courts.[1021]

Proceeds of settlement assignable and may be subject of contractual subrogation. Assignability of the right to sue in tort for personal injuries is governed by the test of survivorship. This right does survive in Nevada, under NRS 41.100, and is therefore assignable. *A fortiori*, proceeds of a settlement are assignable and may be the subject of contractual subrogation.[1022]

A "legal representative" is not personally liable but is authorized to pay claims against the estate. A "legal

---

[1020] *Twaddle v. Winters*, 29 Nev. 88, 85 Pac. 280, 89 Pac. 289 (1906).

[1021] *Zeigler v. Moore*, 75 Nev. 91, 335 P.2d 425 (1959).

[1022] *Davenport v. State Farm Mut. Auto. Ins. Co.*, 81 Nev. 361, 404 P.2d 10 (1965), distinguished, *Maxwell v. Allstate Ins. Co.*, 102 Nev. 502, at 504, 728 P.2d 812 (1986).

representative" against whom a wrongful death action survives by virtue of the provisions of former NRS 41.110 (cf. NRS 41.100) is not personally liable but is one authorized to pay claims against the estate, such as the executor or general administrator, and did not include the special administrator.[1023]

Punitive damage claim did not survive death of tortfeasor. In a personal injury action, punitive damage claim did not survive the death of the tortfeasor and did not fall within the provisions of NRS 41.100, because punitive damages are awarded for the sake of example and by way of punishing defendant (see NRS 42.010) and these purposes cannot be accomplished if the defendant is deceased.[1024]

Subrogation of an insurer to the rights of an insured against public policy. Provision in a policy of automobile insurance which provided that upon the insurer's payment of medical expenses for injuries sustained by an insured in an automobile accident, the insurer was subrogated to the extent of that payment to all of the insured's rights of recovery was void as a violation of public policy.[1025]

Wrongful death cause of action is not preserved in decedent's estate. The provisions of NRS 41.100 do not apply when the representative of a deceased's estate sues for wrongful death and, therefore, the wrongful death cause of action is not preserved in the estate.[1026]

Proceeds of settlement of personal injury action may be assigned to a third party where assignee does not gain control of the action. Claiming that assignment of the proceeds of a settlement of a personal injury action by a client to the respondent was against public policy and that the attorney had a fiduciary duty to the client who requested that the proceeds be turned over to him, the attorney refused to release the proceeds of the settlement to the respondent and turned the proceeds over to the client. Although NRS 41.100 and public policy prohibit assignment of the right of tort action, the client could properly assign a portion of the proceeds from the settlement to the respondent because the client retained full control of the lawsuit and assignee could not pursue action independently. Therefore, because the assignment was validly executed, conveyance of the proceeds by the attorney to the client was in derogation of assignment.[1027]

Federal and Other Cases

Nevada law will apply in a suit for damages brought in another state unless the law of that state does not permit the representative of decedent to be sued. Nevada substantive law is applicable to torts committed within the state. Thus, NCL §§ 240.01 and 240.02 (cf. NRS 41.100), providing for the survival of a cause of action against a deceased tortfeasor, will apply in a suit for damages brought in another state unless the law of such state does not permit the representative of decedent to be sued on such a claim.[1028]

Damages for pain and suffering of the decedent may not be recovered. In a wrongful death action under the provisions of former NRS 41.080, the measure of damages is based upon and limited to the pecuniary loss suffered by the heirs of the decedent, and damages for pain and suffering endured by the deceased may not be recovered. An action under the provisions of former NRS 41.080 (cf. NRS 41.085) is not based on the survival of the decedent's cause of action against the tortfeasor, but is a new and independent cause of action in heirs, in view of NRS 41.100, which provides for the survival of a cause of action for personal injuries only.[1029]

The right to bring a survival action is limited to the appointed representatives of a decedent's estate. The right to bring a survival action pursuant to the provisions of NRS 41.100 is limited to the duly appointed representatives of the decedent's estate. Therefore, in a civil action brought by the mother and minor children of a person who was allegedly killed as a result of excessive forced used by police officers during a fight that occurred in the parking lot of a local bar, the mother and minor children lacked standing to assert a claim under 42 U.S.C. § 1983 where they: (1) failed to allege in their complaint that the claim was brought in a representative capacity on behalf of the decedent's estate; and (2) did not argue or offer any evidence that they had been appointed to represent the decedent's estate.[1030]

See "Statute of Limitations" and "Wrongful Death."

[1023] *Kotecki v. Augusztiny*, 87 Nev. 393, at 394, 487 P.2d 925 (1971), *Jacobson v. Estate of Clayton*, 121 Nev. 518, at 521, 119 P.3d 132 (2005).

[1024] *New Hampshire Ins. Co. v. Gruhn*, 99 Nev. 771, at 773, 670 P.2d 941 (1983), see also *Hansen v. Harrah's*, 100 Nev. 60, at 65, 675 P.2d 394 (1984).

[1025] See NRS 41.100 and 687B.145.) *Maxwell v. Allstate Ins. Co.*, 102 Nev. 502, 728 P.2d 812 (1986), *Canfora v. Coast Hotels and Casinos, Inc.*, 121 Nev. 771, at 778, 121 P.3d 599 (2005).

[1026] *Alsenz v. Clark County School Dist.*, 109 Nev. 1062, 864 P.2d 285 (1993).

[1027] *Achrem v. Expressway Plaza, Ltd.*, 112 Nev. 737, 917 P.2d 447 (1996).

[1028] *Gray v. Blight*, 112 F.2d 696 (10th Cir.), *cert. denied*, 311 U.S. 704, 85 L. Ed. 457, 61 S.Ct. 170 (1940).

[1029] *Borrego v. Stauffer Chem. Co.*, 315 F. Supp. 980 (1970).

[1030] *Moreland v. Las Vegas Metro. Police Dep't*, 159 F.3d 365 (9th Cir. 1998).

Third-Party Beneficiary

An individual obtains third-party-beneficiary status when the contracting parties demonstrate a clear intent to benefit the individual, a third party, by their contract.[1031] A third-party beneficiary has a direct right of action against the promisor in contract.[1032] That right is not necessarily carried forward to claims against a nonparty surety, which are allowable by statute.[1033]

Tortious Breach of the Covenant of Good Faith and Fair Dealing

Every contract in Nevada imposes upon the contracting parties a duty of good faith and fair dealing, which prohibits arbitrary or unfair acts by one party that work to the disadvantage of the other. Each party must act in a manner that is faithful to the purpose of the contract and the justified expectations of the other party.[1034]

While the covenant is in essence an implied contract term, occasionally courts have held that the breach of the implied covenant of good faith and fair dealing can also constitute a tort.[1035] This allows for tort damages as well as contract damages. The tortious breach of the covenant of good faith and fair dealing is generally limited to breaches by insurance companies against the insured.

To establish a contractual breach of the implied covenant of good faith and fair dealing, plaintiff must establish the following:

1. A contract existed between plaintiff and defendant;
2. Defendant performed in a manner that was unfaithful to the purpose of the contract or deliberately contravened the intention and spirit of the contract; and
3. Defendant's conduct was a substantial factor in causing damage to the plaintiff.[1036]

To establish a tortious breach of the implied covenant of good faith and fair dealing, plaintiff must establish the following:

1. Plaintiff and defendant were parties to a contract;
2. There was a special element of reliance or trust between plaintiff and defendant such that defendant was in a superior or entrusted position of knowledge;
3. Defendant performed in a manner that was unfaithful to the purpose of the contract or deliberately contravened the intention and spirit of the contract;
4. Defendant had an actual or implied awareness of the absence of a reasonable basis for not performing under the contract; and
5. Defendant's conduct was a substantial factor in causing damage to the plaintiff.[1037]

In every insurance contract there is an implied obligation of good faith and fair dealing that neither insurer nor the insured will do anything to injure the rights of the other party to receive the benefits of the agreement. The relationship of an insured to an insurer is one of special confidence akin to that of a fiduciary. A fiduciary relationship exists when one has the right to expect trust and confidence in the integrity and fidelity of another. This special relationship exists in part because, as insurers are well aware, consumers contract for insurance to gain protection, peace of mind and security against calamity. To fulfill its implied obligation of good faith and fair dealing, an insurer must give at least as much consideration to the interests of the insured as it gives to its own interests. Bad faith is established where

---

[1031] See *Lipshie v. Tracy Investment Co.*, 93 Nev. 370, 379, 566 P.2d 819, 824-25 (1977).

[1032] *Hemphill v. Hanson*, 77 Nev. 432, 436 n.1, 366 P.2d 92, 94 n.1 (1961).

[1033] See *Morelli v. Morelli*, 102 Nev. 326, 329, 720 P.2d 704, 706 (1986) (providing that, while a third-party beneficiary is generally "subject to the defenses that would be valid as between the parties," the notion that a third-party beneficiary steps into the shoes of a contracting party is a "misstatement of the law"); see also RESTATEMENT (SECOND) OF CONTRACTS § 309 cmt. c (1981) (providing that a third-party beneficiary's right to enforce a contract is "direct, not merely derivative").

[1034] *Falline v. GNLV*, 107 Nev. 1004, 823 P.2d 888 (1991); *Albert H. Wohlers & Co. v. Bartgis*, 114 Nev. 1249, 969 P.2d 949 (1998); *Morris v. Bank of America Nevada*, 110 Nev. 1274, 886 P.2d 454, 457 (1994); *Hilton Hotels Corp. v. Butch Lewis Productions, Inc.*, 109 Nev. 1043. 862 P.2d 1207 (1993); *Hilton Hotels Corp v. Butch Lewis Productions, Inc.*, 107 Nev. 226, 808 P.2d 919 (1991); *Nelson v. Heer*, 123 Nev. 217, 163 P.3d 420 (2007).

[1035] See, e.g., *Crisci v. Security Ins. Co.*, 426 P.2d 173 (Cal. 1967).

[1036] *Perry v. Jordan*, 111 Nev. 943, 900 P.2d 225 (1995); *Hilton Hotels Corp. v. Butch Lewis Production, Inc.*, 107 Nev. 226, 234, 808 P.2d 919 (1991).

[1037] *Great American Ins. Co. v. General Builders, Inc.*, 113 Nev. 346, 934 P.2d 257 (1997); *Falline v. GNLV*, 107 Nev. 1004, 823 P.2d 888 (1991); *Albert H. Wohlers & Co. v. Bartgis*, 114 Nev. 1249, 969 P.2d 949 (1998).

the insurer acts unreasonably and with knowledge that there is no reasonable basis for its conduct.[1038]

The insurance company's duty of good faith and fair dealing cannot be delegated to anyone.[1039]

A special or confidential relationship exists when one party gains confidence of the other and purports to act or advise with the other's interest in mind. It may exist although there is no fiduciary relationship; it is particular likely to exist when there is a family or friendly relationship.[1040]

It is not a breach of the implied covenant of good faith and fair dealing for an insurer to undertake a dispute in good faith. In determining whether the dispute is undertaken in good faith, you may consider all facts and circumstances bearing upon the insurer's conduct including:

1. The reasonableness of the insurer's investigation of the claim;
2. The reasonableness of the insurer's evaluation of the claim;
3. The reasonableness of the insurer's communications with the insured; and
4. The reasonableness of the insurer's interpretation of the contract.[1041]

An insurer has a duty to investigate a claim filed by its insured. When investigating a claim, an insurer has a duty to diligently search for, and to consider, evidence that supports an insured's claimed loss. An insurer may not reasonably and in good faith deny payments to its insured without thoroughly investigating the grounds for denial.[1042] If, in the handling of the claim, the insurer breached the implied covenant of good faith and fair dealing, the payment of the benefits due under the contract does not relieve it from the breach of the implied covenant of good faith and fair dealing.[1043]

The law recognizes certain principles with respect to the interpretation of an insurance policy. Those rules are:

1. An insurance policy is interpreted broadly affording the greatest possible coverage to the insured; and
2. The language in an insurance policy is viewed in its plain, ordinary, and popular meaning.[1044]

An insurance policy is a contract. If the language in the policy is clear and unambiguous, the language is enforced as written in order to accomplish the intent of the parties. However, as the insurer is in complete control of the language of an insurance policy, all doubt is construed against the insurer and in favor of the insured. An ambiguity exists when a policy term is subject to two reasonable interpretations. Any ambiguity in the terms of an insurance contract shall be resolved in favor of the insured and against the insurer.[1045]

An insurer breaches the implied covenant of good faith and fair dealing where it relies upon its own ambiguous

---

[1038] CACI (California Civil Jury Instructions for Judges and Attorneys) 2330; *Ainsworth v. Combined Ins. Co. of America*, 104 Nev. 587, 592, 763 P.2d 673 (1988); *Powers v United Services Auto. Ass'n*, 114 Nev. 690, 962 P.2d 596 (1998); *Albert H. Wohlers & Co. v. Bartgis*, 114 Nev. 1249, 969 P.2d 949 (1998); *Guaranty Nat. Ins. Co. v. Potter*, 112 Nev. 199, 912 P.2d 267, (1996).

[1039] *Albert H. Wohlers & Co. v. Bartgis*, 114 Nev. 1249, 969 P.2d 949 (1999).

[1040] *Perry v. Jordan*, 111 Nev. 943, 900 P.2d 335 (1995).

[1041] *American Excess Ins. Co. v. MGM Grand Hotels, Inc.*, 102 Nev. 601, 604, 729 P.2d 1352 (1986) (reasonable dispute not in bad faith); *Ainsworth v. Combined Ins. Co. of America*, 104 Nev. 587, 592, 763 P.2d 673 (1988) (on the obligation to investigate and evaluate and interpret the policy); *Powers v. United Services Auto. Ass'n*, 114 Nev. 690, 962 P.2d 596 (1998) (on the obligation to investigate and evaluate); *Albert H. Wohlers & Co. v. Bartgis*, 114 Nev. 1249, 969 P.2d 949 (1998) (regarding the duty to be truthful in dealing with the insured and prohibition against interpreting the policy to deprive an insured with "the peace of mind and security for which she had bargained").

[1042] CACI 2332.

[1043] *Guaranty Nat. Ins. Co. v. Potter*, 112 Nev. 199, 912 P.2d 267, 272 (1996).

[1044] *Farmers Ins. Group v. Stonik By and Through Stonik*, 110 Nev. 64, 867 P.2d 389 (1994) (citing to *Harvey's Wagon Wheel, Inc. v. MacSween*, 96 Nev. 215, 219-20, 606 P.2d 1095, 1098 (1980)) (regarding subpart 1). *American Excess Ins. Co. v. MGM Grand Hotels, Inc.*, 102 Nev. 601, 604, 729 P.2d 1352 (1986) (citing to *National Union Fire Ins. Co. of State of Pa., Inc. v. Reno's Executive Air, Inc.* 100 Nev. 360, 682 P.2d 1380 (1984) (regarding subpart 2).

[1045] *Insurance Corp. of America v. Rubin*, 107 Nev. 610, 616, 818 P.2d 389, 392 (1991); *National Union Fire Ins. Co. of State of Pa., Inc. v. Reno's Executive Air, Inc.*, 100 Nev. 360, 365, 682 P.2d 1380 (1984); *Farmers Ins. Exchange v. Young*, 108 Nev. 328, 330, 832 P.2d 376 (1992).

insurance contract as the sole basis for denying a claim.[1046]

The defendant may assert that the plaintiff made a material misrepresentation in the application for insurance or the claims process. A fact is material if it concerns a subject reasonably relevant to the insurance company's investigation, and if a reasonable person would attach importance to that fact. A representation is false when the facts fail to correspond with its assertions.[1047]

NRS 686A.010 *et seq.*, commonly referred to as the Nevada Unfair Insurance Practices Act, prohibits any person in the insurance business from engaging in activities which constitute an unfair or deceptive act or practice. In order to establish a claim for breach of the Nevada Unfair Insurance Practices Act, plaintiff must prove:

1.   That defendant violated a provision of the Nevada Unfair Insurance Practices Act; and
2.   The violation was a substantial factor in causing plaintiff's damages.[1048]

The Nevada Unfair Insurance Practices Act requires the insurance company to comply with the following laws:

1.   Each insurer shall fully disclose to claimants all pertinent benefits, coverages or other provisions of an insurance contract or policy under which a claims is presented;
2.   No agent may conceal from a claimant any of the benefits, coverages or other provisions of any insurance contract or policy when pertinent to a claims;
3.   Every insurer shall acknowledge the receipt of a claim notice within 20 working days after receipt of the claim notice unless payment of the claim is made within that time. If acknowledgement is made by means other than writing, an appropriate dated notation of the acknowledgement must be made in the claim file of the insurer. Notice given to an agent of an insurer is notice to the insurer;

4. An appropriate reply must be made within 20 working days after receipt of any other pertinent communication from a claimant if the communication reasonably suggests that a response is expected;

5. Each insurer, upon receiving notification of claim, shall promptly provide necessary claim forms, instructions and reasonable assistance so that claimants can comply with the policy conditions and the insurer's reasonable requirements. Compliance with the subsection within 20 working days after receipt of notification of a claim constitutes compliance with subsection 1;

6. Each insurer shall establish procedures to begin an investigation of any claim within 20 working days of receipt of notice of the claims. Each insurer shall mail or otherwise provide to each claimant, a notice of all items, statements and forms, if any, which the insurer reasonably believes will be required of the claimant, within 20 days after receiving notice of the claim; believes will be required of the claimant, within 20 days after receiving notice of the claim;

7. Each insurer shall complete an investigation of each claim within 30 days after receiving notice of the claim, unless the investigation cannot reasonably be completed within that time;

8. Within 30 working days after receipt by the insurer of properly executed proofs of loss, the claimant must be advised of the acceptance or denial of the claim by the insurer. No insurer may deny a claim on the grounds of a specific, condition or exclusion unless reference to that provision, condition or exclusion is included in the denial. The denial must be given to the claimant in writing and filed and retained in the insurer's claim file. If the claim of the claimant is accepted, the insurer shall pay the claim within 30 days after it is accepted;

9. If a claim is denied for reasons other than those described in subsection 1, and is made by any means other than writing, an appropriate notation must be made in the claim filed of the insurer, and

10. If the insurer needs more time to determine whether a claim of a claimant should be accepted or denied, it must so notify the claimant within 30 working days after receipt of the proof of loss giving reasons that more time is needed. If the investigation remains incomplete, the insurer shall, 30 days after the date of the initial notification and every 30 days thereafter, send to the claimant a letter setting forth the reasons that additional time is needed for investigation.

Violation of any of the above requirements is a violation of the Nevada Unfair Insurance Practices Act. Engaging in any of the activities does not in and of itself constitute "bad faith" on the part of defendant, but may be considered by you in determining whether the defendant has breach the covenant of good faith and fair dealing.[1049]

The Nevada Unfair Insurance Practices Act also pertains to unfair claims practices of insurance companies. It provides that engaging in any of the following activities is considered to be a violation of the law:

1. Misrepresenting to insureds or claimants pertinent facts or insurance policy provisions relating to any

---

[1046] *Alber H. Wohlers & Co. v. Bartgis*, 114 Nev. 1249, 969 P.2d 949 (1998); *Ainsworth v. Combined Ins. Co. of America*, 104 Nev. 587, 763 P.2d 673 (1988).

[1047] *Powers v. United Services Auto. Ass'n* , 114 Nev. 690, 962 P.2d 596 (1998).

[1048] NRS 686A.020.

[1049] NRS 686A.010–NRS 686A.310; NRS 686A.170; NRS 686A.675.

coverage at issue.

    2. Failing to acknowledge and act reasonably promptly upon communications with respect to claims arising under insurance policies;

    3. Failing to adopt and implement reasonable standards for the prompt investigation and processing of claims arising under insurance policies;

    4. Failing to effectuate prompt, fair and equitable settlements of claims in which liability of the insurer has become reasonably clear;

    5. Compelling insureds to institute litigation to recover amounts due under an insurance policy by offering substantially less that the amounts ultimately recovered in actions brought by such insureds, when the insureds have made a claim for amounts reasonably similar to the amounts ultimately recovered;

    6. Failing to provide promptly to an insured a reasonable explanation of the basis in the insurance policy, with respect to the facts of the insured's claim and the applicable law, for the denial of his claim or for an offer to settle or compromise his claim;

    7. Failing to affirm or deny coverage of claims within a reasonable time after proof of loss requirements have been completed and submitted by the insured;

    8. Failing, upon payment of a claim, to inform insureds or beneficiaries of the coverage under which payment is made.[1050]

    The fact-finder may also consider these standards in determining whether the defendant has breached the implied covenant of good faith and fair dealing.

    See also "Breach of the Implied Covenant of Good Faith and Fair Dealing."

Tortious Interference with Contract

    The elements of a claim of tortious interference with contract are: (1) a contract; (2) defendant's knowledge of the contract; (3) intentional interference by the defendant inducing or causing a breach of the contract; (4) absence of justification; and (5) damages resulting from defendant's conduct.[1051]

Trade Secrets

    Once a covenant not to compete has expired, the injunctive provisions that restricted the employee's business activities based on his likely violations of the Agreement should be dissolved once the Agreement is no longer enforceable. However, that does not necessarily mean that the injunctive provisions that applied to prevent likely trade secret violations should be dissolved.[1052]

    With respect to likely trade-secret violations, an injunction entered under Nevada's Uniform Trade Secrets Act "must be terminated when the trade secret has ceased to exist, but the injunction may be continued for an additional reasonable period of time to eliminate commercial or other advantage that otherwise would be derived from the misappropriation." NRS 600A.040(1). NRS 600A.040(1) requires that an injunction be terminated when the trade secret no longer exists. Assuming that trade secrets are found to exist, an injunction may only be extended for a "reasonable period of time" pursuant to NRS 600A.040(1). The comments to the Uniform Trade Secrets Act indicate that "an injunction should last for as long as is necessary, but no longer than is necessary, to eliminate the commercial advantage or 'lead time' with respect to good faith competitors that a person has obtained through misappropriation."[1053] Accordingly, such a determination should be made on a case-by-case basis by the district courts.[1054]

Trespass to Chattels

    A chattel is movable or transferable property; personal property.[1055] Trespass to chattels is the act of committing, without lawful justification, any act of direct physical interference with a chattel possessed by another. The act must amount to direct forcible injury.

    The RESTATEMENT (SECOND) OF TORTS § 217 defines trespass to chattels as "intentionally... dispossessing another of the chattel, or using or intermeddling with a chattel in the possession of another." Harm to personal property

---

[1050] NRS 686A.010-NRS 686A.310; NRS 686A.170

[1051] *Davis v. Board of Educ. of City of St. Louis*, 963 S.W.2d 679, 691 (Mo. App. 1998). See RESTATEMENT (SECOND) OF TORTS, Sections 766-774.

[1052] *Finkel v. Cashman Professional, Inc.*, 128 Nev. Adv. Op. No. 6 (2012).

[1053] Uniform Trade Secrets Act § 2 cmt., 14 U.L.A. 620 (2005).

[1054] *Id.*

[1055] *Black's Law Dictionary* 268 (9th ed. 2009).

or diminution of its quality, condition or value as a result of a defendant's use can also result in liability under § 218(b) of the RESTATEMENT.

Certain specific circumstances may lend themselves to liability for the action. The RESTATEMENT (SECOND) OF TORTS § 218 states further as follows:

> One who commits a trespass to a chattel is subject to liability to the possessor of the chattel if, but only if, (a) he dispossesses the other of the chattel, or (b) the chattel is impaired as to its condition, quality, or value, or (c) the possessor is deprived of the use of the chattel for a substantial time, or (d) bodily harm is caused to the possessor, or harm is caused to some person or thing in which the possessor has a legally protected interest.

The trespass to chattels cause of action, frequently asserted in recent years against Internet advertisers and email spammers, is often included in complaints against spyware companies. These electronic messaging cases, and their progeny, which have cropped up over the last decade, will typically turn on the situations described in (b) or (d), and, as detailed below, the question of harm caused is a big issue.

In sum, the basic elements of a claim of trespass to chattels are: 1) the lack of the plaintiff's consent to the trespass, 2) interference or intermeddling with possessory interest, and 3) the intentionality of the defendant's actions. Actual damage is not necessarily a required element of a trespass to chattels claim.

Trover

Trover [from Old French, from *trover* to find; see *trouvère*, troubadour] is the act of wrongfully assuming proprietary rights over personal goods or property belonging to another.[1056] There are three distinct methods by which one man may deprive another of his property, and so be guilty of a conversion and liable in an action for trover – (1) by wrongful taking it, (2) by wrongly detaining it, and (3) by wrongly disposing of it. Trover is a remedy of recovery only for the value of whatever was taken, not for the recovery of the property itself (see Replevin).[1057]

The authorities have recognized the evolution of the common law tort of conversion.[1058] At common law, trover was the remedy for conversion, which was limited to tangible personal property, "capable of being identified and taken into actual possession."[1059] The court said, "but the fiction on which the action of trover was founded, namely, that a defendant had found the property of another, which was lost, has become, in the progress of law, an unmeaning thing, which has been by most courts discarded; so that the action no longer exists as it did at common law, but has been developed into a remedy for the conversion of every species of personal property."[1060] The court concluded that the defendant's conversion of shares of stock, an intangible property interest, without converting the share certificates, constituted an actionable conversion.[1061]

[1056] *Collins English Dictionary—Complete and Unabridged* copyright HarperCollins Publishers 1991, 1994, 1998, 2000, and 2003.

[1057] *Black's Law Dictionary* 381 (9th ed. 2009), citing R.F.V. Heuston, *Salmond on the Law of Torts* 94 (17th ed. 1977).

[1058] *Welco Electronics, Inc. v. Mora*, B240626 (Cal.App. Dist.2 01/23/2014).

[1059] *Payne v. Elliot*, 54 Cal. 339, 340 (1880).

[1060] *Id.* at p. 341.

[1061] *Id.* at pp. 341-342.

The Lawyer without Cases Who Pretends to Be Busy
By Honoré Daumier

Uninsured Motorist (UIM)

NRS 687B.145, "Provisions in policies of casualty insurance: Proration of recovery or benefits; uninsured and underinsured motorist coverage; coverage for medical expenses; insurer not entitled to subrogation upon payment made because of underinsured vehicle coverage," provides in relevant part as follows:

> 2. Except as otherwise provided in subsection 5, insurance companies transacting motor vehicle insurance in this State must offer, on a form approved by the Commissioner, uninsured and underinsured vehicle coverage in an amount equal to the limits of coverage for bodily injury sold to an insured under a policy of insurance covering the use of a passenger car. The insurer is not required to reoffer the coverage to the insured in any replacement, reinstatement, substitute or amended policy, but the insured may purchase the coverage by requesting it in writing from the insurer. Each renewal must include a copy of the form offering such coverage. Uninsured and underinsured vehicle coverage must include a provision which enables the insured to recover up to the limits of the insured's own coverage any amount of damages for bodily injury from the insured's insurer which the insured is legally entitled to recover from the owner or operator of the other vehicle to the extent that those damages exceed the limits of the coverage for bodily injury carried by that owner or operator. If an insured suffers actual damages subject to the limitation of liability provided pursuant to NRS 41.035, underinsured vehicle coverage must include a provision which enables the insured to recover up to the limits of the insured's own coverage any amount of damages for bodily injury from the insured's insurer for the actual damages suffered by the insured that exceed that limitation of liability.
>
> . . .
>
> 4. An insurer who makes a payment to an injured person on account of underinsured vehicle coverage as described in subsection 2 is not entitled to subrogation against the underinsured motorist who is liable for damages to the injured payee. This subsection does not affect the right or remedy of an insurer under subsection 5 of NRS 690B.020 with respect to uninsured vehicle coverage. As used in this subsection, "damages" means the amount for which the underinsured motorist is alleged to be liable to the claimant in excess of the limits of bodily injury coverage set by the underinsured motorist's policy of casualty insurance.
>
> 5. An insurer need not offer, provide or make available uninsured or underinsured vehicle coverage in connection with a general commercial liability policy, an excess policy, an umbrella policy or other policy that does not provide primary motor vehicle insurance for liabilities arising out of the ownership, maintenance, operation or use of a specifically insured motor vehicle.

(Added to NRS by 1979, 1090; A 1981, 15; 1983, 1105; 1989, 1567, 1846; 1991, 1943; 1997, 3032; 2003, 3312)

186

There was no cumulation of coverage for bodily injury liability. In an action for wrongful death resulting from a collision of motor vehicles, where the policy of insurance which afforded coverage to defendant provided coverage for three motor vehicles owned by defendant's mother and also provided coverage for bodily injury caused while driving a nonowned vehicle, coverage provided for bodily injury applicable to each insured vehicle could not be tripled, thereby increasing the limits of coverage under the provision in the policy for nonowned vehicles. The cumulation of coverage applicable to uninsured motorists and basic reparation benefits did not apply to the coverage for liability for bodily injury.[1062]

Plaintiff could not recover under coverage for uninsured motorists where the insured also had coverage for liability for bodily injuries; purpose of statute. In an action brought against an insurance company to recover for personal injuries sustained while plaintiff was riding as a passenger on insured's motorcycle, where insured had a policy of automobile insurance which provided coverage for liability for bodily injuries and uninsured motorist coverage, plaintiff could not recover benefits under the latter coverage to increase coverage for bodily injuries because the purpose of NRS 687B.145, which requires an insurer to offer uninsured motorist coverage equal to the limits of coverage for bodily injuries sold to the insured, is to provide an opportunity to procure protection against a tortfeasor who has inadequate insurance and requires tortious involvement of a party and vehicle other than the insured and his vehicle.[1063]

An amendment to a policy to limit the cumulation of coverage was not in clear language and prominently displayed under the circumstances. An amendment to an original policy of insurance which purported to prevent the cumulation of uninsured motorists coverages did not comply with NRS 687B.145, which requires that the limiting provision be expressed in clear language and be prominently displayed in the policy, binder or endorsement, where (1) the amendment was not labeled or lettered correctly and, therefore, did not correspond to the original policy, (2) large, bold-faced print of the amendment appeared throughout the original policy, (3) the amendment had the same type and spacing as the original policy, and (4) the section of the amendment which addressed uninsured motorists coverage emphasized, through the use of darker, bolder type, "covered persons," thereby directing the insureds' attention away from the restricting language. Cumulation of coverages was, therefore, permitted.[1064]

An amendment to a statute that required insurers to offer coverage for uninsured motorists equal to the limits for bodily injury became part of the insured's policy after the effective date of the amendment. Where plaintiff purchased an insurance policy which provided greater coverage for bodily injury than uninsured motorist coverage, and the state statute was then amended to require insurance companies to offer uninsured motorist coverage equal to the limits of insured's coverage for bodily injury (see NRS 687B.145), the increased insurance coverage required by that statute became, by implication of law, part of plaintiff's policy after the effective date of that amendment.[1065]

Where plaintiff settled a claim against a tortfeasor for the maximum amount recoverable under the tortfeasor's insurance policy and then brought an action against her insurer seeking additional compensation under the terms of her own policy which provided underinsured motorist protection, the insurer was liable under NRS 687B.145, which required underinsured motorist coverage to include a provision which enabled the insured to recover any amount of damages for bodily injury which exceeded the limits of coverage for bodily injury carried by the tortfeasor, for those damages not recoverable under the tortfeasor's policy, less that amount plaintiff received in reparation benefits under the provisions of her policy providing no-fault coverage.[1066]

Subrogation of insurer to rights of insured against public policy. The provision in a policy of automobile insurance which provided that upon the insurer's payment of medical expenses for injuries sustained by the insured in an

---

[1062] *Rando v. California State Auto. Ass'n*, 100 Nev. 310, 684 P.2d 501 (1984), *Allstate Ins. Co. v. Pilosof*, 110 Nev. 311, at 315, 871 P.2d 351 (1994).

[1063] *Peterson v. Colonial Ins. Co.*, 100 Nev. 474, 686 P.2d 239 (1984), cited, *Baker v. Criterion Ins. Co.*, 107 Nev. 25, at 26, 805 P.2d 599 (1991).

[1064] *Neumann v. Standard Fire Ins. Co.*, 101 Nev. 206, 699 P.2d 101 (1985), cited, *Maxwell v. Allstate Ins. Cos.*, 102 Nev. 502, at 506, 728 P.2d 812 (1986), Montana *Refining Co. v. National Union Fire Ins. Co.*, 918 F. Supp. 1395, at 1398 (D. Nev. 1996), distinguished, *Allstate Ins. Co. v. Clemmons*, 742 F. Supp. 1073, at 1075 (D. Nev. 1990).

[1065] *Ippolito v. Liberty Mut. Ins. Co.*, 101 Nev. 376, 705 P.2d 134 (1985), cited, *Estate of Delmue v. Allstate Ins. Co.*, 113 Nev. 414, at 418, 936 P.2d 326 (1997).

[1066] *Mid-Century Ins. Co. v. Daniel*, 101 Nev. 433, 705 P.2d 156 (1985), cited, *Maxwell v. Allstate Ins. Cos.*, 102 Nev. 502, at 506, 728 P.2d 812 (1986), see also *Phelps v. State Farm Mut. Auto. Ins. Co.*, 112 Nev. 675, at 680, 917 P.2d 944 (1996).

automobile accident, the insurer was subrogated to the extent of that payment to all of insured's rights of recovery was void as a violation of public policy.[1067]

The minimum statutory coverage was not defeated by the policy exclusions. An automobile insurance policy included an uninsured motorist exclusion for owned but uninsured cars. The insured collided with another car while driving one of his vehicles which was not insured under the policy. He received $15,000, the policy limit, from the other driver. However, his total damages exceeded this amount by $35,000. The insurer contended that the underinsured motorist coverage was limited to $15,000, the minimum required by statute, and paid that amount to the insured. In affirming summary judgment in favor of the insurer, the court held that the exclusion of vehicles not insured under a policy is void to prevent payment of the statutory minimum ($15,000) but valid to restrict the payment of any amount in excess thereof. (See NRS 687B.145 and 690B.020).[1068]

The phrase "must offer" was defined. The term "must offer" as used in NRS 687B.145(2) means that insurance carriers must notify their policyholders that uninsured motorist coverage equal to their bodily injury coverage is available.[1069]

Requirement concerning provisions that limit benefits not applicable to automobile liability coverage because such coverage is not stackable. The requirement of NRS 687B.145 that any provision that limits benefits pursuant to the section must be in clear language and prominently displayed in the policy, binder or endorsement was not applicable to automobile liability coverage because the requirement applies only to insurance coverage, such as uninsured motorist coverage, which is otherwise stackable.[1070]

Under the former provisions of NRS, underinsured motorist coverage was a mere component of uninsured motorist coverage and did not exist separately. The provisions of NRS 690B.020 and the former provisions of NRS 687B.145 did not require that insurers provide separate coverages against uninsured and underinsured motorists, but rather that insurers make uninsured motorist coverage available and that such coverage include coverage against underinsured motorists. Underinsured motorist coverage was merely a component of uninsured motorist coverage and did not exist separately (cf. NRS 687B.145, as amended). Where appellant purchased one coverage for which he paid one premium, he was entitled to only one recovery.[1071]   Restrictions on stacking of medical payments coverage did not satisfy statutory requirements. The restrictions on the stacking of insurance coverage contained in three policies issued to insured by the same insurer, which restrictions consisted of a series of five provisions, none of which standing alone indicated to insured that his medical payments coverage was not stackable, did not satisfy the statutory requirements of clear and prominently displayed stacking limitations contained in NRS 687B.145 and, therefore, insured was entitled to medical payments coverage under all three policies.[1072]

Granting of summary judgment was error where insurer failed to produce both original policy and amendment containing "anti-stacking" provision. Where a clause containing a provision restricting the stacking of insurance coverage was not contained in the insurance policy itself, but rather, in a separate amendment to the policy, it was error for the district court to grant summary judgment for the insurer where insurer failed to produce copies of both the amendment and original policy because a comparison of the original policy with the amendment is necessary in order to assess the validity of such a clause pursuant to NRS 687B.145.[1073]

Language restricting stacking of insurance coverage must be truly comprehensible to the average insured and not merely technically correct. The requirements set forth in NRS 687B.145 for clauses restricting the stacking of coverage in policies of insurance must be strictly construed to require more than a simple lack of ambiguity. The

---

[1067] (See NRS 41.100 and NRS 687B.145.) *Maxwell v. Allstate Ins. Co.*, 102 Nev. 502, 728 P.2d 812 (1986), cited, *Achrem v. Expressway Plaza, Ltd.*, 112 Nev. 737, at 740, 917 P.2d 447 (1996), Martinez v. State, 115 Nev. 9, at 12, 974 P.2d 133 (1999), *Canfora v. Coast Hotels and Casinos, Inc.*, 121 Nev. 771, at 778, 121 P.3d 599 (2005).

[1068] *Zobrist v. Farmers Ins. Exch.*, 103 Nev. 104, 734 P.2d 699 (1987), cited, *Nelson v. California State Auto. Ass'n Inter-Insurance Bureau*, 114 Nev. 345, at 348, 956 P.2d 803 (1998), *Collins v. Farmers Ins. Exch.*, 61 F. Supp. 2d 1124, at 1127 (D. Nev. 1999), *Farmers Ins. Exch. v. Neal*, 119 Nev. 62, at 65, 64 P.3d 472 (2003), *Continental Ins. Co. v. Murphy*, 120 Nev. 506, at 511, 96 P.3d 747 (2004).

[1069] *Quinlan v. Mid Century Ins. Co.*, 103 Nev. 399, 741 P.2d 822 (1987), cited, *Khoury v. Maryland Cas. Co.*, 108 Nev. 1037, at 1039, 843 P.2d 822 (1992), *Breithaupt v. USAA Property & Cas. Ins. Co.*, 110 Nev. 31, at 33, 867 P.2d 402 (1994).

[1070] *Wood v. State Farm Mut. Ins. Co.*, 104 Nev. 735, 766 P.2d 269 (1988), cited, *State Farm Mut. Ins. Co. v. Knauss*, 105 Nev. 407, at 408, 775 P.2d 707 (1989).

[1071] *Hall v. Farmers Ins. Exch.*, 105 Nev. 19, 768 P.2d 884 (1989), cited, *Hartz v. Mitchell*, 107 Nev. 893, at 897, 822 P.2d 667 (1991).

[1072] *State Farm Mut. Ins. Co. v. Knauss*, 105 Nev. 407, 775 P.2d 707 (1989), cited, *Nationwide Mut. Ins. Co. v. Moya*, 108 Nev. 578, at 585, 837 P.2d 426 (1992).

[1073] *Torres v. Farmers Ins. Exch.*, 106 Nev. 340, 793 P.2d 839 (1990).

language must be truly comprehensible to the average insured in order to put him on actual notice of the true effect of such clauses. Where the language used in the policy was technically correct, but the average insured would not realize its significance, the language was not sufficiently clear to satisfy.[1074]

The insurer has the burden to prove the validity of an anti-stacking provision. The burdens of persuasion and production on the issue of the validity of the provision in a policy of automobile insurance prohibiting the stacking of uninsured motorist coverages rest on the insurer. The insured generally has the reasonable expectation that he will receive additional indemnification for each separate premium paid for uninsured motorist coverage, and when he seeks to stack such coverages, the insurer has the burden to defeat that reasonable expectation by proving the validity of the anti-stacking provision pursuant to NRS 687B.145.[1075]

An insured may recover under uninsured and underinsured coverage only if both another person and another vehicle are involved. Where the appellant was injured while riding as a passenger in her own vehicle which was being driven by a permissive user who had no insurance policy of his own, the appellant was not entitled to recover, in addition to the limit of bodily injury coverage of her own policy, compensation pursuant to uninsured and underinsured coverage in her policy because NRS 687B.145, which provides that an insured may recover, up to limits of his uninsured and underinsured coverage, damages for bodily injury from his insurer which he is legally entitled to recover from the owner or operator of the other vehicle to the extent that those damages exceed the limits of coverage for bodily injury carried by that owner or operator, applies only where both a person other than the insured and a vehicle other than the insured's vehicle is involved.[1076]

Lessee of a rental car could not recover from insurer of rental car agency for damages caused by uninsured motorist where insurer had made offer of uninsured motorist coverage to rental car agency. Where an insurance company offered uninsured and underinsured coverage to a rental car agency as required in NRS 687B.145 and the agency rejected such coverage, the insurance company had satisfied its statutory duty and was entitled to summary judgment in an action brought by the survivors of the person who rented the car from the agency and was killed in a collision with the vehicle driven by an uninsured motorist.[1077]

An "exhaustion clause" is void as violating public policy. A clause in a policy of motor vehicle insurance which provided that the insurer would pay under uninsured and underinsured coverage only after the limits of liability under any applicable bodily injury liability bonds or policies had been exhausted by payments of judgments or settlements was void as violative of public policy because such clauses unnecessarily promote litigation costs, increase the number of trials, and unreasonably delay the recovery of underinsured motorist benefits.[1078]

The former provisions placed a burden on insurer to prove by clear and convincing evidence that an offer of uninsured vehicle coverage was made. The former provisions of NRS 687B.145 required an insurer to offer uninsured and underinsured vehicle coverage in the amount equal to the limits of coverage for bodily injury, but did not require the offer to be made on a form approved by the Commissioner. The court interpreted those provisions as placing a burden on the insurer to prove by clear and convincing evidence that the offer was made. In determining whether the insurer has met the burden, the court set forth a four-part test: (1) notification must be in a commercially reasonable manner; (2) the limits of optional coverage must be specified and not set forth in general terms; (3) the insured must be intelligibly advised by the insurer of the nature of the option; and (4) the insurer must advise insured that optional coverage is available for relatively modest premium increases.[1079]

Uninsured motorist coverage limited to compensatory damages for bodily injury; punitive damages not recoverable. In an action by insured against an insurer for payment of punitive damages awarded against a third party, insured was not entitled to seek payment of an award of punitive damages from the insurer under insured's uninsured motorist coverage. The purpose of punitive damages is to punish and deter oppressive, fraudulent or malicious conduct,

---

[1074] *Id.*, cited, *Bove v. Prudential Ins. Co.*, 106 Nev. 682, at 686, 799 P.2d 1108 (1990), *Serrett v. Kimber*, 110 Nev. 486, at 489, 874 P.2d 747 (1994), see also *Breithaupt v. USAA Property & Cas. Ins. Co.*, 110 Nev. 31, at 34, 867 P.2d 402 (1994), *Montana Refining Co. v. National Union Fire Ins. Co.*, 918 F. Supp. 1395, at 1398 (D. Nev. 1996), distinguished, *Farmers Ins. Group v. Stonik*, 110 Nev. 64, at 70, 867 P.2d 389 (1994), *Nationwide Mut. Ins. Co. v. Coatney*, 118 Nev. 180, at 184, 42 P.3d 265 (2002).

[1075] *Torres v. Farmers Ins. Exch.*, 106 Nev. 340, 793 P.2d 839 (1990), cited, *Bove v. Prudential Ins. Co.*, 106 Nev. 682, at 687, 799 P.2d 1108 (1990), see also *Serrett v. Kimber*, 110 Nev. 486, at 489, 874 P.2d 747 (1994)

[1076] *Baker v. Criterion Ins. Co.*, 107 Nev. 25, 805 P.2d 599 (1991), cited, *Farmers Ins. Exch. v. Young*, 108 Nev. 328, at 331, 832 P.2d 376 (1992).

[1077] *Hartz v. Mitchell*, 107 Nev. 893, 822 P.2d 667 (1991).

[1078] (See NRS 687B.145.) *Mann v. Farmers Ins. Exch.*, 108 Nev. 648, 836 P.2d 620 (1992), cited, *Shaw v. Continental Ins. Co.*, 108 Nev. 928, at 930, 840 P.2d 592 (1992), *State Farm Fire & Cas. Co. v. Otto*, 106 F.3d 279, at 283 (9th Cir. 1997), distinguished, *Ray v. Continental W. Ins. Co.*, 920 F. Supp. 1094, at 1098 (D. Nev. 1996).

[1079] *Khoury v. Maryland Cas. Co.*, 108 Nev. 1037, 843 P.2d 822 (1992).

and to allow recovery of punitive damages from an innocent party's own insurer would distort and misdirect that purpose by shifting responsibility for satisfying such awards from deserving tortfeasors to undeserving owners of vehicles in the form of higher insurance premiums. Recovery by insured under uninsured motorist coverage is limited to damages for bodily injury which are compensatory in nature.[1080]

The purpose of uninsured motorist coverage (see NRS 687B.145 and 690B.020) is to mitigate losses sustained by drivers and other insureds who, through no fault of their own, are involved in a collision with a driver who is uninsured or inadequately insured.[1081]

Meaning of the term "legally entitled to recover" as used in section. Under the provision in NRS 687B.145 which provides that uninsured vehicle coverage must enable an insured to recover from his own insurer up to the limits of his own coverage for damages for bodily injury which he is legally entitled to recover from the owner or operator of the other vehicle, the term "legally entitled to recover" means that an insured must be able to establish fault on the part of the uninsured motorist which gives rise to damages and to prove the extent of those damages. However, the insured is not required to obtain judgment against a tortfeasor before the insured is entitled to receive proceeds under the uninsured motorist policy.[1082]

Insurer satisfied its duty under the former provisions of section to notify its insureds of the availability of uninsured motorist coverage equal to bodily injury coverage. Under the former provisions of NRS 687B.145, which required insurers to offer uninsured motor vehicle coverage equal to the limits of bodily injury coverage sold to an individual policyholder, the insurer satisfied its duty to notify its customers where the notice was sufficient to inform the average layman who was untrained in law or the field of insurance that uninsured or underinsured motorist coverage equal to bodily injury coverage was available.[1083]

The Supreme Court did not retroactively apply the amendatory provisions of section under circumstances. In general, the overruling of judicial construction of a statute will not be given retroactive effect. Thus, the Supreme Court declined to apply retroactively the amendatory provisions of NRS 687B.145 where retroactive application would not improve consumer awareness of the benefits of purchasing optional uninsured motorist coverage, would not provide insurers with the opportunity to comply retroactively with the new and more demanding standard of notice, would be highly inequitable to insurers and would do nothing to promote the objectives of the section of imposing a greater duty of notice upon insurers.[1084]

Anti-stacking provision was sufficiently prominent despite the existence of other such provisions which were virtually identical in substance and style. The anti-stacking provision set forth in an amendment to an insurance policy satisfied the requirement of prominence (see NRS 687B.145) where the provision was printed in bold-faced, large letters and was conspicuously different from the balance of the amendment. The existence of two other anti-stacking provisions in the amendment, which were virtually identical in substance and style to the provision in question, did not diminish the prominence of any one of them.[1085]

Anti-stacking provision satisfied the requirement of clarity under circumstances. The anti-stacking provision set forth in an amendment to a insurance policy satisfied the requirement of clarity (see NRS 687B.145) where, although the original policy and the amendment were organized differently, the amendment correctly identified the affected provisions of the policy and left no doubt as to the purpose or effect of the amendment.[1086]

Insurer that wrote umbrella policy which covered the use of a passenger car was required to offer uninsured and underinsured vehicle coverage under the former provisions of section. Where the insured bought an umbrella policy which included coverage for a loss arising out of the occupancy of the vehicle by a teenage son, but did not include uninsured and underinsured vehicle coverage, and the son was subsequently killed while riding as a passenger in the vehicle, the district court erred in finding that the insurer was not required to provide uninsured and underinsured vehicle coverage to the insured in an amount equal to the amount of the umbrella policy. The plain language of the former provisions of NRS 687B.145, which required an insurer to provide uninsured and underinsured vehicle coverage under a policy of insurance covering the use of a passenger car, did not distinguish between a primary automobile coverage policy and an umbrella policy. Therefore, because an umbrella policy covered the use of a passenger car, the insurer was

---

[1080] *Siggelkow v. Phoenix Ins. Co.*, 109 Nev. 42, 846 P.2d 303 (1993), cited, *Lombardi v. Maryland Cas. Co.*, 894 F. Supp. 369, at 372 (D. Nev. 1995).

[1081] *Siggelkow v. Phoenix Ins. Co.*, 109 Nev. 42, 846 P.2d 303 (1993), cited, *Kern v. Nevada Ins. Guar. Ass'n*, 109 Nev. 752, at 758, 856 P.2d 1390 (1993), *State Farm Mut. Auto. Ins. Co. v. Fitts*, 120 Nev. 707, at 710, 99 P.3d 1160 (2004).

[1082] *Pemberton v. Farmers Ins. Exch.*, 109 Nev. 789, 858 P.2d 380 (1993).

[1083] *Breithaupt v. USAA Property & Cas. Ins. Co.*, 110 Nev. 31, 867 P.2d 402 (1994).

[1084] *Id.*

[1085] *Serrett v. Kimber*, 110 Nev. 486, 874 P.2d 747 (1994).

[1086] *Id.*

required to offer uninsured and underinsured vehicle coverage in compliance with NRS 687B.145. (N.B., the case was decided before the amendment of NRS 687B.145 in 1997.)[1087]

An explicit limitation on coverage in a manner that does not violate public policy is not prohibited. The automobile insurance policy insuring two of the insured's vehicles contained a provision excluding uninsured motorist ("UM") coverage for any injury sustained while occupying an owned but uninsured vehicle ("owned but uninsured exclusion") and the insured was injured in an accident with an uninsured motorist while the insured was operating a vehicle not insured under the policy. The insured argued that if the owned but uninsured exclusion operated to prevent the UM coverage from being stacked, then he received no benefit for the additional premium he paid on the second vehicle. In affirming summary judgment for the insurer, the court held that the insured's coverage was expressly limited by the owned but uninsured clause and that while the insurer was required to pay the statutory minimum, an explicit limitation on coverage in a manner that does not violate public policy is not prohibited.[1088]

The commencement of the period for a cause of action for benefits under an underinsured motorist provision of a motor vehicle insurance policy did not begin to run until the insurer refused payment of the insured's claim. Where the insured filed suit against her motor vehicle insurer to recover underinsured motorist coverage benefits (see NRS 687B.145 and NRS 690B.020) 6 years and 2 months after her accident and the insurer argued that the 6-year statute of limitations set forth in NRS 11.190 providing that an action upon a written contract must be commenced within 6 years barred her claim, the court held that the statute of limitations did not begin to run until the insurer refused payment of the insured's claim.[1089] An insurer must be allowed to enforce a provision limiting uninsured motorist recovery to the limits on a single insured vehicle. Restricting uninsured motorist (UM) recovery to the highest amount on a single vehicle is not the only valid anti-stacking method at an insurer's disposal. Provided that the prerequisites set forth in NRS 687B.145(1) are met, an insurer may alternatively restrict UM recovery to the limits on a single insured vehicle.[1090]

A self-insurer was neither uninsured nor underinsured. A motorist was injured in an accident with a street sweeping machine owned by the City of Reno. In relevant part, the motorist's damages allegedly exceeded $50,000 (the liability limit for state and local governments pursuant to NRS 41.035), but the motorist settled his claim with the City for $45,000. The motorist then attempted to claim the damages that allegedly exceeded $50,000 as against his own insurance policy's uninsured motorist and underinsured motorist coverage. As explained by the Supreme Court, a local government may, pursuant to NRS 41.038, self-insure against liability claims up to their maximum limit of $50,000. Furthermore, NRS 485.380 allows a person in whose name more than 10 vehicles are registered in the State of Nevada to qualify as a self-insurer by obtaining a certificate of self-insurance from the Department of Motor Vehicles. As the City of Reno had, in fact, self-insured up to the $50,000 limit, the City was a "qualified self-insured" and, thus, the motorist's insurance company was not obligated to pay uninsured motorist benefits to him. In addition, underinsured motorist coverage as required pursuant to NRS 687B.145 was not at issue, because the City had self-insured to the statutory amount of $50,000. (N.B., the case was decided before the amendment of NRS 687B.145 in 2003.)[1091]

Nonoccupancy exclusion clause for underinsured motorist benefits was void to extent it negated minimum required coverage limits. An automobile insurer brought an action against an insured for a declaratory judgment that the insured's insurance policy excluded underinsured motorist benefits for bodily injuries that the insured sustained while riding a motorcycle that was not covered under the policy. The Nevada Supreme Court held that such an exclusion clause in an insurance policy violates public policy and is, therefore, void, to the extent that it does not satisfy the minimum coverage requirements for insurance policies for motor vehicles found in NRS 687B.145 and NRS 690B.020.[1092]

Federal and Other Cases

Arbitration award in an action by insured against tortfeasor barred subsequent action by insured against insurer pursuant to underinsured motorist coverage. Insured was involved in an automobile accident, sued the driver of the vehicle which had struck hers and agreed to submit the case to binding arbitration. The arbitrator, after an adversarial hearing, found in favor of insured and awarded her approximately $17,000 in damages. The adverse driver's insurance company paid the awarded amount to insured and the state court action was dismissed with prejudice. Insured then

---

[1087] *Estate of Delmue v. Allstate Ins. Co.*, 113 Nev. 414, 936 P.2d 326 (1997).

[1088] See NRS 687B.145 and NRS 690B.020. *Nelson v. California State Auto. Ass'n Inter-Insurance Bureau*, 114 Nev. 345, 956 P.2d 803 (1998), cited, *Collins v. Farmers Ins. Exch.*, 61 F. Supp. 2d 1124, at 1127 (D. Nev. 1999), *Farmers Ins. Exch. v. Neal*, 119 Nev. 62, at 65, 64 P.3d 472 (2003).

[1089] *Grayson v. State Farm Mut. Auto. Ins.*, 114 Nev. 1379, 971 P.2d 798 (1998), cited, *State Farm Mut. Auto. Ins. Co. v. Fitts*, 120 Nev. 707, at 711, 99 P.3d 1160 (2004).

[1090] *Nationwide Mut. Ins. Co. v. Coatney*, 118 Nev. 180, 42 P.3d 265 (2002).

[1091] *White v. Continental Ins. Co.*, 119 Nev. 114, 65 P.3d 1090 (2003).

[1092] *Continental Ins. Co. v. Murphy*, 120 Nev. 506, 96 P.3d 747 (2004), cited, *Griffin v. Old Republic Ins. Co.*, 122 Nev. 479, at 482, 133 P.3d 251 (2006).

brought an action against her own insurer to recover approximately $135,000 pursuant to her underinsured motorist coverage (see NRS 687B.145), and the insurer removed the action to federal court. The court, in granting the insurer's motion for summary judgment, held that the issue of damages had been conclusively determined by the arbitrator and insured was collaterally estopped from relitigating that issue because: (1) when arbitration affords an opportunity for the presentation of evidence and an argument substantially similar in form and scope to the judicial proceedings, the arbitrator's award should have the same effect on the issues necessarily determined as judgment has; and (2) a party not involved in arbitration may use the award in that arbitration to bind his opponent if the party to be bound was before the arbitrator, had full and fair opportunity to litigate the issue, and the issue was actually decided by the arbitrator or was necessary to his decision. (See NRS ch. 38.)[1093]

Insured who received arbitration award from tortfeasor was not entitled to recover compensation from own insurer pursuant to underinsured motorist coverage. Where: (1) underinsured motorist clause of an insurance policy (see NRS 687B.145) provided that the insurer would pay compensatory damages which insured was legally entitled to recover from the owner or operator of the underinsured motor vehicle because of bodily injury; (2) insured chose to litigate a claim against the tortfeasor arising from the automobile accident and agreed to binding arbitration in that litigation; (3) arbitrator conclusively determined amount of damages due insured; (4) insured received payment of those damages; and (5) state court dismissed insured's action against tortfeasor with prejudice, insured was not thereafter legally entitled to recover any damages from the tortfeasor and, therefore, the insurer had no liability to insured pursuant to the underinsured motorist clause of the policy.[1094]   General release signed by insureds did not bar claim under uninsured vehicle coverage provided in umbrella policy. Where insureds, at the time of settling a claim under uninsured vehicle coverage provided by their primary policy of motor vehicle insurance, signed a general release of all claims against their primary insurer and "all other persons, corporate, partnership or individual," insureds were entitled to pursue a claim under uninsured vehicle coverage provided in a separate umbrella policy because there was undisputed evidence which demonstrated that: (1) the insureds did not intend to release their secondary insurer; (2) the primary insurer knew the insureds did not intend to release the secondary insurer; and (3) no part of the settlement could be classified as consideration for the release of the secondary insurer. (See NRS 17.245, NRS 687B.145 and NRS 690B.020.)[1095]

A claim under an umbrella policy was not barred on the ground that the insureds entered into a settlement for less than the limits of coverage provided by primary policy of insurance; liability of secondary insurer. The insureds who settled a claim under the uninsured vehicle coverage provided by their primary policy of motor vehicle insurance for less than the limits of coverage provided by that policy were not barred from making a claim under uninsured vehicle coverage provided by a separate umbrella policy. However, the secondary insurer could be liable only for damages in excess of the limits of coverage provided by the primary policy of insurance. (See NRS 687B.145 and 690B.020.)[1096]

A second action brought by an insured against her insurer for its bad faith denial of her claim for medical payments was barred by the doctrine of res judicata. The plaintiff sued her insurer for breach of contract and for the insurer's bad faith denial of her claim for medical payments under her automobile insurance policy (see NRS 686A.310, NRS 687B.145 and NRS 690B.016 et seq. and former NRS 690B.015). The plaintiff prevailed on her claim for breach of contract, but the trial court granted summary judgment for the insurer on the claim of bad faith. The plaintiff did not appeal the decision of the trial court, but filed a second action against the insurer in which she claimed that she had discovered, while the previous litigation was underway, evidence of "post-filing" bad faith, for which she sought damages in addition to those awarded for breach of contract. The case was removed to federal court on the ground of diversity and dismissed by the federal district court under the doctrine of res judicata. On appeal, the United States Court of Appeals affirmed the decision of the federal district court and held that, although the duty of good faith on the part of an insurer continues after an initial denial of coverage and requires the insurer to consider new evidence brought to its attention after the initial denial, there is no authority to suggest that the Nevada courts would allow a separate bad faith action based on the insurer's refusal to consider new evidence that was uncovered during discovery. The proper remedy for the plaintiff would have been to have appealed the decision of the trial court in her initial action.[1097]

[1093] *Ray v. Continental W. Ins. Co.*, 920 F.Supp. 1094 (D. Nev. 1996).
[1094] *Id.*
[1095] *State Farm Fire & Cas. Co. v. Otto*, 106 F.3d 279 (9th Cir. 1997).
[1096] *Id.*
[1097] *Sosebee v. State Farm Mut. Auto. Ins. Co.*, 164 F.3d 1215 (9th Cir. 1999).

Stacking UIM

NRS 687B.145(1) provides in relevant part as follows:

> Any provision which limits benefits pursuant to this section must be in clear language and be prominently displayed in the policy, binder or endorsement. Any limiting provision is void if the named insured has purchased separate coverage on the same risk and has paid a premium calculated for full reimbursement under that coverage.

Normally, an insured has a reasonable expectation that she will receive additional UIM indemnification for each separate UIM premium paid.[1098] When the insurer attempts to defeat this reasonable expectation, it must prove the validity of its anti-stacking provision in accordance with the requirements of NRS 687B.145(1).[1099] "The burdens of persuasion and production on the issue of the validity of an anti-stacking clause prohibiting stacking of [UIM] coverage limits rest on the insurer."[1100]

Unjust Enrichment

Unjust enrichment occurs whenever a person has and retains a benefit which in equity and good conscience belongs to another.[1101] The statute of limitations for an unjust enrichment claim is four years.[1102] See "Quasi contract."

Unlawful Detention in Violation of the Civil Rights Act of 1866, 42 U.S.C. § 1983

Section 1983 provides a cause of action against any person who, acting under color of state law, "subjects, or causes to be subjected, any citizen of the United States or other person within the jurisdiction thereof to the deprivation of any rights, privileges, or immunities secured by the Constitution and laws[.]" 42 U.S.C. § 1983. Where the Section 1983 defendants are public entities, the plaintiff must demonstrate both an underlying deprivation of a federal right, and that the deprivation "was caused by an official policy or custom."[1103]

A plaintiff may establish that a governmental entity's policy caused a violation of his constitutional rights through one of three ways. A governmental entity may be liable under Section 1983 if the alleged constitutional violations were caused by: (1) an official policy adopted and promulgated by the entity's officers; (2) a governmental practice or custom that, though not officially authorized by law or express policy, is widespread and well settled so as to constitute a custom or usage with the force of law; or (3) an act by an official with final policymaking authority where that act is in conformity with, or in the creation of, governmental policy or rules that essentially have the force of law.[1104] A plaintiff asserts a prima facie claim that an Unlawful Detention Policy violated his Fourth and Fourteenth Amendment rights when he alleges that the Defendants detained him for an unreasonable length of time and in an unreasonable manner after Defendants no longer had probable cause or any right to detain him.[1105]

Unlawful Employment Practices

NRS 613.330, "Unlawful employment practices: Discrimination on basis of race, color, religion, sex, sexual orientation, age, disability or national origin; interference with aid or appliance for disability; refusal to permit service animal at place of employment," provides as follows:

1. Except as otherwise provided in NRS 613.350, it is an unlawful employment practice for an employer:

(a) To fail or refuse to hire or to discharge any person, or otherwise to discriminate against any person with respect to the person's compensation, terms, conditions or privileges of employment, because of his or her race, color, religion, sex, sexual orientation, age, disability or national origin; or

(b) To limit, segregate or classify an employee in a way which would deprive or tend to deprive the employee

---

[1098] *Torres v. Farmers Ins. Exchange*, 106 Nev. 340, 793 P.2d 839, 842-43 (1990).

[1099] *Id.* at 843.

[1100] *Id.* at 842.

[1101] *LeasePartners Corp. v. Brook Trust*, 113 Nev. 747 (1997).

[1102] NRS 11.190(2)(c).

[1103] *Sow v. Fortville Police Dep't*, 636 F.3d 293, 301 (7th Cir. 2011) (citing *Monell v. New York City Dep't of Social Servs.*, 436 U.S. 658, 690 n. 55, 98 S. Ct. 2018, 56 L. Ed. 2d 611 (1978)).

[1104] See *Thomas v. Cook Cnty. Sheriff's Dept.*, 604 F.3d 293, 303 (7th Cir. 2009) (citing *Monell*, 436 U.S. at 690); *Valentino v. Vill. of S. Chi. Heights*, 575 F.3d 664, 674 (7th Cir. 2009)).

[1105] *Otero v. Dart*, No. 12 C 3148, 2012 WL 5077727, at *2 (N.D. Ill. Oct. 18, 2012).

of employment opportunities or otherwise adversely affect his or her status as an employee, because of his or her race, color, religion, sex, sexual orientation, age, disability or national origin.

2. It is an unlawful employment practice for an employment agency to:

(a) Fail or refuse to refer for employment, or otherwise to discriminate against, any person because of the race, color, religion, sex, sexual orientation, age, disability or national origin of that person; or

(b) Classify or refer for employment any person on the basis of the race, color, religion, sex, sexual orientation, age, disability or national origin of that person.

3. It is an unlawful employment practice for a labor organization:

(a) To exclude or to expel from its membership, or otherwise to discriminate against, any person because of his or her race, color, religion, sex, sexual orientation, age, disability or national origin;

(b) To limit, segregate or classify its membership, or to classify or fail or refuse to refer for employment any person, in any way which would deprive or tend to deprive the person of employment opportunities, or would limit the person's employment opportunities or otherwise adversely affect the person's status as an employee or as an applicant for employment, because of his or her race, color, religion, sex, sexual orientation, age, disability or national origin; or

(c) To cause or attempt to cause an employer to discriminate against any person in violation of this section.

4. It is an unlawful employment practice for any employer, labor organization or joint labor-management committee controlling apprenticeship or other training or retraining, including, without limitation, on-the-job training programs, to discriminate against any person because of his or her race, color, religion, sex, sexual orientation, age, disability or national origin in admission to, or employment in, any program established to provide apprenticeship or other training.

5. It is an unlawful employment practice for any employer, employment agency, labor organization or joint labor-management committee to discriminate against a person with a disability by interfering, directly or indirectly, with the use of an aid or appliance, including, without limitation, a service animal, by such a person.

6. It is an unlawful employment practice for an employer, directly or indirectly, to refuse to permit an employee with a disability to keep the employee's service animal with him or her at all times in his or her place of employment.

7. As used in this section, "service animal" has the meaning ascribed to it in NRS 426.097.

Waiver

Waiver requires the intentional relinquishment of a known right.[1106]

Workers' Compensation

Before 1980, the Nevada Industrial Commission was the sole provider of workers' compensation insurance in Nevada.[1107] But, in 1979, recognizing that some employers could fund compensation benefits by themselves, the Legislature allowed employers to opt out of the state industrial insurance system and remain personally liable for the claims of their injured employees.[1108] Thus, the Legislature permitted those qualified employers to "self-insure."[1109] As self-insurers, these employers are exempt from the statutory requirement that employers purchase workers' compensation insurance.[1110]

However, in order to qualify as a "self-insured employer," the employer must be certified by the Commissioner of Insurance, which requires the employer to prove that it is financially capable of assuming the responsibility to pay the claims of its injured workers.[1111] Additionally, the self-insured employer must obtain excess insurance in order to "provide protection against a catastrophic loss."[1112] The excess insurance policy protects the self-insured employer when the specific or total losses in a policy year exceed its deductible.[1113] The Workers' Compensation Act defines "insurer" as

---

[1106] *Nevada Yellow Cab Corp. v. Eighth Judicial District Court of the State of Nevada*, 123 Nev. 44, 152 P.3d 737 (2007).

[1107] Legislative Counsel Bureau, Leg. Comm. on Workers' Compensation, Bulletin No. 01-19 at 5, 71st Leg. (Nev. 2001).

[1108] *Id.*; see generally NRS Chapter 616B.

[1109] *Id.*; NRS 616B.300.

[1110] See generally NRS 616B.300.

[1111] NRS 616A.305; see also NRS 616B.300(1).

[1112] NRS 616B.300(5).

[1113] 23 Eric Mills Holmes, *Appleman on Insurance* § 145.1 at 4 (2d ed., § 145.1 at 4 (2d ed., interim vol., 2003) (stating that "excess coverage" is a second layer of insurance coverage that is generally "triggered on the exhaustion of the limits of the primary policy").

including self-insured employers.[1114]

Nevada recognizes a limited exception to the collateral source rule for workers' compensation payments, whether the payments are made by Nevada or another State.[1115]

Wrongful Death

NRS 41.085, "Heirs and personal representatives may maintain action," provides as follows:

1. As used in this section, "heir" means a person who, under the laws of this State, would be entitled to succeed to the separate property of the decedent if the decedent had died intestate. The term does not include a person who is deemed to be a killer of the decedent pursuant to Chapter 41B of NRS, and such a person shall be deemed to have predeceased the decedent as set forth in NRS 41B.330.

2. When the death of any person, whether or not a minor, is caused by the wrongful act or neglect of another, the heirs of the decedent and the personal representatives of the decedent may each maintain an action for damages against the person who caused the death, or if the wrongdoer is dead, against the wrongdoer's personal representatives, whether the wrongdoer died before or after the death of the person injured by the wrongdoer. If any other person is responsible for the wrongful act or neglect, or if the wrongdoer is employed by another person who is responsible for the wrongdoer's conduct, the action may be maintained against that other person, or if the other person is dead, against the other person's personal representatives.

3. An action brought by the heirs of a decedent pursuant to subsection 2 and the cause of action of that decedent brought or maintained by the decedent's personal representatives which arose out of the same wrongful act or neglect may be joined.

4. The heirs may prove their respective damages in the action brought pursuant to subsection 2 and the court or jury may award each person pecuniary damages for the person's grief or sorrow, loss of probable support, companionship, society, comfort and consortium, and damages for pain, suffering or disfigurement of the decedent. The proceeds of any judgment for damages awarded under this subsection are not liable for any debt of the decedent.

5. The damages recoverable by the personal representatives of a decedent on behalf of the decedent's estate include:

(a) Any special damages, such as medical expenses, which the decedent incurred or sustained before the decedent's death, and funeral expenses; and

(b) Any penalties, including, but not limited to, exemplary or punitive damages, that the decedent would have recovered if the decedent had lived,

but do not include damages for pain, suffering or disfigurement of the decedent. The proceeds of any judgment for damages awarded under this subsection are liable for the debts of the decedent unless exempted by law.

(Added to NRS by 1979, 458; A 1995, 2667; 1999, 1354)

Nevada Cases.

General

An action for wrongful death which occurred in California is transitory and its enforcement is recognized by this State. In an action brought in Nevada for a wrongful death which occurred in California, the trial court did not err in its assumption of jurisdiction, because the cause of action is by statute of California transitory, and enforcement of such cause of action is recognized by the statutes of this State, sec. 1, ch. 48, Stats. 1905 (cf. NRS 41.085).[1116]

Proceeds from a wrongful death action brought by a wife on behalf of a minor child were not within meaning of "acquired" as used in statute defining community property; the husband's negligence was not imputed to wife. The proceeds from the exercise of the right by the wife, under the provisions of NCL § 8553 (cf. NRS 12.080 and 41.085), to maintain an action for the wrongful death or injury of her minor child do not come within the meaning of the word

---

[1114] NRS 616A.270(1); see *MGM Mirage v. Nevada Ins. Guaranty Ass'n,* 125 Nev., Advance Opinion 22 (2009).

[1115] NRS 616C.215(10); see *Tri-County Equipment & Leasing v. Klinke,* 128 Nev. Adv. Op. No. 33 (2012).

[1116] *Christensen v. Floriston Pulp & Paper Co.,* 29 Nev. 552, 92 Pac. 210 (1907), cited, *Forrester v. Southern Pac. Co.,* 36 Nev. 247, at 271, 134 Pac. 753, 136 Pac. 705 (1913), *Leach v. Mason Valley Mines Co.,* 40 Nev. 143, at 150, 161 Pac. 513 (1916).

"acquired" as used in NCL § 3356 (cf. NRS 123.220), defining community property, and the husband's negligence is not imputed to wife to bar her recovery for death or injury of her minor child.[1117]

The basis for an action for wrongful death must be found in the statutes; the remedies in the statutes are exclusive. In an action to recover damages for wrongful death, because no such right of action existed at common law, basis must be found in NCL § 9194, providing that a cause of action in favor of decedent shall survive, 1931 NCL § 9195, providing who may bring this action and how proceeds shall be distributed, and 1931 NCL § 8554, establishing a right of action for wrongful death of an adult by his heirs or by his personal representative or guardian for his heirs (cf. NRS 41.085), and remedies there given are exclusive.[1118]

Common-law rule of parental immunity from suit by child not expressly repealed by former statute. Although 1931 NCL § 8554 (cf. NRS 41.085) gives heirs of deceased person the right to bring an action against a person causing wrongful death and does not expressly preclude a minor from bringing an action by his guardian against one parent for wrongful death of the other, neither does it expressly repeal the common-law rule of parental immunity from suit by child, and in the absence of such express repeal the rule remains in effect.[1119]

The court was justified in using only the appellant's theory of express repeal of parental immunity from suit in considering effect of statute. Where appellant contended that wrongful death statute, 1931 NCL § 8554 (cf. NRS 41.085), did not by implication repeal the common-law rule of parental immunity from an action in tort by a child, but expressly did so by providing that heirs could sue the person causing the wrongful death, without making any limitation upon child suing a parent, the court was justified in using only the appellant's theory of express repeal in considering the effect of the statute.[1120]

An unborn child is a "person" within the meaning of the statute. An unborn child was a "person" within meaning of the Nevada wrongful death statute, the former NRS 41.080 (cf. NRS 41.085).[1121]

Right of action for wrongful death is a personal right, not a community right. In an action under the Nevada wrongful death statute, former NRS 41.080 (cf. NRS 41.085), the family purpose statute, NRS 41.440, did not operate to impute contributory negligence of husband to wife, so as to bar an action by the wife for financial compensation for the wrongful death of her unborn child. Such right of action is a personal, not a community, right.[1122]

Statute of limitations. In an action for wrongful death pursuant to NRS 41.085 brought in 1981, where the decedent received improper medical treatment beginning in 1976 and, as a result thereof, died in 1979, the 2-year statute of limitations provided in NRS 41A.097 did not run before plaintiff filed his complaint because, as used in that statute, "injury" means legal injury and since death is an essential element of a cause of action for wrongful death, there can be no legal injury until death has occurred, and the period of limitation, therefore, does not begin to run until the time of decedent's death or discovery thereof.[1123]

Wrongful death: Choice of law; place where injury is suffered. In a wrongful death action (see NRS 41.085), the "injury" is to the survivors. Thus, for the purposes of the factors set forth in *Motenko v. MGM Dist., Inc.*, 112 Nev. 1038 (1996), used to determine whether a state other than the forum state has an overwhelming interest, the "place where the injury is suffered" is the state in which all or most of the survivors are residents.[1124]

Heirs

The widow and the minor child of the decedent were entitled to bring an action. In an action to recover damages for wrongful death, where plaintiffs were the widow and minor child of decedent, they were entitled to bring an action under 1931 NCL § 8554 (cf. NRS 41.085), affording a right of action to heirs.[1125]

The word "heirs" as used in the wrongful death statute, the former NRS 12.090 (cf. NRS 41.085), to specify persons who may maintain an action includes any person entitled to inherit the estate of decedent.[1126]

[1117] *Los Angeles & S.L.R.R. v. Umbaugh*, 61 Nev. 214, 123 P.2d 224 (1942), cited, *Morrissett v. Morrissett*, 80 Nev. 566, at 571, 397 P.2d 184 (1964) (dissenting opinion).

[1118] *Alsenz v. Clark County School Dist.*, 109 Nev. 1062, at 1064, 864 P.2d 285 (1993).

[1119] *Strong v. Strong*, 70 Nev. 290, 267 P.2d 240 (1954), cited, *Kennedy v. Kennedy*, 76 Nev. 302, at 305, 352 P.2d 833 (1960), distinguished, *Rupert v. Stienne*, 90 Nev. 397, at 404, 528 P.2d 1013 (1974).

[1120] *Id.*

[1121] *White v. Yup*, 85 Nev. 527, 458 P.2d 617 (1969).

[1122] *Id.*

[1123] *Gilloon v. Humana, Inc.*, 100 Nev. 518, 687 P.2d 80 (1984), *State Indus. Ins. Sys. v. Lodge*, 107 Nev. 867, at 869, 822 P.2d 664 (1991).

[1124] See also NRS 1.030; *Northwest Pipe Co. v. Eighth Judicial Dist. Court*, 118 Nev. 133, 42 P.3d 244 (2002), but see *General Motors Corp. v. Eighth Judicial Dist. Court*, 122 Nev. 466, at 472, 134 P.3d 111 (2006).

[1125] *Wells, Inc. v. Shoemake* [sic], 64 Nev. 57, 177 P.2d 451 (1947), cited, *Nevada Paving, Inc. v. Callahan*, 83 Nev. 208, at 213, 427 P.2d 383 (1967) (dissenting opinion).

Right of adopted child was paramount to the rights of surviving brothers and sisters of decedent. Adopted child had the right to maintain an action for wrongful death of his adoptive parent under the provisions of former NRS 12.090 (cf. NRS 41.085), and such right was paramount to the rights of the surviving brothers and sisters of decedent.[1127]

Illegitimate child was a "child" and "heir" within meaning of statute. Minor posthumous illegitimate child had a cause of action for wrongful death of her putative father where paternity was clearly established despite lack of written acknowledgment pursuant to the provisions of former NRS 134.170 (cf. NRS 126.051), because for purposes of a wrongful death action, she was a "child" of decedent within meaning of the term as used in the provisions of former NRS 41.090 (cf. NRS 41.085), and an "heir" within the meaning of former provisions of NRS 12.080, since the equal protection clause prohibits discrimination between legitimate and illegitimate children in wrongful death actions.[1128]

Separate verdicts proper for parents and child of deceased. In a wrongful death action a separate verdict in favor of the parents of deceased was proper because separate causes of action existed for the parents under former provisions of NRS 12.080 and for the child under former NRS 41.080 and 41.090 (cf. NRS 41.085). An allowance of attorney fees under NRS 18.010(2) on the verdict of $10,000 in favor of the parents was proper.[1129]

An action by a widow on behalf of minor heirs was not barred by the statute of limitations applicable to the widow. Where a wrongful death action by the decedent's widow, acting as the guardian ad litem of the minor heirs, was not commenced until after running of the two-year limitation period prescribed by NRS 11.190, the action was not barred by the statute of limitations applicable to the widow because the provisions of former NRS 12.090 (cf. NRS 41.085) created separate causes of action in minor heirs and under NRS 11.250, the running of the statute of limitations as to their claims was suspended during their minority.[1130]

Personal Representatives

"Personal representative" includes temporary, special or ancillary administrators or executors. The term "personal representative" as used in wrongful death statute, former NRS 12.090 (cf. NRS 41.085), is generally considered broad enough to include temporary, special or ancillary administrators or executors.[1131]

A right of action was sufficient to justify the appointment of a special administrator to act as personal representative for purpose of filing suit. Where the estate of the deceased had no assets, but there existed a cause of action for wrongful death, the court did not exceed its jurisdiction in appointing a special administrator. This was so because the right of action, although not an asset of the estate, was sufficient to justify appointing an administrator who could then act as the personal representative for the purpose of filing suit, as authorized by the former NRS 12.090 (cf. NRS 41.085), and hold the proceeds for the benefit of the heirs who suffered loss by reason of the decedent's death.[1132]

Damages

The trial court did not err in refusing to instruct the jury on the present cash value of damages to be suffered in the future. In a wrongful death action, under the provisions of former NRS 41.090 (cf. NRS 41.085), which provided that damages may include compensation for loss of probable future companionship, society and comfort, the trial court did not err in refusing to instruct jury on present cash value of damages to be suffered in the future from defendant's wrongful act, because damages for loss of probable future companionship, society and comfort are subject to the rule relating to future pain and suffering, and the weight of authority is against reduction of damages for such intangible elements.[1133]

The word "pecuniary" is not limited to a tangible financial loss. The provisions of former NRS 41.090 (cf. NRS 41.085), which empowered the court or jury in a wrongful death action to award such pecuniary damages as are fair and just, including damages for loss of probable future companionship, society and comfort, are clear, and do not warrant a jury instruction that word "pecuniary" is limited in meaning to tangible financial loss.[1134]

[1126] *Bower v. Landa*, 78 Nev. 246, 371 P.2d 657 (1962), cited, *Weaks v. Mounter*, 88 Nev. 118, at 126, 493 P.2d 1307 (1972) (dissenting opinion), *Parker v. Chrysler Motors Corp.*, 88 Nev. 560, at 562, 502 P.2d 111 (1972).

[1127] *Bower v. Landa*, 78 Nev. 246, 371 P.2d 657 (1962).

[1128] *Weaks v. Mounter*, 88 Nev. 118, 493 P.2d 1307 (1972).

[1129] *Id.*

[1130] *Parker v. Chrysler Motors Corp.*, 88 Nev. 560, 502 P.2d 111 (1972), cited, *Turner v. Staggs*, 89 Nev. 230, at 240, 510 P.2d 879 (1973) (dissenting opinion), *Gibbs v. Giles*, 96 Nev. 243, at 247, 607 P.2d 118 (1980).

[1131] *Nevada Paving, Inc. v. Callahan*, 83 Nev. 208, 427 P.2d 383 (1967), distinguished, *Klosterman v. Cummings*, 86 Nev. 684, at 690, 476 P.2d 14 (1970).

[1132] *Id.*

[1133] *Porter v. Funkhouser*, 79 Nev. 273, 382 P.2d 216 (1963).

[1134] *Id.*

The court may exclude evidence on collateral issue of a change in defendant's habits between time of accident and time of trial. In a wrongful death action, where punitive damages were sought under the provisions of former NRS 41.090 (cf. NRS 41.085), the evidence of a change in defendant's habits between time of the accident which had caused death and time of the trial concerned a collateral issue, and it was within province of the court to exclude such evidence on the ground that it might be harmful or prejudicial to one party and of little benefit to the other.[1135]

Inclusion of damages for loss of probable future companionship, society and comfort in an award of compensatory damages was not grossly excessive. In a wrongful death action by four adult children for death of their 68-year-old mother, although the only evidence of loss of services of objective monetary value was insufficient to sustain an award of $35,000 compensatory damages, under the provisions of former NRS 41.090 (cf. NRS 41.085), which empowered jury to include damages for loss of probable future companionship, society and comfort, such award was not so grossly excessive as a matter of law that it shocked judicial conscience, and thus was not disturbed upon appeal.[1136]

Damages for loss of probable future companionship, society and comfort are not required to bear reasonable relation to pecuniary loss. Under the provisions of former NRS 41.090 (cf. NRS 41.085), which empowered the jury in a wrongful death action to include damages for loss of probable future companionship, society and comfort, there was no requirement that such damages bear reasonable relation to pecuniary loss.[1137]

Court not required to instruct jury that it may consider reduced purchasing power of dollar in determining amount of damages. In a wrongful death action, under the provisions of former NRS 41.090 (cf. NRS 41.085), which empowered the court or jury to award such damages as are fair and just, an instruction to the jury that they could consider reduced purchasing power of the dollar in determining amount of damages was proper because the court left it in the discretion of the jury whether or not to consider such factor. Refusal to give such instruction would not have been error because the jury need hardly be reminded of what they perceive in daily life.[1138]

The testimony of an economist may be used to prove the loss of probable support. Pursuant to NRS 41.085, in a medical malpractice case, (1) heirs of decedent may prove damages for loss of probable support, (2) such damages, based on decedent's lost earning capacity, may include present as well as future loss of support, and (3) testimony of economist is accepted means of proving loss of probable support.[1139]

Damages recoverable by decedent's estate. In an action brought under NRS 41.085, a decedent's estate cannot recover for lost economic opportunities of decedent or punitive damages.[1140]

Federal and Other Cases

New cause of action created in personal representative. Under B §§ 115 and 116 (cf. NRS 41.085), a new cause of action is created in personal representative of deceased and it is, therefore, immaterial whether deceased died instantly or time intervened between injury and death, as no question of survival of deceased's cause of action is involved.[1141]

It is not necessary to allege the existence of kindred. Under B §§ 115 and 116 (cf. NRS 41.085), which provide for recovery of damages for wrongful death, it is not necessary to allege the existence of kindred unless there is an action for injury to kindred as well as for death of deceased.[1142]

Exemplary damages may be awarded where negligence was willful, wanton or malicious. Under Nevada wrongful death statute, C §§ 3983 and 3984 (cf. NRS 41.085), exemplary damages can be awarded only where negligence causing death was willful, wanton or malicious.[1143]

Only persons named in statute may maintain action. Since the wrongful death action is created by statute, only those persons specifically named in the statute may maintain such action.[1144]

[1135] *Id.*

[1136] *Id.*

[1137] *Id.*

[1138] *Id.*

[1139] *Freeman v. Davidson*, 105 Nev. 13, 768 P.2d 885 (1989), cited, *Gonzales v. Stewart Title*, 111 Nev. 1350, at 1354, 905 P.2d 176 (1995).

[1140] *Alsenz v. Clark County School Dist.*, 109 Nev. 1062, 864 P.2d 285 (1993).

[1141] *Roach v. Imperial Mining Co.*, 7 Fed. 698 (C.C.D. Nev. 1881).

[1142] *Id.*

[1143] *Benner v. Truckee River Gen. Elec. Co.*, 193 Fed. 740 (C.C.D. Nev. 1911).

[1144] *Perry v. Tonopah Mining Co.*, 13 F.2d 865 (D. Nev. 1915).

Nonresident heirs have cause of action under Nevada law which can be sued upon in other jurisdiction. Nonresident heirs of decedent killed in a train wreck in Nevada have a cause of action for wrongful death under NCL § 8554 (cf. NRS 41.085) which can be sued upon in other jurisdictions.[1145]

A foreign personal representative need not obtain ancillary appointment in Nevada to recover for the benefit of decedent's heirs; proceeds not subject to claims of decedent's creditors. Under the provisions of former NRS 12.090, 41.080 and 41.090 (cf. NRS 41.085), a foreign personal representative may maintain a wrongful death action in Nevada against a Nevada resident without obtaining an ancillary appointment in Nevada where he is not suing for the benefit of decedent's general estate, but to recover for the benefit of decedent's heirs, and the proceeds will not be subject to claims of decedent's creditors.[1146]

In a collision between a military aircraft and a commercial airliner, the duty of the United States to passengers was to exercise ordinary care and the duty of the air carrier was to exercise highest degree of care. In a wrongful death action under the provisions of former NRS 12.090 and 41.080 (cf. NRS 41.085), arising out of the collision between a military trainer aircraft and a commercial airliner operating under regulations of the Civil Aeronautics Administration, the duty of the United States toward passengers was to exercise ordinary care for their safety, and the duty of the air carrier was to exercise highest degree of care.[1147]

Nevada limitation on applicability of res ipsa loquitur was not inherent in cause of action. In a wrongful death action arising out of an aircraft collision, the limitation imposed by Nevada law on applicability of res ipsa loquitur as a rule of evidence was not inherent in the cause of action created by former NRS 12.090 and 41.080 (cf. NRS 41.085), and the law of forum was properly applied in instructing the jury on res ipsa loquitur.[1148]

An award under the former statute to heirs based on estimated future earnings of decedent less necessary personal expenditures and taxes was not only adequate but generous. Under the provisions of former NRS 41.090 (cf. NRS 41.085), which at the time of accident did not include a provision for damages for loss of companionship, the wrongful death award to heirs based on estimated earnings of decedent during future working years, less necessary personal expenditures and income tax withholding, was not only adequate but generous.[1149]

Damages for pain and suffering of decedent may not be recovered. In a wrongful death action under the provisions of former NRS 41.080 the measure of damages is based upon and limited to the pecuniary loss suffered by heirs of decedent, and the damages for pain and suffering endured by deceased may not be recovered. An action under the provisions of former NRS 41.080 (cf. NRS 41.085) is not based on the survival of decedent's cause of action against tortfeasor, but is a new and independent cause of action in heirs, in view of NRS 41.100, which provides for survival of a cause of action for personal injuries only.[1150]

The parents were entitled to recover for loss of probable support although they were not dependent upon decedent. In an action for wrongful death brought by the decedent's parents, the parents were entitled to recover for loss of probable support under NRS 41.085 because, although the parents were not dependent on decedent for support, there was a reasonable expectancy that, except for his death, decedent would have contributed gifts and aid having an established pecuniary value to his parents.[1151]

The trial court could make a separate award for damages to each parent of decedent. In an action for wrongful death brought by decedent's parents, the trial court could make a separate award for damages to each parent rather than

---

[1145] *Stone v. Southern Pac. Co.*, 32 F. Supp. 819 (S.D.N.Y. 1940).
[1146] *Sonner v. Cordano*, 228 F. Supp. 435 (D. Nev. 1963).
[1147] *United Air Lines, Inc. v. Wiener*, 335 F.2d 379 (9th Cir. 1964).
[1148] *Id.*
[1149] *United States v. Sommers*, 351 F.2d 354 (C.C.A. 10th 1965).
[1150] *Borrego v. Stauffer Chem. Co.*, 315 F. Supp. 980 (1970).
[1151] *Moyer v. United States*, 593 F. Supp. 145 (D. Nev. 1984).

awarding a lump sum to both parents because NRS 41.085 allows the trier of fact to award each heir pecuniary damages for injuries specified in that statute.[1152]

"Penalties" does not include lost economic benefits. Damages recoverable by personal representatives of decedent on behalf of his estate do not include lost economic benefits because "penalties" as used in NRS 41.085 (5) means civil penalties or perhaps punitive damages.[1153]

To be compensable in wrongful death action, the pain and suffering of the decedent, including the loss of enjoyment of life, must be consciously experienced. In an action for wrongful death pursuant to NRS 41.085, defendant's motion to strike plaintiff's claim for damages for loss of enjoyment of life was granted because (1) the only kinds of pecuniary damages available for wrongful death under Nevada law are those specified in NRS 41.085, (2) the only possible element in NRS 41.085 that could include decedent's loss of enjoyment of life is the provision allowing recovery for pain and suffering of decedent, (3) to be compensable in a wrongful death action in Nevada, pain and suffering must be consciously experienced, and (4) therefore, plaintiffs could only recover for that part of decedent's loss of enjoyment of life that was consciously experienced before death, and such recovery was included in plaintiff's claim for damages for the pain and suffering of decedent.[1154]

Appellants were precluded from asserting a cause of action for wrongful death under the circumstances. On appeal from an order of the district court granting summary judgment in favor of the defendants arising out of the alleged killing of a person as a result of excessive force used by police officers during a fight that occurred in the parking lot of a local bar, the appellants were precluded from asserting a cause of action for wrongful death pursuant to the provisions of NRS 41.085 where: (1) the district court, in granting the defendants' motion for summary judgment, had ruled that the shooting of the decedent was not wrongful; and (2) instead of addressing that ruling on appeal, the appellants argued that they had standing to bring the cause of action. The failure by the appellants to challenge the ruling of the district court waived any argument that the evidence was sufficient to proceed to trial on their cause of action for wrongful death.[1155]

See "Survival of Causes of Action."

Wrongful Execution/ Wrongful Garnishment

An owner whose property is wrongfully seized under execution against another has, ordinarily, an adequate remedy at law for damages, except where his business and credit will be so affected as to make it difficult or impossible to estimate the injury in damages, in which case he may seek injunctive relief.[1156]

Wrongful garnishment refers to improperly obtaining or tortiously employing the remedy of garnishment. A party is entitled to garnish property only where the garnishee in fact owes a debt to the garnishor, and where the garnishee owns a beneficial interest in the property garnished. Where these facts do not appear, a claim for wrongful garnishment arises even where the garnishing party acted without malice and had probable cause to believe garnishment was appropriate. Further, some jurisdictions recognize the applicability of a wrongful garnishment claim where property that belongs to a debtor is statutorily exempted from garnishment.[1157]

***

[1152] *Id.*

[1153] *Hanshew v. United States Fidelity & Guar. Co.*, 746 F. Supp. 55 (D. Kan. 1990).

[1154] *Pitman v. Thorndike*, 762 F. Supp. 870 (D. Nev. 1991).

[1155] *Moreland v. Las Vegas Metro. Police Dep't*, 159 F.3d 365 (9th Cir. 1998).

[1156] *Boone v. Lou Budke's Arrow Finance*, 98 S.W.3d 555 (Mo.App. W.D. 07/16/2002) (Mo. Ct. App. 2002).

[1157] *Vanover v. Cook*, 260 F.3d 1182 (10th Cir. Kan. 2001).

First Considerations

1) Extension: The first act that defense counsel may take, particularly if much of the 20 days has already been taken up by the client's delay in seeking an attorney, is to seek an extension of time in which to answer "or otherwise respond." This language leaves open the possibility of a Rule 12 motion, discussed below.

2) Investigate: Although it helps to have the client go through and "admit" or "deny" each paragraph in writing, defense counsel should also investigate independently the facts and the possible legal defenses.

3) Tender: Because service of a complaint means a claim is being made, counsel should advise the client to tender the defense and coverage to any applicable insurance companies, if this has not already been done.

4) Counterclaim: Next, consider whether the defendant has any possible or even "compulsory" counterclaims. Small but valid legal claims, which on their own would not merit the cost or trouble of litigation, can make an effective counterattack and can be a source of possible offset.

5) Remove/Remand: Should this action be in state court or federal court? The deadline for removal is 30 days from receipt or service of the complaint upon the defendant, per 28 U.S.C. § 1446. A motion to remand back to state court must be made within 30 days after the notice of removal.[1158]

6) Dismiss: Is it possible and advisable to bring a motion to dismiss under Rule 12 in lieu of answering? After *Twombly*[1159] and *Iqbal*,[1160] this tactic is popular.[1161] It does depend on what the claims are. As a practical matter, it can delay service of an answer for months, and possibly result in no answer ever being filed.

7) Motion to Strike: Defendants can also seek relief under Rule 12 other than judgment on the pleadings. For example, a barebones complaint can be met with a motion for a more definite statement under Rule 12(e) or the opposite, an overly detailed complaint, can be addressed with a Motion to Strike under Rule 12(f) of the Federal Rules. Motions to strike are rare, but they are appropriate where the complaint contains "scandalous" or "impertinent" allegations, such as a detailed description of the defendant's sex life that has nothing to do with the breach of contract claim, or gratuitous assertions that the defendant is a dirty, lying scoundrel.

8) Venue: Is it appropriate to seek a change of venue for strategic reasons?

9) Arbitration: Does an arbitration clause apply to the claim?

10) Exhaustion of Administrative Remedies: Is there an administrative venue for the claim that the plaintiff neglected to pursue? "[T]he exhaustion doctrine provides that, before seeking judicial relief, a petitioner must exhaust any and all available administrative remedies, so as to give the administrative agency an opportunity to correct mistakes and perhaps avoid judicial intervention altogether."[1162]

11) Statute of Limitations: What is the applicable limitation period? When did it start?

[1158] 28 U.S.C. § 1447(c).

[1159] *Bell Atlantic Corp. v. Twombly*, 550 U.S. 544 (U.S. 2007).

[1160] *Ashcroft v. Iqbal*, 556 U.S. 662, 129 S.Ct. 1937 (U.S. 2009).

[1161] See "A 'Plausible' Showing After *Bell Atlantic Corp. v. Twombly*," Charles B. Campbell, *Nevada Law Journal* 9.1 (2008): 1-31. Available at: http://works.bepress.com/charles_campbell/1

[1162] *Allstate Ins. Co. v. Thorpe*, 123 Nev. 565, 571-72, 170 P.3d 989, 993-94 (2007).

12) Fraud Claims: Since fraud claims are held to a higher pleading standard under Rule 9 of the state and federal rules, they should almost always be considered for a Rule 12 motion.[1163]

The Defender by Honoré Daumier

AFFIRMATIVE DEFENSES
NRCP 8(c) provides as follows:

> Affirmative Defenses. In pleading to a preceding pleading, a party shall set forth affirmatively accord and satisfaction, arbitration and award, assumption of risk, contributory negligence, discharge in bankruptcy, duress, estoppel, failure of consideration, fraud, illegality, injury by fellow servant, laches, license, payment, release, res judicata, statute of frauds, statute of limitations, waiver, and any other matter constituting an avoidance or affirmative defense. When a party has mistakenly designated a defense as a counterclaim or a counterclaim as a defense, the court on terms, if justice so requires, shall treat the pleading as if there had been a proper designation.

Absolute Immunity
Absolute immunity is a broad immunity that is granted sparingly to individuals performing judicial or quasi-judicial functions.[1164] Party-retained expert witnesses have absolute immunity from suits for damages arising from statements made in the course of judicial proceedings.[1165]

Abstention

Burford Abstention and Thibodaux Abstention
Burford Abstention, derived from *Burford v. Sun Oil Co.*,[1166] allows a federal court sitting in diversity jurisdiction to abstain where the state courts likely have greater expertise in a particularly complex area of state law (the case itself dealt with the regulation of oil drilling operations in Texas). This is closely related to *Thibodaux* abstention, derived from *Louisiana Power & Light Co. v. City of Thibodaux*, 360 U.S. 25 (1959), which occurs when a federal court sitting in diversity jurisdiction chooses to allow a state to decide issues of state law that are of great public importance to that state, to the extent that a federal determination would infringe on state sovereignty. Unlike the abstention doctrines

---

[1163] See "Anatomy of an Answer," V. John Ella, *The Hennepin Lawyer*, 2004.

[1164] *Marvin v. Fitch*, 126 Nev., Advance Opinion 18, 232 P.3d 425 (2010) (en banc).

[1165] *Harrison v. Roitman*, 131 Nev., Advance Opinion 92 (2015).

[1166] 319 U.S. 315 (1943).

raised in federal question cases, there is a strong presumption that federal courts should not apply Burford or Thibodaux Abstention.

Colorado River Abstention

Colorado River abstention, from *Colorado River Water Conservation District v. United States*, 424 U.S. 800 (1976), comes into play where parallel litigation is being carried out, particularly where federal and state court proceedings are simultaneously being carried out to determine the rights of parties with respect to the same questions of law. Under such circumstances, it makes little sense for two courts to expend the time and effort to achieve a resolution of the question.

Unlike other abstention doctrines, application of the Colorado River doctrine is prudential and discretionary, and is based less on comity or respect between different court systems than on the desire to avoid wasteful duplication of litigation. The classification of the doctrine as a form of abstention has been disputed, with some courts simply calling it a "doctrine of exceptional circumstances." Each of the various federal circuits has come up with their own list of factors to weigh in determining whether a federal court should abstain from hearing a case under this doctrine. Typically, such factors include:

> The order in which the courts assumed jurisdiction over property,
> the order in which the courts assumed jurisdiction over the parties,
> the relative inconvenience of the fora,
> the relative progress of the two actions,[1167]
> the desire to avoid piecemeal litigation,
> whether federal law provides the rule of decision,
> whether the state court will adequately protect the rights of all parties, and
> whether the federal filing was vexatious (intended to harass the other party) or reactive (in response to adverse rulings in the state court).

Comity

Comity "is a principle of courtesy by which the courts of one jurisdiction may give effect to the laws and judicial decisions of another jurisdiction out of deference and respect.' "[1168] It is not to be confused with full faith and credit, the constitutional provision that various states within the United States must recognize the laws, acts, and decisions of sister states.

Pullman Abstention

Pullman abstention was the first "doctrine of abstention" to be announced by the Court. It is named for *Railroad Commission v. Pullman Co.*[1169] The doctrine holds that "the federal courts should not adjudicate the constitutionality of state enactments fairly open to interpretation until the state courts have been afforded a reasonable opportunity to pass on them." This doctrine permits a federal court to stay a plaintiff's claim that a state law violates the Constitution until the state's judiciary has had an opportunity to apply the law to the plaintiff's particular case. The hope is to avoid a federal constitutional ruling by allowing the state courts either to construct the law in a way that eliminates the constitutional problem or to rule it void under the state's own constitution.

For Pullman abstention to be invoked, three conditions must be apparent:

1) There must be a state law issue that is potentially dispositive;
2) That state law must be unclear; and
3) That disposing of state law will avoid constitutional questions.

Under Pullman abstention, the federal court retains jurisdiction to hear the constitutional issues in the case if the state court's resolution is still constitutionally suspect. In *Government and Civil Employees Organizing Committee, CIO v. Windsor*[1170] the United States Supreme Court held that litigants must inform the state court that they are contending that the state law violates a federal constitutional provision, so that the state court may take that into consideration when

---

[1167] Added by *Moses H. Cone Memorial Hospital v. Mercury Constr. Corp.* in 1983.
[1168] *Gonzales-Alpizar v. Griffith*, 130 Nev., Advance Opinion 2, p. 10 (2014), quoting *Mianecki v. Second Judicial Dist. Court*, 99 Nev. 93, 98, 658 P.2d 422 424-25 (1983).
[1169] 312 U.S. 496 (1941).
[1170] 353 U.S. 364 (1957).

interpreting the state statute. However, in *England v. Louisiana State Board of Medical Examiners*,[1171] the United States Supreme Court noted that the litigants must not ask the state court to resolve the constitutional issue itself, or the federal court would be bound by res judicata to follow the decision of the state court. In such a case, the litigant seeking a judgment that the law is unconstitutional must usually appeal to the higher courts of the state, rather than seeking review in a federal court.

The federal court was instructed to abstain from ruling on the constitutionality of NRS 31.017 until the state courts construed the statute. On appeal from an action for a declaratory judgment that NRS 31.017 was unconstitutional on the ground that it violated the right to due process guaranteed by the U.S. 14th amendment, the federal district court was instructed to abstain from deciding the federal constitutional issues that were presented pursuant to *Railroad Commission v. Pullman Co.*,[1172] because: (1) the Nevada Supreme Court had not construed the statute and it was possible that the Nevada courts would construe the statute, along with other statutes governing prejudgment writs of attachment, in a manner that would comply with federal constitutional requirements, thereby avoiding the necessity to address the plaintiff's claims; and (2) a pending state court action provided an opportunity for the Nevada courts to resolve the issues presented. (N.B., this case was not appropriate for publication and may not be cited to or by the courts for the Ninth Circuit except as provided in Ninth Circuit Rule 36-3.)[1173]

Rooker-Feldman Doctrine
See "Rooker-Feldman Doctrine."

Younger Abstention
Named for *Younger v. Harris*,[1174] Younger abstention is less permissive to the federal courts, barring them from hearing civil rights tort claims brought by a person who is currently being prosecuted for a matter arising from that claim in state court. For example, if an individual who was charged with drug possession under a state law believes that the search was illegal, and in violation of their Fourth Amendment rights, that person may have a cause of action to sue the state for illegally searching him. However, a federal court will not hear the case until the person is convicted of the crime. The doctrine has been extended to state civil proceedings in aid of and closely related to state criminal statutes, administrative proceedings initiated by a State agency, or situations where the State has jailed a person for contempt of court. The doctrine applies even where the state does not bring an action until after the person has filed a lawsuit in federal court, provided that the federal court has not yet undergone proceedings of substance on the merits of the federal suit.

The three exceptions to Younger abstention are as follows:

1. Where the prosecution is in bad faith (*i.e.*, the State knows the person to be innocent); or
2. Where the prosecution is part of some pattern of harassment against an individual; or
3. Where the law being enforced is utterly and irredeemably unconstitutional (*e.g.*, if the state were to pass a law making it a crime to say anything negative about its governor under any circumstances).

Accord and Satisfaction
See "Accord and Satisfaction" in "Claims."

Acquiescence
Acquiescence is a legal term used to describe an act where a person knowingly stands by without raising any objection to the infringement of their rights, while someone else unknowingly and without malice aforethought makes a claim on their rights. Consequently, the person whose rights are infringed loses the ability to make a claim against the infringer, or succeed in an injunction suit due to the infringer's conduct. The term is most generally "permission" given by silence or passiveness. Acceptance or agreement by keeping quiet or by not making objections.

The common law doctrine of estoppel by acquiescence is applied when one party gives legal notice to a second party of a fact or claim, and the second party fails to challenge or refute that claim within a reasonable time. The second party is said to have acquiesced to the claim, and is estopped from later challenging it, or making a counterclaim. The

---

[1171] 375 U.S. 411 (1964).
[1172] 312 U.S. 496, 61 S.Ct. 643 (1941).
[1173] *Fetish & Fantasy Halloween Ball, Inc. v. Ahern Rentals*, 45 Fed. Appx. 585 (9th Cir. 2002).
[1174] 401 U.S. 37 (1971).

doctrine is similar to, and often applied with, estoppel by laches.

This occurred in the second *Georgia v. South Carolina*, 497 U.S. 376 (1990), when the U.S. Supreme Court ruled that Georgia could no longer make any claim to an island in the Savannah River, despite the 1787 Treaty of Beaufort's assignment to the contrary. The court said that the state had knowingly allowed South Carolina to join the island as a peninsula to its own coast by dumping sand from dredging, and to then levy property taxes on it for decades. Georgia thereby lost the island-turned-peninsula by its own acquiescence, even though the treaty had given it all of the islands in the river.

The doctrine of acquiescence, although typically not found in law, is found a lot in precedent. In U.S. Supreme Court rulings, the doctrine of acquiescence has been mentioned over a thousand times. "Silence is acquiescence" (a.k.a. silent acquiescence and acquiescence by silence) is a related doctrine that can mean, and have the legal effect, that when confronted with a wrong or an act that can be considered a tortious act, where one's silence may mean that one accepts or permits such acts without protest or claim thereby loses rights to a claim of any loss or damage.

Act of God

An Act of God in law is an overwhelming, unpreventable event caused exclusively by forces of nature, such as an earthquake, flood, or tornado.[1175] The definition has been statutorily broadened to include all natural phenomena that are exceptional, inevitable, and irresistible, the effects of which could not be prevented or avoided by the exercise of due care or foresight.[1176]

Adequate Warning

Four elements have been articulated as comprising an adequate warning: (1) notice that a severe hazard exists, (2) a description of the hazard's nature, (3) a description of the hazard's possible consequences, and (4) instructions on how to avoid the hazard.[1177] In addition, the warning must be prominently displayed, and may have to illustrate the nature and severity of the hazard with pictographs.[1178]

In *Rivera v. Philip Morris, Inc.*,[1179] the United States District Court, District of Nevada, certified the question of whether Nevada law recognizes a heeding presumption in strict product liability failure-to-warn cases. A heeding presumption is a rebuttable presumption that allows a fact-finder to presume that the injured plaintiff would have heeded an adequate warning if one had been given. Thus, it shifts the burden of proving the element of causation from the plaintiff to the manufacturer. The Nevada Supreme Court concluded that Nevada law does not recognize a heeding presumption.

In Nevada, it is well-established law that in strict product liability failure-to-warn cases, the plaintiff bears the burden of production and must prove, among other elements, that the inadequate warning caused his injuries. Because a heeding presumption shifts the burden of proving causation from the plaintiff to the manufacturer, it is contrary to Nevada law. Rather than demanding that the plaintiff prove that the inadequate warning caused his injuries, a heeding presumption requires the manufacturer to rebut the presumption that the plaintiff would have heeded an adequate warning by demonstrating that a different warning would not have changed the plaintiff's actions. While other jurisdictions have permitted this shifting of the burden of production, the Nevada Supreme Court was unwilling to do so.

Adhesion Contract

An adhesion contract is a standard-form contract prepared by one party, to be signed by another party in a weaker position, usually a consumer, who adheres to the contract with little choice about the terms.[1180] Insurance policies are contracts of adhesion.[1181] That is, the policies are drafted by the insurer and are offered to the policyholder without any opportunity for the policyholder to negotiate the policy's terms. Thus, in order for an insurer to effectively limit its contractual obligations, the insurance policy's language must unambiguously convey the insurer's intent to do so.[1182] "It follows that 'any ambiguity or uncertainty in an insurance policy must be construed against the insurer and in favor of the insured.' "[1183]

[1175] *Black's Law Dictionary* 39 (9th ed. 2009).

[1176] *Id.*; see 42 U.S.C.A. § 9601(1).

[1177] *Black's Law Dictionary* 1722 (9th ed. 2009).

[1178] *Id.*

[1179] 125 Nev., Advance Opinion 18, 209 P.3d 271 (2009).

[1180] *Black's Law Dictionary* 366 (9th ed. 2009).

[1181] *Farmers Ins. Group v. Stonik*, 110 Nev. 64, 67, 867 P.2d 389, 391 (1994).

[1182] *Id.*

[1183] *United Nat'l Ins. Co. v. Frontier Ins. Co.*, 120 Nev. 678, 684, 99 P.3d at 1156 (2004) (quoting *Vitale v. Jefferson Ins. Co.*, 116 Nev. 590, 594, 5 P.3d 1054, 1057 (2000)).

Adverse Possession

NRS 11.100, "Possession presumed in legal owner unless adversely held," provides as follows:

> In every action for the recovery of real property, or the possession thereof, the person establishing a legal title to the premises shall be presumed to have been possessed thereof within the time prescribed by law; and the occupation of such premises by any other person shall be deemed to have been under and in subordination to the legal title, unless it shall appear:
> 1. That is has been protected by a substantial enclosure; or
> 2. That it has been cultivated or improved in accordance with the usual and ordinary methods of husbandry.

Agency

Agency is a fiduciary relationship created by express or implied contract or by law, in which one party (the agent) may act on behalf of another party (the principal) and bind that other party by words or actions.[1184] Under basic corporate agency law, the actions of corporate agents are imputed to the corporation.[1185]

Alteration of Product / Abnormal Use / Misuse

Under the Uniform Comparative Fault Act, "Misuse of a product" means a misuse giving rise to a danger that could have been reasonably anticipated and guarded against. However, the Act does not apply to a misuse giving rise to a danger that could not reasonably have been anticipated and guarded against by the manufacturer, so that the product was therefore not defective or unreasonably dangerous.

Anticipatory Repudiation

Repudiation of a contractual duty before the time for performance, giving the injured party an immediate right to damages for total breach, as well as discharging the injured party's remaining duties of performance.[1186] A contractual anticipatory repudiation must be clear, positive, and unequivocal.[1187] Whether specific conduct or language is sufficiently clear to constitute an anticipatory repudiation must be decided in light of the total factual context of the individual case.[1188]

A cause of action in contract cases involving a wholly anticipatory repudiation accrues either on the date that performance under the contract is due or, if the plaintiff so elects, on the date that the plaintiff sues upon the anticipatory breach.[1189]

Approval

Sale on approval is a conditional sale, the completion of which depends on acceptance of the goods by a buyer. The sale is complete when the buyer is satisfied with the goods sold. The buyer receives the goods primarily for use with the option to return. When the goods do not meet buyer's approval, s/he can return the goods even though they conform to contract. The buyer need not expressly convey his/her approval. When the buyer keeps the goods beyond a reasonable time, the approval can be implied. Title passes subject to buyer's approval.

Arbitration and Award

Arbitration is a method of dispute resolution involving one or more neutral third parties who are usually agreed to by the disputing parties and whose decision is binding.[1190] Arbitrament and award, or arbitration and award, is a plea that the same matter has already been decided in arbitration.[1191]

[1184] *Id.*, p. 70.

[1185] *Strohecker v. Mut. B. & L. Assn.*, 55 Nev. 350, 355, 34 P.2d 1076, 1077 (1934).

[1186] *Black's Law Dictionary* 1418 (9th ed. 2009).

[1187] *Covington Bros. v. Valley Plastering, Inc.*, 93 Nev. 355, 360, 566 P.2d 814 (1977).

[1188] *Id.*

[1189] NRS 11.190(1)(b).

[1190] *Black's Law Dictionary* 119 (9th ed. 2009).

[1191] *Id.*

Assumption of Risk

Assumption of the risk is a defense raised in personal injury lawsuits. The defense claims that the plaintiff knew that a particular activity was dangerous and thus bears all responsibility for any injury that resulted. In order to show the risk was assumed, the danger assumed must be obvious or the nature of the activity causing injury must be inherently dangerous. Assumption of the risk may be proven by a clause in a contract stating the existence of the danger and the waiver of liability of the defendant for injuries caused, but may be shown by other evidence. Once proven, assumption of risk may bar the plaintiff from any recovery for injuries.

In Nevada, with the single exception of the express assumption of risk, the doctrine of assumption of risk has been subsumed by the State's statute relating to comparative negligence.[1192]

Primary assumption of the risk is not really an affirmative defense; rather, it indicates that the defendant did not even owe the plaintiff any duty of care.[1193]

See "Volenti."

Attorney's Fees Award Not Permissible

Nevada follows the American Rule that attorney fees may not be awarded absent a statute, rule, or contract authorizing such award.[1194]

To recover fees under the substantial benefit doctrine, a successful party must demonstrate that: (1) the class of beneficiaries is small in number and easily identifiable; (2) the benefit [can] be traced with some accuracy; and (3) the costs can be shifted with some exactitude to those benefiting.[1195] To qualify for the substantial benefit exception to the American Rule that parties generally must bear their own attorney fees, the prevailing party must show that the losing party has received a benefit from the litigation.[1196]

The decision to award attorney fees is within the sound discretion of the district court and will not be overturned absent a manifest abuse of discretion.[1197] A party who rejects an offer of judgment yet fails to obtain a more favorable judgment may be ordered to pay attorney fees. NRS 17.115(4)(d); NRCP 68(f)(2). An offeree may accept the offer within ten days, but such offer will lapse after that time. NRS 17.115(2)-(3); NRCP 68(e)-(f). The "offer of judgment pursuant to NRCP 68 and NRS 17.115 is irrevocable during the ten-day period."[1198] If the offer of judgment is not accepted within 10 days after the date of service, then the offer shall be deemed rejected by the party to whom it was made. NRS 17.115(3); NRCP 68(e).

A party that represents itself, however, is not eligible for attorney fees.[1199] The Nevada Supreme Court has stated that another attorney fee provision, NRS 69.030, which provides that a prevailing party shall receive reasonable attorney fees and costs, does not authorize an award of attorney fees to a prevailing proper person litigant, even if that litigant is an attorney.[1200] The reasoning for that decision is that "an attorney proper person litigant must be genuinely obligated to pay attorney fees before he may recover such fees."[1201]

[1192] See NRS 41.141; *Mizushima v. Sunset Ranch, Inc.*, 103 Nev. 259, 737 P.2d 1158 (1987), cited, *Central Telephone Co. v. Fixtures Mfg. Corp.*, 103 Nev. 298, at 299, 738 P.2d 510 (1987), *Auckenthaler v. Grundmeyer*, 110 Nev. 682, at 687, 877 P.2d 1039 (1994), *Woosley v. State Farm Ins. Co.*, 117 Nev. 182, at 190, 18 P.3d 317 (2001).

[1193] *Turner v. Mandalay Bay Sports Entertainment LLC*, 124 Nev. 213, 221 n.27, 180 P.3d 1172 (2008).

[1194] *Thomas v. City of North Las Vegas*, 122 Nev. 82, 90, 127 P.3d 1057 (2006).

[1195] *Id.* at 91.

[1196] *Id.*

[1197] *County of Clark v. Blanchard Constr. Co.*, 98 Nev. 488, 492, 653 P.2d 1217, 1220 (1982).

[1198] *Nava v. Dist. Ct.*, 118 Nev. 396, 398, 46 P.3d 60, 61 (2002). *Settelmeyer & Sons v. Smith & Harmer*, 124 Nev. 1206, 1220, 197 P.3d 1051 (2008).
Settelmeyer & Sons v. Smith & Harmer, 124 Nev. 1206, 1220, 197 P.3d 1051 (2008).

[1200] *Sellers v. Dist. Ct.*, 119 Nev. 256, 259, 71 P.3d 495, 498 (2003).

[1201] *Id.* at 259, 71 P.3d at 497-98.

At-Will Employment

Since employees in Nevada are presumed to be at-will, an employer can dismiss an at-will employee with or without cause, so long as the dismissal does not offend this state's public policy.[1202] The Nevada Supreme Court has recognized certain exceptions to the at-will employment doctrine.[1203] But these exceptions are "severely limited to those rare and exceptional cases where the employer's conduct violates strong and compelling public policy."[1204] Further, the Nevada Supreme Court will not recognize an action for tortious discharge when a plaintiff has an adequate, comprehensive, statutory remedy.[1205]

Authority

Authority is defined as the power to influence or command thought, opinion, or behavior; freedom granted by one in authority; right.

Borrowed Servant or Borrowed Employee

An employee whose services are, with the employee's consent, lent to another employer who temporarily assumes control over the employee's work. Under the doctrine of respondeat superior, the borrowing employer is vicariously liable for the borrowed employee's acts. But the borrowing employer may also be entitled to assert immunity under workers' compensation laws.[1206]

Breach of Express Warranty

In a breach of warranty cause of action, a plaintiff must prove that a warranty existed, the defendant breached the warranty, and the defendant's breach was the proximate cause of the loss sustained.[1207] The Nevada Supreme Court recognizes that purely economic losses can be recovered for breach of warranty.[1208]

Breach of Implied Warranty

A breach of implied warranty is a promise, arising by operation of law, that something that is sold will be merchantable and fit for the purpose for which it is sold.[1209] Every time goods are bought and sold, a sales contract is created: the buyer agrees to pay, and the seller agrees to accept, a certain price in exchange for a certain item or number of items. Sales contracts are frequently oral, unwritten agreements. The purchase of items like a candy bar hardly seems worth the trouble of drafting an agreement spelling out the buyer's expectation that the candy bar will be fresh and edible. Implied warranties protect the buyer whether or not a written sales contract exists.[1210]

[1202] *State of Nevada v. Dist. Ct. (Anzalone)*, 118 Nev. 140, 151, 42 P.3d 233, 240 (2002).

[1203] See *D'Angelo v. Gardner*, 107 Nev. 704, 719, 819 P.2d 206, 216 (1991) (adopting an exception based on "the public policy of this state favor[ing] safe employment practices and the protection of the health and safety of workers on the job").

[1204] *Sands Regent v. Valgardson*, 105 Nev. 436, 440, 777 P.2d 898, 900 (1989) (declining to create an additional exception to the at-will employment doctrine for age discrimination).

[1205] *D'Angelo*, supra, 107 Nev. at 720-22, 819 P.2d at 217-18.

[1206] *Black's Law Dictionary* 602 (9th ed. 2009).

[1207] *Id.*

[1208] *Nevada Contract Servs. v. Squirrel Cos.*, 119 Nev. 157, 161, 68 P.3d 896 (2003).

[1209] *West's Encyclopedia of American Law*, edition 2. Copyright 2008 The Gale Group, Inc. All rights reserved.

[1210] *Id.*

Implied Warranty of Fitness

When a buyer wishes to use goods for a particular, nonordinary purpose, the UCC provides a distinct implied warranty of fitness.[1211] Unlike the implied warranty of merchantability, the implied warranty of fitness does not contain a requirement that the seller be a merchant with respect to the goods sold. It merely requires that the seller possess knowledge and expertise on which the buyer may rely.

For example, one court found that horse buyers who indicated to the sellers their intention to use the horse for breeding were using the horse for a particular, nonordinary purpose.[1212] The buyers soon discovered that the horse they purchased was incapable of reproducing. Because the court found this use of the horse to be nonordinary, the buyers were entitled to an implied warranty of fitness.

Before a court will imply a warranty of fitness, three requirements must be met: (1) the seller must have reason to know of the buyer's particular purpose for the goods; (2) the seller must have reason to know of the buyer's reliance on the seller's skill and knowledge in furnishing the appropriate goods; and (3) the buyer must, in fact, rely on the seller's skill and knowledge. Even when these requirements are met, courts will not imply a warranty of fitness under certain circumstances. A buyer who specifies a particular brand of goods is not entitled to an implied warranty of fitness. Also, a buyer who has greater expertise than the seller regarding the goods generally is precluded from asserting an implied warranty of fitness, as is a buyer who provides the seller with specifications, such as a blueprint or design plan, detailing the types of material to be used in the goods.[1213]

The Nevada Supreme Court has stated as follows: "We perceive no significant policy distinction that would drive us to permit tort-based claims to recover economic losses against design professionals, such as architects and engineers, who provided their professional services in the commercial property development and improvement process, when we have concluded that such claims are barred under the economic loss doctrine if brought against contractors and subcontractors involved in physically constructing improvements to real property."[1214]

Incidentally, California law requires privity for breach of implied warranty of merchantability and breach of implied warranty of fitness claims.[1215]

Implied Warranty of Merchantability

NRS 104.2315, "Implied warranty: Fitness for particular purpose," provides as follows: "Where the seller at the time of contracting has reason to know any particular purpose for which the goods are required and that the buyer is relying on the seller's skill or judgment to select or furnish suitable goods, there is unless excluded or modified under the next section an implied warranty that the goods shall be fit for such purpose."

The Nevada Supreme Court held that contractual privity is not required for the implied warranty of merchantability.[1216] The Court cited NRS 104A.2209, which provides in pertinent part as follows:

> 1. The benefit of the supplier's promises to the lessor under the supply contract and of all warranties, whether express or implied . . . *extends to the lessee* to the extent of the lessee's leasehold interest under a finance lease related to the supply contract . . . .

(Emphasis in original.) The Nevada Supreme Court concluded as follows: "Vacation Village is the lessee under a finance lease with GECC, and as such, the implied warranties of merchantability extend to Vacation Village."[1217]

No warranties were implied under former sales act except merchantability and fitness for a particular purpose.[1218] Under the sales act, the employee of a buyer could not claim benefit of implied warranties.[1219]

[1211] NRS 104.2315, "Implied warranty: Fitness for particular purpose," provides as follows: "Where the seller at the time of contracting has reason to know any particular purpose for which the goods are required and that the buyer is relying on the seller's skill or judgment to select or furnish suitable goods, there is unless excluded or modified under the next section an implied warranty that the goods shall be fit for such purpose."

[1212] *Whitehouse v. Lange*, 910 P.2d 801 (Idaho 1996).

[1213] *Id.*

[1214] *Terracon Consultants v. Mandalay Resort*, 125 Nev., Advance Opinion 8 (2009); see *Calloway v. City of Reno*, 116 Nev. 250, 993 P.2d 1259 (2000); see also *Maine Rubber Intern. v. Environ. Management Group*, 298 F. Supp. 2d 133 (D. Me. 2004) (concluding that negligent design claims present a breach of express or implied warranty issue, properly addressed by contract law).

[1215] *Consolidated Generator v. Cummins Engine*, 114 Nev. 1304, 1308-09, 971 P.2d 1251 (1998).

[1216] *Vacation Village, Inc. v. Hitachi America, Ltd.*, 110 Nev. 481, 486, 874 P.2d 744, 747 (1994).

[1217] *Id.* at 485.

[1218] *Long v. Flanigan Warehouse Co.*, 79 Nev. 241, 382 P.2d 399 (1963).

[1219] *Id.*

Where a specially fabricated carpet conformed in all respects to a sample furnished by the manufacturer and approved by the buyer and to precise specifications provided by the buyer to the manufacturer, implied warranties of merchantability under NRS 104.2314 and fitness under NRS 104.2315 were inapplicable, because the implied warranty of merchantability was limited by the express warranty of conformity to the precise description supplied by the buyer, and the buyer had relied on his own judgment and not that of the seller.[1220]

The implied warranty of merchantability for a business telephone system and related equipment extended to the corporation leasing the system and equipment under a finance lease.[1221]

A county health district is not a "seller of products" and thus cannot be held liable under either the warranty or strict liability theory.[1222]

Implied warranties come in two general types: merchantability and fitness. An implied warranty of merchantability is an unwritten and unspoken guarantee to the buyer that goods purchased conform to ordinary standards of care and that they are of the same average grade, quality, and value as similar goods sold under similar circumstances. In other words, merchantable goods are goods fit for the ordinary purposes for which they are to be used. The Uniform Commercial Code (UCC), adopted by most states, provides that courts may imply a Warranty of merchantability when (1) the seller is the merchant of such goods, and (2) the buyer uses the goods for the ordinary purposes for which such goods are sold (§ 2-314). Thus, a buyer can sue a seller for breaching the implied warranty by selling goods unfit for their ordinary purpose.

There is rarely any question as to whether the seller is the merchant of the goods sold. Nevertheless, in *Huprich v. Bitto*, 667 So.2d 685 (Ala. 1995), a farmer who sold defective horse feed was found not to be a merchant of horse feed. The court stated that the farmer did not hold himself out as having knowledge or skill peculiar to the sale of corn as horse feed, and therefore was not a merchant of horse feed for purposes of determining a breach of implied warranty of merchantability.

The question of whether goods are fit for their ordinary purpose is much more frequently litigated. Thomas Coffer sued the manufacturer of a jar of mixed nuts after he bit down on an unshelled filbert, believing it to have been shelled, and damaged a tooth. Coffer argued in part that the presence of the unshelled nut among shelled nuts was a breach of the implied warranty of merchantability. Unquestionably, Coffer was using the nuts for their ordinary purpose when he ate them, and unquestionably, he suffered a dental injury when he bit the filbert's hard shell. But the North Carolina appellate court held that the jar of mixed nuts was nonetheless fit for the ordinary purpose for which jars of mixed nuts are used.[1223] The court consulted the state agriculture board's regulations and noted that the peanut industry allows a small amount of unshelled nuts to be included with shelled nuts without rendering the shelled nuts inedible or adulterated. The court also noted that shells are a natural incident to nuts.

The policy behind the implied warranty of merchantability is basic: sellers are generally better suited than buyers to determine whether a product will perform properly. Holding the seller liable for a product that is not fit for its ordinary purpose shifts the costs of nonperformance from the buyer to the seller. This motivates the seller to ensure the product's proper performance before placing it on the market. The seller is better able to absorb the costs of a product's nonperformance, usually by spreading the risk to consumers in the form of increased prices.

The policy behind limiting the implied warranty of merchantability to the goods' ordinary use is also straightforward: a seller may not have sufficient expertise or control over a product to ensure that it will perform properly when used for nonstandard purposes.

Cancellation of Contract/Resignation

A seller of land pursuant to a contract of sale is justified in cancelling the contract if the purchaser has failed to perform a material part of the contract which is a condition concurrent or precedent to the seller's obligations to perform.[1224]

Cardinal-Change Doctrine

The cardinal-change doctrine serves to provide a breach remedy for contractors who are directed to perform work which is not within the general scope of the contract, and which is therefore not redressable under the contract.[1225]

[1220] *Mohasco Indus., Inc. v. Anderson Halverson Corp.*, 90 Nev. 114, 520 P.2d 234 (1974), cited, *United States Fidelity & Guar. Co. v. Nevada Cement Co.*, 93 Nev. 179, at 183, 561 P.2d 1335 (1977).

[1221] *Vacation Village, Inc. v. Hitachi America, Ltd.*, 110 Nev. 481, 874 P.2d 744 (1994), cited, *Vacation Village, Inc. v. Hitachi America, Ltd.*, 111 Nev. 1218, at 1219, 901 P.2d 706 (1995).

[1222] See NRS 104.2313, NRS 104.2314 and NRS 104.2315; *Allison v. Merck & Co.*, 110 Nev. 762, 878 P.2d 948 (1994), cited, *Fisher v. Professional Compounding Ctrs. of Am., Inc.*, 311 F.Supp.2d 1008, at 1018 (D. Nev. 2004).

[1223] *Coffer v. Standard Brands*, 30 N.C. App. 134, 226 S.E.2d 534 (N.C. 1976).

[1224] *Goldston v. AMI Investments, Inc.*, 98 Nev. 567, 569, 655 P.2d 521 (1982).

A cardinal change occurs, thus giving rise to a remedy for breach of contract, when the work is so drastically altered that the contractor effectively performs duties that are materially different from those for which the contractor originally bargained.[1226] To prevail under the cardinal-change doctrine, a contractor must prove facts with specificity that support its allegations that a cardinal change occurred.[1227] The cardinal-change doctrine, which provides a breach remedy for contractors who are directed to perform work that is not within the general scope of contract, applies to private contracts that include changes clauses.[1228] For purposes of cardinal-change doctrine, a cardinal change can occur even when there is no change in the final product, because it is the entire undertaking of the contractor, rather than the product, that the court looks to.[1229]

Charitable Immunity

See RESTATEMENT (SECOND) OF CONFLICT OF LAWS § 168 cmt. b (1971) (whether a charitable corporation may assert the defense of charitable immunity may be determined by the local law of the state where the plaintiff is domiciled and defendant corporation has its principal place of business).[1230]

Circuitry of Action

A procedure allowing duplicative lawsuits, leading to unnecessarily lengthy and indirect litigation, as when a defendant fails to bring a counterclaim, but later brings a separate action to recover what could have been awarded in the original lawsuit. [1231]

Claim Preclusion

Claim preclusion protects the finality of decisions and prevents the proliferation of litigation,[1232] but does not apply unless specific requirements are met. When considering whether claim preclusion should apply, the following three-part test is instructive: "(1) the parties or their privies are the same, (2) the final judgment is valid, and (3) the subsequent action is based on the same claims or any part of them that were or could have been brought in the first case."[1233] Claim preclusion applies to preclude an entire second suit that is based on the same set of facts and circumstances as the first suit.[1234] The test established in *Five Star Capital* maintains the well-established principle that claim preclusion applies to all grounds of recovery that "were or could have been brought in the first case."[1235] The Nevada Supreme Court has modified the privity requirement established in *Five Star* to incorporate the principles of nonmutual claim preclusion, meaning that for claim preclusion to apply, a defendant must demonstrate that (1) there has been a valid, final judgment in a previous action; (2) the subsequent action is based on the same claims or any part of them that were or could have been brought in the first action; and (3) the parties or their privies are the same in the instant lawsuit, *or* the defendant can demonstrate that he or she should have been included as a defendant in the earlier suit and the plaintiff fails to provide a "good reason" for not having done so.[1236]

Nevada law rejects the application of claim preclusion in worker's compensation cases.[1237]

See "Collateral Estoppel," "Equitable Estoppel," and "Issue Preclusion."

Collateral Estoppel

Collateral estoppel is also known as issue estoppel, direct estoppel; estoppel by judgment, estoppel by record, estoppel by verdict, cause-of-action estoppel, technical estoppel, or estoppel *per rem judicatam*. See "Issue Preclusion."

Nonmutual, defensive use of collateral estoppel occurs when a defendant seeks to prevent a plaintiff from relitigating an issue the plaintiff has previously litigated unsuccessfully in another action against a different party. Nonmutual, offensive collateral estoppel occurs when a plaintiff seeks to foreclose a defendant from relitigating an issue that

---

[1225] *J.A. Jones Construction Co. v. Lehrer McGovern Bovis*, 120 Nev. 277, 293, 89 P.3d 1009 (2004).
[1226] *Id.*
[1227] *Id.*
[1228] *Id.* at 293-94.
[1229] *Id.* at 295.
[1230] See *Dictor v. Creative Management Services*, 126 Nev., Advance Opinion 4 (2010).
[1231] *Black's Law Dictionary* 276 (9th ed. 2009).
[1232] *Littlejohn v. United States*, 321 F.3d 915, 919 (9th Cir. 2003).
[1233] *Five Star Capital v. Ruby*, 124 Nev. 1048, 1054, 194, P.3d 709, 713 (2008).
[1234] *Id.* at 1055, 194 P. 3d at 713-14.
[1235] *Id.*
[1236] *Weddell v. Sharp*, 131 Nev., Advance Opinion 28 (2015), pp. 2-3.
[1237] *Elizondo v. Hood Machine*, 129 Nev. Advance Opinion 84, pp. 8-10 (Nov. 7, 2013); see *Jerry's Nugget v. Keith*, 111 Nev. 49, 888 P.2d 921 (1995); NRS 616C.390.

the defendant has previously litigated unsuccessfully in another action against a different party. The U.S. Supreme Court has cautioned that non-mutual, offensive collateral estoppel should not be applied where: (1) a plaintiff in the second action could have easily joined in the earlier suit; or (2) where the application of offensive estoppel would be unfair to a defendant.[1238]

See "Equitable Estoppel" and "Issue Preclusion."

Collateral Source Rule

The collateral source rule is a rule of evidence. Evidence of collateral source of payment for an injury may not be admitted into evidence for any purpose; no matter how probative the evidence of a collateral source may be, it will never overcome the substantially prejudicial danger of the evidence.[1239] The collateral source rule is a per se rule that bars the admission of a collateral source of payment for a loss or injury into evidence for any purpose.[1240] The purpose of the collateral source rule is to prevent the jury from reducing the plaintiff's damages on the ground that he received compensation for his injuries from a source other than the tortfeasor.[1241] The collateral source rule provides that where an injured party received some compensation for his injuries from a source wholly independent of the tortfeasor, such payment should not be deducted from the damages which the plaintiff would otherwise collect from the tortfeasor.[1242]

Nevada recognizes a limited exception to the collateral source rule for workers' compensation payments, whether the payments are made by Nevada or another State.[1243]

Conditions Precedent

We also consider in this appeal the circumstances under which a party to a contract may waive a condition precedent to his performance so that he can complete his performance under the contract. We conclude that when a contract contains a condition precedent to a party's performance, that party may waive the condition and tender performance so long as the parties included the condition in the contract for the sole benefit of the party seeking to waive the condition and complete performing his contractual obligations. Whether a condition included in a contract is for the benefit of one or both parties is a question of fact.[1244]

Contract Specification

A contract-specification defense is an affirmative defense that immunizes a contractor and relieves him/her from liability for a defect in a product even when the contractor has manufactured or performed it according to detailed contractual orders. The defense applies to specialized, single-use components and protects a component supplier from claims of negligent design in cases where the component conforms to the contractual specifications. But the defense shall not apply when the specifications are obviously dangerous.[1245]

Contrary to Public Policy

In *Dayside Inc. v. District Court*,[1246] the Nevada Supreme Court addressed whether contractors may waive their statutory rights to a mechanic's lien. In that opinion, the court held that "[a]bsent a prohibitive legislative proclamation, a waiver of mechanic's lien rights is not contrary to public policy" and will be enforced if it is clear and unambiguous.

Contractual jury trial waivers are enforceable because they are neither illegal nor contrary to public policy.[1247]

A transfer of a liquor license as part of the sale of a bar was not rendered illegal between parties or contrary to public policy by a municipal ordinance that required prior city approval of the transfer; the effect of the ordinance was simply to delay completion of the transfer until such time as the city's conditions were satisfied.[1248] It was contrary to public policy to promote the "rising blood alcohol defense" and the concomitant practice of rushing to one's car immediately after ingesting alcohol so as to get home before the alcohol was fully absorbed in the body.[1249]

[1238] definitions.uslegal.com/c/collateral-estoppel; see *United States v. Mendoza*, 464 U.S. 154 (1984).

[1239] *Proctor v. Castelletti*, 112 Nev. 88, 90, 911 P.2d 853 (1996).

[1240] *Winchell v. Schiff*, 124 Nev. 938, 945-46 (2008).

[1241] *Id.* at 946.

[1242] *Id.*

[1243] NRS 616C.215(10); see *Tri-County Equipment & Leasing v. Klinke*, 128 Nev. Adv. Op. No. 33 (2012).

[1244] *Mayfield v. Koroghli*, 124 Nev. 343, 184 P.3d 362 (2008).

[1245] See definitions.uslegal.com.

[1246] 119 Nev. 404, 407, 75 P.3d 384, 386 (2003).

[1247] *Lowe Enterprises v. Dist. Ct.*, 118 Nev. 92, 98 fn.15, 40 P.3d 405, 410 (2002), citing *Smith-Johnson Motor Corp. v. Hoffman Motors Corp.*, 411 F. Supp. 670, 677 (E.D. Va. 1975).

[1248] *Elliot v. Resnick*, 114 Nev. 25, 32, 952 P.2d 961 (1998).

[1249] *Sereika v. State*, 114 Nev. 142, 149, 955 P.2d 175 (1998).

Contribution

To assert the affirmative defense of contribution, the defendant is saying that the damages were the result of unrelated, pre-existing, or subsequent conditions unrelated to the defendant's conduct. See "Indemnity and Contribution" under "Affirmative Defenses."

Contributory Negligence or Comparative Negligence

See NRS 41.141, "When comparative negligence not bar to recovery; jury instructions; liability of multiple defendants," which provides as follows:

> 1. In any action to recover damages for death or injury to persons or for injury to property in which comparative negligence is asserted as a defense, the comparative negligence of the plaintiff or the plaintiff's decedent does not bar a recovery if that negligence was not greater than the negligence or gross negligence of the parties to the action against whom recovery is sought.
> 2. In those cases, the judge shall instruct the jury that:
> (a) The plaintiff may not recover if the plaintiff's comparative negligence or that of the plaintiff's decedent is greater than the negligence of the defendant or the combined negligence of multiple defendants.
> (b) If the jury determines the plaintiff is entitled to recover, it shall return:
> (1) By general verdict the total amount of damages the plaintiff would be entitled to recover without regard to the plaintiff's comparative negligence; and
> (2) A special verdict indicating the percentage of negligence attributable to each party remaining in the action.
> 3. If a defendant in such an action settles with the plaintiff before the entry of judgment, the comparative negligence of that defendant and the amount of the settlement must not thereafter be admitted into evidence nor considered by the jury. The judge shall deduct the amount of the settlement from the net sum otherwise recoverable by the plaintiff pursuant to the general and special verdicts.
> 4. Where recovery is allowed against more than one defendant in such an action, except as otherwise provided in subsection 5, each defendant is severally liable to the plaintiff only for that portion of the judgment which represents the percentage of negligence attributable to that defendant.
> 5. This section does not affect the joint and several liability, if any, of the defendants in an action based upon:
> (a) Strict liability;
> (b) An intentional tort;
> (c) The emission, disposal or spillage of a toxic or hazardous substance;
> (d) The concerted acts of the defendants; or
> (e) An injury to any person or property resulting from a product which is manufactured, distributed, sold or used in this State.
> 6. As used in this section:
> (a) "Concerted acts of the defendants" does not include negligent acts committed by providers of health care while working together to provide treatment to a patient.
> (b) "Provider of health care" has the meaning ascribed to it in NRS 629.031.

Although Nevada used to recognize the complete bar of a plaintiff's recovery under the theory of contributory negligence, NRS 41.141 replaced this harsh rule. The statute permits a plaintiff to recover as long as his or her comparative negligence is not greater than that of the defendant or defendants. For a defendant to prevail, she must prove that the plaintiff's negligence is greater than hers.

Nevada Cases

The statute was not given retroactive application. Where an accident which gave rise to a personal injury action occurred before the enactment of NRS 41.141, but the trial took place after its effective date, it was not error to refuse to instruct the jury on comparative negligence instead of contributory negligence because the statute would not be given a retrospective interpretation in the absence of a clear manifestation of legislative intent that it apply retroactively.[1250]

The last clear chance doctrine is inappropriate under the State's comparative negligence statute. In a wrongful death action where the plaintiffs requested an instruction on the last clear chance doctrine, the trial court's refusal to give the instruction was proper because the doctrine, as a device for assigning the sole responsibility for the injury to the

---

[1250] *Buck v. Greyhound Lines, Inc.*, 105 Nev. 756, at 764, 783 P.2d 437 (1989), AGO 2000-20 (6-8-2000).

defendant, though both the defendant and plaintiff are negligent, was inappropriate under the State's comparative negligence statute.[1251]

Contributory negligence is no defense to the defendant's willful or wanton conduct. In a wrongful death action it was reversible error for the court to refuse an instruction to the effect that contributory negligence is no defense to willful or wanton conduct of the defendant. Although NRS 41.141 makes the principles of comparative negligence applicable where the plaintiff's negligence does not exceed "negligence or gross negligence" of the defendant, the legislature did not extend those principles to instances where the conduct of the defendant is willful or wanton.[1252]

Contributing negligence does not negate the defendant's negligence as a proximate cause. In an action for damages for personal injuries suffered in a motor vehicle accident in which the driver of heavy earthmoving equipment made a right turn into the plaintiff's vehicle, where: (1) the plaintiff alleged negligence of the defendants on several grounds (failure to signal or look, failure to have turn signal or rearview mirror, failure to have escort car) and a finding of negligence on any one of those grounds required a finding of actual causation; (2) there was no intervening force; (3) the type of harm was foreseeable; and (4) the court properly instructed the jury concerning proximate cause, the jury exhibited a manifest disregard for the jury instructions when it found that the defendants were negligent but that their negligence was not the proximate cause of the plaintiff's injuries. Under the doctrine of comparative negligence, contributing fault on the part of the plaintiff, if any, would reduce her recovery but could not negate finding that the defendants' negligence was the proximate cause. The plaintiff's motion for a new trial should have been granted.[1253]

Comparative negligence was not applicable to product liability action. In an action for wrongful death caused by a defective product, where the action was based on the theory of strict liability in tort, the trial court's refusal to instruct the jury that it could use principles of comparative negligence (see NRS 41.141) to reduce the award was proper because (1) no showing of negligence was necessary in such action, (2) the only defenses available were assumption of risk and misuse of the product, and (3) the legislature did not include strict liability for defective products in that class of actions in which comparative negligence may be asserted as a defense.[1254]

The jury should not have been instructed to consider comparative negligence of persons not then defendants or parties to action. In an action for malpractice brought by the sellers of a business against their accountants and their attorneys for failure to liquidate timely their corporation to avoid double taxation, where summary judgment was granted in favor of the attorneys, the jury should not have been instructed to consider the negligence of the attorneys under the statute relating to comparative negligence (see NRS 41.141) or to return a special verdict indicating the attorneys' percentage of negligence, because the attorneys were then neither defendants nor parties to the action.[1255]

The court is required to give instruction on comparative negligence upon request, without limitation. In an action brought to recover damages for personal injuries sustained when a lineman for the telephone company was thrown off a pole owned by the electric company after coming into contact with a primary power line, it was reversible error for the trial court to refuse to give an instruction on comparative negligence as required by NRS 41.141 on the ground that the instruction was unnecessary in a bifurcated trial or where a special verdict was used, because the statute required the court to give an instruction upon request, without limitation.[1256]

The comparative negligence of the victim limits the recovery of the witness. In an action for negligent infliction of emotional distress caused by witnessing harm to another, if the victim's negligence exceeds that of the defendant, the witness cannot recover for emotional distress caused by observing that harm.[1257]

The doctrine of implied assumption of risk was subsumed by the doctrine of comparative negligence. With the single exception of express assumption of risk, the doctrine of assumption of risk has been subsumed by the State's

---

[1251] *Davies v. Butler*, 95 Nev. 763, 602 P.2d 605 (1979), cited, *Woosley v. State Farm Ins. Co.*, 117 Nev. 182, at 190, P.3d 317 (2001).

[1252] *Davies v. Butler*, 95 Nev. 763, 602 P.2d 605 (1979), cited, *Young's Mach. Co. v. Long*, 100 Nev. 692, at 694, 692 P.2d 24 (1984), *Boland v. Nevada Rock & Sand Co.*, 111 Nev. 608, at 613, 894 P.2d 988 (1995).

[1253] *Taylor v. Silva*, 96 Nev. 738, 615 P.2d 970 (1980), cited, *Joynt v. California Hotel & Casino*, 108 Nev. 539, at 544, 835 P.2d 799 (1992).

[1254] *Young's Mach. Co. v. Long*, 100 Nev. 692, 692 P.2d 24 (1984), cited, *Jeep Corp. v. Murray*, 101 Nev. 640, at 648, 708 P.2d 297 (1985), *Central Telephone Co. v. Fixtures Mfg. Corp.*, 103 Nev. 298, at 300, 738 P.2d 510 (1987), *Andrews v. Harley Davidson, Inc.*, 106 Nev. 533, at 537, 796 P.2d 1092 (1990), *General Motors Corp. v. Eighth Judicial Dist. Court*, 122 Nev. 466, at 476, 134 P.3d 111 (2006).

[1255] *Warmbrodt v. Blanchard*, 100 Nev. 703, 692 P.2d 1282 (1984), cited, *Banks v. Sunrise Hosp.*, 120 Nev. 822, at 845, 102 P.3d 52 (2004).

[1256] *Verner v. Nevada Power Co.*, 101 Nev. 551, 706 P.2d 147 (1985).

[1257] *State v. Eaton*, 101 Nev. 705, 710 P.2d 1370 (1985), cited, *Buck v. Greyhound Lines, Inc.*, 105 Nev. 756, at 765, 783 P.2d 437 (1989).

statute relating to comparative negligence.[1258]

The purpose of the comparative negligence statute (see NRS 41.141) is to eradicate the harsh effect of a plaintiff's contributory negligence whenever such negligence is not greater than that of the source against which recovery is sought.[1259]

Several or joint and several liability under former provisions. Where the appellant's car stalled on the highway, a citizen stopped to help but did not push the car off the road, and a bus hit the car, injuring the appellant and his minor children, the appellate court held that (1) the trial court erred in giving a jury instruction on NRS 41.500, Nevada's "Good Samaritan" statute because, as matter of law, there was no emergency when the citizen stopped to assist the appellant, and (2) under the former provisions of NRS 41.141, the liability of the defendants as to the adult appellants was several because their contributory negligence could be properly asserted as a bona fide issue, but the liability as to the minor children was joint and several.[1260]

Where plaintiff settles with one of several defendants, jury must not be informed as to either fact of settlement or amount paid. The plaintiff brought an action against two physicians for medical malpractice, reached a monetary settlement with one and proceeded to trial against the other. At trial, the court instructed the jury concerning the fact of settlement, but informed the jury that the amount of the settlement was confidential. The instruction of the court constituted reversible error because where there has been a settlement between a plaintiff and one of several defendants, the jury must not be informed as to either the fact of the settlement or the amount paid.[1261]

There is no comparative negligence where injury is caused by obvious danger. In an action for negligence, where the danger is obvious and ordinary care does not require a warning from the defendant because the obviousness of the danger is an adequate warning, a determination of the plaintiff's comparative negligence under NRS 41.141 is unnecessary because where there is no negligence on the part of the defendant, there can be no comparative negligence.[1262]

The district court erred in granting summary judgment on ground that pedestrian's negligence exceeded motorist's negligence. In an action to recover damages for injuries sustained when the plaintiff was struck by a vehicle while crossing a street at an intersection outside of an unmarked crosswalk, district court erred in granting defendant's motion for summary judgment on the ground that the plaintiff was negligent per se for failing to yield the right-of-way to the vehicle as required by former NRS 484.327 (cf. NRS 484B.287) and that plaintiff's negligence exceeded that of defendant's (see NRS 41.141) because: (1) defendant may have had a duty under former NRS 484.363 (cf. NRS 484B.603) to decrease his speed as he approached the intersection; (2) the fact that defendant was not violating any traffic laws at the time of the accident did not preclude a finding that he breached his duty of care; and (3) a party's negligence was a question of fact for the jury.[1263]

The term "at fault," as used in NRS 687B.385, must be construed harmoniously with this section. The concepts of fault discussed in NRS 41.141 and 687B.385 are so closely related that they should be construed harmoniously. Thus, as used in NRS 687B.385, "at fault" means a chargeable accident does not occur unless the insured is at least 50 percent at fault.[1264]

A regulation was invalid where it prohibited insurers from defining a "chargeable accident" to include accidents in which an insured was 50 percent at fault. Where the division of insurance adopted a regulation that prohibited an insurer from defining a "chargeable accident" to include accidents in which the insured was 50 percent at fault or less, such a regulation conflicted with both NRS 41.141 and 687B.385. Because NRS 41.141 bars a plaintiff from recovery if the plaintiff's negligence is more than 50 percent, an insurer may be required to pay a judgment under that section where its insured is determined to be 50 percent or more at fault in connection with an accident. Reading NRS 687B.385 *in pari materia* with NRS 41.141, the division's regulation was invalid because it excluded the possibility that

---

[1258] *Mizushima v. Sunset Ranch, Inc.*, 103 Nev. 259, 737 P.2d 1158 (1987), cited, *Central Telephone Co. v. Fixtures Mfg. Corp.*, 103 Nev. 298, at 299, 738 P.2d 510 (1987), *Auckenthaler v. Grundmeyer*, 110 Nev. 682, at 687, 877 P.2d 1039 (1994), *Woosley v. State Farm Ins. Co.*, 117 Nev. 182, at 190, 18 P.3d 317 (2001).

[1259] *Mizushima v. Sunset Ranch, Inc.*, 103 Nev. 259, 737 P.2d 1158 (1987), cited, *Woosley v. State Farm Ins. Co.*, 117 Nev. 182, at 190, 18 P.3d 317 (2001).

[1260] *Buck v. Greyhound Lines, Inc.*, 105 Nev. 756, 783 P.2d 437 (1989), cited, *Stapp v. Hilton Hotels Corp.*, 108 Nev. 209, at 211, 826 P.2d 954 (1992), *Hogle v. Hall*, 112 Nev. 599, at 606, 916 P.2d 814 (1996).

[1261] See NRS 41.141; *Moore v. Bannen*, 106 Nev. 679, 799 P.2d 564 (1990), cited, *Evans v. Dean Witter Reynolds, Inc.*, 116 Nev. 598, at 608, 5 P.3d 1043 (2000), *Banks v. Sunrise Hosp.*, 120 Nev. 822, at 844, 102 P.3d 52 (2004).

[1262] *Harrington v. Syufy Enters.*, 113 Nev. 246, 931 P.2d 1378 (1997).

[1263] *Anderson v. Baltrusaitis*, 113 Nev. 963, 944 P.2d 797 (1997).

[1264] *State, Div. of Ins. v. State Farm Mut. Auto. Ins. Co.*, 116 Nev. 290, 995 P.2d 482 (2000).

an insured could be "at fault" by being exactly 50 percent at fault.[1265]

Res ipsa loquitur: Modification of traditional third element in recognizance of comparative negligence. The traditional third element required before res ipsa loquitur may be invoked (that the event in question must not have been due to any voluntary action or contribution on the part of the plaintiff) does not comport with the statutory rule of comparative negligence (see NRS 41.141). Thus, the third element is revised to provide that res ipsa loquitur may apply as long as the plaintiff's negligence is not greater than that of the defendant.[1266]

The concert of action exception requires more than mere joint negligence or an agreement to act jointly. The "concerted acts" exception referred to in NRS 41.141(5)(d) requires more than mere joint negligence or an agreement to act jointly. To be jointly and severally liable under the concert of action exception set forth in that paragraph, defendants must have agreed to engage in conduct that is inherently dangerous or poses a substantial risk of harm to others. This requirement is met when defendants agree to engage in an inherently dangerous activity, with a known risk of harm, that could lead to the commission of a tort.[1267]

The provisions of NRS 41.133 do not apply to misdemeanor traffic offenses. For the purposes of NRS 41.133, conviction of a "crime" does not include misdemeanor traffic offenses. The history of the legislative measure pursuant to which NRS 41.133 was enacted indicates that the Legislature intended the section to apply to *malum in se* offenses such as crimes of violence and not to *malum prohibitum* acts such as misdemeanor violations of state and local traffic codes. In addition, the application of NRS 41.133 to misdemeanor traffic offenses would conflict with the comparative negligence provisions of NRS 41.141. Thus, because NRS 41.133 does not apply to misdemeanor traffic offenses, convictions entered upon traffic citations may not be used to conclusively establish civil liability.[1268]

Federal and Other Cases

Damages reduced by the amount of negligence attributable to the decedent. In an action for wrongful death brought by the decedent's parents, plaintiffs were not precluded from recovery on the ground that the negligence of the decedent and the defendant each contributed equally to the accident causing the death because NRS 41.141 specifically provides that the contributory negligence of the decedent does not bar recovery if that negligence was not greater than the negligence of the person against whom recovery is sought. The damages recovered by the plaintiffs, however, were reduced by 50 percent because that percentage of negligence was attributable to the decedent.[1269]

In an action to recover damages for personal injuries sustained when plaintiff was struck by a truck driven by defendant, where plaintiff either failed to look up and down the highway before she began to walk across it (see former NRS 484.331; cf. NRS 484B.297) or was so intoxicated that when she looked, she could not see the truck rapidly approaching, and defendant, who was traveling at a reduced speed (see former NRS 484.363; cf. NRS 484B.603) and had no reason to believe that someone would be crossing the highway, immediately applied his brakes when he saw plaintiff and swerved his truck in an attempt to miss her, plaintiff was barred by NRS 41.141 from recovering any damages because her negligence contributed more to the cause of the accident and the resulting injuries than any negligence on the part of defendant.[1270]

Determination of amount of set off against award of compensatory damages. In a civil action brought by the plaintiff against multiple defendants, where: (1) the contributory negligence of the plaintiff was an issue in trial; (2) before the conclusion of the trial, the plaintiff obtained a settlement from one of defendants; and (3) after the settlement was obtained, the jury awarded compensatory damages to the plaintiff against the remaining defendants, provisions of NRS 41.141 rather than provisions of NRS 17.245 applied in determining the set off of the amount of the settlement against the award of compensatory damages.[1271]

The determination of the net sum otherwise recoverable by the plaintiff under special and general verdicts. Pursuant to the plain language of NRS 41.141, the phrase "the net sum otherwise recoverable by the plaintiff pursuant to the general and special verdicts" refers to the net sum otherwise recoverable by the plaintiff pursuant to: (1) the general verdict rendered as to the total amount of compensatory damages as assessed by the trier of fact; and (2) the special verdict indicating the percentage of negligence attributable to each party remaining in the action.[1272]

[1265] *Id.*

[1266] See also NRS 41.130 *et seq.; Woosley v. State Farm Ins. Co.*, 117 Nev. 182, 18 P.3d 317 (2001).

[1267] *GES, Inc. v. Corbitt*, 117 Nev. 265, 21 P.3d 11 (2001).

[1268] *Langon v. Matamoros*, 121 Nev. 142, 111 P.3d 1077 (2005).

[1269] *Moyer v. United States*, 593 F. Supp. 145 (D. Nev. 1984), cited, *State Farm Mut. Auto. Ins. Co. v. Commissioner of Ins.*, 114 Nev. 535, at 542, 958 P.2d 733 (1998).

[1270] *Turnbow v. Wasden*, 608 F. Supp. 237 (D. Nev. 1985).

[1271] *Coughlin v. Hilton Hotels Corp.*, 879 F. Supp. 1047 (D. Nev. 1995).

[1272] *Id.*

A Disgruntled Litigant
By Daumier

A reduction of award for compensatory and punitive damages. In a civil action brought by the plaintiff against multiple defendants, where the plaintiff: (1) was awarded $1,695,000 in compensatory damages and $5,000,000 in punitive damages by the jury; and (2) before the award of damages, obtained a settlement against the former defendant in the amount of $400,000, the district court held that the phrase "compensatory damages awarded" as set forth in NRS 42.005 referred to the amount of the plaintiff's award for compensatory damages after that award was reduced pursuant to NRS 41.141. Accordingly, the district court reduced the plaintiff's award for compensatory damages to $1,295,000 to reflect the $400,000 settlement received by the plaintiff from the former defendant, and reduced the award for punitive damages to $3,885,000 to reflect a statutory limit placed on an award of punitive damages.[1273]

Defense of Property

The question of excessive force in defense of property is for the jury.[1274]

Discharge in Bankruptcy

Once a person has a valid discharge in bankruptcy, she has a prima facie defense against all debts and the burden of proof is then on the creditor to show that the debt is nondischargeable.[1275] A debtor may come within the statute exempting someone from discharge in bankruptcy liability for obtaining of money or property on credit upon a materially false statement reflecting the financial condition made by the debtor with intent to deceive.[1276] The creditor has the burden of proving the necessary elements of fraud by a preponderance of evidence.

The elements of fraud required to be proven by the creditor—under the statute exempting from discharge in bankruptcy liability for obtaining of money or property on credit in reliance upon a false statement respecting financial condition made by debtor with the intent to deceive—are that there were materially false representations in the financial statement, that the borrower made them with intent of deceiving the lender and that the lender relied upon and was misled by the false representations in granting credit to borrower.[1277]

Doctrine of Primary or Exclusive Jurisdiction of Parties

The doctrine of primary jurisdiction occasionally requires courts to refrain from exercising jurisdiction, so that technical issues can first be considered by a governmental body. Two policies underlie this doctrine: (1) a desire for uniform regulation, and (2) the need for a tribunal with specialized knowledge to make initial assessments of certain issues.[1278]

[1273] *Id.*

[1274] *Walker v. Burkham*, 67 Nev. 541, 565, 222 P.2d 205 (1950).

[1275] *Gonzales v. Aetna Finance Co.*, 86 Nev. 271, 275, 468 P.2d 15 (1970).

[1276] *Id.*, Bankr. Act § 17, sub. a(2), 11 U.S.C.A. § 35(a)(2).

[1277] *Aetna Finance* at 275; Bankr. Act, § 17, sub. a(2), 11 U.S.C.A. § 35(a)(2).

[1278] *Clark County School Dist. v. Richardson Construction*, 123 Nev. 382, 392, 168 P.3d 87, 94 (2007).

Where a Master Settlement Agreement (MSA) provided that the parties acknowledged that the federal court had jurisdiction and would retain exclusive jurisdiction for the purposes of implementing and enforcing this Agreement and the Consent Decree as to each Settling State, the MSA's plain language precluded the parties from submitting diligent enforcement disputes to state courts.[1279]

Duress

When a party has satisfied a judgment under coercion, it does not preclude the right to appeal.[1280]

Earmarking

"[T]he earmarking doctrine applies 'when a third party lends money to a debtor for the specific purpose of paying a selected creditor.' "[1281] [T]he earmarking doctrine requires: "(1) the existence of an agreement between the new lender and the debtor that the new funds will be used to pay a specified antecedent debt; (2) performance of that agreement according to its terms; (3) the transaction viewed as a whole . . . does not result in any diminution of the estate."[1282]

Economic Loss Doctrine

The economic loss doctrine is intended to mark the fundamental boundary between contract law, which is designed to enforce the expectancy interests of parties, and tort law, which imposes a duty of reasonable care and thereby generally encourages citizens to avoid causing physical harm to others.[1283] Application of the doctrine protects parties from unlimited economic liability, which could result from negligent actions taken in commercial settings.[1284] Under the economic loss doctrine, there can be no recovery in tort for purely economic loss.[1285] The economic loss doctrine bars negligent misrepresentation claims against commercial construction design professionals where the recovery sought is solely for economic losses.[1286] Exceptions to the economic loss doctrine include economic losses sustained due to defamation, intentionally caused harm, negligent misstatements about financial matters, and loss of consortium.[1287]

Election of Remedies

Election of remedies is:

1 : The act of electing a remedy from those available for an injury;

2 : The doctrine that a plaintiff who elects a remedy for his or her injury is barred from pursuing another remedy that is inconsistent with the one elected.[1288]

Although a party may not assert contradictory theories of recovery such that the assertion of one theory will necessarily repudiate the other, the doctrine of election of remedies applies only to inconsistent remedies.[1289] A party is not required to make an election between breach of contract remedies and rescission before a jury verdict.[1290] No election between theories of recovery based on breach of contract and quantum meruit is required before a jury verdict.[1291]

Equitable Estoppel

Equitable estoppel consists of the following elements: (1) the party to be estopped must be apprised of the true facts, (2) that party must intend that his conduct shall be acted upon or must so act that the party asserting estoppel has the right to believe it was so intended, (3) the party asserting estoppel must be ignorant of the true state of the facts, and (4) the party asserting estoppel must have detrimentally relied on the other party's conduct.[1292]

[1279] *Attorney General v. Dist. Ct. (Philip Morris)*, 125 Nev., Advance Opinion 18, 209 P.3d 271 (2009).

[1280] *Wheeler Springs Plaza, LLC v. Beemon*, 119 Nev. 260, 265, 71 P.3d 1258 (2003).

[1281] *In re Superior Stamp & Coin Co., Inc.*, 223 F.3d at 1008 (quoting *Hansen v. MacDonald Meat Co. (In re Kemp Pac. Fisheries, Inc.)*, 16 F.3d 313, 316 (9th Cir. 1994)).

[1282] *Id.* (quoting *McCuskey v. Nat'l Bank of Waterloo (In re Bohlen Enters., Ltd.)*, 859 F.2d 561, 566 (8th Cir. 1988)).

[1283] *Halcrow, Inc. v. District Court*, 129 Nev., Advance Opinion 42, p. 7 (June 27, 2013).

[1284] *Id.*

[1285] *Jordan v. State, Dep't of Motor Vehicles*, 121 Nev. 44, 74, 110 P.3d 30 (2005).

[1286] *Halcrow, Inc. v. District Court*, 129 Nev., Advance Opinion 42 (June 27, 2013).

[1287] *Id.* at 9.

[1288] *Merriam-Webster's Dictionary of Law* ©1996. Merriam-Webster, Incorporated.

[1289] *J.A. Jones Constr. v. Lehrer McGovern Bovis*, 120 Nev. 277, 288, 89 P.3d 1009 (2004).

[1290] *May v. Watt*, 822 F.2d 896 (9th Cir. 1987).

[1291] *North American Graphite Corp. v. Allan*, 184 F.2d 387 (D.C. Cir. 1950).

[1292] *LVCVA v. Secretary of State*, 124 Nev. 669, 673, 191 P.3d 1138 (2008).

Equitable estoppel is where a court will not grant a judgment or other legal relief to a party who has not acted fairly; for example, by having made false representations or concealing material facts from the other party. This illustrates the legal maxim: "He who seeks equity, must do equity."[1293] Example: Louie Landlord rents space to Dora Dressmaker in his shopping center but falsely tells her a Sears store will be a tenant and will draw customers to the project. He does not tell her a new freeway is going to divert traffic from the center. When she failed to pay her rent due to lack of business, Louie Landlord sues her for breach of lease. Dressmaker may claim he is equitably estopped. See "Collateral Estoppel."

Equitable Indemnity

See "Contribution and Indemnity."

Equitable Recoupment

The Doctrine of Equitable Recoupment

The United States Supreme Court defined and refined the doctrine of equitable recoupment in a series of three cases.[1294] The doctrine is grounded in equity.[1295] It, like the mitigation provisions, relieves the harsh consequences resulting from application of the statute of limitation. The doctrine, however, is not limited to certain circumstances of adjustment.

The doctrine of equitable recoupment prevents unjust enrichment – it is invoked either by the taxpayer to recover a twice paid tax or by the Government to prohibit tax avoidance. It works as a setoff. The Court has explained:

> The essence of the doctrine of recoupment is stated in the *Bull* case: "recoupment is in the nature of a defense arising out of some feature of the transaction upon which the plaintiff's action is grounded." 295 U.S. 247, 262. It has never been thought to allow one transaction to be offset against another, but only to permit a transaction which is made the subject of suit by a plaintiff to be examined in all its aspects, and judgment to be rendered that does justice in view of the one transaction as a whole.[1296]

The doctrine of equitable recoupment applies if "a single transaction constitute[s] the taxable event claimed upon and the one considered in recoupment."[1297] The single transaction must also be subjected to two taxes based on inconsistent legal theories.[1298] Finally, the amount claimed in recoupment must be barred by the statute of limitations, while the asserted deficiency by the government must be timely.[1299] The Court narrowly limits the doctrine's application to avoid seriously undermining the statute of limitations.[1300]

"Recoupment . . . involves a netting out of debt arising from a single transaction."[1301] " 'Its function is to reduce the amount demanded, but only to the extent of the plaintiff's claim.' "[1302] "[R]ecoupment 'is the setting up of a demand arising from the same transaction as the plaintiff's claim or cause of action, strictly for the purpose of abatement or reduction of such claim.' "[1303]

[1293] *Lyerla v. Watts*, 87 Nev. 58, 62 (1971).

[1294] *Bull v. United States*, 295 U.S. 247, 79 L. Ed. 1421, 55 S. Ct. 695 (1935); *Stone v. White*, 301 U.S. 532, 81 L. Ed. 1265, 57 S. Ct. 851 (1937); and *Rothensies v. Electric Storage Battery Co.*, 329 U.S. at (1946).

[1295] *Stone*, 301 U.S. at 534-35.

[1296] *Rothensies*, 329 U.S. at 299.

[1297] *Rothensies*, 329 U.S. at 299; *Los Angeles Shipbuilding & Drydock Corp. v. United States*, 289 F.2d 222, 232-33 (9th Cir. 1961).

[1298] *Rothensies*, 329 U.S. at 300.

[1299] *Stone*, 301 U.S. at 538; *O'Brien*, 766 F.2d at 1049; *Wells Fargo Bank and Union Trust Co. v. United States*, 245 F.2d 524, 535-36 (9th Cir. 1957).

[1300] *Rothensies*, 329 U.S. at 302; *Wells Fargo*, 245 F.2d at 535.

[1301] *Id.* at 425.

[1302] *Id.* (quoting *Long Term Disability Plan of Hoffman-La Roche, Inc. v. Hiler (In re Hiler)*, 99 B.R. 238, 243 (Bankr. D.N.J. 1989)).

[1303] *Newbery Corp. v. Fireman's Fund Ins. Co.*, 95 F.3d 1392, 1399 (9th Cir. 1996) (quoting 5 COLLIER ON BANKRUPTCY ¶ 553.03, at 553-15 (15th ed. 1984)).

Estoppel

See "Equitable Estoppel" and "Promissory Estoppel."

Failure to Exhaust Administrative Remedies

A person generally must exhaust all available administrative remedies before initiating a lawsuit, and failure to do so renders the controversy nonjusticiable.[1304] The exhaustion doctrine gives administrative agencies an opportunity to correct mistakes and it conserves judicial resources, so its purpose is valuable; requiring exhaustion of administrative remedies often resolves disputes without the need for judicial involvement.[1305] A homeowners' association failed to exhaust its administrative remedies by bringing a challenge of the City's building permit for a water treatment plant in its neighborhood to the City's Board of Appeals, and thus, the association could not bring action in district court.[1306]

Generally, a taxpayer must exhaust his administrative remedies before seeking judicial relief from tax assessments and determinations.[1307] NRS 361.420(1) requires a taxpayer who believes that he or she is being taxed "in excess of the amount . . . justly to be due" to notify the Treasurer, in writing, that he or she is paying under protest. After the taxpayer pays under protest, he or she may then bring a complaint before the County Board and, if necessary, appeal to the State Board.[1308] If denied relief, the taxpayer may commence an action in the district court.[1309]

Adversaries
By Honoré Daumier

Failure to Follow Reasonable Commercial Standards

A bank's failure to follow its own normal procedures indicates that bank failed to act in accordance with reasonable commercial standards, for purposes of the statute precluding a person who substantially contributes to a material alteration of an instrument or to making an unauthorized signature from asserting alteration or lack of authority against the holder, drawee, or other payor.[1310] The determination of whether bank conformed to reasonable commercial standards in payment of checks is a question for the trier of fact.[1311] In an action by a credit union to recover the amount disbursed on a fraudulently cashed check, the trial court was required to determine if the credit union acted reasonably in light of commercial standards.

[1304] *Mesagate HOA v. City of Fernley*, 124 Nev. 1092, 1099, 194 P.3d 1248 (2008).

[1305] *Id.*

[1306] *Id.*; see NRS 278.0235, NRS 278.3195.

[1307] *Berrum v. Otto*, 127 Nev., Advance Opinion 30 (2011).

[1308] NRS 361.420(2).

[1309] *Id.*

[1310] *Torino Constr. v. Ensign Fed. Credit Union*, 111 Nev. 1515, 908 P.2d 702 (1995); NRS 104.3406.

[1311] *Id.*

NRS 104.3406, "Negligence contributing to forged signature or alteration of instrument," provides as follows:

> 1. A person whose failure to exercise ordinary care substantially contributes to an alteration of an instrument or to the making of a forged signature on an instrument is precluded from asserting the alteration or the forgery against a person who, in good faith, pays the instrument or takes it for value or for collection.
>
> 2. Under subsection 1, if the person asserting the preclusion fails to exercise ordinary care in paying or taking the instrument and that failure substantially contributes to loss, the loss is allocated between the person precluded and the person asserting the preclusion according to the extent to which the failure of each to exercise ordinary care contributed to the loss.
>
> 3. Under subsection 1, the burden of proving failure to exercise ordinary care is on the person asserting the preclusion. Under subsection 2, the burden of proving failure to exercise ordinary care is on the person precluded.

Failure to Join an Indispensable Party

NRCP 19, "Joinder of Persons Needed for Just Adjudication," provides as follows:

> (a) Persons to Be Joined if Feasible. A person who is subject to service of process and whose joinder will not deprive the court of jurisdiction over the subject matter of the action shall be joined as a party in the action if (1) in the person's absence, complete relief cannot be accorded among those already parties, or (2) the person claims an interest relating to the subject of the action and is so situated that the disposition of the action in the person's absence may (i) as a practical matter impair or impede the person's ability to protect that interest or (ii) leave any of the persons already parties subject to a substantial risk of incurring double, multiple, or otherwise inconsistent obligations by reason of the claimed interest. If the person has not been so joined, the court shall order that the person be made a party. If the person should join as a plaintiff but refuses to do so, the person may be made a defendant, or, in a proper case, an involuntary plaintiff.
>
> (b) Determination by Court Whenever Joinder Not Feasible. If a person as described in subdivision (a)(1)-(2) hereof cannot be made a party, the court shall determine whether in equity and good conscience the action should proceed among the parties before it, or should be dismissed, the absent person being thus regarded as indispensable. The factors to be considered by the court include: first, to what extent a judgment rendered in the person's absence might be prejudicial to the person or those already parties; second, the extent to which, by protective provisions in the judgment, by the shaping of relief, or other measures, the prejudice can be lessened or avoided; third, whether a judgment rendered in the person's absence will be adequate; fourth, whether the plaintiff will have an adequate remedy if the action is dismissed for nonjoinder.
>
> (c) Pleading Reasons for Nonjoinder. A pleading asserting a claim for relief shall state the names, if known to the pleader, of any persons as described in subdivision (a)(1)–(2) hereof who are not joined, and the reasons why they are not joined.
>
> (d) Exception of Class Actions. This rule is subject to the provisions of Rule 23.

In an action ordering a conveyance set aside, the transferee of the property was an indispensable party.[1312] The trial court ordered the conveyance to the husband's present wife to be set aside. The appellate court vacated the order because of the failure to join an indispensable party. Under NRCP 19(a), the present wife, as transferee, should have been joined in an action to set aside the conveyance of transferred property. Entering an order of reconveyance without joining the transferee constitutes taking of property from one and giving it to another without a hearing, and the nonjoined transferee may validly force relitigation of propriety of the conveyance before coming under any legal duty to reconvey the property.[1313] The failure to join an indispensable party may be raised by the appellate court sua sponte, as well as by a party who because of nonjoinder may be subjected to inconsistent or double liability. Similarly, the objection that an indispensable party was not joined is not waived by its nonassertion at the trial level.[1314] An association ordering sanctions imposed by a university against a coach was an indispensable party in an action by the coach against the university to contest the sanctions.[1315] The failure to join a family trust as a party to an action between former spouses

---

[1312] *Johnson v. Johnson*, 93 Nev. 655, 572 P.2d 925 (1977).

[1313] *Id.*

[1314] See *Blaine Equip. Co. v. State, Purchasing Div.*, 122 Nev. 860, at 864, 138 P.3d 820 (2006), see also *Gladys Baker Olsen Family Trust v. Eighth Judicial Dist. Court*, 110 Nev. 548, at 554, 874 P.2d 778 (1994).

[1315] *University of Nevada v. Tarkanian*, 95 Nev. 389, 594 P.2d 1159 (1979), cited, *Crowley v. Duffrin*, 109 Nev. 597, at 602, 855 P.2d 536 (1993).

was fatal to the district court's judgment in action under circumstances.[1316] The successful bidder for a state contract was a necessary party in proceedings against the contracting state agencies.[1317]

Failure to Mitigate Damages

A person who claims damages as a result of another's negligence or breach of contract has a duty under the law to "mitigate" those damages, so that they must take advantage of any reasonable opportunity under the circumstances to reduce or minimize the loss or damage. For example, a person injured due to the negligence of another has a duty to seek treatment for the injuries to prevent the condition from becoming aggravated. In a breach of a lease by a tenant, the aggrieved landlord must make reasonable efforts to relet the property to minimize the lost rent payments due. In a mortgage, a duty may exist to prevent and mitigate the loss, including good faith efforts by the mortgagor to obtain a cure of the default, collect amounts due under the loan, inspect and appraise the property and effectuate the early disposition of the property.

For example, when an employee files a claim for wrongful discharge, he/she may seek to recover damages for lost wages. However, if he/she fails to seek other employment, the court may limit the amount of damages for lost wages to those that the court deems to be a reasonable period of unemployment, under the reasoning that the employee failed to mitigate damages by obtaining other employment. In a further example, when a person is injured in an auto accident he/she may seek damages for injuries. However, if he/she fails to get medical attention and an infection develops, the court may exclude recovery for medical bills, lost wages, and suffering related to the infection.

Evidence of compromise offers is inadmissible for the purpose of demonstrating a failure to mitigate damages because evidence demonstrating a failure to mitigate damages necessarily goes to the "amount" of a claim.[1318]

Failure to Perform

A "failure to perform" exclusion is a provision in some commercial general liability policies, which excludes coverage for the loss of use of undamaged property caused by the insured's delay or failure in performing an obligation, or by a design defect or failure of the performance of a product or service as warranted or represented by the insured. However, this exclusion does not apply to the loss of use of other property arising out of sudden and accidental physical injury to the product or work after it has been put to its intended use.

Failure to Plead Fraud with Particularity

Under NRCP 9(b), a plaintiff must plead the circumstances constituting fraud with particularity. Pleading with particularity is required in order to afford adequate notice to the opposing parties so that they can defend against the charge and not just deny that they have done anything wrong. To plead with particularity, plaintiffs must include in their complaint averments to the time, the place, the identity of the parties involved, and the nature of the fraud. Malice, intent, knowledge and other conditions of the mind of a person may be averred generally.[1319]

A relaxed pleading standard applies in fraud actions in situations where the facts necessary for pleading with particularity are peculiarly within the defendant's knowledge or are readily obtainable by him.[1320] In applying the relaxed pleading standard to fraud actions, a plaintiff must state facts supporting a strong inference of fraud, aver that a relaxed pleading standard is appropriate, and show in his complaint that he cannot plead fraud with more particularity because the required information is in the defendant's possession; if the district court finds that the relaxed standard is appropriate, it should allow the plaintiff time to conduct the necessary discovery.[1321]

Failure to State a Claim upon which Relief May be Granted

An order granting a motion to dismiss under NRCP 12(b)(5) for failure to state a claim is subject to a rigorous standard of review on appeal. The Nevada Supreme Court will regard all factual allegations in the complaint as true and must draw all inferences in favor of the nonmoving party. A complaint should only be dismissed if it appears beyond a reasonable doubt that the plaintiff could prove no set of facts, which, if true, would entitle him to relief. Dismissal is proper where the allegations are insufficient to establish the elements of a claim for relief. The district court's

---

[1316] *Gladys Baker Olsen Family Trust v. Eighth Judicial Dist. Court*, 110 Nev. 548, 874 P.2d 778 (1994), cited, *Guerin v. Guerin*, 114 Nev. 127, at 132, 953 P.2d 716 (1998).

[1317] *Blaine Equip. Co. v. State, Purchasing Div.*, 122 Nev. 860, 138 P.3d 820 (2006).

[1318] *Davis v. Beling*, Nev.Adv. Op. No. 28, 278 P.3d 501 (2012).

[1319] *Rocker v. KPMG LLP*, 122 Nev. 1185, 1192 (2006).

[1320] *Id.* at 1194-95.

[1321] *Id.* at 1195; NRCP 9(b).

conclusions of law are reviewed de novo.[1322]

Failure to Take Advantage of Effective System to Report/Stop Harassment

This affirmative defense, applied in Title VII actions, is called the Faragher-Ellerth defense. The Faragher-Ellerth affirmative defense can help employers avoid liability for alleged unlawful harassment. The United States Supreme Court first articulated the defense in the companion cases of *Faragher v. Boca Raton*, 524 U.S. 775 (1998), and *Burlington Industries, Inc. v. Ellerth*, 524 U.S. 742 (1998). The Faragher-Ellerth affirmative defense is available for claims of harassment under Title VII of the Civil Rights Act of 1964 and the Minnesota Human Rights Act when the employer can prove the following:

That the employer exercised reasonable care to prevent and correct promptly any sexually harassing behavior; and

That the plaintiff employee unreasonably failed to take advantage of any preventive or corrective opportunities provided by the employer or to avoid harm otherwise.

For example, if an employer has a policy prohibiting harassment, and an employee unreasonably fails to report harassment under the policy, the Faragher-Ellerth affirmative defense may be available.[1323]

Fair use (Copyright Law)

The federal statute, 17 U.S.C. § 107, provides as follows:

Notwithstanding the provisions of sections 17 U.S.C. § 106 and 17 U.S.C. § 106A, the fair use of a copyrighted work, including such use by reproduction in copies or phonorecords or by any other means specified by that section, for purposes such as criticism, comment, news reporting, teaching (including multiple copies for classroom use), scholarship, or research, is not an infringement of copyright. In determining whether the use made of a work in any particular case is a fair use the factors to be considered shall include:

the purpose and character of the use, including whether such use is of a commercial nature or is for nonprofit educational purposes;
the nature of the copyrighted work; and
the amount and substantiality of the portion used in relation to the copyrighted work as a whole; and the effect of the use upon the potential market for or value of the copyrighted work.

The fact that a work is unpublished shall not itself bar a finding of fair use if such finding is made upon consideration of all the above factors.

See, *e.g.*, *Campbel, aka Skywalker, et al. v. Acuff-Rose Music, Inc.*, 510 U.S. 569, 590 (1994). The Ninth Circuit has analyzed the fair use factors in detail.[1324]

Filed rate doctrine

The filed rate doctrine is a common-law rule forbidding a regulated entity, usually a common carrier, to charge a rate other than the one on file with the appropriate federal regulatory authority.[1325] For example, in plaintiffs' class action suit on behalf of a nationwide class of raw milk producers seeking monetary and injunctive relief under state law arising from the misreporting of pricing data to the USDA, the district court's dismissal was reversed and remanded, as although the district court properly determined that the filed rate doctrine applied to the Agricultural Marketing Agreement Act of 1937 (AMAA) minimum milk pricing program, it erred by concluding that the filed rate doctrine applied to bar the plaintiffs' state law claims in the case.[1326]

Force Majeure

"Force majeure" [French "a superior force"] is an event or effect that can be neither anticipated nor controlled. The term includes both acts of nature (*e.g.*, floods and hurricanes) and acts of people (*e.g.*, riots, strikes, and wars).[1327]

[1322] *Stockmeier v. State, Dep't of Corrections*, 122 Nev. 385, 389, 135 P.3d 220 (2006).
[1323] See *Jones v. D.C. Dept. of Corrections*, 429 F.3d 276 (D.C. Cir. 2005).
[1324] *Monge v. Maya Magazines, Inc.* (9th Cir. 8/14/12).
[1325] *Black's Law Dictionary* 718 (9th ed. 2009).
[1326] *Carlin v. DairyAmerica, Inc.*, No. 10-16448 (9th Cir. 20120).
[1327] *Id.*

Fraud

See "Fraud" under "Claims."

Frustration of Purpose or Commercial Frustration

The doctrine of commercial frustration applies to discharge a party's contractual obligation when performance remains possible but the expected value of performance to the party seeking to be excused has been destroyed by a fortuitous event, which supervenes to cause an actual but not literal failure of consideration.[1328] The doctrine of commercial frustration does not apply if the unforeseen contingency is one which the promisor should have foreseen, and for which he should have provided.[1329]

Good Faith

Good faith can be an affirmative defense. For example, "good faith" may be a police officer's affirmative defense in a "suicide by cop" case. A "good faith" defense and exceptions exist under the FLSA (Fair Labor Standards Act).[1330]

Government Contractor Defense

The Sixth Circuit observed that other circuits have applied the government contractor defense against the failure to warn claims, but in doing so did not focus on the underlying design defect but instead upon the warnings. "Warning the government of dangers arising from its specific design . . . does not encompass or state a failure to warn claim; it simply encourages contractors to provide the government with all the information required to soundly exercise its discretion."[1331]

The Sixth Circuit continued by stating that, "By contrast, tort law duties to warn accomplish an entirely different objective of helping those who use or otherwise come into contact with a product to protect their own safety."[1332] Thus, design defect and failure to warn claims differ practically, as well as theoretically, and approval of a design does not mean that the government considered the appropriate warnings, if any, that should accompany the product.[1333] The Sixth Circuit has squarely held that the government contractor defense to failure to warn claims is not necessarily established merely by satisfying the government contractor defense as to design defect claims.[1334] The Sixth Circuit further reasoned as follows:

> When the government exercises its discretion and approves designs prepared by private contractors, it has an interest in insulating its contractors from liability for such design defects. . . . Similarly, when the government exercises its discretion and approves warnings intended for users, it has an interest in insulating its contractors from state failure to warn tort liability.[1335]

The Sixth Circuit stated the *Boyle* requirements in failure to warn cases as follows:

> When state law would otherwise impose liability for a failure to warn of dangers in using military equipment, that law is displaced if the contractor can show: (1) the United States exercised its discretion and approved the warnings, if any; (2) the contractor provided warnings that conformed to the approved warnings; and (3) the contractor warned the United States of the dangers in the equipment's use about which the contractor knew, but the United States did not.[1336]

[1328] *Graham v. Kim*, 111 Nev. 1039, 1041, 899 P.2d 1122 (1995).

[1329] *Id.*

[1330] See 29 U.S.C. §§ 207, 260.

[1331] *Tate v. Boeing Helicopters*, 140 F.3d 654 (6th Cir. 1998).

[1332] *Id.* (quoting *Grispo v. Eagle-Picher Industries (In re NY Asbestos)*, 897 F.2d 626, 632 (2d Cir. 1990)).

[1333] *Id.*

[1334] *Id.* at 1157.

[1335] *Id.* (internal citations omitted.)

[1336] *Id.*

Hindrance of Contract

For a case on hindrance of contract, see *Family Snacks of North Carolina, Inc. v. Prepared Products Company, Inc,* 295 F.3d 864 (8th Cir. 2002).

Illegality

See Elliot v. Resnick, 114 Nev. 25, 952 P.2d 961 (1998) (failure to obtain city's prior approval of transfer did not render contract illegal between parties to transaction, but merely conditioned completion of transfer on city's approval).

When a party suffers injury from wrongdoing in which he engaged, the doctrine of *in pari delicto* often prevents him from recovering for his injury.[1337] The rationale underlying the doctrine "is that there is no societal interest in providing an accounting between wrongdoers."[1338] Permitting corporations to sue their coconspirators would not only force courts to apportion blame between wrongdoers, but it would also "diminish[ ] corporate boards' incentives to supervise their own agents."[1339]

Immunity from Liability of Persons Who Engage in Right of Petition

NRS 41.635 to NRS 41.670 concern the liability of persons who engaged in the right to petition. The Nevada Legislature has promulgated statutes that protect and immunize persons who in good faith file petitions and communicate about their petitions. The Reviser's Note provides as follows:

> Ch. 387, Stats. 1997, at p. 1363, which enacts NRS 41.635 and 41.637 and amends NRS 41.640 to 41.670, inclusive, contains the following preamble not included in NRS:
> "Whereas, The framers of the United States Constitution and the constitution of the State of Nevada, recognizing that participation by citizens in government is an inalienable right which is essential to the survival of democracy, secured its protection by giving the people the right to petition the government for redress of grievances in the First Amendment to the United States Constitution and in section 10 of article 1 of the constitution of the State of Nevada; and
> Whereas, The communications, information, opinions, reports, testimony, claims and argument provided by citizens to their government are essential to wise governmental decisions and public policy, the public health, safety and welfare, effective law enforcement, the efficient operation of governmental programs, the credibility and trust afforded government and the continuation of our representative form of government; and
> Whereas, Civil actions are being filed against many citizens, businesses and organizations based on their valid exercise of their right to petition; and
> Whereas, Such lawsuits, called "Strategic Lawsuits Against Public Participation," or "SLAPPs," are typically dismissed, but often not before the defendant is put to great expense, harassment and interruption of their productive activities; and
> Whereas, The number of SLAPPs has increased significantly over the past 30 years; and
> Whereas, SLAPPs are an abuse of the judicial process in that they are used to censor, chill, intimidate or punish persons for involving themselves in public affairs; and
> Whereas, The threat of financial liability, litigation costs and other personal losses from groundless civil actions seriously affects governmental, commercial and individual rights by significantly diminishing public participation in government, in public issues and in voluntary service; and
> Whereas, Although courts have recognized and discouraged SLAPPs, protection of this important right has not been uniform or comprehensive; and
> Whereas, It is essential to our form of government that the constitutional rights of citizens to participate fully in the process of government be protected and encouraged;"

NRS 41.635, "Definitions," provides as follows: "As used in NRS 41.635 to 41.670, inclusive, unless the context otherwise requires, the words and terms defined in NRS 41.637 and 41.640 have the meanings ascribed to them in those sections."

[1337] *Official Comm. of Unsecured Creditors v. R.F. Lafferty & Co., Inc.* 267 F.3d 340, 354 (3rd Cir. 2001); *American Intern. Group,* 976 A.2d 872, 883 (Del. Ch. 2009).

[1338] *American Intern. Group,* 976 A.2d at 882 (Del. 2009).

[1339] *Id.* at 889; see also *Shimrak v. Garcia-Mendoza,* 112 Nev. at 251, 912 P.2d at 825 (1996) ("[T]raditionally neither courts of law nor equity will interpose to grant relief to parties to an illegal agreement."). See *In re AMERCO Derivative Litigation,* 127 Nev. ___, ___ n.6, 252 P.3d 681, 697 n.6 (2011).

(Added to NRS by 1997, 1364; A 1997, 2593)

NRS 41.637, "'Good faith communication in furtherance of the right to petition' defined," provides as follows:

"Good faith communication in furtherance of the right to petition" means any:
1. Communication that is aimed at procuring any governmental or electoral action, result or outcome;
2. Communication of information or a complaint to a Legislator, officer or employee of the Federal Government, this state or a political subdivision of this state, regarding a matter reasonably of concern to the respective governmental entity; or
3. Written or oral statement made in direct connection with an issue under consideration by a legislative, executive or judicial body, or any other official proceeding authorized by law,
which is truthful or is made without knowledge of its falsehood.
(Added to NRS by 1997, 1364; A 1997, 2593)

NRS 41.640, "'Political subdivision' defined," provides as follows: 'Political subdivision' has the meaning ascribed to it in NRS 41.0305."
(Added to NRS by 1993, 2848; A 1997, 1365, 2593)

NRS 41.650, "Limitation of liability," provides as follows:

A person who engages in a good faith communication in furtherance of the right to petition is immune from civil liability for claims based upon the communication.
(Added to NRS by 1993, 2848; A 1997, 1365, 2593)

NRS 41.660, "Attorney General or chief legal officer of political subdivision may defend or provide support to person sued for engaging in right to petition; special counsel; filing special motion to dismiss; stay of discovery; adjudication upon merits," provides as follows:

1. If an action is brought against a person based upon a good faith communication in furtherance of the right to petition:
(a) The person against whom the action is brought may file a special motion to dismiss; and
(b) The Attorney General or the chief legal officer or attorney of a political subdivision of this State may defend or otherwise support the person against whom the action is brought. If the Attorney General or the chief legal officer or attorney of a political subdivision has a conflict of interest in, or is otherwise disqualified from, defending or otherwise supporting the person, the Attorney General or the chief legal officer or attorney of a political subdivision may employ special counsel to defend or otherwise support the person.
2. A special motion to dismiss must be filed within 60 days after service of the complaint, which period may be extended by the court for good cause shown.
3. If a special motion to dismiss is filed pursuant to subsection 2, the court shall:
(a) Treat the motion as a motion for summary judgment;
(b) Stay discovery pending:
(1) A ruling by the court on the motion; and
(2) The disposition of any appeal from the ruling on the motion; and
(c) Rule on the motion within 30 days after the motion is filed.
4. If the court dismisses the action pursuant to a special motion to dismiss filed pursuant to subsection 2, the dismissal operates as an adjudication upon the merits.
(Added to NRS by 1993, 2848; A 1997, 1365, 2593)

NRS 41.670, "Award of reasonable costs and attorney's fees upon grant of special motion to dismiss; person sued for engaging in right to petition may bring separate action for damages," provides as follows:

If the court grants a special motion to dismiss filed pursuant to NRS 41.660:
1. The court shall award reasonable costs and attorney's fees to the person against whom the action was brought, except that the court shall award reasonable costs and attorney's fees to this State or to the appropriate political subdivision of this State if the Attorney General, the chief legal officer or attorney of the political subdivision or special counsel provided the defense for the person pursuant to NRS 41.660.
2. The person against whom the action is brought may bring a separate action to recover:

(a) Compensatory damages;
(b) Punitive damages; and
(c) Attorney's fees and costs of bringing the separate action.
(Added to NRS by 1993, 2848; A 1997, 1366, 2593)

If the plaintiff voluntarily dismisses the action before the defendant filed either an initial responsive pleading or a special motion to dismiss under NRS 41.670, the defendant cannot file an anti-SLAPP suit against the plaintiff based on that action.[1340]

Implied Repeal of Statute
For a case on the implied repeal of a statute, see *In re: Stock Exchanges Options Trading Antitrust Litigation*, 317 F.3d 134 (2d. Cir. 2003).

Implied Waiver
Implied waiver applies when the other party's conduct clearly shows an intention to waive a right or when that party's neglect to insist upon the right prejudices the invoking party.[1341]

Improper Collateral Attack on a Judgment
For a discussion of an improper collateral attack on a judgment, see *Markoff*,[1342] where Plaintiff brought an action against a life insurance company and others for the alleged giving of false testimony and alleged conspiracy to give false testimony in a previous case in which plaintiff had been denied insurance benefits. Motions to dismiss were granted by the district court in favor of some defendants, and summary judgment was granted in favor of others. Plaintiff appealed. The Nevada Supreme Court held that where it was clear that plaintiff had previously had a fair trial upon merits of his claim for benefits and issues previously decided and affirmed were predicated upon the same basic issues raised in the instant action, and where it was clear that the instant action was an attempt to circumvent prior judgments and relitigate entitlement to insurance benefits, the instant action constituted a collateral attack on the prior judgment, not countenanced by traditional principles of res judicata and collateral estoppel.

A final judgment entered with proper jurisdiction is not subject to collateral attack.[1343] However, persons not parties to a judicial proceeding cannot be bound by the court's action therein.[1344]

Improper Notice of Breach
[U] *Gendreau v. Rountree*, No. 97-686 (Mont. 04/23/1998). (Note that this is an unpublished opinion.)

Improper Service
Under the rule permitting certain defenses, including NRCP 12(b)(2) lack of jurisdiction over person, NRCP 12(b)(3) insufficiency of process, and NRCP 12(b)(4) insufficiency of service of process, to be asserted by motion and providing that defenses 2-4 are waived if joined with one or more defenses other than defenses 2-4, a motion by a wife to dismiss her husband's divorce action because of lack of jurisdiction over her person, lack of sufficiency of process, and insufficiency of service of process, and to quash service made on her in Nevada, constituted a "general appearance" invoking the court's general jurisdiction.[1345]

Indemnity and Contribution

"Indemnity" is defined as follows:
1. Indemnity is a duty to make good any loss, damage, or liability incurred by another.
2. Indemnity is the right of an injured party to claim reimbursement for its loss, damage, or liability from a person who has such a duty.

[1340] *Stubbs v. Strickland*, 129 Nev., Advance Opinion 15 (3/14/13).

[1341] *Dickinson v. American Medical Response*, 124 Nev. 460, 468, 186 P.3d 878 (2008).

[1342] *Markoff v. New York Life Ins. Co.*, 92 Nev. 268, 549 P.2d 330 (1976).

[1343] *Ross v. Old Republic Insurance Co.*, 134 P.3d 505 (Colo.Ct.App. 2006).

[1344] *Id.*; see also *Nat'l Farmers Union Prop. & Cas. Co. v. Frackelton*, 662 P.2d 1056 (Colo. 1983) (collateral estoppel cannot be applied to disadvantage a person who has not litigated the issue in question).

[1345] NRCP 12(b). See *Barnato v. District Court*, 76 Nev. 335, 336, 353 P.2d 1103 (1960).

3. Reimbursement or compensation for loss, damage, or liability in tort; especially, the right of a party who is secondarily liable to recover from the party who is primarily liable for reimbursement of expenditures paid to a third party for injuries resulting from a violation of a common-law duty.[1346]

Equitable Indemnity

Equitable indemnity, which allows a defendant to seek recovery from other potential tortfeasors, is generally available to remedy the situation in which the defendant, who has committed no independent wrong, is held liable for the loss of a plaintiff caused by another party.[1347] Nevada's equitable indemnity law has long drawn a distinction between secondary and primary liability.[1348] In order for one tortfeasor to be in a position of secondary responsibility *vis-a-vis* another tortfeasor, and thus be entitled to indemnification, there must be a preexisting legal relation between them, or some duty on the part of the primary tortfeasor to protect the secondary tortfeasor.[1349] Additionally, where a party has committed an "independent wrong," and is thus actively negligent, that party has no right to indemnity from other tortfeasors.[1350]

A claim for equitable indemnity fails as a matter of law based on the lack of any preexisting relationship between the third parties and the third-party plaintiffs' active negligence.[1351]

Dismissal of a contribution claim is improper if the party seeking contribution has not yet paid toward a judgment. The Nevada Supreme Court has concluded that a party need not pay toward a judgment before bringing a claim for contribution. As such, a third-party contribution claim was not properly dismissed on that ground.[1352]

When a claim for contribution is contingent upon a successful showing of medical malpractice, a claimant must satisfy the expert affidavit requirement of NRS 41A.071. Thus, where the third-party plaintiff failed to attach an expert affidavit, that warranted dismissal of their complaint, but such dismissal should be without prejudice.[1353]

The absence of a properly executed jurat does not render a medical expert's written statement insufficient to meet the affidavit requirement of NRS 41A.071.[1354] Because a jurat is merely evidence that the medical expert swore under oath to the veracity of his or her statement before an officer authorized to administer oaths, it is clear that other evidence that the expert's written statement was made under oath can be offered to satisfy NRS 41A.071's affidavit requirement.

Contribution or Right of Contribution

"Contribution" is defined as the right that gives one of several persons who are liable on a common debt the ability to recover proportionately from each of the others when that one person discharges the debt for the benefit of all; the right to demand that another who is jointly responsible for a third party's injury supply part of what is required to compensate the third party.[1355]

NRS 17.225, "Right to contribution," provides as follows:

1. Except as otherwise provided in this section and NRS 17.235 to 17.305, inclusive, where two or more persons become jointly or severally liable in tort for the same injury to person or property or for the same wrongful death, there is a right of contribution among them even though judgment has not been recovered against all or any of them.

2. The right of contribution exists only in favor of a tortfeasor who has paid more than his or her equitable share of the common liability, and the tortfeasor's total recovery is limited to the amount paid by the tortfeasor in excess of his or her equitable share. No tortfeasor is compelled to make contribution beyond his or her own equitable share of the entire liability.

3. A tortfeasor who enters into a settlement with a claimant is not entitled to recover contribution from another tortfeasor whose liability for the injury or wrongful death is not extinguished by the settlement nor in respect to any amount paid in a settlement which is in excess of what was reasonable.

[1346] *Black's Law Dictionary* 837 (9th ed. 2009).
[1347] *Saylor v. Arcotta*, 126 Nev. ___, ___, 225 P.3d 1276, 1278-79. (2010) (citation omitted).
[1348] *Id.*
[1349] *Id.*
[1350] *Id.*
[1351] *Saylor v. Arcotta*, 126 Nev. ___, ___, 225 P.3d 1276, 1278-79. (2010).
[1352] *Id.*
[1353] *Id.*
[1354] *MountainView Hospital v. Dist. Ct.*, 128 Nev. Adv. Op. No. 17 (2012).
[1355] *Black's Law Dictionary* 378 (9th ed. 2009).

NRS 17.235, "Effect of judgment against one tortfeasor," provides as follows:

The recovery of a judgment for an injury or wrongful death against one tortfeasor does not of itself discharge the other tortfeasors from liability for the injury or wrongful death unless the judgment is satisfied. The satisfaction of the judgment does not impair any right of contribution.

NRS 17.245, "Effect of release or covenant not to sue," provides as follows:

1. When a release or a covenant not to sue or not to enforce judgment is given in good faith to one of two or more persons liable in tort for the same injury or the same wrongful death:
(a) It does not discharge any of the other tortfeasors from liability for the injury or wrongful death unless its terms so provide, but it reduces the claim against the others to the extent of any amount stipulated by the release or the covenant, or in the amount of the consideration paid for it, whichever is the greater; and
(b) It discharges the tortfeasor to whom it is given from all liability for contribution and for equitable indemnity to any other tortfeasor.
2. As used in this section, "equitable indemnity" means a right of indemnity that is created by the court rather than expressly provided for in a written agreement.

NRS 17.255, "Intentional tort bars right to contribution," provides as follows: "There is no right of contribution in favor of any tortfeasor who has intentionally caused or contributed to the injury or wrongful death."

NRS 17.265, "Certain rights of indemnity unimpaired," provides as follows:

Except as otherwise provided in NRS 17.245, the provisions of NRS 17.225 to 17.305, inclusive, do not impair any right of indemnity under existing law. Where one tortfeasor is entitled to indemnity from another, the right of the indemnity obligee is for indemnity and not contribution, and the indemnity obligor is not entitled to contribution from the obligee for any portion of his or her indemnity obligation.

NRS 17.275, "Subrogation of insurer," provides as follows:

A liability insurer, who by payment has discharged in full or in part the liability of a tortfeasor and has thereby discharged in full its obligation as insurer, is subrogated to the tortfeasor's right of contribution to the extent of the amount it has paid in excess of the tortfeasor's equitable share of the common liability. This provision does not limit or impair any right of subrogation arising from any other relationship.

NRS 17.285, "Enforcement of right of contribution," provides as follows:

1. Whether or not judgment has been entered in an action against two or more tortfeasors for the same injury or wrongful death, contribution may be enforced by separate action.
2. Where a judgment has been entered in an action against two or more tortfeasors for the same injury or wrongful death, contribution may be enforced in that action by judgment in favor of one against other judgment defendants by motion upon notice to all parties to the action.
3. If there is a judgment for the injury or wrongful death against the tortfeasor seeking contribution, any separate action by the tortfeasor to enforce contribution must be commenced within 1 year after the judgment has become final by lapse of time for appeal or after appellate review.
4. If there is no judgment for the injury or wrongful death against the tortfeasor seeking contribution, the tortfeasor's right of contribution is barred unless the tortfeasor has:
(a) Discharged by payment the common liability within the statute of limitations period applicable to claimant's right of action against him or her and has commenced an action for contribution within 1 year after payment; or
(b) Agreed while action is pending against him or her to discharge the common liability and has within 1 year after the agreement paid the liability and commenced an action for contribution.
5. The judgment of the court in determining the liability of the several defendants to the claimant for an injury or wrongful death shall be binding as among such defendants in determining their right to contribution.

NRS 17.295, "Equitable shares," provides as follows:

> In determining the equitable shares of tortfeasors in the entire liability:
> 1. If equity requires, the collective liability of some as a group constitutes a single share; and
> 2. Principles of equity applicable to contribution generally apply.

NRS 17.305, "Inapplicability to breach of fiduciary relationship," provides as follows: "NRS 17.225 to 17.305, inclusive, do not apply to breaches of trust or of other fiduciary obligation."

Contribution "is an equitable sharing of liability, " whereas indemnity "is a complete shifting of liability to the party primarily responsible."[1356]

Impossibility or Impracticability

The doctrine of impracticability in the common law of contracts excuses performance of a duty, where that duty has become unfeasibly difficult or expensive for the party who was to perform. It is similar in some respects to the doctrine of impossibility because it is triggered by the occurrence of a condition, the nonoccurrence of which was a basic assumption of the contract. The major difference between impossibility and impracticability, however, is that while impossibility excuses performance where the contractual duty cannot physically be performed, the doctrine of impracticability comes into play where performance is still physically possible, but would be very burdensome for the party whose performance is due. Thus, impossibility is an objective condition, whereas impracticability is a subject condition for a court to determine. Typically, the test U.S. courts use for impracticability is as follows (with a few variations between jurisdictions):

There must be an occurrence of a condition, the nonoccurrence of which was a basic assumption of the contract,

The occurrence must make performance extremely expensive or difficult, and

This difficulty was not anticipated by the parties to the contract (note: some jurisdictions require that there be no measure within the contract itself to allocate risk between the parties).[1357]

The RESTATEMENT (SECOND) OF CONTRACTS § 261 does not explicitly define the scope of what is considered impracticable, as it is a fairly subjective and fact-intensive test for the courts. Generally, courts typically do not consider events as increases in prices or costs beyond a normal range to allow for discharge of duties on grounds of impracticability, as such events are normally foreseeable risks of fixed-price contracts.

Uniform Commercial Code

Section 2-615 of the Uniform Commercial Code deals with impracticability in the context of sales of goods, and introduces some additional constraints on the parties. A party whose ability to perform his obligations has only been partially affected must allocate production and delivery among his customers in a manner which is fair and reasonable, affording each of them with partial performance, and must notify all purchasers that there will be delay, partial delivery, or non-delivery. According to note 4 under UCC § 2-615 [see NRS 104.2615 below], increased cost alone does not excuse performance unless the rise in cost is due to some unforeseen contingency which alters the nature of performance. It further explains that a change in market conditions resulting in a rise or drop in prices is not sufficient to claim impracticability, because the parties assumed that risk when the contract was made. The comments indicate that contingencies such as war, embargo, crop failures, or a failure of a major source of supply that causes the market change or prevents a seller from obtaining supplies necessary for his performance would justify a claim of impracticability.

NRS 104.2615, "Excuse by failure of presupposed conditions," provides as follows:

> Except so far as a seller may have assumed a greater obligation and subject to the preceding section on substituted performance:
> 1. Delay in delivery or nondelivery in whole or in part by a seller who complies with subsections 2 and 3 is not a breach of the seller's duty under a contract for sale if performance as agreed has been made impracticable by the occurrence of a contingency[,] the nonoccurrence of which was a basic assumption on

---

[1356] *Medallion Dev., Inc. v. Converse Consultants*, 113 Nev. 27, 32, 930 P.2d 115, 119 (1997), superseded by statute on other grounds as stated in *Doctors Co.*, 120 Nev. at 654, 98 P.3d at 688; NRS 17.245. *Otak Nevada, LLC v. Eighth Judicial District Court of State of Nevada*, 59050 (Nev. 11/07/2013).

[1357] See, *e.g., Transatlantic Financing Corp. v. United States*, 363 F.2d 312 (D.C. Cir. 1966).

which the contract was made or by compliance in good faith with any applicable foreign or domestic governmental regulation or order[,] whether or not it later proves to be invalid.

    2. Where the causes mentioned in subsection 1 affect only a part of the seller's capacity to perform, the seller must allocate production and deliveries among his or her customers but may at his or her option include regular customers not then under contract as well as his or her own requirements for further manufacture. The seller may so allocate in any manner which is fair and reasonable.

    3. The seller must notify the buyer seasonally that there will be delay or nondelivery and, when allocation is required under subsection 2, of the estimated quota.

The Uniform Commercial Code's doctrine of commercial impracticability, NRS 104.2615, was not applicable in a case which involved performance contracts rather than sales contracts.[1358]

The doctrine of impossibility or impracticability is usually invoked to excuse non-performance. However, "there is nothing necessarily inconsistent in claiming commercial impracticability for the method of performance actually adopted; the concept of impracticability assumes performance was physically possible. Moreover, a rule making non-performance a condition precedent to recovery would unjustifiably encourage disappointment of expectations." [1359]

Improper Venue

NRS 13.010 through 13.060 govern where actions may be commenced and other venue issues.

NRS 13.010, "Where actions are to be commenced," provides as follows:

    1. When a person has contracted to perform an obligation at a particular place, and resides in another county, the action must be commenced, and, subject to the power of the court to change the place of trial as provided in this Chapter, must be tried in the county in which such obligation is to be performed or in which the person resides; and the county in which the obligation is incurred shall be deemed to be the county in which it is to be performed, unless there is a special contract to the contrary.

    2. Actions for the following causes shall be tried in the county in which the subject of the action, or some part thereof, is situated, subject to the power of the court to change the place of trial as provided in this Chapter:

    (a) For the recovery of real property, or an estate, or interest therein, or for the determination in any form of such right or interest, and for injuries to real property.

    (b) For the partition of real property.

    (c) For the foreclosure of all liens and mortgages on real property. Where the real property is situated partly in one county and partly in another the plaintiff may select either of the counties, and the county so selected is the proper county for the trial of such action; but, in the case mentioned in this paragraph, if the plaintiff prays in the complaint for an injunction pending the action, or applies pending the action for an injunction, the proper county for the trial shall be the county in which the defendant resides or a majority of the defendants reside at the commencement of the action.

NRS 13.020, "Venue of actions for recovery of penalties and forfeitures; actions against public officers; actions against State of Nevada," provides as follows:

    Actions for the following causes must be tried in the county where the cause, or some part thereof, arose, subject to the power of the court to change the place of trial:

    1. For the recovery of a penalty or forfeiture imposed by statute; except, that when it is imposed for an offense committed on a lake, river or other stream of water, situated in two or more counties, the action may be brought in any county bordering on such lake, river or stream, and opposite to the place where the offense was committed.

    2. Against a public officer, or person especially appointed to execute the duties of a public officer, for an act done by him or her in virtue of the office, or against a person who, by his or her command, or in his or her aid, does anything touching the duties of the officer.

    3. Against the State of Nevada or any agency of the State for any tort action, except that any such tort action may also be brought in Carson City.

[1358] *Helms Constr. v. State ex rel. Dep't of Highways*, 97 Nev. 500, 634 P.2d 1224 (1981).

[1359] *Transatlantic Financing Corp. v. United States*, 363 F.2d 312, 315 n. 1 (D.C.Cir. 1966).

NRS 13.030, "Venue of actions by or against counties," provides as follows:

> 1. Actions against a county may be commenced in the district court of the judicial district embracing the county; but actions between counties shall be commenced in a court of competent jurisdiction in any county not a party to the action.
> 2. Immediately on the service of process, the officer served shall deliver such process and all papers accompanying such service to the district attorney for the county.
> 3. Actions brought for or against the county shall be in the name of the county.

NRS 13.040, "Venue in other cases," provides as follows:

> In all other cases, the action shall be tried in the county in which the defendants, or any one of them, may reside at the commencement of the action; or, if none of the defendants reside in the State, or if residing in the State the county in which they so reside be unknown to the plaintiff, the same may be tried in any county which the plaintiff may designate in the complaint; and if any defendant, or defendants, may be about to depart from the State, such action may be tried in any county where either of the parties may reside or service be had, subject, however, to the power of the court to change the place of trial as provided in this Chapter.

NRS 13.050, "Cases in which venue may be changed," provides as follows:

> 1. If the county designated for that purpose in the complaint be not the proper county, the action may, notwithstanding, be tried therein, unless the defendant before the time for answering expires demand in writing that the trial be had in the proper county, and the place of trial be thereupon changed by consent of the parties, or by order of the court, as provided in this section.
> 2. The court may, on motion, change the place of trial in the following cases:
> (a) When the county designated in the complaint is not the proper county.
> (b) When there is reason to believe that an impartial trial cannot be had therein.
> (c) When the convenience of the witnesses and the ends of justice would be promoted by the change.
> 3. When the place of trial is changed, all other proceedings shall be had in the county to which the place of trial is changed, unless otherwise provided by the consent of the parties in writing duly filed, or by order of the court, and the papers shall be filed or transferred accordingly.

NRS 13.060, "Transfer of cases for trial to other counties within judicial district when actions uncontested; stipulations," provides as follows:

> In any civil action where the complaint or petition is uncontested, or where the parties so stipulate, the court in the county where the action is brought may, upon application of the parties, or of the complainant or petitioner if the action is uncontested and all required notices have been given, transfer the action for trial to another county within the same judicial district.

Injury by Fellow Servant

The fellow servant rule is a common law doctrine that barred or reduced the amount of money an injured employee could recover against an employer if an injury was caused solely by the negligence of a fellow worker. An injured employee had to bring a cause for action against the fellow employee causing the injury, not the employer. It absolves an employer from liability to one engaged in his/her employment for injuries incurred or suffered solely as the result of the negligence, carelessness, or misconduct of others who are in the service of the employer and who are engaged in the same common or general employment as the injured employee. Workers' Compensation laws have nullified the rule for job-related injuries.

In Pari Delicto Doctrine

The in pari delicto doctrine is as an equitable defense in actions between individuals.[1360] When a party suffers injury from wrongdoing in which he engaged, the doctrine of in pari delicto often prevents him from recovering for his injury.[1361] A person may not seek implied indemnity when found *in pari delicto* with the person against whom indemnity

---

[1360] *Shimrak v. Garcia-Mendoza*, 112 Nev. 246, 251-52, 912 P.2d 822, 826 (1996); *Magill v. Lewis*, 74 Nev. 381, 386, 333 P.2d 717, 719 (1958).

[1361] See *In re AMERCO Derivative Litigation*, 127 Nev. ___, ___ n.6, 252 P.3d 681, 697 n.6 (2011).

recovery is sought.[1362]

Insanity is normally a defense in the criminal context, but it may apply in civil suits linked to criminal acts. Insanity is a mental illness of such a severe nature that a person cannot distinguish fantasy from reality, cannot manage his/her own affairs, or is subject to uncontrollable impulsive behavior. In criminal cases, a plea of "not guilty by reason of insanity" will require a trial on the issue of the defendant's insanity (or sanity) when the crime was committed.

In this context, "not guilty" does not mean the person did not commit the criminal act for which he or she is charged. It means that when the person committed the crime, he or she could not tell right from wrong or could not control his or her behavior because of severe mental defect or illness. Such a person, the law holds, should not be held criminally responsible for his or her behavior. The legal test for insanity varies from state to state.

Frequently, a person whose mental illness is not an issue in dispute will still be held responsible despite a mental illness. Such a ruling is known as either a Guilty but Mentally Ill (GBMI) or a Guilty but Insane verdict. It is sometimes involved in cases of crimes committed while a person was intoxicated at the time the crime was committed.

What happens to a defendant after a judge or jury returns a finding of insanity depends on the crime committed, and on the state in which the trial takes place. Usually, those found "not guilty by reason of insanity" are institutionalized in a special hospital for severely mentally ill persons who have committed crimes. After a period of time, the person may request a hearing to determine if he or she is no longer a danger to self or others or no longer mentally ill, and is therefore eligible to be released.

Intervening Cause

An intervening cause is an independent cause that follows another cause in time in producing the result but does not interrupt the chain of causation if foreseeable.[1363] An intervening cause is an event that interrupts the chain of causation by providing an independent cause of the final result, possibly relieving the original actors of liability.[1364]

In *Doud*, to prevail on their negligence claims, plaintiffs had to prove that the defendant was the cause in fact and the foreseeable cause of their harm.[1365] Defendant was the actual cause of appellants' harm if the defendant's actions were a substantial factor in bringing about their injuries.[1366] On the other hand, foreseeability is a policy concern that limits the defendant's liability to only those harms with a reasonably close connection to its breach.[1367] An intervening act will only be superseding and cut off liability if it is unforeseeable.[1368] Thus, under *Doud*, the court must examine whether the third party's acts were foreseeable, such that they were not superseding intervening events that would preclude the defendant's liability.[1369]

To determine whether an intervening cause is foreseeable, the Nevada Supreme Court considers several factors. These include whether (1) the intervention causes the kind of harm expected to result from the actor's negligence, (2) the intervening event is normal or extraordinary in the circumstances, (3) the intervening source is independent or a normal result of the actor's negligence, (4) the intervening act or omission is that of a third party, (5) the intervening act is a wrongful act of a third party that would subject him to liability, and (6) the culpability of the third person's intervening act.[1370] When a third party commits an intentional tort or a crime, the act is a superseding cause, even when the negligent party created a situation affording the third party an opportunity to commit the tort or crime.[1371] In such a scenario, the negligent party will only be liable if he knew or should have known at the time of the negligent conduct that he was creating such a situation and that a third party "might avail himself of the opportunity to commit such a tort or crime."[1372]

[1362] See *Reid v. Royal Insurance Co.*, 80 Nev. 137, 143-46, 390 P.2d 45, 4849 (1964).

[1363] *Merriam-Webster's Dictionary of Law* ©2001.

[1364] *Webster's New World Law Dictionary* Copyright © 2010 by Wiley Publishing, Inc.

[1365] *Doud v. Las Vegas Hilton Corp.*, 109 Nev. 1096 at 1105, 864 P.2d 796 at 801.

[1366] *Id.* at 1105, 864 P.2d at 801.

[1367] *Id.*

[1368] *Id.*

[1369] *Id.* at 1106, 864 P.2d at 801-02. *Bower v. Harrah's Laughlin*, 125 Nev. 37, 215 P.3d 709 (2009).

[1370] *Bower v. Harrah's Laughlin*, 125 Nev. 37, 215 P.3d 709 (2009). RESTATEMENT (SECOND) OF TORTS § 442 (1965).

[1371] *Id.* § 448.

[1372] *Id.*

In order for issue preclusion to apply, each of the following four elements must be met: (1) the issue decided in the prior litigation must be identical to the issue presented in the current action; (2) the initial ruling must have been on the merits and have become final; . . . (3) the party against whom the judgment is asserted must have been a party or in privity with a party to the prior litigation; and (4) the issue was actually and necessarily litigated.[1373]

Whether issue preclusion applies is a mixed question of law and fact.[1374] The party seeking to assert a judgment against another has the burden of proving the preclusive effect of the judgment.[1375] To be in privity, the person must have acquired an interest in the subject matter affected by the judgment through one of the parties, as by inheritance, succession, or purchase.[1376]

In contrast to the doctrine of claim preclusion, the doctrine of issue preclusion does not apply to matters that could have been litigated but were not.[1377] Issue preclusion may be appropriate, even when the causes of action asserted in the second proceeding are substantially different from those addressed in the initial proceeding, as long as the court in the prior action addressed and decided the same underlying factual issues.[1378] When determining whether issue preclusion applies to a given case, courts must scrupulously review the record to determine if it actually stands as a bar to relitigation.[1379] The clients' allegation that an attorney committed malpractice when he failed to state on the record that the clients' settlement agreement was not final until reduced to writing was not barred by collateral estoppel; the court in the prior action did not address the factual bases underlying the malpractice claim.[1380] The clients' allegation that the law firm and attorney committed malpractice by offering the clients bad advice concerning a settlement agreement was not barred by collateral estoppel; the court in the prior action did not address the factual bases underlying the malpractice claim, and the court ruled that the attorneys involved in settlement negotiations could not discuss the details of private conversation that occurred between themselves and their clients.[1381]

The Nevada Supreme Court has emphasized that "only those issues actually addressed and litigated are collaterally barred."[1382] A case is not "actually litigated" when there is no knowledge and participation by both parties and there are no findings of fact established by the evidence.[1383] A confessed judgment, when not actually litigated, even though final, ordinarily fails the "actually litigated" requirement of collateral estoppel.[1384] "When an issue of fact or law is actually litigated and determined by a valid and final judgment, and the determination is essential to the judgment, the determination is conclusive in a subsequent action between the parties, whether on the same or different claim."[1385] Comment (e) states that "[a] judgment is not conclusive in a subsequent action as to issues which might have been but were not litigated and determined in the prior action."[1386] Then it states that "[i]n the case of a judgment entered by confession, consent, or default, none of the issues is actually litigated," and the rule "does not apply with respect to any issue in a subsequent action."[1387]

To satisfy the fourth factor, an issue must have been actually and necessarily litigated. When an issue is properly raised and is submitted for determination, the issue is actually litigated.[1388] Only where the common issue was necessary to the judgment in the earlier suit, will its litigation be precluded.[1389] That it was actually litigated is not enough. It must have been necessarily litigated. In other words, the issue must have been necessary for resolution of the

---

[1373] *In Re Luis Sandoval*, 26 Nev., Adv. Op. 15 (2010).

[1374] *Bower v. Harrah's Laughlin*, 125 Nev. 37, 215 P.3d 709 (2009).

[1375] *Bennett v. Fidelity & Deposit Co.*, 98 Nev. 449, 452, 652 P.2d 1178, 1180 (1982).

[1376] *Paradise Palms v. Paradise Homes*, 89 Nev. 27, 31, 505 P.2d 596, 598-99 (1973).

[1377] *Kahn v. Morse & Mowbray*, 121 Nev. 464, 474, 117 P.3d 227 (2005).

[1378] *Id.* at 474-75.

[1379] *Id.* at 475.

[1380] *Id.*

[1381] *Id.*

[1382] *Id.*

[1383] *In Re Sandoval*, 126 Nev. ___, ____, 232 P.3d 422, 424-25 (2010).

[1384] *United Book v. Maryland Composition*, 786 A.2d 1 (Md. 2001).

[1385] RESTATEMENT (SECOND) OF JUDGMENTS, § 27 (1980).

[1386] *Id.*

[1387] *Id.*; see *Hunter v. Hunter,* 17 B.R. 523, 526 (Bankr. W.D. Mo. 1982) ("But collateral estoppel is inappropriate when the prior judgment was a consent judgment or a confessed judgment without any hearing or determination of the merits by the court itself.")

[1388] See RESTATEMENT (SECOND) OF JUDGMENTS § 27 cut. d (1982).

[1389] *Free v. Goodsell*, 129 Nev. Advance Opinion 43 (July 3, 2013), p. 5, citing *Univ. of Nev. v. Tarkanian*, 110 Nev. 581, 599, 879 P.2d 1180, 1191 (1994).

case.[1390] Where resolution of a case is not dependent on the issue, the issue has not been necessarily litigated.[1391] When either party could have prevailed regardless of the outcome of the issue, then the issue was not necessarily litigated.[1392] Nevada law rejects the application of issue preclusion in worker's compensation cases.[1393]

Joint Venture

All members of a joint venture are jointly and severally liable to third persons for wrongful acts committed in furtherance of the joint enterprise. Moreover, under principles of law related to joint ventures, the negligence or fraud of one venturer, while acting within the scope of the enterprise, may be imputed to coventurers so as to render the latter liable for the injuries sustained by third persons as a result of the negligence or fraud.[1394]

Judicial Estoppel

The doctrine of judicial estoppel may apply when the following five criteria are met: "(1) the same party has taken two positions; (2) the positions were taken in judicial or quasi-judicial administrative proceedings; (3) the party was successful in asserting the first position (*i.e.*, the tribunal adopted the position or accepted it as true); (4) the two positions are totally inconsistent; and (5) the first position was not taken as a result of ignorance, fraud or mistake."[1395] The purpose of the doctrine of judicial estoppel is to protect the integrity of the judiciary, thus permitting the court to invoke the doctrine in its own discretion.[1396] The doctrine is applicable when a party's inconsistent position amounts to an "attempt to gain an unfair advantage."[1397] Judicial estoppel, however, does not preclude a change in position that is not intended to sabotage the judicial process.[1398]

Justification

Justification is 1) A lawful or sufficient reason for one's acts or omissions; any fact that prevents an act from being wrongful; 2) A showing, in court, of a sufficient reason why a defendant acted in a way that, in the absence of the reason, would constitute the offense with which the defendant is charged.[1399]

See *Marschall v. City of Carson*, 86 Nev. 107, 464 P.2d 494 (1970) (justification as an affirmative defense to a claim of false arrest). When an existing contractual relationship is involved, justification for interfering with it is an affirmative defense.[1400] In *Buckaloo*,[1401] the California Supreme Court observed that privilege or justification is an affirmative defense, and the lack thereof need not be shown by the original pleader.[1402] A note of caution, however, crept into the court's formulation of principles at this point. "Perhaps the most significant privilege or justification for interference with a prospective business advantage is free competition," the court wrote. "Ours is a competitive economy in which business entities vie for economic advantage. In a sense, all vendees are potential buyers of the products and services of all sellers in a given line, and success goes to him who is able to induce potential customers not to deal with a competitor."[1403]

Laches

Laches has nothing to do with door latches or the way a dog latches onto her owner. Laches comes from a

---

[1390] *Id.* at pp. 5-7.

[1391] *Id.*

[1392] *Id.*

[1393] *Elizondo v. Hood Machine*, 129 Nev. Advance Opinion 84, pp. 8-10 (Nov. 7, 2013); see *Jerry's Nugget v. Keith*, 111 Nev. 49, 888 P.2d 921 (1995); NRS 616C.390.

[1394] *Radaker v. Scott*, 109 Nev. 653, 660, 855 P.2d 1037 (1993); see also NRS 87.150 (all partners jointly and severally liable).

[1395] *Marcuse v. Del Webb Communities, Inc.*, 123 Nev. 278, 287-88, 163 P.3d 462, 468-69 (2007).

[1396] *Id.*

[1397] *Id.* at 288, 163, P.3d at 469.

[1398] *Southern California Edison v. Dist. Ct.*, 127 Nev., Advance Opinion 22 (2011), p. 9.

[1399] *Black's Law Dictionary* 944 (9th ed. 2009).

[1400] *Rickel v. Schwinn Bicycle Co.*, 144 Cal. App. 3d 648, 192 Cal. Rptr. 732 (Cal.Ct.App.Dist.2 1983).

[1401] *Buckaloo v. Johnson*, 14 Cal. 3d 815 (1975).

[1402] *Id.* at 827-828.

[1403] 14 Cal. 3d at 828.

Latin word that means "negligent" or "lax."[1404] Laches is an equitable doctrine which may be invoked when delay by one party works to the disadvantage of the other, causing a change of circumstances which would make the grant of relief to the delaying party inequitable.[1405] To determine whether a challenge is barred by the doctrine of laches, this court considers (1) whether the party inexcusably delayed bringing the challenge, (2) whether the party's inexcusable delay constitutes acquiescence to the condition the party is challenging, and (3) whether the inexcusable delay was prejudicial to others.[1406]

Lack of Causal Relationship

The affirmative defense of lack of causal relationship was analyzed in an Alabama federal case[1407] as follows:

> The defendant may establish that there is no causal relation in fact between his activities in connection with handling the product and its defective condition. For example, the defendant may show that he is in the business of either distributing or processing for distribution finished products; he received a product already in a defective condition; he did not contribute to this defective condition; he had neither knowledge of the defective condition, nor an opportunity to inspect the product which was superior to the knowledge or opportunity of the consumer.

> "Causal relation," used here in the context of an affirmative defense, is not to be confused with the burden which rests on the plaintiff to prove that his injuries and damages were the proximate result of the defective condition of the product.[1408]

However, this lack of causal relation defense is not available to a "defendant who distributes a product under his own trade name."[1409] The *Sears* court and courts that followed *Sears* relied upon the rule of law stated in the RESTATEMENT (SECOND) OF TORTS § 400 as follows: "One who puts out as his own product a chattel manufactured by another is subject to the same liability as though he were its manufacturer."[1410] As stated by the Court of Appeals of Indiana as follows:

> [T]he reason for imposing such liability is not hard to find. When a vendor puts his name exclusively on a product, in no way indicating that it is the product of another, the public is induced to believe that the vendor was the manufacturer of the product. This belief causes the public to rely upon the skill of the vendor. When products are held out in this manner, the ultimate purchaser has no available means of ascertaining who is the true manufacturer. By this act of concealment, the vendor vouches for the product and assumes the manufacturer's responsibility as his own.[1411]

When the Supreme Court of Alabama established the Alabama Extended Manufacturer's Liability Doctrine, it specifically relied on the holding in *Sears, Roebuck & Co. v. Morris*, 273 Ala. 218, 136 So.2d 883 (Ala. 1961).[1412] Both cases, *Casrell* and *Atkins*, cite *Sears* for the proposition that this particular defense is unavailable to a defendant who distributes a product as if it were his own.[1413] By specifically relying on *Sears*, the *Casrell* and *Atkins* courts not only adopted the rule of law stated therein, but also adopted the rationale for that rule.

[1404] *Webster's New College Dictionary*, p. 799 (2009).
[1405] *Miller v. Burk*, 124 Nev. 56, 188 P.3d 1112 (2008).
[1406] *Id.*
[1407] *Brock v. Baxter Healthcare Corp.*, 96 F.Supp 2d 1352 (S.D.Ala. 2000).
[1408] *Atkins v. American Motors Corp.*, 335 So.2d 134, 143 fn. 4 (Ala. 1976).
[1409] *Id.*, citing *Sears, Roebuck & Co. v. Morris*, 136 So.2d 883 (Ala. 1961).
[1410] *Sears*, 136 So.2d 883 at 885 (Ala. 1961).
[1411] *Dudley Sports Co. v. Schmitt*, 279 N.E.2d 266 (Ind. Ct. App. 1972).
[1412] *Atkins*, 335 So.2d at 140, 143; *Casrell*, 335 So.2d at 132, 134.
[1413] *Atkins*, 335 So.2d at 143; *Casrell*, 335 So.2d at 134.

Reasoning Behind the Rule

In *Sears, Roebuck & Co. v. Morris,* the Supreme Court of Alabama not only adopted the rule of law stated in RESTATEMENT OF TORTS § 400 (liability of one who puts out a product as his own), but the court also specifically incorporated Comment (d) of that Section for the reasoning behind the rule.[1414] Comment (d) reads, "The rule stated in this Section applies only where the chattel is so put out as to lead those who use it to believe that it is the product of him who puts it out. The fact that the chattel is sold under the name of the person selling it may be sufficient to induce such a belief, but this is not always so, as where the goods are marked as made for the seller, without stating the name of the maker, or where the seller is known to carry on only a retail business."[1415]

The Nevada Supreme Court has examined the causation tests that courts have implemented when a plaintiff or decedent alleges that exposure to a defendant's asbestos-containing products caused mesothelioma.[1416] The Nevada Supreme Court adopted a test under which the plaintiff must prove exposure to the defendant's product on a regular basis over some extended period of time and in proximity to where the plaintiff actually worked, such that it is probable, or reasonable to infer, that the exposure caused the mesothelioma.[1417]

Lack of Consent

A recovery of damages may not be had in a civil action for ordinary assault and battery by one who has consented to or participated in the acts causing the injury.[1418] Lack of consent is an essential element of the offense of assault and battery.[1419] Lack of consent being an essential element of a civil action for damages for assault and battery, it is unnecessary that defendant affirmatively plead consent in justification of the acts charged in the complaint and denied in the answer.

Lack of Jurisdiction

Personal Jurisdiction

Nevada may exercise personal jurisdiction over a nonresident defendant only if doing so does not offend due process.[1420] Due process in this context is rooted in a defendant's contacts with the forum state and reflects his or her reasonable expectations about the litigation risk associated with those contacts.[1421] Due process requires a nonresident defendant to have sufficient "minimum contacts" with the forum state" such that the maintenance of the suit does not offend traditional notions of fair play and substantial justice."[1422] Absent the defendant's acquiescence to a forum state's jurisdiction, personal jurisdiction occurs in two forms: general and specific.[1423]

Unlike general jurisdiction, specific jurisdiction is proper only where "the cause of action arises from the defendant's contacts with the forum."[1424] Nevada may exercise specific jurisdiction over a nonresident defendant if the defendant "purposefully avail" himself or herself of the protection of Nevada's laws, or purposefully directs her conduct towards Nevada, and the plaintiff's claim actually arises from that purposeful conduct.[1425] Thus, "the mere unilateral activity of those who claim some relationship with a nonresident defendant cannot satisfy the requirement of contact with the forum State."[1426] Importantly, "[w]hether general or specific, the exercise of personal jurisdiction must also be

---

[1414] *Sears,* 136 So.2d at 885.

[1415] RESTATEMENT OF TORTS § 400, comment (d) (1938).

[1416] *Holcomb v. George Pacific LLC,* 128 Nev. Advance Opinion 56 (12/06/12).

[1417] *Id.*

[1418] *Wright v. Starr,* 42 Nev. 441, 179 Pac. 877 (1919).

[1419] *Id.* at 447.

[1420] *Trump v. Eighth Judicial Dist. Court,* 109 Nev. 687, 698, 857 P.2d 740, 747 (1993); see *Dogra v. Liles,* 129 Nev., Adv. Op. 100 (2013).

[1421] *Id.* at 699, 857 P.2d at 748 ("The defendant must have sufficient contacts with [Nevada] such that he or she could reasonably anticipate being haled into court there.").

[1422] *Int'l Shoe Co. v. Washington,* 326 U.S. 310, 316 (1945) (internal quotation marks and citation omitted).

[1423] *Trump,* 109 Nev. at 699, 857 P.2d at 748.

[1424] *Id.*

[1425] See *World-Wide Volkswagen Corp. v. Woodson,* 444 U.S. 286, 297 (1980).

[1426] *Id.* at 298 (internal quotation marks and citation omitted).

reasonable."[1427]

In car accident cases involving a nonresident's vehicle, courts have determined the nonresident defendant is subject to a forum's jurisdiction when the defendant actually knows his or her car is being operated in the forum state.[1428] But a nonresident defendant is not subject to personal jurisdiction in Nevada when the sole basis asserted is his or her adult child's unilateral act of driving the defendant's vehicle in Nevada.[1429]

A prima facie case of specific personal jurisdiction had been shown for an out-of-state defendant who traveled to Nevada to attend a trade show.[1430] A party made a prima facie showing of specific personal jurisdiction over a defendant with its allegations that meaningful meetings and negotiations regarding a casino investment project took place in Las Vegas, so as to preclude dismissal at the early stage of the proceedings.[1431] After a plaintiff makes, when challenged, a pretrial prima facie showing of jurisdiction, the issue can be raised again at a pretrial evidentiary hearing or at trial itself.[1432] A district court can exercise personal jurisdiction over nonresident officers and directors who directly harm a Nevada corporation.[1433]

Subject Matter Jurisdiction

The Nevada Constitution, article 6, § 1, *et seq.*, and the statutes enacted thereunder establish subject matter jurisdiction in civil actions. Subject matter jurisdiction is the power of the court to hear and determine a particular type of controversy.[1434] Subject matter jurisdiction should be distinguished from personal jurisdiction, which is the power of the court to determine the rights, obligations or status of a particular person.[1435] Subject matter jurisdiction should also be distinguished from *in rem* jurisdiction which is the power of the court to determine the status of particular property.[1436] The rules of venue, often confused with subject matter jurisdiction, govern the propriety of hearing a controversy in a particular county rather than the court's power to determine the controversy.[1437]

Article 6, § 1 of the Nevada Constitution provides that the judicial power of this state shall be vested in a court system comprising a Supreme Court, District Courts, and Justices of the Peace. In addition, the section empowers the legislature to establish Courts for municipal purposes in incorporated towns and cities. *See also* NRS 1.010, "Courts of justice," which provides as follows:

> The following shall be the courts of justice for this State:
> 1. The Supreme Court.
> 2. The district courts.
> 3. Justice courts.
> 4. Such municipal courts as may from time to time be established by the Legislature in incorporated cities or towns.

The legislature may also provide by law for referees in district courts, article 6, § 2(a); and a family court division of any district court. See Nev. Const. article 6, § 2(b).

Where the court lacked jurisdiction to appoint a receiver, all orders of the court were void. Where the court lacked jurisdiction under RL § 5193 (cf. NRS 32.010) to appoint a receiver to take possession of the assets of a corporation, all orders of the court in the receivership proceeding were void, including the order which required the sheriff to show cause why he should not be punished for contempt for refusing to surrender to the receiver the property of the corporation which the sheriff held under a writ of attachment, and a writ of prohibition was made permanent to restrain the court from adjudging the sheriff guilty of contempt.[1438]

[1427] *Emeterio v. Clint Hurt & Assoc., Inc.*, 114 Nev. 1031, 1036, 967 P.2d 432, 436 (1998) (citing *Trump*, 109 Nev. at 703, 857 P.2d at 750).

[1428] *Dogra v. Liles*, 129 Nev., Adv. Op. 100 (2013).

[1429] *Id.*, p. 2.

[1430] *Firouzabadi v. District Court*, 110 Nev. 1348, 1355, 885 P.2d 616, 621 (1994).

[1431] *Tuxedo International Inc. v. Rosenberg*, 127 Nev. Adv. Op. No. 2 (2011).

[1432] See *Fritz Hansen A/S* [sic] *v. Dist. Ct.*, 116 Nev. 650, 655, 6 P.3d 982, 985 (2000). In general, I am indebted to the *Nevada Civil Practice Manual* for this section on jurisdiction.

[1433] *Consipio Holding, BV v. Carlberg*, 128 Nev. Adv. Op. No. 43 (August 9, 2012).

[1434] *Azbarea v. City of North Las Vegas*, 95 Nev. 109, 111, 590 P.2d 161, 162 (1979); *Alexander v. Archer*, 21 Nev. 22, 31, 24 P. 373, 376 (1890).

[1435] *See Perry v. Edmonds*, 59 Nev. 60, 84 P. 2d 711 (1938).

[1436] *Id.*

[1437] *See* Chapter 13 of Nevada Revised Statutes; *see also State ex rel. Elsman v. Second Judicial District Court*, 52 Nev. 379, 397, 287 P. 957 (1930).

[1438] *Ex rel. Nenzel v. District Court*, 49 Nev. 145, 241 Pac. 317 (1925).

FIRREA

FIRREA (the Financial Institutions Reform, Recovery, and Enforcement Act of 1989 (FIRREA), 12 U.S.C. § 1821 (2006), an act that governs the disposition of failed financial institutions' assets, divests a court of jurisdiction to consider any defense or affirmative defense not first adjudicated through FIRREA's claims process. While FIRREA's jurisdictional bar divests a district court of jurisdiction to consider claims and counterclaims asserted against a successor in interest to the FDIC not first adjudicated through FIRREA's claims process, it does not apply to defenses or affirmative defenses raised by a debtor in response to the successor in interest's complaint for collection.[1439]

Municipal Courts

Under the authority of Nevada Constitution, article 6, §§ 1 and 9, the legislature has created a system of municipal courts.[1440]

Under those statutes, municipal courts have subject matter jurisdiction over:

(a) actions relating to violations of a city ordinance,

(b) actions to prevent or abate a nuisance within a city,

(c) offenses committed within the city which violate the peace and good order of the city or which invade any of the police powers of the city or endanger the health of the inhabitants thereof.[1441]

Municipal courts are authorized to hear prosecutions for the collection of city taxes and the enforcement of liens and bonds within the city, recovery of personal property belonging to the city, and the collection of damages by the city.[1442] In all these civil matters, however, the principal amount in issue may not exceed $2,500,[1443] and the action may not require a determination of validity of any tax or the title to real property.[1444] Finally, a municipal court has subject matter jurisdiction to issue warrants, writs and process and to take other actions necessary to the exercise of that jurisdiction, to the protection of that jurisdiction and to the administration of its affairs.[1445]

Justices' Courts

The Nevada legislature sets the subject matter jurisdiction of the justices' courts according to the amount in controversy, the nature of action, the penalty provided, or any combination of these factors.[1446] The legislature has set the limits of the amount in controversy in the justices' courts at $10,000, NRS 4.370(1), and has granted the justices' courts the power to determine matters as follows:

(a) Arising on a contract for the recovery of money only, if the sum claimed, exclusive of interest, does not exceed $10,000;

(b) Actions for damages for injury to the person, or for taking, detaining or injuring personal property, or for injury to real property where no issue is raised by the verified answer of the defendant involving the title to or boundaries of the real property, if the damage claimed does not exceed $10,000;

(c) Except as otherwise provided in paragraph (l), in actions for a fine, penalty or forfeiture not exceeding $10,000, given by statute or the ordinance of a county, city or town, where no issue is raised by the answer involving the legality of any tax, impost, assessment, toll or municipal fine;

(d) In actions upon bonds or undertakings conditioned for the payment of money, if the sum claimed does not exceed $10,000, though the penalty may exceed that sum. Bail bonds and other undertakings posted in criminal matters may be forfeited regardless of amount;

(e) In actions to recover the possession of personal property, if the value of the property does not exceed $10,000;

(f) To take and enter judgment on the confession of a defendant, when the amount confessed, exclusive of interest, does not exceed $10,000;

(g) Of actions for the possession of lands and tenements where the relation of landlord and tenant exists, when damages claimed do not exceed $10,000 or when no damages are claimed;

(h) Of actions when the possession of lands and tenements has been unlawfully or fraudulently obtained or withheld, when damages claimed do not exceed $10,000 or when no damages are claimed;

(i) Of suits for the collection of taxes, where the amount of the tax sued for does not exceed $10,000;

[1439] *Schettler v. RalRon Capital Corporation*, 128 Nev. Adv. Op. No. 20 (2012).

[1440] See NRS 5.010 *et seq.*

[1441] NRS 5.050; NRS 266.550; NRS 266.555.

[1442] NRS 5.050(3); NRS 266.555(3).

[1443] NRS 5.050(3).

[1444] NRS 5.050(4) NRS 266.555(4).

[1445] NRS 5.060; *City of North Las Vegas ex rel. Arndt v. Daines,* 92 Nev. 292, 295, 550 P.2d 399 (1976).

[1446] Nev. Const. art. 6, § 8.

(j) Of actions for the enforcement of mechanics' liens, where the amount of the lien sought to be enforced, exclusive of interest, does not exceed $10,000;

(k) Of actions for the enforcement of liens of owners of facilities for storage, where the amount of the lien sought to be enforced, exclusive of interest, does not exceed $10,000;

(l) In actions for a fine imposed for a violation of NRS 484D.680;

(m) Except as otherwise provided in this paragraph, in any action for the issuance of a temporary or extended order for protection against domestic violence. A justice court does not have jurisdiction in an action for the issuance of a temporary or extended order for protection against domestic violence:

(1) In a county whose population is more than 100,000 and less than 400,000;

(2) In any township whose population is 100,000 or more located within a county whose population is more than 400,000; or

(3) If a district court issues a written order to the justice court requiring that further proceedings relating to the action for the issuance of the order for protection be conducted before the district court;

(n) In an action for the issuance of a temporary or extended order for protection against harassment in the workplace pursuant to NRS 33.200 to 33.360, inclusive;

(o) In small claims actions under the provisions of Chapter 73 of NRS;

(p) In actions to contest the validity of liens on mobile homes or manufactured homes;

(q) In any action pursuant to NRS 200.591 for the issuance of a protective order against a person alleged to be committing the crime of stalking, aggravated stalking or harassment;

(r) In any action pursuant to NRS 200.378 for the issuance of a protective order against a person alleged to have committed the crime of sexual assault;

(s) In actions transferred from the district court pursuant to NRS 3.221; and

(t) In any action for the issuance of a temporary or extended order pursuant to NRS 33.400.

NRS 4.370(1)(g) was amended by the 1991 legislature to include a damage limitation on actions for the possession of land and tenements. The amendment overrules the holding of *K.J.B., Inc. v. Second Judicial District Court*, 103 Nev. 473, 745 P.2d 700 (1987), to the effect the District Court had no jurisdiction over unlawful detainer actions. Original jurisdiction over such matters is now determined by the amount of damages sought.

The justices' courts also have jurisdiction to issue temporary or extended orders of protection against domestic violence in those counties whose population is under 100,000. NRS 4.370(1)(m); *see* Nev. Const. art. 6, § 6; NRS 3.0105 and NRS 3.223. This power is concurrent with that of the family court in counties whose population is greater than 100,000. NRS 3.223(2). Finally, justice courts have jurisdiction over all misdemeanors.[1447]

For the counties that have more than one justice of the peace, the justices have concurrent and coextensive subject matter jurisdiction. See NRS 4.155, which provides as follows: "Townships with more than one justice of the peace," which provides as follows: "In townships where more than one justice of the peace has been provided for by NRS 4.020, such justices of the peace shall have concurrent and coextensive jurisdiction within the territorial limits provided by law, and may make such rules and regulations, not inconsistent with law, as will enable them to transact judicial business in a convenient and lawful manner."

District Courts

The district courts of Nevada's nine judicial districts have both original and appellate subject matter jurisdiction. Nev. Const. art. 6, § 6. Their original jurisdiction is defined by exclusion, *i.e.*, all cases excluded by law from the original jurisdiction of the justices' courts. Nev. Const. art. 6, § 6. *See also* NRS 3.223, giving the family division of the district court certain exclusive jurisdiction. The district courts have final appellate jurisdiction in cases arising in justices' courts and municipal courts,[1448] and have common law and statutory authority to review arbitration awards.[1449]

The district court does not have jurisdiction to entertain a civil action filed by a non-Indian against an Indian [Native American] for events which occurred on Indian land or in Indian country.[1450]

A district court on appeal has the same jurisdiction as the justices' courts or municipal courts from which the appeal was taken.[1451] Therefore, the district court has no authority to render judgment on any matter which is beyond the

---

[1447] NRS 4.370(1)(p).

[1448] Nev. Const. Art. 6 § 6; *Cavanaugh v. Wright*, 2 Nev. 166 (1866).

[1449] NRS 38.135 *et seq.*; *Graber v. Comstock Bank*, 111 Nev. 1421, 905 P.2d 1112 (1995); *New Shy Clown Casino, Inc. v. Baldwin*, 103 Nev. 269, 737 P.2d 524 (1987); *Richardson v. Harris*, 107 Nev. 763, 818 P.2d 1209, 1210 (1991).

[1450] *Snooks v. Ninth Judicial Dist. ex. rel. County of Douglas*, 112 Nev. 798, 919 P.2d 1064 (1996).

[1451] *State ex rel. Harding v. Moore*, 9 Nev. 355 (1874), citing *Peacock v. Leonard*, 8 Nev. 84 (1872).

subject matter jurisdiction of the lower court.[1452] The rules of civil procedure do not extend or limit the jurisdiction of the district courts. See NRCP 82, "Jurisdiction and Venue Unaffected," which provides as follows: "These rules shall not be construed to extend or limit the jurisdiction of the district courts or the venue of actions therein."

The district courts have the power to issue writs of mandamus,[1453] prohibition,[1454] injunctions,[1455] quo warranto,[1456] certiorari,[1457] habeas corpus,[1458] and all other writs proper and necessary to complete exercise of their jurisdiction.[1459] All district courts, including those not designated to be family courts, appear to have the power to issue extended temporary orders in cases of domestic violence pursuant to NRS 33.020, "Requirements for issuance of temporary and extended orders; availability of court; court clerk to inform protected party upon transfer of information to Central Repository," which provides as follows:

1. If it appears to the satisfaction of the court from specific facts shown by a verified application that an act of domestic violence has occurred or there exists a threat of domestic violence, the court may grant a temporary or extended order. A temporary or extended order must not be granted to the applicant or the adverse party unless the applicant or the adverse party has requested the order and has filed a verified application that an act of domestic violence has occurred or there exists a threat of domestic violence.

2. The court may require the applicant or the adverse party, or both, to appear before the court before determining whether to grant the temporary or extended order.

3. A temporary order may be granted with or without notice to the adverse party. An extended order may only be granted after notice to the adverse party and a hearing on the application. A hearing on an application for an extended order must be held within 45 days after the date on which the application for the extended order is filed.

4. The court shall rule upon an application for a temporary order within 1 judicial day after it is filed.

5. If it appears to the satisfaction of the court from specific facts communicated by telephone to the court by an alleged victim that an act of domestic violence has occurred and the alleged perpetrator of the domestic violence has been arrested and is presently in custody pursuant to NRS 171.137, the court may grant a temporary order. Before approving an order under such circumstances, the court shall confirm with the appropriate law enforcement agency that the applicant is an alleged victim and that the alleged perpetrator is in custody. Upon approval by the court, the signed order may be transmitted to the facility where the alleged perpetrator is in custody by electronic or telephonic transmission to a facsimile machine. If such an order is received by the facility holding the alleged perpetrator while the alleged perpetrator is still in custody, the order must be personally served by an authorized employee of the facility before the alleged perpetrator is released. The court shall mail a copy of each order issued pursuant to this subsection to the alleged victim named in the order and cause the original order to be filed with the court clerk on the first judicial day after it is issued.

6. In a county whose population is 47,000 or more, the court shall be available 24 hours a day, 7 days a week, including nonjudicial days and holidays, to receive communications by telephone and for the issuance of a temporary order pursuant to subsection 5.

7. In a county whose population is less than 47,000, the court may be available 24 hours a day, 7 days a week, including nonjudicial days and holidays, to receive communications by telephone and for the issuance of a temporary order pursuant to subsection 5.

8. The clerk of the court shall inform the protected party upon the successful transfer of information concerning the registration to the Central Repository for Nevada Records of Criminal History as required pursuant to NRS 33.095.

Family Courts

The family court is a division of the district court.[1460] The legislature has granted it original, exclusive jurisdiction in the following matters:

[1452] *State ex rel. Abel v. Breen,* 41 Nev. 516, 173 P. 555 (1918).
[1453] Nev. Const. art. 6, § 6; NRS 34.160.
[1454] Nev. Const. art. 6, § 6.
[1455] Nev. Const. art. 6, § 6; NRS 33.010.
[1456] Nev. Const. art. 6, § 6; ; NRS 35.080.
[1457] Nev. Const. art. 6, § 6, NRS 34.020.
[1458] NRS 34.710.
[1459] Nev. Const. art. 6, § 6.
[1460] Nev. Const. art. 6, § 6.

(a) all proceedings within the jurisdiction of juvenile court. NRS 3.223(1)(a) and (d); specifically addressed in NRS 162.020 *et seq.*

(b) proceedings involving domestic relations, including determining the rights of husband and wife, dissolving a marriage, determining custody and visitation issues, determining support obligations, determining parentage, adoptions, terminating parental rights, determinations regarding a minor's disabilities, and proceedings brought pursuant to the Reciprocal Enforcement Support Act; NRS 3.223(1)(a);

(c) proceedings involving guardianships; NRS 3.223(1)(a);

(d) proceedings involving support of dependent children and protection of children from abuse and neglect; NRS 3.223(1)(a);

(e) proceedings brought to facilitate the collection on an obligation for support under Chapter 31A of NRS, although other judicial or administrative procedures may be used to collect the obligation; NRS 3.223(1)(b);

(f) rulings on request for order authorizing abortions; NRS 3.223(1)(b). The family court also has original, exclusive jurisdiction to approve a minor's marriage, NRS 3.223(1)(c); establish the date and place of birth of a minor, NRS 3.223(1)(e); change the name of a minor, NRS 3.223(1)(f); declare the sanity of a minor, NRS 3.223(1)(g); and approve the withholding and withdrawal of life-sustaining procedures for a person as authorized by law, NRS 3.223(1)(h). The family court does not have jurisdiction if the child involved is subject to the jurisdiction of an Indian tribe pursuant to the Indian Child Welfare Act of 1978. 25 U.S.C. § 1901 *et seq.*

In all other matters, the family court judges share equal coextensive and concurrent jurisdiction and power with all other district court judges.[1461]

The Nevada Supreme Court

The subject matter jurisdiction of the Nevada Supreme Court is set forth in Article 6, Section 4 of the Nevada Constitution and NRS 2.090, "Jurisdiction to review on appeal," which provides as follows:

The Supreme Court has jurisdiction to review upon appeal:

1. A judgment in an action or proceeding, commenced in a district court, when the matter in dispute is embraced in the general jurisdiction of the Supreme Court, and to review upon appeal from such judgment any intermediate order or decision involving the merits and necessarily affecting the judgment and, in a criminal action, any order changing or refusing to change the place of trial of the action or proceeding.

2. An order granting or refusing a new trial in such cases; an order in a civil action changing or refusing to change the place of trial of the action or proceeding after motion is made therefor in the cases in which that court has appellate jurisdiction; and from an order granting or refusing to grant an injunction or mandamus in the case provided for by law.

In addition to jurisdiction over appeals, the Nevada Supreme Court has the power to issue writs of mandamus[1462] certiorari,[1463] prohibition,[1464] quo warranto,[1465] habeas corpus,[1466] and all writs necessary and proper to the complete exercise of its appellate jurisdiction is the court's power to grant a stay of judgment, order, or injunction pending appeal and to approve a supersedeas bond.[1467] The Nevada Rules of Appellate Procedure do not extend or limit the jurisdiction of the Nevada Supreme Court as established by law.[1468]

[1461] NRS 3.220.

[1462] NRAP 21 and NRS 34.160.

[1463] NRAP 21 and NRS 34.020.

[1464] NRAP 21.

[1465] NRS Chapter 35.

[1466] NRAP 22.

[1467] NRAP 8.

[1468] NRAP 1(b).

Scope of Objection

The ability to raise the absence of subject matter jurisdiction is never waived and generally may be brought to the court's attention at any time and in almost any manner.[1469] An objection based on the absence of subject matter jurisdiction may be raised at any time.[1470]

How to Raise Objections to Subject Matter Jurisdiction

It is within the inherent powers of all courts to inquire into their own jurisdiction and to determine if jurisdiction over the subject matter exists.[1471] Objections to subject matter jurisdiction may be raised in a pleading allowed by NRCP 12(b) or NJCRCP 12(b), and in a motion, if the defect in jurisdiction is apparent on the face of the pleading.[1472] The absence of subject matter jurisdiction may also be brought to the court's attention by suggestion of the parties or otherwise. NRCP 12(h)(3); NJCRCP 12(h)(3).

Objection to the subject matter jurisdiction of a lower court may be raised by writ of certiorari in a district or the Supreme Court,[1473] by writ of prohibition in the district court or the Supreme Court,[1474] or by direct appeal.[1475] An objection to subject matter jurisdiction must be supported by competent evidence.[1476]

Where a court believes a doubt exists as to jurisdiction, the court has a duty to raise and decide the issue sua sponte,[1477] even though the matter of jurisdiction may be conceded by the parties.[1478]

Subject matter jurisdiction is never waived.[1479] A party may, however, be estopped from challenging the court's jurisdiction, such as where a petition for adoption signed by an individual contained the facts necessary to at least ostensibly confer jurisdiction on the district court to entertain such petition, and there was substantial evidence that the individual acted freely and with understanding in stipulating to such facts, the individual was estopped from subsequently challenging district court's jurisdiction to entertain a petition for adoption.[1480]

Courts have inherent jurisdiction to adopt rules and procedures and to enter orders necessary to the proper administration of justice.[1481] This subject matter jurisdiction exists apart from and in addition to any jurisdiction granted by the constitution or statute, although some of the court's inherent powers have been codified.[1482]

The inherent powers of the courts include the power to adopt rules,[1483] the power to compel expenditures for judicial purposes,[1484] and the power to amend records and orders to remove ambiguity or correct errors.[1485]

The courts also have the inherent power to hire or dismiss judicial personnel,[1486] and to charge and collect reasonable fees.[1487] Judges and justices can also take and certify the acknowledgment of conveyances and the satisfaction of a judgment of any court.[1488]

[1469] *Meinhold v. Clark County School Dist.,* 89 Nev. 56, 59, 506 P.2d 420, 422 (1973); *S. G. & R Bank v. Milisich,* 43 Nev. 373, 390, 233 P. 41, 46 (1925).

[1470] NRCP 12(h)(3); NJCRCP 12(h)(3).

[1471] *In re Estate of Singleton,* 26 Nev. 106 (1901).

[1472] NRCP 12(b)(1); NJCRCP 12(b)(1), *Girola v. Roussille,* 81 Nev. 661, 663, 408 P.2d 918, 919 (1965).

[1473] NRS 34.020; *Jahn v. District Court,* 58 Nev. 204, 213, 73 P.2d 499, 500 (1937).

[1474] NRS 34.330; Nev. Const. art. 6, § 6; *Del Papa v. Steffen,* 112 Nev. 369, 915 P.2d 245 (1996)

[1475] *Parks v. Garrison,* 57 Nev. 480, 482, 67 P.2d 314 (1937).

[1476] *Meinhold v. Clark County School Dist.,* 89 Nev. 56, 506 P.2d 420 (1973).

[1477] *Phillips v. Welch,* 11 Nev. 187 (1876).

[1478] *See also Pengilly v. Rancho Santa Fe Homeowners Ass'n,* 116 Nev. Adv. Op. 75, 5 P.3d 569, 2000 Nev. LEXIS 85 (2000) (holding on appeal from a civil contempt order that the Supreme Court had no jurisdiction over an appeal from a contempt order where no rule or statute provides for such appeal).

[1479] *Phillips v. Welch,* 11 Nev. 187 (1876).

[1480] *Morse v. Morse,* 99 Nev. 387, 663 P.2d 349 (1983).

[1481] *Blackjack Bonding v. City of Las Vegas Municipal Court,* 116 Nev. Adv. Op. 128, 14 P.3d 1275, 20000 Nev. LEXIS 141 (2000); *Goldman v. Bryan,* 104 Nev. 644, 654 764 P.2d 1296, 1302 (1988).

[1482] *State v. Second Judicial District Court,* 116 Nev. Adv. Op. 103, 11 P.3d 1209, 2000 Nev. LEXIS 115 (2000) (to the extent that a statute codifies the court's independent power to regulate procedures, it is valid; to the extent that the statute undermines that power, it is void); *see Lindauer v. Allen,* 85 Nev. 430, 456 P.2d 851 (1969).

[1483] NRS 2.120, NRS 3.020, *State v. Second Judicial District Court,* 116 Nev. Adv. Op. 103, 11 P.3d 1209, 2000 Nev. LEXIS 115 (2000); *Caples v. Central Pacific Railroad,* 6 Nev. 265, 275 (1871).

[1484] *Young v. Board of County Commissioners,* 91 Nev. 52, 530 P.2d 1203 (1975).

[1485] *Grenz v. Grenz,* 78 Nev. 394, 374 P.2d 891 (1962), *Brockman v. Ullom,* 52 Nev. 267, 286 P. 417 (1930).

[1486] *Nunez v. City of North Las Vegas,* 116 Nev. Adv. Op. 63, 1 P.3d 959, 2000 Nev. LEXIS 74 (2000).

Courts have the inherent power to control proceedings before them and to enforce their rulings through using contempt proceedings.[1489] If a district court has personal and subject matter jurisdiction over the parties and matter in dispute, the court may enter judgment against a person or an entity.[1490] The Nevada Supreme Court generally adheres to the proposition that it has jurisdiction to consider an appeal only when the appeal is authorized by statute or court rule.[1491]

The authority of justices of the peace to conduct preliminary hearings in felony and gross misdemeanor cases extends to the limits of their respective counties. Although NRS 1.050 states that Justice Courts are to be held in their respective townships, precincts or cities,[1492] provides, with certain exceptions, that "in criminal cases the jurisdiction of justices of the peace extends to the limits of their respective counties." While Justice Courts do not have jurisdiction to actually try felony or gross misdemeanor charges, Justice Courts may preside over preliminary examinations in felony and gross misdemeanor cases (see NRS 171.196). A justice of the peace has the same geographical authority whether acting as a justice of the peace in misdemeanor cases or as a magistrate in felony or gross misdemeanor preliminary hearings. Thus, in felony and gross misdemeanor cases, justices of the peace have jurisdiction to conduct preliminary hearings to the limits of their respective counties.[1493]

Imposition of certain costs on a garnishee is not appealable. An order of a Justice Court under sec. 132, ch. 112, Stats. 1869 (cf. NRS 31.110), requiring the garnishee to pay the costs of the proceeding to obtain information respecting the amount and description of debt due the defendant, was not an order to pay a tax, an impost or a municipal fine within the meaning of former provisions of Nev. Const. art. 6, § 4, or sec. 5, ch. 19, Stats. 1865, conferring appellate jurisdiction on the Supreme Court in cases at law involving "the legality of any tax, impost, assessment, toll or municipal fine," and the appeal of such an order to the Supreme Court after affirmance by a district court was dismissed for lack of jurisdiction.[1494]

Personal Jurisdiction

Jurisdiction and Fee Disputes

The Nevada Supreme Court has concluded that absent an enforceable charging lien or the client's request or consent to the district court's adjudication of a retaining lien, the district court is without jurisdiction to adjudicate an attorney-client fee dispute in the underlying action.[1495] In the same case the Nevada Supreme Court further concluded that when the client asserts legal malpractice as a defense against the attorney's claim for fees, it is particularly inappropriate to summarily adjudicate the fee dispute in the underlying action. When the district court lacks jurisdiction to adjudicate the fee dispute or the client objects to the court's adjudication of the dispute based on its legal malpractice claim against the attorney, the attorney seeking to recover fees should file a separate action to do so.

How NRCP 41(e) Affects Jurisdiction

NRCP 41(e) states in pertinent part as follows:

Any action heretofore or hereafter commenced shall be dismissed by the court in which the same shall have been commenced . . . on motion of any party . . . after due notice to the parties, unless such action is brought to trial within 5 years after the plaintiff has filed the action, except where the parties have stipulated in writing that the time may be extended.[1496]

NRCP 41(e) requires a district court to dismiss an action if it is not brought to trial within five years after it was

---

[1487] *Blackjack Bonding v. City of Las Vegas Municipal Court,* 116 Nev. Adv. Op. 128, 14 P.3d, 1275, 2000 Nev. LEXIS 141 (2000).

[1488] NRS 2.190; NRS 3.150; NRS 4.180; NRS 5.040.

[1489] NRS 22.010; *Lamb v. Lamb*, 83 Nev. 425, 428, 433 P.2d 265 (1967).

[1490] *C.H.A. Venture v. G.C. Wallace Consulting,* 106 Nev. 381, 383, 794 P.2d 707, 708 (1990).

[1491] *Settelmeyer & Sons v. Smith and Harmer*, 124 Nev. 1206, 1215, 197 P.3d 1051, 1057 (2008).

[1492] NRS 4.370.

[1493] NRS 1.050; AGO 2003-06 (10-17-2003).

[1494] *Wearne v. Haynes*, 13 Nev. 103 (1878).

[1495] *Argentena Consol. Mining Co. v. Jolley Urga,* 125 Nev., Advance Opinion 40 (2009).

[1496] See *Morgan v. Las Vegas Sands, Inc.*, 118 Nev. 315, 320, 43 P.3d 1036, 1039 (2002) (acknowledging only two circumstances in which the prescriptive period of NRCP 41(e) is tolled, namely, the time during which a medical malpractice case is pending before a medical screening panel, and a court-ordered stay of district court proceedings.)

commenced.[1497] The parties' earlier participation in a failed settlement conference does not toll the rule's five-year time limit. The Nevada Supreme Court has concluded that once an NRCP 41(e) motion has been brought, but improperly denied, district courts lack further jurisdiction to take an action to judgment on its merits.[1498] Any subsequent orders entered by district courts going to the merits of an action are in excess of their jurisdiction and, therefore, void.[1499] The Nevada Supreme Court has held that because NRCP 41(e)'s five-year deadline for bringing a case to trial had expired and the defendants properly moved to dismiss the case under that rule, the district court was required to dismiss the case and, thus, lacked jurisdiction in the partition action to order the judicial sale.[1500]

Lack of Ripeness

Ripeness refers to the readiness of a case for litigation. "[A] claim is not ripe for adjudication if it rests upon contingent future events that may not occur as anticipated, or indeed may not occur at all."[1501]

Challenges to voter initiatives, alleging that the procedural requirements for placing a measure on the ballot were not met, are virtually always ripe for preelection judicial review.[1502] Challenges to initiative measures, which invoke the particular constitutional and statutory provisions regulating initiatives, may be reviewed preelection.[1503] Preelection challenges to an initiative's substantive constitutionality are not ripe for judicial review, because they lack a concrete factual context in which a provision may be evaluated, and any harm is highly speculative since the measure may not even pass at election time.[1504]

Although the question of ripeness closely resembles the question of standing, ripeness focuses on the timing of the action rather than on the party bringing the action.[1505] The factors to be weighed in deciding whether a case is ripe for judicial review include: (1) the hardship to the parties of withholding judicial review, and (2) the suitability of the issues for review.[1506]

An alleged harm that is speculative or hypothetical is insufficient to yield a justiciable controversy which is ripe for judicial review; an existing controversy must be present.[1507] While harm need not already have been suffered, it must be probable, for the issue to be ripe for judicial review.[1508]

A business organizations' claims, in a preelection challenge seeking to remove Nevada Clean Indoor Air Act initiative from the general election ballot, that the Act, which would restrict or prohibit smoking in the organizations' business establishments, would, if enacted, violate the Due Process and Equal Protection Clauses of the Federal and State Constitutions, were not ripe for judicial review.[1509]

The issue of whether Nevada Clean Indoor Air Act initiative, which if enacted would restrict or prohibit smoking in business establishments, would apply to hotel and motel rooms, was not ripe for judicial review, in preelection challenge seeking to remove the initiative from general election ballot; the court was presented with a hypothetical set of facts rather than a concrete factual situation, and there was no actual controversy, because the proponents agreed with opponents that the Act would not apply to hotel and motel rooms.[1510]

An action for declaratory relief presented no justiciable controversy ripe for judicial determination where a judgment in a civil action had not been obtained. Plaintiff brought a civil action against defendant alleging that the defendant, while driving a car belonging to another person, negligently struck the plaintiff as she stood in a crosswalk. Before judgment was obtained in the civil action, the plaintiff filed an amended complaint seeking a declaratory judgment (see NRS 30.030) against the defendant's insurer after the insurer denied the plaintiff's claim under the defendant's policy of motorcycle insurance because, according to the insurer, the policy excluded coverage for the defendant's use of the vehicle. The district court dismissed the plaintiff's action against the insurer for failure to state a claim upon which relief could be granted. On appeal, the Supreme Court held that plaintiff's action for declaratory relief

---

[1497] *Cox v. Dist. Ct.*, 124 Nev., Advance Opinion 78 (2008).

[1498] *Id.*

[1499] *Id.*

[1500] *Id.*

[1501] *Texas v. United States*, 523 U.S. 296 (1998), p. 300, (internal quotation marks omitted), quoting *Thomas v. Union Carbide Agricultural Products Co.*, 473 U.S. 568 (1985), p. 581 (quoting 13A C. Wright, A. Miller, & E. Cooper, *Federal Practice and Procedure* § 3532, p. 112 (1984)).

[1502] *Herbst Gaming, Inc. v. Sec'y of State*, 122 Nev. 877, 883, 141 P.3d 1224 (2006).

[1503] *Id.* at 885.

[1504] *Id.* at 886, overruling *Stumpf v. Lau*, 108 Nev. 826, 839 P.2d 120 (1992).

[1505] *Id.* at 887.

[1506] *Id.*

[1507] *Id.*

[1508] *Id.*

[1509] *Id.* at 888, Nev. Const. art. 1, § 8; U.S. Const. Amend. 14.

[1510] *Id.* at 889.

presented no justiciable controversy ripe for judicial determination. Because plaintiff's rights against the insurer were contingent on her successful litigation of the pending civil action against the defendant, the plaintiff could assert no legally protectable interest creating justiciable controversy ripe for declaratory relief.[1511]

Lack of Standing

Standing is the status of being qualified to assert or enforce legal rights or duties in a judicial forum because one has a sufficient and protectable interest in the outcome of a justiciable controversy and usually has suffered or is threatened with of a justiciable controversy and usually has suffered or is threatened with actual injury.[1512] A party must have standing in order to justify the exercise of the court's remedial powers.[1513] Without formally entering an appearance to petition for a relevant legal right to interest pertaining to the parties, an individual who is not a party to an action has no standing to appear and move the Court to act.[1514] "Standing is the legal right to set judicial machinery in motion."[1515]

Where appellant purchased a 12-year-old house and was injured when he fell through a railing of a deck, his action for damages against the original owner was barred by NRS 11.203, the 10-year statute of repose, and appellant lacked standing to challenge the constitutionality of NRS 11.203 because his injuries were not a result of the statute's alleged unconstitutionality, he was not a member of one of the classes who are excluded from protection afforded by the statute of repose and who would benefit from the statute with a broader reach, and the necessary nexus between the injury and the constitutional violation was missing.[1516]

A member of the board of regents of a university had the requisite standing to bring an action for a declaratory judgment challenging the constitutionality of the statute which extended the terms of the members of the board from 4 to 6 years because, pursuant to NRS 30.040, he was a "person . . . whose rights, status or other legal relations are affected by a statute."[1517]

Legal interest is required for standing. Absent evidence of third-party beneficiary status, an assignment of contract rights or delegation of contract duties, the heirs lacked the necessary legal interest in an agreement between the decedent, the family corporation and other stockholders concerning the purchase of decedent's stock to give them standing to challenge an agreement in a declaratory judgment action under NRS 30.040 and 30.130, even though the agreement may have affected their inheritance in a practical–as distinguished from a legal–sense.[1518]

Law-of-the-Case Doctrine

The law-of-the-case doctrine "refers to a family of rules embodying the general concept that a court involved in later phases of a lawsuit should not re-open questions decided (*i.e.*, established as law of the case) by that court or a higher one in earlier phases."[1519] Normally, "for the law-of-the-case doctrine to apply, the appellate court must actually address and decide the issue explicitly or by necessary implication."[1520]

Learned Intermediary Doctrine or Sophisticated User Doctrine

The learned-intermediary doctrine is the principle that prescription-drug manufacturer fulfills its duty to warn of a drug's potentially harmful effects by informing the prescribing physician, rather than the end-user, of those effects.[1521] The Nevada Supreme Court first considered the learned-intermediary doctrine in November 2011 in *Klasch v.*

[1511] *Knittle v. Progressive Cas. Ins. Co.*, 112 Nev. 8, 908 P.2d 724 (1996), cited, *County of Clark ex rel. Univ. Med. Ctr. v. Upchurch*, 114 Nev. 749, at 752, 961 P.2d 754 (1998), *Heller v. Legislature*, 120 Nev. 456, at 473, 93 P.3d 746 (2004), *Herbst Gaming, Inc. v. Heller*, 122 Nev. 877, at 887, 141 P.3d 1224 (2006).

[1512] Findlaw Legal Dictionary.

[1513] *Id.*

[1514] See *Szilagyi v. Testa*, 99 Nev. 834, 838, 673 P.2d 495, 498 (1983) ("Question of standing . . . focuses on the party seeking adjudication rather than on the issues sought to be adjudicated"); see also *Gruber v. Baker*, 20 Nev. 453, 469, 23 P. 858, 862 (1890) ("Landlord and tenant, executors, administrators . . . are all cases in which it is unlawful to give aid in the conduct of a suit before the court of justice."); see also NRCP 17(a); cf. NRS 125C.050 (example of statutory authorization re: standing).

[1515] *Roethlisberger v. McNulty*, 127 Nev. Adv. Op. 48, 256 P.3d 955, 957 (2011) (citations omitted).

[1516] *Elley v. Stephens*, 104 Nev. 413, 760 P.2d 768 (1988).

[1517] *Tam v. Colton*, 94 Nev. 452, 581 P.2d 447 (1978).

[1518] *Wells v. Bank of Nevada*, 90 Nev. 192, 522 P.2d 1014 (1974).

[1519] *Recontrust v. Zhang*, 130 Nev., Advance Opinion 1, p. 8 (2014), citing *Crocker v. Piedmont Aviation, Inc.*, 49 F.3d 735, 739 (D.C. Cir. 1995).

[1520] *Recontrust*, citing *Dictor v. Creative Mgmt. Servs., L.L.C.*, 126 Nev. ___, ___, 223 P.3d 332 (2010).

[1521] *Black's Law Dictionary* 970 (9th ed. 2009).

Walgreen.[1522] The Court adopted the learned-intermediary doctrine in the context of pharmacist/ customer tort litigation and held that pharmacists have no duty to warn of a prescribed medication's generalized risks.[1523] The Nevada Supreme Court next considered whether the learned-intermediary doctrine likewise insulates a pharmacist from liability when he or she has knowledge of a customer-specific risk. Following the modern trend of case law, the Nevada Supreme Court concluded that the learned-intermediary doctrine does not foreclose a pharmacist's potential for liability when the pharmacist has knowledge of a customer-specific risk. Instead, under these circumstances, a pharmacist has a duty to exercise reasonable care in warning the customer or notifying the prescribing doctor of the risk.[1524]

The "mass immunization exception" to the learned intermediary defense applied in an action against a manufacturer of measles, mumps and rubella (MMR) vaccine administered by the county health district. The physician's advice to the infant's mother that "it was time" for the infant to receive a vaccine was not the type of "individualized medical judgment" contemplated by the learned intermediary defense.[1525]

In the prescription drug context, the "learned intermediary doctrine" provides that manufacturers of prescription drugs and medical devices discharge their duty of care to patients by providing warnings to the prescribing physicians.[1526] The justification in this particular context is that consumers cannot buy prescription drugs directly from a manufacturer. The Fourth Circuit Court of Appeals stated as follows:

> Prescription drugs are likely to be complex medicines, esoteric in formula and varied in effect. As a medical expert, the prescribing physician can take into account the propensities of the drug, as well as the susceptibilities of his patient. His is the task of weighing the benefits of any medication against its potential dangers. The choice he makes is an informed one, an individualized medical judgment bottomed on a knowledge of both patient and palliative. Pharmaceutical companies then, who must warn ultimate purchasers of dangers inherent in patent drugs sold over the counter, in selling prescription drugs are required to warn only the prescribing physician, who acts as a "learned intermediary" between manufacturer and consumer.[1527]

Liability Limit

A liability limit is the maximum amount of coverage that an insurance company will provide on a single claim under an insurance policy. It is also termed limit of liability or policy limits.[1528]

License

A permission, usually revocable, to commit some act that would otherwise be unlawful; especially an agreement (not amounting to a lease or *profit à prendre*[1529]) that it is lawful for the licensee to enter the licensor's land to do some act that would otherwise be illegal, such as hunting game.[1530] For example, a physician with a valid medical license can touch people in ways that a non-licensed person cannot.

Limited Liability

Limited liability is liability that is restricted by law or contract; especially, the liability of a company's owners for nothing more than the capital they have invested in the business.[1531]

[1522] 127 Nev. Adv. Op. No. 74 (2011).

[1523] *Id.*

[1524] *Id.*

[1525] *Allison v. Merck and Company*, 110 Nev. 762, 765, 878 P.2d 948 (1994) (per Springer, J., with one Justice concurring, Chief Justice concurring in results and two Justices concurring in part and dissenting in part.)

[1526] See RESTATEMENT (THIRD) OF TORTS: PRODUCTS LIABILITY § 6 cmt. d, reporters' note (1997).

[1527] *Talley v. Danek Med., Inc.*, 179 F.3d 154, 163 (4th Cir. 1999).

[1528] *Id.*, p. 998.

[1529] [French, Right of taking]: The right of persons to share in the land owned by another; a profit à prendre enables a person to take part of the soil or produce of land that someone else owns. It is a right to take from the land, as in the mining of minerals and is, therefore, distinguishable from an easement, which is a nonpossessory interest in land generally giving a person a right of way on the property of another. *West's Encyclopedia of American Law*, edition 2. Copyright 2008 The Gale Group, Inc. All rights reserved.

[1530] *Black's Law Dictionary* 1002 (9th ed. 2009).

[1531] *Id.*, pp. 997-98.

It is a "long-standing common law rule that communications [made] in the course of judicial proceedings [even if known to be false] are absolutely privileged."[1532] In addition, the applicability of the absolute privilege is a matter of law for the court to decide, which the Nevada Supreme Court will review de novo.[1533] Further, because the scope of the absolute privilege is broad, a court determining whether the privilege applies should resolve any doubt in favor of a broad application.[1534]

In *Fink v. Oshins*, the Nevada Supreme Court determined that an attorney's statements made to his client were absolutely privileged after his client began seriously considering commencing proceedings to remove the defendant as cotrustee of a trust.[1535] To support the interpretation of the absolute privilege in *Fink* and in other cases, the Nevada Supreme Court has relied on the RESTATEMENT (SECOND) OF TORTS § 587, which does not limit the application of the absolute privilege to attorney communications.[1536] The purpose of the absolute privilege is to afford all persons freedom to access the courts and freedom from liability for defamation where civil or criminal proceedings are seriously considered.[1537] Therefore, the absolute privilege affords parties the same protection from liability as those protections afforded to an attorney for defamatory statements made during, or in anticipation of, judicial proceedings.[1538]

Thus, where a judicial proceeding has commenced or is, in good faith, under serious consideration, the Nevada Supreme Court has determined there is no need to limit the absolute privilege to communications made by attorneys.[1539] In *Hall v. Smith*, an Arizona Court of Appeals also relied on the RESTATEMENT (SECOND) OF TORTS § 587 to conclude that the absolute privilege applies to both attorneys and parties to litigation. Comment e of RESTATEMENT (SECOND) OF TORTS § 587 explicitly makes clear that the protection from liability for defamation accorded to an attorney under § 586 applies equally to parties to litigation.[1540]

The Nevada Supreme Court has extended the protections of the absolute privilege to instances where a nonlawyer asserts an alleged defamatory communication in response to threatened litigation or during a judicial proceeding.[1541] For the privilege to apply (1) a judicial proceeding must be contemplated in good faith and under serious consideration, and (2) the communication must be related to the litigation.[1542] The outer limits of the litigation privilege are an open issue.

The litigation privilege arises out of common law, tracing its roots back to the 1591 English case of *Buckley v. Wood*, 76 Eng. Rep. 888 (K.B. 1591).[1543] In *Buckley*, the plaintiff brought a defamation action after the defendant alleged in a document filed with a court that the plaintiff was "a maintainer of pirates and murderers." The English court found that the publication of that document was not actionable, holding that "for any matter contained in the bill that was examinable in the said Court, no action lies, although the matter is merely false, because it [the defamatory publication] was in [the] course of justice."[1544] Thus, from early on the litigation privilege provides attorneys with immunity from liability for making alleged defamatory statements so long as they relate to those proceedings.

The purpose of the privilege "is to ensure free access to the court, promote complete and truthful testimony, encourage zealous advocacy, give finality to judgments, and avoid unending litigation."[1545] Courts have repeatedly embraced the privilege because "access to the judicial process, freedom to institute an action, or defend, or participate therein without fear of the burden of being sued for defamation is so vital and necessary to the integrity of our judicial system that it must be made paramount."[1546] In short, the privilege acts as the "backbone to an effective and smoothly

---

[1532] *Circus Circus Hotels v. Witherspoon*, 99 Nev. 56, 60, 657 P.2d 101, 104 (1983).

[1533] *Id.* at 62, 657 P.2d at 105. *Fink v. Oshins*, 118 Nev. 428, 432, 49 P.3d 640, 643 (2002).

[1534] *Fink*, 118 Nev. at 433-34, 49 P.3d at 644.

[1535] *Id.* at 434, 49 P.3d at 644.

[1536] *Fink*, 118 Nev. at 433 n.13, 49 P.3d at 644 n.13; see also *Pope v. Motel 6*, 121 Nev. 307, 316, 114 P.3d 277, 283 (2005); *K-Mart Corporation v. Washington*, 109 Nev. 1180, 1191 n.7, 866 P.2d 274, 282 n.7 (1993), *receded from on other grounds by Pope*, 121 Nev. at 316-17, 114 P.3d at 283.

[1537] RESTATEMENT (SECOND) OF TORTS § 587 cmts. a, e (1977).

[1538] *Id.*, cmt. d (1977).

[1539] See *Hall v. Smith*, 152 P.3d 1192, 1195-96 (Ariz. Ct. App. 2007) ("The privilege applies to both attorneys and parties to litigation").

[1540] RESTATEMENT (SECOND) OF TORTS § 587 cmt. e (1977).

[1541] *Clark County School Dist. v. Virtual Educ.*, 125 Nev., Advance Opinion 31 (2009).

[1542] 118 Nev. at 433-34, 49 P.3d at 644.

[1543] See *The Lawyers' Litigation Privilege* by Robert W. Lucas.

[1544] *Id.* at 889.

[1545] *Wentland v. Wass*, 25 Cal.Rptr.3d 109, 115 (Cal. Ct.App. 2005).

[1546] *Jones v. Trice*, 360 S.W.2d 48, 51 (Tenn. 1962).

operating judicial system."[1547]

American common law early on adopted the protection afforded by the litigation privilege.[1548] The Restatement (Second) of Torts has refined the original common law definition: "An attorney is absolutely privileged to publish defamatory matter concerning another in communications preliminary to a proposed judicial proceeding, or in the institution of, or during the course and as part of, a judicial proceeding in which he participates as counsel, if it has some relation to the proceeding."[1549] Most states have adopted this rule either as part of their common law or by statute. For example in California, Civil Code section 47(b) provides: "A privileged publication . . . is one made . . . in any judicial proceeding . . . or any other official proceeding authorized by law."

The policy of access to the courts requires protection not only for the client, but also for the litigation attorney, because if the attorney's representation is compromised, the client's use of the judicial system is frustrated.[1550] Consequently, public policy recognizes that even the threat of retaliatory action contemporaneous with the attorney's representation may seriously interfere with that representation.[1551] Therefore, the trend is to expand the litigation privilege beyond defamation claims to other conduct arising in the course of litigation with courts increasingly seeing "no reason to distinguish between communications made during the litigation process and conduct during the litigation process."[1552]

While typically all doubts about the privilege are resolved in favor of its recognition, the privilege does not absolutely protect lawyers.[1553] Lawyers cannot use the privilege to shield themselves from either disciplinary proceedings or malpractice actions.[1554] Additionally, the privilege does not bar a malicious prosecution claim against an attorney.[1555] Furthermore, the majority of jurisdictions hold that the privilege does not shield attorneys from fraud claims.[1556] Finally, the privilege provides the attorney with no protection for committing or suborning perjury.[1557]

For the litigation privilege to apply, a judicial proceeding must be contemplated in good faith or be underway.[1558] A judicial proceeding encompasses not only traditional lawsuits in a court of law, but also any other quasi-judicial proceeding, such as administrative actions, so long as "the safeguards that surround judicial proceedings are present."[1559] Likewise, the courts typically consider arbitrations to fall within the rubric of judicial proceedings.[1560]

The privilege not only attaches to communications during the course of the proceeding, but also to communications preliminary to a lawsuit, including threats, demands and efforts to avoid a lawsuit because such acts are an inherent part of the judicial process.[1561] The privilege applies even if the attorney and not the client anticipates the litigation.[1562] Moreover, the attorney does not need to be the attorney who eventually represents the client during litigation.[1563] For the privilege to apply, all that is required is that the communication bear some relation to a judicial proceeding.[1564] Any doubts whether a statement is related to a judicial proceeding should be resolved in favor of the

---

[1547] *Tuff-N-Rumble Mgmt., Inc v. Sugar Hill Music Publ'g Inc.*, 49 F.Supp.2d 673, 680 (S.D.N.Y. 1999).

[1548] *Loigman v. Township Comm. of Tp. of Middletown*, 889 A.2d 428 (N.J. 2006).

[1549] RESTATEMENT (SECOND) OF TORTS § 586.

[1550] *Rubin v. Green*, 847 P.2d 1044 (Cal. 1993); *Hagendorf v. Brown*, 699 F.2d 478 (9th Cir. 1983).

[1551] *Rusheen v. Cohen*, 128 P.3d 713 (Cal. 2006); *Sussman v. Damian*, 355 So.2d 809 (Fla. Dist. Ct.App. 1977).)

[1552] *Clark v. Druckman*, 624 S.E.2d 864, 870 (W.Va. 2005).

[1553] See *Penny v. Sherman*, 684 P.2d 1182, 1185 (N.M. Ct.App. 1984).

[1554] See, *e.g.*, *Bushell v. Caterpillar, Inc.*, 683 N.E.2d 1286, 1289-90 (Ill. App. Ct. 1997) (disciplinary proceedings); *Kolar v. Donahue, McIntosh & Hammerton*, 52 Cal.Rptr.3d 712, 719 (Cal. Ct. App. 2006) (malpractice action).

[1555] See, *e.g.*, *Hagberg v. Cal. Fed. Bank FSB*, 81 P.3d 244, 249 (Cal. 2004); *Dello Russo v. Nagel*, 817 A.2d (N.J. Super. Ct. App. Div. 2003).

[1556] *N.Y. Cooling Towers, Inc. v. Goidel*, 805 N.Y.S.2d 779, 783 (N.Y. Sup. Ct. 2005); *Clark, supra*, 624 S.E.2d at 871-72.

[1557] *Bushell, supra*, 683 N.E.2d at 1289; *Hawkins v. Harris* (661 A.2d 284, 288 (N.J. 1995).

[1558] See *Visto Corp. v. Sproqit Techs., Inc.*, 360 F.Supp.2d 1064, 1069 (N.D. Cal. 2005).

[1559] *Lockheed Inf. Mgmt. Sys Co. v. Maximus, Inc.*, 524 S.E.2d 420, 424 (Va. 2004).

[1560] See, *e.g.*, *AmLifeCare, Inc. v. Wood*, 826 So.2d 646, 49-50 (La. Ct.App. 2002); *W. Mass. Blasting Corp. v. Metro. Prop. & Cas. Ins. Co.*, 782 A.2d 398, 403 (R.I. 2001).

[1561] *Meltzer v. Grant*, 193 F.Supp.2d 373 (D. Mass. 2002); *McBride v. Pizza Hut, Inc.*, 658 A.2d 205 (D.C. 1995).

[1562] *Finkelstein, Thompson & Loughran v. Hemispherx Biopharma, Inc.*, 774 A.2d 332 (D.C. Cir. 2001).

[1563] *Lerette v. Dean Witter Organization, Inc.*, 131 Cal.Rptr. 592 (Cal. Ct. App. 1976).

[1564] *Mossesson v. Jacob D. Fuchsberg Law Firm*, 683 N.Y.S.2d 88, 89 (N.Y. App. Div. 1999).

relation.[1565]

The defense not only protects the lawyer, but also the lawyer's agents.[1566] For instance, an investigator was seeking to find out if the plaintiff's injuries were attributable to his mother's misuse of alcohol during pregnancy.[1567] The court held the privilege to apply even though the investigator falsely told prospective witnesses that there was such evidence. The court concluded that if the conduct would have been privileged by the lawyer, the protection extended to the lawyer's agent. Also, a paralegal who claimed to have witnessed misconduct affecting the outcome of a trial, was entitled to absolute immunity when she was sued for reporting the alleged misconduct to counsel for the losing party.[1568]

Although the privilege still typically involves defamation claims, the purpose of the privilege is not limited to defamation causes of action only, but to a broad variety of torts. For example, a Nevada federal district court applied the privilege to bad faith and breach of fiduciary claims that did not arise from any pleaded defamation claim.[1569]

The privilege has also been applied to causes of action for tortious interference with business relationships and prospective economic advantage, along with civil conspiracy and racketeering.[1570] In short, only malicious prosecution, other claims for initiating litigation for an improper purpose, and fraud have fallen outside the scope of the privilege. As a court explained, "[the privilege] would be nullified if individuals barred from bringing defamation claims could seek damages under other theories of liability."[1571]

Merger Doctrine

The merger doctrine in property law is the absorption of a lesser estate into a greater estate when both become the same person's property.[1572]

Misnomer of Parties

A mistake in naming a person, place, or thing, esp. in a legal instrument. In federal pleading—as well as in most states—misnomer of a party can be corrected by an amendment, which will relate back to the date of the original pleading under NRCP 15(c)(3).[1573]

Mistake

A mistake is an error committed in relation to some matter of fact affecting the rights of one of the parties to a contract.[1574] Mistakes in making a contract are distinguished ordinarily into, first, mistakes as to the motive; secondly, mistakes as to the person, with whom the contract is made; thirdly, as to the subject matter of the contract; and, lastly, mistakes of fact and of law.[1575] In general, courts of equity will correct and rectify all mistakes in deeds and contracts founded on good consideration.[1576] As to mistakes in the names of legatees, see 1 Rop. Leg. 131; Domat, l. 4, t. 2, s. 1, n. 22. As to mistakes made in practice, and as to the propriety or impropriety of taking advantage of them, see Chitt. Pr. Index, h.t. As to mistakes of law in relation to contracts, see 23 Am. Jur. 146 to 166.

In a California case,[1577] Defendant's unilateral mistake of fact provided a basis for rescinding the contract. Rescission was warranted because the evidence established that defendant's unilateral mistake of fact was made in good

---

[1565] *Daystar Residential, Inc. v. Collmer*, 176 S.W.3d 24, 28 (Tex. App. 2004); *Fink v. Oshins*, 49 P.3d 640, 644 (Nev. 2002).

[1566] *Hawkins v. Harris*, 661 A.2d 284, 286-87 (N.J. 1995)

[1567] *Leavitt v. Bickerton*, 855 F.Supp. 455 (D. Mass. 1994).

[1568] *Van Eaton v. Fink*, 697 N.E.2d 490 (Ind. Ct. App. 1998).

[1569] *Crockett & Myers, Ltd. v. Napier, Fitzgerald & Kirby, LLP*, 440 F.Supp.2d 1184 (D. Nev. 2006).

[1570] See *Boca Investors Group, Inc. v. Potash*, 935 So.2d, 273, 274 (business relationships); *Kahala Royal Corp. v. Goodsill Anderson Quinn & Stifel*, 151 P.3d 732, 750-52 (Haw. 2007) (prospective economic advantage); *Jackson v. BellSouth Telecomms.*, 372 F.3d 1250, 1277 (11th Cir. 2004) (civil conspiracy), *Christonson v. United States*, 415 F.Supp.2d 1186, 1196 (D. Idaho 2006) (RICO).

[1571] *Hugel v. Milberg, Weiss, Bershad, Hynes & Lerach, LLP*, 175 F.3d 14, 18 (1st Cir. 1999).

[1572] *Id.*, p. 1078.

[1573] *Id.*, p. 1090.

[1574] *A Law Dictionary, Adapted to the Constitution and Laws of the United States* by John Bouvier, published 1856.

[1575] See Story, Eq. Jur. Sec. 110; Bouv. Inst. Index, h.t.; Ignorance; Motive.

[1576] 1 Ves. 317; 2 Atk. 203; Mitf. Pl. 116; 4 Vin. Ab. 277; 13 Vin. Ab. 41; 18 E. Com. Law Reps. 14; 8 Com. Digest, 75; Madd. Ch. Prac. Index, h.t.; 1 Story on Eq. ch. 5, p. 121; Jeremy's Eq. Jurisd. B. 3, part 2, p. 358. See article Surprise.

[1577] *Donovan v. RRL Corp.*, 26 Cal.4th 261, 27 P.3d 702, 26 Cal.4th 1060, 109 Cal.Rptr.2d 807 (Cal. 2001).

faith, defendant did not bear the risk of the mistake, and enforcement of the contract with the erroneous price would be unconscionable.

See "Mutual Mistake."

Monell Defense

The acts complained of were not done pursuant to a municipal custom, policy or practice.[1578]

Mootness

The mootness doctrine is the principle that American courts will not decide moot cases—that is, cases with which there is no longer any actual controversy.[1579] The question of mootness is one of justiciability.[1580] The Nevada Supreme Court has a duty to "decide actual controversies by a judgment which can be carried into effect, and not to give opinions upon moot questions or abstract propositions, or to declare principles of law which cannot affect the matter in issue . . .."[1581] "[C]ases presenting live controversies at the time of their inception may become moot by the occurrence of subsequent events."[1582] An appeal was moot where a mining company no longer had the claims that were at issue when a quiet title action began.[1583]

In Nevada, a moot case is one which seeks to determine an abstract question which does not rest upon existing facts or rights.[1584] Cases presenting real controversies at the time of their institution may become moot by the happening of subsequent events.[1585] Even if an issue is moot, the court may still consider the case if it is a matter of widespread importance capable of repetition, yet evading review.[1586] If so, then a party must demonstrate that (1) the duration of the challenged action is relatively short, (2) it is likely that a similar issue will arise in the future, and (3) the matter is important.[1587]

Mutual Assent

Agreement by both parties to a contract, usually in the form of offer and acceptance. In modern contract law, mutual assent is determined by an objective standard—that is, by the apparent intention of the parties as manifested by their actions.[1588]

Mutual Mistake

A contract may be set aside based on mutual mistake, which "occurs when both parties, at the time of contracting, share a misconception about a vital fact upon which they based their bargain."[1589] A mutual mistake in one in which each party misunderstands the other's intent. It is also termed "bilateral mistake."[1590] It is a mistake that is shared and relied on by both parties to a contract. Nevada Rule of Civil Procedure 9(b) provides as follows: "In all averments of fraud or mistake, the circumstances constituting fraud or mistake shall be stated with particularity. Malice, intent, knowledge, and other condition of mind of a person may be averred generally."

A court will often revise or nullify a contract based on a mutual mistake about a material term.[1591] Mutual mistake occurs when both parties, at the time of contracting, share a misconception about a vital fact upon which they based their bargain.[1592] "[A] mutual mistake is a basis for an equitable rescission of a contract."[1593]

[1578] See *Monell v. Department of Social Services*, 436 U.S. 658, 694 n.58, 56 L. Ed. 2d 611, 98 S Ct. 2018 (1978).

[1579] *Black's Law Dictionary* 1025 (7th ed. 1999).

[1580] *Personhood Nevada v. Bristol*, 126 Nev. ___, ___, 245 P.3d 572, 574 (2010).

[1581] *NCAA v. University of Nevada*, 97 Nev. 56, 57, 624 P.2d 10, 10 (1981).

[1582] *University Sys. v. Nevadans for Sound Gov't*, 120 Nev. 712, 720, 100 P.3d 179, 186 (2004).

[1583] *Majuba Mining, Ltd. v. Pumpkin Copper, Inc.*, 129 Nev., Advance Opinion 19 (April 4, 2013).

[1584] *Bisch v. Las Vegas Metropolitan Police Department*, 129 Nev., Advance Opinion 36 (May 30, 2013), p. 7.

[1585] *Id.*

[1586] *Id.*, citing *Personhood Nev. v. Bristol*, 126 Nev. ___, ___, 245 P.3d 572, 574 (2010).

[1587] *Id.*

[1588] *Id.*, p. 132.

[1589] *Anderson v. Sanchez*, 131 Nev.Adv.Op. 51 (Ct.App. 2015), citing *Gen Motors v. Jackson*, 111 Nev. 1026, 1032, 900 P.2d 345, 349 (1995).

[1590] *Id.*, 9th ed., p. 1092.

[1591] *Black's Law Dictionary* 1092-93 (9th ed. 2009).

[1592] *Gramanz v. Gramanz*, 113 Nev. 1, 7, 930 P.2d 753 (1997); *General Motors v. Jackson*, 111 Nev. 1026, 1032, 900 P.2d 345, 349 (1995).

[1593] *Id.*

However, where one party bears the risk of the mistake, mutual mistake is not a basis for rescission.[1594] The Nevada Supreme Court has adopted the RESTATEMENT (SECOND) OF CONTRACTS § 154(b) (1981), which provides that a party bears the risk when "he is aware, at the time the contract is made, that he has only limited knowledge with respect to the facts to which the mistakes relates but treats his limited knowledge as sufficient."[1595]

Noerr-Pennington Defense

A Sherman Antitrust Act[1596] defendant can raise the affirmative defense of right to petition for redress, even if they use that right to try to gain an anti-competitive advantage.[1597] The purpose of Nevada's anti-SLAPP statute is similar to the purpose behind the Noerr-Pennington immunity doctrine.[1598] According to this doctrine, "those who petition all departments of the government for redress are generally immune from liability."[1599] The basis of this doctrine is that representative democracy demands that citizens and public officials have the ability to openly engage in discussions of public concern.[1600] As a result, the private or public petitioning of governmental entities is insufficient to violate federal substantive rights.[1601]

The Noerr-Pennington doctrine derives from the Petition Clause of the First Amendment and provides that "those who petition any department of the government for redress are generally immune from statutory liability for their petitioning conduct."[1602] It initially emerged in the antitrust context.[1603] Recognizing that the " 'right to petition extends to all departments of the government' "and includes access to courts, the Supreme Court extended the doctrine to provide immunity for the use of " 'the channels and procedures' " of state and federal courts to advocate causes."[1604]

The U.S. Supreme Court has since held that Noerr-Pennington principles "apply with full force in other statutory contexts" outside antitrust.[1605] In *BE & K*, the Court held that the National Labor Relations Act ("NLRA") did not permit holding an employer liable for unsuccessfully prosecuting retaliatory lawsuits against employees who were exercising rights the NLRA protects.[1606] In doing so, the Court adopted a three-part test to determine whether the defendant's conduct is immunized: (1) identify whether the lawsuit imposes a burden on petitioning rights, (2) decide whether the alleged activities constitute protected petitioning activity, and (3) analyze whether the statutes at issue may be construed to preclude that burden on the protected petitioning activity.[1607]

Not all petitioning activity is immunized, however. Noerr-Pennington immunity does not apply to "sham" cases where a person abuses the government process in order to achieve some benefit.[1608] A "sham" exception to the doctrine developed to prevent the immunization of conduct that used "governmental process . . . as an anticompetitive weapon."[1609] The Ninth Circuit has held that a defendant's activities may fall into this exception if they include making intentional misrepresentations to the court that then "deprive[s] the litigation of its legitimacy."[1610]

The denial of a motion for immunity from liability under the Noerr-Pennington doctrine ("those who petition any department of the government for redress are generally immune from statutory liability for their petitioning conduct:) is not immediately appealable, nor does the court have pendent appellate jurisdiction over the Noerr-Pennington issue, so

---

[1594] *Land Baron Investments v. Bonnie Springs Family Limited Partnership*, 131 Nev., Advance Opinion 69 (2015).

[1595] *Id.*

[1596] 15 U.S.C. §§ 1-7.

[1597] See *Noerr-Pennington Doctrine* (2009), ABA Section of Antitrust Law, p. 107.

[1598] See *Eastern R. Conf. v. Noerr Motors*, 365 U.S. 127 (1961); *Mine Workers v. Pennington*, 381 U.S. 657 (1965).

[1599] *Empress LLC v. City and County*, 419 F.3d 1052, 1056 (9th Cir. 2005).

[1600] *Manistee Town Center v. City of Glendale*, 227 F.3d 1090, 1093 (9th Cir. 2000).

[1601] *Id.*

[1602] *Sosa v. DIRECTV, Inc.*, 437 F.3d 923, 929 (9th Cir. 2006).

[1603] See *E. R.R. Presidents Conference v. Noerr Motor Freight, Inc.*, 365 U.S. 127 (1961); *United Mine Workers v. Pennington*, 381 U.S. 657 (1965).

[1604] *Sosa v. DIRECTV, Inc.*, 437 F.3d 923, 929-30 (9th Cir. 2006) (quoting *Cal. Motor Transp. Co. v. Trucking Unlimited*, 404 U.S. 508, 510-11 (1972)).

[1605] *Id.* at 930 (discussing *BE & K Constr. Co. v. NLRB*, 536 U.S. 516, 525 (2002)).

[1606] 536 U.S. 516.

[1607] See *id.* at 530-33, 535-37.

[1608] *Boulware v. State of Nev., Dept. of Human Res.*, 960 F.2d 793, 797 (9th Cir. 1992); *John v. Douglas County School District*, 125 Nev., Advance Opinion 55 (2009).

[1609] *Kottle v. Nw. Kidney Ctrs.*, 146 F.3d 1056, 1060 (9th Cir. 1998).

[1610] *Id.*

the appeal is dismissed for lack of jurisdiction.[1611]

Non-Liability of Commercial Liquor Vendors in Nevada for Injuries Caused by Intoxicated Patron

It is well settled in Nevada that commercial liquor vendors, including hotel proprietors, cannot be held liable for damages related to any injuries caused by the intoxicated patron, which are sustained by either the intoxicated patron or a third party.[1612] This rule applies equally when the intoxicated patron is a minor.[1613] In other words, Nevada subscribes to the rationale underlying the non-liability principle—that individuals, drunk or sober, are responsible for their torts.[1614]

Novation

See RESTATEMENT (SECOND) OF CONTRACTS § 318 cmt. d (1981) ("An obligor is discharged by the substitution of a new obligor only if the contract so provides or if the obligee makes a binding manifestation of assent, forming a novation. Otherwise, the obligee retains his original right against the obligor.")[1615]

Preemption by Federal or Other Law

Constitutional Law. Preemption is the principle (derived from the Supremacy Clause) that a federal law can supersede or supplant any inconsistent state law or regulation.[1616] The preemption doctrine emanates from the Supremacy Clause of the United States Constitution, pursuant to which state law must yield when it frustrates or conflicts with federal law.[1617] The doctrine is comprised of two broad branches: express and implied preemption.[1618] Express preemption, as its name suggests, occurs when Congress "explicitly states that intent in a statute's language."[1619] Implied preemption arises, in contrast, "[w]hen Congress does not include statutory language expressly preempting state law."[1620]

Implied preemption contains two sub-branches: field and conflict preemption.[1621] Field preemption applies "when congressional enactments so thoroughly occupy a legislative field, or touch a field in which the federal interest is so dominant, that Congress effectively leaves no room for states to regulate conduct in that field."[1622] Conflict preemption, or obstacle preemption, as it is oftentimes called, occurs when "federal law actually conflicts with any state law."[1623] Conflict preemption analysis examines the federal statute as a whole to determine whether a party's compliance with both federal and state requirements is impossible or whether, in light of the federal statute's purpose and intended effects, state law poses an obstacle to the accomplishment of Congress's objectives.[1624]

The United States Supreme Court has set forth "two cornerstones" of preemption that must factor into an analysis.[1625] First, the Court has explained that " 'the purpose of Congress is the ultimate touchstone in every pre-emption case.' "[1626] Second, the Court has instructed that " '[i]n all pre-emption cases, and particularly in those in which Congress has legislated . . . in a field which the States have traditionally occupied, . . . we start with the assumption that the historic police powers of the States were not to be superseded by the Federal Act unless that was the clear and manifest purpose of Congress.' "[1627] The second principle, known as the presumption against preemption, arises out of

---

[1611] *Tanedo v. East Baton Rouge Parish School Board*, No. 11-57064 (9th Cir. 2013).

[1612] *Hamm v. Carson City Nugget, Inc.*, 85 Nev. 99, 101, 450 P.2d 358, 359 (1969); *Snyder v. Viani*, 110 Nev. 1339, 1342-43, 885 P.2d 610, 612-13 (1994), cited in *Rodriguez v. Primadonna Company*, LLC, 216 P.3d 793 (Nev. 10/01/2009).

[1613] *Hinegardner v. Marcor Resorts*, 108 Nev. 1091, 1096, 844 P.2d 800, 803 (1992).

[1614] See *id.* at 1093, 844 P.2d at 802.

[1615] *Easton Bus. Opp. v. Town Executive Suites*, 126 Nev., Advance Opinion 13, fn. 3 (2010).

[1616] *Black's Law Dictionary* 1297 (9th ed. 2009).

[1617] *Nanopierce Tech. v. Depository Trust*, 123 Nev. 362, 370, 168 P.3d 73, 79 (2007).

[1618] *Id.*

[1619] *Id.* at 371, 168 P.3d at 79.

[1620] *Id.*

[1621] *Id.*

[1622] *Id.*

[1623] *Id.* at 371, 168 P.3d at 80.

[1624] *Id.* at 371-72, 168 P.3d at 80.

[1625] *Wyeth v. Levine*, 555 U.S. 555, 565 (2009).

[1626] *Id.* (quoting *Medtronic, Inc. v. Lohr*, 518 U.S. 470, 485 (1996)).

[1627] *Id.* (alterations in original) (quoting *Lohr*, 518 U.S. at 485).

"respect for the States as 'independent sovereigns in our federal system.'"[1628]

With the ADA, Congress has legislated in the area of disability discrimination.[1629] Although states have the "police powers to prohibit discrimination on specified grounds,"[1630] historically states have, at best, played a junior role in this area.[1631] Thus, when a petition does not involve a legislative landscape traditionally occupied by the states, the presumption against preemption does not apply with particular force.[1632]

Privilege

In general, see NRS Chapter 49. One who is required by law to publish defamatory matter is absolutely privileged to publish it.[1633]

Promissory Estoppel

See "Promissory Estoppel" in "Claims."

Punitive Damages Not Permissible

Punitive damages are not permissible for breach of contract claims.[1634] An award for punitive damages cannot be supported by the breach of the implied covenant of good faith and fair dealing when that claim sounds in contract, and not tort.[1635] Where there was no special element of reliance or fiduciary duty here for the implied covenant claim to be based in tort, punitive damages cannot stand.[1636]

Punitive damages are not permissible against a governmental entity.

Qualified Immunity

In *Saucier v. Katz*,[1637] the United States Supreme Court outlined the following sequence for the qualified immunity analysis. First, "[t]aken in the light most favorable to the party asserting the injury, do the facts alleged show the officer's conduct violated a constitutional right?"[1638] If yes, "the next, sequential step is to ask whether the right was clearly established."[1639] The Court explained that in undertaking this second step, the "relevant, dispositive inquiry is whether it would be clear to a reasonable officer that his conduct was unlawful in the situation he confronted."[1640] "The uniformly applied rule is that a search conducted pursuant to a warrant that fails to conform to the particularity requirement of the Fourth Amendment is unconstitutional."[1641]

Qualified Privilege of "Fair Comment" in Defamation Action

In *Diaz v. Espada*, [1642]the court analyzed the qualified privilege of "fair comment" as follows:

[1628] *Id.* at 565 n.3 (quoting *Lohr*, 518 U.S. at 485).

[1629] *Rolf Jensen & Associates v. Dist. Ct.*, 128 Nev. Adv. Op. No. 42 (August 9, 2012).

[1630] *Kroske v. U.S. Bank Corp.*, 432 F.3d 976, 981 (9th Cir. 2005).

[1631] See *Alexander v. Choate*, 469 U.S. 287, 295-96 (1985) (explaining that Congress enacted provisions prohibiting discrimination against disabled persons precisely because such persons had otherwise been neglected).

[1632] See *Wyeth*, 555 U.S. at 565 n.3 (noting that the force given to the presumption against preemption is guided by "the historic presence of state law").

[1633] *Cucinotta v. Deloitte & Touche, LLP*, 129 Nev., Advance Opinion 35 (May 30, 2013), p. 2, citing RESTATEMENT (SECOND) OF TORTS section 592A (1977).

[1634] *Amoroso Const. v. Lazovich and Lazovich*, 107 Nev. 294, 298, 810 P.2d 775, 777-78 (1991).

[1635] See *Hilton Hotels v. Butch Lewis Productions*, 109 Nev. 1043, 1046-47, 862 P.2d 1207, 1209 (1993) (concluding that while "[i]n certain circumstances, breach of contract, including breach of the covenant of good faith and fair dealing, may provide the basis for a tort claim," there is a special element of reliance or fiduciary duty that is required for the claim to sound in tort (quotation omitted)).

[1636] *Road & Highway Builders v. N. Nev. Rebar*, 128 Nev. Adv. Op. No. 36 (August 9, 2012).

[1637] *Saucier v. Katz*, 533 U.S. 194, 200 (2001).

[1638] 533 U.S. at 201, 121 S.Ct. 2151.

[1639] *Id.*

[1640] *Id.* at 202, 121 S.Ct. 2151.

[1641] *Massachusetts v. Sheppard*, 468 U.S. 981, 988 n. 5, 104 S.Ct. 3424, 82 L.Ed.2d 737 (1984).

[1642] 778 N.Y.S.2d 38 (N.Y. 2004).

Statements made regarding a matter of public concern, such as the political campaign at issue here, are generally accorded the qualified privilege of "fair comment" if the statements complained of are (1) a comment, (2) based on facts truly stated, (3) free from imputation of corrupt or dishonorable motives on the part of plaintiff, save insofar as such imputations are warranted by the facts truly stated, and (4) the honest expression of the writer's real opinion.[1643] In order to overcome the qualified privilege and successfully assert that such statements are defamatory, plaintiff in this instance must show that they were made with actual malice.[1644] "Actual malice" requires proof that the statement was made with knowledge that it is false or with a reckless disregard for the truth (*id.* at 382).

Ratification

Generally, contract ratification is the adoption of a previously formed contract, notwithstanding a quality that rendered it relatively void and by the very act of ratification the party affirming becomes bound by it and entitled to all proper benefits from it.[1645] A client can ratify a lawyer's unauthorized act.[1646]

Reasonable Accommodation

Title I of the Americans with Disabilities Act (ADA) requires employers of 15 or more employees to provide an equal opportunity to qualified individuals. It prohibits discrimination in various aspects of employment. Title I restricts employers from asking applicants about health conditions before a job offer. The actual law reads as follows:

> No covered entity shall discriminate against a qualified individual with a disability because of the disability of such individual in regard to job application procedures, the hiring, advancement, or discharge of employees, employee compensation, job training, and other terms, conditions, and privileges of employment.[1647]

Title I of the ADA further discusses discrimination and requires employers to make reasonable accommodations as follows:

> [T]he term "discriminate against a qualified individual on the basis of disability" includes not making reasonable accommodations to the known physical or mental limitations of an otherwise qualified individual with a disability who is an applicant or employee, unless such covered entity can demonstrate that the accommodation would impose undue hardship on the operation of the business.[1648]

Employers are obligated to provide accommodations to the known physical or mental limitations of applicants or employees that are due to the disability. This means that employees might be obligated to tell the employer about the disability and how it limits functioning in order to receive accommodations. In addition, employers are not required to provide accommodations to employees who are not qualified, that is, unable to perform the essential functions of the job with or without reasonable accommodations. What this means is that employers are not obligated to hire unqualified applicants nor keep employees who cannot perform the skills needed to do the main parts of the job.

Where the treating physician of an injured employee determined that the employee was unable to perform the essential functions of his job, the employer of the employee, based on that determination, dismissed the employee because he was not qualified for a reasonable accommodation under the Americans with Disabilities Act, 42 U.S.C. §§ 12101 *et seq.* In an action brought by the employee against the employer for employment discrimination where the physician changed his opinion, the physician's actions constituted "rendering services" for the purposes of the definition of medical malpractice set forth in NRS 41A.009. Therefore, the employer's unsuccessful third party complaint against the physician for negligent misrepresentation was properly characterized as one for medical malpractice and the provisions of former NRS 41A.056 requiring an award of attorney's fees to a prevailing physician were applicable to that claim.[1649]

[1643] *Schneph v. New York Times Co.*, 32 Misc. 2d 237, 239-240, (N.Y. 1961).

[1644] *Rinaldi v. Holt, Rinehart & Winston, Inc.*, 42 N.Y.2d 369, 379, 53 A.D.2d 839 (1976), *cert. denied*, 434 U.S. 969 (1977).

[1645] *Merrill v. DeMott*, 113 Nev. 1390, 1397, 951 P.2d 1040 (1997).

[1646] See RESTATEMENT (THIRD) OF THE LAW GOVERNING LAWYERS § 26(3).

[1647] ADA, Public Law 101-336, § 102(a).

[1648] ADA, Public Law 101-336, Section 102(b)(5)(A).

[1649] *Johnson v. Incline Village Gen. Imp. Dist.*, 5 F. Supp. 2d 1113 (D. Nev. 1998).

Recoupment

Recoup means to get back an equivalent for; make up for (recoup a loss); to regain; to pay back; reimburse.[1650]
Recoupment is:

1: the process or fact of recouping. Example: recoupment of expenses.[1651]

2 a: a keeping back of all or part of a sum sought by a plaintiff in the interest of equity.

b: a reduction in damages because of a demand by the defendant arising out of the same occurrence or transaction.

c: the right of a defendant to have the claim of the plaintiff reduced or eliminated by reason of a breach of contract or duty by the plaintiff in the same occurrence or transaction.

Recoupment involves the type of claim that now must be asserted in a compulsory counterclaim.

A private self-insurer cannot recoup workers' compensation funds properly paid to claimant pending an appeal when funds are later found to be unwarranted. A private self-insurer has no greater rights than State Industrial Insurance System (SIIS) to recoup payments already made.[1652]

See "Equitable Recoupment."

Reformation

Reformation is available as an equitable remedy to a party seeking to alter a written instrument which, because of a mutual mistake of fact, fails to conform to the parties' previous understanding or agreement.[1653]

Rejection of Goods

NRS 104.2602, "Manner and effect of rightful rejection," provides as follows:

1. Rejection of goods must be within a reasonable time after their delivery or tender. It is ineffective unless the buyer seasonably notifies the seller.

2. Subject to the provisions of the two following sections on rejected goods (NRS 104.2603 and 104.2604):

(a) After rejection any exercise of ownership by the buyer with respect to any commercial unit is wrongful as against the seller; and

(b) If the buyer has before rejection taken physical possession of goods in which the buyer does not have a security interest under the provisions of this Article (subsection 3 of NRS 104.2711), the buyer is under a duty after rejection to hold them with reasonable care at the seller's disposition for a time sufficient to permit the seller to remove them; but

(c) The buyer has no further obligations with regard to goods rightfully rejected.

3. The seller's rights with respect to goods wrongfully rejected are governed by the provisions of this Article on seller's remedies in general (NRS 104.2703).

Release

To release is "to relieve or free from obligation, liability, or responsibility," *e.g.*, "the debtor is released from all dischargeable debts."[1654]

Res Judicata

In *Five Star Capital Corp. v. Ruby*,[1655] the Nevada Supreme Court replaced res judicata terminology with claim and issue preclusion. Addressing affirmative defenses, NRCP 8(c) retains res judicata terminology. See "Claim Preclusion" and "Issue Preclusion."

[1650] *Webster's New College Dictionary*, Wiley Publishing: 2007, p. 1198.
[1651] Findlaw Legal Dictionary.
[1652] *Wyphoski v. Sparks Nugget*, 112 Nev. 414, 915 P.2d 261 (1996).
[1653] *Helms Constr. v. State ex rel. Dep't of Highways*, 97 Nev. 500, 503, 634 P.2d 1224 (1981).
[1654] Findlaw Legal Dictionary.
[1655] 124 Nev. 1048, 1051-56, 194 P.3d 709, 711-14 (2008),

Restraint of Trade

In *Hansen v. Edwards*, 83 Nev. 189, 191, 426 P.2d 792, 793 (1967), the Nevada Supreme Court explained as follows:

> An agreement on the part of an employee not to compete with his employer after termination of the employment is in restraint of trade and will not be enforced in accordance with its terms unless the same are reasonable. Where the public interest is not directly involved, the test usually stated for determining the validity of the [non-competition] covenant as written is whether it imposes upon the employee any greater restraint than is reasonably necessary to protect the business and good will [sic] of the employer. A restraint of trade is unreasonable, in the absence of statutory authorization or dominant social or economic justification, if it is greater than is required for the protection of the person for whose benefit the restraint is imposed or imposes undue hardship upon the person restricted. The period of time during which the restraint is to last and the territory that is included are important factors to be considered in determining the reasonableness of the agreement.

Id. at 191-92, 426 P.2d at 793 (citations omitted) (emphasis added); see also *Ellis v. McDaniel*, 95 Nev. 455, 458-59, 596 P.2d 222, 224 (1979) ("There is no inflexible formula for deciding the ubiquitous question of reasonableness. However, because the loss of a person's livelihood is a very serious matter, post employment anti-competitive covenants are scrutinized with greater care . . . .").

Retraction

Retraction is an act of taking back or withdrawing, *e.g.*, her retraction of the defamatory statement.[1656] The sufficiency of the correction and the demand for retraction are questions of fact for the jury to determine by a preponderance of the evidence.[1657] At common law, a retraction was required to be full and unequivocal to be legally sufficient.[1658]

Revocation of Acceptance of Goods

NRS 104.2608, "Revocation of acceptance in whole or in part," provides as follows:

> 1. The buyer may revoke his or her acceptance of a lot or commercial unit whose nonconformity substantially impairs its value to the buyer if the buyer has accepted it:
> (a) On the reasonable assumption that its nonconformity would be cured and it has not been seasonably cured; or
> (b) Without discovery of such nonconformity if his or her acceptance was reasonably induced either by the difficulty of discovery before acceptance or by the seller's assurances.
> 2. Revocation of acceptance must occur within a reasonable time after the buyer discovers or should have discovered the ground for it and before any substantial change in condition of the goods which is not caused by their own defects. It is not effective until the buyer notifies the seller of it.
> 3. A buyer who so revokes has the same rights and duties with regard to the goods involved as if the buyer had rejected them.

NRS 104.2606, "What constitutes acceptance of goods," provides as follows:

> 1. Acceptance of goods occurs when the buyer:
> (a) After a reasonable opportunity to inspect the goods signifies to the seller that the goods are conforming or that the buyer will take or retain them in spite of their nonconformity; or
> (b) Fails to make an effective rejection (subsection 1 of NRS 104.2602), but such acceptance does not occur until the buyer has had a reasonable opportunity to inspect them; or
> (c) Does any act inconsistent with the seller's ownership; but if such act is wrongful as against the seller it is an acceptance only if ratified by the buyer.
> 2. Acceptance of a part of any commercial unit is acceptance of that entire unit.

[1656] *Id.*
[1657] *Nevada Ind. Broadcasting Corp. v. Allen*, 99 Nev. 404, 416, 664 P.2d 337 (1983).
[1658] *Id.*

NRS 104.2607, "Effect of acceptance; notice of breach; burden of establishing breach after acceptance; notice of claim or litigation to person answerable over," provides as follows:

1. The buyer must pay at the contract rate for any goods accepted.
2. Acceptance of goods by the buyer precludes rejection of the goods accepted and if made with knowledge of a nonconformity cannot be revoked because of it unless the acceptance was on the reasonable assumption that the nonconformity would be seasonably cured but acceptance does not of itself impair any other remedy provided by this Article for nonconformity.
3. Where a tender has been accepted:
(a) The buyer must within a reasonable time after the buyer discovers or should have discovered any breach notify the seller of breach or be barred from any remedy; and
(b) If the claim is one for infringement or the like (subsection 3 of NRS 104.2312) and the buyer is sued as a result of such a breach the buyer must so notify the seller within a reasonable time after he or she receives notice of the litigation or be barred from any remedy over for liability established by the litigation.
4. The burden is on the buyer to establish any breach with respect to the goods accepted.
5. Where the buyer is sued for breach of a warranty or other obligation for which the buyer's seller is answerable over:
(a) The buyer may give the seller written notice of the litigation. If the notice states that the seller may come in and defend and that if the seller does not do so the seller will be bound in any action against the seller by his or her buyer by any determination of fact common to the two litigations, then unless the seller after seasonable receipt of the notice does come in and defend the seller is so bound.
(b) If the claim is one for infringement or the like (subsection 3 of NRS 104.2312) the original seller may demand in writing that the seller's buyer turn over to him or her control of the litigation including settlement or else be barred from any remedy over and if the seller also agrees to bear all expense and to satisfy any adverse judgment, then unless the buyer after seasonable receipt of the demand does turn over control the buyer is so barred.
6. The provisions of subsections 3, 4 and 5 apply to any obligation of a buyer to hold the seller harmless against infringement or the like (subsection 3 of NRS 104.2312(3)).

A seller is relieved of liability for breach of warranty if the buyer fails to give notice of breach within a reasonable time.[1659]

NRS 104.2608, "Revocation of acceptance in whole or in part," provides as follows:

1. The buyer may revoke his or her acceptance of a lot or commercial unit whose nonconformity substantially impairs its value to the buyer if the buyer has accepted it:
(a) On the reasonable assumption that its nonconformity would be cured and it has not been seasonably cured; or
(b) Without discovery of such nonconformity if his or her acceptance was reasonably induced either by the difficulty of discovery before acceptance or by the seller's assurances.
2. Revocation of acceptance must occur within a reasonable time after the buyer discovers or should have discovered the ground for it and before any substantial change in condition of the goods which is not caused by their own defects. It is not effective until the buyer notifies the seller of it.
3. A buyer who so revokes has the same rights and duties with regard to the goods involved as if the buyer had rejected them.

Rooker-Feldman Doctrine

The Rooker-Feldman doctrine has some characteristics of an abstention doctrine, because it prohibits federal court review of state court actions. However, it does not require federal courts to abstain from hearing cases pending action in the state court, but instead deems that federal courts lack jurisdiction to hear cases already fully decided in state courts.

The Rooker-Feldman doctrine is a rule of civil procedure set forth by the United States Supreme Court in two cases, *Rooker v. Fidelity Trust Co.*, 263 U.S. 413 (1923) and *District of Columbia Court of Appeals v. Feldman*, 460 U.S. 462 (1983). The doctrine holds that lower United States federal courts other than the Supreme Court should not sit in direct review of state court decisions unless Congress has specifically authorized such relief. In short, a federal court

---

[1659] *Chiquita Mining Co. v. Fairbanks, Morse & Co.*, 60 Nev. 142, 104 P.2d 191 (1940).

must not become a Court of Appeals for a state court decision. The state court plaintiff has to find a state court remedy.

An example of legislation that has been interpreted to this effect is 28 U.S.C. § 2254, which authorizes federal courts to grant writs of habeas corpus. Another explicit legislative exception to this doctrine was the "Palm Sunday Compromise," a statute passed by Congress to permit federal courts to review the decisions of Florida courts in the Terri Schiavo case.

The doctrine has been held to apply to any state court decisions that are judicial in nature. For example, a judge's decision not to hire an applicant for a job is not a "judicial" decision.

In 2005 the United States Supreme Court revisited the doctrine in *Exxon Mobil Corp. v. Saudi Basic Industries Corp.*, 544 U.S. 280. The Court affirmed that the Rooker-Feldman doctrine was statutory (based on the certiorari jurisdiction statute, 28 U.S.C. § 1257), and not constitutional, holding that it applies only in cases "brought by state-court losers complaining of injuries caused by state-court judgments rendered before the district court proceedings commenced and inviting district court review and rejection of those judgments."

The United States Supreme Court has continued to narrow the doctrine, as in *Lance v. Dennis*, 546 U.S. ____, 126 S. Ct. 1198 (2006), and seems to want to minimize the use of the doctrine. For a mock obituary of the doctrine, see Samuel Bray, *Rooker Feldman* (1923-2006) 9 Green Bag 2d 317.

The Rooker-Feldman doctrine is related to the Anti-Injunction Act, a federal statute which prohibits federal courts from issuing injunctions which stay lawsuits that are pending in state courts. The federal law, 28 U.S.C. § 2283 reads: "A court of the United States may not grant an injunction to stay proceedings in a State court except as expressly authorized by Act of Congress, or where necessary in aid of its jurisdiction, or to protect or effectuate its judgments."

Rule 11 (NRCP 11)

A motion for sanctions under Nevada Rule of Civil Procedure 11 (NRCP 11) is not an affirmative defense per se, but it is a way to deter frivolous filings. Such a motion should be used sparingly, if at all. Sometimes the other side has facts and law that you and your client don't know about. Sometimes your client will fail to inform you about facts that harm her case. It can be embarrassing if the other party wins the case. Opposing counsel filed a Rule 11 against Gerry Spence, who went on to win a $25 million jury verdict in the same case.[1660] The jury must have found that Spence's complaint had merit.

Rule 11 does not apply to discovery violations. For discovery violations, see NRCP 26(g).

Under NRCP 11(c)(1)(a), a lawyer who believes that opposing counsel has violated Rule 11 has to send opposing counsel a Rule 11 motion, but the motion is not filed unless opposing counsel, after 21 days, has failed to withdraw or appropriately correct the pleading. After the 21 days have elapsed, if opposing counsel has not withdrawn or appropriately corrected the pleading, the lawyer may file the Rule 11 motion with the court.

Nevada Rule of Civil Procedure 11, "Signing of Pleadings," provides as follows:

(a) Signature. Every pleading, written motion, and other paper shall be signed by at least one attorney of record in the attorney's individual name, or, if the party is not represented by an attorney, shall be signed by the party. Each paper shall state the signer's address and telephone number, if any. Except when otherwise specifically provided by rule or statute, pleadings need not be verified or accompanied by affidavit. An unsigned paper shall be stricken unless omission of the signature is corrected promptly after being called to the attention of the attorney or party.

(b) Representations to Court. By presenting to the court (whether by signing, filing, submitting, or later advocating) a pleading, written motion, or other paper, an attorney or unrepresented party is certifying that to the best of the person's knowledge, information, and belief, formed after an inquiry reasonable under the circumstances,—

(1) it is not being presented for any improper purpose, such as to harass or to cause unnecessary delay or needless increase in the cost of litigation;

(2) the claims, defenses, and other legal contentions therein are warranted by existing law or by a nonfrivolous argument for the extension, modification, or reversal of existing law or the establishment of new law;

(3) the allegations and other factual contentions have evidentiary support or, if specifically so identified, are likely to have evidentiary support after a reasonable opportunity for further investigation or

---

[1660] See *Trial by Fire* by Gerry Spence, Harper Perennial, 1996.

discovery; and

(4) the denials of factual contentions are warranted on the evidence or, if specifically so identified, are reasonably based on a lack of information or belief.
[As amended; effective January 1, 2005.]

(c) Sanctions. If, after notice and a reasonable opportunity to respond, the court determines that subdivision (b) has been violated, the court may, subject to the conditions stated below, impose an appropriate sanction upon the attorneys, law firms, or parties that have violated subdivision (b) or are responsible for the violation.

(1) How initiated.

(A) By Motion. A motion for sanctions under this rule shall be made separately from other motions or requests and shall describe the specific conduct alleged to violate subdivision (b). It shall be served as provided in Rule 5, but shall not be filed with or presented to the court unless, within 21 days after service of the motion (or such other period as the court may prescribe), the challenged paper, claim, defense, contention, allegation, or denial is not withdrawn or appropriately corrected. If warranted, the court may award to the party prevailing on the motion the reasonable expenses and attorney's fees incurred in presenting or opposing the motion. Absent exceptional circumstances, a law firm shall be held jointly responsible for violations committed by its partners, associates, and employees.

(B) On Court's Initiative. On its own initiative, the court may enter an order describing the specific conduct that appears to violate subdivision (b) and directing an attorney, law firm, or party to show cause why it has not violated subdivision (b) with respect thereto.

(2) Nature of Sanction; Limitations. A sanction imposed for violation of this rule shall be limited to what is sufficient to deter repetition of such conduct or comparable conduct by others similarly situated. Subject to the limitations in subparagraphs (A) and (B), the sanction may consist of, or include, directives of a nonmonetary nature, an order to pay a penalty into court, or, if imposed on motion and warranted for effective deterrence, an order directing payment to the movant of some or all of the reasonable attorney's fees and other expenses incurred as a direct result of the violation.

(A) Monetary sanctions may not be awarded against a represented party for a violation of subdivision (b)(2).

(B) Monetary sanctions may not be awarded on the court's initiative unless the court issues its order to show cause before a voluntary dismissal or settlement of the claims made by or against the party which is, or whose attorneys are, to be sanctioned.

(3) Order. When imposing sanctions, the court shall describe the conduct determined to constitute a violation of this rule and explain the basis for the sanction imposed.

(d) Applicability to Discovery. Subdivisions (a) through (c) of this rule do not apply to disclosures and discovery requests, responses, objections, and motions that are subject to the provisions of Rules 16.1, 16.2, and 26 through 37. Sanctions for refusal to make discovery are governed by Rules 26(g) and 37.

"Good faith" is a state of mind consisting in 1) honesty in belief and purpose, 2) faithfulness to one's duty or obligation, 3) observance of reasonable commercial standards of fair dealing in a given trade or business, or 4) absence of intent to defraud or to seek unconscionable advantage.[1661]
In determining whether a paper has been interposed for an improper purposes, the courts typically use an objective standard. The relevant inquiry is whether the existence of an improper purposes may be inferred from the alleged offender's objective behavior. An improper purposes is any purpose other than one to vindicate rights or to put

---

[1661] *Black's Law Dictionary* 762 (9th ed. 2009).

claims of a right to a proper test.[1662] Failure to make the "reasonable inquiry" as required by Rule 11 is tantamount to a finding of frivolousness, which overlaps with the requirement of proper purpose as contemplated by Rule 11.[1663] A district court confronted with solid evidence of a pleading's frivolousness may in circumstances that warrant it infer that it was filed for an improper purposes.[1664]

Where the trial court, after erroneously assuming process to have been served, struck defendant's motion to dismiss as being a sham or otherwise in violation of NRCP 11, without justification under such rule, and ordered a default and judgment thereon entered without allowing time for a responsive pleading in violation of NRCP 12(a), and without notice of hearing in violation of NRCP 55(b)(2), and denied a timely motion to vacate the judgment, the judgment was vacated on appeal with directions to proceed in accordance with rules.[1665]

The signature of the attorney for a defendant on a motion to dismiss the complaint presumptively constituted the certificate required under NRCP 11 as to the propriety of the motion.[1666]

A motion could not have been interposed for delay where the defendant had never been served; so the time was not running against him. Where defendant has never been served with summons and complaint, a motion to dismiss the complaint filed by him could not have been interposed for delay, because his time for appearance was not running against him, and the order to strike the motion on that ground under NRCP 11 was an error.[1667]

Where a motion to dismiss the complaint was properly signed and was not interposed for delay, and there was no indication that it was a sham, false or that it otherwise violated NRCP 11, it was error to strike such motion on the basis of that rule.[1668]

The effect, under NRCP 11, of the attorney's signature on a motion to set aside a default as a certification does not alone constitute a showing of a meritorious defense.[1669] A violation of the rule did not justify an order to strike an ex parte motion without notice to the defendant. In an action to enjoin a nuisance, where the answer did not contain an acknowledgment or the pleader's address as required by NRCP 11, the order to strike answer which was granted on the oral ex parte motion of counsel for plaintiff, without notice to the defendant as required by NRCP 5 and NRCP 7, was erroneous, and it necessarily followed that the default judgment based on such order was erroneous.[1670]

The failure of an answer to contain the defendant's address as required by NRCP 11, is an irregularity capable of being waived and it does not vitiate the answer. This rule applies particularly where the adverse party knows the defendant's address.[1671]

Where an answer failed to contain an acknowledgment as required by NRCP 11, the absence of the acknowledgment was a defect which was not jurisdictional and it did not vitiate the answer.[1672]

A defective answer under the rule should not be treated as a nullity unless the pleader is given an opportunity to correct the default and fails to do so. An answer that was defective with respect to an acknowledgment and address of the pleader under NRCP 11 should not be treated as a nullity unless the pleader is given the opportunity to correct the defect and fails to do so. Such opportunity should be given on a motion to strike.[1673]

An absence of an acknowledgment is a ground for a motion to strike or to set aside the pleading; pleading cannot be treated as nullity. Absence of an acknowledgment in an answer as required by NRCP 11 is a defect in a pleading which is not jurisdictional. Such omission furnishes a ground for a motion to strike or set aside a pleading. An adverse party cannot, without objection, safely disregard a pleading and treat it as a nullity, nor can a court disregard it without affording the opportunity to the pleader to supply an acknowledgment.[1674]

Defendant should be afforded opportunity to cure answer which did not contain acknowledgment or address of

---

[1662] See *McClerin v. R-M Industries, Inc.*, 118 N.C. App. 640, 456 S.E.2d 352, 355 (1995), citing *Mack v. Moore*, 107 N.C. App. 87, 418 S.E.2d 685, 689 (1992). To the same accord, see *Silva v. Witschen*, 19 F.3d 725, C.A. 1 (R.I.), 1994.

[1663] See generally *Townsend v. Holman Consulting Corporation*, 929 F.2d 1358 (9th Cir. 1990)

[1664] *Id.* at 1365.

[1665] *Gull v. Hoalst*, 77 Nev. 54, 359 P.2d 383 (1961), cited, Cheek v. Bell, 80 Nev. 244, at 247, 391 P.2d 735 (1954), see also *Havas v. Engebregson*, 97 Nev. 408, at 411, 633 P.2d 682 (1981).

[1666] *Gull v. Hoalst*, 77 Nev. 54, 359 P.2d 383 (1961).

[1667] *Id.*

[1668] *Id.*

[1669] *Kelso v. Kelso*, 78 Nev. 99, 369 P.2d 668 (1962).

[1670] *Cheek v. Bell*, 80 Nev. 244, 391 P.2d 735 (1964).

[1671] *Id.*

[1672] *Cheek v. Bell*, 80 Nev. 244, 391 P.2d 735 (1964), cited, *Gregerson v. Collins*, 80 Nev. 452, at 453, 396 P.2d 27 (1964).

[1673] *Id.*

[1674] *Id.*

261

defendant. Where answer did not contain acknowledgment or address of defendant as required by NRCP 11, and order to strike was granted on oral ex parte motion of counsel for plaintiff, without notice to defendant as required by NRCP 5 and 7, such order and default judgment based on such order were erroneous, and trial court should have granted motion by defendant to set aside judgment and afford defendant opportunity to cure his defective pleading.[1675]

Under NRCP 11, the signature of attorney to complaint constitutes certificate by him that to the best of his knowledge and belief there is good ground to support allegations contained in complaint.[1676] Where the complaint in a civil action was verified but not acknowledged as required by NRCP 11, the trial court properly granted leave to file an amended complaint and denied defendant's motion for summary judgment. Former D.C.R. 30 (cf. D.C.R. 20), which provides that no effect shall be given to leading in propria persona which is not acknowledged, does not apply to this situation.[1677]

A motion to amend under NRCP 15(a), made after the statute of limitations had run under NRS 137.080, should have been granted and given retroactive effect under NRCP 15(c) to the date of the original proceeding to cure defective pleading under former D.C.R. 30 (cf. D.C.R. 20) and NRCP 11, which requires acknowledgment of pleading in person, because defect was not jurisdictional, was unrelated to the merits of the controversy and without prejudice to the rights of either.[1678]

On appeal from summary judgment for plaintiff in an action to recover a labor claim under NRS 608.150, the fact that the complaint was unverified and no supporting affidavits were filed with the motion for summary judgment did not affect the propriety of the judgment because no statute or special rule required that a complaint filed under NRS 608.150 be verified. Also, under NRCP 11, pleadings need not be verified or accompanied by an affidavit unless to do so is specifically provided by a rule or statute.[1679]

Where a complaint was signed by an out-of-state counsel without his address and was not signed by an active member of the State Bar of Nevada, and the amended complaint signed by Nevada counsel was not filed until more than 18 months later, the action of the district court dismissing complaint, based on the conclusion that the plaintiff or out-of-state counsel, or both, deliberately violated NRCP 11, S.C.R. 42 and former D.C.R. 30 (cf. D.C.R. 20) in an effort to keep lawsuit viable while avoiding the cost of associating Nevada counsel, was not abuse of discretion and was upheld on appeal.[1680]

A party to an action is not entitled to attorney's fees for a frivolous counterclaim under certain circumstances. In action for breach of warranty, fraud and deceptive trade practices, where defendants filed counterclaim seeking damages for breach of alleged accord and satisfaction and malicious abuse of legal process, but consented to dismissal of their counterclaim with prejudice when plaintiff accepted their offer of judgment, plaintiff was not entitled to attorney's fees under NRCP 11 on ground that counterclaim was frivolous and abuse of process because (1) there were sufficient grounds to support it, (2) there was no indication that it was filed for improper purpose, and (3) defendants' consent to its dismissal expressly stated that it was based on acceptance of offer of judgment.[1681]

An award of attorney's fees under NRCP 11 is within sound discretion of district court and will not be disturbed upon appeal absent manifest abuse of that discretion.[1682]

Where the district court erred in deciding a motion to dismiss appellant's claim and had also ruled against appellant's motion for sanctions under NRCP 11 in the form of attorney's fees, the district court was required to reconsider on remand whether an attorney's fee should be awarded.[1683]

Where an attorney's decision to file an action for attorney malpractice before the conclusion of the underlying civil action was warranted by ambiguities in existing law and was founded upon a reasonable belief that the statute of limitations might preclude the action if it were filed at a later date, the imposition of sanctions against the attorney under

---

[1675] *Id.*

[1676] *Dzack v. Marshall*, 80 Nev. 345, 393 P.2d 610 (1964).

[1677] *Gregerson v. Collins*, 80 Nev. 452, 396 P.2d 27 (1964), cited, *Tehansky v. Wilson*, 83 Nev. 263, at 264, 428 P.2d 375 (1967).

[1678] *Tehansky v. Wilson*, 83 Nev. 263, 428 P.2d 375 (1967), distinguished, *Knight v. Witco Chem. Co.*, 89 Nev. 586, at 587, 517 P.2d 792 (1973).

[1679] *Tobler & Oliver Constr. Co. v. Board of Trustees*, 84 Nev. 438, 442 P.2d 904 (1968).

[1680] *Naimo v. Fleming*, 95 Nev. 13, 588 P.2d 1025 (1979), cited, *Barr v. Gaines*, 103 Nev. 548, at 551, 746 P.2d 634 (1987), distinguished, *Ford Motor Credit Co. v. Crawford*, 109 Nev. 616, at 620, 855 P.2d 1024 (1993).

[1681] *Works v. Kuhn*, 103 Nev. 65, 732 P.2d 1373 (1987).

[1682] *Barr v. Gaines*, 103 Nev. 548, 746 P.2d 634 (1987), cited, *Sharpstown Gen. Hosp. v. Laborers Health & Welfare Trust Fund*, 110 Nev. 431, at 434, 874 P.2d 728 (1994), see also *State, Dep't of Motor Vehicles & Public Safety v. Clements*, 106 Nev. 516, at 519, 520, 796 P.2d 588 (1990).

[1683] *Marine Midland Bank v. Monroe*, 104 Nev. 307, 756 P.2d 1193 (1988).

NRCP 11 was improper and was reversed on appeal.[1684]

Where an attorney unsuccessfully attempted in good faith to have the district court recognize a new cause of action for invasion of the right to privacy, the district court abused its discretion in imposing monetary sanctions against attorney under NRCP 11, because while sanctions should be imposed for frivolous actions, to do so in this case would have chilling effect. Sanctions pursuant to NRCP 11 are not intended to chill an attorney's enthusiasm or creativity in reasonably pursuing factual or legal theories, and the court should avoid employing the wisdom of hindsight in analyzing the attorney's action at the time of the pleading.[1685]

As with a decision to award attorney's fees, the Nevada Supreme Court must review a trial court's decision to deny imposition of sanctions pursuant to NRCP 11 under the abuse of discretion standard.[1686]

Sanctions under NRCP 11 should be imposed for frivolous actions. A frivolous claim is one that is both baseless and made without reasonable and competent inquiry. Thus, in determining whether a claim is frivolous, court must determine if pleading is well grounded in fact and is warranted by existing law or good faith argument for extension, modification or reversal of existing law and must determine if attorney made reasonable and competent inquiry.[1687]

Where a judge of the trial court in a civil action threatened plaintiff's counsel with sanctions under NRCP 11 if plaintiff lost the case, and advised the attorneys that the judge was fed up with spurious lawsuits, the threat of sanctions was improper because, although plaintiff's case, in retrospect, was quite marginal, the plaintiff had the right to proceed to trial without being made subject to a threat of sanctions.[1688]

Appellant's argument for sanctions was without merit under the circumstances. Where the appellant requested sanctions against the respondent pursuant to NRCP 11 on the basis of the respondent's alleged failure to properly authenticate certain exhibits, the Supreme Court held that the appellant's argument was without merit because: (1) the alleged defects in authentication had been cured before the final disposition in the court below; and (2) several of the exhibits appeared to have been self-authenticating.[1689]

The imposition of sanctions constituted a manifest abuse of discretion where the district court erroneously interpreted the applicable law. Where the district court erroneously interpreted the applicable law concerning the enforcement by this State of a child support order issued by another state and imposed sanctions against the district attorney pursuant to NRCP 11 for enforcing the child support order, the court held that the district court's erroneous interpretation of the applicable law constituted a manifest abuse of discretion. A writ of mandamus was issued (see NRS 34.160) to vacate the order imposing sanctions.[1690]

A court must use a four-factor analysis when determining whether to impose an order restricting the access of vexatious litigants to court access. First, the litigant must be provided reasonable notice of and an opportunity to oppose a restrictive order's issuance. Second, the district court must create an adequate record for review, including a list of all the cases and documents, or an explanation of the reasons, that led it to conclude that a restrictive order was needed to curb repetitive or abusive activities. Third, the district court must make substantive findings as to the frivolous or harassing nature of the litigant's actions. Finally, the order must be narrowly drawn to address the specific problem encountered.[1691]

The district court improperly awarded attorney's fees as sanctions. A district court granted summary judgment against the plaintiff in a False Claims Act (FCA) action and awarded attorney's fees as sanctions under NRCP 11 and NRS 357.180. In determining that the FCA action was not well grounded in fact or in existing law, the district court's only finding was that the plaintiff had instituted four proceedings alleging misappropriation of funds by the University and Community College System of Nevada (now Nevada System of Higher Education) in regard to part-time instructors' salaries and not one was successful. The Nevada Supreme Court concluded that the district court abused its discretion in awarding attorney's fees. First, the FCA action was not clearly frivolous because the FCA did not expressly state that a plaintiff may not sue the State and no prior Nevada decisional law so interpreted the FCA. Next, the district court made

[1684] *K.J.B., Inc. v. Drakulich*, 107 Nev. 367, 811 P.2d 1305 (1991).

[1685] *Marshall v. Eighth Judicial Dist. Court*, 108 Nev. 459, 836 P.2d 47 (1992), cited, *Bergmann v. Boyce*, 109 Nev. 670, at 676, 856 P.2d 560 (1993), *Lewis v. Second Judicial Dist. Court*, 113 Nev. 106, at 113, 930 P.2d 770 (1997).

[1686] *Bergmann v. Boyce*, 109 Nev. 670, 856 P.2d 560 (1993), cited, *Washoe County Dist. Att'y v. Second Judicial Dist. Court*, 116 Nev. 629, at 636, 5 P.3d 562 (2000), *Richardson Construction, Inc. v. Clark County School Dist.*, 123 Nev. 61, at 64, 156 P.3d 21 (2007).

[1687] *Bergmann v. Boyce*, 109 Nev. 670, 856 P.2d 560 (1993), cited, *Russ v. General Motors Corp.*, 111 Nev. 1431, at 1439, 906 P.2d 718 (1995), *Simonian v. Univ. & Cmty. Coll. Sys.*, 122 Nev. 187, at 196, 128 P.3d 1057 (2006).

[1688] *Horton v. Fritz*, 113 Nev. 824, 942 P.2d 134 (1997).

[1689] *Barmettler v. Reno Air, Inc.* 114 Nev. 441, 956 P.2d 1382 (1998).

[1690] *Washoe County Dist. Att'y v. Second Judicial Dist. Court*, 116 Nev. 629, 5 P.3d 562 (2000).

[1691] *Jordan v. State ex rel. Dep't of Motor Veh. & Pub. Safety*, 121 Nev. 44, 110 P.3d 30 (2005).

no findings of harassment based on the three earlier proceedings. Finally, the merits of the misappropriation issue were addressed in only one of those proceedings, an administrative decision under NRS 281.641 on the plaintiff's allegations of retaliation by a community college. Because the hearing officer was not required to determine the merits of the misappropriation allegations in the retaliation proceeding, and because those allegations did not arise under the FCA, the administrative decision could not be used to show that the plaintiff's FCA claim was unfounded in fact or law. (N.B., this opinion applied the version of NRCP 11 preceding its amendment effective January 1, 2005.)[1692]

A hearing officer's unauthorized determination was not a basis for attorney's fees sanctions. A community college instructor requested a hearing with the Department of Personnel (now Division of Human Resource Management of the Department of Administration) under NRS 281.641, asserting that the community college retaliated against him by refusing to renew his contract because he had alleged that the University and Community College System of Nevada (UCCSN) (now Nevada System of Higher Education) had misappropriated state funds. A hearing officer found that the instructor had not proven his retaliation claim, in part because he had not demonstrated success on the merits of his underlying misappropriation allegations. The Nevada Supreme Court concluded that because the hearing officer was not authorized to determine the merits of those allegations, the determination could not be the basis for a district court's award of attorney's fees against the instructor in an action he later brought against UCCSN. (See NRCP 11 and NRS 357.180.) NRS 281.641 protects a state employee "who discloses information concerning improper governmental action" from retaliatory action.

No statute specifically authorizes hearing officers to independently determine whether the government has actually undertaken improper action. The legislative purpose of NRS 281.641 was to encourage persons to come forward with information of employer wrongdoing, and this could be thwarted if a person was only protected if the allegations are proven correct. And NRS 281.651 separately addresses any improper conduct on a state employee's part, providing that an employee may not use the disclosure provisions to harass and explaining that those provisions do not prohibit proper disciplinary procedures against an employee who discloses untruthful information. Thus, with respect to a retaliation claim, the hearing officer must only determine whether a state employee has engaged in protected activity, *i.e.*, has disclosed information concerning improper governmental action. As a result, the hearing officer's determination in this case regarding whether the instructor's allegations proved correct was unauthorized. (N.B., this opinion applied the version of NRCP 11 preceding its amendment effective January 1, 2005.)[1693]

Safety of Employee (ADA)

The Americans with Disabilities Act (ADA) permits employers to establish qualification standards that will exclude individuals who pose a direct threat–*i.e.*, a significant risk of substantial harm–to the health or safety of the individual or of others, if that risk cannot be eliminated or reduced below the level of a "direct threat" by reasonable accommodation. But an employer may not simply assume that a threat exists; the employer must establish through objective, medically supportable methods that there is significant risk that substantial harm could occur in the workplace. By requiring employers to make individualized judgments based on reliable medical or other objective evidence rather than on generalizations, ignorance, fear, patronizing attitudes, or stereotypes, the ADA recognizes the need to balance the interests of people with disabilities against the legitimate interests of employers in maintaining a safe workplace.

The federal statute, 42 U.S.C. § 12111(3), provides as follows:

> The term "direct threat" means a significant risk to the health or safety of others that cannot be eliminated by reasonable accommodation.

The federal statute, 42 U.S.C. § 12113, "Defenses," provides as follows:

> a) In general − It may be a defense to a charge of discrimination under this Chapter that an alleged application of qualification standards, tests, or selection criteria that screen out or tend to screen out or otherwise deny a job or benefit to an individual with a disability has been shown to be job-related and consistent with business necessity, and such performance cannot be accomplished by reasonable accommodation, as required under this subchapter.

> (b) Qualification standards − The term qualification standards may include a requirement that an individual shall not pose a direct threat to the health or safety of other individuals in the workplace.

[1692] *Simonian v. Univ. & Cmty. Coll. Sys.*, 122 Nev. 187, 128 P.3d 1057 (2006).
[1693] *Id.*

The federal regulation, 29 C.F.R. § 1630.2(r), provides as follows:

> The determination that an individual poses a direct threat shall be based on an individualized assessment of the individual's present ability to safely perform the essential functions of the job. This assessment shall be based on a reasonable medical judgment that relies on the most current medical knowledge and/or on the best available objective evidence.

> In determining whether an individual would pose a direct threat, the factors to be considered include:

> (1) The duration of the risk;
> (2) The nature and severity of the potential harm;
> (3) The likelihood that the potential harm will occur; and
> (4) The imminence of the potential harm.

The federal regulation, 29 C.F.R. § 1630.15(b), "Charges of discriminatory application of selection criteria," provides as follows:

> (1) In general. It may be a defense to a charge of discrimination, as described in Sec. 1630.10, that an alleged application of qualification standards, tests, or selection criteria that screens out or tends to screen out or otherwise denies a job or benefit to an individual with a disability has been shown to be job-related and consistent with business necessity, and such performance cannot be accomplished with reasonable accommodation, as required in this part.

> (2) Direct threat as a qualification standard. The term qualification standard may include a requirement that an individual shall not pose a direct threat to the health or safety of the individual or others in the workplace.

Set-off

Set-off is an equitable remedy that should be granted when justice so requires to prevent inequity.[1694] Set-off is a form of counterclaim that a defendant may urge by way of defense or to obtain a judgment for whatever balance is due.[1695] Set-off is a doctrine used to extinguish the mutual indebtedness of parties who each owe a debt to one another.[1696] The claims that give rise to a set-off need not arise out of the same transaction; they may be entirely unrelated.[1697] Insolvency of one of the parties is not necessary to obtain a set-off between two mutually indebted parties.[1698] Set-off should be allowed in cases where both parties are solvent, but is especially necessary in cases where one party is insolvent to protect the interests of the solvent party.[1699] The purpose behind the doctrine of set-off is to allow mutually indebted parties to apply the debts of the other so that by mutual reduction everything but the difference is extinguished.[1700] Set-off serves the interests of efficiency by allowing two parties with mutual claims of indebtedness to extinguish their debts against one another in a single proceeding.[1701]

Sole Negligence of Co-defendant

Where the defendant claimed that sole negligence on the part of a third person was the proximate cause of plaintiff's injuries. The court said: "A claim on the part of a defendant that plaintiff's injuries were proximately caused by the negligent acts of a person other than the defendant is but another form of a general denial. It does not create a separate issue and does not furnish any basis for the application of the two-issue rule." In an Ohio case,[1702] the court held the rule not applicable when the judgment was for the plaintiff, but only where the judgment was for the defendant.[1703] The cases hereinafter cited uphold the contrary rule, namely, that where two or more material issues are tried and

---

[1694] *Aviation Ventures v. Joan Morris, Inc.*, 121 Nev. 113, 119, 110 P.3d 59 (2005).

[1695] *Id.* at 119-120.

[1696] *Id.* at 120.

[1697] *Id.*

[1698] *Id.* at 121.

[1699] *Id.*

[1700] *Id.*

[1701] *Id.*

[1702] *Cincinnati State Railway Co. v. Keehan*, 186 N.E. 812 (Ohio Ct.App. 1932).

[1703] See also *Bush v. Harvey Transfer Co..*, 67 N.E.2d 851 (Ohio 1946).

submitted to the jury and the verdict is a general one, it cannot be upheld if there was error as to any one of the two or more issues. The reasoning of the cases supporting this rule appears to us to be the better logic, and this is well illustrated by the circumstances of the present case.[1704]

Sovereign Immunity

Sovereign immunity is a government's immunity from being sued in its own courts without its consent.[1705] It is also a state's immunity from being sued in federal court by the state's own citizens.[1706]

NRS 41.032(2) grants the State and its political subdivisions sovereign immunity from civil liability when the challenged act was discretionary in nature.[1707]

NRS 41.031(3) provides as follows: "The State of Nevada does not waive its immunity from suit conferred by Amendment XI of the Constitution of the United States."

Spoliation

"Spoliation" is defined as follows:

1: the destruction, alteration, or mutilation of evidence esp. by a party for whom the evidence is damaging.
2: alteration or mutilation of an instrument (as a will) by one who is not a party to the instrument.[1708]

Nevada does not recognize an independent tort for spoliation of evidence. Although a minority of jurisdictions have recognized an independent cause of action in tort based upon spoliation of evidence, the supreme court of Nevada has declined to do so. The Nevada Supreme Court concurred with the determination of the supreme court of California that the benefits of recognizing such a cause of action "are outweighed by the burden to litigants, witnesses, and the judicial system that would be imposed by potentially endless litigation over a speculative loss, and by the cost to society of promoting onerous record and evidence retention policies."[1709]

But there is rebuttable presumption that evidence of spoliations is adverse to the party who has suppressed or destroyed material evidence. The Court may draw a presumption adverse to the Defendants from their suppression of material evidence.[1710]

NRS 47.250 allows for disputable presumptions to be made by a jury in certain situations. The list includes a presumption "[t]hat evidence willfully suppressed would be adverse if produced." The list provided by that statute "is illustrative, not exclusive."[1711]

The Nevada Supreme Court addressed the issue of spoliation of evidence in *Bass-Davis v. Davis*.[1712] In that case the Court clarified the differences in the trial court's treatment of evidence that is "willfully suppressed" and evidence that is "negligently lost or destroyed."

Where the evidence is willfully suppressed, NRS 47.250(3) applies and a disputable (or rebuttable) presumption is made: When the evidence is negligently lost or destroyed, an adverse inference applies. Good practice is for counsel to obtain and preserve video tapes and DVDs (and other information) when counsel first becomes involved in a case. This minimizes allegations by the adverse party that they did not know a claim or lawsuit might be made in the future.

In general, the Nevada Supreme Court means to punish those who act intentionally to a greater degree than those who act negligently. In *Bass-Davis,* the Nevada Supreme Court held that before a rebuttable presumption that willfully suppressed evidence was adverse to the destroying party applies, the party seeking the presumption's benefit has the burden of demonstrating that the evidence was destroyed with intent to harm.[1713]

When evidence is produced to establish that evidence was destroyed with intent to harm, the presumption that the evidence was adverse applies, and the burden of proof shifts to the party who destroyed the evidence.[1714]

[1704] *Heinen v. Heinen*, 64 Nev. 527, 542 (1947).

[1705] *Black's Law Dictionary* 818 (9th ed. 2009).

[1706] *Id.*

[1707] *Ransdell v. Clark County*, 124 Nev. 847, 854, 192 P.3d 756 (2008).

[1708] Findlaw's Legal Dictionary (at http://dictionary.lp.findlaw.com/index.html).

[1709] *Timber Tech. Eng'd Bldg. Prods. v. The Home Ins. Co.*, 118 Nev. 630, 55 P.3d 952 (2002). See also NRS Chapters 41, 47, and 52.

[1710] See *Fire Ins. Exchange v. Zenith Radio Corp.*, 103 Nev. 648, 747 P.2d 911 (1987).

[1711] See *Privette v. Faulkner*, 92 Nev. 353, 550 P.2d 404 (1976).

[1712] *Bass-Davis v. Davis*, 122 Nev. 442, 451-53, 134 P.3d 103, 109-10 (2006).

[1713] *Id.*

[1714] *Id.* at 448.

To rebut the presumption that destroyed evidence was adverse to the destroying party, the destroying party must then prove, by a preponderance of the evidence, that the destroyed evidence was not unfavorable; if not rebutted, the fact-finder then presumes that the evidence was adverse to the destroying party.[1715]

An intentional or willful destruction of the evidence could support a presumption unfavorable to the destroyer; however, the mere inability to produce the evidence would support an adverse inference rather than a presumption.[1716] Generally, in cases based on negligently lost or destroyed evidence, an adverse inference instruction is tied to a showing that the party controlling the evidence had notice that it was relevant at the time when the evidence was lost or destroyed.[1717]

The prelitigation duty to preserve evidence is imposed once a party is on notice of a potential legal claim.[1718]

A permissible inference that missing evidence would be adverse applied when evidence was negligently lost or destroyed by a party who possessed the evidence, while a rebuttable presumption applied for willful destruction of evidence.[1719]

A person "is under a duty to preserve what it knows, or reasonably should know, is relevant to the action, is reasonably calculated to lead to the discovery of admissible evidence, is reasonably likely to be requested during discovery, and/or is the subject of a pending discovery request."[1720] As you can see, if you (the lawyer) have evidence that is relevant to the factual issues of a case (or a potential case), it is better to keep and preserve it than to risk the Court allowing the other side a presumption that the information would have been favorable to their case.

Statute of Frauds

NRS 111.205, "No estate created in land unless by operation of law or written conveyance; leases for terms not exceeding 1 year," provides as follows:

> 1. No estate or interest in lands, other than for leases for a term not exceeding 1 year, nor any trust or power over or concerning lands, or in any manner relating thereto, shall be created, granted, assigned, surrendered or declared after December 2, 1861, unless by act or operation of law, or by deed or conveyance, in writing, subscribed by the party creating, granting, assigning, surrendering or declaring the same, or by the party's lawful agent thereunto authorized in writing.
>
> 2. Subsection 1 shall not be construed to affect in any manner the power of a testator in the disposition of the testator's real property by a last will and testament, nor to prevent any trust from arising or being extinguished by implication or operation of law.

NRS 111.210, "Contracts for sale or lease of land for periods in excess of 1 year void unless in writing," provides as follows:

> 1. Every contract for the leasing for a longer period than 1 year, or for the sale of any lands, or any interest in lands, shall be void unless the contract, or some note or memorandum thereof, expressing the consideration, be in writing, and be subscribed by the party by whom the lease or sale is to be made.
>
> 2. Every instrument required to be subscribed by any person under subsection 1 may be subscribed by the agent of the party lawfully authorized.

NRS 111.220, "Agreements not in writing: When void," provides as follows:

> In the following cases every agreement is void, unless the agreement, or some note or memorandum thereof expressing the consideration, is in writing, and subscribed by the person charged therewith:
> 1. Every agreement that, by the terms, is not to be performed within 1 year from the making thereof.
> 2. Every special promise to answer for the debt, default or miscarriage of another.
> 3. Every promise or undertaking made upon consideration of marriage, except mutual promises to marry.
> 4. Every promise or commitment to loan money or to grant or extend credit in an original principal

---

[1715] *Id.*

[1716] *Id.* at 449.

[1717] *Id.* at 449-50.

[1718] *Id.* at 450.

[1719] *Id.*, overruling *Reingold v. Wet 'n Wild Nevada, Inc.*, 113 Nev. 967, 944 P.2d 800 (1997), and *Bohlmann v. Printz*, 120 Nev. 543, 96 P.3d 1155 (2004). NRS 47.250(3).

[1720] *Wm. T. Thompson Co. v. General Nutrition Corp.*, 593 F.Supp. 1443, 1455 (C.D. Cal. 1984).

amount of at least $100,000 made by a person engaged in the business of lending money or extending credit.

   5. Every promise or commitment to pay a fee for obtaining a loan of money or an extension of credit for another person if the fee is $1,000 or more.

NRS 111.235, "Grants and assignments of existing trusts to be in writing or are void," provides as follows: "Every grant or assignment of any existing trust in lands, goods or things in action, unless the same shall be in writing, subscribed by the person making the same, or by his or her agent lawfully authorized, shall be void."

   Where the district court admitted a written but unsigned property settlement agreement as a hearing exhibit, the draft otherwise met the requirements for an enforceable contract, and the district court approved the oral stipulation by minute order, the procedure complied with applicable district court rules and obviated any issue as to the statute of frauds.[1721]

   The statute of frauds does not apply to a writing that is subsequently lost or destroyed, and oral evidence is admissible to prove the existence and terms of that lost or destroyed writing.[1722]

Statute of Limitations

   The Nevada Supreme Court has concluded "that, in general, statutory limitations periods may be reduced by contract provided there is no statute to the contrary and the reduced limitations period is reasonable and does not violate public policy."[1723]

   Nevada lawyers probably use NRS 11.190 most often as to issues with the statute of limitations. But the whole section in NRS Chapter 11 is important. Some sections are set forth here. After that, I have set forth the statute on medical malpractice.

NRS 11.010, "Commencement of civil actions," provides as follows: "Civil actions can only be commenced within the periods prescribed in this Chapter, after the cause of action shall have accrued, except where a different limitation is prescribed by statute."

NRS 11.020, "Effect of laws of limitation of other states or countries," provides as follows:

   When a cause of action has arisen in another state, or in a foreign country, and by the laws thereof an action thereon cannot there be maintained against a person by reason of the lapse of time, an action thereon shall not be maintained against the person in this State, except in favor of a citizen thereof who has held the cause of action from the time it accrued.

Real Property

NRS 11.030, "When action cannot be brought by grantee from this State," provides as follows: "No action can be brought for or in respect to real property by any person claiming under letters patent, or grants from this State, unless the same might have been commenced by the State as herein specified in case such patent had not been issued or grant made."

NRS 11.040, "When actions by State or its grantees are to be brought within 7 years," provides as follows:

   When letters patent or grants of real property issued or made by this state are declared void by the determination of a competent court, an action for the recovery of the property so conveyed may be brought, either by the State, or by any subsequent patentee or grantee of the property, his or her heirs or assigns, within 7 years after such determination, but not after that period.

NRS 11.060, "Action for recovery of mining claims: Occupation and possession; other applicable provisions," provides as follows:

   1. No action for the recovery of mining claims, or for the recovery of the possession thereof, shall be maintained, unless it appears that the plaintiff, or those through or from whom the plaintiff claims, were seized

---

[1721] *Grisham v. Grisham*, 128 Nev., Advance Opinion 60 (12/06/12).

[1722] *Khan v. Bakhsh*, 129 Nev., Advance Opinion 57 (2013).

[1723] *Holcomb Condominium Homeowners' Association v. Stewart Venture LLC*, 129 Nev., Advance Opinion 18 (April 4, 2013).

or possessed of such mining claim, or were the owners thereof, according to the laws and customs of the district embracing the same, within 2 years before the commencement of such action.

    2. Occupation and adverse possession of a mining claim shall consist in holding and working the same, in the usual and customary mode of holding and working similar claims in the vicinity thereof.

    3. All of the provisions of this Chapter which apply to other real estate, so far as applicable, shall be deemed to include and apply to mining claims; provided,

    (a) That in such application "2 years" shall be held to be the period intended whenever the term "5 years" is used; and

    (b) That when the terms "legal title" or "title" are used, they shall be held to include title acquired by location or occupation, according to the usages, laws and customs of the district embracing the claim.

NRS 11.070, "No cause of action effectual unless party or predecessor seized or possessed within 5 years," provides as follows:

    No cause of action or defense to an action, founded upon the title to real property, or to rents or to services out of the same, shall be effectual, unless it appears that the person prosecuting the action or making the defense, or under whose title the action is prosecuted or the defense is made, or the ancestor, predecessor, or grantor of such person, was seized or possessed of the premises in question within 5 years before the committing of the act in respect to which said action is prosecuted or defense made.

NRS 11.190, "Periods of limitation," provides as follows:

Except as otherwise provided in NRS 125B.050 and 217.007, actions other than those for the recovery of real property, unless further limited by specific statute, may only be commenced as follows:

    1. Within 6 years:
    (a) An action upon a judgment or decree of any court of the United States, or of any state or territory within the United States, or the renewal thereof.
    (b) An action upon a contract, obligation or liability founded upon an instrument in writing, except those mentioned in the preceding sections of this Chapter.
    2. Within 4 years:
    (a) An action on an open account for goods, wares and merchandise sold and delivered.
    (b) An action for any article charged on an account in a store.
    (c) An action upon a contract, obligation or liability not founded upon an instrument in writing.
    (d) An action against a person alleged to have committed a deceptive trade practice in violation of NRS 598.0903 to 598.0999, inclusive, but the cause of action shall be deemed to accrue when the aggrieved party discovers, or by the exercise of due diligence should have discovered, the facts constituting the deceptive trade practice.
    3. Within 3 years:
    (a) An action upon a liability created by statute, other than a penalty or forfeiture.
    (b) An action for waste or trespass of real property, but when the waste or trespass is committed by means of underground works upon any mining claim, the cause of action shall be deemed to accrue upon the discovery by the aggrieved party of the facts constituting the waste or trespass.
    (c) An action for taking, detaining or injuring personal property, including actions for specific recovery thereof, but in all cases where the subject of the action is a domestic animal usually included in the term "livestock," which has a recorded mark or brand upon it at the time of its loss, and which strays or is stolen from the true owner without the owner's fault, the statute does not begin to run against an action for the recovery of the animal until the owner has actual knowledge of such facts as would put a reasonable person upon inquiry as to the possession thereof by the defendant.
    (d) Except as otherwise provided in NRS 112.230 and 166.170, an action for relief on the ground of fraud or mistake, but the cause of action in such a case shall be deemed to accrue upon the discovery by the aggrieved party of the facts constituting the fraud or mistake.
    (e) An action pursuant to NRS 40.750 for damages sustained by a financial institution or other lender because of its reliance on certain fraudulent conduct of a borrower, but the cause of action in such a case shall be deemed to accrue upon the discovery by the financial institution or other lender of the facts constituting the concealment or false statement.
    4. Within 2 years:

(a) An action against a sheriff, coroner or constable upon liability incurred by acting in his or her official capacity and in virtue of his or her office, or by the omission of an official duty, including the nonpayment of money collected upon an execution.

(b) An action upon a statute for a penalty or forfeiture, where the action is given to a person or the State, or both, except when the statute imposing it prescribes a different limitation.

(c) An action for libel, slander, assault, battery, false imprisonment or seduction.

(d) An action against a sheriff or other officer for the escape of a prisoner arrested or imprisoned on civil process.

(e) Except as otherwise provided in NRS 11.215, an action to recover damages for injuries to a person or for the death of a person caused by the wrongful act or neglect of another. The provisions of this paragraph relating to an action to recover damages for injuries to a person apply only to causes of action which accrue after March 20, 1951.

(f) An action to recover damages under NRS 41.740.

5. Within 1 year:

(a) An action against an officer, or officer de facto to recover goods, wares, merchandise or other property seized by the officer in his or her official capacity, as tax collector, or to recover the price or value of goods, wares, merchandise or other personal property so seized, or for damages for the seizure, detention or sale of, or injury to, goods, wares, merchandise or other personal property seized, or for damages done to any person or property in making the seizure.

(b) An action against an officer, or officer de facto for money paid to the officer under protest, or seized by the officer in his or her official capacity, as a collector of taxes, and which, it is claimed, ought to be refunded.

NRS 11.080, "Seisin within 5 years; when necessary in action for real property," provides as follows: "No action for the recovery of real property, or for the recovery of the possession thereof other than mining claims, shall be maintained, unless it appears that the plaintiff or the plaintiff's ancestor, predecessor or grantor was seized or possessed of the premises in question, within 5 years before the commencement thereof."

NRS 11.090, "Peaceable entry; when not valid as claim," provides as follows: "No peaceable entry upon real estate shall be deemed sufficient and valid as a claim, unless an action be commenced by the plaintiff for possession within 1 year from the making of such entry, or within 5 years from the time when the right to bring such action accrued."

NRS 11.100, "Possession presumed in legal owner unless adversely held," provides as follows:

In every action for the recovery of real property, or the possession thereof, the person establishing a legal title to the premises shall be presumed to have been possessed thereof within the time prescribed by law; and the occupation of such premises by any other person shall be deemed to have been under and in subordination to the legal title, unless it shall appear:

1. That is has been protected by a substantial enclosure; or
2. That it has been cultivated or improved in accordance with the usual and ordinary methods of husbandry.

NRS 11.110, "Occupation under written instrument or judgment; when deemed adverse," provides as follows:

Whenever it shall appear that the occupant, or those under whom the occupant claims, entered into the possession of premises, under claim of title, exclusive of any other right, founding such claim upon a written instrument as being a conveyance of the premises in question, or upon the decree or judgment of a competent court, and that there has been a continued occupation and possession of the premises included in such instrument, decree, or judgment, or of some part of such premises, under such claim, for 5 years, the premises so included shall be deemed to have been held adversely, except that where the premises so included consists of a tract divided into lots, the possession of one lot shall not be deemed a possession of any other lot of the same tract.

NRS 11.120, "What constitutes adverse possession under written instrument or judgment," provides as follows:

For the purpose of constituting adverse possession by any person claiming a title, founded upon a written instrument or judgment or decree, land shall be deemed to have been possessed and occupied in the following cases:

    1. Where it has been usually cultivated or improved.

    2. Where it has been protected by a substantial enclosure.

    3. Where, though not enclosed, it has been used for the supply of fuel, or of fencing timber, for the purpose of husbandry; or for the use of pasturage, or for ordinary uses of the occupant.

    4. Where a known farm or single lot has been partly improved, the portion of such farm or lot that may have been left not cleared, or not enclosed according to the usual course and custom of the adjoining country [sic], shall be deemed to have been occupied for the same length of time as the part improved and cultivated.

NRS 11.130, "Premises actually occupied under claim of title deemed to be held adversely," provides as follows:

Where it appears that there has been an actual continued occupation of premises, under a claim of title, exclusive of any other right, but not founded upon a written instrument, or a judgment or decree, the premises so actually occupied, and no other, shall be deemed to have been held adversely.

NRS 11.140, "What constitutes adverse possession under claim of title not founded on written instrument," provides as follows:

For the purpose of constituting an adverse possession, by a person claiming title, not founded upon a written instrument, judgment or decree, land shall be deemed to have been possessed and occupied in the following cases only:

    1. Where it has been protected by a substantial enclosure.

    2. Where it has been usually cultivated or improved.

NRS 11.150, "Additional requirements for adverse possession: Occupation continuously for 5 years; payment of taxes," provides as follows:

In no case shall adverse possession be considered established unless it be shown, in addition to the requirements of NRS 11.120 or 11.140, that the land has been occupied and claimed for the period of 5 years, continuously, and that the party or persons, their predecessors and grantors have paid all taxes, state, county and municipal, which may have been levied and assessed against the land for the period mentioned, or have tendered payment thereof.

NRS 11.160, "Relation of landlord and tenant as affecting adverse possession," provides as follows:

Whenever the relation of landlord and tenant shall have existed between any persons, the possession of the tenant shall be deemed the possession of the landlord until the expiration of 5 years from the expiration of the tenancy, or, where there has been no written lease, until the expiration of 5 years from the time of the last payment of rent, notwithstanding that such tenant may have acquired another title, or may have claimed to hold adversely to the landlord. But such presumptions shall not be made after the periods herein limited.

NRS 11.170, "Right of possession not affected by descent cast," provides as follows: "The right of a person to the possession of any real property shall not be impaired or affected by a descent being cast in consequence of the death of a person in possession of such property."

NRS 11.180, "Certain disabilities excluded from time to commence actions," provides as follows:

If a person entitled to commence an action for the recovery of real property, or for the recovery of the possession thereof, or to make any entry or defense founded on the title to real property or to rents or services out of the same, be at the time such title shall first descend or accrue, either:

    1. Within the age of majority; or

    2. Insane; or

    3. Imprisoned on a criminal charge, or in execution upon conviction of a criminal offense, for a term

less than for life,

the time during which such disability continues is not deemed any portion of the time in this Chapter limited for the commencement of such actions, or the making of such entry or defense, but such action may be commenced or entry or defense made, within the period of 2 years after such disability shall cease, or after the death of the person entitled, who shall die under such disability, but such action shall not be commenced, or entry or defense made, after that period.

Actions Other Than for the Recovery of Real Property

NRS 11.190, "Periods of limitation," provides as follows:

Except as otherwise provided in NRS 40.4639, 125B.050 and 217.007, actions other than those for the recovery of real property, unless further limited by specific statute, may only be commenced as follows:

1. Within 6 years:

(a) An action upon a judgment or decree of any court of the United States, or of any state or territory within the United States, or the renewal thereof.

(b) An action upon a contract, obligation or liability founded upon an instrument in writing, except those mentioned in the preceding sections of this Chapter.

2. Within 4 years:

(a) An action on an open account for goods, wares and merchandise sold and delivered.

(b) An action for any article charged on an account in a store.

(c) An action upon a contract, obligation or liability not founded upon an instrument in writing.

(d) An action against a person alleged to have committed a deceptive trade practice in violation of NRS 598.0903 to 598.0999, inclusive, but the cause of action shall be deemed to accrue when the aggrieved party discovers, or by the exercise of due diligence should have discovered, the facts constituting the deceptive trade practice.

3. Within 3 years:

(a) An action upon a liability created by statute, other than a penalty or forfeiture.

(b) An action for waste or trespass of real property, but when the waste or trespass is committed by means of underground works upon any mining claim, the cause of action shall be deemed to accrue upon the discovery by the aggrieved party of the facts constituting the waste or trespass.

(c) An action for taking, detaining or injuring personal property, including actions for specific recovery thereof, but in all cases where the subject of the action is a domestic animal usually included in the term "livestock," which has a recorded mark or brand upon it at the time of its loss, and which strays or is stolen from the true owner without the owner's fault, the statute does not begin to run against an action for the recovery of the animal until the owner has actual knowledge of such facts as would put a reasonable person upon inquiry as to the possession thereof by the defendant.

(d) Except as otherwise provided in NRS 112.230 and 166.170, an action for relief on the ground of fraud or mistake, but the cause of action in such a case shall be deemed to accrue upon the discovery by the aggrieved party of the facts constituting the fraud or mistake.

(e) An action pursuant to NRS 40.750 for damages sustained by a financial institution or other lender because of its reliance on certain fraudulent conduct of a borrower, but the cause of action in such a case shall be deemed to accrue upon the discovery by the financial institution or other lender of the facts constituting the concealment or false statement.

4. Within 2 years:

(a) An action against a sheriff, coroner or constable upon liability incurred by acting in his or her official capacity and in virtue of his or her office, or by the omission of an official duty, including the nonpayment of money collected upon an execution.

(b) An action upon a statute for a penalty or forfeiture, where the action is given to a person or the State, or both, except when the statute imposing it prescribes a different limitation.

(c) An action for libel, slander, assault, battery, false imprisonment or seduction.

(d) An action against a sheriff or other officer for the escape of a prisoner arrested or imprisoned on civil process.

(e) Except as otherwise provided in NRS 11.215, an action to recover damages for injuries to a person or for the death of a person caused by the wrongful act or neglect of another. The provisions of this paragraph relating to an action to recover damages for injuries to a person apply only to causes of action which accrue after March 20, 1951.

(f) An action to recover damages under NRS 41.740.

5. Within 1 year:

(a) An action against an officer, or officer de facto to recover goods, wares, merchandise or other property seized by the officer in his or her official capacity, as tax collector, or to recover the price or value of goods, wares, merchandise or other personal property so seized, or for damages for the seizure, detention or sale of, or injury to, goods, wares, merchandise or other personal property seized, or for damages done to any person or property in making the seizure.

(b) An action against an officer, or officer de facto for money paid to the officer under protest, or seized by the officer in his or her official capacity, as a collector of taxes, and which, it is claimed, ought to be refunded.

NRS 11.200, "Computation of time," provides as follows:

The time in NRS 11.190 shall be deemed to date from the last transaction or the last item charged or last credit given; and whenever any payment on principal or interest has been or shall be made upon an existing contract, whether it be a bill of exchange, promissory note or other evidence of indebtedness if such payment be made after the same shall have become due, the limitation shall commence from the time the last payment was made.

NRS 11.202, "Actions for damages for injury or wrongful death caused by deficiency in construction of improvements to real property: Deficiencies resulting from willful misconduct; fraudulently concealed deficiencies," provides as follows:

1. An action may be commenced against the owner, occupier or any person performing or furnishing the design, planning, supervision or observation of construction, or the construction of an improvement to real property at any time after the substantial completion of such an improvement, for the recovery of damages for:

(a) Any deficiency in the design, planning, supervision or observation of construction or the construction of such an improvement which is the result of his or her willful misconduct or which he or she fraudulently concealed;

(b) Injury to real or personal property caused by any such deficiency; or

(c) Injury to or the wrongful death of a person caused by any such deficiency.

2. The provisions of this section do not apply in an action brought against:

(a) The owner or keeper of any hotel, inn, motel, motor court, boardinghouse or lodging house in this State on account of his or her liability as an innkeeper.

(b) Any person on account of a defect in a product.

NRS 11.203, "Actions for damages for injury or wrongful death caused by deficiency in construction of improvements to real property: Known deficiencies," provides as follows:

1. Except as otherwise provided in NRS 11.202 and 11.206, no action may be commenced against the owner, occupier or any person performing or furnishing the design, planning, supervision or observation of construction, or the construction of an improvement to real property more than 10 years after the substantial completion of such an improvement, for the recovery of damages for:

(a) Any deficiency in the design, planning, supervision or observation of construction or the construction of such an improvement which is known or through the use of reasonable diligence should have been known to him or her;

(b) Injury to real or personal property caused by any such deficiency; or

(c) Injury to or the wrongful death of a person caused by any such deficiency.

2. Notwithstanding the provisions of NRS 11.190 and subsection 1 of this section, if an injury occurs in the 10th year after the substantial completion of such an improvement, an action for damages for injury to property or person, damages for wrongful death resulting from such injury or damages for breach of contract may be commenced within 2 years after the date of such injury, irrespective of the date of death, but in no event may an action be commenced more than 12 years after the substantial completion of the improvement.

3. The provisions of this section do not apply to a claim for indemnity or contribution.

NRS 11.204, "Actions for damages for injury or wrongful death caused by deficiency in construction of improvements to real property: Latent deficiencies," provides as follows:

1. Except as otherwise provided in NRS 11.202, 11.203 and 11.206, no action may be commenced against the owner, occupier or any person performing or furnishing the design, planning, supervision or observation of construction, or the construction, of an improvement to real property more than 8 years after the substantial completion of such an improvement, for the recovery of damages for:

(a) Any latent deficiency in the design, planning, supervision or observation of construction or the construction of such an improvement;

(b) Injury to real or personal property caused by any such deficiency; or

(c) Injury to or the wrongful death of a person caused by any such deficiency.

2. Notwithstanding the provisions of NRS 11.190 and subsection 1 of this section, if an injury occurs in the eighth year after the substantial completion of such an improvement, an action for damages for injury to property or person, damages for wrongful death resulting from such injury or damages for breach of contract may be commenced within 2 years after the date of such injury, irrespective of the date of death, but in no event may an action be commenced more than 10 years after the substantial completion of the improvement.

3. The provisions of this section do not apply to a claim for indemnity or contribution.

4. For the purposes of this section, "latent deficiency" means a deficiency which is not apparent by reasonable inspection.

NRS 11.205, "Actions for damages for injury or wrongful death caused by deficiency in construction of improvements to real property: Patent deficiencies," provides as follows:

1. Except as otherwise provided in NRS 11.202, 11.203 and 11.206, no action may be commenced against the owner, occupier or any person performing or furnishing the design, planning, supervision or observation of construction, or the construction of an improvement to real property more than 6 years after the substantial completion of such an improvement, for the recovery of damages for:

(a) Any patent deficiency in the design, planning, supervision or observation of construction or the construction of such an improvement;

(b) Injury to real or personal property caused by any such deficiency; or

(c) Injury to or the wrongful death of a person caused by any such deficiency.

2. Notwithstanding the provisions of NRS 11.190 and subsection 1 of this section, if an injury occurs in the sixth year after the substantial completion of such an improvement, an action for damages for injury to property or person, damages for wrongful death resulting from such injury or damages for breach of contract may be commenced within 2 years after the date of such injury, irrespective of the date of death, but in no event may an action be commenced more than 8 years after the substantial completion of the improvement.

3. The provisions of this section do not apply to a claim for indemnity or contribution.

4. For the purposes of this section, "patent deficiency" means a deficiency which is apparent by reasonable inspection.

NRS 11.2055, "Actions for damages for injury or wrongful death caused by deficiency in construction of improvements to real property: Determination of date of substantial completion of improvement to real property," provides as follows:

Except as otherwise provided in subsection 2, for the purposes of NRS 11.202 to 11.206, inclusive, the date of substantial completion of an improvement to real property shall be deemed to be the date on which:

1.

(a) The final building inspection of the improvement is conducted;

(b) A notice of completion is issued for the improvement; or

(c) A certificate of occupancy is issued for the improvement,
whichever occurs later.

2. If none of the events described in subsection 1 occurs, the date of substantial completion of an improvement to real property must be determined by the rules of the common law.

NRS 11.206, "Actions for damages for injury or wrongful death caused by deficiency in construction of improvements to real property: Limitation of actions not a defense in actions based on liability as innkeeper or for defect in product," provides as follows:

The limitations respectively prescribed by NRS 11.203, 11.204 and 11.205 are not a defense in an action brought against:

     1. The owner or keeper of any hotel, inn, motel, motor court, boardinghouse or lodging house in this State on account of his or her liability as an innkeeper.

     2. Any person on account of a defect in a product.

NRS 11.207, "Malpractice actions against attorneys and veterinarians," provides as follows:

     1. An action against an attorney or veterinarian to recover damages for malpractice, whether based on a breach of duty or contract, must be commenced within 4 years after the plaintiff sustains damage or within 2 years after the plaintiff discovers or through the use of reasonable diligence should have discovered the material facts which constitute the cause of action, whichever occurs earlier.

     2. This time limitation is tolled for any period during which the attorney or veterinarian conceals any act, error or omission upon which the action is founded and which is known or through the use of reasonable diligence should have been known to the attorney or veterinarian.

     The litigation malpractice tolling rule applies to the statute of limitations in NRS 11.207(1). "The two-year statute of limitations in NRS 11.207, as revised by the Nevada Legislature in 1997, is tolled against a cause of action for attorney malpractice, pending the outcome of the underlying lawsuit in which the malpractice allegedly occurred." [1724]

NRS 11.2075, "Malpractice actions against accountants," provides as follows:

     1. An action against an accountant or accounting firm to recover damages for malpractice must be commenced within:

     (a) Two years after the date on which the alleged act, error or omission is discovered or should have been discovered through the use of reasonable diligence;

     (b) Four years after completion of performance of the service for which the action is brought; or

     (c) Four years after the date of the initial issuance of the report prepared by the accountant or accounting firm regarding the financial statements or other information,

     whichever occurs earlier.

     2. The time limitation set forth in subsection 1 is tolled for any period during which the accountant or accounting firm conceals the act, error or omission upon which the action is founded and which is known or through the use of reasonable diligence should have been known to the accountant or the firm.

     3. As used in this section, "accountant" means a person certified or registered as a public accountant pursuant to Chapter 628 of NRS who holds a live permit, as defined in NRS 628.019.

NRS 11.208, "Action by contractor against Department of Transportation upon contract for construction, reconstruction, improvement or maintenance of highway," provides as follows:

     An action by a contractor against the Department of Transportation upon a contract for the construction, reconstruction, improvement or maintenance of a highway must be commenced within 3 years after the date of the:

     1. Completion of the contract; or

     2. Determination of the engineer or decision of the Board of Directors of the Department of Transportation on an appeal of a claim arising from the contract as provided in the standard specifications for construction of roads and bridges adopted by the Department, whichever occurs later.

NRS 11.209, "Actions against principal contractors by employees of subcontractors for wages or benefits," provides as follows:

     1. No action against a principal contractor for the recovery of wages due an employee of a subcontractor or contributions or premiums required to be made or paid on account of the employee may be commenced more than:

[1724] *Brady v. New Albertson's*, 130 Nev., Advance Op. 38 (2014).

(a) Two years, if the principal contractor is located in Nevada; or

(b) Three years, if the principal contractor is located outside this state,

after the date the employee should have received those wages from or those contributions or premiums should have been made or paid by the subcontractor.

2. No action against a principal contractor for the recovery of benefits due an employee of a subcontractor may be commenced more than:

(a) Three years, if the principal contractor is located in Nevada; or

(b) Four years, if the principal contractor is located outside this state,

after the date the employee should have received those benefits from the subcontractor.

(Added to NRS by 1983, 1350)

NRS 11.2095, "Action to recover payment for money owed to hospital," provides as follows:

1. Except as otherwise provided in this section, an action against a person to recover payment for any amount owed to a hospital for hospital care provided to the person at the hospital must be commenced not later than 4 years after the date on which any payment that is due for the services is not paid.

2. The period provided in subsection 1 is tolled during any periods in which the hospital is awaiting a determination concerning eligibility for, or the amount of, benefits from an insurer or public program and during any periods in which payments are being made.

3. As used in this section, "hospital care" has the meaning ascribed to it in NRS 428.155.

NRS 11.210, "Mutual open accounts; accrual of cause of action," provides as follows: "In an action brought to recover a balance due upon a mutual, open and current account, where there have been reciprocal demands between the parties, the cause of action shall be deemed to have accrued from the time of the last item proved in the account on either side."

NRS 11.215, "Actions for damages for injury arising from sexual abuse of minor; exception for actions involving injury arising from appearance of minor in pornography," provides as follows:

1. Except as otherwise provided in subsection 2 and NRS 217.007, an action to recover damages for an injury to a person arising from the sexual abuse of the plaintiff which occurred when the plaintiff was less than 18 years of age must be commenced within 10 years after the plaintiff:

(a) Reaches 18 years of age; or

(b) Discovers or reasonably should have discovered that his or her injury was caused by the sexual abuse,

whichever occurs later.

2. An action to recover damages pursuant to NRS 41.1396 must be commenced within 3 years after the occurrence of the following, whichever is later:

(a) The court enters a verdict in a related criminal case; or

(b) The victim reaches the age of 18 years.

3. As used in this section, "sexual abuse" has the meaning ascribed to it in NRS 432B.100.

NRS 11.220, "Action for relief not otherwise provided for," provides as follows: "An action for relief, not hereinbefore provided for, must be commenced within 4 years after the cause of action shall have accrued."

NRS 11.250, "Disabilities preventing running of statute," provides as follows:

If a person entitled to bring an action other than for the recovery of real property be, at the time the cause of action accrued, either:

1. Within the age of 18 years; or

2. Insane; or

3. In the custodial care of the State, if placed in such care while less than 18 years of age, except when the person is imprisoned, paroled or on probation,

the time of such disability shall not be a part of the time limited for the commencement of the action.

Statute of Limitations for Medical Malpractice

NRS 41A.097, "Limitation of actions; tolling of limitation," provides as follows:

1. Except as otherwise provided in subsection 3, an action for injury or death against a provider of health care may not be commenced more than 4 years after the date of injury or 2 years after the plaintiff discovers or through the use of reasonable diligence should have discovered the injury, whichever occurs first, for:

(a) Injury to or the wrongful death of a person occurring before October 1, 2002, based upon alleged professional negligence of the provider of health care;

(b) Injury to or the wrongful death of a person occurring before October 1, 2002, from professional services rendered without consent; or

(c) Injury to or the wrongful death of a person occurring before October 1, 2002, from error or omission in practice by the provider of health care.

2. Except as otherwise provided in subsection 3, an action for injury or death against a provider of health care may not be commenced more than 3 years after the date of injury or 1 year after the plaintiff discovers or through the use of reasonable diligence should have discovered the injury, whichever occurs first, for:

(a) Injury to or the wrongful death of a person occurring on or after October 1, 2002, based upon alleged professional negligence of the provider of health care;

(b) Injury to or the wrongful death of a person occurring on or after October 1, 2002, from professional services rendered without consent; or

(c) Injury to or the wrongful death of a person occurring on or after October 1, 2002, from error or omission in practice by the provider of health care.

3. This time limitation is tolled for any period during which the provider of health care has concealed any act, error or omission upon which the action is based and which is known or through the use of reasonable diligence should have been known to the provider of health care.

4. For the purposes of this section, the parent, guardian or legal custodian of any minor child is responsible for exercising reasonable judgment in determining whether to prosecute any cause of action limited by subsection 1 or 2. If the parent, guardian or custodian fails to commence an action on behalf of that child within the prescribed period of limitations, the child may not bring an action based on the same alleged injury against any provider of health care upon the removal of the child's disability, except that in the case of:

(a) Brain damage or birth defect, the period of limitation is extended until the child attains 10 years of age.

(b) Sterility, the period of limitation is extended until 2 years after the child discovers the injury.

When subsection 3 and subsection 2 are read in tandem, a plaintiff must satisfy the following two-prong test in order to establish that subsection 2's one-year discovery period should be tolled: (1) that the medical provider intentionally withheld information, and (2) that this withholding would have hindered a reasonably diligent plaintiff from procuring an expert affidavit.[1725]

Other Statutes of Limitation

The Nevada Supreme Court has clarified that NRS 41A.097(2)'s limitations period does not apply to equitable indemnity and contribution claims, and that such claims are instead subject to the limitations periods laid out in NRS 11.190(2)(c) and NRS 17.285, respectively.

NRS 17.285, "Enforcement of right of contribution," provides as follows:

1. Whether or not judgment has been entered in an action against two or more tortfeasors for the same injury or wrongful death, contribution may be enforced by separate action.

2. Where a judgment has been entered in an action against two or more tortfeasors for the same injury or wrongful death, contribution may be enforced in that action by judgment in favor of one against other judgment defendants by motion upon notice to all parties to the action.

3. If there is a judgment for the injury or wrongful death against the tortfeasor seeking contribution, any separate action by the tortfeasor to enforce contribution must be commenced within 1 year after the judgment has become final by lapse of time for appeal or after appellate review.

4. If there is no judgment for the injury or wrongful death against the tortfeasor seeking contribution, the tortfeasor's right of contribution is barred unless the tortfeasor has:

(a) Discharged by payment the common liability within the statute of limitations period applicable to claimant's right of action against him or her and has commenced an action for contribution within 1 year after

---

[1725] *Winn v. Sunrise Hospital & Medical Center*, 128 Nev. Adv. Op. No. 23 (2012).

payment; or

(b) Agreed while action is pending against him or her to discharge the common liability and has within 1 year after the agreement paid the liability and commenced an action for contribution.

5. The judgment of the court in determining the liability of the several defendants to the claimant for an injury or wrongful death shall be binding as among such defendants in determining their right to contribution.

Fraudulent transfers, NRS 112.230.
Order for support of child, NRS 125B.050.
Pets, action for causing injury or death of certain pets, NRS 41.740.
Receipt by victim of proceeds of materials based on crime, NRS 217.007.
Transfer of property to trust, NRS 166.170.

A breach of fiduciary duty is analogous to fraud, and thus, Nevada applies the three-year statute of limitation set forth in NRS 11.190(3)(d).[1726] The statute of limitations for a claim for breach of fiduciary duty does not begin "to run until the aggrieved party knew, or reasonably should have known, of the facts giving rise to the breach."[1727] When a fiduciary "fails to fulfill his obligations" and keeps that failure hidden, the statute of limitations will not begin to run until the failure of the fiduciary is "discovered, or should have been discovered, by the injured party."[1728] "Mere disclosure of a transaction by a director, without disclosure of the circumstances surrounding the transaction, is not sufficient, as a matter of law, to commence the running of the statute."[1729]

See also "Legal Malpractice."

Statute of Repose

There is considerable common ground in the policies underlying statutes of limitation and statutes of repose, which are both used to limit the temporal extent or duration of tort liability. Their specified time periods are measured differently and they seek to attain different purposes and objectives. Statutes of limitation are designed to promote justice by encouraging plaintiffs to pursue claims diligently and begin to run when a claim accrues.[1730]

In contrast to a statute of limitation, which forecloses suit after a fixed period of time following the occurrence or discovery of an injury, a statute of repose bars causes of action after a certain period of time, regardless of whether damage or an injury has been discovered.[1731]

Statutory Compliance

Mandamus is the proper remedy to require statutory compliance. The Nevada Supreme Court has held that the former provisions of NRS 1.230 (cf. NRS 1.235 and S.C.R. 48.1), relating to the disqualification of judges in civil proceedings, were applicable in a contested probate proceeding because, under NRS 155.180, appropriate provisions regulating the proceedings in civil cases apply in estate matters. Mandamus was a proper remedy to require compliance with the former provision of NRS 1.230.[1732]

Statutory Defenses Prerequisites

Basically a statutory defense can be raised in any instance in which a party cannot be shown to have acted purposely, knowingly, recklessly, or negligently, as the law may require, with respect to each material element of the claim. Some representative examples of statutory defenses would be: Mutual consent, such as two drunks deciding they would have a fistfight and then doing so; self-defense; using a reasonable degree of force to defend one's self against injury by assault or physical attack; intoxication, usually only allowed if it can be shown the addiction is pathological; duress, being forced by coercion or intimidation to commit the offense; ignorance or mistake; or justification or necessity.

See *MGM Mirage v. Nevada Ins. Guaranty Ass'n*, 125 Nev., Advance Opinion 22, 209 P.3d 766 (2009), where the issue was whether the claims was a "covered claim" under NRS 687A.033, which requires that either the claimant or

---

[1726] *Nevada State Bank v. Jamison Partnership*, 106 Nev. 792, 799, 801 P.2d 1377, 1382 (1990).

[1727] *Id.* at 800, 801 P.2d at 1382.

[1728] *Golden Nugget, Inc. v. Ham*, 95 Nev. 45, 48-49, 589 P.2d 173, 175 (1979).

[1729] *Id.* at 48, 589 P.2d at 175. See also *In re AMERCO Derivative Litigation*, 127 Nev. ___, ___ n.6, 252 P.3d 681, 697 n.6 (2011).

[1730] *CTS Corp. v. Waldburger*, ___ U.S. ___ (2014).

[1731] *Davenport v. Comstock Hills—Reno*, 118 Nev. 389, 391 46 P.3d 62 (2002).

[1732] *Cf.* NRS 1.235 and S.C.R. 48.1; *Cord v. Second Judicial Dist. Court*, 91 Nev. 260, 533 P.2d 1355 (1975), cited, *Peters v. Peters*, 92 Nev. 687, at 689, 557 P.2d 713 (1976).

insured be a resident of Nevada. In *Williams v. Cottonwood Cove Dev. Co.*, 96 Nev. 857, 858, 619 P.2d 1219 (1980), the defendant raised the defense of a statutory provision (since repealed) which required a limited partner to either give written consent or ratify sale of partnership's business premises. "Fair use" under the "fair use" exception of 17 U.S.C. § 107 is a statutory defense in a copyright infringement case.

A tenant may claim retaliatory eviction on the ground set forth in NRS 118A.510, "Retaliatory conduct by landlord against tenant prohibited; remedies; exceptions," which provides as follows:

1. Except as otherwise provided in subsection 3, the landlord may not, in retaliation, terminate a tenancy, refuse to renew a tenancy, increase rent or decrease essential services required by the rental agreement or this Chapter, or bring or threaten to bring an action for possession if:

(a) The tenant has complained in good faith of a violation of a building, housing or health code applicable to the premises and affecting health or safety to a governmental agency charged with the responsibility for the enforcement of that code;

(b) The tenant has complained in good faith to the landlord or a law enforcement agency of a violation of this Chapter or of a specific statute that imposes a criminal penalty;

(c) The tenant has organized or become a member of a tenant's union or similar organization;

(d) A citation has been issued resulting from a complaint described in paragraph (a);

(e) The tenant has instituted or defended against a judicial or administrative proceeding or arbitration in which the tenant raised an issue of compliance with the requirements of this Chapter respecting the habitability of dwelling units;

(f) The tenant has failed or refused to give written consent to a regulation adopted by the landlord, after the tenant enters into the rental agreement, which requires the landlord to wait until the appropriate time has elapsed before it is enforceable against the tenant; or

(g) The tenant has complained in good faith to the landlord, a government agency, an attorney, a fair housing agency or any other appropriate body of a violation of NRS 118.010 to 118.120, inclusive, or the Fair Housing Act of 1968, 42 U.S.C. §§ 3601 *et seq.*, or has otherwise exercised rights which are guaranteed or protected under those laws.

2. If the landlord violates any provision of subsection 1, the tenant is entitled to the remedies provided in NRS 118A.390 and has a defense in any retaliatory action by the landlord for possession.

3. A landlord who acts under the circumstances described in subsection 1 does not violate that subsection if:

(a) The violation of the applicable building, housing or health code of which the tenant complained was caused primarily by the lack of reasonable care by the tenant, a member of his or her household or other person on the premises with his or her consent;

(b) The tenancy is terminated with cause;

(c) A citation has been issued and compliance with the applicable building, housing or health code requires alteration, remodeling or demolition and cannot be accomplished unless the tenant's dwelling unit is vacant; or

(d) The increase in rent applies in a uniform manner to all tenants.

The maintenance of an action under this subsection does not prevent the tenant from seeking damages or injunctive relief for the landlord's failure to comply with the rental agreement or maintain the dwelling unit in a habitable condition as required by this Chapter.

"Good faith" is a state of mind consisting in 1) honesty in belief and purpose, 2) faithfulness to one's duty or obligation, 3) observance of reasonable commercial standards of fair dealing in a given trade or business, or 4) absence of intent to defraud or to seek unconscionable advantage.[1733]

Real Estate Licensees

NRS 645.251 provides in pertinent part that real estate licensees are "not required to comply with any principles of common law that may otherwise apply to any of the duties of the licensee as set forth in NRS 645.252, 645.253 and 645.254." The Nevada Supreme Court has concluded that although the statute does not, in all instances, shield real estate licensees from common law forms of liability, it precludes such liability when the type of conduct complained of is covered by NRS 645.252, 645.253, or 645.254.[1734]

[1733] *Black's Law Dictionary* 762 (9th ed. 2009).
[1734] *Davis v. Beling*, 128 Nev. Adv. Op. No. 28 (2012).

Statutory Immunity

Through NRS 41.031(1), the Nevada Legislature has waived the State of Nevada's sovereign immunity to liability in civil actions, subject to certain statutory exceptions.[1735] The pertinent exceptions to NRS 41.031(1) in certain cases are set forth in NRS 41.032. Particularly, NRS 41.032 provides that government actors following statutory guidelines or exercising their discretion are immune from common law tort actions in connection with their statutory duties or their discretion:

> Except as provided in NRS 278.0233 no action may be brought under NRS 41.031 or against an immune contractor or an officer or employee of the State or any of its agencies or political subdivisions which is:
> 1. Based upon an act or omission of an officer, employee or immune contractor, exercising due care, in the execution of a statute or regulation, whether or not such statute or regulation is valid, if the statute or regulation has not been declared invalid by a court of competent jurisdiction; or
> 2. Based upon the exercise or performance or the failure to exercise or perform a discretionary function or duty on the part of the State or any of its agencies or political subdivisions or of any officer, employee or immune contractor of any of these, whether or not the discretion involved is abused.

Also, NRS 41.031(3) provides as follows: "The State of Nevada does not waive its immunity from suit conferred by Amendment XI of the Constitution of the United States."

Sudden Emergency Doctrine

The sudden emergency doctrine, a defense to a negligence claim, allows a defendant to argue that he was not negligent insofar as he was confronted with a sudden emergency did not arise due to his own negligence and he acted as a reasonably prudent person would upon being confronted with that emergency.[1736] A "sudden emergency occurs when an unexpected condition confronts a party exercising reasonable care."[1737] Thus, when a party's negligence is what caused the emergency, that party's exercise of reasonable care after the emergency arose will not preclude his liability for the negligent conduct that created the emergency.[1738]

The Court of the Appeals of the State of Nevada has observed as follows:

> For a sudden emergency instruction to be warranted, sufficient evidence must be presented demonstrating that a party was suddenly placed in a position of peril through no fault of his own and that he responded to that emergency as a reasonably prudent person would. Additionally, the emergency must have directly affected the party seeking the instruction, rather than another party involved in the incident, even if the emergency results in indirect consequences for the party seeking the instruction. *See id.* [*Posas*] at 118, 228 P.3d at 461 (concluding that a pedestrian walking into the street in front of a car was not a sudden emergency for the driver of a second car who was following too closely and hit the first car when it stopped short to avoid hitting the pedestrian). Finally, when a sudden emergency instruction is sought in the context of a motor vehicle accident case, evieence must be presented demonstrating that the asserted emergency involved something more than the typical hazards drivers should expect to encounter in the regular course of operaring a vehicle, such as the sudden appearance of obstacles or people, crowded intersections, or sudden stops.[1739]

Suicide

Suicide may be an affirmative defense in some accident or benefits actions.[1740]

[1735] *Boulder City v. Boulder Excavating*, 124 Nev. 749, 756, 91 P.3d 1175 (2008).

[1736] *Frazier v. Drake*, 131 Nev., Advance Opinion 64 (Nev. Ct.App. 2015) at 7, citing *Posas v. Horton*, 126 Nev. 112, 228 P.3d 457 (2010).

[1737] *Posas* at 115, 228 P.3d at 459.

[1738] *Id.*, citing RESTATEMENT (SECOND) OF TORTS § 296 (1965).

[1739] *Frazier v. Drake*, 131 Nev., Advance Opinion 64 (Nev. Ct.App. 2015) at 7, citing *Posas v. Horton*, 126 Nev. 112, 228 P.3d 457 (2010).

[1740] See *Green v. William Penn Life Insurance Co. of New York*, No. 1932 (N.Y.App.Div. 2007) *Evans v. City of Marlin*, 986 F.2d 104 (5th Cir. 1993) and *Gould v. Mutual Life Insurance Co.*, 95 Wash. 2d 722, 629 P.2d 1331 (1981) (en banc).

Supervening Cause or Superseding Cause

A criminal attack by a third party is an intervening act; however, such an intervening act is a superseding cause which breaks the chain of causation only to the extent that it is unforeseeable.[1741] The RESTATEMENT (SECOND) OF TORTS takes the position that a third party crime is a superseding cause of the negligence of the actor who created the situation that afforded the third party the opportunity to commit a crime, unless the actor at the time of the negligence realized or should have realized the likelihood that such a situation might be created and that the third person might avail himself or herself of the opportunity.[1742] Further, if the likelihood that a third party might commit the attack is one of the hazards which makes the actor negligent, the actor is not relieved of liability.[1743] The Nevada Supreme Court finds the RESTATEMENT view to be compatible with its prior decisions regarding the scope of a proprietor's duty to protect a patron from and liability for third party attacks.[1744]

Termination of Employment

In enacting the statutory presumption that an injury that was not reported by a workers' compensation claimant before termination did not arise out of and in the course of employment, the Nevada Legislature intended to create a presumed fact that the injury arose from an event that occurred after the termination of employment.

NRS 616C.150, "Compensation prohibited unless preponderance of evidence establishes that injury arose out of and in course of employment; rebuttable presumption if notice of injury is filed after termination of employment," provides as follows:

> 1. An injured employee or the dependents of the injured employee are not entitled to receive compensation pursuant to the provisions of Chapters 616A to 616D, inclusive, of NRS unless the employee or the dependents establish by a preponderance of the evidence that the employee's injury arose out of and in the course of his or her employment.
>
> 2. For the purposes of Chapters 616A to 616D, inclusive, of NRS, if the employee files a notice of an injury pursuant to NRS 616C.015 after his or her employment has been terminated for any reason, there is a rebuttable presumption that the injury did not arise out of and in the course of his or her employment.

Truth

Truth may be an affirmative defense in a defamation case.[1745] Truth is a complete defense to a claim of defamation.[1746]

Daumier: The Court

Unclean Hands

In determining whether a party's connection with an action is sufficiently offensive to bar equitable relief, two factors must be considered: (1) the egregiousness of the misconduct at issue, and (2) the seriousness of the harm caused by the misconduct.[1747] Only when these factors weigh against granting the requested equitable relief will the unclean

---

[1741] See *Drummond v. Mid-West Growers*, 91 Nev. 698, 705, 542 P.2d 198, 203 (1975).

[1742] See RESTATEMENT (SECOND) OF TORTS §§ 448-49 (1965).

[1743] *Id.* See also *Orlando Executive Park, Inc. v. Robbins*, 433 So.2d 491 (Fla. 1983).

[1744] *Doud v. Las Vegas Hilton Corp.*, 109 Nev. 1096, 1106, 864 P.2d 796 (1993).

[1745] *Raghavan v. Boeing Co.*, 133 Cal.Ct.App.4th 1120, 35 Cal.Rptr.3d 397 (Cal. Ct.App. Dist.2 2005).

[1746] *Diaz v. Espada*, 778 N.Y.S.2d 38 (N.Y. 2004), citing *Dillon v. City of New York*, 261 A.D.2d 34, 704 N.Y.S.2d 1 (N.Y. 1999).

[1747] *Las Vegas Fetish & Fantasy v. Ahern Rentals*, 124 Nev., Advance Opinion 26, 182 P.3d 764 (2008).

hands doctrine bar that remedy.[1748] The district court has broad discretion in applying these factors, and the Nevada Supreme Court will not overturn the district court's determination unless it is unsupported by substantial evidence.[1749]

The unclean hands doctrine should only apply when the egregiousness of the party's misconduct constituting the party's unclean hands and the seriousness of the harm caused by the misconduct collectively weigh against allowing the party to obtain such a remedy.[1750] The unclean hands doctrine generally bars a party from receiving equitable relief because of that party's own inequitable conduct.[1751] The unclean hands doctrine precludes a party from attaining an equitable remedy when that party's connection with the subject matter or transaction in litigation has been unconscientious, unjust, or marked by the want of good faith.[1752] A tortfeasor's unclean hands do not necessarily bar the tortfeasor from obtaining an equitable remedy when the tortfeasor did not act intentionally.[1753]

"Good faith" is a state of mind consisting in 1) honesty in belief and purpose, 2) faithfulness to one's duty or obligation, 3) observance of reasonable commercial standards of fair dealing in a given trade or business, or 4) absence of intent to defraud or to seek unconscionable advantage.[1754]

A partner's actions in bad faith are relevant to that partner's rights against other partners.[1755] The equitable defense of unclean hands "requires inequitable conduct by the plaintiff in connection with the matter in controversy and provides a complete defense to the plaintiff's action."[1756] Whenever a party, who, as actor, seeks to set the judicial machinery in motion and obtain some remedy, has violated conscience, or good faith, or other equitable principle, in his prior conduct, then the doors of the court will be shut against him in limine; the court will refuse to interfere on his behalf, to acknowledge his right, or to award him any remedy.[1757] "The defense of unclean hands does not apply in every instance where the plaintiff has committed some misconduct in connection with the matter in controversy, but applies only where it would be inequitable to grant the plaintiff any relief."[1758] Wrongful dissolution of a partnership, in and of itself, does not establish unclean hands and preclude an accounting.[1759]

"Modern decisions recognize the defense in legal as well as equitable actions."[1760] "A court, discovering the facts of unclean hands, needs no original or amended pleading to justify its refusal to grant relief to the plaintiff. And the defense is, in this respect, more like illegality than laches, for the appellate court may deny relief on this ground, without either pleading or action by the trial court."[1761] A trial court's decision to grant an equitable defense such as unclean hands is reviewed for abuse of discretion.[1762]

[1748] *Id.*

[1749] *Id.*

[1750] *Las Vegas Fetish & Fantasy v. Ahern Rentals*, 124 Nev., Advance Opinion 26, 182 P.3d 764 (2008).

[1751] *Id.*

[1752] *Id.*

[1753] *Banks v. Sunrise Hospital*, 120 Nev. 822, 843, 102 P.3d 52, 66 (2004).

[1754] *Black's Law Dictionary* 762 (9th ed. 2009).

[1755] *Rosenfeld, Meyer & Susman v. Cohen*, 191 Cal.App.3d 1035, 237 Cal.Rptr. 14 (1987).

[1756] *Dickson, Carlson & Campillo v. Pole*, 83 Cal.Ct.App.4th 436, 446 (2000).

[1757] *Id.* at p. 446, fn. 7.

[1758] *Id.* at pp. 446-447.

[1759] *Thomas v. Marvin E. Jewell & Co.*, 440 N.W. 2d 437 (Neb. 1989); *Hoppen v. Powell*, 600 S.W.2d 736, 738-739 (Tenn. 1980).

[1760] 5 Witkin, Cal. Procedure (4th ed. 1997) § 1052, p. 502.)

[1761] 5 Witkin, Cal. Procedure (4th ed.) § 1052, p. 503 (italics omitted).

[1762] *Dickson, Carlson & Campillo v. Pole*, 83 Cal.App.4th at p. 447 (2000).

A painting of the Trial of Bill Burns, showing Richard Martin with the donkey in an astonished courtroom, leading to the world's first known conviction for animal cruelty, a story that delighted London's newspapers and music halls.

Ultra Vires

Ultra vires means unauthorized, or beyond the scope of power allowed or granted by a corporate charter or by law.[1763] Generally, a corporate act is said to be ultra vires when it goes beyond the powers allowed by state law or the articles of incorporation.[1764] The concept of ultra vires acts is not especially well defined, however, particularly given the latitude allowed to chartering members in delineating corporate powers in the articles of incorporation.[1765] Thus, for example, if the corporation's act was within the corporate powers, but was performed without authority or in an unauthorized manner, the act is not ultra vires.[1766]

Unconscionability

"Unconscionable" means the following: 1) (Of a person) having no conscience; unscrupulous; 2) (Of an act or transaction) showing no regard for conscience; affronting the sense of justice, decency, or reasonableness.[1767]

NRS 104.2302, "Unconscionable contract or clause," provides as follows:

> 1. If the court as a matter of law finds the contract or any clause of the contract to have been unconscionable at the time it was made the court may refuse to enforce the contract, or it may enforce the remainder of the contract without the unconscionable clause, or it may so limit the application of any unconscionable clause as to avoid any unconscionable result.
> 2. When it is claimed or appears to the court that the contract or any clause thereof may be unconscionable, the parties shall be afforded a reasonable opportunity to present evidence as to its commercial setting, purpose and effect to aid the court in making the determination.

An adhesion contract has been defined as a standardized contract form offered to consumers of goods and services essentially on a "take it or leave it" basis, without affording the consumer a realistic opportunity to bargain, and under such conditions that the consumer cannot obtain the desired product or service except by acquiescing to the form of the contract. The distinctive feature of an adhesion contract is that the weaker party has no choice as to its terms.[1768]

Both procedural and substantive unconscionability generally must be present for a court to refuse to enforce a contract or clause as unconscionable. If the procedural unconscionability is great, less evidence of substantive

---

[1763] *Id.*, 9th ed., p. 1662.

[1764] *Shoen v. SAC Holding Corp.*, 122 Nev. 621, 643, 137 P.3d 1171 (2002).

[1765] *Id.*

[1766] *Id.*

[1767] *Black's Law Dictionary* 1664 (9th ed. 2009).

[1768] *Farmers Ins. Group v. Stonik*, 110 Nev. 64, at 67, 867 P.2d 389 (1994), see also NRS 104.2302, NRS 104A.2108, NRS 116.1112, NRS 118A.230, NRS 123A.080 and NRS 644.403.

unconscionability may be required to establish unconscionability.[1769]

A contract clause is procedurally unconscionable when a party lacks a meaningful opportunity to agree to the terms of the clause either because of unequal bargaining power (*i.e.*, adhesion contract) or because the clause and its effects are not readily ascertainable upon a review of the contract. Procedural unconscionability often involves the use of fine print or complicated, incomplete or misleading language that fails to inform a reasonable person of the consequences of the contractual language.[1770]

An arbitration provision was unconscionable where the arbitration provision was: (1) procedurally unconscionable since it was inconspicuous, downplayed by representatives of the developer at the time that the homebuyers signed the purchase agreements and failed to advise adequately an average person that important rights were being waived by agreeing to arbitrate any disputes that arose under the purchase agreement; and (2) substantively unconscionable since it imposed a financial penalty on the homebuyers if they chose to forego arbitration, but imposed no such penalty on the developer.[1771]

Undue Influence

Undue influence is the improper use of power or trust in a way that deprives a person of free will and substitutes another's objective.[1772] Consent to a contract, transaction, or relationship or to conduct is voidable if the consent is obtained through undue influence.[1773]

A presumption of undue influence arises when a fiduciary relationship exists and the fiduciary benefits from the questioned transaction.[1774] *Peardon v. Peardon*, 65 Nev. 717, 767, 201 P.2d 309, 333 (1948) (holding that the doctrine of undue influence "reaches every case, and grants relief 'where influence is acquired and abused, or where confidence is reposed and betrayed' . . . but is applied when necessary to conveyances, executory and executed contracts, and wills"); see also *Schmidt v. Merriweather*, 82 Nev. 372, 376, 418 P.2d 991, 993 (1966) (holding that " 'where confidential relations between parent and child are shown to have existed and where a conveyance of property is made by the weaker to the dominant party, a presumption arises that the conveyance was obtained through the undue influence of the dominant party' "[1775]

In Nevada "a fiduciary relationship exists when one has the right to expect trust and confidence in the integrity and fidelity of another."[1776]

Unjust Enrichment

See "Quasi Contract" and "Unjust Enrichment" in "Claims."

Usury

In general, the State of Nevada has no law against usury. See NRS 99.050, "Agreed interest rates; compounding; charges or fees," which provides as follows:

> Except as otherwise provided in section 670 of the John Warner National Defense Authorization Act for Fiscal Year 2007, Public Law 109-364, or any regulation adopted pursuant thereto, parties may agree for the payment of any rate of interest on money due or to become due on any contract, for the compounding of interest if they choose, and for any other charges or fees. The parties shall specify in writing the rate upon which they agree, that interest is to be compounded if so agreed, and any other charges or fees to which they have agreed.

The usurious character of a transaction is determined as of the time of its inception.[1777] The "actual" life of a loan is not to be considered when determining whether the loan is usurious. NRS 99.050. Although the 1973 usury statute provided that a contracted rate of interest could not exceed the rate of 12 percent per annum, that statute did not mean that the interest rate could not exceed 12 percent annually or 12 percent for any one year; the words "twelve percent per annum" referred to the rate of interest and not the time of payment; thus,

---

[1769] See NRS 104.2302, NRS 104A.2108, NRS 116.1112, NRS 118A.230, NRS 123A.080 and NRS 644.403; *Burch v. Second Judicial Dist. Court*, 118 Nev. 438, 49 P.3d 647 (2002), cited, *D.R. Horton, Inc. v. Green*, 120 Nev. 549, at 553, 96 P.3d 1159 (2004).

[1770] *D.R. Horton, Inc. v. Green*, 120 Nev. 549, 96 P.3d 1159 (2004).

[1771] *Id.*, see also *Gonski v. District Court*, 126 Nev., Advance Opinion 51 (2010).

[1772] *Black's Law Dictionary* 1666 (9th ed. 2009).

[1773] *Id.*

[1774] *In re Tiffany Living Trust 2001*, 124 Nev. 74, 78, 177 P.3d 1060 (2008).

[1775] (Quoting *Walters v. Walters*, 188 P. 1105, 1106 (N.M. 1920)).

[1776] *Powers v. United Servs. Auto. Ass'n*, 114 Nev. 690, 700, 962 P.2d 596, 602 (1998).

[1777] See *Collins v. Union Fed. Savings & Loan*, 99 Nev. 284, 286 (1983) and NRS 99.050.

interest payments, for the purpose of usury calculations, were to be prorated over the entire term of the contract.[1778]

Void

Void means "of no legal effect; null." The distinction between void and voidable is often of great practical importance. Whenever technical accuracy is required, void can be properly applied only to those provisions that are of no effect whatsoever–those that are an absolute nullity.[1779] If an invitation to bid and the contract differ materially, then the contract is void. It is void, not voidable, because the local government exceeded its authority and was not authorized to make such a contract.[1780]

Wills and Estates: Where Transfers are Presumed Void

NRS 155.0965, " 'Transferor' "defined," provides as follows: " 'Transferor' means a testator, settlor, grantor of a deed and a decedent whose interest is transferred pursuant to a nonprobate transfer."
(Added to NRS by 2011, 1460)

NRS 155.097, "Validity; circumstances in which transfer is presumed void," provides as follows:

1. To the extent the court finds that a transfer was the product of fraud, duress or undue influence, the transfer is void and each transferee who is found responsible for the fraud, duress or undue influence shall bear the costs of the proceedings, including, without limitation, reasonable attorney's fees.
2. Except as otherwise provided in NRS 155.0975, a transfer is presumed to be void if the transfer is effective on or after a transferor's death and the transfer is to a transferee who is:
(a) The person who drafted the transfer instrument;
(b) A caregiver of the transferor;
(c) A person who arranged for or paid for the drafting of the transfer instrument; or
(d) A person who is related to, affiliated with or subordinate to any person described in paragraph (a), (b) or (c).

NRS 155.0975, "Exceptions to presumption that certain transfers are void," provides as follows:

The presumption established by NRS 155.097 does not apply:
1. To a transfer of property under a will if the transferee is an heir of the testator whose share in the estate of the testator under the terms of the testator's will is not greater than the share the transferee would be entitled to pursuant to Chapter 134 of NRS if the testator had died intestate.
2. Except as otherwise provided in this subsection, if the court determines, upon clear and convincing evidence, that the transfer was not the product of fraud, duress or undue influence. The determination of the court pursuant to this subsection must not be based solely upon the testimony of a person described in subsection 2 of NRS 155.097.
3. If the transfer instrument is reviewed by an independent attorney who:
(a) Counsels the transferor about the nature and consequences of the intended transfer;
(b) Attempts to determine if the intended consequence is the result of fraud, duress or undue influence; and
(c) Signs and delivers to the transferor an original certificate of that review in substantially the following form:

Certificate of Independent Review

I, ... (attorney's name), have reviewed .... (name of transfer instrument) and have counseled my client, ... (name of client), on the nature and consequences of the transfer or transfers of property to .... (name of transferee) contained in the transfer

---

[1778] NRS 99.050.
[1779] *Black's Law Dictionary* 1709 (9th ed. 2009).
[1780] *Orion Portfolio Servs. v. Clark County,* 126 Nev. 39 (2010); see 13 *McQuillin,* supra, § 37:107; 10A *McQuillin,* supra, § 29.104.20 (3d ed. 2009).

instrument. I am disassociated from the interest of the transferee to the extent that I am in a position to advise my client independently, impartially and confidentially as to the consequences of the transfer. On the basis of this counsel, I conclude that the transfer or transfers of property in the transfer instrument that otherwise might be invalid pursuant to NRS 155.097 are valid because the transfer or transfers are not the product of fraud, duress or undue influence.

(Name of Attorney)   (Date)

4. To a transferee that is:
(a) A federal, state or local public entity; or
(b) An entity that is recognized as exempt under section 501(c)(3) or 501(c)(19) of the Internal Revenue Code, 26 U.S.C. § 501(c)(3) or 501(c)(19), or a trust holding an interest for such an entity but only to the extent of the interest of the entity or the interest of the trustee of the trust.
5. A transfer of property if the fair market value of the property does not exceed $3,000.
(Added to NRS by 2011, 1460)

Void ab Initio

In *Fierle v. Perez*,[1781] the Nevada Supreme Court interpreted NRS 41A.071's expert affidavit requirement in medical malpractice actions to apply to a defective pleading served in violation of NRS 11.258. Such a pleading is void ab initio ["from the beginning"] and of no legal effect and, thus, cannot be cured by amendment. Therefore, because the initial pleadings served by certain real parties in interest did not include the attorney affidavit and expert report as required by NRS 11.258, those pleadings were void *ab initio*, and the district court did not have discretionary authority to allow the parties to amend their pleadings to cure their failure to comply with NRS 11.258.[1782]

A medical malpractice suit filed without an expert affidavit is void and cannot be amended. A plaintiff who sued a medical center for alleged negligence failed to file a medical expert affidavit with her complaint, as required by NRS 41A.071. When the medical center moved to dismiss the complaint and after the statute of limitations had expired, the plaintiff filed an amended complaint with an expert affidavit attached. When the medical center sought mandamus relief, the plaintiff argued that NRCP 15(a), which permits a plaintiff to amend a pleading once as a matter of course before a responsive pleading is served, superseded NRS 41A.071's dismissal requirement. The Supreme Court disagreed. Because NRS 41A.071 provides that the district court "shall" dismiss without prejudice a medical malpractice action if it is filed without an expert affidavit, the Court concluded that such a complaint is *void ab initio* and thus cannot be amended but must be automatically dismissed. Therefore, NRCP 15(a)'s amendment provisions are inapplicable.[1783]

Voidable

Voidable means "valid until annulled; especially (of a contract) capable of being affirmed or rejected at the option of one of the parties."[1784] This term describes a valid act that may be voided rather than an invalid act that may be ratified.[1785]

Volenti

Volenti non fit injuria (*Law* Latin "to a willing person it is not a wrong," *i.e.*, a person is not wronged by that to which he or she consents). The principle that a person who knowingly and voluntarily risks danger cannot recover for any resulting injury.[1786] The Nevada Supreme Court analyzed the principle in the context of a cross-country horse race as follows:

One entering into and participating in a cross-country race does assume the risk of injury from the natural hazards necessarily incident to, or which inhere in, such a race. To the extent of natural hazards, the maxim, "*volenti non fit injuria*" applies, which, translated, means, "that to which a person assents is not esteemed in law an injury." The doctrine, or principle, is stated in 38 Am.Jur. 845, as follows: "One who knows, appreciates and deliberately exposes himself to a danger 'assumes the risk' thereof." The natural hazards which the invited participant in a cross-country race may be properly assumed to know and appreciate,

---

[1781] 125 Nev. Adv. Op. No. 54, 219 P.3d 906, 914 (2009).
[1782] *Otak Nevada, LLC v. Dist. Ct.*, 127 Nev., Advance Opinion 53 (2011).
[1783] *Washoe Med. Ctr. v. Second Judicial Dist. Court*, 122 Nev. 1298, 148 P.3d 790 (2006).
[1784] *Black's Law Dictionary* 1709 (9th ed. 2009).
[1785] *Id.* at 1709-10.
[1786] *Id.* at 1710.

in the absence of evidence of actual knowledge thereof, are those which usually are the accompaniment of such a race, such as natural gulleys, natural water-ways or depressions in the surface of the terrain caused by action of the elements, rocky or sandy elevations, bushes and other vegetation growing on the surface. etc. But the participant in such a race is deemed to assume the risk only of such natural, ordinary hazards, and not of extraordinary hazards or dangers artificially created, unless such artificially created hazards are known to such invitee before he enters the race, and he voluntarily assumes the risk thereof.[1787] Such hidden dangers as pitfalls, traps, shafts, holes (so situated as to be partially hidden or obscured), and other excavations artificially created, and the presence of which is known, or by the use of reasonable care should be known, to the owner or occupant, and which are not known to the invitee, or would not be observed by him by the use of ordinary care, do not come within the operation of the doctrine of assumption of risk, nor of the doctrine expressed by the maxim, "volenti non fit injuria."[1788]

See "Assumption of the Risk."

Voluntary Payment Doctrine

The voluntary payment doctrine is a long-standing doctrine of law, which clearly provides that one who makes a payment voluntarily cannot recover it on the ground that he was under no legal obligation to make the payment.[1789] The doctrine is valid in Nevada.[1790] The "voluntary" in the voluntary payment doctrine does not entail the mere payment of the bill or fee.[1791] Instead, it considers the willingness of a person to pay a bill without protest as to its correctness or legality.[1792] This doctrine promotes the policy goals of certainty and stability in transactions.[1793]

Waiver

See "waiver" in claims.

Wrong party

Plaintiff has sued the wrong party, *e.g.*, a company with a name similar to that of the right party.

Younger Abstention

See "Abstention."

Preamble to the Bill of Rights

Congress of the United States begun and held at the City of New-York, on Wednesday the fourth of March, one thousand seven hundred and eighty nine.

THE Conventions of a number of the States, having at the time of their adopting the Constitution, expressed a desire, in order to prevent misconstruction or abuse of its powers, that further declaratory and restrictive clauses should be added: And as extending the ground of public confidence in the Government, will best ensure the beneficent ends of its institution.

RESOLVED by the Senate and House of Representatives of the United States of America, in Congress assembled, two thirds of both Houses concurring, that the following Articles be proposed to the Legislatures of the several States, as

---

[1787] 45 C.J. 837.

[1788] *Hotels El Rancho v. Pray*, 64 Nev. 591, 612, 187 P.2d 568 (1947); see also *Davies v. Butler*, 95 Nev. 763, 774, 602 P.2d 605 (1979).

[1789] *Nevada Ass'n Servs v. Elsinore*, 130 Nev., Advance Opinion 94 (12/04/14), citing *Best Buy Stores v. Benderson-Wainberg Assocs.*, 668 P.3d 1019, 1030 (9th Cir. 2012) (internal quotations omitted.)

[1790] *Nevada Association Services v. Elsinore*, 130 Nev., Advance Opinion 94, p. 1 (12/04/14).

[1791] *Id.* at 6.

[1792] *Id.*

[1793] *Id.*

amendments to the Constitution of the United States, all, or any of which Articles, when ratified by three fourths of the said Legislatures, to be valid to all intents and purposes, as part of the said Constitution; viz.

ARTICLES in addition to, and Amendment of the Constitution of the United States of America, proposed by Congress, and ratified by the Legislatures of the several States, pursuant to the fifth Article of the original Constitution.

Note: The following text is a transcription of the first ten amendments to the Constitution in their original form. These amendments were ratified December 15, 1791, and form what is known as the "Bill of Rights."

United States Bill of Rights

Amendment I
Congress shall make no law respecting an establishment of religion, or prohibiting the free exercise thereof; or abridging the freedom of speech, or of the press; or the right of the people peaceably to assemble, and to petition the Government for a redress of grievances.

Amendment II
A well regulated Militia, being necessary to the security of a free State, the right of the people to keep and bear Arms, shall not be infringed.

Amendment III
No Soldier shall, in time of peace be quartered in any house, without the consent of the Owner, nor in time of war, but in a manner to be prescribed by law.

Amendment IV
The right of the people to be secure in their persons, houses, papers, and effects, against unreasonable searches and seizures, shall not be violated, and no Warrants shall issue, but upon probable cause, supported by Oath or affirmation, and particularly describing the place to be searched, and the persons or things to be seized.

Amendment V
No person shall be held to answer for a capital, or otherwise infamous crime, unless on a presentment or indictment of a Grand Jury, except in cases arising in the land or naval forces, or in the Militia, when in actual service in time of War or public danger; nor shall any person be subject for the same offence to be twice put in jeopardy of life or limb; nor shall be compelled in any criminal case to be a witness against himself, nor be deprived of life, liberty, or property, without due process of law; nor shall private property be taken for public use, without just compensation.

Amendment VI
In all criminal prosecutions, the accused shall enjoy the right to a speedy and public trial, by an impartial jury of the State and district wherein the crime shall have been committed, which district shall have been previously ascertained by law, and to be informed of the nature and cause of the accusation; to be confronted with the witnesses against him; to have compulsory process for obtaining witnesses in his favor, and to have the Assistance of Counsel for his defence.

Amendment VII
In Suits at common law, where the value in controversy shall exceed twenty dollars, the right of trial by jury shall be preserved, and no fact tried by a jury, shall be otherwise re-examined in any Court of the United States, than according to the rules of the common law.

Amendment VIII
Excessive bail shall not be required, nor excessive fines imposed, nor cruel and unusual punishments inflicted.

Amendment IX
The enumeration in the Constitution, of certain rights, shall not be construed to deny or disparage others retained by the people.

Amendment X

The powers not delegated to the United States by the Constitution, nor prohibited by it to the States, are reserved to the States respectively, or to the people.

***

Full-text translation of the 1215 edition of Magna Carta

[Clauses marked (+) are still valid under the charter of 1225, but with a few minor amendments. Clauses marked (*) were omitted in all later reissues of the charter. In the charter itself the clauses are not numbered, and the text reads continuously. The translation sets out to convey the sense rather than the precise wording of the original Latin.]

JOHN, by the grace of God King of England, Lord of Ireland, Duke of Normandy and Aquitaine, and Count of Anjou, to his archbishops, bishops, abbots, earls, barons, justices, foresters, sheriffs, stewards, servants, and to all his officials and loyal subjects, Greeting.

KNOW THAT BEFORE GOD, for the health of our soul and those of our ancestors and heirs, to the honour of God, the exaltation of the holy Church, and the better ordering of our kingdom, at the advice of our reverend fathers Stephen, archbishop of Canterbury, primate of all England, and cardinal of the holy Roman Church, Henry archbishop of Dublin, William bishop of London, Peter bishop of Winchester, Jocelin bishop of Bath and Glastonbury, Hugh bishop of Lincoln, Walter bishop of Worcester, William bishop of Coventry, Benedict bishop of Rochester, Master Pandulf subdeacon and member of the papal household, Brother Aymeric master of the knighthood of the Temple in England, William Marshal earl of Pembroke, William earl of Salisbury, William earl of Warren, William earl of Arundel, Alan of Galloway constable of Scotland, Warin fitz Gerald, Peter fitz Herbert, Hubert de Burgh seneschal of Poitou, Hugh de Neville, Matthew fitz Herbert, Thomas Basset, Alan Basset, Philip Daubeny, Robert de Roppeley, John Marshal, John fitz Hugh, and other loyal subjects:

+ (1) FIRST, THAT WE HAVE GRANTED TO GOD, and by this present charter have confirmed for us and our heirs in perpetuity, that the English Church shall be free, and shall have its rights undiminished, and its liberties unimpaired. That we wish this so to be observed, appears from the fact that of our own free will, before the outbreak of the present dispute between us and our barons, we granted and confirmed by charter the freedom of the Church's elections - a right reckoned to be of the greatest necessity and importance to it - and caused this to be confirmed by Pope Innocent III. This freedom we shall observe ourselves, and desire to be observed in good faith by our heirs in perpetuity.

TO ALL FREE MEN OF OUR KINGDOM we have also granted, for us and our heirs for ever, all the liberties written out below, to have and to keep for them and their heirs, of us and our heirs:

(2) If any earl, baron, or other person that holds lands directly of the Crown, for military service, shall die, and at his death his heir shall be of full age and owe a 'relief', the heir shall have his inheritance on payment of the ancient scale of 'relief'. That is to say, the heir or heirs of an earl shall pay £100 for the entire earl's barony, the heir or heirs of a knight 100s. at most for the entire knight's 'fee', and any man that owes less shall pay less, in accordance with the ancient usage of 'fees'.

(3) But if the heir of such a person is under age and a ward, when he comes of age he shall have his inheritance without 'relief' or fine.

(4) The guardian of the land of an heir who is under age shall take from it only reasonable revenues, customary dues, and feudal services. He shall do this without destruction or damage to men or property. If we have given the guardianship of the land to a sheriff, or to any person answerable to us for the revenues, and he commits destruction or damage, we will exact compensation from him, and the land shall be entrusted to two worthy and prudent men of the same 'fee', who shall be answerable to us for the revenues, or to the person to whom we have assigned them. If we have given or sold to anyone the guardianship of such land, and he causes destruction or damage, he shall lose the guardianship of it, and it shall be handed over to two worthy and prudent men of the same 'fee', who shall be similarly answerable to us.

(5) For so long as a guardian has guardianship of such land, he shall maintain the houses, parks, fish preserves, ponds, mills, and everything else pertaining to it, from the revenues of the land itself. When the heir comes of age, he shall

restore the whole land to him, stocked with plough teams and such implements of husbandry as the season demands and the revenues from the land can reasonably bear.

(6) Heirs may be given in marriage, but not to someone of lower social standing. Before a marriage takes place, it shall be made known to the heir's next-of-kin.

(7) At her husband's death, a widow may have her marriage portion and inheritance at once and without trouble. She shall pay nothing for her dower, marriage portion, or any inheritance that she and her husband held jointly on the day of his death. She may remain in her husband's house for forty days after his death, and within this period her dower shall be assigned to her.

(8) No widow shall be compelled to marry, so long as she wishes to remain without a husband. But she must give security that she will not marry without royal consent, if she holds her lands of the Crown, or without the consent of whatever other lord she may hold them of.

(9) Neither we nor our officials will seize any land or rent in payment of a debt, so long as the debtor has movable goods sufficient to discharge the debt. A debtor's sureties shall not be distrained upon so long as the debtor himself can discharge his debt. If, for lack of means, the debtor is unable to discharge his debt, his sureties shall be answerable for it. If they so desire, they may have the debtor's lands and rents until they have received satisfaction for the debt that they paid for him, unless the debtor can show that he has settled his obligations to them.

* (10) If anyone who has borrowed a sum of money from Jews dies before the debt has been repaid, his heir shall pay no interest on the debt for so long as he remains under age, irrespective of whom he holds his lands. If such a debt falls into the hands of the Crown, it will take nothing except the principal sum specified in the bond.

* (11) If a man dies owing money to Jews, his wife may have her dower and pay nothing towards the debt from it. If he leaves children that are under age, their needs may also be provided for on a scale appropriate to the size of his holding of lands. The debt is to be paid out of the residue, reserving the service due to his feudal lords. Debts owed to persons other than Jews are to be dealt with similarly.

* (12) No 'scutage' or 'aid' may be levied in our kingdom without its general consent, unless it is for the ransom of our person, to make our eldest son a knight, and (once) to marry our eldest daughter. For these purposes only a reasonable 'aid' may be levied. 'Aids' from the city of London are to be treated similarly.

+ (13) The city of London shall enjoy all its ancient liberties and free customs, both by land and by water. We also will and grant that all other cities, boroughs, towns, and ports shall enjoy all their liberties and free customs.

* (14) To obtain the general consent of the realm for the assessment of an 'aid' - except in the three cases specified above - or a 'scutage', we will cause the archbishops, bishops, abbots, earls, and greater barons to be summoned individually by letter. To those who hold lands directly of us we will cause a general summons to be issued, through the sheriffs and other officials, to come together on a fixed day (of which at least forty days notice shall be given) and at a fixed place. In all letters of summons, the cause of the summons will be stated. When a summons has been issued, the business appointed for the day shall go forward in accordance with the resolution of those present, even if not all those who were summoned have appeared.

* (15) In future we will allow no one to levy an 'aid' from his free men, except to ransom his person, to make his eldest son a knight, and (once) to marry his eldest daughter. For these purposes only a reasonable 'aid' may be levied.

(16) No man shall be forced to perform more service for a knight's 'fee', or other free holding of land, than is due from it.

(17) Ordinary lawsuits shall not follow the royal court around, but shall be held in a fixed place.

(18) Inquests of novel disseisin, mort d'ancestor, and darrein presentment shall be taken only in their proper county court. We ourselves, or in our absence abroad our chief justice, will send two justices to each county four times a year, and these justices, with four knights of the county elected by the county itself, shall hold the assizes in the county court, on the day and in the place where the court meets.

(19) If any assizes cannot be taken on the day of the county court, as many knights and freeholders shall afterwards remain behind, of those who have attended the court, as will suffice for the administration of justice, having regard to the volume of business to be done.

(20) For a trivial offence, a free man shall be fined only in proportion to the degree of his offence, and for a serious offence correspondingly, but not so heavily as to deprive him of his livelihood. In the same way, a merchant shall be spared his merchandise, and a villein the implements of his husbandry, if they fall upon the mercy of a royal court. None of these fines shall be imposed except by the assessment on oath of reputable men of the neighbourhood.

(21) Earls and barons shall be fined only by their equals, and in proportion to the gravity of their offence.

(22) A fine imposed upon the lay property of a clerk in holy orders shall be assessed upon the same principles, without reference to the value of his ecclesiastical benefice.

(23) No town or person shall be forced to build bridges over rivers except those with an ancient obligation to do so.

(24) No sheriff, constable, coroners, or other royal officials are to hold lawsuits that should be held by the royal justices.

* (25) Every county, hundred, wapentake, and tithing shall remain at its ancient rent, without increase, except the royal demesne manors.

(26) If at the death of a man who holds a lay 'fee' of the Crown, a sheriff or royal official produces royal letters patent of summons for a debt due to the Crown, it shall be lawful for them to seize and list movable goods found in the lay 'fee' of the dead man to the value of the debt, as assessed by worthy men. Nothing shall be removed until the whole debt is paid, when the residue shall be given over to the executors to carry out the dead man's will. If no debt is due to the Crown, all the movable goods shall be regarded as the property of the dead man, except the reasonable shares of his wife and children.

* (27) If a free man dies intestate, his movable goods are to be distributed by his next-of-kin and friends, under the supervision of the Church. The rights of his debtors are to be preserved.

(28) No constable or other royal official shall take corn or other movable goods from any man without immediate payment, unless the seller voluntarily offers postponement of this.

(29) No constable may compel a knight to pay money for castle-guard if the knight is willing to undertake the guard in person, or with reasonable excuse to supply some other fit man to do it. A knight taken or sent on military service shall be excused from castle-guard for the period of this service.

(30) No sheriff, royal official, or other person shall take horses or carts for transport from any free man, without his consent.

(31) Neither we nor any royal official will take wood for our castle, or for any other purpose, without the consent of the owner.

(32) We will not keep the lands of people convicted of felony in our hand for longer than a year and a day, after which they shall be returned to the lords of the 'fees' concerned.

(33) All fish-weirs shall be removed from the Thames, the Medway, and throughout the whole of England, except on the sea coast.

(34) The writ called precipe shall not in future be issued to anyone in respect of any holding of land, if a free man could thereby be deprived of the right of trial in his own lord's court.

(35) There shall be standard measures of wine, ale, and corn (the London quarter), throughout the kingdom. There shall also be a standard width of dyed cloth, russet, and haberject, namely two ells within the selvedges. Weights are to be standardised similarly.

(36) In future nothing shall be paid or accepted for the issue of a writ of inquisition of life or limbs. It shall be given gratis, and not refused.

(37) If a man holds land of the Crown by 'fee-farm', 'socage', or 'burgage', and also holds land of someone else for knight's service, we will not have guardianship of his heir, nor of the land that belongs to the other person's 'fee', by virtue of the 'fee-farm', 'socage', or 'burgage', unless the 'fee-farm' owes knight's service. We will not have the guardianship of a man's heir, or of land that he holds of someone else, by reason of any small property that he may hold of the Crown for a service of knives, arrows, or the like.

(38) In future no official shall place a man on trial upon his own unsupported statement, without producing credible witnesses to the truth of it.

+ (39) No free man shall be seized or imprisoned, or stripped of his rights or possessions, or outlawed or exiled, or deprived of his standing in any way, nor will we proceed with force against him, or send others to do so, except by the lawful judgment of his equals or by the law of the land.

+ (40) To no one will we sell, to no one deny or delay right or justice.

(41) All merchants may enter or leave England unharmed and without fear, and may stay or travel within it, by land or water, for purposes of trade, free from all illegal exactions, in accordance with ancient and lawful customs. This, however, does not apply in time of war to merchants from a country that is at war with us. Any such merchants found in our country at the outbreak of war shall be detained without injury to their persons or property, until we or our chief justice have discovered how our own merchants are being treated in the country at war with us. If our own merchants are safe they shall be safe too.

* (42) In future it shall be lawful for any man to leave and return to our kingdom unharmed and without fear, by land or water, preserving his allegiance to us, except in time of war, for some short period, for the common benefit of the realm. People that have been imprisoned or outlawed in accordance with the law of the land, people from a country that is at war with us, and merchants - who shall be dealt with as stated above - are excepted from this provision.

(43) If a man holds lands of any 'escheat' such as the 'honour' of Wallingford, Nottingham, Boulogne, Lancaster, or of other 'escheats' in our hand that are baronies, at his death his heir shall give us only the 'relief' and service that he would have made to the baron, had the barony been in the baron's hand. We will hold the 'escheat' in the same manner as the baron held it.

(44) People who live outside the forest need not in future appear before the royal justices of the forest in answer to general summonses, unless they are actually involved in proceedings or are sureties for someone who has been seized for a forest offence.

* (45) We will appoint as justices, constables, sheriffs, or other officials, only men that know the law of the realm and are minded to keep it well.

(46) All barons who have founded abbeys, and have charters of English kings or ancient tenure as evidence of this, may have guardianship of them when there is no abbot, as is their due.

(47) All forests that have been created in our reign shall at once be disafforested. River-banks that have been enclosed in our reign shall be treated similarly.

*(48) All evil customs relating to forests and warrens, foresters, warreners, sheriffs and their servants, or river-banks and their wardens, are at once to be investigated in every county by twelve sworn knights of the county, and within forty days of their enquiry the evil customs are to be abolished completely and irrevocably. But we, or our chief justice if we are not in England, are first to be informed.

* (49) We will at once return all hostages and charters delivered up to us by Englishmen as security for peace or for loyal service.

* (50) We will remove completely from their offices the kinsmen of Gerard de Athée, and in future they shall hold no offices in England. The people in question are Engelard de Cigogné, Peter, Guy, and Andrew de Chanceaux, Guy de Cigogné, Geoffrey de Martigny and his brothers, Philip Marc and his brothers, with Geoffrey his nephew, and all their followers.

* (51) As soon as peace is restored, we will remove from the kingdom all the foreign knights, bowmen, their attendants, and the mercenaries that have come to it, to its harm, with horses and arms.

* (52) To any man whom we have deprived or dispossessed of lands, castles, liberties, or rights, without the lawful judgment of his equals, we will at once restore these. In cases of dispute the matter shall be resolved by the judgment of the twenty-five barons referred to below in the clause for securing the peace (§61). In cases, however, where a man was deprived or dispossessed of something without the lawful judgment of his equals by our father King Henry or our brother King Richard, and it remains in our hands or is held by others under our warranty, we shall have respite for the period commonly allowed to Crusaders, unless a lawsuit had been begun, or an enquiry had been made at our order, before we took the Cross as a Crusader. On our return from the Crusade, or if we abandon it, we will at once render justice in full.

* (53) We shall have similar respite in rendering justice in connexion with forests that are to be disafforested, or to remain forests, when these were first afforested by our father Henry or our brother Richard; with the guardianship of lands in another person's 'fee', when we have hitherto had this by virtue of a 'fee' held of us for knight's service by a third party; and with abbeys founded in another person's 'fee', in which the lord of the 'fee' claims to own a right. On our return from the Crusade, or if we abandon it, we will at once do full justice to complaints about these matters.

(54) No one shall be arrested or imprisoned on the appeal of a woman for the death of any person except her husband.

* (55) All fines that have been given to us unjustly and against the law of the land, and all fines that we have exacted unjustly, shall be entirely remitted or the matter decided by a majority judgment of the twenty-five barons referred to below in the clause for securing the peace (§61) together with Stephen, archbishop of Canterbury, if he can be present, and such others as he wishes to bring with him. If the archbishop cannot be present, proceedings shall continue without him, provided that if any of the twenty-five barons has been involved in a similar suit himself, his judgment shall be set aside, and someone else chosen and sworn in his place, as a substitute for the single occasion, by the rest of the twenty-five.

(56) If we have deprived or dispossessed any Welshmen of land, liberties, or anything else in England or in Wales, without the lawful judgment of their equals, these are at once to be returned to them. A dispute on this point shall be determined in the Marches by the judgment of equals. English law shall apply to holdings of land in England, Welsh law to those in Wales, and the law of the Marches to those in the Marches. The Welsh shall treat us and ours in the same way.

* (57) In cases where a Welshman was deprived or dispossessed of anything, without the lawful judgment of his equals, by our father King Henry or our brother King Richard, and it remains in our hands or is held by others under our warranty, we shall have respite for the period commonly allowed to Crusaders, unless a lawsuit had been begun, or an enquiry had been made at our order, before we took the Cross as a Crusader. But on our return from the Crusade, or if we abandon it, we will at once do full justice according to the laws of Wales and the said regions.

* (58) We will at once return the son of Llywelyn, all Welsh hostages, and the charters delivered to us as security for the peace.

* (59) With regard to the return of the sisters and hostages of Alexander, king of Scotland, his liberties and his rights, we will treat him in the same way as our other barons of England, unless it appears from the charters that we hold from his father William, formerly king of Scotland, that he should be treated otherwise. This matter shall be resolved by the judgment of his equals in our court.

(60) All these customs and liberties that we have granted shall be observed in our kingdom in so far as concerns our own relations with our subjects. Let all men of our kingdom, whether clergy or laymen, observe them similarly in their relations with their own men.

* (61) SINCE WE HAVE GRANTED ALL THESE THINGS for God, for the better ordering of our kingdom, and to allay the discord that has arisen between us and our barons, and since we desire that they shall be enjoyed in their entirety, with lasting strength, for ever, we give and grant to the barons the following security:

The barons shall elect twenty-five of their number to keep, and cause to be observed with all their might, the peace and liberties granted and confirmed to them by this charter.

If we, our chief justice, our officials, or any of our servants offend in any respect against any man, or transgress any of the articles of the peace or of this security, and the offence is made known to four of the said twenty-five barons, they shall come to us - or in our absence from the kingdom to the chief justice - to declare it and claim immediate redress. If we, or in our absence abroad the chief justice, make no redress within forty days, reckoning from the day on which the offence was declared to us or to him, the four barons shall refer the matter to the rest of the twenty-five barons, who may distrain upon and assail us in every way possible, with the support of the whole community of the land, by seizing our castles, lands, possessions, or anything else saving only our own person and those of the queen and our children, until they have secured such redress as they have determined upon. Having secured the redress, they may then resume their normal obedience to us.

Any man who so desires may take an oath to obey the commands of the twenty-five barons for the achievement of these ends, and to join with them in assailing us to the utmost of his power. We give public and free permission to take this oath to any man who so desires, and at no time will we prohibit any man from taking it. Indeed, we will compel any of our subjects who are unwilling to take it to swear it at our command.

If one of the twenty-five barons dies or leaves the country, or is prevented in any other way from discharging his duties, the rest of them shall choose another baron in his place, at their discretion, who shall be duly sworn in as they were.

In the event of disagreement among the twenty-five barons on any matter referred to them for decision, the verdict of the majority present shall have the same validity as a unanimous verdict of the whole twenty-five, whether these were all present or some of those summoned were unwilling or unable to appear.

The twenty-five barons shall swear to obey all the above articles faithfully, and shall cause them to be obeyed by others to the best of their power.

We will not seek to procure from anyone, either by our own efforts or those of a third party, anything by which any part of these concessions or liberties might be revoked or diminished. Should such a thing be procured, it shall be null and void and we will at no time make use of it, either ourselves or through a third party.

* (62) We have remitted and pardoned fully to all men any ill-will, hurt, or grudges that have arisen between us and our subjects, whether clergy or laymen, since the beginning of the dispute. We have in addition remitted fully, and for our own part have also pardoned, to all clergy and laymen any offences committed as a result of the said dispute between Easter in the sixteenth year of our reign (i.e. 1215) and the restoration of peace.

In addition we have caused letters patent to be made for the barons, bearing witness to this security and to the concessions set out above, over the seals of Stephen archbishop of Canterbury, Henry archbishop of Dublin, the other bishops named above, and Master Pandulf.

* (63) IT IS ACCORDINGLY OUR WISH AND COMMAND that the English Church shall be free, and that men in our kingdom shall have and keep all these liberties, rights, and concessions, well and peaceably in their fullness and entirety for them and their heirs, of us and our heirs, in all things and all places for ever.

Both we and the barons have sworn that all this shall be observed in good faith and without deceit. Witness the abovementioned people and many others.

Given by our hand in the meadow that is called Runnymede, between Windsor and Staines, on the fifteenth day of June in the seventeenth year of our reign (i.e. 1215: the new regnal year began on 28 May).

The text in this article is available under the Creative Commons License.

- See more at: http://www.bl.uk/magna-carta/articles/magna-carta-english-translation#sthash.tNB4dJ8X.dpuf

Quotations on Law and Lawyers

1.

As for the attorney Zenas and
    Apollos: do all that you can to help
    Them on their journey so their needs are met.
~Titus 3:13

(This is the only place in the Bible that a lawyer is mentioned by name.)

2.

Far more has been accomplished for the welfare and progress of mankind by preventing bad actions than by doing good ones.
~William Lyon Mackenzie King

3.

In England, justice is open to all—like the Ritz Hotel.
~Sir James Mathew

4.

It is as if the ordinary language we use every day has a hidden set of signals, a kind of secret code.
~William Stafford

5.

Law is the witness and external deposit of our moral life. Its history is the history of the moral development of the race.
~ Oliver Wendell Holmes

6.

Laws are the spider's webs which, if anything small falls into them they ensnare it, but large things break through and escape.
~Solon

7.

Lawyers are the only persons in whom ignorance of the law is not punished.
~Jeremy Bentham

8.

Lawyers spend a great deal of time shoveling smoke.
~Oliver Wendell Holmes

9.

Revenge is a kind of wild justice, which the more man's nature runs to, the more ought law to weed it out.
~Francis Bacon

10.

Without law there is freedom only for the most powerful, and chaos prevails.
~Joseph Rosenfarb

11.

The law of England is a very strange one; it cannot compel anyone to tell the truth. . . . But what the law can do is to give you seven years for not telling the truth.
~Lord Darling

12.

The main work of a trial attorney is to make a jury like his client.
~Clarence Darrow

13.

Let reverence of the law . . . become the political religion of the nation.
~Abraham Lincoln

14.

You are remembered for the rules you break.
~Douglas MacArthur

15.

Law . . . begins when someone takes to doing something someone else does not like.
~Karl Llewellyn

16.

Any fool can make a rule, and every fool will mind it.
~Anonymous

17.

It usually takes 100 years to make a law, and then, after it's done its work, it usually takes 100 years to be rid
of it.

~Henry Ward Beecher

18.

A man may as well open an oyster without a knife, as a lawyer's mouth without a fee.
~Barten Holyday

19.

No matter whether the Constitution follows the flag or not, the Supreme Court follows the election returns.
~Finley Peter Dunne

20.

When you have no basis for an argument, abuse the plaintiff.
~Cicero

21.

The adversary system is a kind of warfare in mufti.
~R. I. Fitzhenry

22.

A jury consists of twelve persons chosen to decide who has the better lawyer.
~Robert Frost

23.

Lawyers are men who hire out their words and anger.
~Martial

24.

Litigant: a person about to give up his skin for the hope of retaining his bone.
~Ambrose Bierce

25.

In America, an acquittal doesn't mean you're innocent; it means you beat the rap. My clients lose even when
they win.

~F. Lee Bailey

26.

Law and order is one of the steps taken to maintain injustice.
~Edward Bond

27.

Whatever is enforced by command is more imputed to him who exacts than to him who performs.
~Michel de Montaigne

28.

The life of the law has not been logic: it has been experience.
~Oliver Wendell Holmes

29.

Every new time will give its law.
~Maxim Gorky

30.

Lawyers and painters can soon change white to black.
~Danish proverb

31.

No man is above the law and no man is below it: nor do we ask any man's permission when we ask him to
obey it.
~Theodore Roosevelt

32.

Fragile as reason is and limited as law is as the institutionalized medium of reason, that's all we have standing
between us and the tyranny of mere will and the cruelty of unbridled, undisciplined feeling.
~Felix Frankfurter

33.

The law of heaven is love.
~Hosea Ballou

References for Elements of Claims and Defenses in Nevada
Black's Law Dictionary, 7th ed. and 9th ed.
Campbell, Charles B., "A 'Plausible' Showing After *Bell Atlantic Corp. v. Twombly,*" *Nevada Law Journal 9.1* (2008):
1-31. Available at: http://works.bepress.com/charles_campbell/1.
definitions.uslegal.com.
Dictionary of American Maxims, David Kin, editor, Philosophical Library: New York (1955)
Chisholm, Hugh, ed., *Encyclopædia Britannica* (11th ed.). Cambridge University Press (1911).
Collins English Dictionary—Complete and Unabridged copyright HarperCollins Publishers 1991, 1994, 1998, 2000, and
2003.
Ella, V. John, "Anatomy of an Answer," *The Hennepin Lawyer*, 2004.
findlaw.com
The Learned Intermediary Doctrine in South Carolina, Brian A. Comer, 2009.
Merriam-Webster's Dictionary of Law ©1996. Merriam-Webster, Incorporated.
Nevada Civil Practice Manual, 5th ed., CLE Committee of the State Bar of Nevada.
Nevada Jury Instructions, Civil, State Bar of Nevada.
Nevada Reports, Nevada Legislative Counsel Bureau.
Nevada Revised Statutes, Nevada Legislative Counsel Bureau.
*Spence, Gerry, *Trial by Fire*, Harper Perennial, 1996.
Versuslaw.com.
Webster's New College Dictionary, Michael Agnes, editor-in-chief, Wiley Publishing: 2009.
West's Encyclopedia of American Law, edition 2. Copyright 2008 The Gale Group, Inc. All rights reserved.

Wikipedia.

305

310

Table of Authorities

Cases

317

325

329

340

345

355

Statutes

Other Authorities

Other Authorities

Treatises

Treatises

Closing Argument
By Honoré Daumier